MW01506079

: 83017

or name: Schultz

of book: Ann Sheridan

number: 0313284822

ANN SHERIDAN

Ann Sheridan
(Author's collection)

ANN SHERIDAN

A Bio-Bibliography

MARGIE SCHULTZ

Bio-Bibliographies in the Performing Arts, *Number 75*
James Robert Parish, Series Adviser

GREENWOOD PRESS
Westport, Connecticut • London

Library of Congress Cataloging-in-Publication Data

Schultz, Margie.
    Ann Sheridan : a bio-bibliography / Margie Schultz.
      p. cm. — (Bio-bibliographies in the performing arts, ISSN
0892–5550 ; no. 75)
    Videography: p.
    Filmography: p.
    Discography: p.
    Includes bibliographical references and index.
    ISBN 0–313–28482–2 (alk. paper)
    1. Sheridan, Ann, 1915–1967. 2. Sheridan, Ann, 1915–1967—
Bibliography. 3. Actors—United States—Biography. I. Title.
II. Series.
PN2287.S3717S38   1997
791.43′028′092—dc21   96–52025
[B]

British Library Cataloguing in Publication Data is available.

Copyright © 1997 by Margie Schultz

All rights reserved. No portion of this book may be
reproduced, by any process or technique, without the
express written consent of the publisher.

Library of Congress Catalog Card Number: 96–52025
ISBN: 0–313–28482–2
ISSN: 0892–5550

First published in 1997

Greenwood Press, 88 Post Road West, Westport, CT 06881
An imprint of Greenwood Publishing Group, Inc.

Printed in the United States of America

The paper used in this book complies with the
Permanent Paper Standard issued by the National
Information Standards Organization (Z39.48–1984).

P

For the many librarians whose work often goes unheralded.
Without their help, a book of this scope could not be written.

CONTENTS

PREFACE

In the 1940s, many epithets or gimmicks were used to help
publicize actresses in the fan magazines. Dorothy Lamour was
known for her sarong, Lauren Bacall had "the Look," and Ann
Sheridan was branded the Oomph Girl. First coined by
columnist Walter Winchell, then adapted by Warner Bros.
publicity man Bob Taplinger, oomph conjured up images of sex
and allure. Warner Bros. publicized Ann Sheridan with a
series of glamorous pictures by photographer George Hurrell,
giving more attention to the oomph campaign than to the roles
in which the studio cast her. The result was that she had to
use the clout she had gained through the publicity to fight
for parts, often taking suspension when the studio refused
her demands. In the end, Miss Sheridan proved her attributes
were more than physical, giving stellar performances in a
variety of genres.

Ann Sheridan came to Hollywood in 1933 as a finalist in
a beauty contest, a publicity stunt for Paramount's Search
for Beauty (F-1). Of the thirty contestants who appeared
in the picture, and the six finalists whom Paramount put
under contract, Ann was the only one to achieve stardom. As
Clara Lou Sheridan, she worked as an extra and bit player at
Paramount, doubling for stars and speaking a few lines of
dialogue. In 1934, she changed her name to Ann and began
playing larger roles. Her most memorable work at Paramount
was in Behold My Wife (1934, F-16). Although her
appearance was brief, her dramatic scene as a jilted woman
who commits suicide garnered much attention. Miss Sheridan
moved to Warner Bros. in 1936. Like Parmaount, the studio
was unsure how to take advantage of her talents. She mostly
was cast in supporting roles in "B" pictures like Black
Legion (1937, F-31), San Quentin (1937, F-33), and
Cowboy from Brooklyn (1938, F-41). The turning point came
with the Hurrell photos and her leading lady role in Angels
with Dirty Faces (Warner Bros., 1938, F-45). After a
publicity push in 1939, in which she was named Oomph Girl by
a number of beauty experts, her career as a pinup and leading
lady was set. She appeared as a dance hall girl in Dodge
City (Warner Bros., 1939, F-47), traded comic repartee with
James Cagney and Pat O'Brien in Torrid Zone (Warner Bros.,
1940, F-54), and proved a dramatic foil for Ida Lupino in

They Drive by Night (Warner Bros., 1940, F-55). Her best
remembered film for Warner Bros. was Kings Row (1942,
F-61), in which she played tomboy Randy Monaghan opposite
Ronald Reagan. Her subtle performance surprised many fans
and critics who did not realize that the Oomph Girl also was
an actress. In the years that followed, she appeared in
comedies, dramas, and musicals, proving her versatility. She
left Warner Bros. in 1948 to free-lance. Some of Miss
Sheridan's best work came during this period, since she was
able to have more control over choosing her roles. Her comic
performance opposite Cary Grant in I Was a Male War Bride
(20th Century-Fox, 1949, F-79) is a classic. She charmed
audiences of all ages in the musical Take Me to Town
(Universal-International, 1953, F-84). Her low-key dramatic
work in Come Next Spring (Republic, 1956, F-86) has made
the film a cult favorite.

     Because of Ann Sheridan's public image, her personal
life was chronicled in the press. In addition to brief
marriages to actors Edward Norris, George Brent, and Scott
McKay, her love life often landed her in the headlines. She
cherished her privacy and even preferred keeping her
charitable work a secret. In addition to appearances at the
Hollywood Canteen during World War II, two U.S.O. tours, and
fundraising for the Mickey Finn Club, she often helped
friends get jobs on her movies, advancing their careers.

     Through the years, Ann Sheridan also appeared on stage
and on many radio and television programs. She enjoyed
spoofing the Oomph Girl image, never letting the publicity
affect her. As with her film career, Miss Sheridan's
broadcasting work was diverse, appearing on dramas, comedies,
talk shows, variety revues, and game shows. In 1965, she
joined the cast of Another World (NBC, T-53), becoming one
of the first movie stars to appear on a soap opera. The role
led to a prime time series, the situation comedy Pistols 'n'
Petticoats (CBS, 1966-67, T-56). She died during
production.

     Modern audiences continue to discover Ann Sheridan on
television and home video. Her earnest, charismatic
performances prove that she was much more than a sex symbol.

     This volume does not purport to be a full-scale
biography, nor an in-depth analysis of Ann Sheridan's films.
It is intended as an overview of her life and career. The
book is divided into eleven sections, as follows:
     (1) a brief biography;
     (2) a chronology;
     (3) a listing of Miss Sheridan's plays and personal
appearances. This chapter includes plays performed on
Broadway and on tour, as well as selected personal
appearances made during World War II and at film premieres.
Each listing is preceded by the letter "P." Cities played,
dates of performances, production and cast credits, a short
synopsis, and reviews are included when available;
     (4) a filmography listing the movies in which Miss
Sheridan appeared. Each feature, short subject, or cartoon
short is preceded by the letter "F." Entries are arranged
chronologically by year of American release. Studio, year of
release, production and cast credits, a short synopsis, and
reviews are included for each film.

        (5)   a listing of Miss Sheridan's national <u>radio</u>
appearances. Each entry is precededed by the letter "R" and
includes episode title, airdate, cast, a brief synopsis, and
selected reviews;
        (6)   a listing of Miss Sheridan's national <u>television</u>
appearances. Entries are preceded by the letter "T" and
include episode title, airdate, cast, brief synopsis, and
selected reviews;
        (7)   a <u>discography</u> of LP records, compact discs, and
commercially-issued cassette tapes featuring Miss Sheridan.
Each listing is preceded by the letter "D" and includes date
of issue, label, number, and songs performed by Miss
Sheridan.
        (8)   a listing of <u>awards and honors</u> bestowed upon Miss
Sheridan. Each entry is preceded by the letter "A."
Listings include the name of the award and the approximate
year of receipt;
        (9)   a list of film <u>song sheets</u> which feature Miss
Sheridan on the cover. Listed chronologically and preceded
by the letter "S," each entry includes published songs from
the film and a brief description of the cover;
        (10) a <u>videography</u> listing the availability of Miss
Sheridan's movies and miscellaneous appearances on home video
and laserdisc. Each entry is preceded by the letter "V" and
includes the company of release and the number, when known;
        (11) a <u>bibliography</u> of writings by and about Miss
Sheridan. This chapter includes reviews, articles, and
announcements from books, newspapers, magazines, tabloids,
and trade papers, showing the diverse publications which have
written about Miss Sheridan's life and career. Each entry is
preceded by the letter "B."
        In addition, the book contains four appendixes:
selected magazine covers which feature Ann Sheridan, ads
using her name or likeness, miscellaneous products which used
her likeness, and archives with outstanding Sheridan
collections. A subject index of names and titles concludes
the volume; index references are keyed to the entry numbers
within the various chapter listings.
        The career and biographical information contained herein
are correct as of October 1, 1996. Any additions or
corrections for future editions may be sent to the author in
care of Greenwood Press.

ACKNOWLEDGMENTS

A book of this scope cannot be written without the help of
archivists, collectors, and other authors. There are many
unsung heroes who helped make this project a reality.
Whether they contributed one article or months of research, I
appreciate their contributions.

Several Ann Sheridan enthusiasts generously loaned items
from their collections so that I could use them in my
research. A heartfelt thanks goes to Ted Coyne, Ray Gain,
Ray Hagen, Allan Herzer, Genevieve Jones, Doug McLelland, and
Jim Meyer.

Special thanks goes to the following individuals and
institutions for providing invaluable resources: Art and
Music Department staff, Public Library of Cincinnati and
Hamilton County; John Cocchi; Richard Finnegan; Larry
Gassman; Richard L. Himmel, University Archivist, University
of North Texas Library; Katha Kievit; Albert Koenig, Jr.; Lou
Ellen Kramer, Reference and Outreach Coordinator, UCLA Film
and Television Archive; JoEllen Martin, secretary to Ralph
Edwards; Madeline F. Matz, Reference Librarian, Library of
Congress; Johnnie Miller; and Antoinette Reinke. I am
particularly grateful to Ned Comstock of the USC
Cinema-Television Library, University of Southern California,
whose assistance was invaluable in my research. He shared
scrapbooks donated by Constance McCormick, as well as
important information about Ann Sheridan's broadcasting
credits.

Many authors took time out from their own projects to
help with my research. I appreciate the efforts of Marsha
Beeman, Connie Billips, Larry Billman, Tom Bourgeois, Beverly
Bare Buehrer, Ann McKee, and Vincent Terrace. Jimmie Hicks
provided a plethora of information from the trade papers and
Los Angeles sources. He was ably assisted by Michael Glenn.
Tom Sharpley, who is writing a full-scale biography of Ann
Sheridan, was particularly helpful with filling in some of
the blanks in the actress' lengthy and sometimes tumultuous
career.

Special thanks to Barry Rivadue, whose friendship and
sense of humor kept me from losing faith when I ran into
obstacles. His research at the New York Public Library at
Lincoln Center was an enormous help in chronicling Ann

Sheridan's stage and television appearances.

I appreciate the advice and patience of my series advisor James Robert Parish and my editor George Butler. Without their help, this book could not have been written.

Finally, a special thanks to my parents, William and Margie. My late father's hard work and love of film continue to inspire me. My mother's friendship, research assistance, and support often went unheralded, but were most appreciated. I could not have written this book without their love and guidance.

BIOGRAPHY

In a 1940 interview, Ann Sheridan described her philosophy.
"What's the use of living if you can't have fun?" she asked
(B-637). The actress made it her credo. From electricians
and wardrobe workers to co-stars and fans, everyone saw Ann
Sheridan as a regular person. Despite her fame as
Hollywood's Oomph Girl, she remained down to earth and
unaffected, keeping her sense of humor about her sex symbol
image. Ann was comfortable with people from all walks of
life. She was frank and open, never a phony. She loved the
slow, simple pace of life in Mexico more than celebrity
parties, surrounding herself with her poodles and livestock
rather than an entourage of hangers-on to stroke her ego.
"She's the kind of girl that wouldn't seem an intruder at a
stag party," Hedda Hopper reported in 1947 (B-243).
     The same naturalness came across onscreen, winning Ann a
devoted legion of fans. She had the unique ability to
perform in period and contemporary dramas, as well as
comedies and musicals, and seem equally at home in each
genre. Whether she was playing the girlfriend of a gangster
in Angels with Dirty Faces (Warner Bros, 1939, F-45), a
flamboyant actress in The Man Who Came to Dinner (Warner
Bros., 1942, F-60), a sympathetic tomboy in Kings Row
(Warner Bros., 1942, F-61), a sharp-tongued WAC in I Was a
Male War Bride (20th Century-Fox, 1948, F-79), or the
long-suffering wife in Come Next Spring (Republic, 1956,
F-86), she came across as earnest and likable. Although
Ann's biggest fame came as a result of a sexy publicity
campaign that dubbed her the Oomph Girl, both sexes admired
her talents. Female fans aspired to be more like the modern,
up front woman Ann presented on and off screen. Males
admired her physical attributes, as well as her ability to be
an equal partner to her leading men.
     During the height of Ann's popularity in the 1940s, she
had many competitors. Actresses like Joan Crawford,
Katharine Hepburn, Barbara Stanwyck, Bette Davis, and Ida
Lupino could handle comedy and drama, but were seldom called
on for musicals or cheesecake photos. Sex symbol Betty
Grable was a musical star, but her dramatic talents were not
taken seriously. Irene Dunne juggled comedy, drama, and
musicals, but never was considered a sex symbol. Although

early critics compared Ann's allure and ease before the camera to that of Jean Harlow, Ann surpassed Harlow in versatility. No other actress had Ann's unique ability to perform in any genre, while maintaining her pinup image. Although current stars like Meryl Streep, Glenn Close, and Demi Moore try to vary their roles, none has achieved the same success as Ann Sheridan in comedy, drama, and musicals. And while Madonna has achieved musical and pinup fame, she has yet to prove herself as an actress. Ann Sheridan remains a unique treasure in film history: a glamour girl who proved her acting talents but never became affected by her own fame and publicity.

Clara Lou Sheridan was born February 21, 1915 in Denton, Texas, a small town outside Dallas. Her parents were Lula Stewart Warren, of the Virginia Warrens, and George W. Sheridan, an alleged great-nephew of Civil War General Philip Sheridan. The family also claimed to have a mixture of Scottish, Irish, and Cherokee blood. Clara Lou was named after her mother and Clara Evans, variously reported as an aunt or neighbor (B-347). As a youngster, she seldom answered to Clara Lou; her nicknames were Lulu and Loudie. The Sheridans had five other children: Kitty (thirteen years older than Clara Lou), Mabel (ten years older), George, Jr. (seven years older), Pauline "Polly" (four years older), and a baby who died before Clara Lou's birth (B-634).

The Sheridans were a straight-laced, southern Baptist family, who tried to instill old-fashioned values in their children. "I finally got over things like 'vanity is bad' and 'marriage is the only way for a woman'," Ann recalled. "That's when I started to fight my own battles. But I guess I started fighting as a kid. Otherwise, I'd never have gotten out of Denton." She compared life in the small Texas town to the fictional Kings Row that she later encountered on screen. Both were full of hypocrisy and narrow-mindedness, in Ann's opinion (B-222). Women were not encouraged to have a career outside the home, religion was full of hellfire and damnation, and show business was frowned upon. Veteran fan magazine writer Ruth Waterbury described the Sheridans as God-fearing people who disapproved of Hollywood and who always hoped their daughter would return to Texas and teach (B-698).

When Clara Lou was three, the Sheridans moved to 304 South Elm Street in Denton (B-347). George owned a ranch, as well as a garage, where he worked as supervisor and mechanic. When Clara Lou was eight, she began attending Robert E. Lee Grammar School. Because the ranch was ten miles from town, Clara Lou lived with her aunt, Julia Sheridan, during the school week, joining her family on weekends (B-531). Despite the fact that the ranch had no plumbing, electricity, or gas, Clara Lou loved it. Always a tomboy, she often played cowboys and Indians, horse thieves, and roping games with her siblings. Although George and Polly were Clara Lou's playmates, she recalled being closest to Mabel, who adopted her as a pet. Mabel would take Clara Lou's side when the other children teased her and, on baking day, would make her little sister a special gingerbread man (B-531). Friends described Clara Lou as outspoken and spirited. In 1957, former neighbor Elizabeth Chitwood recalled that Clara Lou

was an earnest, friendly, straightforward child who was
always eager to do her share. "If she came in while you were
sweeping, she'd say, 'Give me the broom and you go do
something else,'" Chitwood said. "She was brought up at home
to work. She was so full of life that she was kind of noisy,
but she was well liked" (B-527).

Clara Lou busied herself with many interests while
attending Denton Junior High School. In addition to being an
accomplished acrobatic dancer, Clara Lou played football and
basketball (B-637). In eighth grade, she won a musical
appreciation contest, as well as a popularity contest. But
neither honor could erase the disgrace she felt when she was
sent home from a school Halloween party after the teacher
judged her pirate costume indecent. "You take things pretty
seriously when you are sixteen," the actress recalled
(B-531).

Clara Lou was popular, but always preferred male
companionship. In junior high school, she had her first real
boyfriends, Charlie and Truman Turner. When the brothers
became too competitive over her affections, Clara Lou
insisted, "Boys, don't fight over me. I'll go with you both"
(B-627).

After graduating from Denton High School in 1932, Clara
Lou entered the North Texas State Teachers College at Denton.
She later admitted that her enrollment had more to do with
joining her friends than any serious aspirations to become a
teacher. Although a 1943 article claimed she had planned to
go to the Philippines to teach, other interviews insisted her
motives were less altruistic. "We had a lot of fun and I
doubt that any of us ever gave serious thought to the fact
that some day the responsibility of teaching would be staring
us in the face," the actress confided in 1938 (B-603). In
1940, she claimed the college was close to home and
co-educational, adding, "Probably I just hoped to marry and
settle down" (B-637).

There is some debate over Clara Lou's dramatic
ambitions. According to a 1939 Life story, she was
frustrated when she auditioned for school plays and always
was cast as the understudy (B-111). In later interviews, the
actress said that she always had fostered dramatic ambitions,
but her strict, southern Baptist family was against a
theatrical career. She implied that her college dramatics
were done on the sly. Clara Lou enrolled as an art major at
North Texas State Teachers College. However, she soon
switched her major to dramatics because she disliked a
painting class. In the 1933 yearbook, The Yucca, Clara Lou
was listed as a member of the dramatic club. In 1966, she
confided that her secret ambition was to be a professional
band singer, but that her family's attitude about vanity kept
her from pursuing that career. A college speech and drama
course was considered respectable if it led to a teaching
position, she explained (B-222).

Clara Lou's fantasies about becoming a band singer were
realized in early 1933. While visiting her classmate
Gwendolyn Woodford's dancing studio in Denton, Clara Lou was
humming nonchalantly. Most sources say that music professor
Floyd Graham, who conducted the college band, overheard her
and demanded that she audition, although fellow student Bill

Ardis also has been credited with her discovery. Clara Lou
made her singing debut at a college prom and continued to
perform in Saturday night concerts, in and around Denton
(B-531). Clara Lou was not the only singer featured in the
variety shows, although articles in the college's Campus
Chat usually singled her out for mention. During a variety
show entitled Sing and Dance (P-1), Clara Lou's torch style
was described as "singing in her original Harlem manner"
(B-518). Clara Lou performed with the band through August
1933. Gwendolyn Woodford also sang and danced with the band
and remained close to Clara Lou. When the actress went to
Hollywood, Woodford joined her and worked as her secretary,
sharing her home. In addition to singing, Clara Lou kept
active with swimming, basketball, and tennis.
     While Clara Lou was busy with college activities, she
was unaware of the abrupt change that was about to take place
in her life. Paramount Studios had generated reams of
publicity from a nationwide talent search for an actress to
play Panther Woman in Island of Lost Souls (Paramount,
1933). The contest led them to a cache of starlets who
became leading ladies at Paramount, including Gail Patrick,
Kathleen Burke, Grace Bradley, and Gertrude Michael. In
1932, the studio decided to repeat the contest, hoping to
garner more high-profile publicity for a new film, Search
for Beauty (F-1). Thirty finalists from around the world
were promised a trip to Hollywood, a screen test, and roles
in the picture. Across the United States and Europe, men and
women were encouraged to send their photographs to the local
newspapers, whose editors chose the district finalists.
Clara Lou joked about the contest, so she was astounded when
her photo appeared in the Dallas News as a contestant. She
stormed into the office of drama editor John Rosenfield,
berating him for entering her photo without permission. He
explained that her sister Kitty had sent in the picture
without her knowledge in the fall of 1932. Clara Lou did not
expect anything to come of the contest. "I didn't, and still
don't, think I was good-looking enough," the actress said in
a 1966 interview (B-222). During a summer holiday in Waco,
Clara Lou forgot about the contest. She was surprised when
Rosenfield called to tell her that she was a finalist and had
won a trip to Hollywood. On September 15, 1933, Clara Lou
took a train from Dallas to Hollywood to make her screen
debut (B-257).
     Paramount sent a cinematographer to make screen tests of
the newspaper contestants. Although most of the aspirants
had well-rehearsed speeches prepared for the camera, Clara
Lou simply introduced herself. During the test, she stumbled
and almost fell. Despite her poor showing, Clara Lou and the
twenty-nine other contestants were given a one-picture
contract at fifty dollars a week and were guaranteed a role
in Search for Beauty.
     The film took about five weeks to shoot. In addition to
expenses, the contest winners received two hundred dollars
for their work in the movie (B-214). When it was finished,
the players were supposed to return home with tickets
provided by the studio. Many of the contestants refused to
leave Hollywood as promised. They charged big bills to the
studio, prompting Paramount to abolish such contests in the

future (B-474).

Only six of the winners were given Paramount contracts: Alfred Delcambre, Colin Tapley, Eldred Tidbury, Gwenllian Gill, Julian Madison, and Clara Lou Sheridan. Of the six, only Clara Lou ended up with a major film career. At the time, Paramount was known for its sophisticated roster of stars, many of whom started on Broadway. Maurice Chevalier, Jeanette MacDonald, Mae West, and Claudette Colbert were all under contract, appearing mostly in costume dramas and musicals. One of the studio's biggest stars was Marlene Dietrich, whose exotic looks and sexy voice won her fans worldwide. Clara Lou's country background and Texas twang made her more appropriate for the western fare that Paramount was producing for Gary Cooper and Randolph Scott.

Search for Beauty was released on February 2, 1934. Although all the contestants had bit parts, Clara Lou's was exceptionally small. She can be glimpsed peeking over the shoulders of two contest winners and grinning. Clara Lou was disappointed in her less-than-glamorous screen debut. "I thought I was going to look like [Marlene] Dietrich," she said, "But instead I looked like heck" (B-532). Despite her miniscule role, when the movie played in Dallas, the marquee listed Clara Lou as the star (B-257).

Clara Lou was surprised when Paramount hired her after the tiny role in Search for Beauty. She signed a contract in October 1933, with six-month options (B-637). Her contract was more the result of studio necessity than confidence in her acting talents. Paramount needed a woman who could ride and, since Clara Lou had checked that box on her questionnaire, she was hired. "I would ride and ride and ride and ride, then take a hot bath and get massaged and ride some more," the actress recalled. "I'd begin to think I was the only one in the picture; I couldn't see how they'd find room to show anybody else. Then when the picture was finished and shown, I'd be seen riding about fifty yards and dismounting" (B-257).

In the beginning, Clara Lou was little more than a bit player, saying a few lines or doubling for stars. She later claimed that she did not know how many movies she made, as sometimes her hands, feet, or shoulders would be used in close-ups of another actress. She said, "I was paid $50 a week by that studio and all I did for two and a half years was to show my knees in swim suits and play bits in B pictures" (B-195). "I did everything, dubbed hands, legs, everything except make movies," she recalled (B-196). "I used to go to Grauman's Chinese or Pantages and sit there waiting to see my faceless body on the screen" (B-117). During 1934, she appeared in many Paramount films, including Bolero (F-2), Murder at the Vanities (F-4), Shoot the Works (F-5), Kiss and Make-Up (F-6), The Notorious Sophie Lang (F-7), Ladies Should Listen (F-8), You Belong to Me (F-9), Wagon Wheels (F-10), The Lemon Drop Kid (F-11), Ready for Love (F-12), Mrs. Wiggs of the Cabbage Patch (F-13), Limehouse Blues (F-14), College Rhythm (F-15), and One Hour Late (F-17). In some pictures, Clara Lou had a line or two in her small roles as a telephone operator, a wedding guest, a beautician, a chorus girl, and a finishing school student. In others, she was little more than an extra.

During this period, Paramount invested time and money in their contract players. In an effort to lose her Texas accent, Clara Lou underwent vocal training with dramatics coaches Nina Mouise and Phyllis Loughton. Instructors also worked on her posture and movement, so that she would appear more graceful on screen. As she progressed, Clara Lou was asked to join the studio stock company. Contract players not only gained experience by working onstage at the Paramount lot, but it gave producers and directors the opportunity to observe their talents and cast them in future films. Clara Lou played roles in classics like A Doll's House, Romeo and Juliet, and Macbeth (B-532), as well as adaptations of Paramount films, like Double Door, The Pursuit of Happiness, and The Milky Way (P-2). Her work in Double Door led to a supporting role in the film Come On Marines! (F-3) in 1934 (B-536).

Despite the training, Clara Lou's screen exposure continued to be minimal. She spoke to casting directors about trying her in a larger part, but they refused, citing a problem with her attitude. Clara Lou was happy-go-lucky, marveling at her good fortune at being able to earn seventy-five dollars a week during the Depression. However, many interpreted her joie de vivre as disinterest. After being at Paramount for a year, she heard a rumor that her contract would not be renewed because head drama coach Mel Shauer thought she lacked ambition. "This girl fat, lazy and has a tendency to laugh everything off," his report allegedly claimed (B-117). Clara Lou confronted Shauer, quoting dialogue she had memorized in hopes of testing for a role and recalling the hours she had spent in school. She finally convinced Shauer to give her another chance and she stayed at Paramount for another year and a half.

Clara Lou later recalled her years at Paramount with fondness, relishing the fact that she did not have to carry the pictures, as she did later at Warner Bros. She lost weight during this time, thanks to a revolutionary diet secret: wearing corsets. "I laced them in so tight to look slim on the screen that I could barely breathe, let alone eat," the actress later confided to Hedda Hopper. "When you're squeezed up like that there isn't room for food!" (B-254) Clara Lou also endured several serious mishaps while under contract to Paramount. She was hit by a studio lamp, nearly cut off her hand when she pushed it through a window, and almost was killed when a horse fell on her (B-134).

Paramount showed its confidence in Clara Lou's talents by spotlighting her in an ad about potential stars for the 1934-35 season. The three-page spread pictured promising personalities, like Clara Lou, Claude Rains, Lloyd Nolan, Fred MacMurray, and Ben Bernie (B-165). However, it was almost six months before any change was noticeable on screen.

Clara Lou's roles finally began to improve with Behold My Wife (F-16), released December 7, 1934. Although she was in only two scenes, one called for her to commit suicide. Clara Lou believed it was that dramatic action that caused Paramount executives to keep her under contract. She was cast by director Mitchell Leisen, who had become enamored with her when she appeared in Murder at the Vanities (F-4) in 1934

(B-122). Behold My Wife is noteworthy for another reason,
as it is Clara Lou's first film under her new name: Ann
Sheridan. Clara Lou was appearing in a Paramount stock
company production of The Milky Way (P-2) when she was
called into the front office. Paramount recognized that it
had a potential star on its hands and decided her name was
too lengthy for a marquee. The executives vetoed her
suggestion of adopting her middle name, deeming it too
masculine. Since Clara Lou was playing a character named Ann
in The Milky Way, she decided to go with Ann Sheridan. The
studio quickly promoted its newly-christened starlet. On
November 27, 1934, the Hollywood Reporter contained a
half-page ad heralding Ann Sheridan as Mary White in Behold
My Wife (p. 15).

    Despite the promise of Behold My Wife, Ann's career
continued to sag. During 1935, she played small roles at
Paramount in Home on the Range (F-18), Enter Madame!
(F-19), Rumba (F-22), Mississippi (F-24), and The Glass
Key (F-26). Although Ann was Randolph Scott's love
interest in Rocky Mountain Mystery (F-20), the Zane Grey
western was little more than a "B" picture, delegated to
second bills. While Ann was under contract to Paramount, she
was loaned to Ambassador for Red Blood of Courage (F-25), a
1935 murder mystery. During this time, she also appeared in
MGM's celebrity-filled short Star Night at Coconut Grove
(F-21), modeling in a fashion show. Although Paramount named
her as one of its most promising stars in March 1935, the
studio failed to come through with quality roles.

    Ann called Car 99 (F-23) her Waterloo. The film,
released on March 1, 1935, cast her opposite Fred MacMurray
in a crime drama. It marked Ann's first leading role at
Paramount and her first screen kiss. "I was terrible," she
later confessed, "Simply awful. When the word went around
for the second time that I was on the way out, I didn't even
try to fix things up. I folded my tent, like the Arab, and
stole silently away" (B-532).

    Ann's last Paramount film was The Crusades (F-29),
Cecil B. DeMille's 1935 religious epic. Ann appeared as a
Christian woman, wearing a black wig and speaking one line in
a heavy Texas accent. At the same time, Ann was seen in
Hollywood Extra Girl (F-27), a short about the making of
The Crusades and the difficult life of an extra.

    After Ann left Paramount in May 1935, she free-lanced
for a year and a half. Her agent urged her to take any parts
that were offered, including extra work. Ann refused,
realizing that once the studios saw her as an extra, it would
be impossible to play featured roles. She admitted that it
was a perilous time for her. Although she made enough money
to survive, she felt hopeless about her future in movies and
even considered returning to Texas to teach. Ann recalled,
"When I started free-lancing, I lost confidence in myself.
The experience I had at Paramount was valuable, yet it was
months before I completely regained my courage" (B-603).

    During the next year and a half, Ann made only one
feature: Fighting Youth (F-28), a college melodrama
released by Universal on September 30, 1935. In the
programmer, Ann plays a college coed who becomes the pawn of
a communist infiltrator. Billboard noted, "Sheridan is

lovely and miscast, but in the right kind of parts should be able to go places" (November 16, 1935).

Ann spent most of her time testing at different studios. She recalled, "It's a great game. They rush you in, some bird slaps a dab of make-up on you, the lights are bum and you look like hell." She claimed the only part she did not test for was Dracula's mother. "I think I could have got that," she added (B-134).

Ann's personal life also was in upheaval. During the summer of 1936, she met actor Edward "Eddie" Norris in the lobby of her apartment building. A mutual friend introduced them and the couple began dating. Septimus Edward Norris was born March 10, 1911 in Philadelphia, Pennsylvania. The son of a socially prominent doctor, Eddie began his film career doubling for Buddy Rogers in Wings (Paramount, 1928). After gaining experience in stock productions, he came to Hollywood in 1932, making his film debut in Queen Christina (MGM, 1933) with Greta Garbo. By the time Eddie met Ann, he was a contract player at MGM, but he was getting better roles on loan-outs than at his home studio. Although only twenty-five, Eddie already was twice divorced. At sixteen, he had married an older woman. He also was divorced from actress Lona Andre, who had been runner-up in Paramount's Panther Woman contest.

Shortly after Ann and Eddie met, they eloped to Ensenada, Mexico with Eddie's best friends, character actor Ivan Lebedeff and Bruce Pierce. The hotel was overbooked, forcing the couple to delay the wedding for twenty-four hours. They finally were married in a Spanish civil ceremony on August 16, 1936. Ann wore a white slack suit and paisley scarf; Eddie and his friends donned sports clothes. The Norrises settled in an old house in the San Fernando valley (B-532).

Meanwhile, Ann's career was on the upswing. Early in 1936, she made a test for Warner Bros., but was rejected because she looked too much like contract player June Travis. Six months later, the studio executives changed their minds and offered Ann a contract during the summer of 1936. Longtime friend John Engstead recalled that Ann overhauled her appearance during this time, losing weight, capping her teeth, and straightening her wild, curly hair (B-161).

While Paramount had mastered drawing room comedies, period dramas, and sophisticated musicals, spotlighting its cultured stars, Warner Bros. focused on the working man, showing his rise and fall. Players like Humphrey Bogart, James Cagney, Edward G. Robinson, and Pat O'Brien often were showcased in crime dramas. Bette Davis and Joan Blondell were working class women, desperate to get ahead. Adventure was left to dashing Errol Flynn, whose onscreen pairing with Olivia de Havilland was a box office favorite. In the late 1930s, Warner Bros. also became famous for its sharp comedies, many of which were based on Broadway plays. Three Men on a Horse (1936), Boy Meets Girl (1938), and Brother Rat (1938) showed another side of studio contractees. Ann Sheridan seemed much better suited to the proletariat fare being produced at Warner Bros. than the sophisticated films at Paramount. But like its predecessor, Warner Bros. initially was unsure what to do with Ann, wasting her talents as second leads in "B" pictures (B-532).

Ann's first film for Warner Bros. was Sing Me a Love Song (F-30), released January 9, 1937. James Melton and Patricia Ellis star in this "B" romance set in a department store. Although Ann has a supporting role as a girl out to marry Melton, her scenes are cut from most prints seen today. Warner Bros. casting director Max Arnow was so impressed by her work in the musical that he persuaded his bosses at Warner Bros. to sign her to a six-month contract at seventy-five dollars a week.

Black Legion (F-31), released January 30, 1937, was based on a real incident involving Ku Klux Klan activities. The powerful drama shows how Humphrey Bogart's involvement with the organization destroys his life. Ann has the second female lead, the girlfriend of Dick Foran. It marks Ann's first film with Bogart, who would become a close friend.

According to studio publicity, Ann was asked to test for the role of Pat O'Brien's girlfriend, a teacher, in The Great O'Malley (F-32) after the casting director heard that she had studied teaching. Released February 13, 1937, the plot centers around a policeman's troubles with playing by the book. Ann admired her co-star's patience. When nerves caused her to shake, O'Brien told her, "Take it easy, sister, we've got miles and miles of film in the camera. If you don't get it right now, you'll get it next time" (B-204).

Ann was reunited with Pat O'Brien and Humphrey Bogart in San Quentin (F-33), released on August 7, 1937. The gangster drama casts her as Bogart's sister and O'Brien's girlfriend. Ann's role as a cafe singer allows her to sing "How Could You?" Like many Warner Bros. melodramas of the time, San Quentin touts prison reform.

A series of "B" pictures followed. In February 1937, Ann replaced Patricia Ellis in Madcap Heiress, released August 21, 1937 as The Footloose Heiress (F-34). The comedy casts Ann as a society girl intent on marrying quickly. She plays a gambler's girlfriend in Wine, Women and Horses (F-35), a racketeer's girlfriend in Alcatraz Island (F-36), and a fire fighter's girlfriend in She Loved a Fireman (F-37). She is a nurse in two Mignon G. Eberhart mysteries: The Patient in Room 18 (F-38) and Mystery House (F-39).

During this time, Ann's personal life was in turmoil. Despite promising roles in Fox's Show Them No Mercy (1935) and Warner Bros.'s They Won't Forget (1937), Eddie's career was in trouble. He complained about his misuse and was suspended by MGM. When his home studio cast him in more important films, they usually replaced him by better-known, more cooperative stars at the last minute. Eddie turned to alcohol for solace (B-304). He sat at home and brooded as Ann went out to work, causing a strain on the marriage (B-637). The Norrises separated on August 26, 1937. In October 1938, Ann filed for divorce, complaining that Eddie refused to take her out. "He told me several times our marriage was a mistake," Ann said. Her husband did not contest the divorce. Ann received her interlocutory decree on October 5, 1938; the divorce became final on October 6, 1939. In a 1939 interview, Ann said, "I think that I was a jinx to Eddie. He is doing splendidly since we've been

apart. It is better the way it is, I am sure" (B-209).
Despite his ex-wife's optimism, Eddie's career declined,
mostly due to his temperament. He continued playing
character roles in "B" pictures through the 1950s. Following
his retirement from the screen, he raised cattle. Eddie
remarried twice, but remained friends with Ann. In a 1970s
interview, he revealed that he kept her photo on his dresser
and blamed himself for their marital problems (B-304).

Ann returned to Denton during the Christmas holidays in
1937. It was her first trip home since 1933. It marked the
last time she saw her father. A few months later, George was
partially blinded in an accident. He died of a heart attack
on May 20, 1938. Ann was disappointed that he was unable to
share her career success (B-532).

In January 1938, Warner Bros. announced their plans to
turn Ann Sheridan and Humphrey Bogart into a new romantic
team. Torchy in Panama was to be their first vehicle, with
George Bricker writing the script (B-594). The film was
released as Torchy Blane in Panama (Warner Bros., 1938)
with Lola Lane and Paul Kelly. Although Ann and Bogart
worked together in several additional films, they never were
paired romantically on screen.

Warner Bros. continued to cast Ann in "B" pictures in
1938. She played supporting roles as a nightclub singer in
Little Miss Thoroughbred (F-40) and a femme fatale in
Cowboy from Brooklyn (F-41). Ann later claimed, "I did
almost every B picture that was ever made on the Warner lot"
(B-206).

Later that year, Warner Bros. loaned Ann to Universal
for Letter of Introduction (F-42), released August 5, 1938.
Cast as Adolphe Menjou's temperamental mistress and fiancee,
Ann got to wear a sophisticated wardrobe and argue with the
star. Although her role was small, director John Stahl
strung together her five scenes and sent them to Jack Warner
with a note, "I've got a find for you, and she's in your own
studio." Stahl's alert and an increase in Ann's fan mail
eventually led to her being cast in better parts at her home
lot (B-295).

Meanwhile, another factor was influencing Ann's
popularity. When she was between movies, Warner Bros. had
her pose for pinup pictures. "Half of them I never saw," Ann
recalled, "But the studio wanted everybody to earn their
salaries. And believe me, that's just what you did. They
got you as naked as they could for every picture" (B-181).
Impressed by Ann's work in Cowboy from Brooklyn (F-41) and
Letter of Introduction (F-42), during the summer of 1938,
Warner Bros. decided to push her as the studio glamour girl
(B-57). They assigned famed photographer George Hurrell to
take a series of pinup poses of Ann. Though the studio still
was not backing up their faith in their contract player with
substantial roles, the photographs were printed in many fan
magazines, increasing Ann's popularity. Since Jean Harlow's
1937 death, Warners' east coast publicity chief Mitch Rawson
had been looking for a star with the same qualities that not
only made Harlow a sex symbol, but endeared her to millions
of fans of both sexes. He thought Ann had the same kind of
allure, sexy but without an ego. He instructed Ann to
glamorize every still she took. The sexy Hurrell photos and

Rawson's publicity led to comparisons between Ann and Harlow
in the press. When studio visitors began asking about Ann
before Warners' better-known actors, the studio realized it
had been wasting her talents. West coast publicity chief
Charles Einfeld met with Rawson to discuss Ann's potential.
Rawson was impressed with Ann and a major publicity campaign
was launched (B-111).

While the publicity campaign was being put together,
Ann's career continued to have its ups and downs. Warner
Bros. cast her as one of the trio of leading ladies in
Broadway Musketeers (F-44). The film, released October 8,
1938, is a "B" unit remake of Bette Davis's Three on a
Match (Warner Bros., 1933). Ann's role originally was
played by Joan Blondell. The story revolves around three
orphans who renew their friendship. As a nightclub singer,
Ann sings "Has It Ever Occurred to You?" and "Who Said That
This Isn't Love?"

Ann's first "A" picture at Warner Bros. was Angels with
Dirty Faces (F-45), released November 19, 1938. The
gangster film casts her as James Cagney's girlfriend. Cagney
became Ann's first acting teacher, giving her direction
before each scene. "He was the kind of actor who would sit
down and explain the why's and the where-fore's," she
recalled. "He would give you the benefit of everything he
had learned" (B-204). Ann played the role in her stocking
feet, since she and Cagney were both 5'5" and the studio
believed its hero should not be shorter than the leading lady
(B-134).

Warner Bros. began pushing Ann for stardom during this
period. The release of Angels with Dirty Faces coincided
with the distribution of the Hurrell photographs. On
November 10, 1938, Ann appeared on The Kraft Music Hall, a
radio variety show hosted by Bing Crosby (R-1).

Despite the publicity push, Warner Bros. continued
casting Ann in supporting roles. She has a small part in
They Made Me a Criminal (F-46), released January 28, 1939.
She appears briefly in the beginning of the film as John
Garfield's girlfriend. Despite the miniscule size of her
role, when Warner Bros. rereleased the movie in the 1940s,
Ann was second billed.

Warner Bros. was building on its glamour image for Ann
when the studio cast her in Dodge City (F-47), released
April 8, 1939. Errol Flynn and Olivia de Havilland are the
stars of the big-budget western, one of Warner Bros.'s major
releases for 1939. Although Ann's role as a dance hall
hostess is small, she receives third billing. Modern
Movies pointed out the publicity scam, noting, "She's in
the film so briefly it scarcely justifies feature billing"
(B-104). Dodge City marks Ann's first appearance in
Technicolor. On April 1, 1939, Ann joined a trainload of
Warner Bros. players on a junket to Dodge City, Kansas for
the premiere (P-3). By the time the film was released,
another publicity stunt had catapulted Ann to fame. Ann
Sheridan was no longer just a starlet, she was the Oomph
Girl.

Warner Bros. publicity agent Bob Taplinger generally is
credited with giving Ann the Oomph Girl tag. However,
columnist Walter Winchell was really the first to link Ann

with the word, writing that the studio should give her roles
with more "umph," based on the sexy qualities she showed in
the Hurrell photos. Taplinger changed the spelling and began
promoting Ann with the new title, hoping to obtain more
column space in the press for Ann and the studio. It was not
uncommon for stars to have similar epithets. During the
silent years, Theda Bara was the Vamp. In the 1920s, Clara
Bow was known as the It Girl. Later, Dorothy Lamour was
famous for her sarong, Lana Turner her sweater, and Marie
McDonald for her body. In the beginning, Warner Bros. saw
the oomph campaign as routine publicity (B-114). They
figured it would die down after a few months of magazine
photos and column mentions.
     On March 16, 1939, Bob Taplinger and Daisy Parsons,
press agent for the Los Angeles Town House, arranged a dinner
for twenty-five prominent experts on beauty and glamour,
including Lucius Beebe, David Niven, and the Earl of Warwick.
Allegedly, the experts were to select the woman with the most
sex appeal from a dozen actresses picked in a national
college poll, which included Carole Lombard, Hedy Lamarr, and
Alice Faye. The winner would be named the Oomph Girl. Many
of the judges had ties to Warner Bros., like makeup chief
Perc Westmore, actor/singer Rudy Vallee, designer Orry-Kelly,
and director/choreographer Busby Berkeley. They were
instructed to vote for Ann Sheridan. Although the contest
was rigged, Taplinger was amazed by Ann's lack of ego. She
told him, "Fixed or not, honey, keep your fingers crossed"
(B-222). The judges elected Ann and later presented her with
a gold bracelet engraved with their signatures (B-179).
     Ann received a startling amount of press from the stunt.
Screen Guide called her "the most exciting star since
[Jean] Harlow" (April 1939). Life and Look
simultaneously featured her on their covers. Nevin-Seymour
Company, Inc. insured her oomph for $100,000. Fifty
newspapers ran her memoirs. Publicity director Bob Taplinger
had the word oomph copyrighted. Soon there were oomph
automobiles, cigarettes, and gasoline on the market (B-470).
Within six months, Ann's fan mail jumped from thirty-fourth
on the Warner lot to third place. By the time she made It
All Came True (F-53) in 1940, it was up to first place
(B-470). Warner Bros. recognized the importance of
publicity. They added a clause to her contract, requiring
Ann to appear at least three times a week at a Hollywood
nightclub. Ann usually chose expert rumba dancer Cesar
Romero as her escort (B-111). Even an appearance on The
Gulf Screen Guild Show on May 28, 1939 had Ann flirting
with Fibber McGee (Jim Jordan), who jokingly was referred to
as the Oomph Man (R-2). Taplinger said, "The expenditure of
$160 for that dinner gave Warners' a $1,000,000 property"
(B-470).
     What was oomph? Even Ann said she didn't know. Through
the years, she often was quoted as saying it was the noise a
fat man made when he tied his shoes in a phone booth.
Although that answer was fabricated by the publicity
department, Ann had the same irreverence about the title.
She refused to take her glamorous image seriously, calling
out to her makeup woman to "come over and put some oomph on
me" (B-634). Ann allowed friends like Humphrey Bogart to kid

her about the epithet, adapting Oomph Girl to Miss Pushface
of 1893 (B-101). And, although she professed that Bette
Davis was her acting idol, Ann often described herself as
more of a personality than an actress. "I'm just not the
Academy Award type," she admitted, "I don't pretend to be. I
just want to do a good job on a good story. If I can be a
quarter as good as Bette Davis, I'll be happy" (B-347).
Coincidentally, Ann appeared in remakes of four Davis films
during her tenure at Warner Bros., though not always in the
Davis roles. Broadway Musketeers (F-44) is based on Three
on a Match (1932). Castle on the Hudson (F-52) first
appeared as 20,000 Years in Sing Sing (1933). They Drive
by Night (F-55) took some of its inspiration from
Bordertown (1935). The Unfaithful (F-75) was a reworking
of The Letter (1940). Ann finally got to work with her
idol in The Man Who Came to Dinner (F-60) in 1941.
Coincidentally, Ann and Davis also shared leading man George
Brent, who was Ann's husband and Davis's lover.
    Despite the publicity, Ann's ego remained in check.
"The Oomph buildup was a freak," she said, "A highly
publicized young girl with no films to prove whether or not
she had talent" (B-295). She recalled that she did not know
anything about the oomph contest until it was over. "It
wasn't until weeks later, when embarrassing things began to
occur, that I knew what oomph meant," she said (B-470). In
1939, she gave herself a bracelet engraved "From Clara Lou to
Ann. You continue to amaze me, kid!" (B-130). When a
columnist asked her to describe herself in twenty-five words
at the height of the oomph campaign, Ann kept her sense of
humor. "As I see Ann Sheridan she is very average, very
lucky, very bewildered," she said. "Annie had better be good
if she wants me to like her" (B-637). When a critic
commented on the sultry, provocative way she drooped her
eyelids, Ann quickly destroyed his illusions. "I had weak
eyes," she explained. "Those old Klieg lights killed them.
It felt just like needles were being jabbed in them - I had
to droop my eyelids" (B-710). Actor Reginald Gardiner noted,
"I've wondered if Ann Sheridan isn't perhaps the one woman in
the United States who doesn't know what 'Oomph' means. She
has the quality of a chum, not a sizzling siren" (B-639).
    The oomph publicity also resulted in some less
flattering press. Ann's sexy looks and vibrant personality
led to several encounters with jealous wives. On July 24,
1939, Zelma Dewar filed an affidavit concerning late alimony
payments from her ex-husband, director Frank D. Dewar. She
claimed Dewar lavished money on Ann Sheridan and her friend,
Gwendolyn Woodford, and took them to nightclubs, while he was
behind in his alimony (B-656).
    Oddly, oomph survived long after Ann Sheridan. During
the 1940s, North Hollywood was advertised on billboards as
"The Home of the 'Oomph Girl.'" On October 16, 1946, Justice
Sir Raymond Evershed ruled in London that the word be
admitted to Great Britain and Northern Ireland as a trademark
(B-347). In 1996, it continues to be used in commercials for
breakfast cereals. Ann resented the title and bitterly
fought against the publicity until she received a bit of
advice from actor Paul Muni. He told her to use the Oomph
Girl publicity to fight for better roles.

Shortly after the oomph campaign began, Ann received an interesting offer from producer David O. Selznick. In a memo to Warner Bros. executives Jack Warner and Hal Wallis dated April 10, 1939, casting director Steve Trilling revealed that Selznick wanted to borrow Ann for the role of Belle Watling in Gone with the Wind. According to author Rudy Behlmer, who examined the memos for his book Inside Warner Bros. (1935-1951), there was nothing in the files to indicate what happened with negotiations. It is not known if Selznick changed his mind about testing Ann or if Warner refused to loan his Oomph Girl after investing so much in publicizing her. The role was played by Ona Munson (B-88). Film historian James Robert Parish claimed director George Cukor interviewed Ann for the role of Scarlett O'Hara. Parish said Warner Bros. agreed to the interview because it showed Hollywood how much Ann's career had progressed (B-474).

Following Dodge City (F-47), Ann was announced for several Warner Bros. films which she did not make. American Family, mentioned during the summer of 1939, was recast with the Lane Sisters and released as Daughters Couragous (Warner Bros., 1939) (B-134). Three Cheers for the Irish (Warner Bros, 1939) first was heralded as a starring vehicle for Ann, Fred MacMurray, and Pat O'Brien. Priscilla Lane, Dennis Morgan, and Thomas Mitchell were in the final film. Career Man was supposed to co-star Ann and Jeffrey Lynn (B-104). Jane Bryan replaced Ann in Each Dawn I Die (Warner Bros., 1939) when a personal appearance tour kept her from the movie. Ann also was mentioned for the role of Panama in The Roaring Twenties (Warner Bros., 1939), but Gladys George was cast. Columbia wanted to borrow Ann for Golden Boy (1939), but ended up using Barbara Stanwyck (B-474). Ann also was announced for a Warner Bros. film whose title capitalized on the publicity. Variously reported as Oomph Girl and Umph Girl in the summer of 1939, and boasting twelve leading men, the movie was probably only a stunt to keep publicists busy while the studio found Ann a real project (B-134).

Ann next was seen in Naughty But Nice (F-48), a musical comedy released July 1, 1939. The movie stars Dick Powell and Gale Page as a songwriting team. Ann plays a sexy singer who tries to cash in on Powell's fame. She sings "Hooray for Spinach," "Corn Pickin'," "I Don't Believe in Signs," and "In a Moment of Weakness." Although Powell's role clearly is the lead, Ann receives top billing. It was more a nod to studio practicality than encouragement for Ann's career. Warner Bros. preferred promoting a rising contractee rather than Powell, who was making his last film for the studio.

Oddly, Warners initially did little to capitalize on Ann's Oomph Girl image on screen. It took a loan-out to producer Walter Wanger for Winter Carnival (F-49) to cast her as a glamorous star. Wanger had a reputation for creating sex symbols. His promotion helped the careers of Clara Bow, Hedy Lamarr, and Joan Bennett. Winter Carnival revolves around Dartmouth's annual event. Wanger cast Ann as a divorcee and former snow queen who returns to her alma mater and falls in love with her old boyfriend, a professor. Winter Carnival was released by United Artists on July 28,

1939. Wanger placed full-page ads, promoting Ann as "The
Number One Lady of Allure," at a cost of twenty-two thousand
dollars per advertisement (B-653). The New York Times
predicted, "You had better keep your eyes on Miss
Sheridan...since this is her first really big assignment
since she became known as the 'Oomph' girl" (July 28, 1939).
        Back at Warner Bros., Ann was reunited with Pat O'Brien
and Gale Page in Indianapolis Speedway (F-50). Released
August 5, 1939, the racing tale is a remake of The Crowd
Roars (Warner Bros., 1932), which had starred James Cagney
and Joan Blondell. Despite the wealth of oomph publicity,
Ann plays John Payne's wife, a supporting role. Critics were
quick to point out the lack-luster part she had.
        Warner Bros. tried to cash in on the success of Angels
With Dirty Faces (F-45) by reuniting some of the cast in a
low-budget but similarly titled film, The Angels Wash Their
Faces (F-51), released August 26, 1939. Ann plays Ronald
Reagan's girlfriend, but both players are upstaged by the
Dead End Kids.
        In September 1939, Ann's name was linked with two movies
which did not materialize for her. The cast of Dodge City
(F-47) planned to reunite in a sequel about the Nevada silver
mines entitled Virginia City (Warner Bros., 1940).
Although Ann initially was announced to join Errol Flynn,
Olivia de Havilland, Alan Hale, Big Boy Williams, Donald
Crisp, and Frank McHugh in the western, she was not in the
film (B-182). According to Flynn biographer Peter Valenti,
Ann originally was scheduled to be Flynn's leading lady in
Virginia City, but the script was rewritten. The role
ultimately went to Miriam Hopkins (B-686).
        A few weeks later, the Hollywood Reporter announced
Tough Angels was being rushed into production. In addition
to Ann, Warner Bros. planned to use contractees Priscilla
Lane, Rosemary Lane, Jane Bryan, and Jane Wyman in a tale of
air hostesses and the rigorous training they received at a
Chicago flight school. Robert Fellowes was set to produce.
The studio had high aspirations for financial success, as the
film had a relatively low budget (B-697). The melodrama was
released as Flight Angels in 1940, with Jane Wyman,
Virginia Bruce, Dennis Morgan, and Wayne Morris heading the
cast and Edmund Grainger producing.
        Warner Bros. decided to test Ann's popularity by sending
her on a personal appearance tour in the fall of 1939. En
route to Washington, D.C. and New York, Ann stopped in
Chicago to appear at an American Legion convention, where she
presided over the week-long festivities as "Sweetheart of the
Legion" and led a fifteen-hour parade (P-4). After trying
out her act on conventioneers, she opened at Washington's
Earle Theatre on September 29, 1939 and at New York's Strand
Theatre on October 6, 1939 (P-5). Ann promoted Warner Bros.
films by singing songs from Naughty But Nice (F-48), as
well as The Roaring Twenties (Warner Bros., 1939). The
studio sent postcards to fan club members and contest
entrants, hoping to draw a crowd for her arrival at Grand
Central Station. According to the New York Times, over a
thousand fans were present (B-136). When Ann was not busy
filming, she returned to New York for modeling assignments.
        Back in Hollywood, Ann starred in Castle on the Hudson

(F-52) with John Garfield. The prison picture, which was a remake of 20,000 Years in Sing Sing (Warner Bros., 1933), was released February 10, 1940. Ann plays Garfield's girlfriend, a nightclub singer. Her role was played by Bette Davis in the original. Movie-Radio Guide reported, "Ann is at her acting best in this" (April 27, 1940).

In a 1940 interview, Ann claimed the nicest thing that had happened to her in Hollywood was being cast in It All Came True (F-53), a project Bette Davis rejected. It marked the first time Ann received star billing with her name above the title and she was grateful to Jack Warner and Hal Wallis for having faith in her (B-637). Warner Bros. paid Louis Bromfield fifty thousand dollars for the comic story, which casts Ann and Jeffrey Lynn as an aspiring singer and composer whose mothers plot to unite them. Humphrey Bogart is a gangster who threatens their plans. When the feature first was announced in 1939, James Stewart was to play Lynn's role (B-104). The musical gave Ann a chance to sing "Gaucho Serenade" and "Angel in Disguise." The New York Times praised her contralto voice, noting, "...although its range is narrow, Miss Sheridan is quite at home on it" (April 6, 1940). Despite the notices, the movie was a disappointment at the box office.

Ann's career continued to be based more on publicity than acting credits. One such stunt occurred at a preview of It All Came True (F-53). On April 2, 1940, Dick Brunnenkamp, a nineteen-year-old UCLA junior, handcuffed himself to Ann in the theatre lobby and swallowed the key. A locksmith was located and Ann was released within fifteen minutes. Brunnenkamp claimed he did the stunt on a dollar bet from his fraternity house, but some journalists questioned his motives (B-347). The story proved to be harmless publicity for Ann's first starring role.

Ann received more press when the Harvard Lampoon named her the actress least likely to succeed in March 1940. Ann was quick to defend herself in the press, citing that the average Harvard graduate earned less than $5,000 a year, twenty-five years after graduation, while she earned about $100,000 a year, seven years out of North Texas State Teachers College. Harvard responded by saying that if Ann's earnings were that high, "it is further proof of public gullibility" (B-358). Others took advantage of the publicity. Four coeds from Radcliffe picketed the Lampoon office (B-190). The New Jersey Assembly was quick to name Ann an honorary daughter of New Jersey and sister of Princeton, Harvard's longtime rival, and invited her to attend the next Princeton-Harvard game (B-278). Later, Harvard tried to make up with Ann. In 1941, the school's literary journal, The Advocate, named her an honorary editor and invited her to the Advocate's seventy-fifth anniversary Punch banquet on November 20, where she would be inducted into office (B-46).

Torrid Zone (F-54) reunited Ann with James Cagney and Pat O'Brien. It marked her second starring role at Warner Bros. and it proved much more successful than It All Came True (F-53). Released May 25, 1940, Torrid Zone mixes fast-paced comedy with melodrama in a tale about an Honduran banana plantation. Ann plays a nightclub singer who gets

involved with Cagney, the plantation foreman. She sings "Mi
Caballero." She proves her comic abilities with her quick
repartee with Cagney and O'Brien. The New York Times was
surprised by Ann's ability to keep up with her co-stars.
"...Ann Sheridan steps up a notch or two in our
estimation...," the newspaper reported. "...if the males are
two-fisted, Miss Sheridan meets them blow for blow, line for
line" (May 18, 1940).
     Ann's next Warner Bros. film was They Drive by Night
(F-55), released August 3, 1940. The plot centers around the
trucking business and how it affects two brothers, George
Raft and Humphrey Bogart. Ann plays Raft's girlfriend.
Although Ann had appeared in four of Raft's films, dating
back to 1934's Bolero (F-2), They Drive by Night marked
the first time they had played opposite each other. Both the
Hollywood Reporter (July 9, 1940) and Variety (July 10,
1940) called Ann's performance "okay," noting that Ida
Lupino's acting overshadowed her work. To publicize the
movie, Warner Bros. arranged dates for Ann and George Raft
(B-475).
     Ann was reunited with James Cagney in City for
Conquest (F-56), released September 21, 1940. Cagney plays
a fighter who is injured while trying to win back the
affections of his girlfriend, Ann. The Pittsburgh
Post-Gazette [PA] noted that she "gets something more than
just oomph into her role" (October 4, 1940).
     Ann's personal life was taking a new turn. Following
her divorce from Eddie Norris, she often was seen on the town
with actors Cesar Romero, David Niven, Allan Jones, and
Frederick Brisson, as well as directors Anatole Litvak and
Jean Negulesco. However, she was not involved in a serious
romance until she met actor George Brent in November 1939.
The studio arranged a date as a publicity stunt. Within six
months, the actors were dating steadily. Ann and George
seemed the direct antithesis of each other. George was known
as a moody loner who disliked strangers and valued his
privacy. Ann's outgoing personality and casual, laid-back
style seemed ill-suited to him. The press speculated about
whether their opposite personalities would compliment each
other.
     George Brent was born George B. Nolan on March 3, 1904
in Shannonsbridge, Ireland. He came to the United States in
1915, but returned to Dublin to work with the famed stage
troupe the Abbey Players. He settled in the United States in
the 1920s, working mostly on stage. After making several
early talkies, he was signed by Warner Bros. in 1932. Among
his best known films were Jezebel (1938), Dark Victory
(1939), and The Old Maid (1939), all with Bette Davis. By
the time he began dating Ann, he had been divorced three
times. His first marriage, to actress Helen Campbell, lasted
about a month. He spent two years with actress Ruth
Chatterton. His marriage to Constance Worth reportedly ended
during the honeymoon. In between marriages, his name was
linked with many actresses, including Loretta Young, Greta
Garbo, and Bette Davis.
     Warner Bros. took full advantage of Ann and George's
affair by casting them in Honeymoon for Three (F-57).
George is a womanizing novelist; Ann plays the faithful

secretary who catches him in the end. <u>Variety</u> noted,
"[Ann] Sheridan has plenty of [sex appeal], but as a
secretary who has a job on her hands in [George] Brent she
plays it in subdued fashion" (February 12, 1941). By the
time the comedy was released on January 18, 1941, Ann was in
the midst of a controversy with the studio, which kept her
off the screen until the fall of 1941. The dispute concerned
salary, as well as her lack of control over her roles.
     Several projects did not materialize during this time.
Ann turned down ten thousand dollars to work for producer
Billy Rose at the San Francisco exposition during the summer
of 1940 (B-57). In August 1940, Ann was announced for <u>Maid
in Havana</u>, a film about two American hoofers in Cuba.
George Raft was supposed to be her co-star (B-239). The
movie was not made.
     Ann likened the Warner Bros. players to a big family.
She often found herself playing opposite the same actors and
made a point of befriending the crew as well. "We laughed
while we worked," she recalled. "We even laughed at
ourselves and at the script. But everybody had trouble with
the front office" (B-210). The studio was notorious for
fighting with its actors over contract disputes. In 1936,
Bette Davis took Warner Bros. to court and fled to England,
losing the case but gaining better roles. In the late 1930s,
Kay Francis was humiliated by being cast in "B" pictures to
play out her contract. James Cagney, Priscilla Lane, and Ida
Lupino all took studio suspension rather than accepting films
they disliked. In the 1940s, Olivia de Havilland won a
landmark case against the studio, prohibiting them from
tacking additional time onto a seven-year contract if the
actor went on suspension.
     Ann's troubles with Warner Bros. came to a head in the
summer of 1940. Just as the studio was at a loss over what
to do with their Oomph Girl, they also were reluctant to give
her a raise. Though Ann began as a $75-a-week contract
player, working her way up to $350-a-week after several
options on her contract, she felt her salary had not risen
proportionately with her fame. After the oomph campaign, her
salary rose to $500-a-week, but two years were added to her
contract. By August 1940, her salary was $600-a-week, a sum
she felt was inequitable, considering the profits her films
were making (B-586). Her next raise was due April 1, 1941,
and it would increase her salary to only $750-a-week.
Although the studio offered a $250 bonus, Ann went on strike
in the fall of 1940.
     The gesture was a direct result of the oomph campaign.
Ann hated the publicity and felt that the studio was taking
advantage of her. She wanted more control over choosing her
roles without risking suspension every time she disliked a
script. She refused to make <u>The Strawberry Blonde</u> (Warner
Bros., 1941) and demanded that Warner Bros. increase her
salary to two thousand dollars a week. The studio offered
one thousand dollars, which Ann refused, accusing Warners of
trying to starve her. They put her on suspension,
threatening to prevent her from working elsewhere until her
contract ran out in five years. The strike proved to be a
break for Rita Hayworth, who was cast in <u>The Strawberry
Blonde</u> (B-458). Ann admitted that her inability to

compromise with the studio was partially stubbornness.
However, she said, "I couldn't do otherwise and keep my
self-respect" (B-99).

Although Ann's refusal to make The Strawberry Blonde
generally is credited for motivating the strike, another film
also influenced her decision. During the spring of 1940,
Jerry Wald prepared a script for Calamity Jane with Ann in
mind. The project seemed a natural for the girl from Texas
who loved to ride and have fun. However, in June, the
project was turned over to Bette Davis (B-661). Despite
Ann's protests, Davis was queen of the studio and had more
clout in controling her roles. The film eventually was
canceled. In 1953, Doris Day starred in a musical version
of Calamity Jane for Warner Bros.

Ann spent her free time traveling to Texas, relaxing,
and cruising on George Brent's yacht. In December 1940, Ann
offered the studio a compromise. She would return to work
for $1,500 a week, with permission to make one non-Warners
film a year, or $1,750 a week for her exclusive services.
Additionally, Ann insisted that Warner Bros. pay her
four-month salary of $9,600, since she had not received the
notice of suspension that the studio sent (B-8). Despite
negotiations with Ann's agent, Myron Selznick, the strike
lasted six months. Ann returned to work on March 14, 1941,
settling for her original $600-a-week salary. After forty
weeks, her agent could renegotiate (B-458). Ann estimated
that she lost $25,000 in radio appearances and $200,000 in
personal appearances during the strike (B-586). Under her
new agreement, Ann had to take the good with the bad.
Although Ann was promised the dramatic role of Randy in
Kings Row (F-60), first she had to star in a patriotic
musical comedy.

Navy Blues (F-59) was Ann's first movie following the
strike. Released in September 1941, the musical stars Martha
Raye, Jack Haley, and Jack Oakie. Ann plays a singer who
convinces a sailor to reenlist and help her friends win an
artillery contest. Although there is some debate over
whether Ann did her own singing, she appears to perform three
numbers: "Navy Blues," "In Waikiki," and "You're a Natural."
The critics praised her hula, but found the plot implausible.
Ann disliked the musical, a fact the New York World
Telegram pointed out in their review, noting, "...Sheridan
couldn't be any more bored by it all then the spectator"
(September 20, 1941). Ann's next project would make up for
the humiliation of Navy Blues.

Ann first heard about Kings Row (F-61) from Humphrey
Bogart, who advised her to fight for the role of Randy. She
read the Henry Bellamann novel during her strike. Like Grace
Metalious's 1956 small town expose Peyton Place,
Bellamann's controversial book seemed unlikely screen
material, since it dealt with sadism, greed, euthanasia,
promiscuity, and incest. Ann decided Randy was worth a fight
and she ultimately settled her contract dispute so that she
could be in the film. Her reasons for wanting the role were
more than recognizing a meaty part. "Kings Row symbolized
all the hypocrisy and narrow-mindedness I had hated and
fought against in Denton," she recalled in 1966 (B-222). The
film centers on the relationships in a small town. Ann plays

a girl from the wrong side of the tracks who marries a
formerly wealthy playboy, played by Ronald Reagan. Kings
Row was released in April 1942. Critics praised Ann's
dramatic work. Variety called it "one of her most
effective performances thus far" (December 24, 1941).
Liberty noted that Ann was "extremely fine" (January 24,
1942). The Los Angeles Times said, "Her portrayal of Randy
is notably one of her best,...frought with rare sincerity"
(April 2, 1942). The film was nominated for three Academy
Awards and it remains Ann's most acclaimed role.
     Warner Bros. was intent on keeping their stars busy.
Since Ann had been away from the screen for so long, they
were anxious to cast her in as many movies as possible.
Subsequently, Ann found herself shooting the very serious
Kings Row (F-61) at the same time she was playing a comic
role in The Man Who Came to Dinner (F-60). Although she
often had to change costumes, makeup, hairstyles, and
characterizations for two very different parts on the same
day, she was paid her standard salary.
     The Man Who Came to Dinner (F-60) is based on the
Broadway comedy by George S. Kaufman and Moss Hart. Released
January 24, 1942, the movie revolves around an egocentric
critic who takes over the home of an Ohio family after he
falls on their icy steps. Ann plays a flamboyant actress
whom the critic calls to break up his secretary's romance
with a local newsman. Kaufman and Hart based many of their
characters on real celebrities. Ann's Lorraine Sheldon
reportedly had her origins in Gertrude Lawrence. Although
the role is a supporting one, Warner Bros. production
supervisor Hal Wallis insisted Ann appear to boost the film's
box office potential. The New York Times said Ann gave "a
tartly mannered performance" (January 2, 1942). The comedy
marks the only time Ann worked with her acting idol Bette
Davis on screen.
     In 1941, a caricature of Ann appeared in Hollywood
Steps Out (F-58), a Warner Bros. Merrie Melodies cartoon
spoofing many celebrities.
     Following the attack of Pearl Harbor, the studios
rallied to make patriotic war films. On December 22, 1941,
Ann and Dennis Morgan were announced for Aloha Means
Goodbye, a romantic drama about Japanese spy activities in
the Pacific (B-540). The film was canceled. In 1941, Ann
and Morgan also were mentioned for the leads in Saratoga
Trunk. Ann tested for the role, but she was not cast. She
did not photograph well in a blonde wig and her attempts at a
French accent clashed with her Texas drawl (B-475). The
feature was filmed in 1943 with Ingrid Bergman and Gary
Cooper, but was not released until 1945.
     The press often speculated that Ann and George Brent
were secretly married during their two-year courtship. The
couple was engaged twice before a wedding materialized.
Ironically, many columnists believed they permanently had
broken their engagement by the end of 1941. After a Mexican
elopement fell through, the couple outsmarted the press and
traveled separately to Palm Beach, Florida. On January 5,
1942, they were married by County Judge Richard Robbins at
the home of George's sister, China Harris, the widow of
Broadway producer Sam H. Harris. Ann wore a champagne tulle

dinner gown and a white mantilla that belonged to her
grandmother. They had a brief honeymoon in Palm Springs,
thanks to Warner Bros., who wanted the newlyweds back at work
within a week to start work on Shadow of Their Wings
(released as Wings for the Eagle, F-63) and The Gay
Sisters (Warner Bros., 1942). The Brents moved into
George's Toluca Lake home, planning to find a larger house
when his lease expired. Unfounded rumors soon circulated
that the Brents were expecting a baby in October 1942 (B-20).
     Following the success of Kings Row (F-61), Warner
Bros. decided to reteam Ann and Ronald Reagan in Juke Girl,
released May 30, 1942. In this drama set in the Florida
tomato fields, Ann plays a juke joint hostess, a euphemism
for prostitute to appease the censors. Critics praised Ann's
acting, but were less than pleased with the script of the
standard melodrama. The Los Angeles Times noted that the
performances were too good for the material (May 28, 1942).
     When the United States entered World War II, Ann was
anxious to do her part by entertaining the troops. However,
Warner Bros. was reluctant to let its glamour girl go
overseas. They kept promising Ann a U.S.O. army camp tour,
but nothing materialized. In March 1942, Ann finally got
permission to visit camps in Wyoming, Kansas, and Missouri as
part of the U.S.O.'s Funzafire unit (P-7). She vowed to wear
tight dresses and spike heels, no matter how uncomfortable
she felt, realizing that the soldiers wanted to see a pinup
girl in the flesh. And, unlike many stars, she wanted to
mingle with the privates rather than get the celebrity
treatment from officers (B-471).
     During the war, Ann also showed her patriotism by
working at the Hollywood Canteen, making sandwiches, dancing
with soldiers, and performing (P-8). She liked to poke fun
at her oomph image, playing stooge to Jack Carson and Dennis
Morgan and having them announce her as her friend, MGM
actress Ann Sothern (B-163). Humphrey Bogart claimed she
always sought out the shy, homely soldiers who seemed most
likely to be lost in the shuffle (B-101). Between films, the
studio sent Ann on bond drives with Ronald Reagan. On her
ranch, Ann tended a victory garden and raised her own eggs.
She appeared on Armed Forces Radio Service (AFRS) broadcasts,
like Mail Call (R-5 and R-10) and Command Performance
(R-8 and R-11), entertaining the troops. She also starred in
the Red Cross Roll Call trailer, Let's Carry On (F-67),
playing a Red Cross nurse.
     Intent on boosting morale, Warner Bros. cast Ann as a
defense plant worker in Wings for the Eagle (F-63),
released in July 1942. Partially shot at Lockheed Aircraft,
Wings for the Eagle is a domestic drama with a World War II
theme, as Ann's affections waver between her husband   (Jack
Carson) and his friend (Dennis Morgan). The New York Times
reported, "...Miss Sheridan continues to toss crisp retorts
like flapjacks" (August 1, 1942).
     In the months that followed, Ann was announced for two
films in which she was not cast. According to a memo to
casting director Steve Trilling dated February 14, 1942,
producer Hal Wallis suggested Ann to star opposite Humphrey
Bogart in Casablanca (B-88). Through the years, many
rumors surrounding the casting of the classic have surfaced,

with Ann, Ronald Reagan, and George Raft mentioned for the
roles played by Ingrid Bergman, Humphrey Bogart, and Paul
Henreid. It is assumed that Ann's name never went further
than the discussion stage. In May 1942, Warner Bros. planned
to loan Ann to Paramount for Texas Guinan, a musical
biography of the entertainer. In exchange, Paramount would
let Warner Bros. borrow Fred MacMurray for Princess
O'Rourke. However, within two weeks, the deal fell
through. Betty Hutton was cast in the Guinan story,
Incendiary Blonde (Paramount, 1945); Robert Cummings
starred in Princess O'Rourke (Warner Bros., 1943) (B-696).
    Ann returned to comedy with George Washington Slept
Here (F-64), released in November 1942. Based on the play
by George S. Kaufman and Moss Hart, the film chronicles the
adventures of a city couple who buy a dilapidated house in
the country. Although Olivia de Havilland originally was
announced for the role opposite Jack Benny, Ann proved an apt
foil for the comedian. They became friends off screen and
there were rumors that they had an affair (B-91). To promote
the film, Ann appeared on Benny's radio program on May 3,
1942 (R-4). The pair also appeared on the AFRS broadcast
Mail Call (R-5) and a War Department adaptation of George
Washington Slept Here in 1944 (R-9). Ann and Benny
co-starred on two additional radio shows in the 1940s: a 1943
dramatization of "Love Is News" on The Lady Esther Screen
Guild Theatre (R-6) and a 1945 episode of The Jack Benny
Show (R-13).
    Another war theme was developed in Edge of Darkness
(F-65), released by Warner Bros. on April 24, 1943. The plot
concerns a Norwegian resistance group's efforts to fight the
Nazi occupation. Ann co-stars with Errol Flynn, with whom
she was rumored to have had an affair. Harrison's Reports
called Ann and Flynn's performances in Edge of Darkness
"inspired" (March 27, 1943).
    Ann continued to be a favorite with the media in 1943.
The Hollywood Women's Press Club awarded her their Golden
Apple for being the most cooperative actress in Hollywood
(B-50). Her likeness appeared in paint books, juvenile
novels, and paper dolls. Cole Porter mentioned her in the
lyrics of "See That You're Born in Texas" in the Broadway
musical Something for the Boys. As he noted famous
citizens from the Lone Star state, he asked "Say, in a
sweater, who looks better than Missus Sheridan's Ann?"
    Things were less than idyllic on the homefront and the
Brents' marriage began to disintegrate. In the beginning,
Ann had praised George's attentiveness. She vowed that they
would remain happy in their careers and home life, despite
dour predictions from columnists who claimed the stars were
polar opposites. "Too many people lose the things that
brought them together because they try to change each other
the moment the knot is tied," she said. "We aren't going to
let that happen to us" (B-341). On September 28, 1942, Ann
announced their separation and she moved back into her ranch
house in Reseda, California. Although a Warner Bros.
spokesman was quick to point out that there were no plans for
divorce, by October 13, Ann had retained a Las Vegas
attorney. She planned to start divorce proceedings as soon
as she finished filming Edge of Darkness (F-65), however

other movie commitments postponed the suit (B-60). She told
Movieland, "The next time I love, I'm going to make sure my
partner likes me as I am and likes to do the things I like to
do. Whoever wrote that opposites attract was off the beam!"
(B-589).

Sources conflict over the cause of the Brents' breakup.
Some blame it on George's flying. After trying to enlist in
the Air Corps and being turned down because of his age, he
became a civilian flight instructor in Oxnard, California.
According to several sources, Ann worried about him, since
his private plane crashed shortly after he sold it to another
pilot. There were rumors about George and Hungarian actress
Ilona Massey, as well as that he resumed an affair with Bette
Davis while married to Ann (B-475).

At first, Ann claimed it was their diverse careers which
kept them apart (B-341). Later, she said George tried to
change her, becoming possessive and prohibiting her from
seeing her friends. "I thought he wanted me 'as is,' but as
soon as I said 'I do,' it was different somehow," Ann
recalled. "Superficial things, personal habits, and
mannerisms can be changed. BUT YOU CAN'T CHANGE WHAT YOU
ARE" (B-589). According to former Warner Bros. messenger
Stuart Jerome, Ann told Louella Parsons, "Brent bent"
(B-277).

There also were rumors that Errol Flynn was behind the
Brents' breakup. Several 1942 articles claim that the
marriage ended abruptly after George unexpectedly returned to
Hollywood and found Ann had moved out of their home. It was
rumored that George visited Ann on location during the
filming of Edge of Darkness (F-65) and found his wife in
bed with her co-star. The two actors got into a fight, with
Flynn the victor. Several sources report that Ann was
involved with Flynn after her separation from George. While
she was in Mexico obtaining her divorce, Errol was there on
vacation (B-589). Louella Parsons played up the rumors in
her column, speculating whether Ann would wed Errol when her
divorce was final. She reminded readers that Ann also had
denied a relationship with George Brent before their
elopement (B-480). In Flynn's autobiography, he implies that
an affair helped advance Ann's career, but does not mention
the Edge of Darkness incident (B-177). In the 1960s, Ann
insisted that she and Flynn were strictly friends (B-206).

In 1966, with the perspective of wisdom and time, Ann
commented on her divorces from Edward Norris and George
Brent. "With both men, there was no honesty between us," she
recalled. "And if two people living together can't be
honest, then I don't want it" (B-222). She was more succinct
in an interview printed after her death. "I can't stand my
ex-husband [George Brent]," she said. "If I could, I'd still
be married to him" (B-212).

Ann hoped to go overseas on a U.S.O. tour before
embarking on another film, however producer Mark Hellinger
convinced her to appear in an all-star revue, Thank Your
Lucky Stars (F-66), released in September 1943. Warner
Bros. continued their efforts to boost morale, as the thin
plot strings together a cache of musical numbers by an
unlikely array of Warner Bros. stars. Eddie Cantor plays
dual roles as he helps struggling singer Dennis Morgan and

songwriter Joan Leslie crash a charity show. Ann sings "Love
Isn't Born, It's Made." After filming her number for <u>Thank
Your Lucky Stars</u>, Ann flew to Mexico on December 10, 1942
to obtain a divorce. She leased a house in Cuernavaca,
Mexico City, and vacationed with secretary/companion
Gwendolyn Woodford while she waited for the sixteen-day
divorce to become final. Ironically, the divorce was
obtained on January 5, 1943, a year from the date the Brents
eloped.

    After the war, George Brent free-lanced, making such
films as <u>Luxury Liner</u> (MGM, 1948) and <u>Death of a
Scoundrel</u> (RKO, 1956). For many years, he raised horses.
In 1947, he married Janet Michael, with whom he had a son and
a daughter. He died of emphysema on May 26, 1979.

    In late 1942, Ann continued to be announced for movies
that did not materialize. Following the completion of <u>Edge
of Darkness</u> (F-65), Ann and Dennis Morgan were supposed to
star in <u>The Time Between</u>. It was not filmed (B-142). Ann
also was mentioned for <u>A Night at Tony Pastor's</u>, later
known as <u>The Gay Nineties</u>. Jack Chertok planned to direct
the nostalgic look at show business (B-699). <u>Night Shift</u>
was announced for Ann in 1943, following the release of
<u>Thank Your Lucky Stars</u>, but it also was canceled (B-379).
Although there were rumors that she would appear in the
patriotic musical <u>This Is the Army</u> (Warner Bros., 1943), it
is assumed that her role went to Joan Leslie.

    Ann's next movie was <u>Shine On Harvest Moon</u> (F-68), a
musical biography of songwriters/vaudevillians Nora Bayes and
Jack Norworth, released April 8, 1944. The film reunited her
with Dennis Morgan and Jack Carson, but was more fiction than
fact. Although critics praised Ann's singing, her voice was
dubbed by Lynn Martin. Wartime restrictions hampered the use
of color stock, therefore the movie primarily was shot in
black and white, with a ten-minute Technicolor finale. While
this was a novelty when it was used in 1930s films like <u>Kid
Millions</u> (United Artists, 1934), this single color sequence
looks more like a last-minute afterthought.

    Ann rejected the lead in <u>Hollywood Canteen</u> (Warner
Bros., 1944), another wartime extravaganza. The plot centers
around a soldier who falls in love with a star he meets at
the canteen. Ann insisted the premise was an insult to GIs.
She argued that it would lead enlisted men to falsely believe
they could marry celebrities after a brief encounter. Joan
Leslie replaced her (B-475).

    Ann's next film was <u>The Doughgirls</u> (F-69), released in
November 1944. Based on the play by Joseph A. Fields, the
plot centers on four women sharing a hotel bridal suite due
to the wartime housing shortage. Ann co-stars with Jane
Wyman, Alexis Smith, and Eve Arden. Ann had seen the play in
New York and refused to make the movie, insisting that no
role was appropriate for her and worrying that the censors
would cut much of the suggestive script. Warner Bros.
threatened to suspend her if she refused. At the urging of
producer Mark Hellinger, Ann relented. Despite her initial
objections, the critics praised the light comedy. <u>The
Hollywood Reporter</u> noted that Ann "toss[ed] off her lines
with a flair" (August 30, 1944).

    Ann's objections to making <u>The Doughgirls</u> were

dependent on another factor: she wanted to go overseas to
entertain the troops. "I have such a feeling that everyone
of us should be over there, that I just won't make another
picture until I get my way," she vowed. "I will regret it
all my days if I don't have a part in helping lick Hitler and
put Japan in its place" (B-484). Warner Bros. was reluctant
to let its Oomph Girl leave the country, but finally
relented.

In 1944, Ann went on an eight-week U.S.O. tour,
entertaining troops in the China-Burma-India circuit (P-9).
Comedians Ben Blue and Jackie Miles, dancer Mary Landa, and
accordionist Ruth Dennis accompanied her on the sixty
thousand-mile trip. Ann sang "Amor," "Besame Mucho," and
"I'll Be Seeing You," and performed in a comedy skit with
Blue. The group did two shows a day, in addition to making
special visits to hospitals. Although she lost fifteen
pounds during the rigorous tour, Ann was enthusiastic about
performing for the troops. "Gee, it was swell," she told
reporters upon her return on September 6, 1944. "Only
getting back after a trip like ours isn't the big thrill that
it might be, because you wish your own homecoming could be
shared by all those men overseas" (B-194).

Much controversy sprang from the CBI tour. Newsweek
reported on an editorial in the Army newspaper Roundup,
which criticized the celebrities who toured the battlefronts.
The editorial complained about the entertainers "who turn up
in CBI with accompanying ballyhoo, stay around just long
enough to send out their laundry, and then truck off for
home" (B-205). The chief culprits were Ann Sheridan, Joe E.
Brown, Paulette Goddard, Joel McCrea, and Al Jolson, all of
whom took time to respond to the accusations. Ann offered to
"fight boy-fashion, no holds barred, with anybody who thinks
I...dogged it in the overseas theater" (B-205). A letter to
the editor of Newsweek complained about a radio broadcast
in which a tired, thinner Ann said, "I never want to go back
to CBI." Three corporals argued that all they saw of her was
a publicity picture in their theatre paper (B-455). Newsreel
footage of Ann's C.B.I. tour was included in Overseas
Roundup (F-70), a Vitaphone short released March 17, 1945.

Movie audiences next saw Ann in a project that had a
troubled history. Although One More Tomorrow (F-71) was
not released until June 1, 1946, shooting had begun in 1943,
before Ann made Shine On Harvest Moon (F-68). One More
Tomorrow was a reworking of Philip Barry's play The Animal
Kingdom, which had been filmed by RKO in 1932. Ann Harding
played her role in the 1932 version. Ann Sheridan was cast
opposite Dennis Morgan in a romance about a playboy editor
and a leftist photographer and their journalistic ideals.
The set was shut down shortly after filming began when
producer Benjamin Glazer failed to get Production Code
approval. When shooting resumed, both producer Glazer and
director Irving Rapper had been replaced by Henry Blanke and
Peter Godfrey. One More Tomorrow finished filming in
November 1943, but Warner Bros. delayed its release for two
and a half years. Although this was not an uncommon practice
during World War II, when the studio made an overload of
productions, it was apparent that Warner Bros. lacked
confidence in the picture. By the time it was released on

June 1, 1946, supporting players Jane Wyman and Jack Carson
were rising stars. They were top billed on many theatre
marquees rather than Ann and Dennis Morgan (B-369). The
critics praised Ann's looks more than her acting, though the
Hollywood Reporter noted that she "lends all the warmth she
can to her characterization" (May 14, 1946).

During the interim, Ann appeared on many radio programs,
including Burns and Allen (R-7), The Show Goes On (R-12),
Let Yourself Go (R-15), The Raleigh Room (R-16), and
Time to Smile (R-17). Ann's Oomph Girl image was given
gentle parody in the Warner Bros. Merrie Melodies cartoon
Hollywood Daffy (F-72), released June 22, 1946. Daffy Duck
sees Ann, Bette Davis, Bing Crosby, and other stars.

Meanwhile, Ann was concentrating on her personal life
and having more problems with the studio. During the summer
of 1943, she met press agent Steve Hannagan in New York.
Although he was fifteen years her senior and spent most of
his time on the east coast, they soon became a couple. Steve
was a well-known show business figure whose publicity schemes
had established Sun Valley, Idaho and Miami Beach, Florida as
celebrity getaways. His other clients included the Union
Pacific Railroad, the Stork Club, Coca-Cola, and the
Indianapolis Speedway. Steve was twice divorced: from Ruth
Ellery and from model Suzanne Brewster. Ann nicknamed him
O'Toole. Despite their bi-coastal work commitments, the
couple managed to date in New York and Los Angeles. They
spent time at Steve's Park Avenue apartment, his farm in
Connecticut, and his villa in Florida. In June 1944, Steve
began handling publicity for Jack Benny's radio program.

Ann began a second strike from Warner Bros. in December
1944. She refused to make A Night at Tony Pastor's, which
first had been offered in 1942. Dissatisfied with the
scripts she was given, she went on suspension. "I just
couldn't see myself acting in a certain grade of films any
more," she explained. "It isn't that I want a particular
kind of role for myself; it is simply that I do want to be in
good pictures" (B-538).

During her strike, Ann turned down the lead in Mildred
Pierce (Warner Bros., 1945). The film won Joan Crawford an
Oscar and revitalized her career. A biography of composer
Vincent Youmans, entitled Sometimes (Un)Happy, did not
materialize (B-475).

Ann spent her time traveling with Steve Hannagan. She
also journeyed to Mexico, which had been her home away from
home since her 1943 divorce. Ann always had felt an affinity
to Mexico and its people. She learned to speak Spanish as a
child in Texas. She admired the less hectic pace and dreamed
of living there permanently someday. Around 1943, she was
given some land at Nautla, a village on the Gulf Coast near
Vera Cruz, and planned to build a cottage there (B-632). She
became an honorary Mexican citizen and spent most of her
studio vacations there. In the mid 1940s, there were rumors
that Ann was romantically involved with Oscar Brooke, who
worked for Warner Bros. in Mexico (B-725). During a 1947
visit, she toured Estudios Tepeyac, Mexico City's film
studios, with Warner Bros. Mexican executive Michael Sokol
and Estudios Tepeyac head Ted Gildreth. The Mexican studio
offered her several films, but she had to turn them down

because of her Warner Bros. contract (B-18).

Ann also lost her mother during her strike. Lula
Sheridan died in Fort Worth, Texas on· January 27, 1946.

After eighteen months, Ann and the studio patched up
their differences with the help of Steve Hannagan. He hired
Washington trust-buster Thurman Arnold as Ann's attorney.
With Arnold's expert legal advice and power behind her, Ann
convinced Warner Bros. to give her a raise and. script
approval. She agreed to make six films over a three-year
period. In 1947, Hedda Hopper called Ann's strike the
"long-distance star suspension hold-out record" (B-254).

Ann's first feature under her new contract was The
Sentence, released as Nora Prentiss (F-74) on February
22, 1947. Ann plays a singer who is involved with a married
doctor who fakes his own death to be with Ann. The role
allows her to sing "Who Cares What People Say?" and "Would
You Like a Souvenir?" Reviews criticized the credibility of
the story, but praised Ann's acting. The Los Angeles Daily
News said Ann "plays her with complete honesty to the last
moment" (February 22, 1947). Movies noted, "Ann Sheridan,
looking like a million, and talented Kent Smith play the
leads in this well-acted and unusual story" (March 1947).

After settling her dispute with Warner Bros., Ann was
announced for another film in 1946. She told Sheilah Graham
that she would play a Mexican trollop in Serenade, based on
a story by James M. Cain (B-201). Vincent Sherman recalled
that producer Jerry Wald brought the idea to him, with Ann
and Dennis Morgan in mind for the starring roles. Sherman
immediatly questioned the studio's excitement over the
property, since it was filled with censorship problems. A
male singer becomes involved with an older, homosexual man
and his voice changes. The singer runs away to Mexico, where
he has an affair with a prostitute and regains his vocal
skill. Upon his return, he meets the older man again, but
the Mexican woman kills him. To appease the censors, the
story underwent major rewrites, changing the homosexual to a
female. Ann's character became the villainous other woman.
Warner Bros. abandoned the project at that time and Sherman
helped the studio rush The Unfaithful (F-75) into
production (B-298). In a 1960s interview, Ann said that she
repeatedly turned down Serenade because it cast her as a
Mexican woman (B-206). Ten years later, Warner Bros.
reworked Serenade for Mario Lanza and Joan Fontaine.
Sarita Montiel played the role initially intended for Ann.

Ann returned to the screen in The Unfaithful (F-75),
released July 5, 1947. Loosely based on W. Somerset
Maugham's The Letter, which Warner Bros. had filmed in 1940
with Bette Davis, The Unfaithful comments on the
readjustments that returning soldiers and their wives were
making after World War II. Ann plays a wartime wife who
kills an intruder and must deal with complications that arise
when her husband learns she cheated while he was overseas.
The adultery angle initially caused some problems with the
censors, since they believed Ann's character should be
punished. Writer James Gunn resolved the dilemma by pointing
out the evils of divorce (B-715). The press heralded the
film's treatment of a sensitive subject and Ann's portrayal
of the troubled wife. The Los Angeles Evening Herald

called her performance "realistic and poignant" (June 26,
1947). The Hollywood Citizen-News noted that Ann was
"unusually good in a very exciting part" (June 26, 1947).
Variety said, "Miss Sheridan clicks strongly as the wife,
giving a performance that rings true and that will earn her
most favorable mention" (May 28, 1947).

During the filming of The Unfaithful (F-75), Ann was
announced for another project: Flamingo Road. Like
Serenade, this film was plagued by censorship problems.
Ann wanted the role of a fallen woman, which ultimately was
played by Joan Crawford when the movie was released in 1949
(B-243).

In 1947, Ann appeared on two episodes of the radio
series The Smiths of Hollywood (R-18 and R-19). After
making two dramatic films, she told Louella Parsons that she
wanted a comedic role that did not capitalize on her sexy
image. "I'm too old to be an 'oomph' girl any more," Ann
said. "You see, in the beginning, it was all right for me to
do stories of that kind, but I feel I must have benefitted by
my experience or I wouldn't still be on the screen after all
these years - so now I want to act" (B-479).

Ann loved to pull practical jokes on her friends.
Humphrey Bogart was a favorite target and he often repaid her
with stunts of his own. During the oomph campaign, he dubbed
her Miss Pushface of 1893, kidding the glamorous image. She
responded by giving him a Gene Autry toy gun to poke fun at
his gangster typecasting (B-101). Since Bogart had been
right about Kings Row (F-60), Ann was delighted when he
mentioned another project. "He told me the studio had bought
a new property and that I was a natural for the lead and that
I should go to Jack Warner if necessary to get the part," she
recalled. "I began spreading the word that I wanted the part
until somebody explained to me just who Fanny Hill was." The
idea was a practical joke Bogart pulled on his pal, knowing
full well the studio would never make a film about the
notorious madam. "He was a dirty rat, but I loved that man,"
Ann concluded (B-173).

Ann's next screen appearance was the result of a joke
she pulled on Bogart. Conspiring with writer/director John
Huston, Ann donned a padded black satin dress and a wig and
made a cameo appearance as a prostitute in The Treasure of
the Sierra Madre (F-76). The film was released on
January 24, 1948. Huston asked Bogart to reshoot a scene
with a bit player, set on a street of dives. When Bogart
turned to rebuff the hag who was propositioning him, he was
startled by a new piece of business. The actress dressed as
a prostitute lifted her skirt to reveal a painted tattoo with
a butterfly, a fee, and "Annie." He recognized his friend
and had a good laugh (B-262). Although Ann is pictured in
costume in Inside Warner Bros. (1935-1951), there is some
debate over whether the footage really was used in the film
(B-88). The close-ups are definitely another actress, but it
is possible that Ann is used in the long shots.

Ann still was discontent with the scripts being offered
at Warner Bros. She turned down several films, including
The Hasty Heart (Warner Bros., 1950) and Caged (Warner
Bros., 1950). Patricia Neal was cast as the army hospital
nurse in The Hasty Heart, while Eleanor Parker played the

role of the woman falsely imprisoned in <u>Caged</u>. Parker
received an Academy Award nomination for her work.
      Since Ann had a picture deal rather than a standard
contract, Warner Bros. could not suspend her for turning down
scripts. Instead, they loaned her to RKO for <u>Good Sam</u>
(F-78) in 1948. Gary Cooper plays a good Samaratin whose
excessive generosity almost ruins his family. Jean Arthur
was director Leo McCarey's first choice for Cooper's wife,
but she had conflicting contracts. When Arthur suggested
Ann, McCarey made a deal with Warner Bros. Although
audiences were not impressed with the chemistry between Ann
and Gary Cooper, her comic timing was showcased in the film
and it reminded her how her talents were being wasted at her
home studio. <u>The Hollywood Reporter</u> said, "Ann Sheridan
supplies vitality, curves and a loving sense of humor....The
way she tosses the glib lines is a joy to watch" (July 28,
1948). <u>Modern Screen</u> praised Ann's "delicious laugh"
(November 1948).
      <u>Silver River</u> (F-77) proved to be Ann's last film for
Warner Bros. Released May 29, 1948, the routine western
reunited her with Errol Flynn and the two enjoyed playing
practical jokes on the set. When a crew member's wife had a
baby, he passed out cigars to all the males. Ann feigned
jealousy and surprised Flynn by appearing in a scene with his
cigar between her lips. When Ann remarked that her wire
bustle looked like a bird cage, the next morning she found
two parrots in it (B-262). Director Raoul Walsh said her
antics sparked spontaneity in everyone on the set. There
were rumors that Ann and Flynn were drinking heavily
throughout filming and that Walsh demanded that Flynn remain
sober until 5:00 P.M. (B-88). <u>Silver River</u> was a comedown
for both Ann and Flynn after the classic <u>Dodge City</u> (F-47)
of a decade earlier. Critics disliked the film, with
<u>Variety</u> calling Ann's performance "competent" (May 5,
1948).
      Ann's option with Warner Bros. was set to expire on
January 8, 1949. Discontent with the roles being offered,
she bought out the final six months of her contract for
thirty-five thousand dollars in 1948. She wanted to find
better stories and felt the studio was not using her
properly. Ann did not resent the price of freedom, since she
soon was offered a role in <u>I Was a Male War Bride</u> (F-79).
However, she was unhappy with Warner Bros.'s policy toward
other actors. "What really burned me up...was that Barbara
Stanwyck was given her freedom from Warners' right afterwards
without paying one red cent," Ann lamented (B-264). Stanwyck
was released from the studio because they said they could not
find stories for her (B-206).
      In 1949, Ann was in the news again, battling with a new
studio. She had been set to star in <u>Carriage Entrance</u>, an
RKO film with Robert Young, but Young withdrew when the
script was rewritten to diminish his role. Ann maintained
that her contract had been violated when the script was
rewritten and another co-star cast. Although she okayed
several leading men that RKO suggested, the film was shelved
in August 1949 because of casting difficulties and Ann's
contract was terminated. A few months later, Ava Gardner and
Robert Mitchum were cast in the movie, which was released as

My Forbidden Past (RKO, 1951). Gardner was once the love
interest of studio head Howard Hughes, which may have
prompted her casting. On November 21, 1949, Ann sued RKO for
$350,000 damages, alleging breach of contract and bad faith,
and charging that Mitchum had been one of the actors she
approved. On February 6, 1951, a federal jury awarded her
$55,162, representing her salary during her five-month
contract with the studio, as well as interest and court costs
(B-66). The suit also led to Ann being cast in an alternate
RKO film, Appointment in Honduras (F-85) in 1953.
Meanwhile, Ann made a package deal with 20th Century-Fox for
two films: I Was a Male War Bride (F-79) and Stella
(F-80).

    Although I Was a Male War Bride (20th Century-Fox,
1949) turned out to be one of Ann's best comic performances,
the production was beset with problems. Cary Grant developed
yellow jaundice and, as a result, delayed location shooting
in Germany and England. Ann caught an intestinal flu,
pleurisy, and pneumonia, which led to a bronchial disorder
that plagued her for the rest of her life. The film had to
be completed on a Hollywood soundstage after the costly
delays due to the stars' illnesses. The comedy revolves
around a WAC lientenant (Ann) who marries a French army
officer (Grant). Complications ensue when the couple finds
immigration quotas are full and Grant must disguise himself
as a woman to get into the United States. Reviews noted the
chemistry between the stars. The New York Times called Ann
a "nice foil" for Grant (August 27, 1949).

    Audiences were less impressed with Stella (F-80), a
black comedy released in August 1950. In the incredible
plot, Ann helps her shiftless family cover up the accidental
death of a wealthy uncle, while insurance agents Victor
Mature and Leif Erickson vie for her affections. The New
York Times called her performance "competent," noting that
she had "a few sharp scenes with Victor Mature" (August 19,
1950).

    Around this time, Ann spoke of making an independent
film. She acquired the rights to Eleanore Griffin's Second
Lady, a drama with a political background. "We have no
final script and the details are all being ironed out by my
business manager, Andy Hickox," Ann explained in 1949. When
asked why she was considering an independent venture at that
point in her career, Ann said, "I liked the story. I bought
it, I own it and I'll make it" (B-541). Despite her valiant
words, the project never materialized. Ann also was
mentioned for the lead in Ricochet, a gangster story set to
co-star Macdonald Carey (B-249). The film was not made.

    Meanwhile, Ann began working in another medium:
television. On February 11, 1950, she made her TV debut on
the variety program The Ed Wynn Show (T-1). During the
next few years, she became a frequent television guest,
appearing on game shows, variety shows, and dramas, including
Stop the Music (T-2), The Kate Smith Evening Hour (T-3),
and The Colgate Comedy Hour (T-4).

    In 1950, Ann filmed Woman on the Run (F-81), an
independent production released by Universal-International.
In addition to playing the lead in Woman on the Run, she
was an unbilled co-producer. "It's not only the money

angle," she explained, "But it gives you a chance to have
some control over your own career - choose the type of story
you'd like to make, the players you'd like to work with"
(B-286). The film was shot on location in San Francisco and
concerns a wife's search for her estranged husband after he
witnesses a mob killing. The Hollywood Reporter called
Ann's work "excellent," noting, "She gets off her bitterly
flippant lines with finesse, at the same time getting over
her inner discontent" (October 4, 1950). Daily Variety
noted, "[Ann] Sheridan clicks solidly in a straight dramatic
role" (October 4, 1950).

In addition to her movie work, Ann was busy with radio
appearances. She was on The Chesterfield Supper Club
(R-20), Hollywood Calling (R-21), Anacin Hollywood Star
Theatre (R-22), Bill Stern's Colgate Sports Newsreel of
the Air (R-23), Edgar Bergen with Charlie McCarthy
(R-24), and The Big Show (R-25). In the early 1950s, she
also was a candidate for honorary mayor of Encino,
California, running against six male opponents (B-6).

During Ann's long distance affair with Steve Hannagan,
she continued to date other people. She enjoyed the
Hollywood nightlife, frequenting movie premieres and
nightclubs. She often was quoted as saying she had
camaraderie with men, but had few close women friends.
Many dates were studio-arranged to promote her current
projects. Ann's name was linked with set designer Jacques
Mapes, who later produced films with Ross Hunter, producers
Leonard Goldstein and William Cagney, disc jockey Johnny
Grant, and actors Clark Gable, John Conte, and Bruce Cabot.
Around 1951, Ann dated actor Jeff Chandler, who was then
going through a divorce. After he was seen with Ann at
parties, nightclubs, and premieres, the press speculated that
they were serious about each other, but the relationship
ended as quickly as it began (B-84).

Although the fan magazines liked to portray Ann as a
party girl in the 1950s, she also had a more serious side.
She was an active supporter of the Mickey Finn Foundation, a
Los Angeles group organized to keep underprivileged children
off the streets. After hearing about its founder, policeman
Mickey Finn, Ann became active with the organization in 1947.
She raised money, worked with the boys, and donated a station
wagon, a television, and cash, insisting that her acts be
kept secret. In 1950, her generosity was revealed when the
organization's donations slipped because of gang attacks.
Finn convinced her to talk about the group, realizing her
name would bring in the needed contributions (B-335). She
was on hand in December 1952, when the group opened a larger
youth center (P-13).

Despite Ann's public dates with other men, throughout
the 1950s there were consistent rumors that she would marry
Steve Hannagan. Some sources even claimed the couple was
secretly wed, a rumor they hotly denied. Ann told Hedda
Hopper that her two divorces had made her hesitant to
legalize her relationship with Steve. "Why marry and spoil a
perfect friendship?" Ann asked (B-254). When Ann and Steve
ended their romance in 1949, Ann said, "There wasn't a
divorce, so that should prove something" (B-632). Hopper
reported that she spoke to Steve after the split and he

confesssed that he was still very much in love with Ann.
"Maybe in our old age we'll be able to live in the same town
at the same time," he said (B-249).

Some reports claimed that Steve's mother, a devout
Catholic, did not want her son to marry a divorced woman
(B-84). This seems unlikely since Steve himself was twice
divorced. In a 1966 interview, Ann said it was her own
religious beliefs that kept her from marrying Steve (B-222).
Although she had been raised a southern Baptist, she admitted
that the hellfire and damnation of her childhood had scared
her away from organized religion in later years. Hedda
Hopper claimed Ann converted to Catholicism before meeting
Steve, but Ann denied it (B-254). Ann later explained that
she considered converting to Catholicism, but when she
learned she could not marry a divorced man, she changed her
mind. "I was middle-aged. I couldn't rob cradles," Ann
reasoned (B-222). Ruth Waterbury said that it was not so
much Catholicism as Steve's mother that kept Ann and Steve
from marrying. "Insiders said that Hannagan, for all his
seemingly dominant personality, was actually influenced a
great deal by his mother, Hannah," Waterbury reported. "He
dined with her almost every night. He went to mass with her
every day" (B-698). Hannah died in 1950. Other sources
insist that work, not religion, was the problem with Ann and
Steve. Ann refused to give up her career and move to New
York for him so the couple never married.

In 1951, Ann signed a three-picture deal with
Universal-International, which had released <u>Woman on the
Run</u> (F-81). She received a percentage of the films'
grosses rather than a straight salary. All three movies were
relatively low-budget. During this period, actresses like
Jane Wyman, Irene Dunne, and Loretta Young also were working
at the studio in low-budget pictures. All were in their
thirties or older and were passed over for leading roles at
the major studios. Ann insisted Universal-International hire
her friend Ross Hunter as producer. Although Hunter was best
known as an actor and stage producer, the studio agreed to
her demand. Over the next eighteen years, Hunter became the
number one asset at Universal-International, revitalizing
Lana Turner's career with a series of glossy melodramas and
giving his films a big-budget look for a fraction of other
producers' costs (B-469). It was not the first time Ann had
insisted on hiring her friends behind-the-scenes. Wardrobe
woman Martha Giddings Bunch, set designers Jacques Mapes and
Julia Heron, and costume desiger William Travilla all
routinely were used on Ann's movies at her insistence. Ann
liked to be surrounded by friendly faces and knew her friends
knew their jobs.

Ann's first picture under her Universal-International
contract was <u>Steel Town</u> (F-82), released in March 1952.
The Technicolor melodrama is set in a steel mill, where John
Lund and Howard Duff vie for Ann's affections. <u>Daily
Variety</u> noted, "Miss Sheridan delivers one of her snappy
portrayals of a modern young woman with her customary verve"
(March 5, 1952). <u>The Green Sheet</u> said, "Molten steel and
Ann Sheridan in blazing Technicolor make this film all that
might be desired visually" (March 1, 1952). Ann joined Duff
and Lund on a promotional tour to steel centers Atlanta,

Georgia, Detroit, Michigan, Cleveland, Ohio, and Birmingham, Alabama in March 1952 (P-12).

Just Across the Street (F-83) is a black and white romantic comedy, released by Universal-International in June 1952. Ann was reunited with John Lund in this tale of mistaken identity. The critics praised the comedy. The New York Times said Ann was "perfectly cast" (June 28, 1952). Harrison's Reports called the direction and performances "first-rate" (May 24, 1952).

Ann also appeared on several radio broadcasts in 1952. She recreated her role in Good Sam (F-78) on Stars in the Air (R-26), with her Stella co-star David Wayne replacing Gary Cooper. She also appeared on The Kate Smith Show (R-28) and two episodes of The Dean Martin and Jerry Lewis Show (R-27 and R-29).

Ann's final film for Universal-International was Take Me to Town (F-84), released in June 1953. In the Technicolor musical, Ann plays a dance hall hostess on the lam from the law, who reforms after hiding out with a widower and his three sons. It gave Ann the opportunity to sing "Oh, You Redhead" and "Take Me to Town." Critics loved Ann's performance, as well as her sexy costumes. The Los Angeles Examiner noted that "she should do at least a dozen more [films] in the same vein right away" (June 13, 1953). In 1958, Ross Hunter wanted Ann to star in a Broadway musical based on the movie. He suggested she obtain some stage experience before the project was launched. Although Ann toured in several plays, the musical was not produced.

In 1953, Ann appeared in Appointment in Honduras (F-85), part of the settlement in her lawsuit with RKO. The Technicolor melodrama was released on October 16, 1953. Glenn Ford and Zachary Scott co-star in the adventure, which revolves around a trek through the jungle with a band of prisoners. Many reviews pointed out that Ann could have been used to better advantage. Harrison's Reports noted, "The acting is good, and so is the direction, but the color photography leaves much to be desired" (October 24, 1953). Ann later admitted that she took the role because she was tired of fighting with RKO (B-475).

Sometime during the 1950s, Ralph Edwards's This Is Your Life (NBC, 1952-61) planned to surprise Ann with a TV tribute. She found out about the broadcast ahead of time and the show was canceled (B-109). According to longtime Sheridan fan Genevieve Jones, Ann threatened to sue the program if they featured her life. When asked about this, Edwards's executive secretary, JoEllen Martin, said that it was Edwards's policy to cancel a show if the subject found out, since the element of surprise was a backbone of the program. When asked about the possibility of a lawsuit, Martin replied, "Because of the fact Miss Ann Sheridan's 'LIFE' never materialized, we do not have research information we can release." In answer to whether Ann ever appeared on a program honoring another subject, Martin wrote, "No, Miss Sheridan never appeared on a 'This Is Your Life' show." Although Ann often claimed she relished her privacy, it seems she was overly adamant about not being profiled.

During the 1950s, Ann was on the Modern Screen Fashion

Board. She, along with celebrities like Robert Stack,
Vera-Ellen, Terry Moore, and Jean Pierre Aumont, met at the
home of Jeanette MacDonald and Gene Raymond to vote.
    On February 5, 1953, Steve Hannagan suffered a fatal
heart attack during a business trip to Nairobi, Kenya. Ann
attended the funeral mass at St. Patrick's Cathedral in New
York. When his estate was settled some two years later, Ann
was named sole beneficiary of six insurance policies totaling
$218,399. The estate's executors went to court over another
financial matter. Ann agreed to pay the estate $15,000 to
clear up a $40,000 loan from Hannagan and the New York
Surrogate's Court gave her title to two scenarios. Although
the media publicized Ann's inheritance and the forgiving of
her debt, another matter was not mentioned. According to
writer Ruth Waterbury, Steve's financial situation was not
what it seemed. She recalled his giving Ann a new car one
Christmas, only to have it reclaimed by the finance company
shortly thereafter. Waterbury also said that Ann had to sell
an apartment building to cover the losses on some mutual
holdings that she shared with Steve (B-698).
    After Steve Hannagan's death, Ann moved to Mexico City,
taking a three-year break from movies. She always had spoken
of owning a home in Mexico and insisted her move had more to
do with progress than Hannagan's death. "I never thought
[the neighbors] would close in on me," she explained. "I
like the wide open spaces....I want flowers and trees and
dogs around me." With film roles coming less frequently and
operating expenses rising on her ranch, Mexico was also a
less expensive alternative to California. "I didn't work in
those pre-tax days when you could save money," she said.
"Living is so much cheaper in Mexico." When Ann left
Hollywood in July 1953, she announced that she would launch
her own production company, which would make films in both
English and Spanish (B-374). Ann promised, "I'll still be
available for good deals in Hollywood, but they'll have to be
good" (B-543).
    For the next three years, Ann's primary residence was in
Mexico City. She returned to the United States for
television roles, including guest spots on Ford Theater
(T-7), Dunninger (T-8), Lux Video Theatre (T-9), Schlitz
Playhouse of Stars (T-10), All-Star Revue (T-11), Juke
Box Jury (T-12), The Buick-Berle Show (T-13), and The
Eddie Cantor Comedy Theater (T-16).
    In October 1955, Variety announced that Ann and
Mexican actor Rodolfo Acosta Perez, known professionally as
Rudy Acosta, Rodolfo Acosta, and Rudolpho Acosta, were
producing a series of fifty mysteries for Mexican TV (T-17).
Rodolfo, who had appeared in Appointment in Honduras (F-85)
and was living with Ann, planned to star and direct (B-26).
It is not known whether Ann's role was solely behind-
the-scenes or if any episodes actually were produced. Ann's
personal life soon intruded on her business dealings.
    Ann was in New York when the story broke about her
involvement with the married Rodolfo Acosta. On October 31,
1956, Jeanine Cohen Acosta swore out a warrant in Mexico
City, charging Ann and her husband with criminal adultery.
Jeanine claimed that Rodolfo had deserted her in 1953 and
moved into an apartment with Ann in Mexico City. Soon,

Rodolfo was pressuring his wife for a divorce, but she
refused because of their two daughters. Jeanine claimed that
he threatened her with a gun if she did not give him a
divorce (B-118). In December 1956, Mexico City's district
attorney issued a warrant for Ann's arrest after she failed
to answer several subpoenas involving the adultery charge
(B-467). The Los Angeles Times noted that the criminal
charge could lead to a prison sentence (B-352). Ann refused
to comment, but remained in the United States to avoid arrest
(B-118). The story appeared in the scandal magazines, as
well as the mainstream press. Eventually, the charges were
dropped when it was learned that Rodolfo had filed for
divorce before his wife made the complaint. Although Ann
worked with Rodolfo in a TV drama in 1957, it is assumed that
Jeanine's charges cooled the relationship. By 1958, Ann was
involved with someone else. Rodolfo died on November 7, 1974
at the Motion Picture Country Hospital.

     Meanwhile, Ann returned to Hollywood for two films in
1956. Come Next Spring (F-86) was a quiet Republic picture
that cast Ann against type. She plays a simple farm woman
whose alcoholic husband returns after abandoning her and her
children for nine years. Muscular Steve Cochran is her
husband. Ann received some of the best reviews of her
career. The Los Angeles Times called her performance
"sincere" and "worthwhile" (April 4, 1956), while Films in
Review claimed that she had never acted so well in her
career (March 1956). Unfortunately, Come Next Spring did
not receive proper promotion and it performed poorly at the
box office. Ann blamed Republic for letting the "A" picture
appear on double bills (B-206). In recent years, it has
become a minor cult classic.

     From the sensitive, simplistic story of Come Next
Spring (F-86), Ann moved to MGM for The Opposite Sex
(F-87), a big-budget musical version of Clare Boothe's
Broadway comedy The Women. The all-star cast includes June
Allyson, Joan Collins, Dolores Gray, Joan Blondell, and Ann
Miller. The plot revolves around a gossipy set of friends
who ruin one woman's marriage. Ann plays the voice of
reason, a career woman who sees through the phony
friendships. Released in October 1956, the production was
praised for its wide screen, Metrocolor oppulence. Variety
called the movie "high-powered entertainment with a name
cast and a strong boxoffice [sic] potential" (September 19,
1956). The New York Herald Tribune noted, "Ann Sheridan,
Ann Miller, Agnes Moorehead and Joan Blondell form a smart,
well-dressed set of ladies who live luxuriously in the best
MGM tradition" (November 16, 1956). However, most film
historians believe that MGM's 1939 filming of The Women
holds up much better than its musical counterpart. Ann's
role was based on the character played by Joan Fontaine in
the 1939 version.

     The Opposite Sex marked Ann's only appearance with
Joan Blondell and June Allyson, both of whom had been married
to Ann's Cowboy from Brooklyn (F-41) and Naughty But Nice
(F-48) co-star Dick Powell. Coincidentally, Ann had taken
over three of Blondell's roles at Warner Bros. in remakes of
the actress's films. Broadway Musketeers (F-44) had been
Blondell's Three on a Match (1932), Indianapolis Speedway

(F-50) was The Crowd Roars (1932), and Honeymoon for Three (F-57) was previously Goodbye Again (1933).

In 1956, Ann also made a pilot for a situation comedy based in Las Vegas. Ann played a public relations executive for the Flamingo Hotel. "Calling Terry Conway" (T-18) aired on Sneak Preview on August 14, 1956, but was not picked up as a series. "It didn't sell because potential sponsors didn't like the Las Vegas background for selling Wheaties or whatever it is they sell," Ann explained in 1967 (B-295). In other interviews, she claimed that sponsors did not want their products associated with gambling. In the 1950s, another pilot was planned for CBS. According to Sheridan biographer Tom Sharpley, Cafe 101 was the idea of Vincent Sherman, who had directed Nora Prentiss (F-74) and The Unfaithful (F-75). Sherman planned to cast Ann and Martha Raye as truck stop waitresses. Ann was a widow who carried the torch for her late husband, ignoring the passes of the truckers. Martha was interested in the truckers, but none of them wanted her. Sharpley said that Sherman told him that the network gave him $750 to hire a writer for the pilot. Because of the low budget, the script needed a lot of work. Sherman got involved with the feature Lone Star (MGM, 1952) and Cafe 101 was delayed. Sharpley said that Sheridan's letters mention Sherman and an unnamed project in March 1955. As late as 1956, Cafe 101 was noted as a CBS pilot in The Hollywood Reporter. It is not known when the project was abandoned.

In 1956, Ann traveled to Africa in what proved to be her final feature, The Woman and the Hunter (F-88). It was produced by Jack Gross and Phil Krasne, who produced Ann's 1953 Lux Video Theatre appearance (T-9). Ann claimed she took the role because it gave her a trip to Africa. She was disappointed in the final film. Although the actors used makeup meant for color, the movie was shot in black and white, giving them a strange appearance. The Woman and the Hunter was deemed so bad that it was not released theatrically in the United States, but was sold directly to television.

Travel motivated another 1956 appearance. Ann was promised a free trip to England if she would accompany comedian Henry Morgan to Africa in conjunction with the game show I've Got a Secret (T-20). Ann appeared on the show during the fall of 1956, then flew with Morgan to the Belgian Congo and went on to England.

Following Jeanine Cohen Acosta's lawsuit, Ann settled in New York, continuing to act on television. She appeared on dramas like The U.S. Steel Hour (T-21), Lux Video Theatre (T-22), Playhouse 90 (T-23), Ford Theater (T-24), Celebrity Playhouse (T-27), and Pursuit (T-29), as well as variety shows like The Perry Como Show (T-28) and The Arthur Murray Party (T-30 and T-31). In 1957, there were rumors that she would tour in the play Auntie Mame and possibly join the Broadway cast of the comedy. Ann did not appear in either production.

In the 1950s, Ann added another vocation: breeding poodles. The business began as a hobby. After George Brent gave her a poodle during their marriage, Ann acquired another to keep it company. Later, she decided to raise poodles, but admitted that she became so attached to her pets that it was difficult to sell them (B-207). Aided by veterinarian Dr. Laird, the partnership lasted until his death in 1959 (B-206).

During the summer of 1958, Ann made her stage debut, touring in the romantic comedy Kind Sir in summer stock (P-16). Her leading man was Scott McKay, an actor best known for replacing stars on Broadway. Born Carl Chester Gose on May 28, 1915, Scott had been acting since 1937. In the 1940s, he made a few films, but quickly returned to the theatre. He was married to writer Margaret Spickers from 1942 to 1953 and had two sons. In 1953, he married actress Joan Morgan, who was still his wife when he met Ann. During the course of the Kind Sir tour, Ann and Scott began an affair. In August, Scott broke the news to Joan. When he refused to further discuss the matter, Joan tried to commit suicide (B-203).

In October, Ann and Scott were among the all-star cast performing The Time of Your Life for a week at the Brussels Universal and International Exposition (P-17). The Pulitzer-Prize-winning play was part of the American exhibit. The cast included Susan Strasberg, Dan Dailey, and Franchot Tone. Ann played a drunken socialite; Scott was a young lover. When Ann and Scott returned to New York, he left his wife.

In June 1959, it was announced that Ann would make her Broadway debut in Odd Man In (P-19), a French farce adapted by Robin Maugham. Scott McKay was also part of the three-person cast. Rehearsals were set to begin on July 20, with plans for a twenty-five to thirty-week pre-Broadway tour, and a spring opening in New York. Ann appeared thrilled to do the show. "I searched two years for a play, and then this was found for me," she said. "I've always wanted to do something on the stage" (B-679). Before Odd Man In opened, Ann and Scott reprised their roles in Kind Sir at the Grist Mill Playhouse in New Jersey, July 6 through July 11 (P-18).

The Odd Man In tour commenced on October 1, 1959 in Wilmington, Deleware. The show played over fifty cities in five months, garnering mostly negative reviews. Although the producers promised Ann that there would be rewrites, no changes were made. During the tour, she developed a sinus infection, causing her to cough throughout her performances. The show closed in Burlington, Iowa on March 5, 1960, with the producers auctioning off costumes and props to help recoup their loss. Ann recalled, "They never intended to rewrite, or bring it to Broadway. They only intended to make as much money as they could, and they did, from the outlying districts of the country" (B-206). Although the producers announced that they planned to rewrite the show and open it on Broadway in the fall of 1960, only a summer stock production with Marion Mercer at Pennsylvania's Totem Pole Playhouse is chronicled. The Pennsylvania theatre purchased the sets when the original production closed in Iowa.

Ann found her love life in the headlines again in 1960 when Scott's estranged wife Joan filed for a separation and petitioned the court for an increase in alimony. Joan claimed she needed the funds to pay her psychiatric bills,

following two suicide attempts. Scott's lawyer denied the
charges and contended that Scott's nine-hundred-dollar-a-
week salary eminently would end when Odd Man In closed.
Though Joan's attorney accused Scott of "having an affair"
with Ann, he was careful not to use the word "adultery."
Perhaps he feared a counter suit by Ann. Scott tried to make
light of the situation, insisting that Joan was jealous of
all of his leading ladies. "I never had an affair with Miss
Sheridan, then or now," he testified. "I never told my wife
that I did" (B-1). Joan won her case, but commited suicide
on October 11, 1962.

After the debacle of Odd Man In (P-19), Ann settled in
New York, concentrating on television roles. She returned to
California to film episodes of the TV dramas The U.S. Steel
Hour (T-32), Wagon Train (T-34), and Burke's Law (T-40).
She introduced a new dance trio on Celebrity Talent Scouts
(T-33) and returned to that TV show with a singer (T-35).
She became a favorite of the New York-based Goodson and
Todman-produced game shows. In addition to being a regular
panelist on the daytime version of To Tell the Truth (T-36,
T-38, T-39, T-41, T-42, T-44, T-47, T-48, T-49, T-50, and
T-51), Ann appeared on Missing Links (T-37), Get the
Message (T-45), The Match Game (T-46), and The Price Is
Right (T-52). Content to be in the background, Ann
followed Scott McKay on tour, including a 1961 stage
production of Under the Yum Yum Tree.

In early 1962, Ann returned to the stage, starring in
Kind Sir (P-20) at Chicago's Drury Lane Theatre. Although
Elliot Reid was listed as co-star in early Stagebills, it
is believed that Scott McKay eventually replaced him. At the
time, Ann claimed she wanted to do a Broadway musical and was
looking for a suitable property.

In July 1964, Ann was announced as the star of a
Broadway musical based on the life of evangelist Aimee Semple
McPherson, a project which never materialized. According to
spokesman David Hocker, Ann's agent at the time, the untitled
show would cover fifteen years of McPherson's life. Instead
of a conventional score written expressly for the musical, it
would use spirituals. An October opening was planned
(B-429). In a 1965 interview, Ann dispelled the inaccurate
publicity, explaining that she agreed to do the show, only if
McPherson were portrayed honestly. She met with McPherson's
daughter, who wanted to leave out any less-than-savory
aspects of her mother's life. "David [Hocker] was angry with
me for saying it would have to be her real life, that I
wouldn't just stand there and try to sing songs," Ann said.
She was more disturbed by the producers' lack of preparation.
While Hocker was making announcements about the show's
eminent opening, neither the script nor financing had been
taken care of. Eventually, the project was canceled because
the producers were unable to obtain the clearance rights from
the McPherson estate. Rosalind Russell and her husband,
producer Frederick Brisson, also unsuccessfully tried to
secure the rights to do a musical on McPherson (B-206).

In several mid 1960s interviews, Ann mentioned her
affinity for daytime dramas. During the fall of 1965, she
became one of the first movie stars to appear on a soap
opera, creating the role of Catherine Corning on Another

World (T-53). The show gave Ann a grueling schedule,
forcing her to rise at 4:00 A.M. to arrive at NBC's Brooklyn
studio, learn daily lines, rehearse, and perform an episode
live at 3:00 P.M. She described her character as "a woman
looking for a purpose" (B-332) She was fascinated by the
soap opera's ability to stretch a storyline for weeks and
bring in new characters at will. "The role can go any number
of ways and that's another thing that makes daytime TV so
interesting," she said (B-332). Ann signed a thirteen-week
contract, with an option for an additional thirteen weeks.
Her role on Another World, coupled with the rising interest
in vintage movies broadcast on television, brought Ann back
into the limelight. She appeared on The Tonight Show
Starring Johnny Carson (T-55) on January 17, 1966,
discussing the show and her career. The success of Another
World led to offers for a prime time series.
        Ann filmed the pilot for Pistols 'n' Petticoats (T-54)
in December 1965 (B-535). Before departing for California,
she taped several episodes of Another World (T-53) so there
would not be a gap in her storyline. CBS picked up the pilot
for Pistols 'n' Petticoats in March 1966 and Ann left
Another World in April, returning to Hollywood for what
would be her final role.
        On June 5, 1966, Ann married Scott McKay at the Bel Air
home of writer Robert Shaw. Her business manager, Bart
Hackley, and his wife, were the attendants. Since Ann and
Scott had been together since the late 1950s, it is not known
whether health problems or pressure from CBS prompted the
marriage. In 1966, it still would have caused a scandal if
the public learned that the star of a prime time family
series was living with a member of the opposite sex. After a
three-week honeymoon in Hawaii, Ann went to work on Pistols
'n' Petticoats (T-56).
        During this time, Ann gave many interviews, reminiscing
about her career. "There are some films that I'd just as
soon not have done," she confessed. "I see some of them on
television and cringe a bit. I don't share this rosy
nostalgia. You make a lot of movies and there are a lot that
were awful." She admitted that she made some mistakes in the
roles she chose. She said she seldom battled without a
cause. When asked about current movies, Ann said that the
films themselves had not improved since the 1930s, but the
acting had. "The camera and the microphone have demanded a
kind of authenticity which was not always the case previously
in movies," she explained. She admitted that she was not a
Method actress, that she played each part the same. "The
only difference between costume pictures and what I'm doing
now is what I'm wearing," she claimed (B-295).
        Pistols 'n' Petticoats debuted on September 17, 1966.
The western sitcom cast Ann as the matriarch of a gun-toting
frontier family in the 1870s. "The producer, Joe Connelly,
describes it as the Cat Ballou [(Columbia, 1965)] of
television, and that's a pretty good description," Ann said.
"It's a satire on westerns, but the people are real, not
caricatures. It's sort of Bonanza [(NBC, 1959-73)] and
Big Valley [(ABC, 1965-69)] gone crazy" (B-664).
        Three days after the premiere, Ann appeared on Art
Linkletter's House Party (T-57) to promote Pistols 'n'

Petticoats (T-56). Despite Ann's enthusiasm for the
series, critics pointed out the stale jokes and cliched
characters. Although twenty-seven years had passed since the
oomph campaign, many reviews made reference to Ann's image.
Harry Harris of the Philadelphia Inquirer [PA] complained,
"As its utterly unfunny star, Ann Sheridan graduates from
'oomph girl' to 'ouch girl'" (B-125). Frank Judge of the
Detroit News [MI] called it "a befuddled attempt to appeal
to the bucolic humor of corn-ball-loving TV viewers" (B-125).
Variety summed up the series and Ann's participation,
saying, "[She] deserves better" (September 21, 1966).
     But bad reviews were the least of Ann's problems. In
1966, she learned she had terminal cancer. Sources disagree
about when she received the diagnosis. According to
columnist Ruth Waterbury, during her honeymoon, Ann was
thrown from a horse and injured her back. Waterbury claimed
that during a back examination, the doctor discovered Ann had
cancer (B-698). Other sources said that Ann went to the
doctor after finding it difficult to swallow. She was
diagnosed as having an ulcer. Convinced that it was
something more serious, she consulted another doctor, who
discovered an inoperable, very advanced cancer in the
esophagus and liver (B-475). There had been hints of
impending problems for years. During the filming of I Was a
Male War Bride (F-79), she developed pneumonia and bronchial
trouble. She was plagued by respiratory problems throughout
the Odd Man In (P-19) tour. A 1966 TV Guide article
pointed out that Ann smoked three packs a day (B-222). As
early as 1944, she was reportedly trying to cut down to one
cigarette per hour (B-627). During the fall of 1966, Ann
told Sheilah Graham that she had trouble maintaining her
weight since starting Pistols 'n' Petticoats (T-56)
(B-196).
     Despite the severity of her illness, Ann refused to
resign from the series. She hoped her name would keep it
from cancellation and preserve her colleagues' jobs. As
weeks went by, she rapidly began to lose weight, despite
treatments at Cedars of Lebanon Hospital (B-475). When the
cancer made it difficult to walk, she repeated the story of
the honeymoon riding accident, claiming it injured her back,
causing muscle pain and vertigo. Ann remained cheery,
preferring to keep the truth about her illness a secret from
the cast and crew. "Except for the trouble with my back, I
feel great," she told Screen Stories shortly before her
death (B-303).
     In the beginning, some crew members misinterpreted Ann's
symptoms and assumed her staggering around the set was due to
drunkenness (B-475). Eventually, she was so weak, she had to
be carried off the set. The cast and crew noticed a dramatic
difference in her appearance when they returned from
Christmas vacation. "We all knew then how very sick Ann
was," producer Joe Connelly recalled, "But nobody let on. We
had to have her doing most of the scenes sitting down
although she insisted she could walk" (B-117). Connelly
lined up chairs along the set so she could keep her balance
by holding onto them (B-212). Ann's appearance was aided by
costume designer Julia Heron, who padded Ann's clothes so
they would not hang on her frail frame (B-698). Some of her

last scenes had to be redubbed by another actress.

Despite her fraility, Ann managed to film twenty-five episodes of <u>Pistols 'n' Petticoats</u> (T-56). Another script was waiting when she died on January 21, 1967 at her San Fernando Valley home. Although she had missed three weeks of work during this final siege, producer Joe Connelly said her colleagues were unaware of the severity of her illness.

Longtime friend John Engstead shot some publicity stills for the series a few months before Ann's death. He was amazed by her will power, despite her obvious illness. Although she looked weak and gaunt during the photo session, needing help to walk, she was able to gather her strength when he was ready to shoot. Ironically, Engstead's picture of Ann appeared on the cover of the <u>Los Angeles Times'</u> TV magazine the day after her death, a <u>Pistols 'n' Petticoats</u> promotion that had been planned weeks in advance (B-161).

As her doctor certified Ann's death, he spoke out on her gallantry and faith. "Miss Sheridan was not religious in the conventional sense," he said. "She gave orders that she was to have no funeral, that her body was to be cremated. Yet she had faith of such uniqueness, such real goodness that the world should have been told about it" (B-698).

In late 1966, Scott McKay toured in <u>Luv</u>, but he left the play to be with his wife. He was with Ann when she died in their San Fernando Valley home at 3204 Oakley Drive (B-258). Her last words were, "I'm going to be all right" (B-475). Survivors included her three sisters, Kitty, Mabel, and Pauline, all residing in Texas. Her brother George died ten years before Ann. Kitty told the <u>Los Angeles Times</u> that they had not known about Ann's illness, although she claimed the family always kept in close touch (B-258). Ann often spoke out against life in Denton and her family's disapproval of show business.

A private funeral service was held on January 22, 1967 at Pierce Brothers Mortuary in Valhalla, California. There is some mystery about Ann's remains. Several books note that she was cremated, but her ashes continue to be held in a basement holding vault at the Chapel of the Pines crematory, unavailable for viewing (B-137). According to Sheridan biographer Tom Sharpely, whose book on the actress has not been completed at this writing, Ann ordered that the ashes be held in that manner, as she did not want outsiders gawking at her final resting place.

Scott McKay continued to act. He remarried, and died of kidney failure on March 16, 1987 at the age of seventy-one.

In 1967, Universal compiled several episodes of <u>Pistols 'n' Petticoats</u> (T-56) and repackaged them as the film <u>The Far Out West</u> (F-89). It continues to be seen in syndication on TV late shows across the country.

As old movies became more prevalent in revival houses and on television in the 1960s and '70s, Ann Sheridan was rediscovered by a new generation. Although Ann sang in several of her 1930s and '40s films, she never recorded an album. Beginning in the 1970s, several LP records included her songs, taken directly from movie soundtracks. Although these albums are primarily on small, independent labels, even Warner Bros. cashed in on their Oomph Girl, using three of her dramatic scenes on a three-record set, <u>Fifty Years of</u>

Film (D-3), which celebrated the studio's golden
anniversary.

Modern audiences continue to discover Ann nearly thirty
years after her death. In the 1990s, cable stations like TNT
(Turner Network Television), TCM (Turner Classic Movies), and
AMC (American Movie Classics) regularly honor her with
birthday salutes, running her films. Many of her movies are
available on home video and, in recent years, some have been
colorized in an effort to attract younger viewers.

Although Ann Sheridan's name continues to be linked with
the Oomph Girl tag, modern audiences are discovering that
there was much more to her talents than her ability to pose
for cheesecake photos. Despite the fact that Ann often was
wasted in supporting roles, her acting holds up well next to
co-stars like James Cagney, Pat O'Brien, and John Garfield.
Her natural style does not appear over-done or hammy like
many of her contemporaries. Her best-known performances in
Kings Row (F-61) and I Was a Male War Bride (F-79) show
her as a woman who is not afraid to stand up for her
principles or go head-to-head against a man. Her quick-
thinking, no-nonsense roles are the precursors of modern,
independent screen heroines like those portrayed by Winona
Ryder, Demi Moore, and Sally Field. And with so many of
Ann's films easily accessible, modern audiences can see just
how versatile she was. Her movie legacy traces her
maturation as a performer. From her beauty contest
beginnings, her rise from "B" movie extra to serio/comic
leading lady, and finally to her sensitive, dramatic
performances in Kings Row (F-61) and Come Next Spring
(F-86), Ann Sheridan proved she was more than a sex symbol.
The warmth and joie de vivre that many of her coworkers
recalled is apparent in her work. Like Mitch Rawson first
noticed in the 1930s when launching Ann's initial glamour
campaign, she had a quality that endears her to members of
both sexes. Her performances will continue to endure because
of her talent and charisma.

CHRONOLOGY

1915   February 21: Clara Lou Sheridan is born in Denton, Texas to Lula (nee Warren) and George Sheridan.

1932   Spring: graduates from Denton High School.

        Fall: enrolls in the North Texas State Teachers College, Denton, Texas.

1933   January: begins singing with the North Texas State Teachers College Stage Band. She appears at college functions and travels through Texas. Continues through August 1933 (P-1).

        Finalist in Search for Beauty contest (A-1).

        September 15: goes to Hollywood to appear in film Search for Beauty (F-1).

        October: signs first film contract with Paramount.

        Appears in plays with Paramount stock company, including Double Door, The Pursuit of Happiness, and The Milky Way (P-2).

1934   February 2: Search for Beauty (F-1) is released, marking Clara Lou Sheridan's film debut.

        February 23: Bolero (F-2) is released.

        March 23: Come On Marines! (F-3) is released.

        May 25: Murder at the Vanities (F-4) is released.

        June 29: Shoot the Works (F-5) is released.

        July 6: Kiss and Make-Up (F-6) is released.

        July 20: The Notorious Sophie Lang (F-7) is released.

August 3: <u>Ladies Should Listen</u> (F-8) is released.

August 24: <u>You Belong to Me</u> (F-9) is released.

September 21: <u>Wagon Wheels</u> (F-10) is released.

September 28: <u>The Lemon Drop Kid</u> (F-11) is released.

October 12: <u>Ready for Love</u> (F-12) is released.

October 19: <u>Mrs. Wiggs of the Cabbage Patch</u> (F-13) is released.

November 9: <u>Limehouse Blues</u> (F-14) is released.

November 23: <u>College Rhythm</u> (F-15) is released.

Changes name to Ann Sheridan during Paramount stock company production of <u>The Milky Way</u> (P-2)

December 7: <u>Behold My Wife</u> (F-16) is released. It is her first film as Ann Sheridan.

December 14: <u>One Hour Late</u> (F-17) is released.

December 21: <u>Home on the Range</u> (F-18) is released.

1935   January 4: <u>Enter Madame!</u> (F-19) is released.

February 1: <u>Rocky Mountain Mystery</u> (F-20) is released.

Is seen in <u>Star Night at Coconut Grove</u> (F-21), an all-star short.

February 8: <u>Rumba</u> (F-22) is released.

March 1: <u>Car 99</u> (F-23) is released. Ann Sheridan receives her first screen kiss from Fred MacMurray.

March 8: <u>Mississippi</u> (F-24) is released.

March: Paramount names Ann Sheridan as one of six starlets most likely to succeed in 1935 (A-2).

April 20: <u>Red Blood of Courage</u> (F-25) is released.

May: completes Paramount contract and begins free-lance film work.

May 31: <u>The Glass Key</u> (F-26) is released.

Makes a test for Warner Bros., but is turned down because of her resemblance to June Travis.

July: Warner Bros. reconsiders and casts her in <u>Sing Me a Love Song</u> (F-30), leading to a six-month contract with the studio. She remains at Warner Bros. until 1948.

August 16: Ann Sheridan marries Edward Norris in Ensenada, Mexico.

Appears in Hollywood Extra Girl (F-27), a short about the making of The Crusades (F-29).

September 30: Fighting Youth (F-28) is released. It is Ann Sheridan's only movie made between her Paramount and Warner Bros. contracts.

October 25: The Crusades (F-29) is released, marking her last film for Paramount.

1937   January 9: Sing Me a Love Song (F-30) is released. It is her first Warner Bros. movie.

January 30: Black Legion (F-31) is released.

February 13: The Great O'Malley (F-32) is released.

August 7: San Quentin (F-33) is released.

August 21: The Footloose Heiress (F-34) is released.

August 26: Ann Sheridan and Edward Norris separate.

September 11: Wine, Women and Horses (F-35) is released.

November 6: Alcatraz Island (F-36) is released.

December 18: She Loved a Fireman (F-37) is released.

1938   January 8: The Patient in Room 18 (F-38) is released.

May 20: Ann's father George Sheridan dies of a heart attack in Denton, Texas. She flies home for funeral.

May 21: Mystery House (F-39) is released.

June 4: Little Miss Thoroughbred (F-40) is released.

July 9: Cowboy from Brooklyn (F-41) is released.

Made an honorary member of the Lake Arrowhead police force (A-3).

August 5: Letter of Introduction (F-42) is released. It is the first time Warner Bros. loans Ann Sheridan to another studio.

September 19: appears in unreleased Hearst newsreel footage titled <u>35,000 Legion Vistors Are Guests of Warner Bros. Film Studio--Burbank, California</u> (F-43).

October: files for divorce from Edward Norris.

October 5: receives interlocutory decree of divorce from Edward Norris.

October 8: <u>Broadway Musketeers</u> (F-44) is released.

November 10: appears on the variety show <u>The Kraft Music Hall</u> (R-1).

November 19: <u>Angels with Dirty Faces</u> (F-45) is released.

1939   January 28: <u>They Made Me a Criminal</u> (F-46) is released.

March 16: is named Oomph Girl at a banquet arranged by Warner Bros. (A-4). The epithet is associated with her for the rest of her life.

April 1: goes to Dodge City, Kansas with trainload of Warner Bros. stars for <u>Dodge City</u> (F-47) premiere (P-3).

April 8: <u>Dodge City</u> (F-47) is released.

May 28: appears on the variety program <u>The Gulf Screen Guild Show</u> (R-2).

July 1: <u>Naughty But Nice</u> (F-48) is released. Ann Sheridan receives top billing for the first time.

July 28: <u>Winter Carnival</u> (F-49) is released. On loan to producer Walter Wanger, the role boosts Ann's Oomph Girl image better than her Warner Bros. parts at this time.

August 5: <u>Indianapolis Speedway</u> (F-50) is released.

August 26: <u>The Angels Wash Their Faces</u> (F-51) is released.

September: appears at American Legion convention in Chicago (P-4).

September 29: begins personal appearance tour, performing vaudeville act at movie theatres in New York and Washington, D.C. (P-5).

October 6: divorce from Edward Norris becomes final.

Named as Max Factor's "Girl of the Year" for 1939 (A-8).

1940   February 10:   Castle on the Hudson (F-52) is
        released.

        March: is chosen as the movie actress "most unlikely
        to succeed" by the Harvard Lampoon (A-6).

        March 11: is appointed "a daughter of New Jersey and
        sister of Princeton" in response to Harvard's dubious
        award (A-7).

        April 6: It All Came True (F-53) is released.

        April 14: possibly appears in "Elmer the Great" on
        The Gulf Screen Guild Show (R-3). Some sources
        credit Rita Hayworth.

        May 25: Torrid Zone (F-54) is released.

        August 3: They Drive by Night (F-55) is released.

        September 21: City for Conquest (F-56) is released.

        Fall: goes on salary strike from Warner Bros.

        Is rated eighteenth in the top twenty box office
        personalities for 1940 (A-9).

1941   January 18: Honeymoon for Three (F-57) is
        released. It is her only film with future husband
        George Brent.

        March 14: settles strike with Warner Bros. and
        returns to work.

        May 24: likeness appears in the Warner Bros. Merrie
        Melodies cartoon Hollywood Steps Out (F-58).

        August 14: acts as captain in Seventh Annual
        Comedians and Leading Men Baseball Game (P-6), a
        charity event for Mount Sinai Hospital.

        September: Navy Blues (F-59) is released. It is
        the first film made after her studio strike.

        Is chosen "Sweetheart of the U.S. Marines" by the
        Leathernecks at League Island Navy Yard in
        Philadelphia (A-10).

        October: is named honorary editor of the Harvard
        Advocate (A-10).

1942   January 5: marries George Brent in Palm Beach,
        Florida at the home of his sister.

        January 24: The Man Who Came to Dinner (F-60) is
        released.

        February: is voted glamour beauty of the month by

Photoplay (A-12).

March 23: begins eight-day U.S.O tour of army camps called Funzafire (P-7).

March: receives plaque naming her "Novio del Aire" (Sweetheart of the Air) from pilots at Camp Francis Warren (A-13).

April: Kings Row (F-61) is released. It becomes one of Ann Sheridan's best remembered roles.

May 3: appears on The Jack Benny Show (R-4).

May 30: Juke Girl (F-62) is released.

July: Wings for the Eagle (F-63) is released. The cast goes to Lockheed Aircraft to sell war bonds.

August 27: appears on the variety show Mail Call (R-5).

September 28: announces separation from George Brent.

October 3: attends opening of the Hollywood Canteen (P-8). She continues to support the retreat for servicemen throughout World War II, performing, dancing with GIs, and making sandwiches.

Is named an honorary officer by a New Zealand fighting division (A-14).

October 13: retains Las Vegas lawyer to divorce George Brent, but shooting schedule delays her plans.

November: George Washington Slept Here (F-64) is released.

December 10: flies to Mexico to divorce George Brent.

1943   January 5: receives divorce from George Brent in Cuernavaca, Mexico. Coincidentally, they were married on the same date a year earlier.

Given land in Mexico.

April 24: Edge of Darkness (F-65) is released.

June 14: appears in "Love Is News," a comedy on The Lady Esther Screen Guild Theatre (R-6).

September: Thank Your Lucky Stars (F-66) is released.

September 28: appears on radio comedy Burns and Allen (R-7).

Plays a Red Cross nurse in Red Cross Roll Call trailer

Let's Carry On (F-67).

December 19: receives the Golden Apple award from the
Hollywood Women's Press Club (A-15).

1944   January: appears on armed forces variety show
Command Performance (R-8).

April 8: Shine On Harvest Moon (F-68) is released.

July: entertains troops in the China-Burma-India
theatre (P-9). She loses sixteen pounds during the
trip. She returns September 6, 1944.

Appears in War Department radio dramatization of
George Washington Slept Here (R-9).

Hosts armed forces variety program Mail Call (R-10).

November: The Doughgirls (F-69) is released.

Appears on armed forces variety show Command
Performance (R-11).

December 6: appears on radio variety series The
Show Goes On (R-12).

December: receives the Golden Apple award from the
Hollywood Women's Press Club (A-16).

1945   January 28: appears on The Jack Benny Show (R-13).

March 17: Overseas Roundup (F-70) is released. In
the short, Ann Sheridan is seen entertaining the
troops in the China-Burma-India theatre (P-9).

Is named Best Dressed Woman in Motion Pictures by New
York's Fashion Academy (A-17).

May 16: appears on radio game show Let Yourself Go
(R-15), which is hosted by Milton Berle.

May 22: appears on The Raleigh Room with
Hildegarde (R-16).

June 20: appears on Eddie Cantor's radio program,
Time to Smile (R-17).

December: goes on second salary strike from Warner
Bros.

1946   January 27: Ann Sheridan's mother, Lula Stewart
Warren Sheridan, dies in Fort Worth, Texas.

June 1: One More Tomorrow (F-71) is released after
being finished for three years.

June 22: Warner Bros. Merrie Melodies cartoon

Hollywood Daffy (F-72) is released. A caricature of Ann Sheridan is included.

Settles eighteen-month strike with Warner Bros. Her new contract gives her a raise and script approval.

August 10: unreleased Hearst newsreel footage entitled _Bob Ripley's Party--New York City_ (F-73) is filmed.

1947   February 14: appears on radio drama _The Smiths of Hollywood_ (R-18) in an episode titled "Cancer Fund Drive."

February 22: _Nora Prentiss_ (F-74) is released, marking Ann's first film since her studio strike.

June 22: returns to radio drama _The Smiths of Hollywood_ (R-19).

July 5: _The Unfaithful_ (F-75) is released.

Appears at Cancer Fund benefit at Ciro's (P-10).

1948   January 24:   _The Treasure of the Sierra Madre_ (F-76) is released. Ann Sheridan films a cameo as a practical joke, but it is doubtful her footage appears in the release print.

Is listed as one of Warner Bros. makeup chief Perc Westmore's favorite stars (A-22).

May 29: _Silver River_ (F-77) is released, marking Ann's last film for Warner Bros.

Summer: buys out the final six months of her Warner Bros. contract for thirty-five thousand dollars. Her contract option would have been up on January 8, 1949.

Summer: _Good Sam_ (F-78) is released. The movie is made prior to her release from Warner Bros. and her services are loaned to RKO.

September 4: Appears with the Ringling Brothers and Barnum & Bailey Circus in a fundraiser for St. John's Hospital (P-11).

1949   Catches pneumonia while filming _I Was a Male War Bride_ (F-79) in Germany.

August: _I Was a Male War Bride_ (F-79) is released.

September 22: appears on radio musical program _Chesterfield Supper Club_ (R-20).

November 21: sues RKO for $350,000 damages because the studio replaced her in _Carriage Entrance_, released as _My Forbidden Past_ (RKO, 1951).

December 18: appears on radio quiz <u>Hollywood</u>
<u>Calling</u> (R-21).

Receives plaque from Mickey Finn Youth Foundation for
her charitable work (P-23).

1950   February 4: hosts radio anthology <u>Anacin Hollywood</u>
<u>Star Theatre</u> (R-22).

February 11: makes television debut on the variety
program <u>The Ed Wynn Show</u> (T-1).

August: <u>Stella</u> (F-80) is released.

October: <u>Woman on the Run</u> (F-81) is released.

October 13: appears on radio sports show <u>Bill</u>
<u>Stern's Colgate Sports Newsreel of the Air</u> (R-23).

October 26: appears on television game show <u>Stop</u>
<u>the Music</u> (T-2).

1951   February 6: is awarded $55,162 in her suit against
RKO and a role in an upcoming film. She settles for
<u>Appointment in Honduras</u> (F-85) in 1953.

<u>Dodge City</u> (F-47) rereleased in black and white on
the bill with <u>Virginia City</u> (Warner Bros., 1940).

May 20: plays herself on radio comedy <u>Edgar Bergen</u>
<u>with Charlie McCarthy</u> (R-24).

November 11: appears on radio variety program <u>The</u>
<u>Big Show</u> (R-25).

November 21: appears on the Thanksgiving episode of
<u>The Kate Smith Evening Hour</u> (T-3).

1952   March: <u>Steel Town</u> (F-82) is released. It is the
first of a three-picture deal with Universal-
International. The cast travels to Atlanta, Detroit,
Cleveland, and Birmingham to promote the film (P-12).

March 13: appears in radio adaptation of <u>Good Sam</u>
(F-78) on <u>Stars in the Air</u> (R-26).

April 25: appears on radio comedy program <u>The Dean</u>
<u>Martin and Jerry Lewis Show</u> (R-27).

April 27: guests on radio variety program <u>The Kate</u>
<u>Smith Show</u> (R-28).

May 25: appears on the television variety show <u>The</u>
<u>Colgate Comedy Hour</u> (T-4).

June: <u>Just Across the Street</u> (F-83) is released.

July 20: appears as a Mystery Guest on the

television game show What's My Line? (T-5).

October 21: makes another appearance on radio program
The Dean Martin and Jerry Lewis Show (R-29).

November 16: returns to The Colgate Comedy Hour
(T-6) for another guest appearance.

December 18: attends Mickey Finn Youth Clubs Holiday
Party, celebrating the opening of a larger facility
(P-13).

1953   February 5: longtime friend and escort Steve Hannagan
dies of a heart attack.

June: Take Me to Town (F-84) is released.

June 18: makes dramatic television debut in "Malaya
Incident" on Ford Theater (T-7).

July: moves to Mexico, returning to the United States
for occasional acting roles.

Appears on Dunninger (T-8), a syndicated series
hosted by mentalist Joseph Dunninger.

August 13: appears in "The Lovely Day" on Lux Video
Theatre (T-9).

October 2: appears in "The Prize" on the television
anthology Schlitz Playhouse of Stars (T-10).

October 16: Appointment in Honduras (F-85) is
released.

November 28: appears on the variety show All-Star
Revue (T-11).

Appears as a panelist on the game show Juke Box
Jury (T-12).

1954   May 25: guests on the comedy series The Buick-Berle
Show (T-13).

September 29: attends premiere of A Star Is Born
(P-14) and appears in television coverage of the event
(T-14).

1955   Ford Theater's "The Malaya Incident" (T-7) is
repeated on Henry Fonda Presents The Star and the
Story (T-15).

Named sole beneficiary of six of Steve Hannagan's
insurance policies totaling $218,399.

September 26: appears on anthology series The Eddie
Cantor Comedy Theater (T-16).

October: allegedly begins producing fifty television shorts in Mexico (T-17).

1956   Come Next Spring (F-86) is released.

August 14: "Calling Terry Conway," an unsold television pilot, airs on Sneak Preview (T-18).

September 2: appears on prime time variety series The Steve Allen Show (T-19).

Fall: appears on the game show I've Got a Secret (T-20) and announces she will accompany panelist Henry Morgan to Africa.

Travels to Africa with Henry Morgan.

Goes to London following trip to Africa.

October: The Opposite Sex (F-87) is released.

October 31: is accused of criminal adultery by Jeanine Cohen Acosta in a warrant issued in Mexico City. Mrs. Acosta claims Ann Sheridan stole her husband, actor Rodolfo Acosta.

December 5: appears in "Hunted" on the television anthology The U.S. Steel Hour (T-21).

December: a warrant is issued for Ann Sheridan's arrest in Mexico City after she fails to answer several subpoenas in the Acosta case. Charges are dropped when it is learned Rodolfo Acosta filed for divorce prior to his wife's accusations.

1957   The Woman and the Hunter (F-88) is released. In the United States, it is sold directly to television. It is Ann Sheridan's last feature film.

May 2: appears in "The Hard Way" on Lux Video Theatre (T-22).

June 6: appears in "Without Incident" on the anthology Playhouse 90 (T-23).

June 12: appears in "Cross Hairs" on the anthology Ford Theater (T-24).

September 20: Ford's Theater's "Cross Hairs" (T-24) is repeated on Undercurrent (T-25).

October 23: travels to Chicago for Raintree County midwestern premiere (P-15).

November 10: A 1953 episode of Schlitz Playhouse of Stars (T-10) entitled "The Prize" is repeated on Bulova Showtime (T-26).

1958   April 2: appears on <u>Celebrity Playhouse</u> (T-27).

June 28: begins summer tour of <u>Kind Sir</u> with Scott McKay (P-16).

September 27: appears on variety program <u>The Perry Como Show</u> (T-28).

October 8: appears in <u>The Time of Your Life</u> (P-17) at the Brussels Universal and International Exposition. The play closes October 15. Scott McKay is also in the cast.

December 31: appears in "The Dark Cloud" on the television drama <u>Pursuit</u> (T-29).

1959   February 9: appears on the variety program <u>The Arthur Murray Party</u> (T-30).

July 6: appears in New Jersey summer stock production of <u>Kind Sir</u> (P-18) with Scott McKay.

July 20: begins rehearsals for <u>Odd Man In</u> (P-19) with Scott McKay.

October 1: launches pre-Broadway tour of <u>Odd Man In</u> (P-19). The play closes on the road on March 5, 1960.

1960   March: is named as "other woman" in Joan Morgan McKay's request for an increase in alimony from estranged husband Scott McKay.

April 26: makes a second appearance on <u>The Arthur Murray Party</u> (T-31).

June 15: appears in "The Imposter" on <u>The U.S. Steel Hour</u> (T-32).

August 1: guests on <u>Celebrity Talent Scouts</u> (T-33).

1962   January 25: opens in <u>Kind Sir</u> (P-20) at Chicago's Drury Lane Theatre.

October 11: Scott McKay's estranged wife, Joan Morgan McKay, commits suicide.

October 24: stars in "The Mavis Grant Story" on <u>Wagon Train</u> (T-34).

1963   August 6: appears on <u>Talent Scouts</u> (T-35).

September 9: begins a week as panelist on daytime game show <u>To Tell the Truth</u> (T-36).

October 21: begins a week as panelist on daytime game show <u>Missing Links</u> (T-37).

November 4:   starts another week as panelist on <u>To Tell the Truth</u> (T-38).

December 23:   returns as panelist on <u>To Tell the Truth</u> (T-39).

1964   Plays a reporter on <u>Burke's Law</u> (T-40).

February 10:   returns to <u>To Tell the Truth</u> (T-41) for another week as panelist.

March 30:   appears on <u>To Tell the Truth</u> (T-42) for another week.

May 11:   is seen in "Sirens, Symbols and Glamor Girls," a documentary airing on television on <u>Hollywood and the Stars</u> (T-43).   The two-part show concludes May 18.

July 13:   begins another week as panelist on <u>To Tell the Truth</u> (T-44).

July 20:   begins a week of appearances as a panelist on daytime game show <u>Get the Message</u> (T-45).

July: is announced for a Broadway musical about evangelist Aimee Semple McPherson, due to open in October 1964.   The show never materializes.

August 31:   starts a week of appearances on daytime game show <u>The Match Game</u> (T-46).

September 7:   returns to <u>To Tell the Truth</u> (T-47) for another week as panelist.

November 16:   begins another week of appearances on <u>To Tell the Truth</u> (T-48).

1965   January 4:   returns to <u>To Tell the Truth</u> (T-49) for another week as panelist.

March 22:   begins another week as panelist on <u>To Tell the Truth</u> (T-50).

May 17:   starts another week on <u>To Tell the Truth</u> (T-51).

May 31:   appears on the daytime game show <u>The Price Is Right</u> (T-52) for a week.

November 11:   begins appearing on the daytime drama <u>Another World</u> (T-53).   She continues to act on the program until April 15, 1966, taping sequences to be used while she is in California filming the pilot for <u>Pistols 'n' Petticoats</u> (T-54).

December: pilot for <u>Pistols 'n' Petticoats</u> (T-54) is filmed.

1966   January 17:   appears on <u>The Tonight Show Starring Johnny Carson</u> (T-55).

March: CBS picks up pilot for <u>Pistols 'n' Petticoats</u> (T-54). Two characters are recast.

April 15: appears on <u>Another World</u> (T-53) for the last time.

Moves to California to film television series <u>Pistols 'n' Petticoats</u> (T-56).

April: is diagnosed with inoperable cancer of the esophagus and liver.

June 5: marries Scott McKay in Bel Air, California.

September 17: television series <u>Pistols 'n' Petticoats</u> (T-56) premieres.

September 20: appears on daytime variety show <u>Art Linkletter's House Party</u> (T-57).

1967   January 21: dies of cancer at her home in the San Fernando valley at the age of fifty-one.

January 22: a private funeral service is held at Pierce Brothers Mortuary in Valhalla, California.

March 11: last original episode of <u>Pistols 'n' Petticoats</u> (T-56) airs. Reruns continue through August 26.

April 3: a five-day film retrospective salutes Ann Sheridan's career at Chicago's Clark Theatre (A-25).

Several episodes of <u>Pistols 'n' Petticoats</u> (T-56) are combined to make <u>The Far Out West</u> (F-89), a feature which is syndicated to television.

1974   November 7: ex-boyfriend Rodolfo Acosta dies.

1979   May 26: ex-husband George Brent dies of emphysema.

1987   March 16: husband Scott McKay dies of kidney failure.

1996   August: is named "Star of the Month" by TCM (Turner Classic Movies) and is honored with a month-long movie salute (A-26).

PLAYS AND PERSONAL APPEARANCES

This chapter features information on plays and personal appearances made by Ann Sheridan. Each entry includes cities played, performance dates, credits, synopsis, and a brief note about Ann Sheridan's participation. As it is impossible to chronicle all of the appearances she made during her college career, the Paramount stock company, World War II, and at film premieres, only a sampling of those public appearances are given.

P-1   North Texas State Teachers College Stage Band

Cities played: Denton, TX (circa January 1933-August 1933, North Texas State Teachers College Auditorium), other Texas cities.

CAST: Professor Floyd Graham, Clara Lou Sheridan, Gwendolyn Woodford, Virginia Craig, Jim Ashburne, Bill Ardis, Louise Hutcheson, Emily Ann McCallan, Evelyn Wise, Lois Dickson, the Vitz Sisters, Guy Bush, Hymie Laufer, Hobart McLaughlin, Debbs Reynolds, Bryant Holland, Pete Gates, J.B. Woodrum, Bob Marquis, Stewart Jernigan, Annaloyd Cardwell, Winifred Wheeler, Leffel Simmons, the Teachers College Stage Band.

REVIEWS AND PREVIEWS:
Campus Chat, February 16, 1933: "Making her first reappearance since her brilliant debut of several weeks ago, Clara Lou Sheridan will be presented in a new number."

Campus Chat, March 2, 1933: "For this week...the Professor has arranged that hot Harlem torch song (his own phraseology), 'Going! Going Gone!' [sic]. And it is to be featured by none other than Clara Lou Sheridan and her big little voice."

Campus Chat, April 27, 1933: "Clara Lou Sheridan, standard favorite of [Teachers College] audiences, will again be presented singing in her original Harlem manner."

Campus Chat, August 4, 1933: "Clara Lou Sheridan, torch singer who appeared frequently with the Band during the winter season, will appear featuring 'Stormy Weather.'"

Campus Chat, August 11, 1933: "Clara Lou Sheridan will
sing 'Sunday Down in Caroline,' and 'I've Got to Sing a Torch
Song.'"

Campus Chat, August 18, 1933: "Clara Lou Sheridan,
possibly appearing for the last time with the band this
summer, gave the audience 'Sunday Down in Caroline,' and an
encore with 'I've Got to Sing a Torch Song.' Sheridan was
lovely; never before has she been so charming - even at her
debut before [Teachers College] audiences."

NOTES: According to conflicting reports, Clara Lou Sheridan
was discovered by fellow student Bill Ardis or professor
Floyd Graham while Clara Lou was visiting friend and fellow
student Gwendolyn Woodford's dancing studio. Clara Lou made
her debut singing with Graham's Teachers College Stage Band
in early 1933 while she was attending North Texas State
Teachers College. The group performed variety shows on
Saturday nights at the university and traveled to other
near-by Texas cities. The cast varied from show to show,
with Graham helming the band most of the time and singer
Clara Lou and tap dancer Gwendolyn Woodford headlining.
Graham recalled Clara Lou's first review after an engagement
in Sherman, Texas. "The critic on the paper there referred
to her singing of 'Going, Going, Gone,'" Graham remembered.
"'She didn't learn that in college,' the critic said" (B-7).
All reviews and previews are from the North Texas State
University newspaper.

P-2   Paramount Stock Company

City played: Hollywood, CA (1933-35).

CAST: Julian Madison, Lona Andre, Alfred Delcambre, Larry
"Buster" Crabbe, Barbara Fritchie, John Engstead, Ida Lupino,
Gwenllian Gill, Colin Tapley, Eldred Tidbury, Clara Lou
Sheridan, others.

Double Door (horror drama)
Play: Elizabeth McFadden.
BROADWAY: 138 performances, 1933, starring Anne Revere.
FILM: Paramount, 1934, starring Anne Revere.

SYNOPSIS: An over-bearing, fanatical grande dame has a fit
when her brother marries beneath his station. After numerous
attempts to split the couple, she locks the bride in a secret
room in hopes of killing her. The bride is rescued and the
grande dame is incapacitated by an epileptic stroke.

The Pursuit of Happiness (comedy)
Play: Lawrence Langner and Armina Marshall.
BROADWAY: 248 performances, 1933, starring Tonio Selwart
  and Peggy Conklin. Musicalized as Arms and the Girl,
  134 performances, 1950, starring George Guetary and
  Nanette Fabray.
FILM: Paramount, 1934, starring Francis Lederer and Joan

Bennett.

SYNOPSIS: A Hessian soldier falls in love with a colonial
woman during the American Revolution.

The Milky Way   (comedy)
Play: Lynn Root and Harry Clork.
BROADWAY: 63 performances, 1934, starring Brian Donlevy
  and Gladys George.
FILMS: Paramount, 1936, starring Harold Lloyd and Adolphe
  Menjou. Remade as The Kid from Brooklyn (RKO, 1946),
  starring Danny Kaye and Virginia Mayo.

SYNOPSIS: A mild-mannered milkman is recruited by an
ambitious fight promoter after the milkman accidentally
knocks out the middleweight champion of the world.

A Doll's House   (drama)
Play: Henrik Ibsen.
STAGE: First Copenhagen production in 1879. Many Broadway
  revivals after this period.
FILMS: Paramount, 1973, starring Claire Bloom and Anthony
  Hopkins; Tomorrow Entertainment/World Film Services, 1973,
  starring Jane Fonda and David Warner.

SYNOPSIS: A suppressed wife decides to leave her husband and
be her own person.

Romeo and Juliet   (drama)
Play: William Shakespeare.
STAGE: First London production circa 1595. Many Broadway
  revivals after this period.
FILMS: MGM, 1936, starring Leslie Howard and Norma Shearer;
  Verona/United Artists, 1954, starring Laurence Harvey and
  Susan Shentall; Mosfilm, 1955, starring Jdanov and
  Oulanova (ballet); Poetic/Embassy Pictures Corp., 1966,
  starring Rudolf Nureyev and Margot Fonteyn (ballet);
  Impreone-Hispaner-World Entertainment, 1968, starring
  Gerald Meynier and Rosemarie Dexter; British Home
  Entertainments-Verona, 1968, starring Leonard Whiting and
  Olivia Hussey.

SYNOPSIS: Star-crossed lovers marry, despite their feuding
families, and come to a tragic end.

Macbeth   (drama)
Play: William Shakespeare.
STAGE: First recorded London production in 1611. Many
  Broadway revivals after this period.
FILMS: Mercury/Republic, 1948, starring Orson Welles; Grand
  Prize Films/Prominent, 1963, starring Maurice Evans
  (originally broadcast on television); Playboy/Columbia,
  1971, starring Jon Finch.

SYNOPSIS: A Scottish nobleman lusts for power, spurred on by
prophecies and his obsessive wife.

NOTES: As a contract player at Paramount, Clara Lou Sheridan

was part of a studio acting troupe that put on plays, from
the classics to properties Paramount had acquired for future
films. Actors were able to gain experience in a variety of
roles and perform for other Paramount personnel who might
consider them when casting features. Clara Lou's work in
Double Door led to her screen role in Come on Marines!
(F-3), which began production in January 1934 (B-536).
     During rehearsals for the Paramount stock company's
version of The Milky Way, Clara Lou was called to the
Paramount front office. Deciding her name was too long for a
marquee, the studio asked her to change it. Clara Lou wanted
to adopt her middle name, but the executives vetoed her
suggestion, deeming it too masculine. Since Clara Lou was
playing a character named Ann in The Milky Way, she decided
to go with Ann Sheridan.

P-3   Dodge City Premiere

City played: Dodge City, KS (April 1, 1939-April 2, 1939).

CAST: Gloria Dickson, Errol Flynn, Hoot Gibson, Alan Hale,
Buck Jones, Priscilla Lane, Rosemary Lane, Lya Lys, Frank
McHugh, Jean Parker, Gilbert Roland, Slapsie Maxie
Rosenbloom, Ann Sheridan, Jack Warner, Guinn "Big Boy"
Williams.

NOTES: To publicize Dodge City (F-47), Warner Bros. sent a
sixteen-car train filled with stars from Hollywood through
Santa Fe, New Mexico to Dodge City, Kansas to attend the
film's premiere. The train made twelve stops, where the
stars signed autographs and waved to the crowds. Aboard the
Dodge City special, the studio recreated a replica of the
film's Gay Lady saloon in the baggage car. It was the only
bar open on April 1 and April 2, since Kansas was dry. Dodge
City residents threw a parade for the stars. The premiere
was held simultaneously at three Dodge City theatres, where
admission ranged from one to six dollars. An all-night
showing allowed the entire population of Dodge City to view
the film before dawn.

P-4   American Legion Convention

City played: Chicago, IL (September 1939, Soldier Field).

NOTES: Warner Bros. launched Ann Sheridan's personal
appearance tour with a spot at the American Legion convention
in Chicago. After being voted "Sweetheart of the Legion" by
more than three hundred posts, Ann was chosen to lead the
fifteen-hour parade and preside over the week-long
festitivies. Vaudeville producer Will J. Harris put together
a variety show at Soldier Field on September 24, 1939. Other
stars who appeared at the convention were Eddie Cantor (at an
Americanization rally), Jack Benny, and Kate Smith. While
Ann was in Chicago attending the convention, Harry Anger,
producer of the Warner Bros.'s Earle Theatre in Washington,
D.C., met her and laid the groundwork for the act she did on
her subsequent personal appearance tour.

P-5   Personal Appearance Tour

Cities played: Washington, D.C. (September 29, 1939-
October 5, 1939, Earle Theatre); New York, NY (October 6,
1939-October 12, 1939, Strand Theatre).

CAST: Ann Sheridan, Earl Oxford (both dates); magician
Gwynne, trumpeter Billy Blake, ballroom dancers Duval, Merle
& Dee, comedian A. Robins, sixteen Roxyettes, film What a
Life (Washington); Ted Weems Orchestra with singer Marvel
Maxwell, singer Perry Como, whistler Elmo Tanner, and comedy
clarinetist Red Ingle, dance team Ruth and Billy Ambrose,
comic acrobats Cass, Owen and Topsy, film Dust Be My
Destiny (New York).

REVIEWS:
Washington Post [D.C.], September 30, 1939: "Wearing a
backless black gown and her copper-colored hair high, Ann
looked 'oomphy' enough to meet the most exacting
requirements....Ann is so utterly natural and unaffected that
she is instinctively liked. And besides that, the girl can
sing."

Variety, October 4, 1939: "Rehearsed talk is unfunny, but
[Ann] Sheridan's smile, her titian hair, low-cut black velvet
dress and her pleasing, if unspectacular, throaty warbling,
done with plenty rhythm, get her off satisfactory with one
good bow."

Variety (New Acts), October 4, 1939: "Impression she is
making offstage chores, plus occasional ad libs behind the
footlights, indicate she has potentially sock stage
personality, but she's too uncertain as yet to try to improve
the act her studio gave her - or failed to give her."

Variety, October 11, 1939: "...a few banal questions and
answers...entirely nullify whatever [sex appeal] impression
[Ann Sheridan] makes in a very low cut, black velvet gown,
latter highlighting her red hair. Vocally, she's quite all
right..., but she needs plenty of coaching in speaking lines
on a stage. Her flair for going into the high registers at
the punches is amateurish."

Billboard, October 14, 1939: "...[Ann] Sheridan handles
herself in a manner tha makes one wonder if her wooden
characterizations in films weren't played by two other
people. As far as personal appearances go, this is probably
the best to hit a vaude house in some time. Miss Sheridan
sings, if not brilliantly certainly pleasingly, and handles
lines and bits of business with admirable grace, poise and a
sense of humor. Her self-derogation about her trade-mark
[sic] falls pleasantly on the ears and a parody of 'Are You
Havin' Any Fun?' is perhaps the cleverest material ever
included in a Hollywooden [personal appearance]."

NOTES: Warner Bros. sent Ann Sheridan on a personal
appearance tour to capitalize on the oomph campaign.
Following the wealth of publicity she garnered from her

American Legion convention stint, two movie house dates were
booked. Ann was given only two days to rehearse before her
opening in Washington, causing critics to complain about
Warner Bros.'s lack of preparation and Ann's material.

   Ann's seven-minute act included plugs for her own
movies, as well as other Warner products. She sang a medley
of "Hooray for Spinach" and "Corn Pickin'" from Naughty But
Nice (F-48), and promoted friend James Cagney's The
Roaring Twenties (Warner Bros., 1939) with a medley of
three songs, "Melancholy Baby," "It Had to Be You," and "I'm
Just Wild About Harry." Earl Oxford served as master of
ceremonies and straight man, feeding her questions about
oomph. After the show successfully played movie houses in
Washington and New York, several other Warner Bros. theatres
tried to convince the studio to extend the personal
appearance tour. Ann was scheduled to begin filming on
November 1, 1939 (B-688). Although she was announced for an
engagement with Ted Weems at the Stanley Theatre in
Pittsburgh during the week of October 20, she returned to
Warner Bros. to start work on It All Came True (F-53).

P-6   Seventh Annual Comedians and Leading Men Baseball
       Game

City played: Hollywood, CA (August 14, 1941, Wrigley Field).

Ann Sheridan and Martha Raye, then appearing onscreen in
Navy Blues (F-59), were the rival captains of the Leading
Men and the Comedians in this celebrity baseball game.
Edward Sutherland and Frank Lloyd were credited as general
directors of the game, which included many scripted gags.
More than 125 celebrities participated in a "Parade of Stars"
before the game. Proceeds from the event went to Mount Sinai
Hospital and Free Medical Clinic.

P-7   Funzafire U.S.O. Tour

Cities played: Cheyenne, WY (March 23, 1942, Fort Francis E.
Warren); Kansas (March 1942, Fort Riley); Missouri (April 2,
1942, Fort Wood).

NOTES: Shortly after Ann Sheridan's marriage to George
Brent, Warner Bros. mogul Jack Warner ordered her to go on a
U.S.O. tour of army camps around the country. Warner figured
the publicity would be good for the studio, while enforcing a
patriotic image. Variety reported that Ann's eight-day
tour with the Funzafire troupe saw her performing before
15,868 soldiers (B-283). Silver Screen ran a photo of her
in a chef hat, helping soldiers with KP duty at Fort Riley
(B-611). Movies showed her playing pool with a private and
fraternizing with some South American pilots (B-82). Despite
the positive publicity, Jack Warner was not so eager to send
his Oomph Girl outside the country when Ann requested an
overseas tour. He cast her in film after film until she
refused to make another until after she visited the troops.
He finally relented and let her go to China, Burma, India,
and French Morocco in 1944 (P-9).

P-8   Hollywood Canteen

City played: Hollywood, CA (October 3, 1942, Hollywood
Canteen).

CAST: Bud Abbott, Constance Bennett, Joan Bennett, Eddie
Cantor, Lou Costello, Joan Crawford, Bette Davis, Marlene
Dietrich, Duke Ellington's Band, Judy Garland, Greer Garson,
Betty Grable, Rita Hayworth, Betty Hutton, Kay Kyser's Band,
Hedy Lamarr, Eleanor Powell, Santa Ana Air Base Band, Col.
Harold B. Shanon, Ann Sheridan, Dinah Shore, Ginny Simms,
Rudy Vallee's Coast Guard Band, Loretta Young.

NOTES: With the success of New York's Stage Door Canteen,
Bette Davis and John Garfield organized a similar west coast
retreat for servicemen. After enlisting studio craftsmen to
help renovate a former nightclub called the Rancho Grande,
Davis and Garfield called on their fellow actors to
entertain the servicemen, wash dishes, bus tables, and
mingle at the canteen. The opening, on October 3, 1942, was
a chaotic, star-filled evening. Although two thousand
servicemen filled the airy club, nearly five thousand were
turned away. Rudy Vallee's Coast Guard Band set up shop in
a filling station lot on the next corner to appease the
crowd. Other bands alternated throughout the evening.
Inside the canteen, Eddie Cantor hosted a variety show.
Admission was free to service personnel. However, the stars
were forced to pay for the opening, which raised ten
thousand dollars for the canteen. Ann Sheridan continued to
appear at the canteen throughout World War II.

P-9   C.B.I. Tour

Countries played: China, India, Burma, French Morocco (June
1944-September 6, 1944).

CAST: Ann Sheridan, comedian Ben Blue, master of ceremonies
Jackie Miles, dancer Mary Landa, accordionist Ruth Dennis.

NOTES: After nine months of promises, Jack Warner finally
let Ann Sheridan do a two-month U.S.O. tour in the orient. He
continued to pester her on the front, threatening to suspend
her when she did not return on time. For security reasons,
Ann and the company were not given their orders before they
left, but learned of their destination as they flew over the
Atlantic Ocean. The tour took them to Burma, China, India,
and French Morocco.
     The troupe performed two shows a day, as well as
additional performances in army hospitals. "The show ran
anywhere from an hour and a half to two hours, depending upon
encores," Ann recalled (B-528). Audiences ranged from
seventy-five to five thousand men. Ann sang "Amor," "Besame
Mucho," and "I'll Be Seeing You," and appeared as the
straight woman in a skit with Ben Blue. Although the
officers often tried to monopolize the celebrities' time, Ann
was outraged that they could not spend more time with the
GIs.
     After four months of extreme heat, sleeping on planes

and floors, and surviving on K-rations, Ann's weight dropped
from 128 to 112 pounds. Upon returning to New York, she
rushed out for milk and ice cream, the two amenities she
had missed most. She had trouble readjusting to a bed and
spent her first night on the floor, sleeping for eighteen
hours.

The tour received a lot of negative publicity in the
service newspapers, with soldiers complaining about Ann, as
well as other celebrities. Ann countered the criticism by
offering to wrestle with anyone who did not believe she
roughed it while overseas.

P-10   Cancer Fund Benefit

City played: Hollywood, CA (Ciro's, 1947).

NOTES: Ann Sheridan was one of the celebrity auctioneers who
helped raise money for the Damon Runyon Cancer Fund at a
benefit at Ciro's. The benefit was held in memory of the
writer, whose stories of Broadway and gangsters inspired the
1950 Broadway musical Guys and Dolls. Runyon was a friend
of Ann's frequent escort Steve Hannagan.

P-11   Circus Benefits

Cities played: Los Angeles, CA (September 4, 1948); Grand
Rapids, MI; others.

NOTES: Longtime circus fan Ann Sheridan made several
personal appearances with the Ringling Brothers and Barnum &
Bailey Circus, riding an elephant during the performances as
a publicity stunt. The Los Angeles appearance was part of an
all-star fundraiser for St. John's Hospital. It marked her
first public ride, although she had been training on circus
grounds without an audience (B-342). An uncredited clipping
in the Constance McCormick Collection, USC Cinema-Television
Library, shows Ann appearing with three clowns at the
Ringling Brothers and Barnum & Bailey Circus in Grand Rapids,
Michigan. It notes that it had been a childhood ambition of
Ann's to perform in a circus.

P-12   Steel Town Junket

Cities played: Atlanta, GA; Detroit, MI; Cleveland, OH
(March 17, 1952-March 18, 1952); Birmingham, AL.

CAST: Ann Sheridan, John Lund, Howard Duff, Gloria Murphy
(Ann's secretary), Adele Parmenter (Universal-International
wardrobe coordinator), Rae Forman (assistant studio
hairdresser), Frank McFadden (company manager), Universal-
International officials.

NOTES: Ann Sheridan, John Lund, Howard Duff, and a
Universal-International entourage traveled to four steel
centers to promote Steel Town (F-82). During the Cleveland
junket, the stars made TV and radio appearances and
participated in St. Patrick's Day festivities, but did not
attend the premiere.

P-13   Mickey Finn Youth Clubs Holiday Party

City played: Los Angeles, CA (December 18, 1952).

CAST: Patrolman Mickey Finn, Ann Sheridan, Palm Springs
restaurateur George Strebe, the Guadalajara Boys, Harry
Carey, Jr., Stan Jones, Frank Miller, thirteen Burbank High
School students, three hundred underprivileged children.

NOTES: Ann Sheridan helped Mickey Finn and three hundred
underpriviliged children celebrate the opening of an expanded
Mickey Finn Club. Ann was active with the group, which
provided a recreation program for poor boys.

P-14   A Star Is Born World Premiere

City played: Hollywood, CA (September 29, 1954, Pantages
Theatre).

CAST: George Fisher, Jack Carson, Larry Finley (Masters of
ceremonies), Rosemarie Bowe, Paula Raymond, Amanda Blake, Ann
Robinson (Starlet assistants), Louella Parsons, Jimmy McHugh,
Mamie Van Doren, Dean Martin, Gloria Grahame, Cy Howard,
Edward Arnold, Jon Hall, Hedda Hopper, Raymond Burr, Evelyn
Russell, Jean Hersholt, Edward G. Robinson, Donald Crisp,
Virginia Mayo, Marilyn Maxwell, Elizabeth Taylor, Michael
Wilding, Liberace, Dennis Morgan, Debbie Reynolds, Kim Novak,
Suzan Ball, Richard Long, Gordon Macrae, Sheila Macrae,
Dorothy Lamour, Andy Devine, Peggy Lee, Ray Bolger, Mitzi
Gaynor, Danny Thomas, William Bendix, Sophie Tucker, George
Jessell, Joan Crawford, Cesar Romero, Marie Wilson, Jack
Palance, Doris Day, Marty Melcher, Vera-Ellen, Fred
MacMurray, June Haver, Judy Garland, Sid Luft, Jack Warner,
Van Heflin, Pat O'Brien, Ben Alexander, Shelley Winters,
Sonja Henie, Ann Sheridan, Jacques Mapes, Lauren Bacall,
Janet Leigh, Tony Curtis, Sue Carol, Alan Ladd, Lucille Ball,
Desi Arnaz, Claire Trevor, Greer Garson, Sheilah Graham, Earl
Wilson (Celebrity attendees), others.

NOTES: Ann Sheridan and Jacques Mapes attended the
star-studded premiere of A Star Is Born (Warner Bros.,
1954) and were interviewed by Larry Finley.

See also T-14, V-29.

P-15   Raintree County Midwestern Premiere

City played: Chicago, IL (October 23, 1957, McVickers
Theatre).

NOTES: Ann Sheridan, George Murphy, and Myrna Hansen were
among the celebrities attending the midwestern premiere of
MGM's Raintree County. WGN did radio interviews in the
lobby, as well as color commentary about the premiere. The
stars and civic leaders in attendance were invited to a
cocktail and buffet party at the Ambassador East before the
film.

P-16 <u>Kind Sir</u>

Cities played: East Hampton, Long Island, NY (June 28, 1958-July 5, 1958, John Drew Theatre); Fayetteville, NY (July 7, 1958-July 12, 1958, Famous Artists Country Playhouse); Bristol, PA (July 15, 1958-July 20, 1958, Grand Theater); Ivoryton, CT (July 21, 1958-July 26, 1958, Ivoryton Playhouse); Detroit, MI (July 30, 1958-August 1958, Northland Playhouse); Chicago, IL (two weeks beginning August 4, 1958, Edgewater Beach Playhouse).

Producer: Ross Hunter. Director: Gus Schirmer, Jr. Play: Norman Krasna. Costumes: Travilla.

CAST: Ann Sheridan (Jane Kimball), Scott McKay (Philip Clair), Hildegarde Halliday (Annie Miller), Jack Davis (Alfred Munson), Louise Larabee (Margaret Munson), Sorrell Booke (Carl Miller).

SYNOPSIS: Jane Kimball is a glamorous actress who tries to romance Phillip Clair, a suave banker/diplomat, who tells her he has a wife in another state. When Jane learns he is really single, she plots diabolical revenge. In the end, she wins his heart.

REVIEWS:
<u>Detroit Times</u> [MI], July 31, 1958: "With her flaming red hair, her lithe body and an undeniably strong stage presence, [Ann Sheridan] moves gracefully on the stage and her nervousness was betrayed only by a tendency toward over-emphasizing trivial lines and, quite often, hurrying over scenes that could profit by better timing. But there's a decisive talent there."

<u>Chicago Daily News</u>, August 5, 1958: "It is a pleasure to be able to report that [Ann] Sheridan cuts a charming figure in a variety of dazzling gowns. (Should I mention the negligee?) Also she heads a delightfully competent cast in the performance of Norman Krasna's frothy comedy, <u>Kind Sir</u>."

<u>Chicago Sun-Times</u>, August 6, 1958: "In looks, flaming-haired Ann Sheridan is more of a dazzler on a stage than in any movie in which this admirer of hers has ever seen her. But in acting ability before a live audience...she is lamentably limited....Miss Sheridan utters lines as if reciting them during a practice session to her diction teacher."

<u>Chicago Tribune</u>, August 5, 1958: "As the actress, Ann Sheridan is a handsome redhead with a figure so fine she even looks attractive when she sits down in a short, tight dress. Her wardrobe is extensive...and she sounds like Tallulah Bankhead if Miss Bankhead had been born in Texas....What trapped [Ann Sheridan and Scott McKay] in <u>Kind Sir</u> I couldn't even guess, unless it was the salary."

NOTES: Most sources say that, on the advice of Ross Hunter,

Ann Sheridan performed Kind Sir in summer stock, hoping to
gain some stage experience so that she could star in a
Broadway version of Take Me to Town (F-84). However, Ann
told the Chicago Daily News that she did·Kind Sir
because there was a chance it would be made into a Broadway
musical for her. "Never having appeared on Broadway, I
thought I had better get my feet wet in summer stock first!"
she said (B-356).
    Mary Martin and Charles Boyer starred in the ·original
Broadway production of Kind Sir, which opened on
November 4, 1953 and ran for 166 performances. Cary Grant
and Ingrid Bergman were in the renamed film version,
Indiscreet (Warner Bros., 1958). Ann Sheridan claimed the
summer stock script was updated, stressing the comic
situations more than the Broadway production had.

P-17   The Time of Your Life

City played: Brussels, Belgium (October 8, 1958-October 15,
1958, American Pavilion Theatre, Brussels Universal and
International Exposition).

U.S. Commissioner General: Howard S. Cullman. Deputy
Commissioners General: Katherine G. Howard and James S.
Plaut. Coordinator, Performing Arts Program: Jean
Dalrymple. Producer: New York City Center Theatre Company.
Director: Jean Dalrymple. Play: William Saroyan. Music:
Max Marlin and Eddie Barefield. Sets: Watson Barratt.
Costumes: Watson Barratt. Lighting: Watson Barratt.

CAST: Art Ostrin (The newsboy), Franchot Tone (Joe), Will
Kuluva (Arab), Billy M. Greene (The drunkard), Myron
McCormick (Nick), Fred Kareman (Willie), Lonny Chapman (Tom),
Susan Strasberg (Kitty Duval), Dan Dailey (Harry), Scott
McKay (Dudley), Samuel Benskin (Wesley), Claire Waring
(Lorene), Howard Smith (Blick), Ann Sheridan (Mary L.), Larry
Blyden (Krupp), George Mathews (McCarthy), Rosana San Marco
(Nick's Ma), Len Doyle (Kit Carson), Charles K. Robinson III
(Sailor), Florence Mitchel (Anna), Rita Gam (Elsie), Betty
Bartley (The killer), Hildy Parks (The killer's sidekick),
Paula Laurence (A society lady), Arnold Moss (A society
gentleman), Clifton James (First cop), Michael Kasdan (Second
cop).

SYNOPSIS: A bizarre assortment of characters visit Nick's
Pacific Street Saloon, Restaurant, and Entertainment Palace
in San Francisco in October 1939. They celebrate the joy of
life and their faith in mankind.

REVIEW:
Variety, October 15, 1958: "[Ann] Sheridan and [Rita] Gam
are stymied by tiny parts, and expectant playgoers are
thereby frustrated....Those who came to this show to see the
best of Broadway were sent home drenched with
disappointment."

NOTES: The Time of Your Life was one of many productions
having a brief run at the Brussels Universal Exposition in

1958. Performed at the 1,120-seat American Pavilion Theatre,
the show drew capacity crowds during its one-week run. The
New York Times noted that the opening night audience,
filled with ambassadors and socially prominent guests, gave
the performers eight curtain calls. "Newspaper critics
unanimously described the performance as art of the highest
order," the paper said (B-685).
    Ann Sheridan played the drunken socialite, Mary L., a
character described in the program as "an unhappy woman of
great quality and great beauty." Ann's future husband, Scott
McKay, played opposite Rita Gam as a pair of young lovers.
There are rumors that the play was televised in London, but
they cannot be verified.
    The Pulitzer Prize-winning comedy opened on Broadway on
October 25, 1939 and ran for 185 performances. Among the
stars in the original cast were Eddie Dowling (Joe), Celeste
Holm (Mary L.), and William Bendix (Krupp). Broderick
Crawford played Krupp in the 1948 film, distributed by United
Artists. Bendix was recast as Nick. Ann Sheridan's friends
and former Warner Bros. colleagues James Cagney and Gale Page
played Joe and Mary L. in the movie. Franchot Tone, who
headlined the Brussels cast, also appeared in a 1955 revival
at New York's City Center.

P-18 Kind Sir

City played: Andover, NJ (July 6, 1959-July 11, 1959, Grist
Mill Playhouse).

Producer: Harold J. Kennedy. Director: Scott McKay. Play:
Norman Krasna. Sets: Herbert Neilsen. Production stage
manager: David L. Kaufman. Technical director: Ray Gowen.

CAST: Ann Sheridan (Jane Kimball), Scott McKay (Phillip
Clair), Barbara Benziger (Annie Miller), Louise Larabee
(Margaret Munson), Roy Munsell (Alfred Munson), Wilson Brooks
(Carl Miller).

REVIEW:
Newark Star-Ledger [NJ], July 7, 1959: "A radiant, dynamic
Ann Sheridan proved last night that she is as talented an
actress as she is a lovely woman....Miss Sheridan gives the
phrase 'sheer delight' a double meaning. It sums up the
three-act comedy perfectly and also describes the
unforgetable vision of her in a black negligee in the final
uproarious scene."

NOTES: After a successful summer tour in 1958, Ann Sheridan
returned to the stage in Kind Sir the following year.
Scott McKay and Louise Larabee reprised their roles from the
1958 tour. McKay also directed.

P-19 Odd Man In

Cities played: Wilmington, DE (October 1, 1959, the
Playhouse); Baltimore, MD (October 5, 1959-?, Ford's
Theatre); Rochester, NY (October 15, 1959-October 17, 1959,
Auditorium Theater); Atlanta, GA (October 27, 1959-

October 29, 1959, Tower Theatre); Pittsburgh, PA (November 2, 1959-November 7, 1959, Nixon Theatre); Montgomery, AL (November 9, 1959, Lanier High School); Columbus, GA (November 10, 1959, Royal Theatre); Savannah, GA (November 11, 1959, City Auditorium); Springfield, MA (November 16, 1959, Paramount Theatre); Worcester, MA (November 17, 1959, Loew's Poli Theatre); New Bedford, MA (November 18, 1959, Empire Theatre); Manchester, NH (November 19, 1959, Palace Theatre); Providence, RI (November 20, 1959-November 21, 1959, Vets Memorial Auditorium); Philadelphia, PA (November 23, 1959-November 28, 1959, New Locust Theatre); Charlotte, NC (November 30, 1959-December 1, 1959, Ovens Auditorium); Roanoke, VA (December 2, 1959, American Theatre); Norfolk, VA (December 3, 1959-December 5, 1959, Center Theatre); Schenectady, NY (December 7, 1959); Buffalo, NY (December 8, 1959); Akron, OH (December 9, 1959, Colonial); Huntington, WV (December 10, 1959); Lansing, MI (December 12, 1959, Sexton High School); Grand Rapids, MI (December 14, 1959-December 15, 1959, Regent Theatre); South Bend, IN (December 16, 1959-December 17, 1959, Palace Theatre); Louisville, KY (December 18, 1959-December 19, 1959, Memorial Auditorium); Detroit, MI (December 21, 1959-January 2, 1960); Evansville, IN (January 4, 1960, Memorial Auditorium); Memphis, TN (January 5, 1960-January 7, 1960, Ellis Auditorium); Little Rock, AR (January 8, 1960-January 9, 1960, Robinson Memorial Auditorium); New Orleans, LA (January 11, 1960-January 15, 1960, Municipal Auditorium); Beaumont, TX (January 16, 1960, City Auditorium); San Antonio, TX (January 18, 1960-January 19, 1960); Corpus Christi, TX (January 20, 1960-January 21, 1960, Del Mar); Harlingen, TX (January 22, 1960, Municipal Auditorium); Austin, TX (January 23, 1960, Municipal Auditorium); Amarillo, TX (January 26, 1960); Oklahoma City, OK (January 27, 1960-January 28, 1960); Tulsa, OK (January 29, 1960-January 30, 1960); Shreveport, LA (February 1, 1960-February 2, 1960); Houston, TX (February 3, 1960-February 5, 1960); Dallas, TX (February 6, 1960-February 7, 1960); Wichita, KS (February 9, 1960-February 10, 1960); Topeka, KS (February 11, 1960); St. Louis, MO (February 15, 1960-February 20, 1960, American Theatre); Springfield, MO (February 21, 1960); Lincoln, NE (February 23, 1960); Sioux City, IA (February 24, 1960); Waterloo, IA (February 25, 1960); Omaha, NE (February 26, 1960-February 27, 1960, Music Hall); Davenport, IA (February 29, 1960-March 1, 1960, RKO Orpheum Theatre); Springfield, IL (March 2, 1960); Peoria, IL (March 3, 1960-March 4, 1960); Burlington, IA (March 5, 1960, Memorial Auditorium).

Executive producer: Dennis McDonald. Producers: Theatrical Interests Plan (Ted Ritter, Dennis McDonald, and John Gerstad) in association with Henry Sherek. Director: Ira Cirker. Based on the play Monsieur Masure by Claude Magnier. Adaptation: Robin Maugham. Sets: John Boyt. Costumes: Travilla. General manager: C. Edwin Knill. Company manager: Boris Bernardi. Press: Glen Allvine. Stage manager: James Hagerman.

CAST: Ann Sheridan (Jane Maxwell), Scott McKay (Mervyn Browne), Michael Clarke-Laurence (George Maxwell), Bella Jarrett, Edward Claymore (Understudies).

SYNOPSIS: When Mervyn Browne's car breaks down in front of Jane and George Maxwell's English cottage, Mervyn asks Jane if he can use her telephone.   While Jane is calling the garage, Mervyn drinks her sleeping draught, mistaking it for water.   Both fall into bed, knocked out by the sleeping potion.   When George arrives, he finds them in bed.   Jane tries to explain her innocence, but rogue Mervyn insists they had an affair.   Realizing he is only trying to preserve his reputation, Jane makes him think she wants to continue the fling.   Mervyn leaves quickly, much to George's amusement.

REVIEWS:
Variety, October 7, 1959:   "[Ann] Sheridan displays a nice sense of comedy, which is no surprise.   She handles her lines with ease and good timing....As it is now, Odd Man In is light-weight farce suitable for summer stock, but below par for Broadway."

New Orleans Times-Picayune [LA], January 12, 1960:   "With work,...some of the drawn-out situations could be condensed into neat packages of nonsense which would be easier on the box office customers.   The actors have the ability to make the play considerably funnier than it is now, if they wouldn't try so hard."

Dallas Morning News [TX], February 7, 1960:   "...[Ann] Sheridan showed snappy timing, an assured and unabashed stage presence, and an ability to project the Sheridan qualities that have intrigued millions and still titillate.   As for the 'Oomph,' it is still there in quantity, chestnut hair and a siren's figure even slimmer than we recall.... Although not in best voice Saturday, Miss Sheridan has a good one, darkly colored and powerful.   And usually she watches her enunciation, sometimes too carefully."

Kansas City Times [KS], February 13, 1960:   "Ann Sheridan...looks stylish, natty and smart as the heroine of the play, speaks in a throaty, husky voice which turns out to be attractive, and holds up her part of the action well."

NOTES: Odd Man In initially was announced as a twenty-five to thirty week pre-Broadway tour.   Rehearsals began July 20, 1959.   During its five-month, sixty-seven-city route, the show encountered many problems.   The schedule changed drastically, often after it was publicized.   Although the play was announced for a two-week run in La Jolla, California, beginning August 10, 1959, it never made it that far west.   Cincinnati, Ohio and Indianapolis, Indiana were among the erroneously announced dates in Theatre Arts. During the grueling tour, which was mostly one-night stands traveled by automobile, Ann developed a sinus infection, causing her weight to drop to 112 pounds.

   Shortly after the tour was launched, Ann Sheridan described Odd Man In as "a delightful French sex comedy," adding that "with a long road tour, all of the kinks will be ironed out before Broadway" (B-350). Her enthusiasm was short-lived. Although the producers promised Ann that the play would be rewritten before it hit Broadway, it closed before reaching New York. By the time the show played Davenport, Iowa on March 1, 1960, Ann attacked the management in the press. "The show stinks," she said bluntly, blaming director Ira Cirker for deserting the company shortly after the premiere, as well as Robin Maugham for refusing to rewrite the show with its present cast (B-80). In 1965, Ann labeled the play an "atrocity," recalling that her first review said the best thing about the show was when she had to leave the stage due to a coughing fit (B-206).

By the time the show closed in Burlington, Iowa on March 5, 1960, things had hit bottom. The management of the show sued Morris A. Mechanic and Ford's Theatre Corp. in Baltimore Superior Court. Theatrical Interests Plan, the sponsor of the tour, claimed Mechanic, owner of Ford's Theatre, owned them $4,617 under a contract for a one-week engagement of Odd Man In in October 1959. Ann Sheridan and Scott McKay were not involved in the suit. In Burlington, executive producer Dennis McDonald arranged with the local sponsor, the Hawk-Eye Gazette, to auction off props and costumes in order to reduce transportation and storage expenses in a New York warehouse. The auction returned $186, with 35% of the take going to the Players Workshop, a Burlington community theatre group. The set was sold to the Totem Pole Playhouse in Carlisle, Pennsylvania (B-80).

Despite its lack of success in the United States, Odd Man In had proved more popular abroad. It was based on Claude Magnier's French farce Monsieur Masure, which ran for six months in Paris in 1956. Robin Maugham, a nephew of playwright W. Somerset Maugham, translated and adapted the play, which became Odd Man In. Maugham's version ran for over a year in London. During the American tour, Maugham rewrote the third act, based on audience reaction to the play. After the Iowa closing, there were rumors that Maugham planned a complete rewrite before a summer tryout and a Broadway opening in the fall of 1960. The only production chronicled is a summer stock performance at the Totem Pole Playhouse with Marion Mercer in Ann's role.

P-20 Kind Sir

City played: Chicago, IL (beginning January 25, 1962, Drury Lane Theatre).

Producer: Carl Stohn, Jr. Director: Vernon Schwartz. Playwright: Norman Krasna.

CAST: Ann Sheridan (Jane Kimball), Sidney Breese (Alfred Munson), Elliott Reid (Philip Clair), Ruth Bailey (Margaret Munson), Joan Lewis (Annie Miller), Charles Booth (Carl Miller).

NOTES: After the disasterous results of Odd Man In (P-19), Ann Sheridan returned to a familiar property: Kind Sir. Although some sources claim Scott McKay was in the show, the

72   Ann Sheridan

<u>Stagebill</u> from February 4, 1962 does not list him.

FILMOGRAPHY

This chapter lists feature films, short subjects, and cartoon shorts in which Ann Sheridan or her likeness appears. Films are arranged chronologically by release date. Each entry includes title, studio, date of release, length, credits, synopsis, selected reviews, and background data. Movies made prior to 1935 are credited to Clara Lou Sheridan, as they were made before her name change. Since much of her early work was as an extra, every effort has been made to document her roles as completely as possible. All films are black and white unless a color process is noted.

F-1   Search for Beauty   (Paramount, February 2, 1934)
       77 mins.

Producer: E. Lloyd Sheldon. Executive producer: Emanuel Cohen. Director: Erle C. Kenton. Choreographer: LeRoy Prinz. Screenplay: David Boehm, Maurine Watkins, Frank Butler, Claude Binyon, and Sam Hellman. Based on the play Love Your Body by Schuyler Grey and Paul Milton. Songs: Ralph Rainger and Leo Robin. Photography: Harry Fischbeck. Editor: James Smith. Art direction: Hans Dreier and John Goodman. Sound: Joel Butler.

CAST: Larry "Buster" Crabbe (Don Jackson), Ida Lupino (Barbara Hilton), Toby Wing (Sally Palmer), James Gleason (Dan Healey), Robert Armstrong (Larry Williams), Gertrude Michael (Jean Strange), Roscoe Karns (Newspaper reporter), Verna Hillie (Susie), "Pop" Kenton (Caretaker), Frank McGlynn, Sr. (Reverend Rankin), John Anderson (Contestant), Nora Cecil (Miss Pettigrew), Virginia Hammond (Mrs. Archibald Henderson Judge), Eddie Bribbon (Adolph Knockler), Bradley Page (Joe), Harry Stubbs (Fat man in bed), Ara Haswell (Blonde in bed), Phil Dunham (Heinie), Del Henderson (Mac), Tammany Young (Formation director), Vigne (First author), Monya Andre (Second author), Arthur Rankin (Third author), Charles Williams (Cameraman), William Norton Bailey (Cement foreman), Earl Pingree (Prison clerk), thirty Search for Beauty contest winners including Clara Lou Sheridan.

SYNOPSIS: Con artists Dan Healey, Larry Williams, and Jean

Strange hire Olympic diver Barbara Hilton and swimmer Don
Jackson as editors of a health magazine. Don and Barbara
take their positions seriously, unaware that they are part of
a racket. While Don is on a world tour, promoting a beauty
contest, Larry turns the magazine into a sexy confessional.
When Don and Barbara protest the changes in the magazine,
Larry buys them off with shares in a run-down health farm.
Don and Barbara plan to turn it into a resort where the
contest winners can work as instructors. Jean plots to get
control of the resort by flirting with Don. After she
finances a stadium, Don gives her a percentage of the resort,
making Jean and Larry have controlling interest. Larry and
Dan see the resort as a place for lascivious parties. They
invite a host of undesirables to the opening. Don and the
contestants teach the guests a lesson by insisting on early
hours and plenty of exercise. When Larry and Dan try to oust
Barbara and Don by revealing that Jean controls the resort,
Barbara explains that Jean's shares are worthless, thanks to
a purposeful typing error. A department of justice officer
reveals he has been tailing the con artists and they are
forced to give up their scam. Barbara and Don reconcile and
take full control of the resort.

REVIEWS:
Billboard, January 13, 1934: "This is the flicker
Paramount made with the 30 winners of the Search for Beauty
Contest....While it's pretty risque in parts, this should
please.... About the only way you can put this one across is
to play up the 30 winners, even tho [sic] they have mediocre
parts."

Variety, February 13, 1934: "Idea was to provide a
reasonable medium for exhibition of the 30 members of
Paramount's United States-United Kingdom beauty contest. The
beauts, of both sexes, are in focus but briefly, but their
presence is a principal part of the story....There are some
eye-filling girls whose shapes are not exactly kept under
cover, as well as some well built boys..."

Harrison's Reports, February 17, 1934: "Pretty good
program entertainment; it will be enjoyed more by the younger
element....A colorful display of fine looking young men and
women comes in the closing scene in which there is held a
pageant of healthful exercises, done rhythmically to music."

Cincinnati Enqurier [OH], March 26, 1934: "The sole reason
for being possessed by this photoplay is the parade of
femininity and masculinity collected by Paramount in its
'Search for Beauty' contest....It is in a scene in this
resort that the squad of heroes and heroines of the world
perform in abreviated costume. Their work consists of
marches and exercises."

NOTES: Search for Beauty began filming in late October
1933 after an extensive publicity stunt. Paramount sponsored
a newspaper contest in the United States and the United
Kingdom, offering thirty winners a trip to Hollywood, a role
in the movie Search for Beauty, and a chance at a Paramount

contract. Paramount had offered similar exploitation in a search for Panther Woman for <u>Island of Lost Souls</u> (1933), combing the coasts for a star and creating a plethora of publicity before filming ever began. The Panther Woman stunt brought the studio several starlets who went on to become leading ladies at Paramount: Kathleen Burke, Grace Bradley, Gertrude Michael, and Gail Patrick. Paramount hoped to make similar discoveries in the <u>Search for Beauty</u> contest.

Clara Lou Sheridan made her film debut in <u>Search for Beauty</u> along with twenty-nine other contest winners. The contestants are seen leaving for California and in a Busby Berkeley-esque "Symphony of Health" vignette. Although some contestants are introduced by name in short scenes at the spa, Clara Lou is announced only during a parade as the Texas winner. Despite her brief appearance, when <u>Search for Beauty</u> played in Dallas, the local theatre marquee listed Clara Lou Sheridan as the star (B-475). Six of the contestants were signed by Paramount after the film: Alfred Delcambre, Gwenllian Gill, Julian Madison, Colin Tapley, Eldred Tidbury, and Clara Lou Sheridan. Only Clara Lou went on to achieve film stardom, following a name change and a move to Warner Bros. <u>Search for Beauty</u> also is noteworthy as Ida Lupino's first American film.

F-2   <u>Bolero</u>   (Paramount, February 23, 1934)   83 mins.

Producer: Benjamin Glazer. Executive producer: Emanuel Cohen. Director: Wesley Ruggles. Screenplay: Horace Jackson, Carey Wilson, and Kubec Glasmon. Based on an idea of Ruth Ridenour. Song "Raftero": Ralph Rainger. Composition "Bolero": Maurice Ravel. Music: Ralph Rainger. Musical director: Nathaniel Finston. Photography: Leo Tover. Editor: Hugh Bennett. Art direction: Hans Dreier and Ernst Fegte. Sound: Earl Hayman.

CAST: George Raft (Raoul DeBaere), Carole Lombard (Helen Hathaway), Sally Rand (Annette), Frances Drake (Leona), Gertrude Michael (Lady D'Argon), William Frawley (Mike DeBaere), Raymond [Ray] Milland (Lord Robert Coray), Gloria Shea (Lucy), Del Henderson (Theatre manager), Frank G. Dunn (Hotel manager), Martha Beaumattre (Belgian landlady), Paul Panzer (Bailiff), Adolph Milar (German beer garden manager), Anne Shaw (Young matron), Phillips Smalley (Leona's angel), John Irwin (Porter), Gregory Golubeff (Orchestra leader), Clara Lou Sheridan.

SYNOPSIS: Aspiring dancer Raoul DeBaere leaves New York in 1910, looking for fame in Europe. Raoul teams with Leona and becomes a success in French nightclubs. Leona is jealous when Raoul flirts with other women; she threatens to quit the act. Raoul's ego and ambition swells. He fires Leona and hires pushy American dancer Helen Hathaway to perform with him. Raoul explains that he likes to keep his partnerships platonic. He asks Helen to stop him if he tries to romance her. Raoul is jealous when he learns that Lord Robert Coray is in love with Helen. Although Raoul loves her too, he hides his feelings. Helen postpones her wedding to dance the bolero with Raoul in Paris. Raoul tries to tell Helen that

he loves her, but she stops him. On opening night, World War
I is declared before Helen and Raoul can introduce their new
dance. Raoul enlists as a publicity stunt, believing the war
will end quickly. Helen is furious when she learns that his
motive was more mercenary than patriotic. While he is gone,
she marries Robert. Raoul's heart and lungs are damaged in
the war. Despite doctors' warnings, he reopens his
nightclub, determined to dance the bolero. Helen and Robert
attend the opening. When Raoul's partner gets drunk, Helen
dances with him. The bolero is a big success and Raoul makes
plans for a future with Helen. However, before the encore,
he has a fatal heart attack. Helen admits their love never
would have worked and she returns to her husband.

REVIEWS:
New York Times, February 17, 1934: [George] Raft is a
vivid and pictorially interesting type, rather than an actor
in the technical sense, and consequently he proves unequal to
the full implications of the fame-hungry dancer....Bolero
is also helped by the performances of William Frawley,...
Carole Lombard,...and...Frances Drake."

Variety, February 20, 1934: Bolero is a studio
conference product....On paper the idea probably was good.
On the screen,...it's a little enervating. Characterization
is notably weak throughout. For the box office, despite
efforts and some success toward rigging the production for
sex appeal, the picture is not promising."

Harrison's Reports, March 3, 1934: "Pretty good
entertainment. The interest is held better in the first half
than in the second; the second half, however, has its lavish
atmosphere which should make up for the slower pace."

NOTES: Bolero is based on the life of French dancer
Maurice Mouvet (1888-1927). Filming began on November 14,
1933. The Hollywood Reporter claimed that Paramount paid
composer Maurice Ravel for the rights to use the title of his
composition as the title of the film. However, when the
studio learned that the title was in public domain, they
decided to use the composition in the film as well, without
any further compensation to Ravel (B-211).
     Miriam Hopkins was the original choice for the role that
ultimately went to Carole Lombard. Paramount was so pleased
with the chemistry between Lombard and George Raft, they were
reteamed in Rumba (F-22) in 1935 (B-211). Although both
Lombard and Raft prided themselves on their dancing
abilities, some of their choreographic chores were dubbed by
professional dancers Alan Fisher and Ruth Harrison.
     The backstage story about the life and loves of a dancer
was not without controversy. Portions of fan dancer Sally
Rand's routine often was cut by state censors. The Detroit
Legion of Decency banned Bolero for its Catholic membership
(B-211).
     In a 1948 interview, George Raft called Bolero one of
his favorite roles, since it featured dancing and was based
on the life of a real performer (B-211). In 1959, Raft
unsuccessfully tried to obtain the film and television rights

to the story so that he could remake <u>Bolero</u>. It was considered such a high point in his career that the Bolero dance number was recreated by Ray Danton in his film biography <u>The George Raft Story</u> (Allied Artists Pictures Corporation, 1961).

  <u>Bolero</u> usually is credited as one of Clara Lou Sheridan's early films. It is assumed that she is an extra appearing in one of the nightclub scenes.

F-3   <u>Come On Marines!</u>   (Paramount, March 23, 1934)
   64 mins.

Producer: Albert Lewis. Director: Henry Hathaway. Screenplay: Byron Morgan and Joel Sayre. Based on a story by Philip Wylie. Songs: Ralph Rainger and Leo Robin. Music: Ralph Rainger. Photography: Ben Reynolds. Editor: James Smith. Art direction: Earl Hedrick and Hans Dreier. Sound: Jack Goodrich.

CAST: Richard Arlen (Lucky Davis), Ida Lupino (Esther Cabot), Roscoe Karns (Terrence V. "Spud" McGurke), Grace Bradley (JoJo LaVerne), Toby Wing (Dolly), Virginia Hammond (Susie Raybourne), Lona Andre (Shirley), Leo Chalzel (Bumpy), Pat Flaherty (Peewee), Fuzzy Knight (Wimpy), Monte Blue (Lieutenant Allen), Emil Chautard (Priest), Gwenllian Gill (Katherine), Julian Madison (Brick), Edmund Breese (General Cabot), Roger Gray (Celano/Brooklyn), Jean Chatburn (First girl), Jenifer Gray (Second girl), Kay McCoy (Third girl), Mary Blackwood (Fourth girl), Clara Lou Sheridan (Loretta), Colin Tapley, Eldred Tidbury, Yancy Lane (Marines), Gil Berry, Richard Gray.

SONGS: "Hula Holiday" (Rainger, Robin), "Tequila" (Rainger). "Oh Baby, Obey" (Rainger, Robin) was written for the film but was not used (B-100).

SYNOPSIS: Womanizing marine sergeant Lucky Davis becomes involved in a scandal while on leave. He is demoted to private and sent to duty in the Philippines. Lucky convinces Terrence V. "Spud" McGurke, a taxi driver and former marine deserter, to go with him because of his part in the scandal. In the Philippines, the marines are sent to rescue a group of shipwrecked children. Lucky is surprised to find the "children" are really beautiful Esther Cabot and a group of Parisian finishing school companions who are stranded on the island after their cruise ship sinks in the Pacific. Lucky leads his battalion to rescue them. Lucky falls in love with Esther. The marines fight off bandit Celano, but cannot capture him. Lucky refuses to obey orders to arrest Spud for deserting. When he finds that Spud has escaped during the night, Lucky goes after his friend. Together, they fight a band of guerilla natives. One native speaks English and calls himself Brooklyn. He insists that Celano is dead and offers to lead Lucky and Spud through the jungle. On the way back to the marine camp, Brooklyn tries to escape. He stabs Lucky and Spud, but they knock him out. When they bring him to the marine camp the next morning as their prisoner, they are surprised to learn Brooklyn is Celano in disguise. Lucky

and Spud are exonerated by Lieutenant Allen for their role in
capturing the bandit.   Back in the United States, Spud drives
Lucky and Esther to the church for their wedding.

REVIEWS:
Hollywood Reporter, March 1, 1934:   "Rough, rowdy,
boisterous, Come on Marines [sic] is a far better than
average picture, with foolproof comedy angle balanced by
really dramatic tenseness and a human, believable love
story....all the girls [Gwenllian Gill, Clara Lou Sheridan,
Toby Wing, and Lona Andre] enter heartily into the spirit of
the thing."

Cincinnati Enquirer [OH], March 24, 1934:   "This photoplay
isn't extraordinary in any particular detail, but like its
kind, has sufficient action and humor to warrant it some
attention....[Ida] Lupino leads a group of well-formed
(physically) young ladies, including Virginia Hammond,
Gwenllian Gill, Clara Lou Sheridan, Toby Wing, Lona Andre and
Jean Chatburn."

New York Times, March 24, 1934:   "It is no noteworthy
cinematic achievement..., but nevertheless its boisterous
humor evidently found favor with an audience..."

Harrison's Reports, March 31, 1934:   "This comedy is
fast-moving and fairly entertaining; however, much of the
comedy is rowdyish....The scene that shows the girls bathing
in flimsy undergarments was dragged in by the ear; it is very
vulgar. Some of the girls appear as if being nude....
Children will not understand some of the vulgar talk;
however, adolescents will. For this reason is unsuitable for
them, or for Sunday showing."

NOTES: Come On Marines! underwent many changes before
production began on January 15, 1934. Paramount had the
script for three years before they decided to film it.
Though it passed through several writers' hands during that
time, scenarists Byron Morgan and Joel Sayre completed their
version of the script in just five weeks so that the comedy
could start production. When filming began, a leading man
had not been cast. Paramount considered Buster Crabbe and
Richard Arlen, with the latter winning the role. Oddly,
comedian "Skeets" Gallagher was announced to star in Come
On Marines! in August 1931. Within a few weeks of the
announcement, the 1931 production was canceled. Gallagher
was best known for his vaudeville routines with the Marx
Brothers' uncle Al Sheen.
     Clara Lou Sheridan plays one of the shipwrecked
finishing school students in Come On Marines!. Sources
disagree on her character's name, with reviews in the New
York Times and Variety listing her as Shirley and the
American Film Institute Catalog of Motion Pictures in the
United States, Feature Films, 1931-1940 calling her Loretta
(B-211). Since researchers at the American Film Institute
viewed the film during the preparation for the book, it is
assumed that the reviews confused Ann and Lona Andre and
credited them for the wrong roles. The author was unable to

view Come On Marines!

F-4   Murder at the Vanities   (Paramount, May 25, 1934)
       95 mins.

Producer: E. Lloyd Sheldon. Director: Mitchell Leisen.
Choreographers: Larry Ceballos and LeRoy Prinz. Screenplay:
Carey Wilson, Joseph Gollomb, and Sam Hellman. Based on the
play by Earl Carroll and Rufus King. Songs: Arthur Johnston
and Sam Coslow. Photography: Leo Tover. Editor: Billy
Shea.

CAST: Jack Oakie (Jack Ellery), Kitty Carlisle (Ann Ware),
Carl Brisson (Eric Lander), Victor McLaglen (Bill Murdock),
Gertrude Michael (Rita Ross), Jessie Ralph (Elsie Singer/
Helene Smith), Charles B. Middleton (Homer Boothby), Gail
Patrick (Sadie Evans), Donald Meek (Dr. Saunders), Otto
Hoffman (Walsh), Charles McAvoy (Ben), Beryl Wallace (Beryl),
Barbara Fritchie (Vivien), Toby Wing (Nancy), Dorothy
Stickney (Norma Watson), Lona Andre (Lona), Colin Tapley
(Stage manager), William Arnold (Treasurer), Arthur Rankin
(Assistant treasurer), Teru Shimada (Koto), Roy Crane
(Assistant stage manager), Ted Oliver (Murdock's chauffeur),
Mildred Gover (Pearl), Cecil Weston (Miss Bernstein), Hal
Greene (Call boy), Stanley Blystone (Policeman), Mike Pat
Donovan (Sergeant), Howard Mitchell (Detective), Betty
Bethune (Fat charwoman), Clara Lou Sheridan (Lou), Gwenllian
Gill (Gwen), Duke Ellington's Orchestra (Themselves), Billie
Huber, Winnie Flint, Virginia Davis, Ernestine Anderson,
Marion Callahan, Dorothy Dawes, Ruth Hilliard, Constance
Jordan, Evelyn Kelly, Leda Necova, Wanda Perry, Laurie
Shevlin, Anya Taranda (Earl Carroll girls), Dave O'Brian
(Chorus boy).

SONGS: "Cocktails for Two," "Marihuana," "Lovely One,"
"Where Do They Come from (Now)," "Live and Love Tonight,"
"Ebony Rhapsody/The Rape of the Rhapsody," "My Gigolo"
(Johnston, Coslow).

SYNOPSIS: Earl Carroll's Vanities stars Eric Lander and
Ann Ware plan to elope after the performance. Maid Norma
Watson tells actress Rita Ross about the elopement, although
she knows it will make her boss jealous. Eric's mother,
Elsie Singer, who works as a wardrobe woman under the alias
Helene Smith, warns him that jealous Rita may spoil the
opening. Ann nearly is killed by a falling spotlight, which
is deemed an accident. When a sandbag line is cut,
endangering Ann again, stage manager/press agent Jack Ellery
calls homicide inspector Bill Murdock to investigate. Eric
hires private detective Sadie Evans to retrieve some material
from Rita's apartment that Rita planned to use to blackmail
Helene. He reveals that Helene, a former opera singer, is
wanted for murder in Austria. When Sadie is murdered with
Rita's hat pin, Jack insists that Bill investigate while the
performance continues. Rita implicates Helene, claiming
Helene tried to kill her too. When Rita is fatally shot
during a song involving a prop gun, Bill suspects Helene and
Eric. Helene confesses to protect Eric, but Jack proves she

is innocent. Norma admits that she killed Rita because the
actress had abused her. Norma explains that Rita murdered
Sadie because Sadie tried to stop her from throwing acid on
Ann during the show. Free of suspicion, Ann and Eric plan
their elopement and help Norma find a lawyer.

REVIEWS:
Variety, May 22, 1934: "Herein they mix up the elements of
a musical show and a murder mystery, with effective comedy to
flavor, and, keeping the cutter's hands off as much as
possible, come out with 95 minutes of entertainment that
should genuinely satisfy....The 'Vanities' girls are costumed
sparingly for eye appeal and in the press book this is
stressed for exploitation."

Cincinnati Enquirer [OH], May 26, 1934: "There is small
value in debating whether Murder at the Vanities would be a
better film if it were just Earl Carroll's Vanities without
the cohesiveness given by the murder plot. However, in
spectacle there is some shine."

Harrison's Reports, May 26, 1934: "A fairly good
combination murder mystery melodrama and musical comedy; it
should satisfy the masses. It has been produced very well,
although not in as spectacular a fashion as some of the late
musical pictures....Parts of it are vulgar - the chorus
numbers in which the girls are practically nude are more so
than in any other picture of this type; also there is some
suggestive dialogue."

NOTES: Murder at the Vanities is a backstage tale, based
on a 1933 play written by entrepreneur Earl Carroll. The
showman was best known for the scantily-clad show girls who
abounded in his Vanities revues. Before the movie was
filmed, the censors were concerned about potential nudity, as
well as the song "Marihuana." Although the lyrics mentioned
the drug, Paramount producer A.M. Botsford insisted that the
movie did not glorify its use. The film was deemed
acceptable with the song in tact, however the lyrics
continued to haunt Paramount. In 1935, the State Department
interceded after the United States was attacked in Geneva by
the Opium Advisory Committee of the League of Nations.
Paramount ordered that the song be deleted from all prints
and negatives of Murder at the Vanities, although prints of
the controversial footage regularly appear today (B-211).
Some versions run only eighty-nine minutes, instead of
ninety-five. Clara Lou Sheridan can be glimpsed as a chorus
girl in a dressing room scene.

See also V-1.

F-5   Shoot the Works   (Paramount, June 29, 1934)
       64 mins.

Producer: Albert Lewis. Director: Wesley Ruggles.
Screenplay: Howard J. Green and Claude Binyon. Based on the
play The Great Magoo by Ben Hecht and Gene Fowler. Songs:
Ralph Rainger, Leo Robin, Mack Gordon, Harry Revel, Ben

Bernie, Walt Bullock, Harold Adamson, and Al Goering.
Photography: Leo Tover. Art direction: Hans Dreier and
Robert Usher.

CAST: Jack Oakie (Nicky Nelson), Ben Bernie (Joe Davis),
Dorothy Dell (Lily Raquel), Arline Judge (Jackie Donovan),
Alison Skipworth (The Countess), Roscoe Karns (Sailor Burke),
William Frawley (Larry Hale), Paul Cavanaugh (Alvin "Bill"
Ritchie), Lew Cody (Axel Hanratty), Jill Dennett (Wanda), Lee
Kohlmar (Professor Jonas), Monte Vandergrift (Man from Board
of Health), Tony Merlo (Headwaiter), Ben Taggart (Detective),
Charles McAvoy (Cop), Frank Prince (Crooner), Clara Lou
Sheridan (Hanratty's secretary), Ben Bernie's Lads (Joe
Davis's Band).

SONGS: "Do I Love You?" (Rainger, Robin), "Were Your Ears
Burning?," "With My Eyes Wide Open I'm Dreaming" (Gordon,
Revel), "A Bowl of Chop Suey and You-ey" (Goering, Bernie,
Bullock). "In the Good Old Wintertime" (Gordon, Adamson,
Revel) and "Take a Lesson from the Larks" (Rainger, Robin)
were not used (B-100).

SYNOPSIS: Nicky Nelson runs a second-rate sideshow, which
features flagpole sitter Sailor Burke, Sailor's two-timing
girlfriend Jackie Donovan, the ticket-taking Countess, and
Joe Davis's Band. In financial straights, Nicky decides to
take his vaudeville act on the road. He teams with singer
Lily Raquel. Nicky gambles the money he was supposed to use
to buy an act. Disgruntled with Nicky's poor business sense,
his friends walk out on him. Jackie, Sailor, and Joe get
jobs at the Yellow Dragon Cafe. Lily sings with them while
she rehearses her act with Nicky. Lily and Nicky fall in
love. Hoping to win enough money to buy her a ring, Nicky
gambles the rights to their song. When Lily finds out, she
breaks up with him and accepts a radio contract. Nicky's
sideshow closes, while Joe and Lily are a hit in nightclubs
and radio. Producer Alvin "Bill" Ritchie courts Lily.
Jealous radio reporter Larry Hale promotes a feud with Joe's
troupe. Lily realizes she still loves Nicky, but he pretends
he never loved her, afraid he will ruin her career. He
decides to leave town. Alvin convinces Lily to quit singing
and marry him. When Larry learns that Lily was involved with
Nicky, he plans to report the details to destroy Alvin's
career. Nicky beats Larry to stop the story. Nicky
postpones his trip after Sailor is blamed for the beating.
Larry refuses to press charges against Nicky and encourages
him to fight for Lily. Larry helps Lily and Nicky reconcile.
Joe hires Nicky as the announcer in his show.

REVIEWS:
Cincinnati Enquirer [OH], June 28, 1934: "Shoot the
Works does exactly that. This heavy melodrama to music
goes off at a great pace, but when the force of the explosion
is spent, there's scarcely sufficient energy left to draw the
curtains."

Variety, July 10, 1934: "Jack Oakie and Ben Bernie carry,
will have to, and probably will carry Shoot the Works to

acceptable [box office] returns....Plenty of footage unreels setting the atmosphere with nothing happening up front."

Harrison's Reports, July 14, 1934: "The picture offers just fair entertainment, somewhat slow in the first half, and picking up some speed in the second half....in its transference to the screen it has been cleaned up considerably, except for some of the dialogue given to Arline Judge....most of her remarks are suggestive."

NOTES: Shoot the Works is based on the 1932 play The Great Magoo by Ben Hecht and Gene Fowler, however the new title, Shoot the Works, came from a 1931 revue written by Heywood Broun. In Great Britain, the film was released as Thank Your Stars. Both The Great Magoo and Thank Your Stars were considered as titles in the United States before the film's release. Much of the play had to be rewritten to appease the censors, to many critics' disappointment. In its review of Shoot the Works, The New York Times notes "The Great Magoo has now been scrubbed, rinsed and dried in the California sunshine with such heartiness that not only its stench but also its humor has been washed out" (July 7, 1934).
    Shoot the Works began production on April 4, 1934. It marks the film debut of orchestra leader Ben Bernie. Bernie had gained fame on the radio with a pretend feud with columnist Walter Winchell. The publicity stunt is parodied in the movie, with Bernie's character feuding with a columnist played by William Frawley. Clara Lou Sheridan has a small role as an agent's secretary. Leading lady Dorothy Dell died shortly after completing the film, as did character actor Lew Cody.
    The sideshow is set at Hubert's Museum, a nightspot which gained notoriety in the 1960s for giving singer Tiny Tim his start. Shoot the Works was remade as Some Like It Hot (Paramount, 1939) with Bob Hope and Shirley Ross in the Jack Oakie and Dorothy Dell roles. That film has no connection to the 1959 Marilyn Monroe movie of the same title.

F-6   Kiss and Make-Up   (Paramount, July 6, 1934)
       78 mins.

Producer: B.P. Schulberg. Executive producer: Emanuel Cohen. Director: Harlan Thompson. Associate director: Jean Negulesco. Second unit director: Ralph Ceder. Screenplay: Harlan Thompson, George Marion, Jr., and Jane Hinton. Based on the play Kozmetika by Stephen Bekeffi. Songs: Ralph Rainger and Leo Robin. Photography: Leon Shamroy. Art direction: Hans Dreier and Ernst Fegte. Sound: Jack Goodrich.

CAST: Cary Grant (Dr. Maurice Lamar), Helen Mack (Annie), Genevieve Tobin (Eve Caron), Edward Everett Horton (Marcel Caron), Lucien Littlefield (Max Pascal), Mona Maris (Countess Rita), Henry Armetta (Chairman of banquet), Rafael Storm (Rolondo), Mme. Bonita Weber (Mme. Severac), Doris Lloyd (Mme. Durand), Milton Wallace (Maharajah of Baroona), Sam Ash

(Plumber), Helena Phillips (Landlady), Toby Wing (Consuelo Claghorne), George Andre Beranger (Jean, the valet), Clara Lou Sheridan (Beauty operator), Dorothy Christy (Greta), Rita Gould (Mme. Dupont), Chick Collins, John Sinclair (Taxi drivers), Betty Bryson, Jacqueline Wells [Julie Bishop] (Beauty clinic patients), Judith Arlen, Jean Gale, Hazel Hayes, Lu Ann Meredith, Dorothy Drake (Beauty clinic nurses), Ann Hovey (Lady Rummond-Dray), Gigi Parrish (Radio listener), Helene Cohan (Radio announcer), Jean Carmen (Maharajah's wife), Lucille Lund (Magda), Katherine [Kay] Williams (Vilma).

SONGS: "Corn Beef and Cabbage I Love You," "Love Divided by Two" (Robin, Rainger).   "The Mirror Song" (Robin, Rainger) was not used (B-100).

SYNOPSIS: Dr. Maurice Lamar operates a beauty hospital in Paris that attracts women from all over the world. He romances many of his clients, but ignores his faithful secretary Annie, who has a long-standing crush on him. Maurice's prized creation is Eve Caron, a plain woman who he turns into a raving beauty. Eve's husband Marcel dislikes the changes in his wife's looks and temperament. He names Maurice as corespondent in their divorce. Maurice is too caught up in the fame and fortune of his beauty business to help his friend Max Pascal with an important serum. Eve chases Maurice, despite his claim that he sees her as his creation, not a potential wife. He eventually relents and marries her, but finds there is little beneath Eve's beauty. Meanwhile, the jilted Annie befriends Marcel on vacation. Maurice returns to Paris and finds his salon in chaos with Annie away. Disgusted with the shallowness of his customers, he agrees to help Max with the serum and files for divorce. Eve marries Rolondo, who loves her for her looks. Annie quits her job and plans to marry Marcel. Maurice realizes that he always has loved Annie. He chases the couple in Max's car. The automobiles collide and Annie discovers that Marcel's "naturally curly hair" is really a toupe. She reconciles with Maurice.

REVIEWS:
New York Times, June 29, 1934: "...Kiss and Make-Up is a first-class lingerie bazaar and a third-class entertainment. It represents a triumphant attempt to achieve pictorial allure without disturbing its pious editorial point of view on the impersonal worship of feminine beauty. It crowds the screen so thickly with silk, satin and nymphs that it is with some difficulty that such agreeable players as Edward Everett Horton, Cary Grant and Genevieve Tobin succeed in projecting themselves at all."

Variety, July 3, 1934: "A nice picture lacking sufficient strength to wow but should do all right."

Harrison's Reports, July 7, 1934: "This supposedly sophisticated comedy might amuse class audiences, but the masses will be bored. There is no human interest, and the characters are not of the type to arouse any sympathy....Not even the good acting on the part of the entire cast can save it from being just ordinary entertainment, frequently foring [sic]."

Cincinnati Enquirer [OH], September 17, 1934: "Kiss and Make-Up...purports to show the rhythmic goings-on in a gay temple of beauty art in Paris."

NOTES: The working title of Kiss and Make-Up was Cosmetics, an Americanization of Kozmetika, the title of the 1933 play on which it was based. The new title took advantage of the two meanings of makeup, alluding to both the reconciliation and beauty themes in the film.
    Kiss and Make-Up began production on April 3, 1934. Carole Lombard originally was considered for the role that went to Genevieve Tobin. The film features the Wampas Baby Stars of 1934: Judith Arlen, Betty Bryson, Jean Carmen, Helene Cohan, Dorothy Drake, Jean Gale, Hazel Hayes, Ann Hovey, Lucille Lund, Lu-Anne Meredith, Gigi Parrish, Jacqueline Wells, and Katherine Williams. The starlets were part of a Paramount publicity campaign, not unlike the Search for Beauty (F-1) contest that brought Clara Lou Sheridan to Hollywood in 1934. Coincidentally, both Lombard and Katherine Williams went on to marry Clark Gable.
    Clara Lou Sheridan has a bit part as a beauty operator in Kiss and Make-Up. The comedy is noteworthy for marking Cary Grant's singing debut. Fifteen years later, he would star opposite Ann Sheridan in I Was a Male War Bride (F-79).

F-7   The Notorious Sophie Lang   (Paramount, July 20, 1934)   64 mins.

Producer: Bayard Veiller. Director: Ralph Murphy. Screenplay: Bayard Veiller. Based on the novel The Notorious Sophie Lang by Frederick Irving Anderson. Photography: Al Gilks. Editor: James Smith. Art direction: Hans Dreier and Robert Odell. Costumes: Travis Banton. Sound: Harry Lindgren.

CAST: Gertrude Michael (Sophie Lang/Elisa Morgan), Paul Cavanaugh (Max Bernard/Sir Nigel Crane), Alison Skipworth (Aunt Nellie), Arthur Byron (Inspector Stone/Parr) Leon Errol (Stubbs/Peltz), Norman Ainsley (Robin), Arthur Hoyt, Edward McWade (Jewelers), Ferdinand Gottschalk (Augustus Telfen), Lucio Villegas (French marshal), Ben Taggart (Captain Thompson), Mme. Jacoby (Countess De Cesca), Del Henderson (House detective), Stanhope Wheatcroft (Floor-walker), Adrian Rosley (Oscar), Joe Sawyer (Building guard), Jack Pennick (Bystander), Jack Mulhall, William Jeffries, Perry Ivins, Alphonse Martell (Clerks), Colin Tapley, Alfred Delcambre, Gwenllian Gill, Julian Madison, Adamae Vaughn, Peggy Graves, Clara Lou Sheridan (Extras).

SYNOPSIS: Police inspector Stone wants to catch Sophie Lang, a notorious American jewel thief who has been absent from the crime scene for five years. Stone hopes that Max Bernard, a European thief who is Sophie's chief competitor, will lead

him to Sophie. The thieves constantly outwit Stone and his
health-conscious associate, detective Stubbs. Sophie and Max
lie about their identities, but make a date. Both plot to
steal a famous set of pearls from a jewelry store before they
go out. Stone attempts to outwit the thieves by replacing
the pearls with fakes and using a hidden camera. Sophie
eludes the camera by using a disguise. On their date, Sophie
and Max realize the other's identity, but keep up their
aliases. Max steals the pearls from Sophie's neck during a
kiss. Stone catches Max and arrests him. Sophie pretends to
be shocked when Stone tells her Max's occupation. She steals
the pearls from Stone and hides them in her goldfish bowl.
Stone pursues her. Max escapes and steals a limosine from a
Russian marshal. Sophie's accomplice, Nellie, retrieves the
pearls, but gets the fish bowl stuck on her hand. She
smashes the bowl on Stubbs's head and he takes possession of
the pearls. Sophie joins Max in the stolen limosine and they
escape, sailing for England. When Stubbs finds jewelry
hidden in the pipes in Sophie's hotel room, Stone warns
Scotland Yard that two jewel thieves are headed for England.

REVIEWS:
New York Times, July 21, 1934:   "...Paramount's new film
proves to be a witty and exuberant entertainment. Performed
with light-hearted gaiety by an excellent cast, it pulls no
long faces over the whereabouts of the booty, arranging its
hectic meetings between the bulls and the fleeing scofflaws
with a proper informality."

Harrison's Reports, July 28, 1934:   "This crook melodrama
is fast-moving but implausible and, because of its theme,
demoralizing. However, if not taken seriously, it should
amuse adults fairly well because there are plentiful laughs
provoked by the clever way in which the crooks fool the
nonsensical detectives."

Cincinnati Enquirer [OH] September 22, 1934:   "The
Notorious Sophie Lang...is the tale of a pair of crooks who
just couldn't bear to give the spotlight of sensationalism
and police activity to each other....The laugh lines of the
film are plenty..."

NOTES: The Notorious Sophie Lang was the first of three
movies which cast Gertrude Michael as the wanted criminal who
was being chased by the police. Production began on May 9,
1934. During filming, director Ralph Murphy altered a scene
to include a mishap suffered on the set. Gertrude Michael
accidentally fell through a glass window and, when it was
learned that she was unhurt, Murphy decided to use the
footage (B-211). Clara Lou Sheridan and her fellow Search
for Beauty (F-1) contest winners Gwenllian Gill, Alfred
Delcambre, Colin Tapley, and Julian Madison all appear in
bits in the film. The Notorious Sophie Lang was based on a
1925 novel of the same title by Frederick Irving Anderson.
    Contemporary sources disagree on two characters' names.
The Motion Picture Guide lists Arthur Byron as Inspector
Parr and Leon Errol as Peltz (B-431). The American Film
Institute Catalog of Motion Pictures Produced in the United

States, Feature Films, 1931-1940 calls Byron "Inspector Stone" and Errol "Stubbs" (B-211). The author was unable to view a print of the film. One name may be used in the credits and another on screen as in Black Legion (F-31).

F-8   Ladies Should Listen   (Paramount, August 3, 1934)
       62 mins.

Producer: Douglas MacLean. Executive producer: Emanuel Cohen. Director: Frank Tuttle. Screenplay: Frank Butler and Claude Binyon. Based on the play Ladies Should Listen by Guy Bolton and the French play Le demoiselle de Passy by Alfred Savoir. Photography: Henry Sharp. Editor: Eda Warren. Art direction: Ernst Fegte and Hans Dreier. Sound: Earl Hayman.

CAST: Cary Grant (Julian de Lussac), Frances Drake (Anna Mirelle), Edward Everett Horton (Paul Vernet), Nydia Westman (Susie Flamberg), Rosita Moreno (Marguerite Cintos), George Barbier (Joseph Flamberg), Charles Ray (Henri, the doorman), Charles Arnt (Albert, the manservant), Rafael Corio (Ramon Cintos), Clara Lou Sheridan (Adele, the telephone operator), Henrietta Burnside (Operator), Joe North (Butler).

SYNOPSIS: French businessman Julian de Lussac is unaware that girlfriend Marguerite Cintos is only interested in his option on a Chilean nitrate concession. During a phony suicide attempt, Julian learns that hotel telephone operator Anna Mirelle is in love with him. Anna confesses that she eavesdrops on Julian's calls. She warns him that Marguerite and her jealous husband Ramon want his nitrate contract. Julian refuses to listen. Undaunted, Anna calls Susie Flamberg, the pesty daughter of a millionaire, to keep Julian from going away with Marguerite. When Susie's father catches Julian with Susie, he insists they must marry. Julian's friend Paul Vernet accuses Julian of trying to marry Susie so her father will finance the nitrate project. Ramon coerces Julian to sign away the nitrate rights. Julian takes the phone off the hook so Anna will hear Ramon's threats and bring the authorities. When Anna rescues Julian, he realizes he loves her. To test his love, Anna pretends to be engaged to the doorman. Paul confesses his long-standing crush to Susie and she breaks her engagement. Julian convinces Anna that he loved her all along, despite her interference.

REVIEWS:
Variety, July 31, 1934: "Basically there may have been enough comedy and farce possibility in this story, but, as handled, it emerges a much too highly strained attempt at farce. A good deal of it is actually unfunny, and all of it is too synthetic. No real marquee strength either..."

Harrison's Reports, August 4, 1934: "This French farce is strictly adult fare, and at that more suitable for sophisticated audiences. The production is excellent, but the story is thin, and although it provokes hearty laughter from time to time it is mostly of the risque type, the dialogue having double meaning....It is just light summer entertainment, not to be taken seriously."

NOTES: Ladies Should Listen is based on the play of the
same name, which opened in Long Island, New York on July 3,
1933. The play, in turn, is based on Le demoiselle de
Passy, a French farce of undetermined production. The
romantic comedy attempts to play like a French farce, but the
style is too heavy-handed. In her second film with Cary
Grant, Clara Lou Sheridan appears in a scene as a telephone
operator. Although the New York Times erroneously lists
her character as Blanche, in the film she is called Adele.

F-9   You Belong to Me   (Paramount, August 24, 1934)
       67 mins.

Producer: Louis D. Lighton. Executive producer: Emanuel
Cohen. Director: Alfred Werker. Assistant director:
George Templeton. Screenplay: Walter DeLeon, Grover Jones,
and William Slavens McNutt. Based on the story "Fifty-two
Weeks for Florette" by Elizabeth Alexander. Songs: Sam
Coslow and Leo Robin. Photography: Leo Tover. Editor:
Doane Harrison. Art direction: Hans Dreier and Robert
Usher. Costumes: Edith Head. Sound: Harry D. Mills.

CAST: Lee Tracy (Bud Hannigan), Helen Morgan (Bonnie Kay),
Lynne Overman (Mr. Brown), David Jack Holt (Jimmy Faxon),
Helen Mack (Florette Faxon), Arthur Pierson (Hap Stanley),
Edwin Stanley (Principal), Dean Jagger (Instructor), Irene
Ware (Lila Lacey), Lou Cass (Joe Mandel), Max Mack (Jack
Mandel), Mary Owen (Maizie Kelly), Rev. Neal Dodd (Minister),
Irving Bacon (Stage manager), Hugh McCormick (Ventriloquist),
Allen Fox, Eddie Borden (Ushers), Willie Fung (Waiter), Jerry
Tucker, Wally Albright, Jr. (Schoolboys), Bernard Suss
(Doctor), Frank Rice (Stagehand), Margaret Daggett, Al Shaw,
Billy Bletcher, Gwenllian Gill, Clara Lou Sheridan, Sam Lee,
Charles Dorety, Harry Depp, Al Gordon, Lulu Beeson, Sam Rice,
Tom Plank, Earle Foxe (Wedding guests), Junior Herschfeld
(David Holt's stand-in).

SONGS: "Laughing the Clouds Away," "When He Comes Home to
Me" (Robin, Coslow). "I Ain't Gonna Carry No Torch" (Coslow)
was written for Helen Morgan, but was not used (B-100).

SYNOPSIS: Alcoholic vaudevillean Bud Hannigan helps Florette
Faxon and her seven-year-old son Jimmy after the death of her
husband. Bud takes her to see singer Bonnie Kay in hopes she
can learn to perform in a single act. Bud is upset by the
performance, since Bonnie is his estranged wife. Opportunist
Hap Stanley sees Florette as a way to get back in vaudeville.
Jimmy dislikes Hap and is upset when he becomes Florette's
partner and husband. Hap mistreats his wife and forces
Florette to put Jimmy in military school. Jimmy begs Bud to
rescue him. Bud subtly tries to convince Florette to bring
her son home. When Hap learns the act has been canceled, he
tells Florette he is leaving her for another woman.
Devastated, Florette falls from a swing during a performance
and dies. Bud goes to the school to tell Jimmy. By
coincidence, Bonnie is appearing at the school's parents'

day program. Jimmy tells Bonnie about Bud taking him to see
her show and bonds with her. Bonnie and Bud discuss their
marriage and admit they still care for each other. She
insists that he should not have walked out because he felt he
was holding back her career. Bonnie urges Bud to tell Jimmy
the truth about Florette. Instead, Bud tells him that
Florette is on a fifty-two-week tour. Bud and Bonnie decide
to reconcile and give Jimmy a second family.

REVIEWS:
Harrison's Reports, August 25, 1934: "You Belong to Me
is a fairly entertaining picture, more because of the
excellence of the performances, then of the story. It is a
little too thickly coated with sentiment, particularly in the
closing scenes, which become draggy."

New York Times, September 13, 1934: "...the minor show
people who form the population of [You Belong to Me]
present an unusually attractive target for the sentimental
dramatists. Their glib mediocrity, empty pride and ten-cent
glamour are both terribly human and terribly obvious....
After a beginning which promises a fresh approach to these
dramatic riches, [the movie] collapses into tedium and the
clumsy pursuit of tears."

Variety, September 18, 1934: "Though loaded down with
faults, You Belong to Me should be salable to family
audiences. Making it chiefly so is eight-year-old David Jack
Holt."

Cincinnati Enquirer [OH], October 22, 1934: "You Belong
to Me is another tear jerker. With Lee Tracy talking down
a putty nose in the role of a vaudeville actor..., and with
Helen Morgan singing one good song, but only one, the play
slithers across the screen."

NOTES: Portions of You Belong to Me were filmed at the
Black-Foxe Military Institute in Hollywood, California and at
the Mason Theatre in Los Angeles. The working title was
Honor Bright. Dickie Moore originally was cast as Jimmy,
but illness caused him to withdraw from the picture. He was
replaced by David Jack Holt, whose performance garnered the
best reviews. After the child actor received a flurry of
publicity, Variety compared him to Shirley Temple.
Although Holt worked steadily in supporting roles in many
films from the 1930s to the 1950s, he never became a star.
     Clara Lou Sheridan is an extra in You Belong to Me,
appearing as a wedding guest at Florette's reception. The
movie had no relation to the 1941 Columbia picture of the
same title.

F-10   Wagon Wheels   (Paramount, September 21, 1934)
       56 mins.

Producer: Harold Hurley. Director: Charles Barton.
Screenplay: Jack Cunningham, Charles Logue, and Carl A.
Buss. Adapted from the story "Fighting Caravans" by Zane
Grey. Songs: Peter DeRose, Billy Hill, and Manuel Ponce.

Photography: William C. Mellor.   Editor: Jack Dennis.   Art
direction: Earl Hedrick.

CAST: Randolph Scott (Clint Belmet), Gail Patrick (Nancy
Wellington), Billy Lee (Sonny Wellington), Jan Duggan (Abby
Masters), Leila Bennett (Hetty Masters), Monte Blue (Kenneth
Murdock), Raymond Hatton (Jim Burch), Olin Howland (Bill
O'Meary), J.P. McGowan (Couch), James A. Marcus (Jed), Helen
Hunt (Mrs. Jed), James B. "Pop" Kenton (Masters), John
Marston (Orator), Sam McDaniel (Black coachman), Howard
Wilson (Permit officer), Michael S. Visaroff (Russian),
Julian Madison (Lester), Eldred Tidbury (Chauncey), E. Alyn
Waren (The Factor), Fern Emmett (Settler), Clara Lou Sheridan
(Extra), Lew Meehan (Listener), Harold Goodwin (Nancy's
brother), Colin Tapley (Mountaineer), Alfred Delcambre (Ebe),
Pauline Moore.

SONGS: "Wagon Wheels" (DeRose, Hill), "Estrellita" (Ponce),
"Under the Daisies" (Unknown).

SYNOPSIS: In 1840, widow Nancy Wellington heads west to
Oregon with her little boy Sonny. She clashes with wagon
train leader Clint Belmet, who tries to convince her that a
stagecoach is much safer than a wagon. Half-breed fur trader
Kenneth Murdock conspires with other fur traders to stop the
settlers from encroaching on their territory. During the
trip, Sonny befriends Clint, but Nancy remains cool. Murdock
sparks an Indian attack on the wagon train, but Clint refuses
to turn back. As the caravan heads west, Nancy becomes
friendlier to Clint. She confesses that she is going to
Oregon because her in-laws tried to take Sonny after her
husband's death. They slowly fall in love. Murdock plots
with the Indians to attack the wagon train again, but Clint
follows him and overhears the plan. Clint moves the caravan
out ahead of schedule, but the Indians attack. Murdock tries
to kidnap Nancy, but Clint saves her. The caravan arrives
safely in Oregon, where Nancy and Clint decide to marry.

REVIEWS:
New York Times, October 4, 1934: "Another story - or is it
the same one? - of the covered wagon days....while it rates a
better classification than 'horse opera,' [Wagon Wheels]
has not quite the epic sweep that its producers intended it
should have....The film does possess much that is interesting
and entertaining. The regrets are mostly for what it might
have been."

Variety, October 9, 1934: "While picture charts no new
courses, it offers enough action, romance and comedy to merit
mass approval. In gross results it should top the average
western."

Cincinnati Enquirer [OH], November 3, 1934: "Wagon
Wheels is adventure filled and carries in it the nostalgia
for this form of entertainment. It is the complete and
sweeping melodrama. The song of the same name as the show
echoes as background."

Motion Picture Herald, June 1, 1935: "How in the world
Paramount ever let this get by as a program picture is a
mystery to me. If they realized it they have a Covered
Wagon [(Famous Players-Lasky, 1923)] or better. This
picture properly handled would have made the best outdoor
picture since sound started."

NOTES: _Wagon Wheels_ began production on August 8, 1934.
It is a remake of _Fighting Caravans_ (Paramount, 1931), a
western that stars Gary Cooper. Both films are based on a
Zane Grey story of the same title, which ran in _Country
Gentleman_ November 1928-March 1929. The working title of
Wagon Wheels also was _Fighting Caravans_. The popularity
of the song "Wagon Wheels," which first appeared in _The
Ziegfeld Follies of 1934_, led Paramount to acquire the
rights and use it as a title theme (B-211). Part of _Wagon
Wheels_ was filmed at a ranch near Cooperstown, California.
According to many modern sources, unused footage from
Fighting Caravans also was utilized.
    Clara Lou Sheridan is an extra in this film. She later
recalled that when Paramount put her under contract, she was
asked if she could ride (B-206). _Wagon Wheels_ marks the
first of many westerns. The picture also is known as
Caravans West.

F-11   _The Lemon Drop Kid_   (Paramount, September 28, 1934)
       71 mins.

Producer: William LeBaron. Director: Marshall Neilan.
Assistant director: James Dugan. Screenplay: Howard J.
Green. Adapted from a story by Damon Runyon. Photography:
Henry Sharp. Editor: Richard Currier. Art direction: Hans
Dreier and John B. Goodman. Sound: Earl C. Sitar.

CAST: Lee Tracy (Wally Brooks), Helen Mack (Alice Deering),
William Frawley (The Professor/William Dunhill), Minna
Gombell (Maizie), Baby LeRoy (Wally, Jr.), Robert McWade (Mr.
Griggsby), Henry B. Walthall (Jonas Deering), Clarence H.
Wilson (Martin Potter), Charles Wilson (Warden), Kitty Kelley
(Cora Jennings), Edward J. LeSaint (Doctor), Del Henderson
(Judge Forrest), Robert E. Homans (Sheriff), Grace Godall
(Griggsby's secretary), William B. Davidson (Police captain),
Edward Gargan (Sullivan), James Burke, Jules Cowles, C.L.
Sherwood (Tramps), Bee McCune, Jean McCune (Twins), Lillian
West (Nurse), Tammany Young, Al Hill (Mugs), Tempe Pigott
(Old lady), Charles McEvoy, Edwin Baker (Road cops), Walter
McGrail (Tout), Lee Shumway, Stanley Blystone (Policemen),
Eddie Peabody (Banjo player), Marshall Ruth (Fat man at
party), Nell Craig (Miss Murgatroy), Clara Lou Sheridan (Girl
at track), Sam McDaniel.

SYNOPSIS: Fast-talking racetrack bum Wally Brooks is known
as the Lemon Drop Kid because of his love of candy. Wally
offers wheelchair-bound millionaire Griggsby a lemon drop as
a placebo and convinces him to bet one hundred dollars on a
horse. When the money is stolen from Wally's pocket and the
horse wins, Wally is forced to leave town since he cannot pay
Grisby his winnings. While on the run, Wally befriends

alcoholic Jonas Deering. Wally falls in love with Jonas's
daughter Alice. Wally tries to tell Alice about his past
before they marry, but she assures him that she loves him
unconditionally. Complications arise when Alice gets
pregnant. The doctor orders Wally to take her to a
specialist in the city. After Wally's boss refuses to give
him a loan, a desperate Wally robs him. Wally arrives too
late with the money. Alice delivers Wally, Jr. and dies.
The police arrest Wally for robbery, as he revealed his
identity by eating a lemon drop during the theft. Wally
becomes bitter and makes life in prison difficult. With the
help of a kindly warden, he gets to know Wally, Jr. and
changes his attitude. He dreams of spending more time with
his son after his release. Unbeknownst to Wally, Jonas dies
of alcoholism and the baby is put up for adoption. When
Wally gets out of jail, he is heartbroken about the adoption.
His misery is short-lived, as he finds his partner and his
wife are caring for the boy until Wally's release. He also
learns that Griggsby has appointed himself Wally, Jr.'s
foster father, since the lemon drops cured his arthritis.
Grigsby gives Wally a check for five thousand dollars, minus
the one hundred dollars he was supposed to bet, and together
they go to visit Wally, Jr.

REVIEWS:
Harrison's Reports, October 13, 1934: "Fairly good
entertainment for the masses. Although the story is simple,
it has human interest, emotional appeal, and some comedy."

New York Times, October 27, 1934: "In the words of the
racetrack from which its story springs, The Lemon Drop Kid
is no Man o' War. It breaks its stride trying to go the full
feature distance and its pedigree is open to suspicion. But
the spectator who follows its course down the projection room
is reasonably sure of enjoying a few good chuckles..."

Variety, October 30, 1934: "A genuinely diverting and at
times touching screen interval....It is packed with human
interest, humor and action. Not to mention snappy dialog
[sic], a swell performance by Lee Tracy, and a plot treatment
which enriches the story for galloping celluloid."

Cincinnati Enquirer [OH], November 10, 1934: "Lee Tracy,
verbal cannonball of motion picture players, is starred as a
race track [sic] tout who learns life's biggest lesson in a
'one-horse' town, in Damon Runyon's tale..."

NOTES: The Lemon Drop Kid began production on July 31,
1934. Racetrack scenes were filmed on location at Tanforan
Racetrack in San Bruno, California. Clara Lou Sheridan has
several lines as a girl at the track. Gertrude Michael was
supposed to co-star in the film with Lee Tracy and Helen
Mack, however she did not appear in the final movie (B-211).
Paramount remade The Lemon Drop Kid in 1951 with Bob Hope
and a slightly different storyline.

F-12 Ready for Love (Paramount, October 12, 1934)
      77 mins.

Producer: Albert Lewis. Executive producer: Emanuel Cohen. Director: Marion Gering. Screenplay: J.P. McEvoy and William Slavens McNutt. Based on the novel The Whipping by Roy Flannagan. Photography: Leon Shamroy. Editor: Eda Warren. Art direction: Hans Dreier and Earl Hedrick. Sound: Jack Goodrich.

CAST: Ida Lupino (Marigold Tate), Richard Arlen (Julian Barrow), Marjorie Rambeau (Goldie Tate), Trent [Junior] Durkin (Joey Burke), Beulah Bondi (Louella Burke), Esther Howard (Aunt Ida), Ralph Remley (Chester Burke), Charles E. Arnt (Sam Gardner), Henry Travers (Judge Pickett), Charles Sellon (Caleb Hooker), Irving Bacon (Milkman), Oscar Smith (Pullman porter), Ben Taggart (Pullman conductor), Franklyn Ardell (Dean), Fredric Santley (Farnum), James C. Burtis (Blaine), David Loring (Skyscraper), Wilbur Mack (Davis), Louise Carter (Mrs. Thompson), Eleanor Wesselhoeft (Mrs. Black), Ralph Lewis (Mr. Thompson), Bernard Suss (Mr. Black), Burr Caruth (Stage doorman), Henry Dunkinson, Howard Brooks, Lucille Ward, Joseph J. Franz, A.S. "Pop" Byron, Cecil Weston, Blanche Rose, Clara Lou Sheridan (Villagers).

SYNOPSIS: Aspiring actress Marigold Tate runs away from boarding school in hopes that her mother Goldie will allow her to join her traveling stage show. Instead, Goldie sends her to New England to stay with her aunt. When Marigold's dog runs away as she is getting off the train, the citizens mistake the tearful girl for the grieving mistress of Nathaniel Burke, whose casket arrives on her train. Marigold is shunned by the local women, but receives special attention from the men. Nathaniel's family threatens to sue after journalist Julian Peters runs a story about Marigold in the newspaper. She pretends to be Nathaniel's mistress to protect Julian. Nathaniel's nephew, Joey Burke, falls in love with Marigold, despite his family's objections. The citizens misinterpret a mishap during a town picnic, causing Marigold to be ostracized further. The women tie Marigold to an antique dunking stool and dip her in the lake. Julian saves her, but the story appears in newspapers around the country. Julian proposes to Marigold. Goldie convinces Marigold to cash in on the publicity and go on tour. Julian breaks their engagement and accepts a job on a New York newspaper. After Marigold convinces her mother that she loves Julian, Goldie has the newspaper print her apology. Julian responds in a headline of his own. Many headlines later, Julian and Marigold reconcile.

REVIEWS:
Harrison's Reports, October 27, 1934: "A fair program comedy. It is a little far-fetched, and the story is thin, but it is well acted and for the most part amusing."

Variety, December 4, 1934: "A light family picture, of no more entertainment weight than to suggest that it will have another feature as company almost everywhere it shows."

NOTES: Ready for Love began production on July 31, 1934. The movie is based on Roy Flannagan's 1930 novel The

Whipping. According to the pressbook, some scenes were
filmed at Sherwood Lake, a location near Los Angeles. Clara
Lou Sheridan has a bit part as one of the townspeople.

F-13 **Mrs. Wiggs of the Cabbage Patch**   (Paramount,
      October 19, 1934)   80 mins.

Producer: Douglas MacLean. Director: Norman Taurog.
Assistant director: Edgar Anderson. Choreographer: LeRoy
Prinz. Screenplay: William Slavens McNutt and Jane Storm.
Based on the novel by Alice Hegan Rice and the play by Anne
Crawford Flexner. Songs: Lilla Cayley Robinson, Paul
Lincke, Andrew B. Sterling, Harry Von Tilzer, Alice
Hawthorne, Stephen Foster, Robert Burns, Harry H. Williams,
and Egbert Van Alstyne. Photography: Charles Lang. Editor:
Anne Bauchens. Art direction: Hans Dreier and Robert Odell.
Sound: Eugene Merritt.

CAST: W.C. Fields (C. Ellsworth Stubbins), Pauline Lord
(Elvira Wiggs), ZaSu Pitts (Tabitha Hazy), Evelyn Venable
(Lucy Olcott), Kent Taylor (Bob Redding), Charles Middleton
(Mr. Bagby), Donald Meek (Hiram Wiggs), Jimmy Butler (Billy
Wiggs), Virginia Weidler (Europena Wiggs), George Breakston
(Jimmy Wiggs), Edith Fellows (Australia Wiggs), Carmencita
Johnson (Asia Wiggs), George Reed (Julius, the servant),
Mildred Gover (Priscilla, the maid), Arthur Housman (Dick
Harris, drunk), Sam Flint (Railroad agent Jenkins), James
Robinson (Mose), Bentley Hewlett (Box office man), Edward
Tamblyn (Eddie, the usher), Clara Lou Sheridan (Girl),
Lillian Elliott (Mrs. Bagby), Earl Pingree (Brakeman), George
Pearce (Minister), Del Henderson (House manager), Al Shaw,
Sam Lee (Comedians), Walter Walker (Dr. Barton), Tyler Brooks
(Ticket taker), Dorothy Ross, Daisy Rooney, Gladys Young
(Dancers).

SONGS: "The Glow Worm" (Robinson, Lincke), "Wait till the
Sun Shines, Nellie" (Sterling, Von Tilzer), "Listen to the
Mockingbird" (Hawthorne), "Old Folks at Home" (Foster),
"Comin' Thro' the Rye" (Burns), "In the Shade of the Old
Apple Tree" (Williams, Van Alstyne), "Beulah Land."

SYNOPSIS: Elvira Wiggs lives in a shantytown shack with her
five children. She dreams of the return of her husband
Hiram, who deserted her three years earlier to search for
gold in the Klondike. Mr. Bagby criticizes the Wiggses and
constantly reminds Elvira that she still owes twenty-five
dollars on her mortgage. Wealthy Lucy Olcott and her fiance,
newspaperman Bob Redding, try to help the Wiggses. Although
Bob sees that Jimmy Wiggs is hospitalized for his hacking
cough, he dies. Elvira tries to contact Hiram, but he cannot
be found. Elvira helps her spinster friend Tabitha Hazy
snare hungry bachelor C. Ellsworth Stubbins. Tabitha fools
Stubbins with Elvira's cooking and he proposes. Bob runs
newspaper ads across the country in an effort to locate
Hiram. When Bagby learns the railroad wants the Wiggses'
land, he decides to foreclose unless they can pay the
twenty-five dollars immediatly. Billy confesses their
financial troubles to Bob and Lucy and they race to save the

Wiggses' home. As all is about to be lost, Hiram returns.
Bob plants twenty-five dollars in Hiram's suit so he can be a
hero and save his family. Reunited, the Wiggses are happy at
last. After Tabitha confesses her deception to her husband,
Stubbins learns to cook.

REVIEWS:
Harrison's Reports, October 20, 1934: "Except for the last
fifteen minutes, which are somewhat slow and a little far-
fetched, Mrs. Wiggs of the Cabbage Patch should appeal to
every one, because of the comedy and human interest....An
excellent family entertainment."

Cincinnati Enquirer [OH], October 22, 1934: "Mrs. Wiggs
of the Cabbage Patch is one of those happy creations which
suits the tastes of all but the most hard of hard-boiled film
goers....The cast [is] large and capable..."

Variety, October 30, 1934: "Out of town reports give
'Mrs. Wiggs' top grosses, and no reason why this should not
be continued down the line....Women and children are going to
rave over it, and whoever gets it Christmas week can raise
the mortgage, or a good part of it, for it is a perennially
popular story given a production that is a credit to all
concerned....Nothing artistic or subtle, but loaded with the
good old-fashioned hoke..."

NOTES: By 1934, Mrs. Wiggs of the Cabbage Patch had a
long history. Based on Alice Hegan Rice's 1901 novel of the
same title, it was adapted for the stage by Anne Crawford
Flexner in 1904, then filmed as a silent picture in 1919. A
silent sequel, Locwy Mary, was made by MGM in 1926. In
addition to the 1934 version of Mrs. Wiggs of the Cabbage
Patch, the story was filmed again in 1942 with Fay Bainter
in the title role.
      Production began in early June 1934. Some of the film
was shot in Calabasas and Lasky Mesa, California. Mrs.
Wiggs of the Cabbage Patch marks the film debut of Pauline
Lord, best known for stage roles like the title character in
the 1921 production of Eugene O'Neill's Anna Christie.
Mrs. Wiggs usually is credited as one of Clara Lou
Sheridan's early pictures. It is assumed that she is a
neighbor.

F-14 Limehouse Blues (Paramount, November 9, 1934)
      65 mins.

Producer: Arthur Hornblow, Jr. Executive producer: Emanuel
Cohen. Director: Alexander Hall. Second unit director:
William Shea. Screenplay: Arthur Phillips and Cyril Hume.
Based on a story by Arthur Phillips. Songs: Sam Cowlow,
Douglas Furber, and Philip Braham. Music: Sam Coslow.
Photography: Harry Fischbeck. Editor: William Shea. Art
direction: Hans Dreier and Robert Usher. Makeup: Wally
Westmore.

CAST: George Raft (Harry Young), Jean Parker (Toni), Anna
May Wong (Tu Tuan), Kent Taylor (Eric Benton), Montagu Love

(Pug Talbot), Billy Bevan (Herb), John Rogers (Smokey),
Robert Loraine (Inspector Sheridan), E. Alyn Warren (Ching
Lee), Eily Malyon (Woman who finds Pug), Forrester Harvey
(McDonald), Robert "Bob" A'Dair (Alfred), Elsie Prescott
(Employment agent), James May (Taxi driver), Colin Kenny
(Davis), Eric Blore (Slummer), Colin Tapley (Man fighting
with wife), Rita Carlyle (Wife), Desmond Roberts (Constable),
Tempe Pigott (Maggie), Otto Yamaoka (Chinese waiter on boat),
Dora Mayfield (Flower woman), Clara Lou Sheridan (Girl with
couples), Keith Kenneth (Policeman in Pug's house), Louis
Vincenot (Rhama), Wyndham Standing (Commissioner Kenyon),
Angelo Bianchi (Street organist), Lillian Kilgannon (Jean
Parker's stand-in).

SONGS: "Limehouse Nights" (Coslow), "Limehouse Blues"
(Furber, Braham).

SYNOPSIS: Chinese-American Harry Young operates a cafe and
smuggling business in London's Limehouse district. When
pickpocket Toni is arrested for stealing a watch, Harry
provides an alibi. He offers Toni a job, although her brutal
step-father Pug Talbot is his enemy. When Harry refuses to
give Pug a cut of the smuggling operation, Pug tips off the
police. Harry has Pug killed after he learns that Pug beat
Toni for warning Harry. Toni protects Harry by telling the
police that Harry and Pug had settled their differences
before his death. Harry hires Toni to work as a smuggler and
invites her to live with him. Tu Tuan, Harry's mistress, is
jealous as Harry showers Toni with gifts and attention. Tu
Tuan confronts him and predicts doom from an interracial
romance. Distrustful of the caucasian, Tu Tuan has Toni
followed. While Toni is grateful for Harry's attentions, she
does not return his feelings of love. She falls in love with
Canadian pet shop owner Eric Benton and tries to quit her
job. Harry has her blackballed from working in Limehouse,
hoping it will make her remain with him. Toni confesses her
past to Eric. When Eric confronts Harry about releasing
Toni, Harry orders his henchman to kill him. Toni begs Harry
to call off the murder, promising to give up Eric. Harry
realizes the hopelessness of his romance and he tries to call
off the hit. Jealous Tu Tuan tells Inspector Sherman of
Scotland Yard about Harry's smuggling operation and commits
suicide. Sherman chases Harry, believing he is on a job.
Harry is fatally shot, but lives long enough to save Eric and
clear Toni of any suspicions. Eric and Toni are free to
marry.

REVIEWS:
Harrison's Reports, December 1, 1934: "Poor! An
antiquated story with only one redeeming feature - good
production....It moves along listlessly and without
exceitement."

New York Times, December 12, 1934: "...even those
filmgoers who are most successful in fighting off [George]
Raft's overpowering personal allure can hardly blame hin for
the frailities of Limehouse Blues. It owns the most
childlike scenario that the grown-up Broadway area has seen

in many weeks and its chief virtue is to remind some of us
novagenarians of the Yellow Peril literature of an earlier
day."

Variety, December 18, 1934: "Weak picture except for its
support cast. Though exciting in spots, this offshoot of the
East is East and West is West theme never comes within the
ken of gripping drama. Won't satisfy the average fan but the
George Raft name may help...picture will need help."

NOTES: Limehouse Blues underwent several changes before
coming to the screen in 1934. The working title was
Limehouse Nights, which explains the inclusion of Sam
Coslow's song of the same name. Paramount originally cast
Sylvia Sidney in the role of Toni, but she refused to make
the film. Heather Angel tested for the role before Jean
Parker ultimately was borrowed from MGM (B-211).
    During the 1930s, many studios cast occidental actors in
oriental roles, with mixed results. Although Paul Muni won
praise for his performance in The Good Earth (MGM, 1937),
George Raft was less-than-convincing as the Chinese smuggler
in Limehouse Blues. The melodrama includes a now-
embarrassing central theme, comparing the mixing of races to
breeding thoroughbred dogs and mongrels. Clara Lou Sheridan
can be glimpsed as an extra in a scene with several couples.
The film was rereleased as East End Chant and it is under
that title that it usually appears on television.

F-15 College Rhythm   (Paramount, November 23, 1934)
       75 mins.

Producer: Louis B. Lighton. Director: Norman Taurog.
Choreographer: LeRoy Prinz. Screenplay: Walter DeLeon,
John McDermott, and Francis Martin. Based on a story by
George Marion, Jr. Songs: Mack Gordon and Harry Revel.
Photography: Leo Tover and Ted Tetzlaff. Editors: LeRoy
Stone and Edward Dmytryk. Art direction: Hans Dreier, Earl
Hedrick, and Robert Usher. Sets: Ray Moyer. Sound: Eugene
Merritt.

CAST: Jack Oakie ("Love and Kisses" Finnegan), Joe Penner
(Joe), Lyda Roberti (Mimi), Lanny Ross (Larry Stacey), Helen
Mack (June Cort), Mary Brian (Gloria Van Dayham), George
Barbier (J.P. Stacey), Franklin Pangborn (Peabody), Mary
Wallace (Peggy Small), Dean Jagger (Coach), Joseph Sauers
(Spud Miller), Julian Madison (Jimmy Poole), Robert McWade
(Herman Whimple), Clara Lou Sheridan (Glove saleswoman),
Harold Minjir (Witherspoon), Dutch Hendrian (Taylor, Whimple
football team captain), Bradley Metcalfe (Sonny Whimple),
Eric Alden (Stacey quarterback), Lee Phelps (Timekeeper),
Gilbert Wilson (Whimple quarterback), Alfred Delcambre (First
substitute), Howard Wilson (Colton end), Morgan Wallace,
Douglas Wood, Arthur Hoyt (Tramps), Patrick Moriarity (Irish
peanut vendor), Harry Strang (Taxi driver), Lillian Harmer,
Helen Dixon, Charles Irwin, Francis Sayles (Customers), Hal
Raynor (Gag man), Patsy Bellamy, Katharine Snell, Laura
Morse, Pinkie Reynolds, Harriette Haddon, Dorothy Dayton,
Grace Davies, Mary Fairweather, Helen Hawley, Bobby Joyce,

June Karlin, Sheila Rae, Eileen Thomas, Mary Croft, Frances
Lehman, Virginia Debney, Margot Sage, Joyce Murray, Virginia
George, Sally Haines, Lovene Sheehan, Amy Sureau, Aimee
David, Mary Daly, Marguerite Caverley, Crystal Keate, Colleen
Ward, Geneva Hall, Martha Fields, Mildred Dixon, Alma Ross,
Rita Dunn, Dorothy White, Mickey MacKillop, "Peaches" Ahlman,
Ethel Bryant, Adele Cutler Jerome, Paula DeCarlo, Jean Fursa,
Emily LaRue, Rosalie Lissner, Mildred Morris, Bobbe Cronin,
Sydna Black, Jeanette Fuller, Jean Joyce, Ethel Pressman,
Bonita Barker, Edna Lawrence, Carol Carmen, Eva Reynolds,
Cassie Hanley, Theo De Voe, Jeanette Dickson, Celeste
Edwards, Patsy King, Bee Stevens, Kay Gordon, Betty Gordon,
Myra Mason, Vivian Faulkner, Thaya Foster, Dorothy Thompson,
Kathryn Hankin, Mary Jane Hodge, Betty McMahon, Vina Gale,
Pokey Champion, Dixie Martin, Virginia Kleinberger, Regana De
Liguora, Isabel Coffrey (Chorus girls), Freddy Welch (Joe
Penner's stand-in).

SONGS: "College Rhythm," "Stay As Sweet As You Are,"
"Goo-Goo I'm Ga-Ga Over You," "Let's Give Three Cheers for
Love," "Take a Number from One to Ten," "Victory Song,"
"We're Here to State," "Love and Kisses Finnegan," "Stacey
Cheer" (Gordon, Revel).

SYNOPSIS: Studious Larry Stacey is jealous when his fiancee
Gloria Van Dayham praises brash, All-American football star
"Love and Kisses" Finnegan.   Larry predicts the athlete will
be unsuccessful when he graduates from State College.   Two
years later, Finnegan remains unemployed and revels in his
former glory days.   Swallowing his pride, he visits Larry,
who is now general manager of his father's department store.
Larry hires Finnegan to work at the ribbon counter, hoping to
humiliate his former rival.   When Larry's father, J.P.
Stacey, returns from a trip, he finds that Larry's high ideas
have driven away all the customers.   J.P. insists that the
store needs a publicity stunt to make money.   He decides to
cash in on Finnegan's football stardom and conceited
personality, making Finnegan his assistant.   Larry resigns
and takes a job in the music department.   J.P. and Finnegan
remodel the store to resemble a college-themed nightclub and
form a football team.   Larry's former secretary, June Cort,
urges him to stand up to Finnegan when Finnegan tries to
steal Gloria.   Larry vows to prove himself on the football
field to win back his girlfriend.   June helps him train,
while harboring a secret crush on her boss.   A rival
department store challenges Stacey's team to a football game.
When their mascot is late, it looks like Stacey's team will
lose.   Finnegan steps in and wins the game with Larry's help.
They make up.   Larry realizes that he loves June, leaving
Finnegan free to romance Gloria.

REVIEWS:
Harrison's Reports, November 17, 1934:   "Very good.   It is
a mixture of romance, football, comedy, and music, and they
have all been blended in a lavish production excellently."

New York Times, November 24, 1934:   "...College Rhythm is
a mad and generally merry concoction, unbelievable,

nonsensical and designed solely for eye and ear amusement....
the plot hangs by less than a thread and the saving grace of
the film is its ability to capitalize on the singing talents
of [Lanny] Ross, the charm of [Lyda] Roberti, the
handsomeness of [Mary] Brian and [Helen] Mack and [Joe]
Penner's clowning."

Variety, November 27, 1934: "...College Rhythm
recaptures much of the charm of [the early talker days] to
rate as a highly entertaining semi-musical. It has a well
balanced set of cast names and carries a punch, so shouldn't
have much trouble at the box office."

Real Screen Fun, February 1935: "A rollicking musical
built around the story of two college enemies....and for
feminine loveliness, there's Lyda Roberti, Helen Mack and a
bevy of beauties known as the Stacey Salesgirls."

NOTES: College Rhythm began production on August 14, 1934.
The film marks the debut of radio comedian Joe Penner, best
known for his popular catch phrase "Want to buy a duck?"
Penner's feathered pal Goo-Goo plays himself in the film.
Goo-Goo was replaced by a mechanical stand-in during some
scenes because the duck had stage fright (B-211). Clara Lou
Sheridan appears in two scenes, as a glove saleswoman and a
spectator at the department store football game. She
allegedly filled in for Lyda Roberti when the singer/
comedienne became ill (B-211). Roberti died in 1938.

F-16   Behold My Wife   (Paramount, December 7, 1934)
       78 mins.

Producer: B.P. Schulberg. Executive producer: Emanuel
Cohen. Director: Mitchell Leisen. Screenplay: Grover
Jones and Vincent Lawrence. Adaptation: William R. Lipman
and Oliver LaFarge. Based on the novel The Translation of
a Savage by Sir Gilbert Parker. Photography: Leon
Shamroy. Art direction: Hans Dreier and Bernard Herzbrun.

CAST: Sylvia Sidney (Tonita Storm Cloud), Gene Raymond
(Michael Carter), Juliette Compton (Diana Carter-Curzon),
Laura Hope Crews (Catherine Carter), H.B. Warner (Hubert
Carter), Monroe Owsley (Bob Prentice), Kenneth Thomson (Jim
Curzon), Ann Sheridan (Mary White), Dean Jagger (Pete),
Charlotte Granville (Mrs. Sykes), Eric Blore (Benson),
Charles B. Middleton (Juan Storm Cloud), Ralph Remley
(Jenkins), Cecil Weston (Gibson), Dewey Robinson (Bryan),
Edward Gargan (Connolly), Olin Howland (Mattingly), Greg
Whitespear (Medicine man), Jim Thorpe (Indian chief), Otto
Hoffman (Minister), Evelyn Selbie, Lillianne Leighton
(Neighbors), Raymond Turner (Porter), Nella Walker (Mrs.
Copperwaithe), Gwenllian Gill (Miss Copperwaithe), Charles
Wilson (Police captain), Fuzzy Knight (News photographer),
Countess Rina De Liguoro (Countess Slavotski), Virginia
Hammond (Mrs. Lawson), Jack Mulhall, Martin Malone, Pat
O'Malley, Neal Burns (Reporters at train), Phillips Smalley,
Edmund Mortimer, Cyril Ring (Society men), Celeste Ford
(Society woman), Mabel Forrest (Society dowager), Rhea

Mitchell (Female reporter), Phil Tead, Eddie Anderson, Matt
McHugh, Rafael Storm (Chauffeurs), Cosmo Kyrle Bellew (Mr.
Lawson), Frank Dunn (Footman), Arnold Korff (Mr. Lawson's
companion), Joseph Sauers (Morton, Michael's chauffeur), Joan
Standing (Miss Smith), Kate Price (Mrs. MacGregor), Mike
Morita (Fuji), Charles Stevens (Apache herder), Whitedove
Clemens (Indian girl at meal), Billy Lee (Indian boy at
meal), Howling Wolf (Indian father at meal), Mrs. Choree
(Indian mother at meal).

SYNOPSIS: The Carters are a wealthy society family who
cherish their reputation. Although daughter Diana is
cheating on her husband with Bob Prentice, the Carters are
more concerned with son Michael, who is engaged to poor
stenographer Mary White. The Carters disapprove of the union
because of Mary's lower social standing. Diana tries to buy
off Mary, claiming that Michael's intentions are insincere.
Distraught, Mary commits suicide. Michael blames his
family's interference for Mary's death. He heads west,
determined to get revenge by disgracing the Carters. When
Michael accidently is shot, Native American Tonita Storm
Cloud nurses him at a secluded cabin. The tribe exiles
Tonita for living with a caucasian man. When Tonita
confesses that she loves Michael, he decides to marry her to
disgrace his family. As expected, the Carters are outraged
by the marriage. However, after Diana gives Tonita a
makeover, she charms the Carters' society friends. Michael
is furious over Tonita's acceptance. He confesses the motive
behind their marriage and Tonita is devastated. She leaves
Michael, vowing to get revenge. Diana is jealous when Bob
flirts with Tonita. When he refuses to resume their affair,
Diana shoots him in Tonita's presence. Tonita confesses to
the crime, feeling her life is useless. She tells Michael
the truth, hoping he will feel guilty for marrying her and
ruining her life. Michael realizes he loves his wife and he
also confesses to shooting Bob. The police put Michael and
Tonita in a room with a microphone and discover both are
innocent. Michael and Tonita realize that they love each
other. They are released to resume their marriage.

REVIEWS:
Cincinnati Enquirer [OH], December 14, 1934: "Behold My
Wife meanders. It has Gene Raymond as a spoiled playboy,
angry at his family for interfering in his love affair with
Ann Sheridan and sending the distracted girl to suicide....
The story...does not hold to a true course."

Harrison's Reports, December 22, 1934: "A fairly good
program comedy-drama. It is slow in getting started but
gradually picks up speed."

Variety, February 20, 1935: "There's a girl in an early
sequence bit, Ann Sheridan, who should be an important screen
personality some day if her work here is any criterion, and
that despite the fact that the sound goes screwy on her just
when it shouldn't."

New York Times, February 21, 1935: "The fact is that the

Roxy's new photoplay is so abnormally improbable and so
crudely arranged that it lacks any sort of distinction except
the dubious one of harboring the most wild-eyed scenario of
the new year."

NOTES: Behold My Wife is based on the 1893 novel The
Translation of a Savage by Sir Gilbert Parker. It first
was filmed by Famous Players-Lasky Corp. in 1920. The silent
film starred Milton Sills and Mabel Julienne Scott as the
wealthy man and his Indian bride. Maude Wayne played Sills's
fiancee who married another instead of committing suicide in
the 1920 version. One of the working titles for the 1934
film was Red Woman (B-211).
     Director Mitchell Leisen was responsible for casting
Clara Lou Sheridan in Behold My Wife. Having befriended
her during Murder at the Vanities (F-4), he insisted on
giving her the small but pivotal role as the fiancee who
commits suicide. The movie provided her with her best screen
exposure at Paramount (B-122). Clara Lou believed the
dramatic suicide scene was responsible for Paramount renewing
her option. She was quoted as saying, "Committing suicide is
a great thing...to have in a picture. It's something that
draws your eye to the girl" (B-475).
     Clara Lou Sheridan changed her name to Ann during
production of Behold My Wife. It marks the first use of
her new name on screen. She receives seventh billing.

F-17   One Hour Late   (Paramount, December 14, 1934)
       75 mins.

Producers: Albert Lewis and Bayard Veiller. Director:
Ralph Murphy. Assistant director: Charles Wending.
Screenplay: Kathryn Scola and Paul Gerard Smith. Based on a
story by Libbie Block. Songs: Sam Coslow, Leo Robin, Harry
Revel, Mack Gordon, Val Burton, Will Jason, Billy Hill, and
Lewis Gensler. Photography: Ben Reynolds. Art direction:
Hans Dreier and John Goodman. Sound: P.G. Wisdom.

CAST: Joe Morrison (Eddie Blake), Helen Twelvetrees (Bessie
Dunn), Conrad Nagel (Stephen Barclay), Arline Judge (Hazel),
Ray Walker (Cliff Miller), Edward Craven (Maxie), Toby Wing
(Maizie), Gail Patrick (Eileen Barclay), Charles Sellon
(Simpson), George E. Stone (Benny), Jed Prouty (Mr. Finch),
Jack Mulhall (Whittaker), Edward Clark (Mr. Meller), Raymond
[Ray] Milland (Tony St. John), Bradley Page (Jim), Sidney
Miller (Orville), Gladys Hulette (Gertrude), Billy Bletcher
(Smith), Betty Farrington (Miss Jones), Arthur Hoyt (Barlow),
Matty Fain (Crook), Hallene Hill (Sick woman), Diana Lewis
(Her daughter), Frank Mayo (Kearney), Eddie Phillips
(Elevator starter), Phil Tead (Wally), James P. Burtis (Art),
Maxine Elliot Hicks (Elsie Kelsey), Jack Norton (Manager),
Frank Losee, Jr., Alfred Delcambre (Friends), Sam Ash (Phil
Romaine), William Norton Bailey (Clayton), William H. Strauss
(Man who is robbed), Carol Holloway (Nurse), George Lloyd
(Collier), Frank Rice (Engineer), Robert Kent (Soda clerk),
Harry Depp (Fiddle player), Billy Dooley (Attendant in radio
station), Rhea Mitchell (Stage mother), Shirley Jeanne
Rickert (Child), Douglas Blackley (Soda clerk), Charles

Morris (Man outside radio room), William Jeffrey (M.C.),
Genevieve Phillips (Information girl), Buck Mack (Property
man), Jack Raymond (Musician), Robert Littlefield (Orchestra
leader), Ann Sheridan (Girl), Monte Vandergrift, Lee Shumway
(Detectives), Francis Sayles, Duke York (Mixers).

SONGS: "The Last Roundup" (Hill), "A Little Angel Told Me
So" (Coslow), "Me Without You" (Gensler, Robin), "With My
Eyes Wide Open I'm Dreaming" (Revel, Gordon), "Penthouse
Serenade" (Burton, Jason).

SYNOPSIS: Eddie Blake is an aspiring singer who works as an
assistant file clerk at a radio station. He is upset when
his girlfriend, stenographer Bessie Dunn, delays answering
his marriage proposal. Bessie is asked to fill in as a
secretary for the radio station's electrical engineer,
Stephen Barclay. Stephen insults Bessie's secretarial skills
and makes her cry. As an apology, he takes her to lunch.
Eddie sees them and misinterprets the scene as a romantic
rendevous and a rejection of his proposal. Eddie quits and
goes to a radio audition, determined to prove his talents.
Unbeknownst to Eddie, the station's star singer refuses to go
on the air that night or sign his contract unless station
owner Zeller gives him an exorbitant raise. Stephen tells
Bessie about his troubled marriage and invites her away for
the weekend. Eddie overhears her plans and, on the rebound,
proposes to Hazel, another station coworker. Stephen's
estranged wife Eileen stops by to tell him that she is
leaving him for her lover. Eileen, Bessie, and Eddie all end
up in the same elevator, which crashes and delays them an
hour for their appointments. When another passenger has a
heart attack, Eddie enters the elevator shaft to get help.
To calm his nerves, Eddie sings. Zeller hears him and
realizes Eddie can replace his temperamental star. Eddie
saves the passengers and Zeller offers him a contract. Bessie
realizes she loves Eddie and cancels her plans with Stephen.
Eileen has second thoughts about leaving her husband when she
overhears Bessie say Eileen has neglected him. The Barclays
reconcile. When Eddie is late, Hazel accepts a date with
someone else, leaving Eddie free. He makes his radio debut
and makes up with Bessie.

REVIEWS:
Harrison's Reports, January 5, 1935: "An ordinary program
picture. Although there is some comedy and music, the story
is so silly that it barely holds one's interest."

Variety, February 5, 1935: "Picture is rather long, and on
occasion draggy, but still checks as mild amusement."

NOTES: Production began on One Hour Late on September 24,
1934. The working title was Me Without You. Leading man
Joe Morrison was a popular radio singer of the day.
Assistant director Charles Wending was the brother of actress
Claudette Colbert, then a major star at Paramount. Clara Lou
Sheridan can be glimpsed in a bit part as a girl.
     Because of its infidelity theme, Harrison's Reports
deemed the film unsuitable for children, adolescents, or

Sundays (January 5, 1935). The New York Times erroneously
lists Helen Twelvetrees's character as "Betty Dunn" rather
than "Bessie Dunn."

F-18 Home on the Range   (Paramount, December 21, 1934)
      54 mins.

Producer: Harold Hurley. Executive producer: Emanuel
Cohen. Director: Arthur Jacobson. Screenplay: Ethel
Doherty and Grant Garrett. Adaptation: Charles Logue.
Based on the novel Code of the West by Zane Grey. Song
"Home on the Range": Daniel E. Kelly and Dr. Brewster M.
Higley. Photography: William Mellor. Editor: Jack Dennis.
Art direction: Hans Dreier and Earl Hedrick.

CAST: Jackie Coogan (Jack Hatfield), Randolph Scott (Tom
Hatfield), Evelyn Brent (Georgie Haley), Dean Jagger (Boyd
Thurman), Addison Richards (Beady Pierce), Fuzzy Knight
("Cracker" Williams), Clara Lou Sheridan (Elsie Brownly),
Ralph Remley (Brown), Philip Morris (Benson), Francis Sayles
(Hotel clerk), Allen Wood ("Flash" Roberts), Howard Wilson
(Bill Morris), Albert Hart (Undertaker), Richard Carle (James
Butts), C.L. Sherwood (Shorty), Jack Clark (Sheriff), Alfred
Delcambre (Lem), Joe Morrison.

SYNOPSIS: Boyd Thurman is arrested for a land scam, but his
partners Beady Pierce and Georgie Haley escape. They get
jobs in a hotel lunch room in Green Valley, Arizona. Beady
wins at gambling and takes over the hotel. Georgie and her
friend, Elsie Brownly, open a dance hall. Meanwhile,
brothers Tom and Jack Hatfield worry about losing their ranch
when they cannot pay the mortgage. Certain that their prize
horse Midnight can win enough to pay their debts, they sell
eight thousand dollars in cattle to finance Midnight's entry
in the big race. The brothers argue when Tom hires jockey
Flash Roberts to ride the horse. Jack worries that the
jockey will spoil Midnight's chances of winning. Georgie
tires of a criminal life and falls in love with Tom. When
Boyd is released from jail, he goes to Green Valley where
Beady enlists his help to get control of the Hatfields'
ranch. Boyd steals Tom's eight thousand dollars so the
Hatfields will not be able to race Midnight. Georgie
confronts Boyd and Beady about the theft, but they deny any
involvement. Beady kills Boyd to get him out of the way.
His henchman starts a fire on the ranch, which allows Beady
to steal Midnight. Georgie helps Tom fight the fire. She
confesses her sordid past, but he forgives her. They
convince the racetrack manager to let Midnight race without
the entry fee. Jack knocks out Flash and takes his place as
jockey. Midnight wins the race, saving the ranch. Tom
confronts Beady with a gun and demands his money. Beady is
arrested for Boyd's murder. Tom and Georgie marry.

REVIEWS:
Variety, February 12, 1935: "[Home on the Range is] a
picture which...follows tried and well-beaten paths,
developing its menace in the same old way. This goes for
both its western and its racetrack aspects. Picture is short

on running time...and pans out as fair entertainment."

<u>New York Times</u>, February 13, 1935: "...<u>Home on the
Range</u> is a Western only by courtesy. The shooting-irons
might just as well be toy pistols for all the good that the
new film...makes of them. The narrative progresses by fits
and starts, with depressing interims during which you have
the suspicion that the scenarists are just behind the camera
working up something for the next scene."

NOTES: <u>Home on the Range</u> is the second film based on Zane
Grey's western novel <u>Code of the West</u>, first published in
1934. Famous Players-Lasky produced a silent version called
<u>Code of the West</u> in 1922. Owen Moore and Constance Bennett
starred in the roles played by Randolph Scott and Evelyn
Brent in the remake. The working title of <u>Home on the
Range</u> also was <u>Code of the West</u>. However, when the
producers obtained the rights to the well-known song, the
title was changed and new footage was filmed to incorporate
the western ballad. Some of the movie was shot on location
in Malibu Lake, California. Clara Lou Sheridan plays a dance
hall girl in the film.

F-19   <u>Enter Madame!</u>   (Paramount, January 4, 1935)
        83 mins.

Producer: Benjamin Glazer. Director: Elliott Nigent.
Screenplay: Charles Brackett and Gladys Lehman. Based on
the play <u>Enter Madame!</u> by Gilda Varesi Archibald and
Dorothea Donn-Byrne. Songs: Pietro Mascagni, Guido Menasci,
Giovanni Targioni-Tozzetti, Giacomo Puccini, Giuseppe
Giacosa, Luigi Illica, Giuseppe Verdi, and Salvatore
Cammarano. Musical director: Nathaniel Finston.
Photography: Theodor Sparkuhl and William C. Mellor.
Editor: Hugh Bennett. Art direction: Hans Dreier and Ernst
Fegte. Costumes: Travis Banton. Sound: M.M. Paggi.

CAST: Elissa Landi (Lisa Della Robbia), Cary Grant (Gerald
Fitzgerald), Lynne Overman (Mr. Farnham), Sharon Lynne (Flora
Preston), Michelette Burani (Bice), Frank Albertson (John
Fitzgerald), Cecilia Parker (Aline Chalmers), Paul Porcasi
(Archimede), Adrian Rosley (The doctor), Diana Lewis
(Operator), Wilfred Hari (Tamamoto), Torben Meyer (Carlson),
Harold Berquist (Bjorgenson), Richard Bonnelli (Scarpia on
stage), Matt McHugh, Mildred Booth (Reporters), Nina Koshetz
(Elissa Landi's voice double), Wallis Clark (Mr. Massey),
Fred Malatesta (Hotel clerk), Tony Merlo (Ship's operator),
Dick Kline (Stage manager), Gino Corrado (Waiter), Frank G.
Dunn (Second stage manager), Jack Byron (Cameraman), Bud
Galea (Spoletta on stage), Gabriel Leonoff (Spoletta's voice
double), Lorimer Johnston, Clara Lou Sheridan.

SONGS: <u>Cavalleria rusticana</u> (Mascagni, Menasci,
Targioni-Tozetti), <u>Tosca</u> (Puccini, Giacosa, Illica), "The
Anvil Chorus" and "Miserare" from <u>Il trovatore</u> (Verdi,
Cammarano).

SYNOPSIS: American millionaire Gerald Fitzgerald marries

Italian opera star Lisa Della Robbia. Their happiness is
short-lived when Lisa returns to work. As they tour Europe,
Gerald finds he is just another member of the entourage.
Lisa refuses to cancel any engagements, despite her husband's
protests. Tiring of Lisa's indifference, Gerald returns to
New York alone. Lisa promises to join him for six months of
uninterrupted marital bliss after she finishes a tour in
Scandanavia. Gerald meets old flame Flora Preston, who talks
him into filing for divorce when Lisa keeps delaying her
return. Lisa rushes home to fight for her husband. Although
she still loves Gerald, Lisa lies about having a lover and
wanting a divorce. She invites Gerald and Flora to a
performance and rekindles her husband's feelings as she sings
an aria to him. Gerald admits he never stopped loving Lisa.
The Fitzgeralds reconcile. To avoid reporters, they leave
the apartment via the dumbwaiter and run off to South
America.

REVIEWS:
Harrison's Reports, January 5, 1935: "Fair entertainment
for class audiences. It is a light domestic comedy-drama,
but with little human interest; the characters do not arouse
one's sympathy."

Cincinnati Enquirer [OH], January 7, 1935: "Enter
Madame, several years back, had a very successful Broadway
run. As a film play it should find equal favor, for the
comicalities [sic] of its plot are conducive to laughter."

New York Times, January 12, 1935: "This latest attempt to
merge the cinema with the opera is developed along farce
lines. The effort, while fairly entertaining, finds its
players more animated than their dialogue....Although the
theme is not exactly novel and its execution much short of
brilliant, it has the advantages of a swift pace, general
good-humor and the presence of a hard-working cast."

Variety, January 15, 1935: "Apparently a story that will
not draw large grosses to most spots, but none-the-less a
brisk story, well adapted, with good dialog [sic], good
acting and intelligent direction....The League of Decency may
object to the divorce angle, but no good reason why it
should."

NOTES: Enter Madame! opened on Broadway on August 16, 1920
with its playwright Gilda Varesi in the title role. It ran
for 366 performances. Samuel Zierler Photoplay Corp.
produced a silent film starring Clara Kimball Young in 1922.
Since the story is set in an opera company, the 1934 version
utilizes selections from Cavalleria rusticana, Tosca, and
Il trovatore. Metropolitan Opera baritone Richard Bonelli
made his film debut in Enter Madame!. Singers from the Los
Angeles Opera Company were employed as background voices in
the operatic sequences. Elissa Landi's voice was dubbed by
Nina Koshetz. Michelette Burani originated the role of Bice
on stage (B-211).
        Enter Madame! usually appears as one of Clara Lou
Sheridan's early film credits. It is assumed she is an

extra, however the author was unable to view a print.

F-20 <u>Rocky Mountain Mystery</u>   (Paramount, February 1, 1935)   63 mins.

Producer: Harold Hurley. Executive producer: Emanuel Cohen. Director: Charles Barton. Screenplay: Edward E. Paramore, Jr. and Ethel Doherty. Based on the story "Golden Dreams" by Zane Grey. Photography: Archie Stout. Editor: Jack Dennis. Art direction: Hans Dreier and Dave Garber. Sound: George Sutton.

CAST: Randolph Scott (Larry Sutton), Charles "Chic" Sale (Tex Murdock), Mrs. Leslie Carter (Mrs. Borg), Kathleen Burke (Flora), George Marion, Sr. (Jim Ballard/Adolph Borg), Ann Sheridan (Rita Ballard), James C. Eagles (John Borg), Howard Wilson (Fritz Ballard), Willie Fung (Ling Yat), Florence Roberts (Mrs. Ballard).

SYNOPSIS: Aged recluse Jim Ballard summons his relatives to his deathbed to distribute shares of his radium mine. When the mine's chief engineer, Adolph Borg, is murdered, Larry Sutton arrives to replace him and help solve the crime. Larry befriends deputy sheriff Tex Murdock, who is in charge of the investigation. Although Jim reveals that his will includes a clause prohibiting the redistribution of shares if a relative predeceases him, the murders continue. His niece Flora and nephew Fritz die mysteriously. Tex is bothered by the murders, as all the suspects have alibis. Larry romances Jim's niece, Rita. Jim's condition worsens and Larry sends a telegram to Mrs. Ballard, summoning her to his bedside. Housekeeper Mrs. Borg tries to prevent her from seeing Jim. Larry and Mrs. Ballard discover that Adolph is still alive and that it is Jim who initially was murdered. Adolph has been impersonating Jim, since the Borgs killed him during an attempt to take over the mine. Adolph struggles with Larry and falls to his death. Mrs. Borg, son John, and Chinese servant Ling Yat are sentenced to twenty years in prison for Jim's murder. Tex is named sheriff for his role in solving the crimes. Larry and Rita marry and buy a ranch in Hawaii.

REVIEWS:
<u>Harrison's Reports</u>, March 30, 1935: "This may appeal to the followers of murder mystery melodramas; but it is unpleasant entertainment for the ordinary picture-goer because of the many murders and the horrible way in which they are committed....There is little human appeal, and the love interest, although pleasant, is only incidental."

<u>Variety</u>, April 3, 1935: "Tendency to get away from the conventional oats opera has brought forth <u>Rocky Mountain Mystery</u>, more of a murder mystery than anything else. In spite of minor shortcomings it is good entertainment....Ann Sheridan is very good opposite [Randolph] Scott."

<u>Cincinnati Enquirer</u> [OH], April 12, 1935: "Heading the cast is Randolph Scott, veteran of many Zane Grey outdoor action stories, who is coupled with Ann Sheridan, Texas

beauty, in the romantic leads."

NOTES: Rocky Mountain Mystery is based on an unpublished
Zane Grey story titled "Golden Dreams." Paramount first
filmed it as The Vanishing Pioneer in 1928 with Jack Holt
and Sally Blane in the roles taken by Randolph Scott and Ann
Sheridan. The 1935 version also was called The Vanishing
Pioneer before its release. Ann Sheridan plays Randolph
Scott's love interest. The film also is known as The
Fighting Westerner and it is this title which appears on
most TV and video prints.

See also V-2.

F-21 Star Night at Coconut Grove   (MGM, 1935)   2 reels
      Technicolor

Producer: Louis Lewyn. Photography: Ray Rennahan and
William V. Skall.

CAST: Leo Carrillo (Host), Gary Cooper, Richard Cromwell,
Jack Oakie, Mary Brian, Arline Judge, El Brendel, Sir Guy
Standing, Toby Wing, Mary Pickford, Johnny Mack Brown, Mrs.
Johnny Mack Brown (Celebrity patrons), Ted Fio Rito and His
Orchestra, Candy Candido, Bing Crosby (Themselves), Ann
Sheridan (Fashion show model), Lloyd Hamilton (Hawaiian
chieftain in floor show).

SYNOPSIS: Leo Carrillo hosts an evening at the famed
Hollywood nightspot, Coconut Grove. He points out the
celebrities in the audience and introduces musical
performers, including Ted Fio Rito and His Orchestra, Candy
Candido, and Bing Crosby. Ann Sheridan is among a group of
young women modeling fashions from various eras, from
Cleopatra's time to the Gay '90s.

NOTES: According to film historian Leonard Maltin, producer
Louis Lewyn had a remarkable talent for convincing actors
from rival studios to appear in his shorts. During this
period, performers' services belonged exclusively to the
studios; only the studios could loan them to another company.
What makes this Colortone musical short particularly unusual
is the fact that Bing Crosby sings "With Every Breath I Take"
from Here Is My Heart (Paramount, 1934) and Candy Candido
sings "She's Way Up Thar" from Stand Up and Cheer (Fox,
1934), songs that belonged to MGM's rivals (B-338). Star
Night at Coconut Grove was copyrighted on January 30, 1935.

F-22 Rumba   (Paramount, February 8, 1935)   77 mins.

Producer: William LeBaron. Executive producer: Emanuel
Cohen. Director: Marion Gering. Choreographers: LeRoy
Prinz, Veloz and Yolanda. Screenplay: Howard J. Green,
Harry Ruskin, and Frank Partos. Based on an idea by Guy
Endore and Seena Owen. Songs: Ralph Rainger. Spanish
lyrics: Francois B. de Valdes. Music: Andrea Setaro, S.K.
Wineland, and Maurice Lawrence. Musical director: Nathaniel
Finston. Photography: Ted Tetzlaff. Editor: Hugh Bennett.

Art direction: Hans Dreier and Robert Usher. Costumes:
Travis Banton and Lily Del Barrio. Sound: J.A. Goodrich.

CAST: George Raft (Jose Martinez/Joe·Martin), Carole Lombard
(Diana Harrison), Margo (Carmelita), Lynne Overman (Flash),
Monroe Owsley (Hobart Fletcher), Iris Adrian (Goldie Allen),
Gail Patrick (Patsy Fletcher), Samuel S. Hinds (Henry B.
Harrison), Virginia Hammond (Mrs. Harrison), Jameson Thomas
(Jack Solanger), Soledad Jimenez (Maria), Paul Porcasi
(Carlos), Raymond McKee (Dance director), Akim Tamiroff
(Tony), Hallene Hall (Wardrobe woman), Bud Flannigan (Man in
Diana's party), Mack Gray (Assistant dance instructor),
Dennis O'Keefe (Man in Diana's theatre party), Eldred Tidbury
(Watkins), Peggy Watts (Girl in Diana's party), Bruce Warren
(Dean), Hugh Enfield (Bromley), Rafael Corio (Alfredo),
Rafael Storm, Paul Lopez (Cashiers), Charles Stevens (Ticket
vendor), M. Luna (Driver), Victor Sabini (Waiter), Carli
Taylor (Steward on yacht), James Burke, Eddie Dunn, James P.
Burtis (Reporters), Dick Rush (Policeman), Bud Shaw (Ticket
taker), E.H. Calvert (Police captain), Frank O'Connor (Police
sergeant), Alfred P. Jones (Stage doorman), Mason Litson
(Stage manager), Paul Ellis (Waiter at Cafe Elefante), Hooper
Atchley (Doctor), Dick Alexander (Policeman), Don Brodie,
Charlie Sullivan, Jack Raymond (Gangsters), Frank Mills
(Bouncer), Clara Lou Sheridan (Dancer), Olga Barrancos, Luis
Barrancos, Lara Puente, Ambrosio Sardinias, Carmita Curbelo,
Zora (Rumba dancers), Brooks Benedict (Extra in audience),
Jane Wyman (Chorus girl), Veloz and Yolanda (Dancing doubles
for George Raft and Carole Lombard), Frank Leyva.

SONGS: "I'm Yours for Tonight," "The Rhythm of the Rumba,"
"Your Eyes Have Said" (Rainger). "The Magic of You" and "If
I Knew" (Rainger) were not used (B-100).

SYNOPSIS: Joe Martin is a half-Cuban, half-American dancer
working in Havana. He blames vacationing American heiress
Diana Harrison when his winning lottery number is proven to
be counterfeit. Worried that Joe needs the money, Diana
visits his dressing room and offers him the five thousand
dollar prize. Joe misunderstands and flirts with her. Her
jealous boyfriend, Hobart Fletcher, starts a fight, causing
Joe to get fired. Recognizing the rumba as the latest dance
craze, Joe opens a club in Havana, where he teams with his
girlfriend Carmelita. She realizes the hopelessness of their
relationship, since he loves Diana. Joe teaches Diana to
rumba and she falls in love with him. Diana's mother is
furious over newspaper reports about Diana and Joe. She
orders her daughter to announce her engagement to Hobart,
Diana's social equal. Joe thinks Diana is toying with his
affections and he plots to humiliate her. He soon realizes
that her intentions are sincere. Diana is devastated when
Carmelita reveals Joe's original plan. Diana returns to New
York. The Harrisons hire a detective to investigate Joe. He
reveals Joe fears for his safety in New York because he once
double-crossed the mob after they tried to frame him.
Distraught over his breakup with Diana, Joe accepts a
Broadway offer, despite his fears of the mob. In New York,
Joe tries to reconcile with Diana, but she refuses to listen.

When Joe receives a death threat, the press builds up the
story of him risking his life to dance. The stress causes
Carmelita to faint before the opening. Diana volunteers to
take Carmelita's place onstage. After Diana and Joe score a
big success, they decide to marry and remain dancing
partners. Joe's press agent reveals that the entire gangster
scare was a publicity stunt.

REVIEWS:
Harrison's Reports, February 2, 1935: "This should
entertain the masses fairly well because of the lavish
production, the music, and the dancing. But the story is
neither exciting nor novel. And parts of it are
unpleasant..."

Cincinnati Enquirer [OH], February 9, 1935: "With the
seductive rhythms of Cuban gourds as a background, Rumba...
combines musical innovations and poignant love story."

New York Times, February 25, 1935: "No more appropriate
title could have been selected, except, possibly, Too Much
Rumba. The narrative is a modest little blossom which
timidly raises its head now and then above the rhythmic
convolutions of its cast....The question reduces itself to
this: either you are perfectly happy watching [George] Raft
and his partners do the rumba for hours, or you are not.
This corner...can think of lots more interesting pastimes."

Variety, February 27, 1935: "An attractive title and some
fascinating studio work behind it are what Rumba has
chiefly to offer. It's a good looking production that
doesn't rate high in a literary way, but has managed to
capture quite a lot of the spirit of the dance for which it
is named. It listens and looks like a better than moderate
grosser."

NOTES: Hoping to recapture the success of Bolero (F-2),
Paramount reteamed George Raft and Carole Lombard in another
film with a dance background. Rumba underwent several
changes in storyline during production. Before filming
began, the studio rejected the novel they had bought for the
basis of the movie and hired novelist Edgcumb Pinchon to
write an original story. After shooting began, Guy Endore
was hired to adapt the story for the screen. The film was
shut down in December 1934 so that further revisions could be
made (B-211). Most of Raft and Lombard's routines were
performed by the professional dance team of Veloz and
Yolanda. Clara Lou Sheridan appears as a dancer in the
"Birth of the Rumba" number. Coincidentally, her future
Warner Bros. co-star and friend, Jane Wyman, also has a bit
part as a chorus girl.

F-23 Car 99 (Paramount, March 1, 1935)   60 mins.

Producer: Bayard Veiller. Director: Charles Barton.
Screenplay: Karl Detzer and C. Gardner Sullivan. Based on
the short stories "Hue and Cry," "A Still Small Voice," "One
Good Turn, and "He Also Serves" by Karl Detzer. Photography:

William C. Mellor.   Editor: Eda Warren.   Art direction:
Hans Dreier and John Goodman.   Sound: A.W. Singley.
Technical advisor: Karl Detzer.

CAST: Fred MacMurray (Ross Martin), Sir Guy Standing
(Professor Anthony), Ann Sheridan (Mary Adams), Frank Craven
(Sheriff Pete Arnot), William Frawley (Sergeant Barrel),
Douglas Blackley (Recruit Blatsky), John Cox (Recruit
Carney), Eddy Chandler (Recruit Haynes), Alfred Delcambre
(Recruit Jamison), Dean Jagger (Recruit Jim Burton), Nora
Cecil (Granny), Marina Schubert (Nan), Joe Sauers (Whitey),
Mack Gray (Smoke), Howard Wilson (Dutch), Charles Wilson
(Police captain), Russell Hopton (Operator Harper), John
Howard, Robert Kent (Recruits), Eddie Dunn (Mac, the
servant), Peter Hancock (Eddie), Al Hill (Hawkeye, the hood),
Hector Sarno (French Charlie), Jack Cheatham (Sergeant
Meyers), Ted Oliver (Sergeant), Harry Strang (Dispatch
sergeant), Charles Sullivan (Green gang hood), Malcolm
McGregor (Pilot), Sam Flint (Bank president), John Sinclair
(Crook), Gordon Jones (Mechanic).

SYNOPSIS: Sheriff Pete Arnot and the Michigan state police
refuse to take recruit Ross Martin seriously, even after he
catches his first criminal. Bank robber Anthony poses as a
criminology professor in order to observe the latest law
enforcement practices. He befriends the sheriff, who shows
Anthony how the intricate police radio system operates. Ross
tries to catch Anthony's gang, who hide out in Michigan after
a bank job. Anthony's daughter Nan flirts with Ross to throw
him off track. When Ross notices that Anthony's car carries
license plates from different states which can be changed at
the touch of a button, he arrests Anthony and Nan. They
knock out Ross and escape, causing Ross to be kicked off the
force. Ross works as a mechanic while waiting for the police
board to vote on his permanent dismissal. His girlfriend,
telephone operator Mary Adams, urges him to face the board
and fight for his badge. With Ross out of the way, Anthony
plans a large bank robbery. He tricks Mary into thinking he
wants to help Ross get his job back, then kidnaps her,
paralyzing the communications system. Ross convinces
Sergeant Barrel to use the Massachusetts state police system
to relay the police calls, since they use the same radio
frequency as Michigan. Ross begs Barrel to let him join the
search, but Barrel refuses. After Ross learns Anthony's gang
has Mary, he steals a police motorcycle and pursues them.
Ross's partner broadcasts a clue to Ross about where the gang
is headed. Ross catches the criminals and is reinstated.

REVIEWS:
New York Times, February 23, 1935: "A fast-moving
adaptation..., it is played to the hilt by such excellent
veterans as Sir Guy Standing, Frank Craven and William
Frawley and by a group of promising newcomers, including Fred
McMurray [sic], Marina Schubert, Dean Jagger and Ann
Sheridan."

Variety, February 27, 1935: "Away above the average action
picture that seeks to glorify some arm of the law....Other

players that gain for themselves special attention are Ann
Sheridan as [Fred] MacMurray's love interest, William
Frawley..., Frank Craven..., and Marina Schubert...."

Liberty, March 23, 1935: "Though there are many faulty
spots in Car 99 that cannot be cut out, wise picturegoers
will wait until this film appears in neighborhood theaters.
For by that time it may be rid of much of its unnecessary
padding."

Cincinnati Enquirer [OH], April 1, 1935: "Sir Guy
Standing, Fred MacMurray, and Ann Sheridan are starred in
this latest product of Hollywood's mighty intellects, which,
aside from its simplicity of plot, is an exciting series of
episodes, sure to please lovers of Western thrillers and
ancient melodrama."

NOTES: Car 99 marks Ann Sheridan's first leading lady role
at Paramount, as well as her first screen kiss. Although
Car 99 is a "B" picture, the size of Ann's role indicates
that Paramount was gaining confidence in her work after her
role in Behold My Wife (F-16). Car 99 is based on four
stories by Karl Detzer that ran in the Saturday Evening
Post in 1933 and 1934. Detzer, a criminology buff, based
his articles on the adventures of the radio cars of the
Michigan state police. Detzer also served as technical
advisor for the film.

F-24 Mississippi   (Paramount, March 8, 1935)   73 mins.

Producer: Arthur Hornblow, Jr. Directors: A. Edward
Sutherland and Wesley Ruggles. Screenplay: Francis Martin
and Jack Cunningham. Adaptation: Claude Binyon, and Herbert
Fields. Based on the play Magnolia by Booth Tarkington.
Songs: Richard Rodgers, Lorenz Hart, and Stephen Foster.
Photography: Charles Lang. Editor: Chandler House. Art
direction: Hans Dreier and Bernard Herzbrun. Sound: Eugene
Merritt. Technical director: Irvin S. Cobb.

CAST: Bing Crosby (Tom Grayson/Colonel Steele), W.C. Fields
(Commodore Orlando Jackson), Joan Bennett (Lucy Rumford),
Queenie Smith (Alabam), Gail Patrick (Elvira Rumford), Claude
Gillingwater, Sr. (General Rumford), John Miljan (Major
Patterson), Edward Pawley (Joe Patterson), Fred Kohler, Sr.
(Captain Blackie), John Larkin (Rumbo), Libby Taylor (Lavinia
Washington), Harry Myers (Joe, the stage manager), Paul Hurst
(Hefty), Theresa Maxwell Conover (Miss Markham), Al Richmond,
Francis McDonald, King Baggott, Mahlon Hamilton, Stanley
Andrews, Eddie Sturgis, George Lloyd (Gamblers), Bruce
Covington (Colonel), Jules Cowles (Bartender), Harry Cody
(Abner, the bartender), Lew Kelly, Matthew Betz (Men at bar),
Jack Mulhall (Duelist), Victor Poetl (Guest), Bill Howard
(Man in auditorium), Jack Carlyle (Referee), Richard Scott
(Second), Jan Duggan (Showboat customer), James Burke
(Passenger in pilot house), Helene Chadwick, Jerome Storm
(Extras at opening), the Cabin Kids (the Inky Kids),
Molasses, January (Themselves), Charles L. King (Desk clerk),
Mabel Van Buren, Bill Harwood (Party guests), J.P. McGowan

(Dealer), Clarence Geldert (Hotel proprietor), Fred
"Snowflake" Toones (Valet), Forrest Taylor (Bar customer who
orders sarsaparilla), Warner Richmond (Bar customer who pulls
a gun), Oscar Smith (Valet), Robert McKenzie (Show patron),
Jean Rouverol, Mildred Stone, Mary Ellen Brown, Ann Sheridan
(Students at girls' school), Arthur Millett (First leadsman),
Clarence L. Sherwood (Relay man), Bert Lindley (Second
leadsman), Roy Bailey (Pianist), Dennis O'Keefe, Warren
Rogers, Jean Clarendon, Dan Crimmins, William Howard Gould.

SONGS: "It's Easy to Remember," "Down by the River," "Roll
Mississipi," "Soon" (Rodgers, Hart), "Old Folks at Home"
(Foster), "Little David, Play on Your Harp" (Unknown).
"Pablo, You Are My Heart" (Rodgers, Hart) was not used
(B-100).

SYNOPSIS: Commodore Orlando Jackson is the drunken captain
of a showboat on the Mississippi River in the 1800s. The
Commodore's troupe is asked to entertain at Tom Grayson and
Elvira Rumford's engagement party. Elvira's father, General
Rumford, complains to younger daughter Lucy that he would
prefer that Elvira marry a military man like Major Patterson
rather than a peaceful northerner like Tom. Pacifist Lucy is
upset when her father gives Tom a set of dueling pistols.
Patterson challenges Tom to fight for Elvira's hand, but Tom
refuses. Although Lucy sees Tom's actions as heroic, Elvira
breaks the engagement, labeling her beau a coward. Lucy
confesses her long-standing love to Tom, but he sees her as a
child. He leaves town on the Commodore's showboat. Captain
Blackie threatens to take away the boat when the Commodore
fails to pay his debts. To frighten Blackie, the Commodore
bills Tom as "The Notorious Colonel Steele, the Singing
Killer." Undeterred, Blackie disrupts the show and starts a
brawl. Tom accidently kills Blackie during the fight. The
Commodore capitalizes on Tom's new celebrity by spreading
rumors that Tom also killed Lucy's cousin. Tom meets the
adult Lucy and is attracted to her. Lucy is devastated to
learn that Tom is Colonel Steele. Tom goes to the Rumfords'
plantation to explain that the killing stories are lies. He
proves his bravery to the family by confronting Patterson.
Tom and Lucy reconcile and sail off on the showboat.

REVIEWS:
Cincinnati Enquirer [OH], March 30, 1935: "W.C. Fields...
steers his river packet into a flood of laughter in
Mississippi...."

Harrison's Reports, March 30, 1935: "Pleasing! The action
is fast enough to hold one's interest....There is nothing
objectionable in the picture, even though it deals with
gamblers and killers....Consequently, it is good for the
entire family."

New York Times, April 18, 1935: "Mississippi is a
tuneful and diverting show even when it isn't being
particularly hilarious, and it is madly funny at sufficient
length to satisfy us [W.C.] Fields idolators."

Variety, April 24, 1935:   "Bing Crosby, W.C. Fields and
Joan Bennett may prove sufficient [box office] magnets for
this weak musical."

NOTES: Mississippi was the third film adaptation of Booth
Tarkington's play Magnolia, which opened August 27, 1923.
Famous Players-Lasky filmed a silent version called The
Fighting Crowd in 1924, starring Ernest Torrence and Mary
Astor in the Bing Crosby and Joan Bennett roles. Buddy
Rogers and Mary Brian were cast in River of Romance
(Paramount, 1929), an early talkie. Mississippi began
filming with singer Lanny Ross in the lead. After Paramount
executives viewed a few days' rushes, they decided Ross could
not carry the picture and he was replaced by Bing Crosby.
Director A. Edward Sutherland was ill during the filming and
some scenes were shot by Wesley Ruggles. Only Sutherland
receives screen credit (B-211).
     Ann Sheridan plays Joan Bennett's boarding school
classmate in Mississippi. She appears in several scenes,
including a dormitory setting and a party. Although
Mississippi was a major film, this very minor role is a
comedown after Ann's leading lady status in previous "B"
pictures.

F-25   Red Blood of Courage   (Ambassador, April 20, 1935)
        55 mins.

Producers: Maurice Cohn and Sigmund Neufield. Director:
Jack English. Screenplay: Barry Barringer. Based on a
story by James Oliver Curwood. Photography: Arthur Reed.
Editor: Richard G. Wray. Sets: Louis Rachmil. Sound:
Corson Jowett.

CAST: Kermit Maynard (Jim Sullivan/James Anderson), Ann
Sheridan (Beth Henry), Reginald Barlow (Mark Henry/Pete
Drago), Ben Hendricks, Jr. (Bart Slager), George Regas
(Frenchy), Nat Carr (Dr. Meyer), Charles King (Joe), "Rocky"
(Horse), Carl Mathews (Indian in store/mountie), Milt Morante
(Gunman), Art Dillard (Henchman).

SYNOPSIS: Northwest Mounted Policeman Jim Sullivan goes
undercover to look for his partner, Buck Taylor, who
disappeared while working incognito. Pete Drago and his
henchmen, Bart Slager and Frenchy, try to run Jim out of
town, but Jim is undeterred by their threats. Pete
masquerades as wealthy land owner Mark Henry, hoping to get
control of Mark's oil-rich land from his niece Beth. Since
Beth has not seen her uncle in many years, she does not know
about the oil or realize that Pete is impersonating him. He
holds the real Mark hostage. Pete conspires to have Beth
marry Bart so he can kill Mark and get control of the oil.
When Beth overhears Pete and Bart making plans, she gets
scared and runs away. Jim rescues her and she confides in
him. Frenchy and Bart kidnap Beth and Jim. When Pete
mistakes Jim for a wanted murderer, he decides to blackmail
Jim into cooperating with the criminals. Since Beth prefers
Jim to Bart, Pete decides to let Jim marry her. While Pete
consults with a geologist about the oil deposits, Beth

realizes Jim is not a killer and urges him to escape.
Jealous that his role is being usurped, Bart shoots Pete in
the back and accuses Jim of the crime. He ties up Jim and
holds him hostage. Mark helps Jim escape. Jim calls the
Mounties, but is recaptured. After Bart sets the building on
fire, Mark helps Jim escape again. Bart and Frenchy kidnap
Beth, and Jim pursues them. The Mounties capture the crooks
and Jim rescues Beth. She is reunited with her real uncle.
Although Jim realizes the gang killed Buck, he tells the
Mounties that he is going to stay and continue his
investigation, implying that he will be seeing more of Beth.

REVIEW:
Variety, June 12, 1935: "There is plenty of good fighting
and fast riding streaming through the film....Cast does
exceptionally good work....[Ann] Sheridan is a newcomer who
is acceptable in a shadowy role."

NOTES: Red Blood of Courage marks Ann Sheridan's only
loan-out while under contract to Paramount. Her onscreen
credit states that she appears courtesy of the studio.
Kermit Maynard performed his own stunts in the film. He was
almost burned alive when the log cabin set caught fire
prematurely during filming (B-211). James Oliver Curwood's
story previously was filmed in a two-reel Selig Polyscope in
1915.

F-26 The Glass Key   (Paramount, May 31, 1935)   80 mins.

Producer: E. Lloyd Sheldon. Executive producer: Henry
Herzbrun. Director: Frank Tuttle. Assistant director:
Russell Matthews. Screenplay: Kathryn Scola, Kubec Glasmon,
and Harry Ruskin. Based on the novel The Glass Key by
Dashiell Hammett. Photography: Henry Sharp. Editor: Hugh
Bennett. Sound: J.A. Goodrich.

CAST: George Raft (Ed Beaumont), Claire Dodd (Janet Henry),
Edward Arnold (Paul Madvig), Rosalind Culli (Opal Madvig),
Ray Milland (Taylor Henry), Robert Gleckler (Shad O'Rory),
Guinn "Big Boy" Williams (Jeff), Tammany Young (Clarkie),
Harry Tyler (Henry Sloss), Charles C. Wilson (Farr), Emma
Dunn (Mom), Matt McHugh (Puggy), Patrick Moriarity
(Mulrooney), Mack Gray (Duke), Frank Marlowe (Walter Ivans),
Herbert Evans (Senator's butler), George H. Reed (Black
serving man), Percy Morris (Bartender), Irving Bacon
(Waiter), Ann Sheridan (Nurse), Henry Roquemore (Rinkle),
Frank O'Connor (McLaughlin), Michael Mark (Swartz), Alfred
Delcambre (Reporter), Veda Buckland (Landlady), George Ernest
(Boy), Charles Richman (Senator John Henry).

SYNOPSIS: Political boss Paul Madvig yields much power, but
makes many enemies. When he refuses to help Henry Schloss
free his brother-in-law on a drunken driving rap, Schloss
vows revenge. Paul's henchman, Ed Beaumont, questions his
boss's allegiance with crooked Senator John Henry. Ed
disapproves of Paul's plans to marry John's daughter Janet.
Crime boss Shad O'Rory threatens Paul when Paul closes his
gambling casinos, but Paul refuses to back down. Paul vows

to break up the relationship between his daughter Opal and
John's son Taylor, who owes gambling debts to Shad. When
Taylor is murdered, Shad frames Paul for the killing. Ed
advises Paul to reopen the casinos so Shad will stop planting
implicating stories in the press, but Paul refuses.
Determined to find the killer, Ed gains the confidence of
Shad and his men. Shad confesses that Schloss and Janet are
helping him trap Paul. When Ed tries to destroy evidence,
Shad's henchman beats him and locks him up. Ed escapes and
warns Paul about Schloss. Janet convinces Opal to accuse her
father of murder in the press. Ed disguises himself as a
reporter to get into the Henrys' home, where he finds a clue
to the murderer's identity. He convinces Opal of Paul's
innocence. Paul worries he will be blamed when Schloss is
murdered. Ed gets Shad's henchman to admit he killed Schloss
in a drunken rage. John confesses that he killed Taylor
following an argument about Opal. An honest politican is
named as his successor. Ed begins dating Opal with Paul's
blessing.

REVIEWS:
Harrison's Reports, June 1, 1935: "A fast-moving melodrama
of crooked politics, and a good mass entertainment."

New York Times, June 15, 1935: "A salty tale of violence
and secret murder, [The Glass Key] has been excellently
produced..., and it becomes as crisply exciting a melodrama
as Broadway has seen lately."

Variety, June 19, 1935: "Murder mystery in a setting of
politics and gangster tactics which gets by."

Cincinnati Enquirer [OH], June 22, 1935: "Unbelievable
that such a small thing as a metal top off of a murderer's
walking stick could be the instrument of salvation for a man
in the shadow of blasted romance and the electric chair.
Unbelievable it is, and impossible it would be, but the thing
that gets into the hands of the nonchalant George Raft during
his portrayal of one of those snoopy, toughy roles he does so
well, and - well, you know how it is."

NOTES: Paramount paid author Dashiell Hammett a then-
exorbitant twenty-five thousand dollars for the rights to
film his 1931 novel The Glass Key. However, the studio
found that it had to deal with many problems before bringing
the tale of political corruption and violence to the screen.
When the film first was announced in September 1932, Harry
d'Abbadie D'Arrast was director and B.P. Schulberg was
producer. They encountered trouble with the censors and the
script was banned by the Hays Office. By 1934, the project
resumed with E. Lloyd Sheldon producing and Frank Tuttle
directing. The censors insisted they eliminate any
references to the politician's gambling connections, tone
down the violence, and make George Raft's character
sympathetic. The movie is best remembered for a brutal scene
in which Guinn "Big Boy" Williams beats George Raft, a test
to censorship rules. Much of the violence is left to the
audience's imagination, with the action being heard instead

of seen. According to the Motion Picture Almanac, The Glass Key was one of the box office champions for the 1936-37 season (B-211).

Ann Sheridan portrays a nurse who tends to Raft in a hospital scene. Paramount remade The Glass Key in 1942 with Brian Donlevy, Alan Ladd, and Veronica Lake in the roles taken by Edward Arnold, George Raft, and Claire Dodd in 1935. Frances Gifford played the nurse in the 1942 version.

F-27 Hollywood Extra Girl   (Paramount, 1935)   10 mins.

Producers: Adolph Zukor and William H. Pine. Director: Herbert Moulton. Continuity: John Flory. Dialogue: Herman Hoffman. Photography: Harry Fishbeck. Special effects: Gordon Jennings.

CAST: Cecil B. DeMille, Suzanne Emery, Clara Kimball Young, Ann Sheridan, Katherine DeMille, Joseph Schildkraut, C. Aubrey Smith, William Farnum, Henry Wilcoxon, Hobart Bosworth, Ian Keith, George Barbier, Montagu Love, Alan Hale, C. Henry Gordon, Loretta Young.

NOTES: This Paramount Variety short was used to promote The Crusades (F-29). In it, director Cecil B. DeMille instructs extra Suzanne Emery on the difficult road she chose as an actress. The short was copyrighted on August 22, 1935. A copy of the short is in the film collection at the UCLA Film and Television Archive.

F-28 Fighting Youth   (Universal, September 30, 1935)
      85 mins.

Producer: Fred S. Meyer. Associate producer: Ansel Friedberger. Director: Hamilton Macfadden. Assistant directors: George Blair and Victor Noerdlinger. Screenplay: Henry Johnson, Florabel Muir, and Hamilton Macfadden. Based on an idea by Stanley Meyer. Musical director: Constantin Bakaleinikoff. Photography: Edward J. Snyder. Editor: Bernard Burton. Art direction: Ralph Berger. Sound: Gilbert Kurland.

CAST: Charles Farrell (Larry Davis), June Martel (Betty Wilson), Andy Devine (Cy Kipp), J. Farrell Macdonald (Coach Parker), Ann Sheridan (Carol Arlington), Edward Nugent (Tony Tonnetti), Herman Bing (Herman), Phyllis Fraser (Dodo Gates), Alden Chase (Louis Markoff/Boris Marovich), Glenn Boles (Paul), Murray Kinnell (Dean Churchill), David Worth (Captain Blake), Jeff Cravath (Assistant coach), Charles Wilson (Bull Stevens), Walter Johnson (Buck), Larry "Moon" Mullins, Jim Purvis, Paul Schwegler, Dale Van Sickel, Jim Thorpe, Leslie Cooper, Howard "Red" Christie, Dick Lukats, Frank Baker, "Dutch" Fehring, Frank Sully (Football players), Clara Kimball Young (Mrs. Stewart, house mother), Ralph Brooks (Student manager), Bob Hale (Trainer), Del Henderson (Detective), Russell Wade (Buck's roommate), Clyde Dilson (Manchester alumnus), David O'Brien (Rooter), William Moore (Busboy), Mickey Bennett (Newsboy), Charles Tannen (Radical student), Parker McConnell (Army major), William R. Arnold

(Army captain), Colonel McDonnell (Army colonel), Roberta
Gale (Betty's roommate), George Humbert (Ice cream man), Lew
Kelly (Policeman), Tiny Sandford (Truck driver), Al Williams
(Freshman), Jack Mower (Station owner), Jack Gratten, John
Morley (Students), Wade Boteler, Harry Adams, Babe Lawrence,
Edmund Cobb, Vance Carroll (Detectives), Marcia Remy
(Secretary), Kay Hughes, Mary Bovard, Constance Lee, Helen
Valkis, Chloe Elrod (Sorority girls), Jean Rogers, John King,
Auguste Tollaire.

SYNOPSIS: State College students Larry Davis and Betty
Wilson plan to marry after graduation. Their plans are
disrupted when wealthy Carol Arlington transfers to State to
infiltrate a liberal student organization. Communist Louis
Markoff arranges for Carol to become president of the group.
In an effort to take the commercialization out of football,
he urges Carol to seduce Larry and disrupt the team. Betty
and Larry attend a meeting, where Carol urges the radicals to
get rid of the commercialization of football. Larry promises
to help the group, despite Betty's protests. When Larry
accuses Betty of trying to run his life, they break their
engagement. Upset about the breakup, Larry's football skills
decline. The coach and Captain Blake accuse Larry of
throwing the game when they hear about his speech at the
meeting. The coach brings in former player Bull Stevens to
shake up the team. When Larry's roommate is injured during
practice because of Bull's rough tactics, Larry quits.
Markoff realizes that his room is being watched so he plots
to have someone remove a list of radical students. He
convinces Betty to steal the papers to keep Larry from being
expelled. Betty tells the dean about her suspicions about
Markoff. Radical student Tony Tonnetti reveals that he is a
government agent who was sent to catch Markoff. With Betty's
information, he is able to deport Markoff and expell Carol.
Larry rejoins the team, but the coach refuses to let him
play. Betty leads the stands in a cheer for Larry during the
final minutes of the game. The coach relents and Larry
scores two touchdowns. Betty and Larry reconcile.

REVIEWS:
Hollywood Reporter, September 9, 1935: "At best it's only
a programmer, but, it's of the better type in its class and
should fare well as the top feature on double bills....[Ann]
Sheridan is immense in her role."

New York Times, November 2, 1935: "In short, Fighting
Youth is neither impressive in its stand for Americanism
nor as an expose of the extra-curicular [sic] activities of
Left Wing students:

Variety, November 6, 1935: "Some very good material in
this picture and some that is not so good. It is deficient
in [box office] name value, and its weave of radicalism and
campus football somehow doesn't mix....June Martel and Ann
Sheridan, competitive femmes, do nicely..."

Billboard, November 16, 1935: "[Ann] Sheridan is lovely
and miscast, but in the right kind of parts should be able to

go places....Picture should never have been produced, with a
vapid, thoughtless story. Only good features are some nice
football shots."

NOTES: Fighting Youth began production on July 25, 1935.
The film's working title was Off Side. According to the
Hollywood Reporter, Fighting Youth was considered timely
because of publicity on commmunist activity in schools
(September 9, 1935). Much of the movie was shot at the Los
Angeles Coliseum. Nine real college players were utilized in
the film's football scenes.
     Ann Sheridan received a salary of $125 per week for her
three weeks' work as the femme fatale communist supporter in
the "B" picture. Although released prior to The Crusades
(F-29), Fighting Youth was filmed after she left Paramount.
It is the only free-lance movie she made between her
contracts with Paramount and Warner Bros.

F-29   The Crusades   (Paramount, October 25, 1935)
       123 mins.

Producer: Cecil B. DeMille. Executive producer: Henry
Herzbrun. Director: Cecil B. DeMille. Assistant directors:
George Hippard and David MacDonald. Screenplay: Harold
Lamb, Waldemar Young, and Dudley Nichols. Based on the book
The Crusades: Iron Men and Saints by Harold Lamb. Song
"Song of the Crusades": Harold Lamb, Jeanie MacPherson,
Richard A. Whiting, Leo Robin, and Rudolph Kopp. Music:
Rudolph Kopp. Photography: Victor Milner. Editor: Anne
Bauchens. Art direction: Roland Anderson. Costumes:
Travis Banton, Joe Kaplan, and Edna Shotwell. Sound:
"Curley" Nelson. Special effects: Gordon Jennings.

CAST: Loretta Young (Berengaria, princess of Navarre), Henry
Wilcoxon (Richard, king of England), Ian Keith (Saladin,
sultan of Islam), Katherine DeMille (Alice, princess of
France), C. Aubrey Smith (The Hermit), Joseph Schildkraut
(Conrad of Montferrat), Alan Hale (Blondel), C. Henry Gordon
(Philip II, king of France), George Barbier (Sancho, king of
Navarre), Montagu Love (Blacksmith), Hobart Bosworth
(Frederick, duke of Germany), William Farnum (Hugo, duke of
Burgundy), Lumsden Hare (Robert, earl of Leicester), Ramsey
Hill (John, prince of England), Pedro de Cordoba (Karakush),
Paul Satoff (Michael, prince of Russia), Mischa Auer (Monk),
Maurice Murphy (Alan, Richard's squire), Jason Robards, Sr.
(Amir), J. Carroll Naish (Arab slave seller), Oscar Rudolph
(Philip's squire), Albert Conti (Leopold, duke of Austria),
Sven-Hugo Borg (Sverre, the Norse king), Fred Malatesta
(William, king of Sicily), Hans von Twardowski (Nicholas,
count of Hungary), Anna Demetrio (Duenna), Perry Askam
(Soldier), Edwin Maxwell (Ship's master), Winter Hall
(Archibishop), Emma Dunn (Alan's mother), Georgia Caine
(Nun), Robert Adair (English chamberlain), Pat Moore
(Leicester's squire), Ann Sheridan, Jean Fenwick (Christian
girls), Josef Swickard (Buyer), Edgar Dearing (Cart man),
Alphonse Ethier (Priest), Gilda Oliva (First lady-in-waiting
to Alice), Mildred Van Buren (Second lady-in-waiting to
Alice), John Rutherford (Knight), Colin Tapley (Stranger/

messenger), Harry Cording, Stanley Andrews, Maurice Black,
William B. Davidson (Amirs), Addison Richards (Sentry), Guy
Usher (Grey beard/templar), Boyd Irwin, Gordon Griffith
(Templars), Kenneth Gibson (Captain of English men-at-arms),
Vallejo Gantner (Chanting monk), George MacQuarrie (Captain
of templars), Sam Flint (Captain of hospitalers), Harold
Goodwin (Wounded man).

SYNOPSIS: In 1187, Saladin leads the Saracens of Asia in an
attack against Jerusalem, killing Christians or selling them
as slaves. The Hermit, a zealot, vows to return with a band
of crusaders to reclaim the holy land in the name of Christ.
To protect his throne, King Philip of France forces his
cousin King Richard the Lion Hearted of England to go through
with his betrothal to Philip's sister Alice. Despite
Richard's lack of faith, he joins the crusade, knowing it
will break his engagement. En route to Jerusalem, the troops
need provisions. The king of Navarre agrees to sell them
what they need if Richard will marry his daughter Berengaria.
She dislikes Richard's violence, but agrees to the marriage
for the sake of the crusade. Richard forces Berengaria to go
with him, but she refuses to consummate the marriage. The
crusaders declare war on Saladin. Richard's marriage causes
trouble between him and Philip. Although Philip offers to
help Richard reclaim his throne from his brother John if
Richard gives up Berengaria, Richard makes his wife queen.
Philip threatens to quit the crusade. Richard vows to open
the gates of Jerusalem, even if he is alone. Berengaria
falls in love with Richard after his heroic actions, but
warns him that if he breaks with Philip, he is going against
God. At troublemaking Conrad's suggestion, she decides to
commit suicide to unite the cousins. Saladin disguises
himself as a Christian to get an army from Jerusalem. When
Berengaria is shot and kidnapped, Saladin nurses her. The
Saracens capture the Hermit, threatening to kill him if the
crusaders attack. The Hermit insists the crusaders carry on
their fight. Saladin realizes Berengaria planned to commit
suicide for the crusade. He pledges his love, explaining
that his kingdom does not accept Christian marriages. Conrad
offers to kill Richard in exchange for being named king of
Jerusalem, but Saladin refuses. Berengaria begs Saladin to
warn Richard about the traitors. She agrees to marry Saladin
in exchange for saving Richard's life. Saladin offers
Richard control of Jerusalem if he will give up Christianity
and the fight. Despite Richard's lack of faith, he refuses.
Berengaria begs her husband to compromise and save his life.
Saladin agrees to free the Christian captives and let all but
Richard pass through the gates of Jerusalem unarmed. Richard
and Berengaria sacrifice their love for the sake of peace.
As Jerusalm is free, Richard finds faith and prays for
Berengaria's return. When Saladin realizes that Berengaria
always will love Richard, he releases her. Berengaria is
thrilled to hear Richard found faith and they reconcile.

REVIEWS:
New York Times, August 22, 1935: "The Crusades is a
grand show. Displaying all of that healthy contempt for
icebox pedantry which distinguishes the master showman in his

bouts with history, [Cecil B.] De Mille provides two hours of tempestuous extravaganza. On his clamorous screen you will discover the most impressive mass excitement that the screen has offered in years."

Variety, August 28, 1935: "Probably only [Cecil B.] DeMille could make a picture like Crusades - and get away with it. It's long, and the story is not up to some of his previous films, but the production has sweep and spectacle. And one of these production splurges occasionally is all right. It will do nicely in the theatres."

Harrison's Reports, August 31, 1935: "The Crusades is a boisterous spectacle, a massive one, but it is a 'mechanical' picture: big bodies of soldiers battling effectively....It is doubtful if a picture has been produced to this day where there was more deafening activity."

NOTES: The Crusades is an epic, produced and directed by the master, Cecil B. DeMille. Though he hired author Harold Lamb to adapt his 1933 book, The Crusades: Iron Men and Saints, DeMille was more concerned with making an entertaining film than an accurate portrayal of history. "The Crusades is a good example of what I call telescoping history," DeMille said. "Audiences are not interested in dates, but in events and their significance. And they do not want to be educated, but entertained" (B-431). He called The Crusades "one of the best pictures I have ever made" (B-211). Although the 1936-37 Motion Picture Almanac lists the film as a "box office champion" of 1935, the film lost more than $700,000 during its initial release. The epic's high costs kept it from recouping its investment, despite high grosses during its initial run (B-431).

Ann Sheridan plays a Christian captive who is auctioned off during the first five minutes of The Crusades. Years later, she laughed about her one line of dialogue, which she delivered with a heavy Texas accent. It was a most unusual interpretation of "The cross, the cross, let me kiss the cross." Although Ann had been thrilled about the opportunity to wear a black wig, she was disappointed by her first experience with an epic. She recalled, "I didn't know they take [the wigs] out of stock and they slam 'em on your head and it doesn't fit and the hair lace comes loose and they come up and glue it on just before the take and it falls off again - I was so horrible looking!" (B-206). The Crusades marked Ann's last movie under her Paramount contract. In May 1935, she became a free-lance actress (B-675).

F-30 Sing Me a Love Song (Warner Bros., January 9, 1937)
      78 mins.

Producer: Sam Bischoff. Executive producers: Jack L. Warner and Hal B. Wallis. Director: Raymond Enright. Assistant director: Lee Katz. Dialogue director: Gene Lewis. Choreographer: Bobby Connolly. Screenplay: Sig Herzig and Jerry Wald. Based on a story by Harry Sauber. Songs: Harry Warren, Al Dubin, Gus Kahn, Walter Blaufuss, Carson J. Robinson, and Egbert Van Alstyne. Musical

director: Leo Forbstein. Photography: Arthur Todd.
Editor: Thomas Pratt. Art direction: Anton Grot.
Costumes: Milo Anderson.

CAST: James Melton (Jerry Haines/Jerry Handley), Patricia
Ellis (Jean Martin), Hugh Herbert (Sigfried Hammerschlag/
Papa Hammerschlag/Sigfried's brothers), ZaSu Pitts (Gwen
Logan), Allen Jenkins (Christopher Cross), Nat Pendleton
(Red, the chauffeur), Ann Sheridan (Lola Parker), Walter
Catlett (Sprague), Hobart Cavanaugh (Mr. Barton), Charles
Halton (Mr. Willard), Charles Richman (Mr. Malcolm), Dennis
Moore (Ronald Blakeley), Georgia Caine (Mrs. Parker),
Granville Bates (Goodrich), George Guhl (Policeman), Betty
Farrington (Customer), Adrian Rosley (Waiter), George Sorel
(Head waiter), Linda Perry (Miss Joyce, the secretary),
Gordon Hart (Caldwell), Robert Emmett O'Connor, Harry
Hollingsworth (Detectives), Emett Vogan (Floorwalker).

SONGS: "Summer Night," "The Little House that Love Built,"
"That's the Least You Can Do for a Lady" (Warren, Dubin),
"Your Eyes Have Told Me So" (Kahn, Blaufuss, Van Alstyne),
"Carry Me Back to the Lone Prairie" (Robinson).

SYNOPSIS: Wealthy playboy Jerry Haines is ordered to take
over the management of his family's failing department store.
Determined to learn the business from the bottom, he uses an
assumed name and takes a job as a music clerk at the store.
He romances saleswoman Jean Martin and befriends coworkers
Gwen Logan and Christopher Cross. Unaware of Jerry's real
identity, elevator operator Chris brags that he is a close
friend of the department store heir. Jerry uses Chris's
tales to make changes in store policy. Chris overhears two
executives plotting to run the store into bankruptcy and take
over. Jerry borrows an elaborate outfit from the store and
gives it to Jean to wear on a date. The floorwalker has them
arrested for shoplifting. Chris tells Jerry about the
takeover plot, still unaware of Jerry's identity. When Jerry
is released from jail, he confronts the traitors and examines
the store's books. Jean is angry when she learns Jerry lied
to her about his identity. She quits and goes into hiding.
Jerry tries to borrow money to stall his creditors, but the
bank refuses to give him a loan. When Jerry realizes that a
habitual shoplifter is related to a prominent family that
owns a railroad, he agrees not to prosecute in exchange for
use of a train. Jerry utilizes Jean's idea for saving the
store from bankruptcy, using the car to bring the store's
products to customers outside the city. Jerry finds Jean
working at a rival store and they reconcile.

REVIEWS:
Harrison's Reports, December 26, 1936: "Although this
musical picture stars James Melton...it is Hugh Herbert who
raises it above the level of ordinary entertainment....The
production is good, but the plot is routine. The love affair
is pleasant, though not exciting."

New York Times, December 26, 1936: "Sing Me a Love Song
is definitely [Hugh] Herbert's picture, though he graciously

surrenders the stage now and then to Floorwalker Walter
Catlett and to Merchant Prince Incognito James Melton....the
film is really pretty gay fare."

Variety, December 30, 1936: "Story isn't much and the
dialog [sic] fails to sparkle, yet there's a constant stream
of laughs, thanks to an incidental running gag in the hands
of Hugh Herbert."

NOTES: Sing Me a Love Song began production on July 6,
1936. The film went through several title changes before its
release, including Always Leave Them Laughing, Come Up
Smiling, and Let's Pretend. The Variety review noted
the poor grammar used in the final title (December 30, 1936).
In England, the film is known as Come Up Smiling. Marie
Wilson originally was cast in the role that went to ZaSu
Pitts. The producers decided Wilson was too young for the
assignment (B-211). Although radio singer James Melton is
the leading man and has the most screen time, comedian Hugh
Herbert garnered the best reviews. His quadruple role as a
kleptomaniac, his father, and two brothers, steals the
picture.
      Sing Me a Love Song usually is listed as Ann
Sheridan's first Warner Bros. credit. Although she is
seventh billed in the Variety review, she does not appear
in the print viewed by the author, nor in that viewed by
editors of the American Film Institute Catalog of Motion
Pictures Produced in the United States, Feature Films,
1931-1940 (B-211). Many sources refer to a scene in which
Ann and her matchmaking mother, played by Georgia Caine,
pursue James Melton. In the author's copy, Ann's character
is mentioned several times, implying that she is chasing
Melton. Reviews also credit Bobby Connolly with
choreographing non-existent production numbers. Since
sources disagree on the movie's running time, it is assumed
that Ann's scenes and at least one musical number were cut
after the film's initial release. Neither she nor Connolly
are credited onscreen.
      Despite Ann's missing footage, Sing Me a Love Song led
to her Warner Bros. contract. Impressed by her performance
in the film, casting director Max Arnow persuaded his Warner
Bros. bosses to sign her to a six-month contract at
seventy-five dollars a week. Ann later called Sing Me a
Love Song's Ray Enright her favorite director.

F-31   Black Legion   (Warner Bros., January 30, 1937)
       83 mins.

Producer: Robert Lord. Executive producers: Jack L. Warner
and Hal B. Wallis. Director: Archie L. Mayo. Assistant
director: Jack Sullivan. Screenplay: Abem Finkel and
William Wister Haines. Based on a story by Robert Lord.
Music: Bernhard Kaun. Photography: George Barnes. Editor:
Owen Marks. Art direction: Robert Haas. Costumes: Milo
Anderson. Sound: C.A. Riggs. Special effects: Fred
Jackson and H.F. Koenekamp.

CAST: Humphrey Bogart (Frank Taylor), Dick Foran (Ed

Jackson), Erin O'Brien-Moore (Ruth Taylor), Ann Sheridan
(Betty Grogan), Robert Barrat (Brown), Helen Flint (Pearl
Danvers/Davis), Joseph Sawyer (Cliff Summers/Moore), Addison
Richards (Prosecuting attorney), Eddie Acuff (Metcalf),
Clifford Soubier (Mike Grogan), Paul Harvey (Billings),
Samuel S. Hinds (Judge), John Litel (Tommy Smith), Charles
Halton (Osgood), Francis Sayles (Charlie), Harry Hayden
(Jones), Alonzo Price (Alf Hargrave), Dickie Jones (Buddy
Taylor), Dorothy Vaughan (Mrs. Grogan), Henry Brandon (Joe
Dombrowski), Pat C. Flick (Nick Strumpas), Paul Stanton (Dr.
Barham), Egon Brecher (Old Man Dombrowski), Ed Chandler,
Robert E. Homans (Policemen), William Wayner (Counterman),
Frederick Lindsley ("March of Time" voice), Fred MacKaye,
Frank Nelson, John Hiestand, Ted Bliss (Radio announcers),
Larry Emmons (Man in drugstore), Don Barclay (Drunk), Emmett
Vogan (News commentator), John Butler (Salesman), Frank Sully
(Helper), Max Wagner (Truck driver), Carlyle Moore, Jr,
Dennis Moore, Milt Kibbee (Reporters), Lee Phelps (Guard),
Wilfred Lucas (Bailiff), Jack Mower (County clerk), Millard
Mitchell.

SYNOPSIS: Factory worker Frank Taylor feels cheated when a
studious Polish employee beats him out of a promotion.
Stirred up by a radio speech against immigrants, Frank joins
the Black Legion, a brutal secret group that tortures and
intimidates anyone whose views differ from theirs. Frank
helps the legion run his coworker's family out of town and
destroy businesses run by immigrants. Frank gets the
promotion and lavishes gifts on his wife Ruth and son Buddy.
When he neglects his work for legion business, he is demoted.
The legion flogs his replacement, Frank's Irish neighbor.
When Ruth learns that Frank is involved in the violence, she
leaves him. Frank tries to quit the legion, but cannot. He
loses his job and has an affair with Pearl Danvers, his best
friend Ed Jackson's ex-girlfriend. When Ed tries to
intercede, Frank accidently tells him about the legion.
Frank worries that the legion will kill them both if Ed tells
police. Ed wires Ruth to return. Jealous of Ed's engagement
to Betty Grogan, Pearl claims Ed beat her. Prompted by
Pearl's accusations, as well as Frank's leak, the legion
kidnaps Ed. Frank fatally shoots him. Ed's murder prompts a
national investigation of the legion. Ruth stands by her
husband. A legion boss threatens to kill Frank's family
unless he pleads self-defense. Pearl substantiates the
self-defense claim, vilifying Ed's character and upsetting
Betty. Frank's conscience keeps him from lying on the
witness stand. He tells the truth about the legion and names
its members. Frank and the legionaires receive life
sentences for Ed's murder. As Frank goes off to jail, he
realizes that his jealousy and prejudice have not only ruined
his own life, but those of his wife and son.

REVIEWS:
New York Times, January 18, 1937: "...there are soundly
executed portrayals by Dick Foran, Helen Flint, Ann Sheridan,
Clifford Soubier, John Litel and many others."

Variety, January 20, 1937: "Warners has taken yesterday's

headlines and fashioned a melodrama which gives the emotions
a rough going over. With an effective blend of good drama
and timely propaganda in its favor, Black Legion should
gather heaps of critical plaudits."

Harrison's Reports, January 23, 1937: "A powerful
melodrama centering around the activities of a hooded
legion;....The same topic was covered in Columbia's Legion
of Terror [(1936)], but this is far superior both in
production and content."

Cincinnati Enquirer [OH], February 19, 1937: "A cast
imbued with the indignation of the director and writers
carries out the portrayal with clear-cut impersonations....
Ann Sheridan [is] the girl friend [sic] of [Dick] Foran....
As a piece of melodrama and propaganda Black Legion makes
its own case."

NOTES: Black Legion began production in August 1936.
According to internal memos found in the Warner Bros.
Collection at the USC Cinema-Television Library, executive
producer Hal Wallis originally wanted to cast Edward G.
Robinson in the lead. However, writer Robert Lord disagreed,
claiming Robinson looked too foreign. Lord wanted a
"distinctly American looking actor to play this part" and
Humphrey Bogart was cast. Glenda Farrell was considered for
the role that ultimately went to Erin O'Brien-Moore. Some of
the film was shot on location at the Warner Bros. ranch in
Calabasas, California and the Providencia Ranch (B-211).
     Despite the usual disclaimer that the characters and
events were fictional, Black Legion mirrors the burgeoning
growth of the Ku Klux Klan in the midwest during the mid
1930s. The movie is based on a story by Robert Lord which
dramatized the Michigan Black Legion killing of Charles Poole
and the testimony of Dayton Dean, the legion executioner who
was state's evidence at the trial. The Ku Klux Klan sued
Warner Bros. for patent infringement when the movie showed
their insignia of a white cross on a background of red with a
black square (B-211). Despite the controversy, the National
Board of Review chose Black Legion as Best Film for 1937
and named Humphrey Bogart Best Actor. Writer Robert Lord was
nominated for an Academy Award for Best Original Story, but
lost to William A. Wellman and Robert Carson for A Star Is
Born (United Artists, 1937).
     Ann Sheridan's role as Dick Foran's fiancee is small and
thankless. Black Legion marks her first film with Humphrey
Bogart, who became a close friend offscreen. Although The
Great O'Malley (F-32) actually began filming before Black
Legion, Ann and Bogart's characters had little interaction.
Two characters' names vary in the actual film and the closing
credits of Black Legion. Helen Flint is billed as Pearl
Davis, but is called Pearl Danvers. Similarly, Joseph
Sawyer's character, Cliff, whose name is listed as Moore, is
called Cliff Summers in the movie.

F-32 The Great O'Malley   (Warner Bros., February 13,
      1937)   71 mins.

Executive producers: Jack L. Warner and Hal B. Wallis.
Associate producer: Harry Joe Brown.   Director: William
Dieterle.   Assistant director: Frank Shaw.   Dialogue
director: Irving Rapper.   Screenplay: Milton Krims and Tom
Reed.   Based on the story "The Making of O'Malley" by Gerald
Beaumont.   Music: Heinz Roemheld.   Musical director: Leo F.
Forbstein.   Photography: Ernest Haller.   Editor: Warren
Low.   Art direction: Hugh Reticker.   Costumes: Milo
Anderson.   Special effects: James Gibbons, Fred Jackman,
Jr., and H.F. Koenekamp.

CAST: Pat O'Brien (James Aloysius O'Malley), Sybil Jason
(Barbara Phillips), Humphrey Bogart (John Phillips), Frieda
Inescort (Mrs. Phillips), Hobart Cavanaugh (Pinky Holden),
Ann Sheridan (Judy Nolan), Donald Crisp (Captain Cromwell),
Henry O'Neill (Attorney for the defense), Mary Gordon (Mrs.
O'Malley), Mabel Colcord (Mrs. Flaherty), Frank Sheridan
(Father Patrick), Delmar Watson (Tubby), Craig Reynolds
(Motorist), Gordon Hart (Doctor), Lillian Harmer (Miss
Taylor), Frank Reicher (Dr. Larson), Jack Mower, Arthur
Millet (Detectives), Max Wagner (Bus driver), Charles Wilson
(Cop), Bob Perry (Man getting shoe shine), James Farley
(Jones, desk sergeant), Jack Gamel, George Bookasta, Basil
Bookasta, Frank Lombardi (Bootblacks), Armand "Curly" Wright
(Vegetable peddler), George Humbert (Junkman), Granville
Bates (Bar proprietor), Raymond Brown (Timekeeper), Egon
Brecher (Pawnshop proprietor), Cliff Saum, Glen Cavender,
Charles Wilson (Policemen), W.H. Clauson (Police announcer),
John Sheehan, Edward Gargan (Radio car cops), Robert E.
Homans (Dugan), John Butler (Prosecuting attorney), Thomas
Pogue (Judge), Thomas L. Brower (Sergeant), Jerry Mandy
(Italian umbrella salesman), Virginia Sanborne, Francesca
Rotoli, Lottie Williams, Myrtle Stedman (Nurses), Perc Teeple
(Motorist), Joseph Allen (Warden), Huey White, Stanley Fields
(Convicts), Ralph Dunn (Police stenographer), Georgie
Billings, Leonard Kibrick.

SYNOPSIS: Over-zealous policeman James O'Malley makes a
laughing stock of the department by issuing ordinances for
out-of-date laws.   He refuses to listen to Captain
Cromwell's order to make friends with the citizens.   James
detains John Phillips over a broken muffler, causing John to
lose his job.   Desperate for money to support his wife and
lame daughter Barbara, John robs a pawnbroker.   James stops
John again, more concerned with the muffler than the
robbery.   John's lawyers make a fool of James in court.
John is sentenced to the penitentiary.   The press blames
James's persecution for making John turn to crime.   When
James refuses to resign, Cromwell demotes him to school
crossing guard.   The press and police harrass James.   As
time passes, he is charmed by the school children and begins
to act more humanely.   He befriends Barbara and clashes with
her teacher, Judy Nolan.   When James realizes that Barbara
is John's daughter, he feels guilty about his role in her
father's imprisonment.   James secretly arranges for a
prominent surgeon to operate on her lame leg.   He also
arranges for John's parole and finds a job for him.   When
James visits the Phillipses' apartment, paranoid John

assumes the policeman has come to harrass him. Drunk, John
shoots James. The policeman hovers near death. When Judy,
Cromwell, and John learn that James paid for Barbara's
operation, they realize James has changed. James refuses to
press charges. John donates blood for a transfusion and
James recovers completely. He returns to his beat, where he
is the most popular cop in the neighborhood. A changed man,
James courts Judy.

REVIEWS:
Harrison's Reports, February 6, 1937: "A good human-
interest picture of program grade;....The romantic interest
is subdued."

New York Times, March 6, 1937: "The conversion of a thick
cop, who writes summonses as fast as some authors write
screen plays, into a regular guy...by the power of love and
Sybil Jason is described with considerable economy,
especially of ideas....the picture steers its way to a
denouement as familiar as the route it takes to get there."

Variety, March 10, 1937: "One of Hollywood's pat formulas
for cop pictures, but with less action than usual....Fact
that [Pat] O'Brien gets shot by [Humphrey] Bogart is an added
tear-jerker for the finale as well as paving the way for the
romantic finish with schoolmarm Ann Sheridan....There's
practically no action for the first 40 minutes, and
subsequent footage hardly is in the very exciting class....
Performances on the whole are good."

NOTES: The Great O'Malley is based on "The Making of
O'Malley," a short story by Gerald Beaumont that appeared in
Red Book Magazine in October 1924. A silent version of
The Making of O'Malley was filmed by First National in
1925, with Milton Sills and Dorothy Mackaill in the roles
taken by Pat O'Brien and Ann Sheridan in the remake.
     The Great O'Malley began production in July 1936. Its
working title was The Making of O'Malley. The movie marks
Humphrey Bogart's first star billing, following acclaimed
performances in Black Legion (F-31) and The Petrified
Forest (Warner Bros., 1936). Bogart felt The Great
O'Malley was a comedown after the stirring dramas. He
recalled, "It was terrible, but it was one of those things we
did at that goddamned sweatship [Warner Bros.]. Pat
[O'Brien] was very good. Pat was never bad" (B-431). Ann
Sheridan's role as the teacher who becomes O'Brien's love
interest is small. Fan magazines of the time claimed that
she was cast because she had studied teaching before coming
to Hollywood, a blatant attempt by Warner Bros. to use
whatever angle they could to promote the film.

F-33 San Quentin   (Warner Bros., August 7, 1937)
      70 mins.

Producer: Samuel Bischoff. Executive producers: Jack L.
Warner and Hal B. Wallis. Director: Lloyd Bacon. Assistant
director: Dick Mayberry. Screenplay: Peter Milne and
Humphrey Cobb. Based on a story by Robert Tasker and John

Bright. Songs: Harry Warren, Al Dubin, Jean Kenbrovin, and
John William Kellette. Music: Heinz Roemheld, Charles
Maxwell, and David Raksin. Musical directors: Leo F.
Forbstein and Ray Heindorf. Photography: Sid Hickox.
Editor: William Holmes. Art direction: Esdras Hartley.
Costumes: Howard Shoup. Special effects: James Gibbons and
H.F. Koenekamp. Technical advisor: Doc Stone.

CAST: Pat O'Brien (Captain Stephen Jameson), Humphrey Bogart
(Joe "Red" Kennedy), Ann Sheridan (May Kennedy/Mae De
Villiers), Barton MacLane (Lieutenant Druggin) Joseph Sawyer
("Sailor Boy" Hansen), Veda Ann Borg (Helen), Joseph King
(Warden Taylor), James Robbins (Mickey Callahan), Gordon
Oliver (Captain), Garry Owen (Dopey), Marc Lawrence
(Venetti), Emmett Vogan (Lieutenant), William Pawley, Al
Hill, George Lloyd, Frank Faylen, Paul W. Panzer, Doc Stone,
Herman Marks, Eddie Gribbon (Convicts), Max Wagner (Prison
runner), Ernie Adams (Fink), Raymond Hatton (Pawnbroker), Hal
Neiman (Convict No. 38216), Glen Cavender (Convict Hastings),
William Williams (Convict Conklin), George Offerman, Jr.
(Young convict), Lane Chandler, Bruce Mitchell, Eddy Chandler
(Guards), Edward Piel, Sr. (Deputy), Dennis Moore (Convict
Simpson), John Ince (Old convict), Ralph Byrd (Policeman on
phone), Ray Flynn (Police officer), Claire White, Jack Mower
(Couple in car), Douglas Wood (Chairman of prison board),
Ernest Wood (Attorney), Saul Gorsa (Clerk), Jerry Fletcher
(Hoffman), Ralph Dunn (Head guard), Frank Fanning (Cop in
radio car), Bob Wilkie (Young convict in riot), Max Hoffman,
Jr. (Wall guard), Harry Hollingsworth (First guard), Dick
Wessel (Trusty), Edward Keane, Lee Phelps (Detectives), Pat
Flaherty (Policeman), Joe Cunningham (Doctor), Gennaro Curci
(Proprietor).

SONGS: "How Could You?" (Warren, Dubin), "I'm Forever
Blowing Bubbles" (Kenbrovin, Kellette).

SYNOPSIS: After a series of riots, Stephen Jameson replaces
brutal Lientenant Druggin as captain of the yard at San
Quentin. Stephen tries to bring military order and social
reforms to the prison. He falls in love with nightclub
singer May Kennedy, but keeps his job a secret when he learns
May's brother Red is in San Quentin for attempted robbery.
When May learns Stephen is captain of the yard, she breaks up
with him. Stephen's humane treatment and prison reform earns
the respect of the prisoners. With Stephen's guidance, Red
tries to work his way out of jail. He is assigned to the
road crew because of his good behavior. When the prisoners
who do not get road assignments plan a strike, Stephen locks
them up to thwart any violence. Jealous of Stephen's
popularity, Druggin reports the strike to the press, which
causes the parole board to investigate charges of favoritism.
Stephen explains how he thwarted the riot and the board gives
him free reign. When May learns of Stephen's prison reforms,
she reconsiders her feelings. The prisoners tease Red about
May and Stephen's relationship, making Red think Stephen is
using both Kennedys. Red escapes with Sailor, taking Druggin
as hostage. Sailor and Druggin are killed. Stephen worries
about his job after the incident, since he hoped to use Red

as an example of his reform ideas. Red hides at May's
apartment without her knowledge. He shoots Stephen, accusing
him of using May. Stephen convinces Red of his love for May
and his belief in prison reform. Stephen tries to protect
Red from the police, but Red is shot. Red hitchhikes back to
San Quentin. He dies at the prison gates, pleading with the
prisoners to give Stephen a chance.

REVIEWS: ·
Variety, July 28, 1937: "Romantic leads are Pat O'Brien
and Ann Sheridan....Miss Sheridan, in the first reel, capably
sings 'How Could You,' from a cabaret floor..."

New York Times, August 4, 1937: "It also provides Ann
Sheridan an opportunity to sing rather pleasantly, unless the
dubbing artists have been trifling with us again."

Harrison's Reports, August 14, 1937: "Good entertainment.
It is a fast-moving prison melodrama, with plentiful
action....Mixed in with melodrama is human interest and an
appealing romance."

NOTES: San Quentin began production in November 1936. It
was one of a series of gangster pictures Warner Bros. made
touting prison reform, suggesting that convicts should be
treated humanely and that firsttime offenders should be
isolated from repeat criminals. Much of the movie was shot
in and around San Quentin, with director Lloyd Bacon using
Doc Stone, a former convict, as technical advisor. Several
scenes had to be refilmed after character actor Tom Manning
died of a heart attack on the set (B-211). Ann Sheridan's
role as a cafe singer gave her the opportunity to sing "How
Could You?" in a nightclub scene.

See also S-1.

F-34   The Footloose Heiress   (Warner Bros., August 21,
        1937)   61 mins.

Executive producers: Jack L. Warner and Hal B. Wallis.
Associate producer: Bryan Foy. Director: William Clemens.
Assistant director: Drew Eberson. Dialogue director: Harry
Seymour. Screenplay: Robertson White. Based on a story by
Robertson White. Photography: Arthur Edeson. Editor: Lou
Hesse. Art direction: Hugh Reticker. Costumes: Howard
Shoup.

CAST: Craig Reynolds (Bruce "Butch" Baeder), Ann Sheridan
(Kay Allyn), Anne Nagel (Linda Pierson), William Hopper (Jack
Pierson), Hugh O'Connell (John C. Allyn), Teddy Hart (Charlie
McCarthy), Hal Neiman (Luke Peaneather), Frank Orth (Justice
Cuttler), William Eberhardt (Wilbur Frost), Lois Cheaney
(Sarah Cuttler).

SYNOPSIS: Advertising agency head John Allyn worries about
his madcap, marriage-minded daughter Kay and a radio program
that an oil company wants to sponsor. While trying to stop
Kay from eloping, John befriends hobo Bruce "Butch" Baeder.

Butch stops the wedding by pretending that he and Kay already
are married. She realizes her father is behind the charade
and she encourages Butch's attentions. Butch offers to try
and tame the impulsive Kay by using psychology. Kay tries to
get revenge on Butch, but he continually outsmarts her. When
John learns that Butch is the son of a wealthy Boston
advertising executive, he enlists Butch's help on the oil
program. Kay challenges his identity when Butch's father
denies his parentage because Butch insulted his ideas.
Convinced Butch is a phony, John throws him out. Kay admits
to her father that she is in love with him. Thinking Butch
is insolvent, she has the chauffeur plant five hundred
dollars in his coat. After the oil executives are impressed
with Butch's ideas, John realizes he needs Butch to make the
program work. John and Kay chase Butch's train. Kay sends
the sheriff to stop the train, claiming Butch stole five
hundred dollars from John. She is unaware that Butch has
traded coats with a hobo on the train, leading to a case of
mistaken identity. Kay confesses about planting the money and
wanting Butch to return. The sheriff releases Butch, who
insists he arrest the Allyns for their plot to falsely
imprison him. The sheriff locks up the Allyns, Butch, and
the hobo, hoping they will work out the problems by
themselves. They all collaborate on a script for the oil
program. Kay and Butch escape and stow away on a train to
Boston. Admitting their love, they plan to marry and tell
off Butch's father.

REVIEWS:
Harrison's Reports, August 21, 1937: "Just mild program
entertainment. The story is familiar; and it lacks novelty
treatment....There's little human appeal, for the actions of
the heroine are such as to annoy one."

New York Times, October 9, 1937: "If you are shopping for
quantity rather than quality, then the Palace should be your
market place this week. For on the basement bargain counter
you will find such slightly damaged items as...That Certain
Woman [(Warner Bros., 1937)], an Educational short called
The Big Apple,...and something called Footloose
Heiress."

Variety, October 13, 1937: "This is the kind of a picture
that might have been made off the arm and for that type of
picture not bad, considering that it's intended only for
multiple programs....Craig Reynolds and Ann Sheridan both are
ingratiating."

NOTES: Ann Sheridan plays the title role and receives second
billing in this "B" unit attempt at madcap comedy. The
film's working title was The Madcap Heiress. Patricia
Ellis originally was cast in the movie. However, when
commitments at Columbia kept her from starting the picture in
February 1937, Ann was called in to replace her (B-595).
Co-star William Hopper was the son of columnist Hedda Hopper,
whom Ann Sheridan later befriended.

F-35 Wine, Women and Horses   (Warner Bros., September 11,

1937)   64 mins.

Executive producers: Jack L. Warner and Hal B. Wallis.
Associate producer: Bryan Foy.   Director: Louis King.
Assistant director: Arthur Lueker.   Dialogue director:
Reggie Hammerstein.   Screenplay: Roy Chanslor.   Based on the
novel Dark Hazard by W.R. Burnett.   Photography: James Van
Trees, Sr.   Editor: Jack Saper.   Art direction: Esdras
Hartley.   Costumes: Howard Shoup.

CAST: Barton MacLane (Jim Turner), Ann Sheridan (Valerie),
Dick Purcell (George Mayhew), Peggy Bates (Marjorie Mayhew),
Walter Cassell (Pres Barrow), Lottie Williams (Mrs. Mayhew),
Kenneth Harlan (Jed Bright), Eugene Jackson (Eight Ball),
Charles Foy (Broadway), James Robbins (Joe), Nita (Lady
Luck), Addison Richards (Bit).

SYNOPSIS: Chicago gambler Jim Turner shares his love of
horses with his friend Valerie.   When he places a series of
losing bets, he heads for Saratoga, hoping his luck will
change.   En route to New York, he befriends gambler George
Mayhew, who invites him to move into the family boarding
house.   Jim is lucky at the track and falls in love with
George's sister Marjorie.   She insists that Jim get a steady
job and give up gambling before they marry.   Jim and Marjorie
go to Chicago, where he tries to conform, taking a job as a
hotel desk clerk.   Jim is drawn back to gambling when a guest
pays him for track tips.   The guest offers Jim a job at Santa
Anita.   Jim convinces Marjorie to move to California, despite
her feelings about gambling.   There, Jim runs into Valerie,
who is suprised to hear about his marriage and gambling
abstinence.   Marjorie is jealous when Valerie pursuades Jim
to go gambling.   Disgusted and pregnant, Marjorie goes home
to her mother.   After a year and a half, Marjorie begins
dating Pres Barrow, her childhood sweetheart.   Jim loses his
money and goes to visit his son.   He is saddened to learn the
baby died.   Despite Marjorie's love for Pres, she convinces
Jim to stay and get a job.   Jim tries to reform, however when
his favorite horse is injured, he insists on buying her to
save her life.   Jim's mother-in-law confides that Marjorie is
in love with Pres and that she took Jim back out of pity.
Jim urges Marjorie to divorce him so he can go back to the
track where he belongs.   The horse recovers and becomes a
winner.   Jim realizes he has loved Valerie all along and they
marry.

REVIEWS:
Harrison's Reports, September 11, 1937:   "This remake is
even less entertaining than [Dark Hazard]; it is just mild
program fare....it is not edifying either to children or to
adults, for it glorifies gambling;....Moreover, the players
are not strong box-office attractions."

Variety, September 29, 1937:   "Even the horses aren't much
good in what they slapped together for Barton MacLane, Ann
Sheridan and some lesser players.   That's less than can be
said for most westerns....Miss Sheridan plays the second
wife, but it is only a minor matter for her scrapbook."

NOTES: <u>Wine, Women and Horses</u> began production in March
1937. Its working title was <u>Lady Luck</u>. The film is a
remake of <u>Dark Hazard</u> (Warner Bros., 1934), a dog track
tale based on W.R. Burnett's 1933 novel. Edward G. Robinson,
Glenda Farrell, and Genevieve Tobin played the parts taken by
Barton MacLane, Ann Sheridan, and Peggy Bates in the remake.
Character actor Charles Foy, who plays Broadway in <u>Wine,</u>
<u>Women and Horses</u>, was the brother of Warner Bros. "B" unit
producer Bryan Foy, who produced the movie.

F-36 <u>Alcatraz Island</u>   (Warner Bros., November 6, 1937)
      64 mins.

Producer: J.J. Cohn. Associate producer: Bryan Foy.
Director: William McGann. Assistant directors: Elmer
Decker and Claude E. Archer. Dialogue director: Harry
Seymour. Screenplay: Crane Wilbur. Based on the story
"Alcatraz" by Crane Wilbur. Photography: L.W. O'Connell.
Editor: Frank Dewar. Art direction: Esdras Hartley.
Costumes: Howard Shoup. Sound: Francis J. Scheid.
Technical advisor: Charles Perry.

CAST: Ann Sheridan (Flo Allen), John Litel (Gat Brady), Mary
Maguire (Annabel Brady), Gordon Oliver (George Drake), Dick
Purcell (David "Harp" Santell), Vladimir Sokolof (Flying
Dutchman), Addison Richards (Fred MacClane), Ben Welden (Red
Carroll), George E. Stone (Tough Tony Burke), Peggy Bates
(Miss Tolliver), Doris Lloyd (Miss Marquand), Anderson Lawlor
(Whitey Edwards), Charles Trowbridge (Warden Jackson), Edward
Keane (Crandall), Walter Young (Federal judge), Ed Stanley
(U.S. attorney), Veda Ann Borg (The red head), Ellen Clancy
(Sally Carruthers), Matty Fain (Butch), Lane Chandler
(Federal officer), Patricia Walthal, Cliff Saum, Stuart
Holmes, Edward Price, Bert Ross, Johnny Harron, Sol Gorss,
Milton Kibbee, Bill Gavier, Pat O'Malley, Jack Gardner, Sam
Bennett, William Worthington, Myrtle Steadman, Granville
Owen, Dick Rich, Henry Otho, Tommy Bupp, Willard Parker, Spec
O'Donnell, Earl Dwire, Francis Sayles, Ralph Dunn, Galan
Galt, Ted Oliver, Paul Panzer, Guy Usher, Helen Valkis,
Carole Landis, Sammy Cohen, John Ogatty, Gwen Seager, Gene
Hart, Connie Andre, Jack Wagner, Douglas Williams, George P.
Meyers, Glen Cavender, Don Turner, Phil Ryley.

SYNOPSIS: Racketeer Gat Brady is against murder under any
circumstances. His henchman Red Carroll vows to get revenge
when Gat refuses to help his brother, a murder fugitive. Gat
tries to keep his business dealings a secret from his teenage
daughter Annabel. She insists that his racketeering does not
change her feelings for him. As Gat and Annabel prepare to
sail to Europe, he is arrested for income tax evasion. He is
sentenced to five years at Leavenworth. Gat asks Annabel's
governess, Flo Allen, to take Annabel on the trip and keep
her away from the prison. When they return from Europe, Red
kidnaps Annabel, claiming that Gat escaped and is hiding at
his home. Annabel is anxious to see her father so she goes
with Red. However, when she finds out the truth, she
escapes. Red is sent to Leavenworth for kidnapping. He
picks a fight with Gat, causing the guards to transfer Gat to

Alcatraz Island. Meanwhile, Annabel tells prosecuting attorney George Drake about her father's mistreatment in prison. Although George was responsible for Gat's prosecution, he promises to help. Still seeking revenge, Red arranges a transfer to Alcatraz and schemes to get Gat in trouble so Gat cannot be paroled. Gat is the chief suspect when his knife is used to kill Red. George proves that Gat's knife was stolen during a diversion caused by the China Clipper flying over the prison. Red's killer, the Flying Dutchman, gives an undercover agent a taped confession, then hangs himself. Gat is aquitted and returns to Leavenworth to serve the last six months of his sentence.

REVIEWS:
Variety, October 13, 1937: "Ann Sheridan, John Litel and Mary Maguire, freshmen in films, are all excellent, but Miss Sheridan has had better roles in her brief career, including in San Quentin."

New York Times, October 14, 1937: "...the film has a compact plot, smooth performances by John Litel and the little-known others, and a good bit of interesting material on the present residence of Al Capone. Whether the Alcatraz scenes are accurate or not is beside the point; they do make good watching. And so, for all its Class B-ishness, does the picture."

Billboard, October 30, 1937: "Ann Sheridan, as Gat's girl friend [sic], appears too briefly to do any real harm."

Harrison's Reports, October 30, 1937: "A fairly good program melodrama; the title offers unusual exploitation possibilities....There are two romances, each one mildly pleasant."

NOTES: Alcatraz Island began production on May 24, 1937. It was produced by Cosmopolitan Pictures, a Warner Bros.'s "B" unit headed by communications mogul William Randolph Hearst. The plot capitalized on gangster Al Capone's 1931 conviction for income tax evasion. Prior to the film's release, there was much controversy over the crime in the movie. Censors criticized the violence, the open display of liquor, and the depiction of a fixed jury. A story in the Hearst-owned San Francisco Examiner brought the Attorney General's office into the foray, fearing it would misrepresent the penal system. Warner Bros. agreed to let Attorney General Homer S. Cummings view the film prior to its release. Alcatraz Island was banned in Sweden, Finland, and Trinidad (B-211).
     Alcatraz Island also landed the studio in court. Screenwriter Milton Herbert Gropper sued Warner Bros., claiming the film was adapted from his unproduced play Ex-Racketeer. The studio insisted it was based on Crane Wilbur's original story. In January 1941, the matter went to court, where the judge ruled in favor of the studio.
     In 1946, Warner Bros. announced plans to rerelease Alcatraz Island because of new interest in the prison after five men were killed and fifteen injured during an incident.

The studio said they would add newsreel footage of the recent riot, a new opening, and three additional sequences (<u>Daily Variety</u>, May 8, 1946). No further information can be found on this unlikely rerelease.

F-37 <u>She Loved a Fireman</u>   (Warner Bros., December 18, 1937)   57 mins.

Producer: Bryan Foy. Executive producers: Jack L. Warner and Hal B. Wallis. Director: John Farrow. Assistant director: Elmer Decker. Dialogue director: Jo Graham. Screenplay: Carlton C. Sand and Morton Grant. Based on the story "Two Platoons" by Carlton C. Sand. Song "He Thinks He's a Fireman": M.K. Jerome and Jack Scholl. Photography: L. William O'Connell. Editor: Thomas Pratt. Art direction: Hugh Retticker. Costumes: Howard Shoup. Sound: Stanley Jones. Technical advisor: Captain Orville J. Emory.

CAST: Dick Foran (Red Tyler), Ann Sheridan (Margie Shannon), Robert Armstrong (Smokey Shannon), Eddie Acuff (Skillet Michaels), Veda Ann Borg (Betty), May Beatty (Mrs. Michaels), Eddie Chandler (Callahan), Lane Chandler (Patton), Ted Oliver (Lieutenant Grimes), Pat Flaherty (Duggan), Leo White (Barber), Kathrin Clare Ward (Mrs. Murphy), Myrtle Stedman (Mrs. Brown), Brick Sullivan (Man at dance), Janet Shaw (Girl at dance), Russ Powell (Barman), Jack Mower (Bell captain), Cy Kendall (Chief deputy), Hal Craig (Examining officer), Fred "Snowflake" Toones (Joe), Minerva Urecal (Nurse Purdy), Huey White (Turtle), Allen Mathews (Junior officer), Wilfred Lucas (Captain), Eddie Hart (McDermott), Paul Panzer (Night watchman), Monte Vandergrift (Ben).

SYNOPSIS: Captain Smokey Anderson tries to dissuade former bookie Red Tyler from joining the fire department. He dislikes Red's arrogance and poor attitude. When Smokey steals Red's girlfriend, Red vows to join the force and get revenge. During his training, Red befriends fellow recruit Skillet Michaels. They are assigned to Smokey's firehouse. Red continues his grudge against Smokey, vowing to steal the captain's pretty girlfriend. Red is unaware that she is really Margie Shannon, Smokey's sister. Despite Red's initial motives, he falls in love with Margie. Smokey is furious about the relationship and continues to give Red a difficult time at work. Red abuses his friendship with Skillet, convincing him to take Red's place at the firehouse so he can go out with Margie. She gets angry at Red's laziness and breaks up with him. Skillet breaks his leg when he falls from a ladder which Red failed to attach in his haste to leave for his date. Red feels guilty and is brought before the board for negligence. He asks to stay in the fire department so he can help Skillet financially. At Margie's insistence, Smokey recommends that the commissioner transfer Red to another firehouse. Reformed by the incident, Red takes his job seriously. During a four-alarm fire, he further redeems himself by risking his life to save Smokey. Realizing that Red has changed, Smokey gives his consent for Red to marry Margie. The wedding is interrupted by a fire call and Red and Smokey race off to do their duty.

REVIEWS:
Variety, November 17, 1937: "Ann Sheridan has much to say
but little to do in her role. Okay as the romantic foil."

Harrison's Reports, December 18,.1937: "Moderately
entertaining program fare. The picture is hampered by a
trite plot and excessive dialogue."

New York Times, January 21, 1938: "...the film is merely a
succession of warehouse fires out of whose crucible Dick
Foran emerges a better boy and worthier of the arms of Ann
Sheridan. Our advice would be to look around for the nearest
exit."

Billboard, February 5, 1938: "The heart interest, Ann
Sheridan, isn't bad at all, and should be tossed a better
bone next time."

NOTES: She Loved a Fireman began production in July 1937.
Its working title was Two Platoons. This "B" picture
reunited Ann Sheridan with Dick Foran, her fiance in Black
Legion (F-31). Both later had·supporting roles in Cowboy
from Brooklyn (F-41). The American Film Institute Catalog
of Motion Pictures in the United States, Feature Films,
1931-1940 notes that the plot of She Loved a Fireman is
very similar to Warner Bros.'s Here Comes the Navy, a 1934
film that starred James Cagney, Pat O'Brien, and Gloria
Stuart (B-211).

F-38   The Patient in Room 18   (Warner Bros., January 8,
       1938)   58 mins.

Producer: Bryan Foy. Executive producers: Jack L. Warner
and Hal B. Wallis. Directors: Bobby Connolly and Crane
Wilbur. Assistant director: Fred Tyler. Dialogue director:
Harry Seymour. Screenplay: Eugene Solow and Robertson
White. Based on a novel by Mignon G. Eberhart. Photography:
James Van Trees. Editor: Lou Hesse. Art direction: John
Hughes. Costumes: Howard Shoup. Sound: Leslie G. Hewitt.

CAST: Patric Knowles (Lance O'Leary), Ann Sheridan (Sara
Keate), Eric Stanley (Bentley, the valet), John Ridgely (Jim
Warren), Rosella Towne (Maida Day), Jean Benedict (Carol
Lethany), Harland Tucker (Dr. Arthur Lethany), Edward
Raquello (Dr. Fred Harker), Charles Trowbridge (Dr. Balman),
Vicki Lester (Nurse), Cliff Clark (Inspector Foley), Ralph
Sanford (Inspector Donahue), Frank Orth (John Higgins), Greta
Meyer (Hilda), Walter Young (Coroner), Ralph Dunn (Hotel
clerk), George Offerman, Jr., Dick Paxton, Julius Molnar,
Jr., George Hickman (Newsboys), Glen Cavender (Doorman), Jack
Richardson (Cabbie), Cliff Saum, Jack Mower (Policemen), Spec
O'Donnell (Elevator operator), William Hopper (Grabshot),
Owen King (Day clerk), John Harron (Orderly), Allan Conrad
(Night clerk).

SYNOPSIS: Private detective Lance O'Leary is on the verge of
a nervous breakdown after he fails to solve a case. Dr.
Arthur Lethany insists Lance check into his private hospital

to rest. Lance worries about meeting nurse Sara Keate, his
former girlfriend. During Lance's hospital stay, wealthy
patient Frank Warren is murdered and $100,000 worth of radium
is stolen from his chest. The suspects include James,
Frank's financially-strapped nephew, and Dr. Balman, the
physician who thought the radium should be used to treat the
masses rather than one wealthy patient. Although Dr. Lethany
orders Lance to avoid any discussion of crime during his
recovery, Lance insists that solving a case and redeeming his
reputation is the best cure for his nerves. Inspector Foley
allows Lance to help with the investigation. When Dr.
Lethany disappears, he is blamed for the crimes. Sara
insists the doctor is innocent. Lance questions Lethany's
cheating wife and her boyfriend, Dr. Harker, when Dr.
Lethany's body is found. Before the Warren murder's only
apparent witness can reveal the killer, he also is murdered.
Lance solves the crimes and calls together the suspects to
review their motives. Dr. Lethany appears, explaining that
Lance told him to fake his own death, since he witnessed Dr.
Balman stealing the radium. Lance accuses Dr. Balman of the
murders. Balman pulls a gun on Lance, but Foley apprehends
him. Lance lets Foley take credit for solving the case,
considering his reconcilation with Sara as his reward.

REVIEWS:
Harrison's Reports, January 8, 1938: "This murder mystery
melodrama is only mild program fare, for the plot is trite
and the action drags....Two romances are woven in the plot,
but they are of secondary importance."

Variety, January 26, 1938: "...the femme portion is ably
represented by Ann Sheridan, as head nurse..."

New York Times, April 22, 1938: "...if you feel yourself
slipping - or if you just want to kill an hour - this little
item may be your meat. Otherwise, it is an obvious (and
harmless) run-of-the-mill detective film, with Patric Knowles
as the handsome ace and Ann Sheridan as his nurse
girlfriend."

Motion Picture, May 1938: "This will keep you on the edge
of your seat until Patient in Room 18 discovers the
perpetrators of the crime. Patric Knowles and Ann Sheridan
score in the leading roles."

NOTES: The Patient in Room 18 began production on
August 29, 1937. It is based on Mignon G. Eberhart's 1929
novel of the same title. Eberhart, whose name mistakenly is
spelled "Minon" in the film credits, wrote a series of
mysteries about detective Lance O'Leary and his girlfriend,
nurse Sara Keate. According to The Warner Bros. Story,
seven films were based on Eberhart's five novels (B-226).
Ann Sheridan repeated her role as Sara Keate in Mystery
House (F-39).

F-39 Mystery House   (Warner Bros., May 21, 1938)
      56 mins.

Supervising producer: Bryan Foy. Executive producers: Jack
L. Warner and Hal B. Wallis. Director: Noel Smith.
Assistant director: Chuck Hansen. Dialogue director: John
Langan. Screenplay: Sherman L. Lowe and Robertson White.
Based on the novel The Mystery of Hunting's End by Mignon
G. Eberhart. Photography: L. William O'Connell. Editor:
Frank Magee. Art direction: Stanley Fleischer. Costumes:
Howard Shoup. Sound: Leslie G. Hewitt.

CAST: Dick Purcell (Lance O'Leary), Ann Sheridan (Sarah
Keate), Anne Nagel (Gwen Kingery), William Hopper (Lal
Killian), Anthony Averill (Julian Barre), Dennie Moore
(Annette), Hugh O'Connell (Newell Morse), Ben Welden (Gerald
Frawley), Sheila Bromley (Terice Von Elm), Elspeth Dudgeon
(Aunt Lucy Kingery), Anderson Lawlor (Joe Page), Trevor
Bardette (Bruker), Eric Stanley (Huber Kingery), Jean
Benedict (Helen Page), Jack Mower (Coroner), Stuart Holmes
(Jury foreman), Loia Cheaney (Secretary), John Harron
(Director).

SYNOPSIS: Banker Huber Kingery invites his colleagues to his
hunting lodge to find out who has been embezzling funds. He
gives the embezzler until the next morning to confess his
identity. That night, Huber is murdered. Although the
coroner rules the death a suicide, Huber's daughter Gwen
hires a detective to solve the crime. Nurse Sarah Keate, who
tends Gwen's wheelchair-bound aunt Lucy, recommends her
boyfriend Lance O'Leary. Gwen invites the same guests back
to the lodge so Lance can retrace the crime. Two guests are
murdered. Suspicion falls on a cheating husband, aunt Lucy,
the chauffeur who once stole from Huber's company, and
several of Huber's colleagues. When Lance discovers a gun
set up to shoot automatically, he realizes he must catch the
killer before any more murders can take place. Lance finds a
note in the safe accusing Julian Barre of embezzlement. He
traps Julian with the help of the Kingerys' German shepherd
and the guests. Julian reveals he killed all three victims
to cover up his embezzlement.

REVIEWS:
Harrison's Reports, May 14, 1938: "A typical program
murder mystery melodrama, developed along familiar lines....
The romance is of minor importance."

Variety, June 1, 1938: "Situations aren't cleanly cut, nor
are motives established with much clarity. Dialog [sic] is
often hackneyed and run-of-mill. Humor gets about a complete
overlooking."

New York Times, June 29, 1938: "...Mystery House [is
weak in spots] and the spots are pretty big."

NOTES: Mystery House began production in November 1937.
Prior to release, it used the title of its source, Mignon G.
Eberhart's 1930 novel The Mystery of Hunting's End. Ann
Sheridan reprised her role as Sarah Keate from The Patient
in Room 18 (F-38), though the credits spell her character's
name differently in the two films. Both movies are based on

Eberhart's books.

F-40 <u>Little Miss Thoroughbred</u>   (Warner Bros., June 4,
1938)   65 mins.

Supervising producer: Bryan Foy. Executive producers: Jack
L. Warner and Hal B. Wallis. Director: John Farrow.
Assistant director: Elmer Decker. Dialogue director: Jo
Graham. Screenplay: Albert DeMond and George Bricker.
Based on the story "Little Lady Luck" by Albert DeMond.
Photography: L. William O'Connell. Editor: Everett Dodd.
Art direction: Ted Smith. Costumes: Howard Shoup. Sound:
Stanley Jones.

CAST: John Litel (Nelson "Nails" Morgan), Ann Sheridan
(Madge Perry), Frank McHugh (Todd Harrington), Janet Kay
Chapman (Janet Smith), Eric Stanley (Colonel Whitcomb),
Robert E. Homans (Officer O'Reilly), Charles Wilson (Becker),
John Ridgely (Slug), Jean Benedict (Sister Margaret), Maureen
Rodin-Ryan (Sister Patricia), Lottie Williams (Mother
Superior), James Nolan (Intern), Cy Kendall (District
attorney Sheridan), Paul Everton (Judge Stanhope), Dorothy
Vaughn (Katie O'Reilly), Frank Orth (Marriage clerk), Loia
Cheaney (Apartment house manager).

SYNOPSIS: Orphan Janet Smith believes her father is still
alive. She runs away from the orphanage to look for him.
Overwhelmed by the traffic and noise of the city, she faints
in the middle of the street and is taken to the hospital.
Meanwhile, gamblers Nails Morgan and Todd Harrington hurry to
the racetrack to place a bet. When they are stopped by
Officer O'Reilly for speeding, Todd claims Janet is Nails's
daughter and they are following the ambulance. O'Reilly
escorts them to the hospital. When Janet hears that her
father has been found, she recovers immediatly. Because
O'Reilly is standing nearby, Nails cannot refuse her request
to go home. Janet charms Todd and neighbor Madge Perry, who
is in love with Nails. Todd suggests that the child is good
luck, hoping Nails will keep her. Nails insists they must
return her to the orphanage as soon as possible. When Nails
continuously wins while accompanied by Janet, he is convinced
that she is his lucky charm. He decides to move to
California with Todd and Janet, hiring Madge to act as her
nurse. Madge is disgusted that he sees the child as a
business opportunity, but agrees to accompany them. When
O'Reilly learns that Nails and Madge are not married, he
forces them to wed for Janet's sake. After Nails departs for
California, O'Reilly learns that Janet is not his daughter.
O'Reilly gets permission to pursue him. Bookie Becker also
goes after Nails, hoping to get a cut of his winnings. Janet
gives Colonel Whitcomb a tip on Talisman and the horse wins.
To thank her for breaking its losing streak, the colonel
gives her the horse. With Todd as trainer, Talisman is a
winner. Becker blackmails Nails into fixing a big race,
threatening to report that Nails kidnapped Janet. Nails
considers sending Janet back to the orphanage, breaking her
heart but pocketing the money from the race. When he
realizes how much Janet loves him, he throws the race. The

officials notice Talisman's jockey pulling the horse to slow him down and call Nails to the office. Before he can answer their charges, O'Reilly arrests Nails, Madge, and Todd for kidnapping. In court, the jury is swayed by Janet's love for Nails. Everyone is exonerated. The judge orders Nails to get a steady job and stay away from gambling. Nails agrees to settle down and be a proper father and husband.

REVIEWS:
Harrison's Reports, May 28, 1938: "Fair program entertainment; it mixes comedy with heart appeal....The love interest is pleasant."

Cincinnati Enquirer [OH], May 27, 1938: "Little Miss Thoroughbred is a nice, light, wholesome family picture. It's a program picture that rates a B-plus for its entertainment value."

Variety, June 15, 1938: "Ann Sheridan plays straight in the girl routine..."

NOTES: Little Miss Thoroughbred began production in January 1938. Its working title was Little Lady Luck. The film marks the screen debut of six-year-old Janet Chapman, whom Warner Bros. hoped to turn into another Shirley Temple. Reviews compare the film to Temple's Little Miss Marker (Paramount, 1934), which also revolves around a child reforming a gambler. Although Chapman made several additional films for Warner Bros., including Heart of the North (1937) and On Trial (1939), her career never reached the peaks the studio had hoped. Ann Sheridan plays Chapman's adoptive mother in Little Miss Thoroughbred. Later that year, she was reunited with Chapman and co-star John Litel in Broadway Musketeers (F-44), adopting Champman a second time.

F-41 Cowboy from Brooklyn   (Warner Bros., July 9, 1938)
      80 mins.

Executive producers: Jack L. Warner and Hal B. Wallis. Associate producer: Lou Edelman. Director: Lloyd Bacon. Assistant director: Dick Mayberry. Screenplay: Earl Baldwin. Based on the play Howdy Stranger by Louis Pelletier, Jr. and Robert Sloane. Songs: Johnny Mercer, Richard A. Whiting, Harry Warren, Brewster Higley, and Dan Kelly. Musical director: Leo. F. Forbstein. Orchestrations: Adolph Deutsch. Photography: Arthur Edeson. Editor: James Gibbons. Art direction: Esdras Hartley. Costumes: Milo Anderson. Sound: Dolph Thomas and David Forrest.

CAST: Dick Powell (Elly Jordan), Pat O'Brien (Roy Chadwick), Priscilla Lane (Jane Hardy), Dick Foran (Sam Thorne), Ann Sheridan (Maxine Chadwick), Johnnie "Scat" Davis (Jeff Hardy), Ronald Reagan (Pat "Speed" Dunn), Emma Dunn (Ma Hardy), Granville Bates (Pop Hardy), James Stephenson (Professor Landis), Hobart Cavanaugh (Mr. Jordan), Elisabeth Risdon (Mrs. Jordan), Dennie Moore (Abby Pitts), Rosella

Towne (Panthea), May Boley (Mrs. Krinkenheim), Harry Barris
(Louie), Candy Candido (Spec), Donald Briggs (Star
reporter), Jeffrey Lynn (Chronicle reporter), John Ridgely
(Beacon reporter), William B. Davidson (W.P. Alvey), Mary
Field (Myrtle Semple), Monte Vandergrift, Eddy Chandler
(Brakemen), Cliff Saum (Conductor), Sam Hayes (News
commentator), Jack Wise, Eddie Graham (Reporters), Don Marion
(Bellboy), Jack Mower (Station manager), John Harron
(Technician), Wen Niles (Announcer), John T. Murray (Colonel
Rose), George Hickman (Newsboy), Dorothy Vaughan (Fat woman),
Jimmy Fox (Photographer), Stuart Holmes (Doorman), Mary
Gordon (Chambermaid), Emmett Vogan (Loudspeaker announcer),
James Nolan (Alvey's secretary), John Hiestand (Radio
announcer), Jack Moore (First timekeeper), Ben Hendricks
(First judge).

SONGS: "I've Got a Heart Full of Music," "I'll Dream
Tonight," "Ride, Tenderfoot, Ride," "Howdy Stranger" (Mercer,
Whiting), "Cowboy from Brooklyn" (Mercer, Warren), "Git Along
Little Doggies" (traditional), "Home on the Range" (Higley,
Kelly).

SYNOPSIS: Despite a deathly fear of animals, Brooklyn-born
Elly Jordan becomes a singing cowboy at a Wyoming dude ranch
owned by Ma and Pop Hardy. The Hardys' daughter Jane coaches
him on western behavior to fool the tourists. She falls in
love with Elly and urges him to fight his fear of animals by
trying to impress a woman. Practical joker Sam Thorne is
jealous of Elly's attentions to Jane, as well as his singing
talents. When fast-talking theatrical agent Roy Chadwick
hears Elly sing at the ranch, he hires Elly for a radio spot.
Changing Elly's name to Wyoming Steve Gibson, Roy promotes
him as an authentic cowboy singer. Elly becomes a radio
star. Roy arranges a date with his sexy sister Maxine,
hoping it will boost Elly's romantic image. Back in Wyoming,
Jane misses Elly. Her family urges her to participate in a
rodeo at Madison Square Garden so she can see Elly in New
York. Tired of lying about his Brooklyn background, Elly
tells Roy the truth. Roy insists Elly keep up the scam until
he signs a movie contract. Jealous of Jane's feelings for
Elly, Sam tells the press that Elly is a phony. Roy tries to
salvage the situation by having the Hardys masquerade as
Elly's family. Despite the charade, the press reveals Elly
is from Brooklyn. Producer W.P. Alvey agrees to give Elly a
movie contract anyway, if he can prove his skills at the
rodeo. Elly panics at the idea of coming in contact with
animals. Although Jane thinks Elly is in love with Maxine,
she hires a hypnotist to rid Elly of his phobia. At the
rodeo, Elly wins the bulldogging contest, but a fall brings
him out of hypnosis. Alvey gives Elly the movie contract.
Elly realizes he loves Jane.

REVIEWS:
Variety, June 15, 1938: "Not all the opportunities for a
different and unusual picture are realized because the
farcial situations get out of hand and the actors take to
clowning."

<u>Harrison's Reports</u>, June 25, 1938: "This burlesqued
Western, with music, is fairly good entertainment. The first
half is somewhat slow; but it picks up speed in the second
half, ending in an extremely comical manner."

<u>New York Times</u>, July 14, 1938: "To have built a standard-
length comedy out of the almost piteously frail satirical
idea embodied in <u>Cowboy from Brooklyn</u>...was an engineering
achievement equivalent...to the reconstruction of a giant
dilpodocus from a fossil great toe....The best of the film's
comic passages are slapstick, and the best, incidentally -
are none too good."

NOTES: <u>Cowboy from Brooklyn</u> began production in January
1938. It was based on the Broadway play <u>Howdy Stranger</u>,
which opened January 14, 1937 and ran for seventy-seven
performances. <u>Cowboy from Brooklyn</u> had several working
titles, including <u>Dude Rancher</u>, <u>Howdy Stranger</u>, and <u>The
Brooklyn Cowboy</u> (B-211). The film marks Ann Sheridan's
first appearance with Ronald Reagan, whom she later played
opposite in <u>Kings Row</u> (F-61) and <u>Juke Girl</u> (F-62). Ann's
role as Pat O'Brien's femme fatale sister is secondary.
<u>Cowboy from Brooklyn</u> was remade as the musical <u>Two Guys
from Texas</u> (Warner Bros., 1948) with Dennis Morgan, Jack
Carson, and Dorothy Malone in the parts originated by Dick
Powell, Pat O'Brien, and Priscilla Lane.

See also S-14, V-27.

F-42   <u>Letter of Introduction</u>   (Universal, August 5, 1938)
       104 mins.

Producer: John M. Stahl. Director: John M. Stahl.
Assistant directors: Joseph A. McDonough and Charles Gould.
Screenplay: Sheridan Gibney and Leonard Spigelgass. Based
on a story by Bernice Boone. Musical director: Charles
Previn. Photography: Karl Freund. Editors: Ted Kent and
Charles Maynard. Art direction: Jack Otterson and John
Ewing. Sets: R. A. Gausman. Costumes: Vera West. Sound:
Bernard B. Brown and Joseph Lapis. Hairstylists: Emily
Moore and Helen Stoeffler. Makeup: Jack Pierce and Tom
Karnagle.

CAST: Adolphe Menjou (John Mannering), Andrea Leeds (Kay
Martin), Edgar Bergen and Charlie McCarthy (Themselves),
George Murphy (Barry Paige), Rita Johnson (Honey), Ann
Sheridan (Lydia Hoyt), Eve Arden (Cora), Ernest Cossart
(Andrews), Jonathan Hale (Woodstock), Frank Jenks (Joe),
Walter Perry (Backstage doorman), Frances Robinson (Hatcheck
girl), Constance Moore (Autograph seeker), Eleanor Hansen
(Stagestruck girl), Raymond Parker (Call boy), May Boley
(Mrs. Meggs), Armand Kaliz (Jules, the barber), Russell
Hopton (Process server), Stanley Hughes (Kibitzer), William
B. Davidson (Mr. Raleigh), Kathleen Howard (Aunt Jonnie),
Esther Ralston (Mrs. Sinclair), Irving Bacon, Ray Walker
(Reporters), Leonard Mudie (Critic), Doris Lloyd (Charlotte),
Morgan Wallace (Editor), Richard Tucker (Gossip), George
Humbert (Musician on stage), Frank Reicher, Theodore Von

Eltz, Chester Clute (Doctors), Natalie Moorhead (Mrs. Raleigh), Crauford Kent (Mr. Sinclair), Gordon "Bill" Elliott (Backgammon man), Sam Hayes (Announcer), Wade Boteler (Policeman), Donald "Red" Barry, Philip Trent (Men at party), Dick Winslow (Elevator boy), Rolfe Sedan (Fitter), Alphonse Martell (Maitre d'hotel), Sharon Lewis (Bridge player), Edith Craig, Kitty McHugh (Girl singers), Claire Whitney (Nurse), Sandy Sanford (Fireman), John Archer, Allan Fox (Photographers), Charlie Sherlock, Don Brodie (Reporters), Kane Richmond (Man), Inez Courtney, Dorothy Granger (Women at party), Mortimer Snerd (Himself), Russell Hopton (Process server), Bert Hendrickson, Kay Stanley, Dick Buck, V. Corbin, M. Wagner, D. Barry, William Lundigan, May Boley, George Davis, Yvonne Brusseau, Anthony Hughes, Bobby Teefts, Grace Hayle, Hayden Stevenson, Harry Bradley, Dora Clement, Alan Davis, Grace Goodall, Ray Johnson, Richard Tucker, Helen Millard, Frank Elliott, Hugh Huntley.

SYNOPSIS: Aspiring actress Kay Martin risks her life in a fire to retrieve a letter of introduction to matinee idol John Mannering. She tells boyfriend Barry Page about the letter, but does not admit John is her father. John is stunned by Kay's appearance, unaware that he fathered a child with the first of his three wives. Out of vanity, he keeps his relationship to Kay a secret, introducing her as his protegee. John's jealous fiancee, Lydia Hoyt, suspects John of cheating. Kay's friends also jump to conclusions about her relationship with the older man. When Lydia catches John dining with Kay, Lydia causes a scene and breaks their engagement. John helps Kay's friend Edgar Bergen get a job with his ventriloquist act. Edgar misinterprets John's fatherly affection for love and tells Barry. Jealous Barry punches John in the nose. When Kay defends John, Barry thinks she is breaking their engagement. On the rebound, Barry proposes to his dance partner Honey. Kay plans to tell Barry the truth, but decides to keep her parentage a secret after she hears Honey happily making plans. John launches a stage comeback with Kay as his leading lady. They plan to announce their relationship in a curtin speech. However, on opening night, John gets drunk to ease his nerves. Kay is heartbroken when the manager stops the play. Upset about his failing career, John steps in front of a taxi. He insists on telling reporters that he is Kay's father, but dies before he can make his announcement. Kay refuses to capitalize on John's fame by doing another play or revealing her parentage to the public. As she prepares to leave town, Barry confesses he still loves her. Kay lets Barry read her letter and they reconcile.

REVIEWS:
Harrison's Reports, August 6, 1938: "An excellent entertainment. It has comedy, romance, human appeal, and pathos."

Variety, August 10, 1938: "The three girls who are important to the action are Rita Johnson, [George] Murphy's dancing partner; Ann Sheridan, fiancee of [John] Mannering, and Eve Arden as a sophisticated, hard-boiled showgirl. All turn in fine performances."

New York Times, September 1, 1938:   "...it is a
surprisingly fresh, uncommonly diverting, remarkinbly [sic]
well-done film....Eve Arden, Rita Johnson, Ernest Cossart and
Ann Sheridan do very nicely, too."

NOTES: Letter of Introduction began production on
March 23, 1938.   It marks Ann Sheridan's first loan-out under
her Warner Bros. contract.   She plays the secondary role of
Adolphe Menjou's jealous fiancee, which allows her to show
off her temperament and wear a stylish wardrobe.   Variety
and Harrison's Reports devote much of their reviews to
Edgar Bergen, whose dummy Mortimer Snerd made his screen
debut in the film.   Variety even suggests that Snerd might
replace Bergen's Charlie McCarthy in popularity.
Coincidentally, one of Ann's co-stars was Eve Arden, who
later joined Ann on the Warner Bros. lot, appearing with her
in The Doughgirls (F-69) and The Unfaithful (F-75).

See also V-3.

F-43   35,000 Legion Vistors Are Guests of Warner Bros. Film
       Studio--Burbank, California   (filmed September 19,
       1938 for Hearst newsreels)   7 mins.

CAST: Jack Warner, Paul Muni, Joan Blondell, Dick Powell,
Ann Sheridan, Pat O'Brien, French Legion commander Daniel
Doherty, California governor Frank Merriam, French general
Paul Boe, Senator Walsh.

NOTES: This unreleased newsreel footage is part of the
Hearst Vault material in the film collection at the UCLA Film
and Television Archive.   Ann Sheridan is one of several
Warner Bros. stars introduced to visiting French Legion
dignitaries during their visit to the studio.

F-44   Broadway Musketeers   (Warner Bros., October 8, 1938)
       62 mins.

Producer: Brian Foy.   Executive producers: Jack L. Warner
and Hal B. Wallis.   Director: John Farrow.   Assistant
director: Russ Saunders.   Dialogue director: Frank
Beckwith.   Screenplay: Don Ryan and Kenneth Gamet.   Songs:
M.K. Jerome and Jack Scholl.   Photography: L. William
O'Connell.   Editor: Thomas Pratt.   Art direction: Stanley
Fleischer.   Costumes: Howard Shoup.   Sound: David Forrest.

CAST: Margaret Lindsay (Isabel Dowling), Ann Sheridan (Fay
Reynolds), Marie Wilson (Connie Todd), John Litel (Stanley
Dowling), Janet Chapman (Judy Dowling), Dick Purcell (Vincent
Morrell), Richard Bond (Phil Peyton), Horace MacMahon (Gurk),
Dewey Robinson (Milt), Dorothy Adams (Anna), James Conlon
(Skinner), Jan Holm (Teacher), Anthony Averill (Nick), John
Ridgely (M.C.), Howard Mitchell, Ted Oliver (Detectives),
Eddie Graham (Arthur, the chauffeur), Gordon Hart
(Magistrate), Nat Carr (Clerk), Myra Marsh (Matron), Dudley
Dickerson (Porter), Sol Gorss (Driver), Janet Shaw (Nurse),

Marian Alden (Floor nurse), Leo White (Waiter), Stuart Holmes
(Bartender), John Harron (Croupier), Vera Lewis (Landlady),
Eddy Chandler, Charles Hickman (Detectives), Wen Niles (Radio
announcer), Francis Sayles, Claude Payton, Hal Craig, Ralph
Sanford, Cliff Saum (Policemen), John Hiestand (News
announcer).

SONGS: "Has It Ever Occurred to You?," "Who Said That This
Isn't Love?" (Jerome, Scholl).

SYNOPSIS: Wealthy wife Isabel Dowling, nightclub singer Fay
Reynolds, and secretary Connie Todd meet for an annual
birthday toast after growing up together in an orphanage.
They renew their friendship after Fay is arrested for
stripping during her act. Isabel reveals that she is
unhappy, despite her husband Stanley and young daughter Judy.
At Fay's next nightclub opening, gambler Phil Peyton flirts
with Isabel. While Stanley is away on business, Isabel
neglects Judy and begins an affair with Phil. Their car
crashes, causing a scandal. Connie and Fay concoct an alibi
to save Isabel's marriage, but Judy's nanny tells Stanley
about the affair. Stanley agrees to Isabel's request for a
divorce, but demands sole custody of Judy. When Fay realizes
a reconciliation is hopeless, she befriends Stanley and Judy.
Isabel marries Phil, who gambles away most of her divorce
settlement. Fay marries Stanley and becomes a devoted step-
mother to Judy. When Phil passes a bad check to racketeer
Vincent Morrell, Isabel borrows money from Fay so they can
leave town. Isabel convinces Fay to let her spend the
afternoon with Judy, fearing it may be the last time she sees
her daughter. Morrell's henchmen kill Phil and kidnap Judy
and Isabel. As the police close in on the racketeers,
Morrell's men decide to kill Judy and Isabel because they
know too much. To protect Judy and bring the police to the
hideout, Isabel jumps out the window with a headline about
the kidnapping in her hand. The police rescue Judy and kill
the racketeers. Connie announces her engagement to her boss.
Connie and Fay let Judy join them for their annual birthday
toast, hoping for a happier future.

REVIEWS:
Harrison's Reports, October 8, 1938: "An unpleasant
program drama....One feels little sympathy for the
characters, particularly for the heroine, who deserts her
child and devoted husband....Unsuitable for children or
adolescents."

New York Times, October 14, 1938: "Alas, this is no job
for a mere reviewer. What Broadway Musketeers needs is a
psychoanalyst."

Variety, October 19, 1938: "Two songs, 'Has It Ever
Occurred to You?' and 'Who Said That This Isn't Love,'...are
sung effectively by [Ann] Sheridan."

NOTES: Broadway Musketeers is a "B" unit remake of Three
on a Match (Warner Bros., 1933), which had starred Bette
Davis as the secretary, Ann Dvorak as the wealthy wife, and

Joan Blondell as the actress. In the original movie, Dvorak
had a son instead of a daughter. During filming, Broadway
Musketeers was known as Three Girls on Broadway. Ann
Sheridan's role as a nightclub singer allowed her to sing two
songs: "Has It Ever Occurred to You?" and "Who Said That
This Isn't Love?."

F-45 Angels with Dirty Faces   (Warner Bros., November 19,
       1938)   97 mins.

Producer: Sam Bischoff. Executive producers: Jack L.
Warner and Hal B. Wallis. Director: Michael Curtiz.
Assistant directors: Sherry Shourds and Emmett Emerson.
Dialogue director: Jo Graham. Screenplay: John Wexley and
Warren Duff. Based on a story by Rowland Brown. Music: Max
Steiner. Musical director: Leo F. Forbstein.
Orchestrations: Hugo Friedhofer. Photography: Sol Polito.
Editor: Owen Marks. Art direction: Robert Haas. Costumes:
Orry-Kelly. Sound: E. A. Brown.

CAST: James Cagney (William "Rocky" Sullivan), Pat O'Brien
(Jerry Connolly), Humphrey Bogart (James Frazier), Ann
Sheridan (Laury Ferguson Martin), George Bancroft (Mac
Keefer), Billy Halop (Soapy), Bobby Jordan (Swing), Leo
Gorcey (Bim), Gabriel Dell (Patsy), Huntz Hall (Crab),
Bernard Punsley (Hunky), Joe Downing (Steve), Edward Pawley
(Guard Edwards), Adrian Morris (Blackie), Frankie Burke (Teen
Rocky), William Tracey (Teen Jerry), Marilyn Knowlden (Teen
Laury), Oscar O'Shea (Guard Kennedy), William Pawley (Bugs
the gunman), Charles Sullivan, Theodore Rand (Gunmen), John
Hamilton (Police captain), Earl Dwire (Priest), St. Brendan's
Church Choir (Themselves), William Worthington (Warden),
James Farley (Railroad yard watchman), Pat O'Malley, Jack C.
Smith (Railroad guards), Roger McGee, Vince Lombardi, Sonny
Bupp, A.W. Sweatt (Boys), Chuck Stubbs (Red), Eddie Syracuse
(Maggione boy), George Sorel (Headwaiter), Robert Homans
(Policeman), Harris Berger (Basketball captain), Lottie
Williams (Woman), Harry Hayden (Pharmacist), Dick Rich,
Stevan Darrell, Joe A. Devlin (Gangsters), Donald Kerr, Jack
Goodrich, Al Lloyd, Jeffrey Sayre, Charles Marsh, Alexander
Lockwood, Earl Gunn, Carlyle Moore (Reporters), Lee Phelps,
Jack Mower (Detectives), Belle Mitchell (Mrs. Maggione),
William Edmunds (Italian storekeeper), Charles Wilson
(Buckley, the police chief), Vera Lewis (Soapy's mother),
Eddie Brian (Newsboy), Billy McClain (Janitor), Claude
Wisberg (Hanger-on), Frank Hagney, Dick Wessel, John Harron
(Sharpies), Wilbur Mack (Croupier), Frank Coughlan, Jr.,
David Durand (Boys in poolroom), Mary Gordon (Mrs. Patrick
McGee), George Offerman, Jr. (Older boy in poolroom), Joe
Cunningham (Managing editor), James Spottswood (Record
editor), John Dilson (Chronicle editor), Charles Trowbridge
(Norton J. White), Tommy Jackson (Press city editor), Ralph
Sanford, Galan Galt (Policemen at call box), Emory Parnell,
Wilfred Lucas, Elliott Sullivan (Police), William Crowell
(Whimpering convict), Lane Chandler, Ben Hendricks (Guards),
Sidney Bracey, George Taylor, Oscar G. Hendrian, Dan Wolheim,
Brian Burke (Convicts), John Marston (Well dressed man),
Poppy Wilde (Girl at gaming table).

SYNOPSIS: A juvenile arrest leads Rocky Sullivan to reform
school and a life of crime. His friend Jerry Connolly evades
police and becomes a priest. Jerry works with delinquents,
hoping to give them a positive role model. When Rocky is
released from prison after a big robbery, he moves back to
Jerry's parish. Rocky befriends a street gang and soon
becomes their idol. Jerry is impressed with the change in
Rocky, as he proves a good influence on the boys. Social
worker Laury Martin is skeptical of Rocky's reform. She is
bitter about her late husband, who also was a criminal.
Rocky blackmails his former partner, lawyer James Frazier,
into giving him $100,000 and a cut of a nightclub James owns
with racketeer Mac Keefer. When Rocky realizes that James
plans to kill him instead of giving him his share, he kidnaps
James and steals the lawyer's extortion ledgers. Afraid
Rocky will implicate them, Keefer convinces police that the
kidnapping was a misunderstanding. Rocky gives the gang a
cut for hiding the ledgers and money during police
questioning. Jerry realizes that he must teach the gang that
crime does not pay. He vows to fight for the truth about
James's kidnapping and expose the racketeers, even if it
means bringing down Rocky. Keefer and James feel threatened
by Jerry's radio appearances and a press investigation.
Rocky overhears them plotting Jerry's murder and he shoots
them. Rocky is apprehended and sentenced to the electric
chair. The gang continues to idolize Rocky, glamorizing his
arrest. Shortly before Rocky's execution, Jerry appeals to
him to act the coward to turn the gang against him. Rocky
refuses. As he heads for the electric chair, Rocky
reconsiders and begs for life. When the press reports his
cowardice, the gang loses respect for him. Reassured of
Rocky's real heroism, Jerry asks the gang to pray for his
friend.

REVIEWS:
Variety, October 26, 1938: "Ann Sheridan walks through the
two-dimensional part of [James] Cagney's girl..."

Harrison's Reports, November 5, 1938: "A powerful gangster
melodrama. Although it is not very different in story
content from other pictures of its type, it is unusual in
other respects - the acting...is brilliant, the comedy
involving the 'Dead End' boys is at times hilariously
comical, the action is fast and extremely exciting, and to
top it off, there are situations that have strong emotional
appeal."

New York Times, November 26, 1938: "Besides [James]
Cagney, [Pat] O'Brien and the Dead End Kid hooligans...,
there are Humphrey Bogart, George Bancroft, Ann Sheridan and
Frankie Burke...in a panel of effective supplementary
characterizations."

Movie Mirror, January 1939: "If you've been waiting for a
picture with power and punch or a Cagney with all his oldtime vim and vigor, here they are all rolled in one terrific
story....it remains socko entertainment for adults with
[James] Cagney and [Pat] O'Brien at their tip-top best."

NOTES: Angels with Dirty Faces began production on
June 27, 1938. Audiences had come to expect expert gangster
melodramas from Warner Bros., after such hits as Little
Caesar (Warner Bros., 1930) and Public Enemy (Warner
Bros., 1931). Angels with Dirty Faces proved to be one of
the most popular of the genre, becoming one of the top
moneymaking films of the 1938/39 season (B-650). Ironically,
Variety predicted fair business, calling the film "no
bonfire" and "hokey" (October 26, 1938). The review also
pointed out that the same set was used for two different
locales.
     Angels with Dirty Faces is the quintessential James
Cagney picture, showing that even tough characters have a
human side. Cagney used several mannerisms that
impressionists later adopted for their impersonations of the
actor, including twisting his neck, lifting his shoulders,
and biting his bottom lip. Cagney claimed he based the ticks
on a New York pimp he had observed as a child. Cagney's work
won praise from the New York Film Critics and the National
Board of Review, who named him Best Actor in 1938. Cagney
also received his first Academy Award nomination for Best
Actor for his performance in Angels with Dirty Faces, but
lost to Spencer Tracy in Boys Town (MGM, 1938). Director
Michael Curtiz lost to Frank Capra for It's a Wonderful
Life (Columbia, 1938). Screenwriter Rowland Brown was
nominated for Best Original Story, but lost to Eleanore
Griffin and Dore Schary for Boys Town. Despite its
acclaim, Angels with Dirty Faces was rejected by censors in
Quebec, France, Jamaica, Denmark, Geneva, Poland, Finland,
China, and Norway (B-211).
     According to many contemporary sources, director Michael
Curtiz insisted real bullets be used during the warehouse
chase. Special effects technicians had not mastered the
effect of bursting bullets. Although Cagney almost had been
killed during a similar bullet rainfall in Public Enemy
(Warner Bros., 1931), he agreed to the live ammunition, but
refused to be in front of the window during the gunfire in
Angels with Dirty Faces. When the bullets knocked out a
pane of glass where Curtiz had wanted him to stand, Cagney
was thankful he had not listened to the director. Liberty
disagrees with the live ammunition story, insisting that the
gunfire is all special effects created by exploding dynamite
caps hidden on the stairs and a master marksman firing an air
rifle from off camera (Beverly Hills, "A Last Mile...And a
Moral," Liberty, November 19, 1938).
     The Dead End Kids also caused some trouble on set,
trying to intimidate James Cagney and Humphrey Bogart.
Although they tore off Bogart's pants, Cagney stood up to the
young actors and insisted they behave more professionally.
According to Dead End Kid Bernard Punsley, Cagney resorted to
violence to keep Billy Halop and Leo Gorcey in line during
production. When Gorcey continually repeated his lines under
his breath, Punsley recalled, "Cagney stopped production,
grabbed Gorcey by the hair and let him have it" (B-217).
     Angels with Dirty Faces marks Ann Sheridan's first
featured role in an "A" picture for Warner Bros. It was a
turning point in her career, making critics and audiences
take notice of the actress who had been working in Hollywood

for four years. Around the time of the film's release, the
George Hurrell photographs of Ann were making the rounds of
the magazines and columnists. While her work in Angels
with Dirty Faces was exemplary, it was the publicity
surrounding the photographs and Warner Bros.'s succeeding
oomph campaign that catapulted Ann to instant national
attention.
    Fred Fisher and Maurice Spitalny wrote a song called
"Angels with Dirty Faces," which was published with a photo
of Cagney and O'Brien on the cover. The song is not
performed in the movie. In recent years, the film has been
colorized and often appears that way on television.

See also V-4.

F-46 They Made Me a Criminal   (Warner Bros., January 28,
      1939) 92 mins.

Executive producer: Hal B. Wallis. Associate producer:
Benjamin Glazer. Director: Busby Berkeley. Assistant
director: Russ Saunders. Screenplay: Sig Herzig. Based on
the play Sucker by Bertram Millhauser and Beulah Marie Dix.
Music: Max Steiner. Musical director: Leo F. Forbstein.
Photography: James Wong Howe. Editor: Jack Killifer. Art
direction: Anton Grot. Costumes: Milo Anderson. Sound:
Oliver S. Garretson.

CAST: John Garfield (Johnnie Bradfield/Jack Dorney), Billy
Halop (Tommy Rafferty), Bobby Jordan (Angel), Leo Gorcey
(Spit), Huntz Hall (Dippy), Gabriel Dell (T.B.), Bernard
Punsley (Milt), Claude Rains (Detective Monty Phelan), Ann
Sheridan (Goldie), May Robson (Grandma Rafferty), Gloria
Dickson (Peggy Rafferty), Robert Gleckler (Doc Ward), John
Ridgely (Charlie Magee), Barbara Pepper (Budgie), William B.
Davidson (Inspector Ennis), Ward Bond (Lenihan, the fight
promoter), Robert Strange (Malvin, the lawyer), Louis Jean
Heydt (Smith), Ronald Sinclair (J. Douglas Williamson), Frank
Riggi (Gaspar Rutchek), Cliff Clark (Doc Wood, Rutchek's
manager), Dick Wessel (Collucci), Raymond Brown (Sheriff),
Sam Hayes (Fight announcer), Irving Bacon (Speed, the gas
station attendant), Sam McDaniel (Splash), Bert Roach
(Hendricks), Charles Randolph, Larry McGrath (Referees),
Mushy Callahan (Schwimmer), Janet Shaw, Sally Sage (Girls),
John Harron (Announcer), Georgie Cooper (Elderly lady), Joe
Cunningham (Columnist), Dorothy Varden (Woman), Eddy
Chandler, Hal Craig (Detectives), Jack Austin, Frank Meredith
(Cops), Richard Bond, Nat Carr (Reporters), Arthur Houseman
(Drunk), Elliott Sullivan (Hoodlum), Tom Dugan, Frank Mayo,
Cliff Saum, Al Lloyd, John Sheehan (Men), Leyland Hodgson
(Mr. Williamson), Doris Lloyd (Mrs. Williamson), Stuart
Holmes (Timekeeper), Bob Perry (Cawley), Nat Carr (Haskell),
Clem Bevans (Ticket taker), Jack Wise (Ticketman), Reid
Kilpatrick (Sports commentator), Ed Brian (Newsboy), Tom
Wilson (Kid Tacoma), Charles Sullivan (Trainer), John Dilson
(Doctor), Dave Roberts (Police announcer), Donald Kerr, Jack
Mower, Arthur Housman.

SYNOPSIS: Although prizefighter Johnnie Bradfield has a

clean-living image, he is really a cynical, womanizing drunk.
During a celebration with his girlfriend Goldie and manager
Doc Ward, an inebriated Johnnie reveals the truth to a
reporter. Doc accidently kills the reporter while Johnnie is
passed out. Doc convinces Goldie that Johnnie will implicate
them so they flee with his money, car, and identification.
When Doc and Goldie are killed in a car accident, the press
assumes the male corpse is Johnnie. A lawyer advises him to
assume a new identity and leave town, since the newspapers
blame him for the reporter's death. He warns Johnnie not to
fight, since his stance will identify him. Detective Monty
Phelan believes Johnnie is still alive. Since Monty once
sent an innocent man to the electric chair, he sees the case
as a chance to redeem his reputation. Johnnie changes his
name to Jack Dorney and hides out at an Arizona date ranch
owned by Peggy Rafferty and her grandmother. Jack empathizes
with Peggy's brother Tommy and his reform school buddies who
work at the ranch. He soon falls in love with Peggy. When
Jack learns that she may lose the ranch, he signs up for a
boxing match to earn money to buy a gas pump for the ranch.
Monty sees Jack's photo in the newspaper and heads for
Arizona. Jack changes his stance during the fight so Monty
will not recognize him. He wins enough to buy the gas pump.
Monty realizes that Jack has turned his life around with
Peggy and the boys. When Jack surrenders, Monty releases
him, claiming he may have made another mistake. He warns
Jack to stay out of the papers if he wants to continue his
new life. Jack heads back to the ranch and Peggy.

REVIEWS:
New York Times, January 21, 1939: "...a generous cast
and...an ample production have been flatteringly assembled
about [John] Garfield's ingratiating personality, and the
result...is a better-than-average workout for a rising
star....It's an elderly plot, all right, but Mr. Garfield is
young; he will live it down."

Variety, January 25, 1939: "...Ann Sheridan clicks in the
brief role of the champ's sirenish gal."

Harrison's Reports, January 28, 1939: "A strong melodrama,
with very good box-office possibilities....The strength of
this picture lies, not so much in the story, as in the
excellent performances....One situation at the beginning is
pretty sexy; also a murder is committed."

Modern Screen, April 1939: "If you like your drama in
strong doses, They Made Me a Criminal will supply plenty of
excitement and tense moments....Ann Sheridan, the girl who
walks out on the champ, is spectacular in her brief role..."

NOTES: They Made Me a Criminal began production in August
1938. It was based on the 1933 play Sucker, which was
filmed by First National as The Life of Jimmy Dolan in
1933. Douglas Fairbanks, Jr., Loretta Young, and Shirley
Grey originated the roles taken by John Garfield, Gloria
Dixon, and Ann Sheridan in the remake. They Made Me a
Criminal tried to capitalize on John Garfield's sudden

success in <u>Four Daughters</u> (Warner Bros., 1938), offering
him his first starring role on screen. It is one of the few
non-musical films directed by Busby Berkeley, best known for
his elaborate production numbers. He added a private joke in
a shower scene that had Huntz Hall singing "By a Waterfall"
to the showering Garfield, a nod to Berkeley's directorial
effort in <u>Footlight Parade</u> (Warner Bros., 1933), where it
is rumored that Garfield is an extra.
     Ann Sheridan receives fourth billing, under John
Garfield, the Dead End Kids, and Claude Rains, for her small
role as Garfield's girlfriend. Despite the size of her part,
when Warner Bros. rereleased <u>They Made Me a Criminal</u> in the
1940s, she and the Dead End Kids were the only ones billed on
promotional materials.

See also V-5.

F-47   <u>Dodge City</u>   (Warner Bros., April 8, 1939)
       105 mins.   Technicolor

Producer: Robert Lloyd. Executive producer: Hal B. Wallis.
Director: Michael Curtiz. Assistant director: Sherry
Shourds. Dialogue director: Jo Graham. Screenplay: Robert
Buckner. Songs: Daniel Decatur Emmett, Joseph E. Winner,
C.A. White, and Henry Clay Work. Music: Max Steiner.
Musical director: Leo F. Forbstein. Photography: Sol
Polito and Ray Rennahan. Editor: George Amy. Art
direction: Ted Smith. Costumes: Milo Anderson. Sound:
Oliver S. Garretson. Makeup: Perc Westmore. Special
effects: Byron Haskin and Rex Wimpy. Color director:
Natalie Kalmus. Associate color director: Morgan Padelford.

CAST: Errol Flynn (Wade Hatton), Olivia de Havilland (Abbie
Irving), Ann Sheridan (Ruby Gilman), Bruce Cabot (Jeff
Surrett), Frank McHugh (Joe Clemens), Alan Hale (Algernon
"Rusty" Hart), John Litel (Matt Cole), Henry Travers (Dr.
Irving), Victor Jory (Yancey), William Lundigan (Lee Irving),
Guinn "Big Boy" Williams (Tex Baird), Bobs Watson (Harry
Cole), Gloria Holden (Mrs. Cole), Douglas Fowley (Munger),
Georgia Caine (Mrs. Irving), Charles Halton (Surrett's
lawyer), Ward Bond (Bud Taylor), Cora Witherspoon (Mrs.
McCoy), Russell Simpson (Orth), Monte Blue (Barlow, the
Indian agent), Henry O'Neill (Colonel Dodge), Nat Carr
(Crocker), Clem Bevans (Charlie, the barber), Joe Crehan
(Hammond), Thurston Hall (Twitchell), Chester Clute
(Coggins), James Burke (Cattle auctioneer), Robert Homans
(Mail clerk), George Guhl (Jason, the marshall), Spencer
Charters (Clergyman), Bud Osborne (Stagecoach driver/
waiter), Pat O'Malley (Conductor), Wilfred Lucas (Bartender),
Milton Kibbee (Printer), Vera Lewis (Woman), Ralph Sanford
(Brawler), William Merrill McCormick (Man), Fred Graham (Al),
Henry Otho (Conductor), Richard Cramer (Clerk), Earle Hodgins
(Spieler), Pat Flaherty (Cowhand), James Farley (Engineer),
Jack Mower, Horace Carpenter, Francis Sayles, Ky Robinson,
William Crowell, Earl Dwire, Bob Stevenson, Bruce Mitchell,
Hal Craig, Howard Mitchell, George Chesebro, Frank Pharr, Ed
Peil, Sr., Frank Mayo, Guy Wilkerson, Steve Clark.

SONGS: "Little Brown Jug" (Winner), "Marching through
Georgia" (Work), "Dixie" (Emmett), "Ise Gwine Back to Dixie"
(White).

SYNOPSIS: As the first railroad cuts through the west in
1866, Colonel Dodge makes plans for the growth of Dodge City,
Kansas.   He offers cattleman Wade Hatton and his friends jobs
in Dodge City, but Wade refuses to settle down.   By 1872,
Dodge City is a bustling, crime-ridden town full of gamblers
and gunmen.   Wade's rival, Jeff Surrett, runs the town,
cheating and killing anyone who crosses him.   Wade leads a
wagon train to Dodge City, which includes Abbie Irving and
her brother Lee.   Wade warns Lee about his drunken shooting
sprees, which threaten to cause a stampede. Lee ignores the
warnings, forcing Wade to shoot him in self-defense.   Abbie
blames Wade when Lee is trampled to death.   In Dodge City,
Wade learns that Jeff and his henchman Yancey killed Matt
Cole in a cattle dispute.   A citizens' committee begs Wade to
take the law into his hands and clean up the town.   Wade
refuses until Matt's young son is killed.   As sheriff, Wade
makes the town safe for families.   Abbie gains a new respect
for Wade for his peace efforts.   When Abbie and editor Joe
Clemens learn that Jeff cheated Matt's widow, they plan to
expose Jeff in the newspaper.   Yancey kills Joe and steals
the file on Jeff to keep the story from running.   Abbie tells
Wade that she remembers enough from the file to hang Jeff.
Wade confesses that he loves Abbie and orders her to leave
town to protect herself.   He arrests Yancey for Joe's murder.
Yancey blackmails Jeff into saving him.   As Wade, Yancey, and
Abbie head for Wichita on the same train, Jeff and the
outlaws take over and have a gunfight.   Wade saves Abbie and
regains control of the train.   He and his men kill Jeff,
bringing peace to Dodge City.   As Wade prepares to marry
Abbie, Colonel Dodge asks him to clean up Virginia City.
Abbie overhears and insists they go where they are needed.

REVIEWS:
New York Times, April 8, 1939:   "The supporting cast...
seemed competent enough.   Of course, it was hard to tell
sometimes, with all that gunsmoke and dust about."

Variety, April 12, 1939:   "Dodge City is a lusty western,
packed with action, including some of the dandiest melee
stuff screened, superbly lensed in Technicolor, and with
Errol Flynn, Olivia de Havilland and Ann Sheridan topping a
sturdy cast....Ann Sheridan as the dancehall [sic] girl
rounds out the top marquee names."

Harrison's Reports, April 22, 1939:   "A very good Western,
photographed in Techniclor.   Produced with lavishness, and
acted with skill by a large and capable cast, it offers
entertainment that should go over exceedingly well with the
masses."

Liberty, May 20, 1939:   "This is a Western with epic
pretensions - but it turns out to be just another story of a
handsome, courageous, hard-riding young cowboy - an Irishman
this time - who wanders into the pioneer Kansas settlement,

remains to clean up the place in the unhealthy job of
sheriff."

NOTES: Dodge City was Warner Bros.'s major release for
1939 and they spared no expense in shooting or promoting it.
Production began in November 1938, with much of the footage
filmed on location at Warner Bros.'s ranch in Calabasas,
California and around Modesto and Sonora, California. While
promoting the film, Warner Bros. was proud to report many
statistics. To create the effect of rolling prairie, the
studio had to take down 12 miles of barbed wire range fencing
and 6,348 posts. It took five days to film the ten-minute
saloon brawl in Dodge City. They used 150 extras, 73
breakaway chairs, and 392 breakaway bottles (B-149). Dodge
City was shot in Technicolor, a process then used solely
for films of epic proportions that were expected to be big
moneymakers for the studio. Errol Flynn and Olivia de
Havilland were one of Warner Bros.'s most popular romantic
teams, having co-starred in Captain Blood (1935), The
Charge of the Light Brigade (1936), and The Adventures of
Robin Hood (1938). Their pairing also indicated the
studio's confidence in the picture. The expense proved
worthwhile. Dodge City not only became a classic western,
it was one of the top moneymaking films of the 1938/39 season
(B-650).
    Ann Sheridan plays a dance hall girl in Dodge City.
The role allows her to sing "Ise Gwine Back to Dixie,"
"Little Brown Jug," and "Marching Through Georgia" with the
chorus girls and saloon patrons. She receives third billing,
more the result of the Hurrell photo campaign than the size
of her role. Dodge City marks Ann's first color feature.
She later recalled that the intense lighting needed for
Technicolor films in those days almost blinded her (B-475).
Dodge City also is the first of Ann's four movies with
Errol Flynn, who became a friend off screen. In his
autobiography, the actor implies that he helped Ann's career
after they had an affair. Presumably, he is referring to
having her cast in Dodge City (B-177).
    Warner Bros. enthusiastically promoted the film, sending
a caravan of stars to the premiere in Dodge City, Kansas on
April 1, 1939 (P-3). Ann Sheridan, Errol Flynn, Frank
McHugh, Guinn "Big Boy" Williams, and Alan Hale were among
the movie's stars who took the sixteen-car train to Dodge
City for the premiere and parade. Olivia de Havilland had to
get off in Pasadena, California so that she could report for
work on Gone with the Wind (MGM, 1939). The Dodge City
stunt brought the film a cache of publicity, including a
Life article (B-149), and stories generated by the
thirty-six reporters on board. Warner Bros. sent a
Technicolor crew to film the premiere.
    The movie was tremendously popular, despite intense
competition from memorable westerns like Stagecoach (United
Artists, 1939), Destry Rides Again (Universal, 1939), and
Union Pacific (Paramount, 1939). Although there was talk
of making a sequel, Virginia City, Warner Bros.'s 1940 film
of that name was a Civil War western with little connection
to the original. Errol Flynn returned, but neither Olivia de
Havilland nor Ann Sheridan were cast in the 1940 film. In

1951, <u>Dodge City</u> was rereleased in black and white and played on a double bill with <u>Virginia City</u>. According to Leonard Maltin, <u>Dodge City</u> was the principal inspiration for Mel Brooks's comic western <u>Blazing Saddles</u> (Warner Bros., 1974) (B-337).

See also V-6.

F-48   <u>Naughty But Nice</u>   (Warner Bros., July 1, 1939)
       90 mins.

Executive producer: Hal B. Wallis. Associate producer: Sam Bischoff. Director: Ray Enright. Assistant director: Jesse Hibbs. Dialogue director: Hugh Cummings. Screenplay: Richard Macaulay and Jerry Wald. Based on the story "Always Leave Them Laughing" by Richard Macaulay and Jerry Wald. Songs: Johnny Mercer and Harry Warren, with acknowledgments to Richard Wagner, Franz Liszt, Wolfgang Amadeus Mozart, and Johann Sebastian Bach. Musical director: Leo F. Forbstein. Orchestrations: Ray Heindorf. Photography: Arthur L. Todd. Editor: Thomas Richards. Art direction: Max Parker. Costumes: Howard Shoup. Sound: Francis J. Scheid and David Forrest.

CAST: Ann Sheridan (Zelda Manion), Dick Powell (Professor Donald Hardwick), Gale Page (Linda McKay), Helen Broderick (Aunt Martha Hogan), Ronald Reagan (Ed Clark), Allen Jenkins (Joe Dirk), ZaSu Pitts (Aunt Penelope), Maxie Rosenbloom (Killer), Jerry Colonna (Allie Gray), Luis Alberni (Stanislaus Pysinski), Vera Lewis (Aunt Annabella), Elizabeth Dunne (Aunt Henrietta), Bill Davidson (Sam Hudson), Granville Bates (Judge), Halliwell Hobbes (Dean Burton), Peter Lind Hayes (Band leader), Bert Hanlon (Johnny Collins), John Ridgely (Hudson's assistant), Herbert Rawlinson (Plaintiff's attorney), Selmer Jackson (Defense attorney), Hobart Cavanaugh (Piano tuner), Grady Sutton (Mankton), Sally Sage (Miss Danning), Elise Cavanna, Daisy Bufford (Maids), Jack Mower, Wedgwood Nowell, Sidney Bracy (Professors), Ed McWade (Professor Trill), Bob Sherwood (Announcer), Ernest Wood (Headwaiter), Stuart Holmes (Capt. Gregory Waddington-Smith), Jerry Mandy, Al Herman (Waiters), Daisy Dufford (Maid), Tom Dugan (Man with seals), Billy Newell (Arranger), Harrison Greene, Garry Owen (Bartenders), Jimmy Conlin (Pedestrian), Cliff Saum (Man), Frank Mayo, William Gould (Bailiffs), John Harron (Clerk), Maurice Cass (First witness), the National Jitterbug Champions (Themselves).

SONGS: "Hooray for Spinach," "Corn Pickin'," "I Don't Believe in Signs," "I'm Happy about the Whole Thing," "In a Moment of Weakness" (Warren, Mercer).

SYNOPSIS: Straight-laced music professor Donald Hardwick is upset when lyricist Linda McKay and publisher Ed Clark turn his symphony into a popular song. Despite Linda and Ed's insistence that he could be a successful songwriter, Donald prefers to return to his classical music, his college, and his three maiden aunts. During a drunken binge, Donald agrees to stay in New York and collaborate with Linda. When

he is sober, he refuses to go back on his word. Linda and
Donald write several hits. Rival publisher Sam Hudson
resents the success of Ed's company, thanks to Donald and
Linda's songs. Sam offers singer Zelda Manion a cut of the
profits if she persuades Donald to switch publishers. Zelda
romances Donald, then gets him drunk so he will sign a
contract with Sam. Although Linda loves Donald, she refuses
to leave Ed's firm. Sam teams Donald with unscrupulous
songwriter Joe Dirk. When Donald refuses to turn a well-
known classical melody into a pop song, Joe tapes the music
and gives Donald credit for the composition. When the
composer's heirs sue Donald for plagiarism, Sam cancels his
contract and threatens to have him blackballed. Donald
realizes he loves Linda and she gives him the courage to face
the lawsuit. At the trial, Donald's aunts prove the
classical composition was borrowed from an earlier work in
public domain. The judge dismisses the case. Donald
proposes to Linda and a classical conductor reconsiders
performing his symphony.

REVIEWS:
New York Times, June 23, 1939:   "...Ann Sheridan, who is
billed as co-star, appears in about a half-dozen sequences
and sings a couple of songs. That gives you an idea of the
'oomph' in it."

Variety, June 28, 1939:   "[Ann] Sheridan is the slight
menace here, a mike siren who would break up the songwriting
team just to be cut-in on his future songs."

Harrison's Reports, July 1, 1939:   "Just a fair comedy with
music. It is somewhat amusing in spots, but for the most
part the silly plot developments and trite dialogue tend to
tire one....Whatever entertainment value the picture has is
due more to the efforts of the players than to the material."

Hollywood Reporter, July 13, 1939:   "The Warner picture is
particularly interesting as affording a copious view of
vastly exploited Ann Sheridan. Miss Sheridan here appears to
justify the studio's expectations, for she photographs with
devastating effect and handles her lines and singing
assignments with ease and profound effect."

NOTES: Naughty But Nice began production in October 1938.
Its working titles were Professor Steps Out and Always
Leave Them Laughing. Although Ann Sheridan's name still is
listed below the title, Naughty But Nice marks the first
film in which she receives top billing. It also was Dick
Powell's last movie for Warner Bros., after six years of
musicals at the studio. Powell's departure was one of the
reasons Ann was top billed, with Warner Bros. preferring to
build up a star they had under contract rather than one who
was leaving. Her role as a singer gave her the chance to
perform "Hooray for Spinach," "Corn "Pickin'," "I Don't
Believe in Signs," and "In a Moment of Weakness." The plot
spoofs popular songs which were adapted from the classics.
It had become a trend in the late 1930s, when songs like "My
Reverie" (based on Debussy's "Reverie") and "Moon Love"

(based on the second movement of Tchaikovsky's Symphony No. 5) were on the Hit Parade.

Naughty But Nice was Ann's first film with Warner Bros. contract player Gale Page. The two became close friends off screen, with Ann often refering to Page as "my favorite Cherokee girl friend," alluding to both actresses' Indian roots.

The pressbook played up Ann's sexy image, suggesting theatre owners choose a Miss Oomph to wander through the shopping district promoting the movie. A poster offered Ann's advice on how to be popular with men. "Not too much fire...Not too much ice...It's best to be just a bit... 'Naughty but Nice.'" She also gave marriage tips. "I think there would be a lot more happy marriages if women tried to be companions more than wives," Ann was quoted as saying (B-689).

See also S-2, S-14.

F-49 Winter Carnival   (United Artists, July 28, 1939)
      105 mins.

Producer: Walter Wanger. Director: Charles F. Riesner. Second unit director: Ray Hines. Assistant directors: Charles Kerr and Edward Montagne. Screenplay: Budd Schulberg, Lester Cole, Maurice Rapf, and (uncredited) F. Scott Fitzgerald. Based on the story "Echoes That Old Refrain" by Corey Ford. Song "Winter Blossoms" by L. Wolfe Gilbert and Werner Janssen. Music: Werner Janssen. Musical director: Werner Janssen. Photography: Merritt Gerstad. Editors: Dorothy Spencer and Otho Lovering. Art direction: Alexander Toluboff and Richard Irvine. Sound: Fred Lau.

CAST: Ann Sheridan (Jill Baxter), Richard Carlson (Professor John Weldon), Helen Parrish (Ann Baxter), James Corner (Mickey Allen), Robert Armstrong (Tiger Reynolds), Alan Baldwin (Don Reynolds), Joan Brodel [Leslie] (Betsy Phillips), Virginia Gilmore (Margie Stafford), Cecil Cunningham (Miss Ainsley), Robert Allen (Rocky Morgan), Marsha Hunt (Lucy Morgan), Susan and Molly McCash (Baby Morgan), Morton Lowry (Count Olaf Von Lundborg), Jimmy Butler (Larry Grey), Kenneth Stevens (Male soloist), Benny Drohan (Bartender), Martin Turner (Pullman porter), Robert E. Homans (Conductor), John Wray (Poultry truck driver), Emory Parnell (New York Mercury editor Williams), Al Hill, George Magrill (Mercury reporters), Robert Walker (Wes), Cyril Ring, John Berkes (Terminal reporters), Florence Pepper (Ethel), Mary Jane Barnes (Aileen), Phyllis Howell (Rose), Eleanor Riley (Helen), Roberta Wilson (Shirley), Jean Lucius (Mildred), Jean Broughton (Katherine), Alyne Sherry (Myrna), Peggy Moran (Viola), Dick Durrell (Tom), Stephen Whitney (Jack), Joe Roberts (Martin), Winton Reynolds (Eddie), Dale Fellows (Jim), Douglas Meins (Russ), Pat Hurst (Bobby), Edward Brian (Art), Paul Portanova (Duke), Lois Ranson (Patsy), Carlyle Black, Jr., Dick Winslow and His Orchesta, the Tudor Williams Male Chorus.

SYNOPSIS: Following a highly publicized divorce, former Snow

Queen Jill Baxter escorts her sister Ann to Dartmouth
College. Jill plans to sail for Europe, but she gets caught
up in plans for Dartmouth's impending winter carnival and
renews her friendship with professor John Weldon, her college
boyfriend. Although John was upset that Jill left him for a
wealthy, titled marriage, he realizes he still loves her.
They rekindle their romance when Jill decides to stay for the
carnival. Jill worries when Ann copies her mistakes,
ignoring her dependable boyfriend, Mickey Allen, when a
flashy Norwegian ski champion gives her attention. John
convinces Jill to give up her glamorous life and marry him.
However, when Jill learns that her ex-husband is bringing a
train of reporters to Dartmouth, she breaks the engagement.
She decides to leave town, afraid the adverse publicity will
ruin John's reputation and career. Ann reconciles with
Mickey after he beats the Norwegian in the ski competition.
They are surprised to find Jill and John at the fraternity
house after the contest. Jill admits that her love for John
is greater than her fear of publicity. She confesses that
she jumped off the train so that she and John can settle down
at last.

REVIEWS:
Hollywood Reporter, July 20, 1939: "The only redeeming
feature of the picture is a beautiful close-up of Ann
Sheridan, which appears on the screen spasmodically. Try as
they would to lift the Oomph crown from her head, the gal
stills holds first claim to the title."

Variety, July 29, 1939: "Ann Sheridan, who's currently
getting a Warners buildup, has a complimentary role as the
divorced glamor girl. It doesn't require any acting and
displays her in a succession of becoming situations and
clothes. She's an eyeful, all right."

Time, July 31, 1939: "Although Producer [Walter] Wanger's
expert hand keeps things moving, he cannot keep the Oomph
Girl from looking embarrassed throughout, fails to teach her
any trick of self-expression more meaningful than a habit of
wrinkling her forehead when speaking."

Movie Mirror, August 1939: "Walter Wanger has given Ann
Sheridan her first starring role and she ably justifies his
confidence in her....Your reviewer says: Cool off and get a
lift from this amusing movie."

NOTES: Producer Walter Wanger tried to cash in on the oomph
campaign by casting Ann Sheridan in Winter Carnival, the
second loan-out during her Warner Bros. contract. The film
began production in April 1939. It was based on Corey Ford's
story "Echoes That Old Refrain," which had been published in
The Saturday Evening Post May 29, 1937. Wanger, who had
advanced the careers of Hedy Lamarr in Algiers (United
Artists, 1938) and his future wife Joan Bennett in Trade
Winds (United Artists, 1938), did the same for Ann in
Winter Carnival. The part and Wanger's publicity campaign
capitalized on Ann's Oomph Girl image better than any of her
previous Warner Bros. films. She returned to her home studio

with her career as a sexy leading lady on track. It was
almost a year later that Warner Bros. began casting Ann in
leading roles that played up the image they had created in
the oomph campaign.
     Kay Kyser and his band wanted seventy-five thousand
dollars to appear in Winter Carnival so they were not used.
The movie marks the screen debut of Virginia Gilmore and Alan
Baldwin (B-211). Winter Carnival is noteworthy to film
historians because it was another example of author F. Scott
Fitzgerald trying to conform to Hollywood standards and churn
out a script. Producer Walter Wanger personally hired
Fitzgerald, who was dismissed from the movie when he went on
a drinking binge after writing several scenes. It marked one
of Fitzgerald's last scriptwriting assignments before his
death in 1940. Co-writer Budd Schulberg later turned his
experience researching Dartmouth's winter carnival with
Fitzgerald into the 1950 novel The Disenchanted. Wanger,
Schulberg, co-writer Maurice Rapf, and composer Werner
Janssen were all Dartmouth alumni.
     Some of the carnival scenes, as well as campus
background footage, were filmed at Dartmouth's 1938 event.
The principals shot their scenes on a refrigerated stage in
Hollywood. According to Liberty, they had to spend twenty
minutes acclimatizing themselves to the cold in special rooms
instead of going from the California heat to a few degrees
above freezing. The cold stage was used to get a natural
steaming winter breath (Beverly Hills, "From Jail to
Dartmouth," Liberty, September 2, 1939, p. 53).
     As Joan Leslie, starlet Joan Brodel became a leading
lady at Warner Bros. in the early 1940s. Coincidentally, she
replaced Ann Sheridan in Hollywood Canteen (Warner Bros.,
1944) when Ann refused to make the picture.

See also S-3.

F-50   Indianapolis Speedway   (Warner Bros., August 5,
       1939)   82 mins.

Executive producers: Hal B. Wallis and Jack L. Warner.
Associate producer: Max Siegel. Director: Lloyd Bacon.
Assistant director: Elmer Decker. Dialogue director: Jo
Graham. Screenplay: Sig Herzig and Wally Klein. Based on
the story "The Roar of the Crowd" by Howard and William
Hawks. Music: Adolph Deutsch. Musical director: Leo F.
Forbstein. Photography: Sid Hockox. Editor: William
Holmes. Art direction: Esdras Hartley. Costumes:
Orry-Kelly. Sound: Frank J. Scheid. Technical advisors:
E.A. "Babe" Stapp and Arthur Klein.

CAST: Pat O'Brien (Joe Greer), Ann Sheridan (Frankie
Merrick), John Payne (Eddie Greer), Gale Page (Lee Mason),
Frank McHugh (Spud Connors), Grace Stafford (Martha Connors),
Granville Bates (Mr. Greer), John Ridgely (Ted Horn), Regis
Toomey (Dick Wilbur), John Harron (Red), William Davidson
(Duncan Martin), Ed McWade (Tom Dugan), Irving Bacon (Fred
Haskill), Tommy Bupp (Haskill's son), Robert Middlemass
(Edward Hart), Charles Halton (Mayor), Patsy O'Byurne
(Vinegary female), Creighton Hale, Eddy Chandler, Jeffrey

Sayre (Officials), Evelyn Mulhall (Mrs. Martin), Georges
Renavent (Headwaiter), Billy Wayne (Stubby), Sam Hayes, John
Conte, Wendell Niles, Reid Kilpatrick (Announcers), Ed Parker
(Man), Monroe Lee (Baby), Nat Carr, Jack Wise, Sidney Bracy
(Spectators), Claude Wisberg (Bellboy), Ralph Dunn, Ted
Oliver (Referees), Ed Parker (Pit man), Elliott Sullivan
(Jimmy), Hal Craig (Mechanic), Sol Gorss, Paul Phillips
(Drivers), William Gould (Doctor), Garland Smith (Reporter).

SYNOPSIS: Eddie Mason dreams of being an auto racer like his
brother Joe. Despite Joe's misgivings, he agrees to train
Eddie if he continues his college education as well. Joe's
girlfriend, Lee Mason, begs him to settle down and quit
racing, but Joe insists he must help his brother. Eddie
falls in love with Frankie Merrick, Lee's attractive but
promiscuous friend. Joe thinks Frankie is a gold digger and
a bad influence on his brother. The night before the big
race, the Masons fight about Frankie. Eddie signs up to
drive a rival car. Joe breaks up with Lee, blaming her for
introducing Eddie to Frankie. Joe vows to teach his brother
a lesson by running him off the track. Joe's best friend,
driver Spud Connors, tries to separate the cars, but is
killed when his racer crashes and bursts into flames.
Devastated and guilty, Joe gives his savings to Spud's widow
and leaves town. Eddie marries Frankie and continues on the
racing circuit. He makes a name for himself as an expert
driver and racing car inventor. He receives an offer to race
at the Indianapolis Speedway. Despite the friction between
the brothers, Joe attends the race. A friend reunites him
with Lee, who urges Joe to race again. Joe confides that he
lost his courage after Spud's death. Eddie leads the race
until he has an accident. Joe overcomes his fear and jumps
in Eddie's car. The brothers win the race together and
reconcile at the finish line. Joe proposes to Lee and
accepts a job with a car manufacturer, promising to settle
down.

REVIEWS:
New York Times, July 15, 1939: "...we won't say any more
about the story except to deny stoutly the Warner
advertisements that this is the picture that gives their
'oomph girl,' Ann Sheridan, the 'big part you've wanted to
see her play.' It isn't a big part and, so far as we are
concerned, we don't remember wanting to see her play it....
Besides, she doesn't play it any too well, seeming to mistake
sulkiness for sultryness and being of much less service to
the melodrama than Gale Page who isn't an 'oomph girl' but
knows what to do when the camera's looking."

Harrison's Reports, July 22, 1939: "Aside from the thrills
of automobile racing, with its attendant crashes and deaths,
it offers little that is outstanding. The plot...unfolds
just as one expects....Men may enjoy the racing, but it is
doubtful if women will be interested in it, for it is wearing
on the nerves."

Variety, July 29, 1939: "[Ann] Sheridan...is not flattered
by the camera, the angles on her nose being wrong. She's

being built up as an 'oomph' girl, with the result that the
first flash of her is in a nightgown, then under a shower
and, third, in shorts."

NOTES: Indianapolis Speedway began production on
January 16, 1939. Both Ronald Reagan and Wayne Morris were
considered for the role that ultimately went to John Payne.
Indianapolis Speedway record breaker Arthur Klein served as a
technical advisor on the racing sequences (B-211).
    Indianapolis Speedway is a remake of The Crowd
Roars (Warner Bros., 1932). James Cagney, Joan Blondell,
Eric Linden, and Ann Dvorak created the parts played by Pat
O'Brien, Ann Sheridan, John Payne, and Gale Page in the 1939
version. Coincidentally, Frank McHugh plays the role of the
racer's friend who gets killed in both movies. Reviews point
out the similarity between Indianapolis Speedway and Warner
Bros.'s Wings of the Navy (1938), which has a plot about
rival brothers training to be fighter pilots. Both John
Payne and Frank McHugh also are in that film, which stars Ann
Sheridan's future husband George Brent and Olivia de
Havilland. In Great Britain, Indianapolis Speedway is
known as Devil on Wheels, one of its working titles in the
United States. Prior to release, Indianapolis Speedway
also was known as The Roaring Road.
    Ann Sheridan's role was a disappointment to many fans
and critics, who expected much more out of the actress in the
midst of Warner Bros.'s oomph publicity blitz. The studio
played up her sexy image in the film, showing her in a
nightgown, shorts, and shower. However, Indianapolis
Speedway did little to advance her acting career.

F-51   The Angels Wash Their Faces   (Warner Bros.,
       August 26, 1939)   84 mins.

Executive producers: Jack L. Warner and Hal B. Wallis.
Associate producer: Max Siegel. Director: Ray Enright.
Dialogue director: Hugh Cummings. Screenplay: Michael
Fessier, Niven Busch, and Robert Buckner. Based on an idea
by Jonathan Finn. Music: Adolph Deutsch. Musical director:
Leo F. Forbstein. Orchestrations: Ray Heindorf.
Photography: Arthur L. Todd. Editor: James Gibbon. Art
direction: Ted Smith. Costumes: Milo Anderson. Sound:
Dolph Thomas.

CAST: Ann Sheridan (Joy Ryan), Billy Halop (Billy Shafter),
Bernard Punsley (Sleepy Arkelian), Leo Gorcey (Leo Finnegan),
Huntz Hall (Huntz), Gabriel Dell (Luigi), Bobby Jordan
(Bernie Smith), Ronald Reagan (Pat Remson), Bonita Granville
(Peggy Finnegan), Frankie Thomas (Gabe Ryan), Henry O'Neill
(A. H. Remson), Eduardo Ciannelli (Martino), Berton Churchill
(Mayor Dooley), Bernard Nedell (Kroner), Dick Rich (Shuffle),
Jack Searl (Alfred Goonplatz), Margaret Hamilton (Miss
Hannaberry), Marjorie Main (Mrs. Arkelian), Minor Watson
(Maloney), Cyrus Kendall (Haines), Grady Sutton
(Gildersleeve), Aldrich Bowker (Turnkey), Robert Strange
(Simpkins), Egon Brecher (Mr. Smith), Sarah Padden (Mrs.
Smith), Frank Coughlin, Jr. (Boy), Claude Wisberg (Al), Nat
Carr, Garry Owen (Drivers), Jack Wagner (Marsh), Harry Strang

(Assistant turnkey), John Ridgely, John Harron, Max Hoffman, Jr. (Reporters), Jack Clifford, Tom Wilson, Eddy Chandler (Cops).

SYNOPSIS: After being released from reform school, Gabe Ryan joins a gang called the Termites. When several suspicious fires break out in the neighborhood, gangster Kroner implicates Gabe because Gabe's sister Joy rebuffed him. The district attorney's son, Pat Remson, realizes Gabe's innocence and vows to find the arsonist. When one of the Termites is hit by a car after Kroner closes the playground, Joy urges civic league leader Martino to join with parents to make a safe environment for the children. Although Martino is a secret partner of Kroner in an arson/insurance fraud ring, he pretends to support her ideas. Martino plots to frame Gabe so Joy will be too preoccupied to pursue her citizens' committee. Gabe decides to redeem his reputation by running for honorary mayor during boys' week. His plans are destroyed after Kroner's men implicate Gabe in a fire that killed one of the Termites. Joy is devastated when he is convicted and sent to prison. She tries to discourage Pat from romancing her, knowing she will be a detriment to his career until Gabe is proven innocent. The Termites vow to get Gabe released by electing a member as honorary mayor. They help Pat catch the arsonists by going through the fire commissioner's records. They bring evidence to the district attorney, proving the arson ring is involved in insurance fraud. Pat gets Kroner to confess Martino's role in the arson ring. The Termites catch the fire commissioner, who also is involved in the crimes. Pat arranges for Gabe's release. The arsonists are convicted and a new playground is built. Pat invites the Termites to his and Joy's wedding.

REVIEWS:
Harrison's Reports, August 26, 1939: "Very good. Although the story is far-fetched, the melodramatic action is exciting, holding one's attention well throughout....The romance is incidental."

New York Times, September 4, 1939: "...susceptible as we are to 'Oomph,' in [Ann] Sheridan's case 'Oomph' is not enough."

Variety, September 6, 1939: "Surefire boxoffice [sic] in spots where they like Ann Sheridan and the 'Dead End' kids....Ann Sheridan doesn't have much chance to advance as a glamorous figure but this film proves that she is a first-rate little thespian, with or without the 'oomph' tag."

NOTES: In an effort to cash in on the success of Angels with Dirty Faces (F-45) and the rising popularity of the Dead End Kids, Warner Bros. made The Angels Wash Their Faces. Although many contemporary sources call it a sequel, none of the characters from the previous film are included. Production began on March 13, 1939 and it took only a month to film. Working titles for the low-budget picture were Battle Cry of City Hall and The Battle of City Hall.

Despite the publicity Warner Bros. was giving Ann
Sheridan in the oomph campaign, the studio refused to follow
up with quality roles. Though she plays the romantic lead in
The Angels Wash Their Faces, it is a "B" picture, with the
focus markedly on the antics of the Dead End Kids. As in
previous movies, the Dead End Kids wreaked havoc on the
Warner Bros. lot during the filming of The Angels Wash
Their Faces. After they painted obscene murals on the
executives' office walls, threw a lighted firecracker into
Humphrey Bogart's dressing room, and set off fire sprinklers
in the wardrobe department, the studio hired ex-football
player Russ Saunders to act as their guardian. Dead End Kid
Leo Gorcey recalled that Saunders knew how to handle their
antics. "[When] the kids really got out of line, Russ
ordered a fire hose out, and let us have it full force,"
Gorcey said. "Anyone who has ever been hit point blank with
the water from a full-size, high-pressure fire hose can
understand that we were very nice kids while working on the
rest of that picture" (B-217).

F-52   Castle on the Hudson   (Warner Bros., February 10,
       1940)   77 mins.

Producer: Anatole Litvak. Executive producer: Hal B.
Wallis. Associate producer: Samuel Bischoff. Director:
Anatole Litvak. Assistant director: Chuck Hansen. Dialogue
director: Irving Rapper. Screenplay: Seton I. Miller,
Brown Holmes, and Courtney Terrett. Based on the book
20,000 Years in Sing Sing by Warden Lewis E. Lawes. Music:
Adolph Deutsch. Musical director: Leo F. Forbstein.
Orchestrations: Ray Heindorf. Photography: Arthur Edeson.
Editor: Thomas Richards. Art direction: John Hughes.
Costumes: Howard Shoup. Sound: Robert B. Lee. Makeup:
Perc Westmore. Special effects: Byron Haskin and Edwin
DuPar.

CAST: John Garfield (Tommy Gordan/Gordon), Ann Sheridan (Kay
Manners), Pat O'Brien (Warden Long), Burgess Meredith (Steven
Rockford), Henry O'Neill (District attorney), Jerome Cowan
(Ed Crowley), Guinn "Big Boy" Williams (Mike Cagle), John
Litel (Chaplain), Margot Stevenson (Ann Rockford), Willard
Robertson (Ragan), Edward Pawley (Black Jack), Billy Wayne
(Pete), Nedda Harrigan (Mrs. Long), Wade Boteler (Principal
keeper), Barbara Pepper (Goldie), Robert Strange (Joe
Morris), Grant Mitchell (Dr. Ames), Robert Homans (Clyde
Burton), Joseph Downing, Sol Gross (Gangsters), Charles
Sherlock, Mike Lally, Jack Mower, Frank Mayo, Pat O'Malley,
Walter Miller, Harry Strang, James Richard, Eddy Chandler, Ed
Gargan, James Flavin, Cliff Saum (Guards), Pat Flaherty
(Stretcher attendant), Ed Kane (Club manager), Claude
Wisberg, Michael Conroy (Newsboys), Frank Faylen (Guard who
is slugged), Nat Carr, William Telark, Bill Hopper
(Reporters), Lee Phelps (Guard in visitor's room), James
Flavin (Guard in Death Row), George Sorel (Waiter), Howard
Hickman (Judge), Stuart Holmes (Foreman), Ralph Dunn (Court
clerk), Thomas Jackson, Emmett Vogan (Reporters), Clyde
Courtwright (Conductor), John Ridgely, Eddie Acuff, Alan
Davis (Clerks), Cliff Clark (Sergeant), Howard Mitchell

(Officer), Dutch Hendrian, Frank Sully, Adrian Morris, Max
Marx, Jack Richardson, Charles Sullivan (Prisoners), John
Lester, Ernest Whitman (Negroes), John Kelly (Convict), Ernie
Adams (Kelner), Dick Wessel (Trusty), Philip Morris (Joe,
detective), Julie Stevens (Operator), Brenda Fowler (Nurse),
Richard Clayton (Elevator boy), Max Hoffman, Jr. (Warden's
clerk), Robert Stevenson (Sailor), Frank Puglia (Tony), Sugar
Willie Keeler (Joe), Loia Cheaney.

SYNOPSIS: Jewel thief Tommy Gordan thinks he is invincible
to the law. When he is arrested, he is sure his crooked
lawyer, Ed Crowley, will get him released from Sing Sing.
Warden Long refuses Ed's bribe and Tommy becomes an
uncooperative prisoner. After three months in solitary
confinement, Tommy befriends Steven Rockford, an educated
prisoner who organizes a break. Tommy plans to escape with
Steven, but changes his mind when it is set for his unlucky
day. The warden thinks Tommy's good behavior is a sign that
he has reformed. When Tommy's girlfriend Kay Manners is
critically injured in an auto accident, the warden permits
Tommy to visit her, providing he returns to prison. Kay
tells Tommy that she was injured when she jumped from a
moving car, trying to fight off Ed's advances. She plans to
blackmail Ed for ten thousand dollars, hoping the money will
buy Tommy's release. She takes Tommy's gun, begging him not
to harm Ed and spoil his chances for parole. When Ed and
Tommy get into a fight, Kay shoots Ed to protect her
boyfriend. She begs Tommy to flee so he will not be
implicated. Although Kay confesses to the shooting, Ed
accuses Tommy. The district attorney blames Long's honor
policy. Tommy plans to leave the country until he hears that
Long is going to resign over the incident. Tommy returns to
Sing Sing to face murder charges. Although Kay tells the
district attorney the truth, he thinks she is protecting
Tommy. Despite appeals, Tommy is sentenced to the electric
chair. As his execution grows near, Tommy changes. Kay
tries to convince the warden of Tommy's innocence, but Tommy
takes the blame to protect her. As Tommy goes to the chair,
the warden has a new respect for him.

REVIEWS:
Variety, February 28, 1940: "Starring trio of John
Garfield, Ann Sheridan and Pat O'Brien gives marquee impetus
to drawing values of the picture, which will click better in
the action houses....Miss Sheridan provides a strong
characterization as the gangster's girl."

Harrison's Reports, March 2, 1940: "Like [20,000 Years
in Sing Sing], it is a strong prison melodrama, unpleasant
in some respects, but gripping for the most part. It is,
however, strictly adult fare, for some of the situations and
dialogue are pretty suggestive."

New York Times, March 4, 1940: "Ann Sheridan is [John
Gafield's] night-clubby moll....You have met [all the
characters] before, and whether you care to renew the
acquaintance or not, here is an excellent opportunity."

<u>Movie-Radio Guide</u>, April 27, 1940: "Ann [Sheridan] is at her acting best in this."

NOTES: <u>Castle on the Hudson</u> began production on July 10, 1939. It was based on Warden Lewis E. Lawe's 1932 book <u>20,000 Years in Sing Sing</u>. Warner Bros. filmed the property under that title in 1933, with Spencer Tracy and Bette Davis originating the roles taken by John Garfield and Ann Sheridan in 1940. According to many modern sources, background footage from the 1933 film was used in <u>Castle on the Hudson</u>, with many of the sets designed expressly to match the originals. Working titles were <u>City of Lost Men</u> and <u>Years without Days</u> (B-211).
     <u>Castle on the Hudson</u> is Ann Sheridan's second film with John Garfield. Although reviews praise her role as the gangster's girlfriend, her part is secondary, since most of the action takes place in the prison. Inexplicably, Garfield's character's last name is spelled "Gordan" in headlines in the film, but "Gordon" in the credits.

See also D-3.

F-53   <u>It All Came True</u>   (Warner Bros., April 6, 1940)
       97 mins.

Executive producers: Jack L. Warner and Hal B. Wallis. Associate producer: Mark Hellinger. Director: Lewis Seiler. Assistant director: Russ Saunders. Dialogue director: Robert Foulk. Choreographer: Dave Gould. Screenplay: Michael Fessier and Lawrence Kimble. Based on the story "Better than Life" and the novelette <u>And It All Came True</u> by Louis Bromfield. Songs: Kim Gannon, Stephen Weiss, Paul Mann, James Cavanaugh, John Redmond, Nat Simon, Gus Kahn, Egbert Van Alstyne, Richard Whiting, Stanley Murphy, Percy Wenrich, Chauncey Olcott, Seymour Brown, Nat D. Ayer, Monty C. Brice, Walter Donaldson, Slim Gaillard, Sam Stewart, Bud Green, Otto Harbach, Karl Hoschna, Bobby Heath, Charles O'Donnell, Eben E. Rexford, Hart Pease Danks, and George Graff, Jr. Music: Heinz Roemheld. Musical director: Leo F. Forbstein. Orchestrations: Ray Heindorf and Frank Perkins. Photography: Ernie Haller. Editor: Thomas Richards. Art direction: Max Parker. Costumes: Howard Shoup. Sound: Dolph Thomas. Makeup: Perc Westmore. Special effects: Byron Haskin and Edwin B. DuPar.

CAST: Ann Sheridan (Sarah Jane "Sally" Ryan), Jeffrey Lynn (Tommy Taylor), Humphrey Bogart (Grasselli/Chips Maguire), ZaSu Pitts (Miss Flint), Una O'Connor (Maggie Ryan), Jessie Busley (Mrs. Nora Taylor), John Litel (Mr. Roberts), Grant Mitchell (Rene Salmon), Felix Bressart (The Great Boldini), Charles Judels (Henri Pepi de Bordeaux), Brandon Tynan (Mr. Van Diver), Howard Hickman (Mr. Prendergast), Herbert Vigran (Monks), Tommy Reilly, The Elderbloom Chorus, Bender and Daum, White and Stanley, the Lady Killers' Quartet (Vaudeville acts).

SONGS: "Angel in Disguise" (Gannon, Weiss, Mann), "Gaucho Serenade" (Cavanaugh, Redmond, Simon), "Pretty Baby,"

"Memories" (Kahn, Van Alstyne), "Ain't We Got Fun" (Whiting), "Put On Your Old Grey Bonnet" (Murphy, Wenrich), "When Irish Eyes Are Smiling" (Olcott, Graff), "Oh You Beautiful Doll" (Brown, Ayer), "The Daughter of Rosie O'Grady" (Brice, Donaldson), "Flat Foot Floogie" (Gaillard, Stewart, Green), "Cuddle Up a Little Closer, Lovey Mine" (Harbach, Hoschna), "My Pony Boy" (Heath, O'Donnell), "Silver Threads Among the Gold" (Rexford, Danks).

SYNOPSIS: Widows Maggie Ryan and Nora Taylor run a theatrical boarding house for elderly tenants. They hope that their children, singer Sarah Jane Ryan and pianist/composer Tommy Taylor, will marry someday. When Tommy's boss, gangster Chips Maguire, kills a man with a gun registered in Tommy's name, Tommy brings Chips to the boarding house to hide. Chips uses an alias and pretends he needs privacy to recover from a nervous breakdown. Sarah Jane and Tommy bond over music and decide to team up and audition. She recognizes Chips and confronts Tommy about his involvement with the gangster. Tommy lies to her, claiming that Chips promised to help him get his music published. The boarders put on a performance for Chips as an audition. Tommy is jealous of Chips's attention to Sarah Jane. When she learns about the impending foreclosure, Sarah Jane asks Chips for a loan. Bored and sympathetic to Nora and Maggie's plight, Chips helps them open a nightclub in the house to support the tennants and showcase Tommy and Sarah Jane's talents. On opening night, one of the boarders mistakenly tells the police where Chips is hiding. Chips stalls the police, promising to give them some startling information after the show. He plans to implicate Tommy, citing the gun as evidence, so he can have Sarah Jane for himself. Tommy confesses the truth to Sarah Jane, including the fact that he has been in love with her for years. She vows to stand by him. When Nora thanks Chips for his generosity and tells him about Tommy and Sarah Jane's happiness, he weakens and surrenders to police. The Roaring 90s Club is a big success and Sarah Jane and Tommy are free to marry, just as their mothers always dreamed.

REVIEWS:
New York Times, April 6, 1940: "It also affords Ann Sheridan practically the first opportunity she has had to demonstrate anything at all except her talent for exuding abstract 'oomph'; it now appears that she also has a contralto voice and that, although its range is narrow, Miss Sheridan is quite at home on it."

Los Angeles Times, April 10, 1940: "[Ann] Sheridan is exceptionally successful, too, enjoying the benefits of a role that lives up to the far-flung exploitation which has kept her in the spotlight. The casting is very sagacious, the sincerity of her acting in sympathetic scenes is telling and her singing evokes favorable response."

Variety, April 10, 1940: "Ann Sheridan, as a femme loaded with [sex appeal], and Ann Sheridan, as a dramatic actress, are two things distinctly apart. She fits the first, but the

second is beyond her present capabilities. She holds
attention when displaying her chassis, as for instance when
fitting a corset, but is only fairish at best when speaking
lines."

Liberty, May 11, 1940:   "You'll probably like Ann Sheridan
as the hot-tempered, torrid rumba-dancing daughter of the
household. The comedy is entirely too long, except for the
Oomph Girl's rumba."

NOTES: Writer Louis Bromfield was paid fifty thousand
dollars for the rights to his story "Better than Life," which
ran in Hearst's National Cosmopolitan in January 1936.
Warner Bros. first offered the project to Bette Davis, but
she rejected it. With Ann Sheridan's growing popularity and
her hard work for the studio, director Lewis Seiler and
executive producer Hal Wallis decided to offer her the lead.
It marks the first time Ann was called on to carry an "A"
picture and shows the studio's growing confidence in her
ability to draw audiences.
    It All Came True began production on November 29,
1939. Working titles included The Roaring Nineties and
And It All Came True. Ann was reunited with friend and
frequent co-star Humphrey Bogart in the film. Playing a
nightclub singer gave Ann the opportunity to sing "Angel in
Disguise" and "Gaucho Serenade," as well as a medley of old
favorites with the club patrons and Jeffrey Lynn. Theodore
of the Dancing Theodores taught her to do the rumba for the
film.

See also D-2, S-4.

F-54   Torrid Zone   (Warner Bros., May 25, 1940)
       88 mins.

Executive producer: Hal B. Wallis. Associate producer:
Mark Hellinger. Director: William Keighley. Assistant
director: Frank Heath. Screenplay: Jerry Wald and Richard
Macaulay. Song "Mi Caballero": M.K. Jerome and Jack Scholl.
Music: Adolph Deutsch. Musical director: Leo F. Forbstein.
Photography: James Wong Howe. Editor: Jack Killifer. Art
direction: Ted Smith. Sets: Edward Thorne. Costumes:
Howard Shoup. Sound: Oliver S. Garretson. Makeup: Perc
Westmore. Special effects: Byron Haskin and H.F. Koenekamp.
Technical advisor: John Mari.

CAST: James Cagney (Nick Butler), Ann Sheridan (Lee Donley),
Pat O'Brien (Steve Case), Andy Devine (Wally Davis), Helen
Vinson (Gloria Anderson), Jerome Cowan (Bob Anderson), George
Tobias (Rosario), George Reeves (Sancho), Victor Kilian
(Carlos), Frank Puglia (Juan Rodriguez), John Ridgley
(Gardner), Grady Sutton (Sam, the secretary), Paul Porcasi
(Garcia), Frank Yaconnelli (Lopez), Dick Boteler (Hernandez),
Frank Mayo (Shaffer), Jack Mower (McNamara), Paul Hurst
(Daniels), George Regas (Police sergeant), Elvira Sanchez
(Rita), George Humbert (Hotel manager), Paul Renay (Jose),
Rafael Corio (Man), Trevor Bardette, Ernesto Piedra
(Policemen), Don Orlando (Employee), Manuel Lopez (Chico),

Joe Cominguez (Manuel), Joe Molinas (Native), Tony Paton (Charley), Max Blum, Betty Sanko, Victor Sabuni.

SYNOPSIS: Banana company manager Steve Case revels in controlling the Honduran town and its citizens. When he finds singer Lee Donley cheating his workers, he convinces police to deport her. While waiting in jail, Lee befriends Rosario, a revolutionary awaiting execution. Rosario escapes and plots to reclaim his land. Steve is disgruntled with plantation foreman Bob Anderson and tries to convince his womanizing predecessor, Nick Butler, to return. Steve thinks of a series of plans to keep Nick on the plantation indefinitely. Nick befriends Lee, who follows him to the plantation. She pretends to be involved with Nick so Bob will not be suspicious of Nick's relationship with Gloria, Bob's wife and Nick's former girlfriend. Lee and Nick fall in love and she tries to convince him to stay on the plantation. Steve is ungrateful when Nick captures Rosario. Nick threatens to leave immediatly. Steve tries to get Nick to stay by arresting Lee and firing Bob. Rosario escapes and threatens Bob, Gloria, Nick, Steve, and Lee. Nick overpowers Rosario, but lets him escape. Lee pretends to be shot in the melee. Nick agrees to stay on the plantation, realizing how much he cares for her. After the others leave, Nick proves his love, revealing he really was shot by Rosario and knew Lee was acting. Lee and Nick marvel that they finally outsmarted Steve.

REVIEWS:
San Francisco Chronicle [CA], March 30, 1940: "Whether [Ann] Sheridan can really act in a crisis is a detail still to be decided. Frankly I don't know whether her appeal is the result of extremely astute direction, a tantalizing wardrobe, or provocative photography; a good guess would be that it's all of them."

New York Times, May 18, 1940: "...Ann Sheridan steps up a notch or two in our estimation as the femme fatale of the piece....But if the males are two-fisted, Miss Sheridan meets them blow for blow, line for line. And, quite aside from a modicum of acting ability displayed, Miss Sheridan is not an unlikely cause for tropical contretemps."

Los Angeles Times, May 24, 1940: "Torrid Zone makes no pretentions at being serious which is fortunate. The comedy is fast-moving....[Ann Sheridan will] make a lot of new friends with her work in this picture."

Screenland, July 1940: "Ann Sheridan really comes into her own here. She's not only more oomph-ish than usual, but gives a tangy performance of the girl whose morals, despite her way with cards and [James] Cagney, are above reproach.... It's Ann's film, but for George Tobias as an ingratiating bandit."

NOTES: Torrid Zone marks Ann Sheridan's second starring role with her name above the title, the first being the disappointing It All Came True (F-53). Production began

February 8, 1940. Ann receives second billing below James
Cagney. Critics were surprised to see that she could steal
the picture from screen veterans Cagney and Pat O'Brien. The
comedy includes many snappy exchanges of risque dialogue and
Ann's comic timing was tested. She proved an adept foil for
her co-stars. Cagney's role first was offered to George
Raft. Reviews called the film a cross between What Price
Glory (Fox, 1926), The Front Page (United Artists, 1931),
and The Badman (Warner Bros., 1941).
     The movie was shot in forty-one days. In order to give
the film a realistic feel, Warner Bros. planted 950 banana
trees on their 30-acre backlot. Ann Sheridan sings "Mi
Caballero" during a scene at the saloon. The last line of
the film is an "in" joke, with Cagney cracking to Ann, "You
and your fourteen-carat oomph." Blowing Wild (Warner
Bros., 1953), loosely was based on Torrid Zone, recycling
the complicated romantic entanglements (B-211). Barbara
Stanwyck is the wife (Helen Vinson's character in Torrid
Zone), Gary Cooper the man she wants (James Cagney), Ruth
Roman the new girlfriend (Ann Sheridan), and Anthony Quinn
the cuckolded husband (Jerome Cowan).

See also S-5, V-7.

F-55 They Drive by Night   (Warner Bros., August 3, 1940)
      93 mins.

Producer: Mark Hellinger. Executive producer: Hal B.
Wallis. Director: Raoul Walsh. Assistant director: Elmer
Decker. Dialogue director: Hugh MacMullen. Screenplay:
Jerry Wald and Richard Macaulay. Based on the novel The
Long Haul by Albert Isaac Bezzerides. Music: Adolph
Deutsch. Musical director: Leo F. Forbstein. Photography:
Arthur Edeson. Editors: Oliver S. Garretson and Thomas
Richards. Art direction: John Hughes. Costumes: Milo
Anderson. Sound: Oliver S. Garretson. Makeup: Perc
Westmore. Special effects: Byron Haskin and H.F. Koenekamp.

CAST: George Raft (Joe Fabrini), Humphrey Bogart (Paul
Fabrini), Ann Sheridan (Cassie Hartley), Ida Lupino (Lana
Carlsen), Alan Hale (Ed Carlsen), Gale Page (Pearl Fabrini),
Roscoe Karns (Irish McGurn), John Litel (Harry McNamara),
George Tobias (George Rondolos), Charles Halton (Farnsworth),
Paul Hurst (Pete Haig), John Ridgely (Hank Dawson), George
Lloyd (Barney), Henry O'Neill (District attorney), Joyce
Compton (Sue Carter), Charles Wilson (Mike Williams), Norman
Willis (Neves), George Lloyd (Barney), Lillian Yarbo (Chloe),
Pedro Regas (Mexican helper), Eddy Chandler, Frank Faylen,
Ralph Sanford, Sol Gorss, Michael Harvey, Eddie Featherston,
Alan Davis, Dick Wessel, Al Hill, Charles Sullivan, Eddie
Acuff, Pat Flaherty, Mike Lally, Don Turner, Ralph Lynn,
Charles Sherlock, Frank Mayo, Dutch Hendrian (Drivers),
George Haywood (Policeman), Claire James (Party guest), Marie
Blake (Waitress), Vera Lewis (Landlady), Dorothea Kent (Sue),
Frank Wilcox, J. Anthony Hughes (Reporters), Joe Devlin
(Fatso), William Haade (Tough driver), Phyllis Hamilton
(Stenographer), Jack Mower (Deputy), Carl Harbaugh
(Mechanic), Mack Gray (Mike), Richard Clayton (Young man),

Max Wagner (Sweeney), Demetrius Emanuel (Waiter), Dorothy
Vaughan, Brenda Fowler (Matrons), Billy Wayne, Matt McHugh
(Electricians), Howard Hickman (Judge), Wilfred Lucas
(Bailiff), John Hamilton (Defense attorney).

SYNOPSIS: Brothers Joe and Paul Fabrini are struggling
independent truckers. When financial success seems imminent,
Paul falls asleep at the wheel and loses an arm. Joe becomes
an assistant at Ed Carlsen's trucking firm to support Paul
and his wife Pearl. Ed's ambitious wife Lana urges Joe to
have an affair, but he rebuffs her. Paul is depressed by his
unemployment and resents Joe's financial help. Joe proposes
to waitress Cassie Hartley, but she insists that he has too
many responsibilities to consider marriage. At the Carlsens'
anniversary party, Lana confronts Joe and he gives her a
final rebuff. Desperate to have Joe at any cost and
disgusted with Ed's drinking, Lana leaves her inebriated
husband in the garage with the motor running and he is killed
by carbon monoxide fumes. The district attorney labels the
death accidental. Lana hires Joe as her partner, hoping to
win his affections as they work. He gives Paul a
supervisory job in the garage, making him feel independent.
Lana is furious when she learns about Joe's engagement.
Consumed by guilt about Ed's death and jealousy over Cassie,
Lana tells Joe that she killed Ed. When he is unimpressed by
her efforts to be with him, she decides to destroy his
happiness. She tells the district attorney that Joe
blackmailed her into killing her husband and giving him a
share of the business. Circumstantial evidence incriminates
Joe. On the witness stand, Lana loses her mind and
confesses. Joe is released and plans to return to the road.
Cassie and the drivers convince him to stay on as boss. As
Joe and Cassie make marriage plans, Paul announces his
impending fatherhood.

REVIEWS:
Hollywood Reporter, July 9, 1940: "Ann Sheridan is in a
tough spot because of little [Ida] Lupino. Annie looks
great, and before Miss Lupino comes on the screen with so
much the better of the parts, the redhead stands out. But
after Ida gets working, she steals all the attention. But
'Miss Oomph' is okay."

Variety, July 10, 1940: "[Ann] Sheridan is okay, mainly
for love interest, overshadowed by the stellar performance of
[Ida] Lupino."

New York Times, July 27, 1940: "As usual, the Warners are
delivering in A-1 shape another of their fast action
dramas....And, smartly, they have chosen to play it the cream
of their ungrammatical roughnecks, starting with George Raft
and Humphrey Bogart, and their ace baggage, Ann Sheridan."

Liberty, August 31, 1940: "The story becomes theatric;
owes its vigor to its graphic picturing of the hardy night
riders who bring a great city's produce market....Ann
Sheridan's little waitress is wise and sympathetic....The
whole cast, in fact, is authentically real."

NOTES: Production began in April 1940. They Drive by
Night marks Ann Sheridan and George Raft's fifth picture
together, but it is the first time they played opposite each
other.   Their scene in the truckstop is reprinted in many
sources and appears on Warner Bros.'s fiftieth anniversary
album (D-3).   The film also reunited Ann with Ida Lupino.
In the six years since Search for Beauty (F-1), the two
leading ladies had progressed remarkably from their roles as
an ingenue and a contest winner.
     They Drive by Night is based on Albert Isaac
Bezzerides's 1938 novel The Long Haul.   It also is a
partial reworking of Bordertown (Warner Bros., 1935),
whichhad starred Bette Davis as the predatory wife (Ida
Lupino in They Drive by Night), Paul Muni as the man she
wanted (George Raft), and Margaret Lindsay as his patient
girlfriend (Ann Sheridan).   Although the first half of They
Drive by Night concentrates on the Fabrini brothers'
independent trucking adventures, the entanglements with the
boss's wife and the courtroom confession mirror Bordertown.
They Drive by Night later served as inspiration for
Blowing Wild (Warner Bros., 1953), a love triangle
involving maverick oil drillers in Mexico (B-431). Blowing
Wild recycles the plot device of a wife killing her husband
to be with her lover.   The roles played by Barbara Stanwyck,
Anthony Quinn, Gary Cooper, and Ruth Roman match up to those
essayed by Ida Lupino, Alan Hale, George Raft, and Ann
Sheridan in They Drive by Night.
     Before becoming an actor, George Raft had delivered
bootleg liquor shipments for his underworld pal, Owney
Madden.   The experience came in handy during the filming of
They Drive by Night when Raft was called upon to drive a
truck down a steep California mountain with Ann Sheridan and
Humphrey Bogart as his passengers.   The brakes failed and
Raft had to control the truck down the twisted road, finally
managing to stop it on an embankment.
     In addition to the black and white original, a computer
colorized version of They Drive by Night often is shown on
television.   In Great Britain, the film is known as Road to
Frisco.

See also D-3, V-8.

F-56 City for Conquest   (Warner Bros., September 21,1940)
      101 mins.

Producer: Anatole Litvak.   Executive producer: Hal B.
Wallis.   Associate producer: William Cagney.   Directors:
Anatole Litvak and (uncredited) Jean Negulesco. Assistant
directors: Sherry Shourds and Chuck Hansen. Dialogue
director: Irving Rapper.   Choreographer: Robert Vreeland.
Screenplay: John Wexley.   Based on the novel City for
Conquest by Aben Kandel. Music: Max Steiner. Musical
director: Leo F. Forbstein.   Orchestrations: Hugo
Friedhofer and Ray Heindorf. Photography: James Wong Howe
and Sol Polito. Editor: William Holmes. Art direction:
Robert Haas.   Costumes: Howard Shoup.   Sound: E.A. Brown.
Makeup: Perc Westmore.   Special effects: Byron Haskin and
Rex Wimpy.

CAST: James Cagney (Danny Kenny), Ann Sheridan (Peggy Nash),
Frank Craven ("Old Timer"), Arthur Kennedy (Eddie Kenny),
Elia Kazan ("Googi"), Donald Crisp (Scotty McPherson), Lee
Patrick (Gladys), Frank McHugh ("Mutt"), Anthony Quinn
(Murray Burns), Jerome Cowan ("Dutch"), Blanche Yurka (Mrs.
Nash), George Lloyd ("Goldie"), Joyce Compton (Lily), George
Tobias ("Pinky"), Bob Steele (Callahan), Thurston Hall (Max
Leonard), Ben Welden (Cobb), John Arledge (Salesman), Selmer
Jackson, Joseph Crehan (Doctors), Billy Wayne (Henchman), Pat
Flaherty (Floor guard), Charles Lane (Al, the agent), Sidney
Miller (M.C.), Ed Keane (Gaul), Ethelreda Leopold (Dressing
room blonde), Lee Phelps, Charles Wilson, Ed Gargan, Howard
Hickman, Murray Alper, Dick Wessel, Bernice Pilot, Dana Dale,
Margaret Hayes, Ed Pawley, William Newell, Lucia Carroll.

SYNOPSIS: Truck driver Danny Kenny turns professional boxer
to help finance his brother Eddie's musical training and
impress his girlfriend Peggy Nash. Ambitious Peggy teams
with dancer Murray Burns, in hopes of becoming a star.
Although she promises to settle down with Danny when her tour
ends, dreams of fame and fortune make her cancel the wedding.
Embittered, Danny recklessly decides to compete in the
welterweight championship, hoping his success will bring back
Peggy. During the fight, Danny is blinded when his opponent
hits him with gloves that were soaked in rosin. His manager
blames Peggy for Danny's fate and refuses to let Danny see
her. Eddie earns a living composing popular songs, but
dreams about classical music. Danny encourages Eddie to
finish his symphony, working in a newsstand to support his
brother. Peggy realizes how foolish she was to sacrifice
Danny's love for a career. She attends the premiere of
Eddie's Magic Isle symphony at Carnegie Hall. Danny listens
on the radio at the newsstand, afraid his presence will jinx
his brother. The music reminds Peggy of Danny and she breaks
down. Eddie's symphony is a big success. In a curtin
speech, he thanks Danny for his sacrifices and inspiration.
Peggy visits Danny at the newsstand and they reconcile,
realizing how much time they wasted.

REVIEWS:
Variety, September 11, 1940:   "[Ann] Sheridan is excellent
as the girl, displaying dancing abilities in several ballroom
numbers with [Anthony] Quinn."

New York Times, September 27, 1940:   "Any picture that has
[James] Cagney and [Ann] Sheridan is bound to be tough and
salty, right off the city's streets. And this one is. Miss
Sheridan waxes quite emotional..."

Pittsburgh Post-Gazette [PA], October 4, 1940:   "Miss Ann
Sheridan, the girl, gets something more than just oomph into
her role."

Modern Screen, December 1940:   "It has been many years
since this particular reviewer of films has been so thrilled
and excited by a movie....it is a sock, a smash, a click, a
whiz, or whatever else you can think of....[James] Cagney and
[Ann] Sheridan are topnotch..."

NOTES: James Cagney first wanted to film Aben Kandel's
novel City for Conquest after he read it in 1936 (Beverly
Hills, "Gunfire and the Jersey Lily," Liberty, November 2,
1940, p. 42).   There were many production changes before
City for Conquest went before the cameras four years
later.   Raoul Walsh originally was scheduled to direct, but
he was replaced by Anatole Litvak.   Warner Bros. first
wanted Ginger Rogers for the female lead, but they signed
Sylvia Sidney.   By the time production began on May 31,
1940, Litvak and James Cagney decided the role was better
suited to Ann Sheridan.   Ann recalled, "It was a very good
part, and of course it was Cagney again.   He sold like
wildfire.   To be in a picture with him was just the
greatest" (B-476).   Cesar Romero and George Raft both wanted
the role as Ann's sleazy dance partner, but the part went to
Anthony Quinn.   When director Litvak suffered an eye injury
during the filming, Jean Negulesco took over (B-211).   The
film marks Arthur Kennedy's screen debut.   Associate
producer William Cagney was James Cagney's brother.

Although most of City for Conquest was shot on Warner
Bros. soundstages, cameraman Bunny Haskins and a technical
crew spent three weeks shooting background footage on
location in New York.   Liberty claimed Aben Kandel was
working on a sequel, continuing the saga of his characters
(November 2, 1940).   Although Kandel wrote other books and
screenplays, no evidence of a sequel can be found.

Variety notes several similarities between City for
Conquest and real and fictional devices.   Eddie conducting
his own symphony at Carnegie Hall mirrors George Gershwin's
debut (September 11, 1940).   The film is framed by narrator
Frank Craven, in a role similar to his stint in Our Town
(United Artists, 1940).

See also V-9.

F-57   Honeymoon for Three   (Warner Bros., January 18,
        1941)   77 mins.

Executive producer: Hal B. Wallis. Associate producer:
Henry Blanke. Director: Lloyd Bacon. Dialogue director:
Hugh Cummings. Screenplay: Earl Baldwin, Julius J. Epstein,
and Philip G. Epstein. Based on the play Goodbye Again by
Allan Scott and George Haight. Music: H. Roemheld. Musical
Director: Leo F. Forbstein. Orchestrations: Ray Heindorf.
Photography: Ernie Haller. Editor: Rudi Fehr. Art
direction: Max Parker. Costumes: Orry-Kelly. Sound:
Oliver S. Garretson. Makeup: Perc Westmore.

CAST: Ann Sheridan (Anne Rogers), George Brent (Kenneth
Bixby), Charlie Ruggles (Harvey Wilson), Osa Massen (Julie
Peterson Wilson), Jane Wyman (Elizabeth Clochessy), William
T. Orr (Arthur Westlake), Lee Patrick (Mrs. Pettijohn),
Walter Catlett (Waiter), Herbert Anderson (Floyd T. Ingram),
Johnny Downs (Chester T. Farrington III).

SYNOPSIS: Womanizing novelist Kenneth Bixby is disturbed
when his college girlfriend, Julie Peterson, appears during a
book tour. Julie insists that she is the inspiration for his

latest book, <u>Miriam</u>, and announces plans to leave her
husband Harvey Wilson. Kenneth's secretary/fiancee Anne
Rogers tries to keep Kenneth away from Julie and out of
scandal. Anne is furious when she catches Kenneth and Julie
having dinner at a secluded inn. He tries to win Anne's
sympathy by faking illness, but she sees through his ploy.
Harvey sues Kenneth for $100,000 and names him in the
Wilsons' divorce suit. Kenneth plans to flee before the suit
comes to trial. Angry and jealous, Anne quits. Harvey
offers to cancel his suits if Kenneth marries Julie,
explaining that he has wanted to get rid of his wife for
years. Anne tries to dissuade Julie from marrying Kenneth,
insisting it may hurt his career. Kenneth tries to delay
things by feigning illness. Anne sees the opportunity to
save her ex-boss when a fan arrives with a baby named after
Kenneth. Anne and Kenneth imply that he is Kenneth's son and
that his mother was the real inspiration for <u>Miriam</u>. The
Wilsons reconcile. Kenneth proposes to Anne, but she
refuses. When he fakes suicide, she realizes she loves him
and they get back together.

REVIEWS:
<u>Hollywood Reporter</u>, January 16, 1941: "Ann Sheridan does
just about her finest work to date as the loving and long-
suffering secretary, a performance which will unquestionably
increase her already great popularity."

<u>New York Times</u>, February 8, 1941: "Ann Sheridan plays the
secretary in one key of bored tolerance, which is not
surprising in view of her employer's juvenile behavior..."

<u>New Orleans Times-Picayune</u> [LA], February 14, 1941: "A
romantic comedy which provides many amusing situations, the
film is a light and frothy affair in which [Ann] Sheridan
gives an excellent account of herself in a new type of role."

<u>Liberty</u>, March 22, 1941: "Even George Brent as the best-
seller novelist and Ann Oomph Sheridan as the secretary can't
help this much. Just a minor opus."

NOTES: Hoping to cash in on the real-life romance of Ann
Sheridan and George Brent, Warner Bros. teamed them in
<u>Honeymoon for Three</u>. It marks their only film together.
<u>Honeymoon for Three</u> is based on Allan Scott and George
Haight's Broadway play <u>Goodbye Again</u>, which opened
December 28, 1932. Osgood Perkins and Sally Bates starred in
the comedy, which ran 212 performances. It was filmed under
that title by Warner Bros. in 1933, with Warren William and
Joan Blondell in the parts taken by George Brent and Ann
Sheridan in the remake. Despite the popularity of Sheridan
and Brent, <u>Honeymoon for Three</u> was a disappointment at the
box office. Twin screenwriters Julius J. and Philip G.
Epstein fared much better on their next assignment,
<u>Casablanca</u> (Warner Bros., 1942).

F-58   <u>Hollywood Steps Out</u>   (Warner Bros., May 24, 1941)
       cartoon short

Supervision: Fred Avery. Musical director: Carl W.
Stalling.

NOTES: This Merrie Melodies cartoon spoofs many film stars,
including Greta Garbo, Groucho Marx, and Dorothy Lamour. Set
at Ciro's, a caricature of Edward G. Robinson is seen
greeting the Oomph Girl.

F-59   Navy Blues   (Warner Bros., September 1941)
        108 mins.

Executive producer: Hal B. Wallis. Associate producers:
Jerry Wald and Jack Saper. Director: Lloyd Bacon. Dialogue
director: Eddie Blatt. Choreographer: Seymour Felix.
Screenplay: Jerry Wald, Richard Macaulay, Sam Perrin, and
Arthur T. Horman. Based on a story by Arthur T. Horman.
Songs: Arthur Schwartz and Johnny Mercer. Music: Arthur
Schwartz. Musical director: Leo F. Forbstein.
Orchestrations: Ray Heindorf. Photography: Tony Gaudio and
James Wong Howe. Editor: Rudi Fehr. Art direction: Robert
Haas. Costumes: Howard Shoup. Makeup: Perc Westmore.
Special effects: H.F. Koenekamp. Technical advisor: J.J.
Giblon.

CAST: Ann Sheridan (Margie Jordan), Jack Oakie (Cake
O'Hara), Martha Raye (Lillibelle Bolton), Jack Haley
(Powerhouse Bolton), Herbert Anderson (Homer Mathews), Jack
Carson (Buttons Johnson), Richard Lane (Rocky Anderson),
William T. Orr (Mac), Jackie Gleason (Tubby), John Ridgely
(Jersey), Howard da Silva (First petty officer), Ray Cooke
(Lucky), Richard Travis (Tex), William Hopper (Ensign
Walters), Hardie Albright, Frank Wilcox (Officers),
Marguerite Chapman, Leslie Brooks, Peggy Diggins, Georgia
Carroll, Katharine [Kay] Aldridge, Claire James (Navy Blues
Sextet), Ralph Byrd (Lieutenant), Jean Ames, Lucia Carroll,
Maris Wrixon (Girls), Tom Dugan (Hot dog stand proprietor),
Gaylord Pendleton, Don Rowan, Pat McVeigh, Walter Sande
(Marines), Dick Wessel, Victor Zimmerman (Petty officers),
Charles Drake, Emmett Vogan (Officers), Selmer Jackson
(Captain Willard), Harry Strang (Chief petty officer Lane),
Gig Young, Murray Alper, Lane Allen, Will Morgan, Garland
Smith, George O'Hanlon, Arthur Gardner (Sailors).

SONGS: "In Waikiki," "You're a Natural," "Navy Blues," "When
Are We Going to Land Abroad?" (Schwartz, Mercer).

SYNOPSIS: Sailors Powerhouse Bolton and Cake O'Hara look for
a way to make money while on leave in pre-Pearl Harbor
Honolulu. When they learn that excellent marksman Homer
Mathews is transferring to their ship, they see the navy
gunnery contest as a way to get rich quick. They plan to bet
on their ship, but keep Homer's transfer a secret to insure
better odds. The sailors confide in Powerhouse's ex-wife
Lillibelle and and her friend Margie, promising the plan will
get Lillibelle her back alimony. The sailors' dreams are
dashed when they learn Homer's enlistment is up before the
contest and he plans to return to his Iowa pig farm. Cake
and Powerhouse persuade Margie to flirt with Homer to

encourage him to reenlist. She pretends to be a farm girl
who admires Homer's patriotism. Homer reenlists, but
questions Margie's integrity when sailors from a rival ship
accuse her of being a spy. During target practice, he is so
upset about Margie that he cannot aim. Cake and Powerhouse
try to convince Homer that Margie is sincere. They send
Margie a message on shore. Realizing she loves Homer, Margie
flies over the ship to let him know with a hog call.
Encouraged by the sign of support, Homer earns a perfect
score during the contest. Cake and Powerhouse win their bets
and Lillibelle collects her support. All join for a
patriotic finale.

REVIEWS:
Variety, August 13, 1941: "The boys are going to like
[Ann] Sheridan. She is, often enough, in hula costume to
emphasize that chassis. It's enough to stop a flotilla. And
Miss Sheridan sings, too, quite pleasantly; also, she does
some hog-calling, although Honolulu, the yarn's setting,
would certainly be remote under ordinary circumstances from
such paradoxes. But that's the story department for you."

New York Times, September 20, 1941: "... [Ann] Sheridan is
on hand to sing a couple of songs and wear a grass skirt
(which ain't hay!)....the worst that can be said for Navy
Blues is that it works hard without much to show..."

New York World Telegram, September 20, 1941: "...the day
has passed when oomph alone can carry a film for nearly two
hours, especially when the owner of that oomph is so
definitely bored by the whole business. Even so, [Ann]
Sheridan couldn't be any more bored by it all then the
spectator."

Liberty, October 4, 1941: "[Ann Sheridan] is up on her
toes all the time in Navy Blues. What I like especially
about her performance is the fact that she is really trying
to put over a part, instead of merely being a sultry
siren....A bit better script and this show might have been
good going all the way."

NOTES: Navy Blues marks Ann Sheridan's first film since
going on suspension over a salary dispute with Warner Bros.
in September 1940. She reached a compromise only after the
studio agreed to give her the plum role of Randy Monoghan in
Kings Row (F-60). The deal also included a comedy for
Warner Bros., which ended up being Navy Blues. Ann was
less than happy with the film, but wanted Kings Row enough
to compromise.
     Ann's role as a nightclub singer lets her perform in
several production numbers. She sings the title song in a
nightclub scene with Martha Raye, the Navy Blues Sextet, and
the customers. At a luau for the navy officers, she performs
a hula and sings "In Waikiki" with the Navy Blues Sextet. In
a picnic scene, she extols Herbert Anderson's virtues in the
duet "You're a Natural." Ann also joins the cast for a
patriotic finale, reprising "You're a Natural" with Anderson.
Although some sources say that her voice was dubbed in Navy

Blues (B-475), the author and Sheridan biographer Tom
Sharpley believe it is Ann singing.
    Screenwriter Stuart Jerome, who was a mailboy at Warner
Bros. in the early 1940s, recalled that it wasn't all work on
the Navy Blues set. He remembered drinking binges in Ann's
trailer with co-stars Jack Haley and Jackie Gleason. One
afternoon Jerome was ordered to pick up a bottle of brandy
for Gleason. He chose a cheap brand, pocketing the change
from a five-dollar bill. The set had to be closed down when
the stars got sick from the liquor (B-277).
    The reviews focus more on the cheesecake aspects of Ann
Sheridan's appearance than her acting. Publicity for the
film includes shots of Ann in a short skirt and with stars
and stripes, a sailor's top with bare midriff, and a sailor's
hat. The ad line reads, "Sailor, beware! Sheridan at work"
(B-475).

See also D-2, D-6, D-7, S-6.

F-60   The Man Who Came to Dinner   (Warner Bros.,
       January 24, 1942)   112 mins.

Executive producer: Hal B. Wallis. Associate producers:
Jack Saper and Jerry Wald. Director: William Keighley.
Screenplay: Julius J. Epstein and Phillip G. Epstein. Based
on the play by George S. Kaufman and Moss Hart. Original
production produced by Sam H. Harris. Music: Frederick
Hollander. Musical director: Leo F. Forbstein.
Photography: Tony Gaudio. Editor: Jack Killifer. Art
direction: Robert Haas. Costumes: Orry-Kelly. Sound:
Charles Lang. Makeup: Perc Westmore.

CAST: Monty Woolley (Sheridan Whiteside), Bette Davis
(Maggie Cutler), Ann Sheridan (Lorraine Sheldon), Jimmy
Durante (Banjo), Richard Travis (Bert Jefferson), Billie
Burke (Daisy Stanley), Grant Mitchell (Ernest Stanley),
Elisabeth Fraser (June Stanley), Russell Arms (Richard
Stanley), Ruth Vivian (Harriett Stanley), Mary Wickes (Miss
Preen), George Barbier (Dr. Bradley), Reginald Gardiner
(Beverly Carlton), Edwin Stanley (John), Betty Roadman
(Sarah), Charles Drake (Sandy), Nanette Vallon (Cosette),
John Ridgely, Herbert Gunn, Creighton Hale (Radio men), Pat
McVey (Harry), Frank Coghlan, Jr. (Telegram boy), Vera Lewis
(Woman), Frank Moran (Michaelson), Roland Drew
(Newspaperman), Sam Hayes (Announcer), Ernie Adams
(Haggerty), Eddy Chandler (Guard), Hank Mann, Cliff Saum
(Expressmen), Billy Wayne (Vendor), Dudley Dickerson
(Porter), Jack Mower, Frank Mayo (Plainclothesmen), Fred
Kelsey (Man), Georgia Carroll, Lorraine Gettman [Leslie
Brooks], Peggy Diggins, Alix Talton (Girls). Chester Clute
(Mr. Gibbons) and Laura Hope Crews (Mrs. Gibbons) were cut
from the final print.

SYNOPSIS: During a lecture tour in Ohio, temperamental
critic Sheridan Whiteside breaks his hip on Ernest and Daisy
Stanley's icy steps. The accident forces him to move in for
an extended period. Sheridan takes over the Stanleys' house,
tying up the phone lines, entertaining crowds of strangers,

and exiling Ernest and Daisy to the second floor. Sheridan
befriends newspaperman Bert Jefferson, who has written a
play. Sheridan's devoted secretary, Maggie Cutler,
encourages Bert's writing and they fall in love. When she
reveals her plans to quit and marry Bert, jealous Sheridan
plots to stop her. Desperate to keep Maggie in his employ,
Sheridan pretends his hip has not recovered so he can stay in
town. He convinces flamboyant actress Lorraine Sheldon to
flirt with Bert, implying that she needs to seduce him to get
cast in his play. Maggie quits after she learns Sheridan is
behind Lorraine's visit. Sheridan realizes how much he hurt
his secretary. He gets rid of Lorraine and gives Maggie and
Bert his blessing. Sheridan admits he has recovered and he
departs for New York. As he starts down the Stanleys' steps,
he falls again. Ernest bangs his head against the wall and
Daisy faints at the realization that their nightmare is
beginning again.

REVIEWS:
Hollywood Reporter, December 23, 1941: "...[director]
William Keighley...never favors [Bette] Davis as a ranking
star, or gives pointed attention to Ann Sheridan. The
latter's role of a conniving stage actress is much flashier
than the patient secretary part upon which Miss Davis is
wasted. The show is still all [Monty] Woolley and a yard
wide."

New York Times, January 2, 1942: "Ann Sheridan..., as an
actress of definitely feline breed, gives a tartly mannered
performance..."

Liberty, January 3, 1942: "...Ann Sheridan does some
flamboyant and striking acting as a flyblown actress whom the
lecturer calls on to break up his secretary's romance."

Variety, January 7, 1942: "Ann Sheridan, the third
starring name, is a pip as the beautiful and hammy actress
menace imported by [Monty] Woolley to snatch his secretary's
love interest so he won't lose her services."

NOTES: The Man Who Came to Dinner was based on the hit
Broadway play by George S. Kaufman and Moss Hart, which ran
for 739 performances, beginning October 16, 1939. Warner
Bros. payed the then-exorbitant sum of a quarter of a million
dollars for the screen rights. The project proved to be
worth the investement, as the movie became one of the top
moneymaking films of the 1941/42 season. Although John
Barrymore was the original choice for the role of the
narcissistic critic who becomes the unwelcome houseguest, he
had trouble with his lines, and Monty Woolley, who created
the role on Broadway, was tapped for the movie. Mary Wickes
also reprised her stage role. Bette Davis had seen the show
on Broadway and requested to play the secondary part of the
secretary, which had been created by Edith Atwater.
     Warner Bros. production supervisor and executive
producer Hal Wallis decided he wanted Ann Sheridan to boost
the box office potential of The Man Who Came to Dinner.
After testing her for the role of the flamboyant actress,

created by Carol Goodner on stage, he cast Ann, despite the
fact that she already was filming Kings Row (F-60). The
working situation was further complicated by the presence of
Bette Davis, who had a reputation of disagreeing with her
female co-stars. In a 1960s interview, Ann revealed that she
and Davis were friends, however their relationship was chilly
during the filming of The Man Who Came to Dinner. Ann
blamed Davis's much-publicized clash with co-star Miriam
Hopkins in The Old Maid (Warner Bros., 1939) for her
reluctance to warm up to Ann during the film (B-206). Ann
told John Kobal that she adored Bette Davis and refused to
fight with her. "She was just - temperamental," Ann
explained. "Who isn't now and then? She probably hated her
role" (B-298). Ann is billed below Davis in the credits.
Although Ann appeared in remakes of many Davis films, The
Man Who Came to Dinner was the only time she appeared on
screen with her acting idol. Coincidentally, Davis had been
romantically involved with her frequent leading man George
Brent, who was then dating Ann.
      Like many of George S. Kauffman and Moss Hart's plays,
some of the characters in The Man Who Came to Dinner have
their roots in real show business personalities. Sheridan
Whiteside, Lorraine Sheldon, Beverly Carlton, and Banjo
reportedly were based on critic Alexander Woollcott, actress
Gertrude Lawrence, actor/playwright/composer Noel Coward, and
comedian Harpo Marx. Three TV productions of the play have
been produced on CBS: January 16, 1949 with Edward Everett
Horton (Sheridan), Judith Parrish (Maggie), and Vicki
Cummings (Lorraine); October 13, 1954 with Monty Wooley
(Sheridan), Merle Oberon (Maggie), and Joan Bennett
(Lorraine); and November 29, 1972 with Orson Welles
(Sheridan), Lee Remick (Maggie), and Joan Collins (Lorraine).
A Broadway musical version called Sherry! ran for
seventy-two performances, beginning March 27, 1967. Clive
Revill (Sheridan), Elizabeth Allen (Maggie), and Dolores Gray
(Lorraine) were the stars.

See also V-10.

F-61 Kings Row   (Warner Bros., April 1942)   127 mins.

Executive producer: Hal B. Wallis. Associate producer:
David Lewis. Director: Sam Wood. Screenplay: Casey
Robinson. Based on the novel Kings Row by Henry Bellamann.
Music: Erich Wolfgang Korngold. Musical director: Leo F.
Forbstein. Orchestrations: Hugo Friedhofer. Photography:
James Wong Howe. Editor: Ralph Dawson. Art direction:
Carl Jules Weyl. Production designer: William Cameron
Menzies. Costumes: Orry-Kelly. Sound: Robert B. Lee.
Makeup: Perc Westmore. Special effects: Robert Burks.

CAST: Ann Sheridan (Randy Monaghan), Robert Cummings (Parris
Mitchell), Ronald Reagan (Drake McHugh), Betty Field
(Cassandra Tower), Charles Coburn (Dr. Henry Gordon), Claude
Rains (Dr. Alexander Tower), Judith Anderson (Mrs. Harriet
Gordon), Maria Ouspenskaya (Madame von Eln), Nancy Coleman
(Louise Gordon), Kaaren Verne (Elise Sandor), Harry Davenport
(Colonel Skeffington), Ernest Cossart (Pa Monoghan), Pat

Moriarity (Tod Monoghan), Ilka Gruning (Anna, the maid),
Minor Watson (Sam Winters), Ludwig Stossel (Dr. Berdorff),
Erwin Kalser (Mr. Sandor), Egon Brecher (Dr. Candell), Ann
Todd (Young Randy), Douglas Croft (Young Drake), Scotty
Beckett (Young Parris), Mary Thomas (Young Cassandra), Joan
Duval (Young Louise), Danny Jackson (Benny Singer), Henry
Blair (Willie), Leah Baird (Aunt Mamie), Eden Gray (Mrs.
Tower), Julie Warren (Poppy Ross), Mary Scott (Ginny Ross),
Bertha Powell (Esther), Walter Baldwin (Deputy constable),
Jack Mower (Freight conductor), Frank Mayo (Conductor),
Thomas W. Ross (Patterson Lewes), Frank Milan (Teller), Hank
Mann (Livery stable keeper), Fred Kelsey (Bill Hockinson),
Herbert Heywood (Arnold Kelly), Emory Parnell (Harley Davis),
Elizabeth Valentine (Nurse), Ludwig Hardt (Porter), Hattie
Noel (Gordon's maid), Hermine Sterler (Secretary).

SYNOPSIS: Wealthy orphan Parris Mitchell is raised by his
grandmother in the turn-of-the-century midwestern town Kings
Row. His best friends are fun-loving Drake McHugh, tomboy
Randy Monaghan, snobby Louise Gordon, and shy Cassandra
Tower. Parris prepares for his entrance exams to medical
school by studying with Cassie's father. Dr. Tower takes a
fatherly interest in Parris and introduces him to psychology.
Although Dr. Tower prohibits Parris from seeing Cassie, they
become secret lovers. After Parris's grandmother dies,
Cassie begs Parris to run away with her. Drake convinces him
that he cannot give up his dream of medicine. The town is
shocked when Dr. Tower poisons Cassie and shoots himself.
Drake pretends that he was involved with Cassie to protect
Parris's reputation. When Dr. Gordon discovers Cassie was
pregnant, he blames playboy Drake and prohibits Louise from
dating him.   Dr. Tower leaves his estate to Parris, who
learns that Dr. Tower killed Cassie because he noticed signs
of insanity in her. Parris goes to Vienna to study
psychology. Louise loves Drake, despite her parents'
objections. Drake dates Randy to make Louise jealous, but
soon falls in love with her. A bank officer embezzles funds,
leaving Drake destitute. He gets a job on the railroad and
is crushed by a freight car. To punish Drake for his
womanizing ways, Dr. Gordon unnecessarily amputates his legs.
Randy nurses Drake and insists on marrying him. Parris gives
them the Tower estate for a new beginning. With Randy's
encouragement, Drake starts a real estate development.
Parris returns to Kings Row to practice medicine. Mrs.
Gordon asks him to treat Louise, who has lost her mind.
Parris is horrified when Louise reveals that her father
sadistically performed many needless operations to punish
people. Parris considers leaving Kings Row since it holds so
many painful memories. While visiting his childhood home, he
meets pianist Elise Sandor. She helps him erase his
unpleasant memories and they fall in love. Despite the
success of the real estate development, Drake refuses to
leave his room. Randy worries that the truth about his
operation will devastate him. Parris considers committing
Louise to an asylum to silence her. Elise urges Parris to
treat Drake and Louise objectively, instead of as his
friends. Parris tells Drake the truth about his legs. The
news gives Drake courage to overcome his handicap and face

society, proving Dr. Gordon cannot defeat him.   Parris rushes
to tell Elise about his success.

REVIEWS:
Hollywood Reporter, December 23, 1941:   "No awards short of
Academy recognition can properly evaluate the achievements of
production..., direction..., screenplay...and just about as
perfect a set of performances as have ever distinguished a
Hollywood attraction....Careers are advanced through the
appearances of Robert Cummings as Parris, Ronald Reagan as
Drake, Ann Sheridan as Randy, and Betty Field as Cassie, each
giving a superior performance."

Variety, December 24, 1941:   "Ann Sheridan, in one of her
most exacting roles to date, seems too casual in the early
sequences as the clear-eyed, wholesome girl from the slums.
Her makeup for these scenes is also a handicap, having
apparently been planned more for boxoffice [sic] than
characterization.   However, Miss Sheridan rises admirably to
the emotional demands of the later scenes and gives one of
her most effective performances thus far."

Time, February 2, 1942:   "But the surprise of Kings Row
is beauteous, lazy Ann Sheridan, who manages her shanty Irish
role with credible facility.   Somebody (probably [director
Sam] Wood) has very nearly de-oomphed her."

Screenland, April 1942:   "Surprise is not to find the
lustrous name of Ann Sheridan in the cast, but to see her
playing her first serious part, and playing it beautifully.
Minus all oomphy aids, Ann is quietly convincing always, and
in several scenes genuinely moving, and if you're a Sheridan
fan you'll go to Kings Row for her performance alone."

NOTES: When Henry Bellamann's controversial 1940 novel was
announced as a film project, there was much speculation about
how it could be adapted for the screen.   The plot deals with
sadism, incest, greed, promiscuity, and mental illness,
subjects that the censors did not allow to be presented.
Among the incidents left out of the screenplay are Parris's
mercy killing of his grandmother and Drake's death from
cancer in the end.   Dr. Tower's incestuous feelings for his
daughter are explained away by having Tower kill his daughter
after seeing her insanity, thus keeping her from marrying
Parris and ruining his life.   The novel was a precurser to
small town exposes like Grace Metalious's 1956 best seller
Peyton Place.
        Humphrey Bogart first brought Kings Row to Ann
Sheridan's attention, encouraging her to fight for the role
of Randy Monaghan.   She read the book and decided Bogart was
right.   She settled her contract dispute with Warner Bros. in
exchange for the part.   It proved to be one of her best
films.   The studio originally wanted Tyrone Power for the
role played by Robert Cummings, however 20th Century-Fox
refused to loan the actor.   According to Rudy Behlmer's book
of Warner Bros. memos, Olivia de Havilland, Ida Lupino, Joan
Leslie, Susan Peters, and Priscilla Lane were among the
actresses considered for the role of for Cassie.   He also

notes that Ginger Rogers was sent a script, although it is not indicated if she would have played Cassie or Randy (B-88). Ronald Reagan was not the first choice for the part of Drake either. Among the actors considered were Dennis Morgan, Jack Carson, Jeffrey Lynn, Eddie Albert, Franchot Tone, and Robert Preston. The film ended up being Reagan's most memorable. He used his famous line, "Where's the rest of me?" as the title of his 1965 autobiography (B-526).

Reagan recalled filming the famous scene where he discovered his legs had been amputated. He spent days worrying about shooting the scene, losing sleep and going without makeup to help his performance. He remembered Ann Sheridan bursting through the door after his cries, although she was not in the shot they were filming. "[She] normally wouldn't have been on hand until we turned the camera around to get her entrance, but she knew it was one of those scenes where a fellow actor needed all the help he could get and at that moment in my mind, she was Randy answering my call" (B-526).

Ann Sheridan's one complaint about making Kings Row was that Warner Bros. forced her to film The Man Who Came to Dinner (F-60) at the same time. The shooting schedule often called for her to create two very different characterizations, with vastly different costumes, makeup, and hairstyles, on the same day. But even more upsetting to Ann was the fact that she was paid her standard salary, despite her concurrent work on two films.

Although Kings Row won wide acceptance from audiences, the inital review in the New York Times was less than complimentary, calling it "gloomy and ponderous" (February 3, 1942). Harrison's Reports deemed it a "powerful but somewhat depressing drama" that was "morally unsuitable for all" (December 27, 1941). Despite the criticism, it was nominated for three Academy Awards: Best Picture, Best Director (Sam Wood), and Best Black and White Cinematography (James Wong Howe). Mrs. Miniver (MGM, 1942) won the Oscars in all three categories. Kings Row became one of the top moneymaking films of the 1941/42 season (B-650). A colorized version often is shown on television.

Author Henry Bellaman began a sequel to his novel entitled Parris Mitchell of Kings Row, but died in 1945 before it was finished. His widow Katherine completed the book, which was published in 1948.

See also D-3, V-11.

F-62 Juke Girl (Warner Bros., May 30, 1942)   90 mins.

Executive producer: Hal B. Wallis. Associate producers: Jerry Wald and Jack Saper. Director: Curtis Bernhardt. Dialogue director: Hugh Cummings. Screenplay: A.I. Bezzerides. Adaptation: Kenneth Gamet. Based on the story "Jook Girl" by Theodore Pratt. Song "I Hates Love": M.K. Jerome and Jack Scholl. Music: Adolph Deutsch. Musical director: Leo F. Forbstein. Photography: Bert Glennon. Editor: Warren Low. Art direction: Robert Haas. Costumes: Milo Anderson. Sound: Charles Lang. Makeup: Perc Westmore.

CAST: Ann Sheridan (Lola Mears), Ronald Reagan (Steve
Talbot), Richard Whorf (Danny Frazier), Gene Lockhart (Henry
Madden), Faye Emerson (Violet "Murph" Murphy), George Tobias
(Nick Garcos), Alan Hale ("Yippee"), Betty Brewer (Skeeter),
Howard da Silva (Cully), Donald MacBride ("Muckeye" John),
Fuzzy Knight (Ike Harper), Willie Best (Jo-Mo), Willard
Robertson (Mister Just), Spencer Charters (Keene), William B.
Davidson (Paley), Frank Wilcox (Truck driver), William Haade
(Watchman), Eddy Waller (Man in car), Alan Bridge, Jack
Gardner, Fred Kelsey, Frank Pharr, Ray Teal, Bill Phillips,
Guy Wilkerson, Milton Kibbee, Ed Peil, Sr., Glenn Strange,
Victor Zimmerman (Men), Paul Burns (Ed), Frank Darien
(Elderly farmer), William Edmunds (Travitti), Dewey Robinson,
Kenneth Harlan (Dealers), Joan Fitzgerald (Juke girl), Sol
Gorss, William Gould (Deputies), William Hopper (Clerk),
Frank Mayo (Detective), Pat Flaherty (Mike), Forrest Taylor,
Clancy Cooper, Pat McVey (Farmers).

SYNOPSIS: Drifters Steve Talbot and Danny Frazier go to
Florida to find jobs in a packing plant. They take opposite
sides when crooked plant owner Henry Madden clashes with
farmer Nick Garcos. Danny takes a job in Henry's plant,
while Steve helps Nick become an independent farmer. Steve
romances juke joint hostess Lola Mears. When Henry learns
that Lola is encouraging pickers to sell their crops
independently, he has her fired. Lola is reluctant to marry
Steve because of her shady past. She takes a job in Atlanta,
insisting that Steve is better off without her. Nick gets
drunk to celebrate selling his crop. He sneeks out to make
peace with Henry. Nick begs Henry to put the past behind
them, but Henry refuses, blaming Nick for ruining his
business. During an arguement, Henry kills Nick in
self-defense. Henry panics and dumps the body in a swamp.
Henry implicates Steve in the murder, mailing Lola the money
from Nick's pocket and pointing out that Steve has the most
to gain from Nick's death. A lynch mob goes after Lola and
Steve. Danny persuades Henry to stop the mob, knowing he
controls the town. Intimidated, Henry confesses to the
murder and offers Danny a promotion to keep his secret.
Danny stops the mob by forcing Henry to tell them the truth.
Danny's wanderlust returns and he leaves town. Lola and
Steve settle down on the farm.

REVIEWS:
Variety, April 8, 1942: "Outstanding in the film is the
high degree of acting skill. [Ann] Sheridan has come far,
far from the 'oomph girl' stage."

Los Angeles Times, May 28, 1942: "Portrayals by [Ann]
Sheridan, [Ronald] Reagan, [Richard] Whorf and [Gene]
Lockhart are good enough for the material. As a matter of
fact, they are probably too good for it."

New York Times, June 20, 1942: "[Ann] Sheridan is also
able as the self-deprecating girl. But the whole smacks too
much of the synthetic. It's like a tune that comes out of a
juke box."

<u>Miami News</u> [FL], September 28, 1958: "<u>Juke Girl</u> sounds
like a poor film but if you see it, you may be pleasantly
surprised. The acting of Ann Sheridan, Ronald Reagan and
Richard Whorf is both personable and polished and the Florida
locales will have great interest for many local viewers."

NOTES: Although Ida Lupino originally was announced for the
lead in <u>Juke Girl</u>, Warner Bros. decided to cash in on the
success of <u>Kings Row</u> (F-61) and re-pair Ann Sheridan and
Ronald Reagan. Despite the stars involved, the result was a
standard "B" melodrama. Since much of the movie was filmed
at night, the actors had to rub glycerine on their faces to
simulate perspiration in the cool California air. Many of
the actors were asked to smoke cigarettes to explain the
vapor in the air. Ann's role as a juke joint hostess allowed
her to sing "I Hates Love." Her occupation was a euphemism
for prostitute.

F-63 <u>Wings for the Eagle</u>   (Warner Bros., July 1942)
      85 mins.

Producer: Robert Lord. Director: Lloyd Bacon. Dialogue
director: Hugh Cummings. Screenplay: Byron Morgan, B.H.
Orkow, and Richard Macaulay. Based on the story "Shadow of
Their Wings" by Byron Morgan and B.H. Orkow. Music:
Frederick Hollander. Musical director: Leo F. Forbstein.
Photography: Tony Gaudio. Editor: Owen Marks. Art
direction: Max Parker. Costumes: Milo Anderson. Sound:
Francis J. Scheid. Makeup: Perc Westmore. Special effects:
Byron Haskin and H.F. Koenekamp.

CAST: Ann Sheridan (Roma Maple), Dennis Morgan (Corky
Jones), Jack Carson (Brad Maple), George Tobias (Jake Hanso),
Don DeFore (Gil Borden), Russell Arms (Pete Hanso), Tom
Fadden (Tom "Cyclone" Shaw), John Ridgely (Johnson), Frank
Wilcox (Stark), George Meeker (Personnel man), Fay Helm (Miss
Baxter), Billy Curtis (Eddie), Emory Parnell (Policeman),
Edgar Dearing (Motorcycle officer), Frank Faylen (Orchestra
leader).

SYNOPSIS: Corky Jones hopes to avoid the draft by getting a
job at the Lockheed-Vega defense plant before the United
States enters World War II. He moves in with his college
friend, Brad Maple, and his wife Roma. Brad becomes
depressed and moody when he learns he has been attending a
non-accredited engineering school. He refuses to take a
menial job at the plant and fights with Corky. Roma leaves
Brad and gets a secretarial job at Lockheed. Corky befriends
coworkers Pete Hanso and his immigrant father Jake. Pete
studies hard to become a pilot and serve his country. Corky
moves in with the Hansos and dates Roma. Brad buries his
pride and gets a factory job at Lockheed. When a federal
order forbids the employment of alien defense plant workers,
Jake is dismissed. Pete wants to quit flying school in
protest, but Corky convinces him to change his mind. Jake is
proud when Pete joins the army air corps. Brad and Corky vie
for Roma's attention. Brad begs Roma to reconcile, but she
refuses. After Jake becomes a citizen, Lockheed rehires

him as supervisor. The Pearl Harbor attack leads to an
increase in production at the defense plant. Jake inspires
workers to get the two thousandth bomber off the assembly
line in record time. Corky works hard, but revels in the
fact that his essential job in an essential industry will
keep him from the draft. When Corky realizes Roma and Brad
still love each other, he helps them reconcile. With a
newfound patriotism, Corky enlists in the air corps. On the
day the two thousandth plane is finished, Jake learns that
Pete was killed in the Philippines. Inspired by his son's
death and Corky's patriotism, Jake encourages the workers to
double their efforts to win the war. In Australia, Corky
shoots down a Japanese plane in memory of Pete.

REVIEWS:
Variety, June 3, 1942: "With Ann Sheridan and Dennis
Morgan, both of whom have given excellent account of
themselves lately, in the leads, picture looks headed for
profitable takings....Ann Sheridan...furnishes just the
proper amount of femme lure to an otherwise strictly factory
yarn. It's the sort of role she does up brown."

New York Times, August 1, 1942: "...[Ann] Sheridan
continues to toss crisp retorts like flapjacks."

Modern Screen, August 1942: "Against the reality of
Lockheed, Wings for the Eagle can only pit a cooked-up plot
which has been served before in dozens of other pictures.
It's a triangle story....Angle two (rather nicely curved) is
Ann Sheridan, hard-minded, loyal and good to look at."

Movies, August 1942: "Ann Sheridan, the girl who said, 'I
regret I have but one salary to give to my country,' makes
her stellar contribution to civilian morale in this portrayal
of the personal problems of defense workers in an aircraft
plant."

NOTES: With World War II raging, Warner Bros. followed the
other studios by making patriotic films about the homefront.
This one deals with defense plant aircraft workers and urges
citizens to do their bit to help win the war. Wings for
the Eagle is dedicated to airplane factory workers.
Background footage was shot at Lockheed Aircraft Corporation.
Upon the film's release, the cast made a promotional stop at
Lockheed to urge workers to buy war bonds. The movie's
working title was Captains of the Clouds.
     Wings for the Eagle marks Ann Sheridan's first film
with Dennis Morgan, who would go on to be her leading man in
Shine On Harvest Moon (F-68) and One More Tomorrow
(F-71).

F-64 George Washington Slept Here   (Warner Bros.,
      November 1942)   93 mins.

Producer: Jerry Wald. Director: William Keighley.
Screenplay: Everett Freeman. Based on the play by George S.
Kaufman and Moss Hart. Original production produced by Sam
H. Harris. Music: Adolph Deutsch. Musical director: Leo

F. Forbstein. Photography: Ernie Haller. Montages: Don Siegel. Editor: Ralph Dawson. Art direction: Max Parker. Sets: Casey Roberts. Costumes: Orry-Kelly. Sound: Charles Lang. Makeup: Perc Westmore.

CAST: Jack Benny (Bill Fuller), Ann Sheridan (Connie Fuller), Charles Coburn (Uncle Stanley), Hattie McDaniel (Hester), Percy Kilbride (Mr. Kimber), William Tracy (Steve Eldridge), Joyce Reynolds (Madge), Lee Patrick (Rena Leslie), Charles Dingle (Mr. Prescott), John Emery (Clayton Evans), Douglas Croft (Raymond), Harvey Stephens (Jeff Douglas), Franklin Pangborn (Mr. Gibney), Chester Clute (Man), Isabel Withers (Woman), Hank Mann, Cliff Saum (Moving man), Sol Gorss, Glenn Cavender (Well diggers), Dudley Dickerson (Porter), Jack Mower (Passenger), Gertrude Carr (Wife).

SYNOPSIS: Businessman Bill Fuller is content living in a Manhattan apartment with his antique-loving wife Connie and her boy-crazy sister Madge. When their dog destroys the building's rug, they are evicted. Although Bill wants to find another apartment in New York, Connie buys a ramshackle colonial cottage in Pennsylvania without his knowledge. Connie is attracted by a legend that George Washington once slept there. Reluctantly, Bill moves to the country, finding the house even worse than he imagined, with rotting floors, missing walls, and a dry well. At every turn, the inept caretaker, Mr. Kimber, offers unsolicited advice and more expenses. After a few months, Bill's resources are tapped, with remodeling, taxes, repairs, and Kimber's constant drilling for water. Bill is upset when Connie's mischievous nephew Raymond and wealthy uncle Stanley come for extended visits. Even more daunting is a neighbor's threat to foreclose on the Fullers' home unless they can pay the five thousand-dollar mortgage in two days. Bill admits that he likes the country. They try to borrow against their inheritance, but Stanley confesses that his wealth is a myth. Defeated, the Fullers plan to return to New York. Their dog saves the house when he discovers a letter from George Washington in an old boot Kimber found while digging a well. The letter not only authenticates Washington's stay, but its value more than pays for the mortgage. As the seventeen-year locusts arrive, the Fullers find water on their farm, much to Kimber's delight.

REVIEWS:
Harrison's Reports, September 19, 1942: "Considering the drawing power of Jack Benny and Ann Sheridan, and the fame the play gained as a Broadway stage hit, this picture should do good business. It is a pretty good comedy, patterned in a manner that does justice to Jack Benny's type of humor. The story lacks a substantial plot, but some of the dialogue is bright, and several of the situations extremely comical."

Variety, September 23, 1942: "[Ann] Sheridan performs nicely as [Jack] Benny's wife, evoking sympathy now and then because of her intense desire for things rustic and antique, a desire that almost meets with complete frustration."

New York Times, October 31, 1942:   "[Ann] Sheridan plays
straight to [Jack Benny's] foibles, but does so quite
fetchingly..."

Screenland, February 1943:   "Jack Benny and Ann Sheridan
prove a piquant team as Mr. and Mrs. in this amusing
picturization of the [George S.] Kaufman-[Moss] Hart stage
play.....This will give you some hearty laughs."

NOTES: George Washington Slept Here was Ann Sheridan's
second film based on a play by George S. Kaufman and Moss
Hart. The show ran 173 performances, beginning October 18,
1940. Coincidentally, the original stage production was
produced by George Brent's brother-in-law, Sam H. Harris.
Several changes were made in transfering the comedy to the
screen. The most obvious was the reversing of the roles,
with the husband wanting to move to the country in the stage
version. The characters also were older in the play.
Onstage, Madge was their daughter, rather than the wife's
sister. Percy Kilbride created his part of Mr. Kimber on
Broadway. He later became best known for his role as Pa
Kettle in a series of Universal films.
      Ann Sheridan replaced Olivia de Havilland, who
originally was scheduled to star in George Washington Slept
Here. It gave Ann the chance to work with Jack Benny, who
remained a friend through the years. Benny's wife Mary
Livingstone was suspicious that the relationship was more
than platonic. In her autobiography, Livingstone said she
was suspicious that Benny had an affair with Ann.
Livingstone recalled that George Brent was upset when the
comedian sent his wife flowers. Livingstone invited Ann to a
party and confronted her. "Miss Sheridan," she said, "I
don't know whether you like Jack or he likes you, but you are
making a picture together and I wanted to remind you of
something. Jack wouldn't give my little finger for your
whole body." When Ann reported Livingstone's outburst to
Benny, he told his wife that she did not have to worry
(B-91). Ironically, Livingstone almost was cast opposite her
husband when Ann was delayed during an army camp tour (P-7).
Ann returned and the film was able to start on time (B-92).
Ann and Benny reprised their roles on several radio
broadcasts (R-4 and R-9).
      Max Parker, Mark-Lee Kirk, and Casey Roberts were
nominated for an Academy Award for Best Art Direction. They
lost to Richard Day, Joseph Wright, and Thomas Little for
This Above All (20th Century-Fox, 1942).

See also R-4, R-9, V-12.

F-65 Edge of Darkness   (Warner Bros., April 24, 1943)
      120 mins.

Producer: Henry Blanke. Director: Lewis Milestone.
Dialogue director: Herschel Daugherty. Screenplay: Robert
Rossen. Based on the novel by William Woods. Music: Franz
Waxman. Musical director: Leo F. Forbstein.
Orchestrations: Leon Radd. Photography: Sid Hickox.
Montages: Don Siegel and James Leicester. Editor: David

Weisbart. Art direction: Robert Haas. Sets: Julia Heron.
Costumes: Orry-Kelly. Sound: Everett A. Brown. Makeup:
Perc Westmore. Special effects: Lawrence Butler and
William Van Enger. Technical advisors: Frank U. Peter
Pohlenz, E. Wessel Klausen, and Gerard Lambert.

CAST: Errol Flynn (Gunnar Brogge), Ann Sheridan (Karen
Stensgard), Walter Huston (Dr. Martin Stensgard), Nancy
Coleman (Katja), Helmut Dantine (Capt. Haumptman Koenig),
Judith Anderson (Gerd Bjarnesen), Ruth Gordon (Anna
Stensgard), John Beal (Johann Stensgard), Roman Bohnen (Lars
Malken), Charles Dingle (Kaspar Torgerson), Morris Carnovsky
(Sixtus Andresen), Art Smith (Knut Osterholm), Richard Fraser
(Pastor Aalesen), Tom Fadden (Hammer), Henry Brandon (Major
Ruck), Tonio Selwart (Paul), Helene Thimig (Frida), Frank
Wilcox (Jensen), Francis Pierlot (Mortensen), Lottie Williams
(Mrs. Mortensen), Monte Blue (Petersen), Dorothy Tree
(Solveig Brategaard), Virginia Christine (Hulda), Henry
Rowland (Helmut), Kurt Katch (German captain), Kurt Kreuger
(German aviator), Peter Van Eyck (German soldier), Vera Lewis
(Woman), Torben Meyer (Clerk), Walt LaRue (Villager), William
Edmunds (Elderly sailor), Vic Potel, Richard Kipling (Men),
Fred Giermann, Rolf Lindau, Peter Michael (German soldiers).

SYNOPSIS: Fisherman Gunnar Brogge and his fiancee Karen
Stensgard lead the Norwegian resistance against the Nazis.
Karen's brother Johann is forced to spy on the resistance by
his uncle, a Nazi activist who runs the town cannery. When
the resisters catch Johann spying, he is ostracized into the
Nazi headquarters. Nazi captain Hauptman Koenig tries to
defeat the Norwegians by confiscating their supplies,
enforcing strict curfews, and torturing an elderly teacher.
The atrocities unite the citizens, who plan to take over the
city with British-supplied weapons. After Karen is raped by
one of the Nazis, her father kills her attacker. Hauptman
sentences all the resistance leaders to death for his crime.
As the leaders dig their own graves, the other citizens fight
the Nazis, unafraid to die. They rush to regain control of
their city before the Nazi patrol arrives. The Nazis kill
Johann after he warns the Norwegians about a Nazi trap. As
the Norwegians attack the garrison, Hauptman commits suicide.
Although the Nazi patrol concludes a Nazi victory, Karen
establishes the real victors, shooting a Nazi soldier who
tries to replace the Norwegian flag with the German one.
Gunnar, Karen, and the others take to the hills to continue
their fight for their country.

REVIEWS:
Variety, March 24, 1943: "Best feature of the film is its
cast. Errol Flynn and Ann Sheridan, as the stars, provide
the proper romantic note, plus the necessary dash as the
leaders of the Trollness underground....There isn't a single
weak performance in the picture..."

Harrison's Reports, March 27, 1943: "Excellent! Of the
numerous films produced recently, dealing with Norway's
struggle against the Nazi invader, none surpass, and few
approach, this picture's powerful and grim depiction of the

Nazi's ruthlessness and bestiality, and of the Norwegian
people's dogged determination to resist oppression. It is
the type of picture audiences will not forget soon, for its
dramatic impact makes a deep impression on one. Lewis
Milestone's direction is masterful, and the performances,
from the stars to the bit players, are superb....Errol
Flynn...and Ann Sheridan...turn in inspired performances."

New York Times, April 10, 1943: "If its flavor is strongly
melodramatic, if its conflict is simple and direct and if
Errol Flynn, Ann Sheridan and others in it seem odd sort of
folk for Norway, it is still a finely jointed motion
picture....Mr. Flynn and Miss Sheridan...act mainly by
looking alert."

NOTES: Edge of Darkness is based on William Wood's 1942
novel. Filmed in Monterey, California, the production was
plagued with delays, including intense fog, which made the
shooting extend over schedule. Judith Anderson and Ruth
Gordon were due in New York for a Broadway production of The
Three Sisters so they were especially anxious to wind up the
movie before their opening in December 1942.
     During the filming of Edge of Darkness, Errol Flynn
was accused of statutory rape by two young women with whom he
had consensual sex in 1941 and 1942. Ann Sheridan remembered
the actor entertaining the cast and crew with tales about the
trial, which ended in an acquittal. Despite Flynn's
reputation as a hell-raiser, Ann enjoyed working with him,
calling him "always strictly fun" (B-475).
     Ann separated from George Brent during Edge of
Darkness. There are unsubstantiated rumors that George
caught Ann in bed with her co-star during the filming. The
actors fought, with Errol Flynn the victor. The Brents were
divorced on January 5, 1943.
     In recent years, Edge of Darkness has been colorized.

See also V-13.

F-66   Thank Your Lucky Stars   (Warner Bros., September
       1943)   127 mins.

Producer: Mark Hellinger. Director: David Butler.
Dialogue director: Herbert Farjeon. Choreographer: LeRoy
Prinz. Screenplay: Norman Panama, Melvin Frank, and James
V. Kern. Based on a story by Everett Freeman and Arthur
Schwartz. Songs: Arthur Schwartz, Frank Loesser, Johnny
Mercer, Al Sherman, Al Lewis, and Harold Arlen. Musical
director: Leo F. Forbstein. Orchestrations: Ray Heindorf.
Vocal arrangements: Dudley Chambers. Photography: Arthur
Edeson. Editor: Irene Morra. Art direction: Anton Grot
and Leo E. Kuter. Sets: Walter F. Tilford. Costumes:
Milo Anderson. Sound: Francis J. Scheid and Charles David
Forrest. Makeup: Perc Westmore. Special effects: H.F.
Koenekamp.

CAST: Eddie Cantor (Joe Simpson/himself), Dennis Morgan
(Tommy Randolph), Joan Leslie (Pat Dixon), Dinah Shore
(Herself), S.Z. Sakall (Dr. Schlenna), Edward Everett Horton

(Farnsworth), Ruth Donnelly (Nurse Hamilton), Richard Lane
(Barney Jackson), Don Wilson (Himself), Henry Armetta
(Angelo), Humphrey Bogart, Jack Carson, Bette Davis, Olivia
de Havilland, Errol Flynn, John Garfield, Alan Hale, Ida
Lupino, Ann Sheridan, Alexis Smith, George Tobias, Spike
Jones and His City Slickers (Specialties), Frank Faylen
(Sailor), Creighton Hale, Jack Mower (Engineers), Noble
Johnson (Charlie, the Indian), Ed Gargan (Doorman), Billy
Benedict (Busboy), Hank Mann (Assistant photographer), Don
Barclay (Pete), Stanley Clements, James Copedge (Boys), Leah
Baird, Joan Matthews, Phyllis Godfrey, Lillian West, Morgan
Brown, George French (Bus passengers), Joe De Rita
(Milquetoast type), Eleanor Counts (Sailor's girlfriend),
Charles Soldani, J.W. Cody (Indians), Harry Pilcer (Man in
broadcasting station), Mike Mazurki (Olaf), Bennie Bartlett
(Page boy), Marjorie Hoshelle, Anne O'Neal (Maids), Jerry
Mandy (Chef), Betty Farrington (Assistant chef), William
Haade (Butler), Lou Marcelle (Commentator), Mary Treen (Fan),
Juanita Stark (Secretary), Paul Harvey (Dr. Kirby), Bert
Gordon (Patient), David Butler, Mark Hellinger (Themselves),
Billy Wayne (Chauffeur), Howard Mitchell, James Flavin
(Policemen), Dick Rich (Fred), Ralph Dunn (Marty), James
Burke (Bill, the intern guard), Frank Mayo (Dr. Wheaton),
Angi O. Poulos (Waiter), Boyd Irwin (Man), Helen O'Hara (Show
girl), Harriette Haddon, Harriett Olsen, Joy Barlowe, Nancy
Worth, Janet Barrett, Dorothy Schoemer, Dorothy Dayton,
Lucille LaMarr, Mary Landa, Sylvia Opert (The Lucky Stars),
Matt McHugh (Fireman in Bogart sequence); "Love Isn't Born,
It's Made" number: Georgia Lee Settle, Virginia Patton
(Girls), Joyce Reynolds (Girl with book); "Ice Cold Katie"
number: Hattie McDaniel (Gossip), Rita Christiani (Ice Cold
Katie), Willie Best (Soldier), Jess Lee Brooks (Justice),
Ford, Harris and Jones (Trio), Matthew Jones (Gambler);
"That's What You Jolly Well Get" number: Monte Blue
(Bartender), Art Foster, Fred Kelsey, Elmer Ballard, Buster
Wiles, Howard Davies, Tudor Williams, Alan Cook, Fred McEvoy,
Bobby Hale, Will Stanton, Charles Irwin, David Thursby, Henry
Ibling, Earl Hunsaker, Hubert Hend, Dudley Kuzello, Ted
Billings (Pub characters); "You're Either Too Young or Too
Old" number: Jack Norton (Drunk), Henri DeSoto (Maitre
d'hotel), Dick Elliott, Dick Earle (Customers), Harry Adams
(Doorman), Sam Adams (Bartender), Conrad Wiedell (Jitterbug),
Charles Francis, Harry Bailey (Bald men), Joan Winfield
(Cigarette girl), Nancy Worth, Sylvia Opert (Hatcheck girls);
"Good Night, Good Neighbor" number: Igor DeNavrotsky
(Dancer), Brandon Hurst (Cab driver), Angelita Mari (Duenna),
Lynne Baggett (Miss Latin America), Mary Landa (Miss Spain).

SONGS: "They're Either Too Young or Too Old," "That's What
You Jolly Well Get," "Ice Cold Katie," "Love Isn't Born, It's
Made," "Thank Your Lucky Stars," "The Dreamer," "I'm Ridin'
for a Fall," "We're Staying Home Tonight," "Goin' North," "No
You, No Me," "How Sweet You Are," "Good Night, Good Neighbor"
(Schwartz, Loesser), "Blues in the Night" (Mercer, Arlen),
"Otchi Tchorniya"/"Hotcha Cornia" (Russian folk song), "Now's
the Time to Fall in Love" (Sherman, Lewis).

SYNOPSIS: Egocentric comedian Eddie Cantor refuses to let

his protegee Dinah Shore appear in an all-star charity
benefit unless he can appear as well. Producers Schlenna and
Farnsworth try to outsmart Cantor, but· he soon takes over
their show. Meanwhile, dramatic actor Joe Simpson laments
that his resemblance to Cantor keeps him from getting acting
roles. Joe's friends, songwriter Pat Dixon and singer Tommy
Randolph, try to get Tommy a role in the benefit, but Cantor
refuses. Pat and Tommy convince Joe to masquerade as Cantor
at the benefit so Tommy can sing. They arrange for Cantor to
be kidnapped so the switch can take place. The producers are
thrilled with the new, charming Cantor, whose only demand is
for Tommy to sing. The real Cantor escapes and hides in an
asylum, where he is mistaken for a mental patient. Tommy is
offered a Warner Bros. contract after his song scores a big
success at the benefit. Cantor brings the police to the
theatre to interrupt the show. Pat convinces Joe to continue
his charade as Cantor. Dinah Shore and Cantor's assistant
identify Joe as their boss. Cantor is evicted while Joe
finishes the show.

REVIEWS:
Variety, August 18, 1943: "With virtually all the stars
and featured performers on the Warner lot written into the
script for bit sequences, the new Eddie Cantor-Dinah Shore WB
musical Thank Your Lucky Stars is a [box office] natural
that'll garner top grosses everywhere....Ann Sheridan also
[is] spotted for a vocalization of one of the better numbers,
'Love Isn't Born, It's Made.'"

Harrison's Reports, August 21, 1943: "Good mass
attraction. The expensive production and the combination of
Eddie Cantor and virtually all the Warner Brothers' [sic]
stars and featured players should assure excellent box-office
returns. The story is ordinary and unimportant; it is used
as a framework for Cantor's gags and to tie together the
musical numbers and the stars' specialty routines. It has a
few slow moments, but for the most part it is a peppy
entertainment with plentiful comedy, music, and dancing."

New York Times, October 2, 1943: "It does seem that Warner
Bros. could have thought up a better device for getting their
stars before the camera to do their acts than this rather
testy one....Overlook it and you have a conventional all-star
show which has the suspicious flavor of an 'amateur night' at
the studio. But at least it is lively and genial. All the
'benefit performers' have fun....Ann Sheridan gives a saucy
once-over to the ditty 'Love Isn't Born, It's Made.'"

Photoplay, January 1944: "Dennis Morgan and Joan Leslie
attempt to crash the benefit, in which such stars as Bette
Davis, Errol Flynn, Ann Sheridan, Jack Carson and Olivia de
Havilland shine brightly."

NOTES: Thank Your Lucky Stars was one of Warner Bros.'s
entries in the all-star extravaganza race meant to boost
morale during World War II. Most of the studio's stars were
utilized in the benefit sequence, with even the most dramatic
performers doing song and dance routines. Where else could

audiences see Errol Flynn spoofing his own image in "That's
What You Jolly Well Get," Bette Davis singing and
jitterbugging to "They're Either Too Young or Too Old," and
George Tobias, Ida Lupino, and Olivia de Havilland (with a
voice dubbed by Lynn Martin) singing and dancing to a jazzy
rendition of "The Dreamer?" Each of the stars were paid
fifty thousand dollars for their cameos, which was supposed
to be turned over to the Hollywood Canteen for war efforts
(B-431). The movie became one of the top moneymaking films
of the 1943/44 season (B-650).
     Ann Sheridan appears in a bedroom scene, advising a
group of girls that "Love Isn't Born, It's Made." She also
is seen in the all-star finale, which combines joint
performances from some of the stars with clips of others.
Ann's snippet obviously was filmed at another time, since she
does not interact with any of the other actors. Although Ann
had hoped to go on a U.S.O. tour before comitting to any more
movies, she appeared in Thank Your Lucky Stars as a favor
to producer Mark Hellinger. As soon as her scenes were shot,
she flew to Mexico to divorce George Brent.

See also D-9, S-7, V-14.

F-67 Let's Carry On   (1943)

NOTES: Ann Sheridan appears in a Red Cross Roll Call
trailer, playing a Red Cross nurse. She talks about the
organization's work and urges moviegoers to join.

F-68   Shine On Harvest Moon   (Warner Bros., April 8,
      1944)   112 mins.   black and white and Technicolor

Producer: William Jacobs. Director: David Butler.
Dialogue director: Hugh Cummings. Choreographer: LeRoy
Prinz. Screenplay: Sam Hellman, Richard Weil, Francis
Swann, and James Kern. Based on a story by Richard Weil.
Songs: Jack Norworth, Nora Bayes, M.K. Jerome, Kim Gannon,
Harry Gifford, Huntley Trevor, Tom Mellor, Harry Williams,
Henry I. Marshall, C.W. Murphy, Hugh Owen, Dan Lipton, Jean
Schwartz, William Jerome, Gus Edwards, Vincent Bryan, Egbert
Van Alstyne, Gus Kahn, Tony Jackson, Cliff Friend, Charles
Tobias, Otto Harbach, Karl Hoschna, Seymour B. Simons, Albert
Von Tilzer, Haven Gillespie, Richard A. Whiting, Harry Dacre,
Stanley Murphy, Seymour Brown, Nat D. Ayer, Stanislaus
Stange, and Julian Edwards. Musical adaptation: H.
Roemheld. Musical director: Leo F. Forbstein. Vocal
arrangements: Dudley Chambers. Orchestrations: Frank
Perkins. Photography: Arthur Edeson. Montages: James
Leicester. Editor: Irene Morra. Art direction: Charles
Novi. Sets: Jack McConaghy. Costumes: Milo Anderson.
Sound: Dolph Thomas and David Forrest. Makeup: Perc
Westmore. Special effects: Edwin A. DuPar.

CAST: Ann Sheridan (Nora Bayes), Dennis Morgan (Jack
Norworth), Jack Carson (The Great Georgetti), Irene Manning
(Blanche Mallory), S.Z. Sakall (Poppa Karl), Marie Wilson
(Margie), Robert Shayne (Dan Costello), Bob Murphy (Police
sergeant), the Four Step Brothers, the Ashburns (Dance

teams), William B. Davidson (Tim Donovan), Will Stanton
(Drunk), James Bush (William Fowler), Joseph Crehan (Harry
Miller), Betty Bryson (Soubrette), Don Kramer, George Rogers
(Dancers), Harry Charles Johnson (Juggler), Walter Pietilla
(Acrobat), Paul Panzer (Doorman), Al Hill (Captain of
waiters), Mike Mazurki, Frank Hagney (Bouncers), Jack Norton,
Bert Roach (Drunks), Nestor Paiva (Romero, the chef), Charles
Marsh, Tom Quinn, Jack Boyle, Duke Johnson, Billy Bletcher,
Peggy Carson, Anita Pike, Doria Caron (Vaudevillians), Gino
Corrado (Cook), Brandon Hurst (Watchman), Johnnie Berkes,
Bill Young (Tramp ambassadors in "My Own United States"
number), Jack Daley, Mike Donovan, Frank McCarroll, Charles
McAvoy, Kernan Cripps, Thomas Murray, George McDonald, Bob
Reeves, Bill O'Leary, Charles McMurphy, Allen D. Sewell
(Policemen in "It Looks to Me Like a Big Night Tonight"
number), Doodles Weaver (Elevator operator).

SONGS: "So Dumb But So Beautiful," "We're Doing Our Best,"
"Don't Let the Rainy Days Get You," "Thank You for the
Dance," "I Go for You" (M.K. Jerome, Gannon), "Shine On
Harvest Moon" (Norworth, Bayes), "When It's Apple Blossom
Time in Normandy" (Gifford, Trevor, Mellor), "What's the
Matter with Father?," "It Looks Like a Big Night Tonight,"
"San Antonio" (Williams, Van Alstyne), "Pretty Baby" (Kahn,
Jackson), "Time Waits for No One" (Friend, Tobias), "Every
Little Movement Has a Meaning of Its Own" (Harbach, Hoschna),
"Just Like a Gypsy" (Simons, Bayes), "Take Me Out to the Ball
Game" (Norworth, Von Tilzer), "Along with the Breeze"
(Gillespie, Simons, Whiting), "A Bicycle Built for Two"
(Dacre), "Be My Little Baby Bumblebee" (Murphy, Marshall),
"Oh You Beautiful Doll" (Brown, Ayer), "My Own United States"
(Stange, J. Edwards), "How Can They Tell That I'm Irish?"
(Murphy, Bayes, Norworth), "Mister Dooley" (Schwartz, W.
Jerome), "He's Me Pal," "In My Merry Oldsmobile" (G. Edwards,
Bryan), "I've a Garden in Sweden" (Murphy, Owen, Lipton,
Bayes, Norworth), "Who's Your Honey Lamb?" (M.K. Jerome,
Scholl).

SYNOPSIS: Vaudevillian/songwriter Jack Norworth helps
singers Blanche Mallory and Nora Bayes form a sister act.
Blanche quits because she is jealous of Nora's success, as
well as her relationship with Jack. Despite Jack's
reluctance to have a partner, he teams with Nora and finds
success. They marry and prepare to sign a lucrative
vaudeville contract. The act is blacklisted from a powerful
theatre chain, which is owned by Nora's former boss. Jack
tries to convince Blanche to sing his composition "Shine On
Harvest Moon" in her act, but she refuses unless Jack will be
her partner. Nora leaves Jack, afraid she is holding back
his career. Devastated, Jack works alone in vaudeville,
still refusing to team with Blanche. Friend and agent Poppa
Karl tries to reunite the Norworths. After he explains that
Jack refused to work with Blanche because he loves his wife,
Nora attends Jack's vaudeville opening. When Jack forgets
his lyrics, Nora joins him onstage. A Ziegfeld scout spots
them and hires them for the <u>Follies of 1907</u>. Successful
and reconciled, Nora and Jack happily sing "Shine On Harvest
Moon" in the <u>Follies</u>.

REVIEWS:
Harrison's Reports, March 11, 1944: "The individual
performances are good, but the story...presents nothing
novel....In contrast with most musicals, however, it has
human interest, awakened by the affection between Ann
Sheridan and Dennis Morgan....Miss Sheridan...does well; her
singing voice has a sympathetic, throaty quality, which is
reminiscent of [Nora] Bayes' voice."

Variety, March 15, 1944: "[Ann] Sheridan displays a good
soundtrack singing 'voice' for solos and harmonies with
[Dennis] Morgan....Morgan and Miss Sheridan excellently team
to maintain interest in their characterizations, and pair
gets major support from [Irene] Manning, [Jack] Carson, and
[Marie] Wilson."

New York Times, March 16, 1944: "...this musical film in
which [Nora Bayes] and her second husband, Jack Norworth, are
supposedly represented in their joint and devoted careers is
no more veracious to the real thing than if it were a story
of Alice Faye....As for the performances of [Ann] Sheridan
and [Dennis] Morgan in the pseudo-biographical roles, we can
only say that history does not repeat itself."

Screenland, September 1944: "The pictures sees fit to call
the girl 'Nora Bayes' and the man 'Jack Norworth,' although
neither Ann Sheridan nor Dennis Morgan lends much credence to
recollections of these famed real-life entertainers."

NOTES: Shine On Harvest Moon was a highly fictionalized
account of the careers of husband-and-wife entertainers Nora
Bayes and Jack Norworth. Bayes was one of the best known
singers in vaudeville; Norworth was a prolific composer who
wrote "Shine On Harvest Moon" and "Take Me Out to the Ball
Game." Together, they were known as "The Happiest Married
Couple of the Stage." However, their billing as "Nora Bayes,
Assisted and Admired by Jack Norworth" indicates the egotism
and inequality in the partnership. The real lives of Bayes
and Norworth did not end as happily as the Technicolor finale
suggests. According to film and theatre historian Anthony
Slide, Bayes's career declined due to her own temperament.
And, while the film suggests the couple reconciled and lived
happily ever after, the real Bayes and Norworth divorced in
1913. She went on to marry three times and died of cancer
in 1928. Norworth died in 1959 (B-635). Warner Bros. played
with other facts for dramatic purposes as well. Although
Bayes appeared in Ziegfeld's first Follies in 1907, "Shine
On Harvest Moon" was introduced in the Ziegfeld Follies of
1908, not 1907 as the film suggests. Even the score mixed
in many songs that were written by other composers.
     The majority of the movie was shot in black and white,
but the ten-minute musical finale was filmed in Technicolor.
While the same technique had been a novelty ten years earlier
in Kid Millions (United Artists, 1934), giving a scene set
in an ice cream factory a fantasy feeling, the Technicolor
bit in Shine On Harvest Moon looks like it was tacked on at
the last minute. Even with wartime restrictions on color
film, it left audiences wondering why Warner Bros. had not

given <u>Shine On Harvest Moon</u> more financial backing and allowed the whole film to be shot in color.

According to records at the Warner Bros. Archive of Historical Papers, USC School of Cinema-Television, Ann's voice is dubbed by Lynn Martin. The plot calls for her to perform many songs in a variety of settings. At the honkytonk, she sings "My Own United States" and "Time Waits for No One." In the sister act, she performs "We're Doing Our Best" and "Don't Let the Rainy Days Get You" with Irene Manning and does a solo on "How Can They Tell That I'm Irish?" She sings a medley with Dennis Morgan, illustrating the Bayes/Norworth act, including "When It's Apple Blossom Time in Normandy," "Take Me Out to the Ball Game," "Along with the Breeze," and "Who's Your Honey Lamb?." Morgan fantasizes about performing "I Go for You." As a song plugger, Ann demonstrates "Just Like a Gypsy." In the Technicolor finale, Ann and Dennis Morgan sing "Shine On Harvest Moon," while the chorus, Jack Carson, Marie Wilson, and the Four Step Brothers reprise other songs.

See also S-8.

F-69   **The Doughgirls**   (Warner Bros., November 1944)
        102 mins.

Producer: Mark Hellinger. Director: James V. Kern. Dialogue director: Jack Gage. Screenplay: James V. Kern and Sam Hellman. Additional dialogue: Wilkie Mahoney. Based on the play by Joseph A. Fields. Music: Adolph Deutsch. Musical director: Leo F. Forbstein. Photography: Ernest Haller. Montages: Jack Leicester. Editor: Folmer Blangsted. Art direction: Hugh Reticker. Sets: Clarence Stensen. Costumes: Milo Anderson. Sound: Stanley Jones. Makeup: Perc Westmore. Special effects: William McCann. Technical adviser: Nicholas Kobliansky.

CAST: Ann Sheridan (Edna Stokes), Alexis Smith (Nan Curtis), Jane Wyman (Vivian Marsden), Eve Arden (Natalia Moskarova), Jack Carson (Arthur Halstead), Charles Ruggles (Stanley Slade), Alan Mowbray (Breckenridge Drake), Irene Manning (Sylvia Cadman), John Ridgely (Julian Cadman), John Alexander (Buckley), Craig Stevens (Tom Dillon), Barbara Brown (Elizabeth Brush Cartwright), Stephen Richards [Mark Stevens] (Lieutenant Keary), Francis Pierlot (Mr. Jordan), Donald MacBride (Judge Franklin), Regis Toomey (Timothy Walsh), Joe De Rita (Stranger), John Walsh (Bellhop), Grandon Rhodes, Tom Quinn (Clerks), Fred Kelsey (Man with suitcase), Dink Trout (Young husband), John Hamilton (Businessman), Almira Sessions, Minerva Urecal (Hatchet-faced women), Earle Dewey (Fat man), Dolores Conlon, Dorothy Reisner, Helen Gerald, Joan Breslaw, Yoland Baiano, Julie Arlington (Schoolgirls), Harry Tyler (Angular man), Marie de Becker, Anita Bolster (Maids), Joan Winfield (Slade's secretary), Oliver Blake (Porter), Elmer Jerome (Elderly waiter), Lou Marcelle (Announcer's voice), Warren Mills, Dick Hirbe, William Frambes (Bellboys), Ralph Sanford (Workman), Jack Mower, John O'Connor (Technicians), Larry Rio (Attendant in baths), Carlyle Blackwell, Jr. (Messenger), Nick Kobliansky (Father

Nicolai), Will Fowler (Lieutenant), Walter DePalma (Justice of the peace).

SYNOPSIS: Newlywed Arthur Halstead is upset when his wife Vivian Marsden invites her friends to share their honeymoon suite because of the room shortage in wartime Washington, D.C. Coincidentally, both Edna Stokes and Nan Curtis also are new brides. When all three learn their marriages are invalid, they evict Arthur from the suite. Guerilla fighter Natalia Moskarova visits from the Russian embassy and moves in with the women. Arthur refuses to remarry Vivian or pay the hotel bill until she gets rid of her friends. Vivian is forced to pawn her earrings to pay the hotel bill. Arthur's boss, Stanley Slade, proposes to Vivian, despite her involvement with Arthur. Vivian pawns Stanley's ring in order to reclaim her earrings and win back Arthur. Nan's fiance returns from a heroic war mission and they rush to legalize their marriage before a White House luncheon. Edna's fiance learns his divorce is valid after all, making him free to marry Edna. Natalia brings a Russian priest to marry both couples. When Arthur learns Vivian is not interested in Stanley, they make it a triple wedding. Everyone leaves and the Halsteads finally have the suite to themselves.

REVIEWS:
Hollywood Reporter, August 30, 1944: "It's zany. It's farcical. It's rowdy. It is one of the funniest pictures of this or any year and is a practically flawless job in its field from every angle....Without exception the cast is superlative. Ann Sheridan...[is] the slightly hard-boiled ex-chorine, tossing off her lines with a flair..."

Newsweek, September 4, 1944: "Least benefited by this misguided tolerance [of first-time director James V. Kern] is Ann Sheridan who has developed into a competent actress, but who lacks the comedienne's light touch."

Los Angeles Examiner, November 24, 1944: "Zany, crazy, but with a lot of laughs on the sex-y [sic] side, 'Doughgirls' opened...yesterday to resounding guffaws. A little naughty, with such charmers as Ann Sheridan, Alexis Smith and Jane Wyman to make everything oomphful, this Warner comedy follows the popular stage play almost intact to the screen....Cast is tops, with Ann Sheridan perhaps the top-est [sic] as the slightly hardboiled ex-chorine with some wonderful lines to speak."

Motion Picture, November 1944: "Ann Sheridan, Jane Wyman and Alexis Smith are the unwed matrons and their partners in sin are Jack Carson, John Ridgely and Craig Stevens....The girls look gorgeous and use their talents effectively while trying to evolve plans that will make them honest women."

NOTES: The Doughgirls was based on the hit Broadway comedy, which opened December 30, 1942 and ran for 671 performances. Virginia Field, Doris Nolan, Arleen Whelan and Arlene Francis created the roles respetively played by Ann

Sheridan, Alexis Smith, Jane Wyman, and Eve Arden in the movie. Ann Sheridan was in New York when Warner Bros. decided to cast her in The Doughgirls. Since the play still was running on Broadway, she went to see it, immediatly deciding that there was not an appropriate part for her. She also worried about the censors pruning the script, which dealt with infidelity. The studio threatened to suspend her if she refused the film. In the end, she agreed to do it because she liked producer Mark Hellinger. Her character, who had been a mistress onstage, was now a bride who learned her marriage was invalid. Ann had to convince co-star Jane Wyman to do the comedy. According to biographers Joe Morella and Edward Z. Epstein, Wyman thought of risking suspension because she did not think the film or fourth billing could advance her career, despite its "A" picture status (B-369). Screen spouses Alexis Smith (Nan) and Craig Stevens (Tom) married in real life on June 8, 1944.

F-70   Overseas Roundup   (Vitaphone, March 17, 1945)
       10 mins.

CAST: America's Gas Bag Fleet, Merrill's Mauraders, Ann Sheridan, Ben Blue, U.S.O. troupe.

REVIEW:
The Exhibitor, April 18, 1943: "Most of this is familiar, and is not presented with any degree of freshness. Nor are there any new angles except that it is wholly devoted to happenings in the service."

NOTES: This Vitaphone Varieties short utilizes newsreel footage from the fighting fronts during World War II. Ann Sheridan appears in a segment about her U.S.O. visit to the China-Burma-India theatre (P-9). Other sections focus on blimps in America's Gas Bag Fleet, camp activities at Bougainville, a secret road to Russia, and a raid on Burma with Merrill's Mauraders.

F-71   One More Tomorrow   (Warner Bros., June 1, 1946)
       88 mins.

Producer: Henry Blanke. Director: Peter Godfrey. Screenplay: Charles Hoffman, Catherine Turney, Julius J. Epstein, and Philip G. Epstein. Based on the play The Animal Kingdom by Philip Barry. Song "One More Tomorow": Ernesto Lecuona, Eddie DeLange, and Josef Myrow. Music: Max Steiner. Musical director: Leo F. Forbstein. Photography: Bert Glennon. Editor: David Weisbart. Art direction: Anton Grot. Sets: George James Hopkins. Costumes: Milo Anderson. Sound: Dolph Thomas. Makeup: Perc Westmore.

CAST: Ann Sheridan (Christie Sage), Dennis Morgan (Tom Collier), Jack Carson (Pat Regan), Alexis Smith (Cecelia Henry), John Loder (Owen Arthur), Jane Wyman (Frankie Connors), Reginald Gardiner (Jim Fisk), Marjorie Gateson (Edna), Thurston Hall (Rufus Collier), John Abbott (Joseph Baronova), Sig Arno (Poppa Diaduska), Marjorie Hoshelle (Illa Baronova), William Benedict (Office boy), John Alvin

(Announcer), Henri DeSoto (Headwaiter), Hal K. Dawson
(Guest), Otto Hoffman (Stationmaster), Mary Field (Maude
Miller), Frances Morris (Young woman), Fred Essler (Picard),
Danny Jackson (Orson Curry), Frank Coghlan, Jr. (Telegraph
boy), Lynne Baggett, Gertrude Carr, Robert Hutton, Juanita
Stark, Lottie Williams, Joan Winfield (Party guests).

SYNOPSIS: Wealthy playboy Tom Collier is intrigued by
photographer Christie Sage, whom he meets in 1939. Charmed
by Christie and her artistic friends, Tom buys The Bantam,
a liberal magazine that exposes civic wrongdoings. Although
Christie is more concerned about the impending war in Europe
than Tom's society connections, she falls in love with him as
he becomes more politically aware. However, she turns down
his proposal, insisting that the differences in their social
standings will cause unhappiness. She goes to Mexico to find
herself. On the rebound, Tom marries Cecelia Henry, a gold
digging socialite who plots with Tom's father Rufus to
convince Tom to give up The Bantam. Christie returns to
New York, realizing she loves Tom. Cecelia manipulates her
husband, pretending to want children and keeping him from his
friends. She lies to Tom about Rufus's involvement in a
copper company scandal to keep Tom from running an expose.
Christie confronts Cecelia about her lie, insisting that
leaving the articles unpublished will destroy Tom's self
esteem and integrity. Butler Pat Regan overhears Cecelia
talking to Rufus and Pat tells Tom the truth. Tom confronts
Cecelia and he realizes their marriage is based on lies. He
leaves Cecelia and runs the expose. When Christie learns
Cecelia is getting a divorce, she reconciles with Tom.

REVIEWS:
Hollywood Reporter, May 14, 1946: "Ann Sheridan, who
enacts the girl photographer, should be pardoned for shooting
whoever gave her that hat to wear in the big scene when she
calls upon the wife. For the most part Miss Sheridan lends
all the warmth she can to her characterization."

New York Times, May 25, 1946: "Ann Sheridan and Alexis
Smith are equally fetching and competent as the photographer
and wife, respectively..."

Newsweek, May 27, 1946: "...[Ann] Sheridan is still [Ann]
Sheridan, and the subsequent crises are not to be taken very
seriously."

Screen Guide, August 1946: "Ann Sheridan...and Dennis
Morgan...have little to do except be attractive, but Alexis
Smith has one of her finest parts as the scheming blueblood
who loses her man."

NOTES: One More Tomorrow is a reworking of Philip Barry's
play The Animal Kingdom, which ran for 171 performances on
Broadway, beginning January 12, 1932. William Gargan played
the publisher and Frances Fuller his socially conscious
girlfriend. RKO filmed The Animal Kingdom in 1932 with Ann
Harding, Leslie Howard, and Myrna Loy in the roles later
taken by Ann Sheridan, Dennis Morgan, and Alexis Smith. Both

films were controversial, since Barry's play deals with a
free-spirited artist's involvement with a married man.
    One More Tomorrow had a troubled road to the screen.
The movie began filming in 1943, but shut down after a few
weeks when it was discovered that producer Benjamin Glazer
had failed to get Production Code approval from the Johnston
Office. Since the play concerned the then-sensitive topic of
infidelity, as well as hints of communism, approval from the
censors was mandatory. In the meantime, Ann Sheridan began
work on Shine On Harvest Moon (F-68). When One More
Tomorrow resumed production, producer Benjamin Glazer had
been dismissed, with Henry Blanke taking over, and director
Peter Godfrey replacing Irving Rapper. A revised script
avoided the sensitive censorship issues, implying an affair
between characters played by Dennis Morgan and Ann Sheridan,
softening the major theme of radical versus conservative, and
omitting a role intended for Dane Clark. Filming finally
ended in November 1943, however the picture was not released
until May 1946, a clear indication that Warner Bros.
executives thought the movie would be a box office failure.
By the time the studio released the movie, supporting players
Jane Wyman and Jack Carson were hot properties and often were
billed above Sheridan and Morgan on theatre marquees (B-369).
The Hollywood Reporter notes that the film threw out the
intention of Philip Barry's play: questioning radical and
conservative values. Its review concludes, "When
[censorship] worries are paramount, such thoughtful
properties as this should not be approached" (May 14, 1946).

See also S-9.

F-72 Hollywood Daffy   (Warner Bros., June 22, 1946)
      cartoon short

Director: I. Freleng. Story: Michael Maltese. Animation:
Ken Champin, Virgil Ross, Gerry Chiniquy, and Manuel Perez.
Layouts and backgrounds: Hawley Pratt and Paul Julian.
Voice characterization: Mel Blanc. Musical direction: Carl
W. Stalling.

NOTES: Daffy Duck stars in this Merrie Melodies cartoon,
which spoofs a host of stars. Among those caricatured are
Bette Davis, Johnny Weismuller, Charlie Chaplin, Jimmy
Durante, Bing Crosby, and Bud Abbott and Lou Costello. Ann
Sheridan appears twice. Midway, she is surrounded by bear
traps and barbed wire. At the end, she is among the stars
Daffy sees after he is beaten on the head.

F-73 Bob Ripley's Party--New York City (filmed
      August 10, 1946 for Hearst newsreels)   5 mins.

CAST: Robert Ripley, Steve Hannagan, Ann Sheridan, Anna May
Wong, Chinatown Mayor Shady Lee, girls from the China Doll
show.

NOTES: This unreleased newsreel footage can be found in the
Hearst Vault in the film collection at the UCLA Film and
Television Archive. Ann Sheridan and Steve Hannagan are seen

walking away from a boat in Mamaroneck, New York. The scenes
are from a party hosted by Robert Ripley, best known for his
"believe it or not" column.

F-74 <u>Nora Prentiss</u>   (Warner Bros., February 22, 1947)
      111 minutes

Producer: William Jacobs. Director: Vincent Sherman.
Screenplay: N. Richard Nash. Based on "The Man Who Died
Twice" by Paul Webster and Jack Sobell. Songs: M.K. Jerome,
Jack Scholl, and Eddie Cherkose. Music: Franz Waxman.
Musical director: Leo F. Forbstein. Orchestrations: Leonid
Raab. Photography: James Wong Howe. Montages: James
Leicester. Editor: Owen Marks. Art direction: Anton Grot.
Sets: Walter Tilford. Costumes: Travilla. Sound: Charles
Lang. Makeup: Perc Westmore. Special effects: Harry
Barndollar and Edwin DuPar.

CAST: Ann Sheridan (Nora Prentiss), Kent Smith (Dr. Richard
Talbot/Robert Thompson), Robert Alda (Phil Dinardo), Bruce
Bennett (Dr. Joel Merriam), Rosemary DeCamp (Lucy Talbot),
John Ridgley (Walter Bailey), Robert Arthur (Gregory Talbot),
Wanda Hendrix (Bonita Talbot), Helen Brown (Miss Judson),
Rory Mallinson (Fleming), Harry Shannon (Police lieutenant),
James Flavin (District attorney), Douglas Kennedy (Doctor),
Don McGuire (Truck driver), Clifton Young (Policeman), John
Newland, John Compton, Ramon Ros (Reporters), Jack Mower
(Sheriff), Philo McCullough (Warden), Fred Kelsey (Turnkey),
Louise Quince (Judge), Lottie Williams (Agnes), Gertrude Carr
(Mrs. Dobie), Richard Walsh (Bystander), Tiny Jones (Flower
woman), Georgia Caine (Mrs. Sterritt), Dean Cameron (Rod, the
piano player), Roy Gordon (Oberlin), David Fresco (Newsboy),
Jack Ellis, Lee Phelps (Doormen), Creighton Hale (Captain of
waiters), Ed Hart, Clancey Cooper, Alan Bridge (Policemen),
Ross Ford (Billie, the chauffeur), Adele St. Maur (Nurse),
Ralph Dunn, Ed Chandler (Detectives), Charles Marsh
(Bailiff), Matt McHugh, Wallace Scott (Drunks), George
Campeau (Man), Charles Jordan (Clerk at court), John Elliott
(Chaplain), Herb Caen, Bill McWilliams, Mike Musura, Jerry
Baulch, Fred Johnson, Jack Dailey, Bill Best, Seymore Snaer,
James Nickle (Newspapermen at ferry building).

SONGS: "Who Cares What People Say?" (Scholl, Jerome), "Would
You Like a Souvenir?" (Scholl, Cherkose, Jerome).

SYNOPSIS: Dedicated doctor Richard Talbot treats singer Nora
Prentiss. Although he loves his wife and family, Nora shows
him how predictable his life is and they have an affair.
When Nora realizes that his family always will come first,
she breaks up with him and goes to New York to work for
nightclub owner Phil Dinardo. Unable to face his wife,
Richard writes a letter, requesting a divorce. When a
patient dies in his office after hours, Richard decides to
use the corpse to fake his own death. Richard joins Nora in
New York, pretending he left his wife. When Richard's
colleague finds the remains of Richard's letter and learns
that six thousand dollars is missing from his bank account,
he tells the police. Richard becomes paranoid about being

recognized after he learns that his "death" is being
investigated as a blackmail and murder case. He shaves off
his moustache and uses the alias Robert Thompson. He
confesses the truth to Nora. Although she realizes he cannot
practice medicine or marry, she promises to stand by him.
She sings at Phil's club to support them. Richard loses his
mind as he stays locked in the apartment. In a jealous rage,
he knocks out Phil and flees, fearing he killed the nightclub
owner. During a police chase, Richard's face is injured in
an automobile wreck. He has plastic surgery and looks to the
future, realizing his family and old friends can no longer
recognize him. The police are suspicious of his bank book,
which is in the name of Robert Thompson and shows a six
thousand-dollar deposit. They arrest him for his own murder
since Robert's fingerprints match those found in the office.
Richard refuses to defend himself, knowing he cannot go back
to his family or stay with Nora. He urges Nora to keep his
secret. Richard is convicted and sentenced to death. Phil
stands by Nora, offering hope for her future happiness.

REVIEWS:
Hollywood Reporter, February 4, 1947: "Something can be
made of the resumption of Ann Sheridan's film career at
Warners. Yet this vehicle to mark her return belongs less to
her than it does to Kent Smith, who plays the doctor....
Smith and Miss Sheridan, splendidly photographed by James
Wong Howe, lend reality to their characterizations. Not they,
but the characters, fall short of entertaining."

Variety, February 5, 1947: "Nora Prentiss is an overlong
melodrama that will have to depend considerably on Ann
Sheridan's draw value....Miss Sheridan makes much of her role
but the personal achievement isn't enough to balance general
shortcomings."

Los Angeles Daily News, February 22, 1947: "The role of
the entertainer is played by Ann Sheridan with a blend of
superficial hardness and inner warmth that is thoroughly
convincing. It is a character which elicits a good deal of
sympathy, and Miss Sheridan plays her with complete honesty
to the last moment..."

Cue, March 22, 1947: "For nearly two hours the trials and
tribulations of unhappy, husband-stealing Ann Sheridan
squeeze the screen dry of tears and you of patience. Will
her misery - or yours, for that matter - ever end?...The
acting is rheumatic, the direction unimaginative, and the
script a bumbling series of starts, stops and anti-climaxes."

NOTES: Nora Prentiss marked Ann Sheridan's first film
following an eighteen-month suspension after the completion
of One More Tomorrow (F-71) in 1943. Ann's new three-year,
six-film contract gave her better control in choosing her
roles. Ann said she liked the story of Nora Prentiss,
which was brought to her by director Vincent Sherman (B-206).
Although many label the film a "woman's picture" because of
its melodramatic plot, it also falls into the film noir
class. The tone is set by James Wong Howe's expert

photography, which details Kent Smith's increasing paranoia and the general moodiness in the movie. <u>Nora Prentiss</u> was one of the top moneymaking films for 1946/47 (B-650).

See also D-2, S-10.

F-75   <u>The Unfaithful</u>   (Warner Bros., July 5, 1947)
        110 minutes

Producer: Jerry Wald. Director: Vincent Sherman. Dialogue director: Felix Javoves. Screenplay: David Goodis and James Gunn. Based on the play <u>The Letter</u> by W. Somerset Maugham. Music: Max Steiner. Musical director: Leo F. Forbstein. Orchestrations: Murray Cutter. Photography: Ernest Haller. Editor: Alan Crosland, Jr. Art direction: Leo K. Kuter. Sets: William Wallace. Costumes: Travilla. Sound: Francis J. Scheid. Makeup: Perc Westmore. Special effects: William McGann and Robert Burks.

CAST: Ann Sheridan (Chris Hunter), Lew Ayres (Larry Hannaford), Zachary Scott (Bob Hunter), Eve Arden (Paula), Jerome Cowan (Prosecuting attorney), Steven Geray (Martin Barrow), John Hoyt (Detective lieutenant Reynolds), Peggy Knudsen (Claire), Marta Mitrovich (Mrs. Tanner), Douglas Kennedy (Roger), Claire Meade (Martha), Frances Morris (Agnes), Jane Harker (Joan), Joan Winfield (Girl), Maude Fealy (Old maid), Cary Harrison (Seedy man), Dick Walsh, Betty Hill, Charles Marsh, Bob Lowell (Reporters), John Elliott (Judge), George Hickman, Bob Alden (Newsboys), Paul Bradley (Mr. Tanner), Ray Montgomery (Secretary), Mary Field (Receptionist), Monte Blue (Businessman), Jack Mower (Plainclothesman), Jean De Briac (Maitre d'hotel), Lois Austin (Middle-aged woman), Ross Ford (Young man), Even Whitney (Young woman), Dorothy Christy (Mrs. Freedley), Charles Jordan (Attendant).

SYNOPSIS: Former war bride Chris Hunter kills an intruder while her husband Bob is away on business. Lawyer Larry Hannaford insists it was justifiable homicide after Chris claims the unarmed stranger tried to rob her. The police doubt her story when the corpse is identified as Michael Tanner, a sculptor with no criminal record. An art dealer tries to blackmail Larry with a bust of Chris sculpted by the dead man, which proves she knew Michael. Chris admits to Larry that she had an affair with Michael while Bob was away during World War II. She rebuffed him after Bob's return and killed him when he tried to attack her. She insists she lied to the police to prevent a scandal. The art dealer gives the bust to Michael's widow, convincing her that telling Bob will cause Chris more suffering than prosecution. Bob confronts Chris, who tries to explain that Michael seduced her when she was most lonely and vulnerable. Bob plans to pay the blackmail and quietly divorce Chris after the scandal dies down. The police arrest Chris after Mrs. Tanner reveals the bust. Chris goes on trial for murder. While the jury deliberates, Bob's divorced cousin Paula convinces him that Chris is not to blame for all the marital problems and that women also need to readjust to marriage after the war. Chris

is acquitted, but her reputation is ruined. She prepares to
leave Bob. Larry realizes how much the Hunters still love
each other. He denounces divorce, convincing them that they
will regret their decision. Chris and Bob decide to give
their marriage another chance.

REVIEWS:
Harrison's Reports, May 31, 1947: "A gripping adult
drama, masterfully directed and flawlessly performed....Ann
Sheridan gives an exceedingly fine performance and is
completely convincing in a difficult role; she speaks her
lines so well, and acts with such emotional understanding,
that the spectator is held spellbound and is at all times
sympathetic towards her."

Los Angeles Evening Herald, June 26, 1947: "The answer to
Ann Sheridan's prayer for a strong dramatic role comes in
The Unfaithful, a considerably less than perfect film but
one that will whip up controversy....Miss Sheridan's
performance, at least is realistic and poignant."

Screenland, August 1947: "At last Ann Sheridan has been
given a role that gives her a great deal more to do than sing
a torchy song and look glamorous. She still has potent eye
appeal in this dramatic story....It's Ann's dramatic
triumph."

Esquire, September 1947: "Here's the picture which the
adult woman must turn to for an intelligent discussion of
real women and real problems....This picture restores Ann
Sheridan to the top ranks of stardom and promotes Zachary
Scott from the ranks of villainy to an important place among
leading men."

NOTES: The Unfaithful loosely was based on W. Somerset
Maugham's play The Letter, which opened September 26, 1927
and ran for 104 performances with Katharine Cornell. It had
been filmed twice: with Jeanne Eagels (Paramount, 1929) and
Bette Davis (Warner Bros., 1940). In 1982, The Letter was
remade as a telefilm with Lee Remick. In all four versions
of The Letter, an adulteress accused of murder tries to
prove her innocence by pleading self-defense. A letter from
the deceased is the evidence that implicates her. In The
Unfaithful, the letter is replaced by a sculpture. The
Unfaithful also focuses on a matter that post-World War II
audiences were experiencing: readjusting to marriage after
the war. Instead of showing only the returning soldiers'
difficulties, The Unfaithful acknowledges that the women at
home also needed time to adapt.
     The Unfaithful proved to be another controversial film
for Ann Sheridan because of its theme of adultery. Warner
Bros. tried to deal with any criticism by stressing the
importance of the cooperation of the Johnston Office in
allowing them to let Ann's character be portrayed as a
sympathetic adulteress who goes unpunished. It was an
unexpected move from the censorship office. Among the
options considered for the ending were divorce and the
husband shooting his wife. Writer James Gunn explained the

censor's philosophy for a peaceful ending. "Obviously, it couldn't recommend that everybody go around shooting somebody, so it decided to permit the adultery in the picture if we would say that divorce was bad. So that's the way we settled it to keep the admission of adultery in" (B-715).

Ironically, director Vincent Sherman said The Unfaithful was rushed into production when another controversial production encountered censorship problems. He recalled that Warner Bros. planned to make Serenade with Ann Sheridan and Dennis Morgan until Sherman pointed out that the censors would never approve the story, which dealt with sex and homosexuality. He suggested they proceed with The Unfaithful, which began filming with only twenty pages of completed script. After the movie was finished, Jack Warner called Sherman to his office and renegotiated his contract because he was so pleased with the film (B-298). A drastically rewritten Serenade was made in 1956 with Mario Lanza and Eleanor Parker.

Lew Ayres was given the choice of playing the attorney or the husband in The Unfaithful. He later regretted choosing the attorney, since the other role would have made him more a part of the action. Ayres recalled feeling like a stranger while working with Ann Sheridan in The Unfaithful. "She was very cool to me," he said. "Maybe it was our different lifestyles. She seemed to take her role... very lightly; her attention span was quite short." Ayres remembered wondering how she would be able to deal with such a serious role when she constantly was joking on the set. "Somehow, she wound up doing a very good job," he admitted (B-331).

F-76   The Treasure of the Sierra Madre   (Warner Bros., January 24, 1948)   124 mins.

Producer: Henry Blanke. Director: John Huston. Screenplay: John Huston. Based on the novel by B. Traven [Berwick Traven Torsvan]. Music: Max Steiner. Musical director: Leo F. Forbstein. Orchestrations: Murray Cutter. Photography: Ted McCord. Editor: Owen Marks. Art direction: John Hughes. Sets: Fred M. MacLean. Sound: Robert B. Lee. Makeup: Perc Westmore. Special effects: William McGann and H.F. Koenekamp. Technical advisors: Ernesto A. Romero and Antonio Arriaga.

CAST: Humphrey Bogart (Fred C. Dobbs), Walter Huston (Howard), Tim Holt (Curtin), Bruce Bennett (James Cody), Barton MacLane (McCormick), Alfonso Bedoya (Gold Hat), A. Soto Rangel (Presidente), Manuel Donde (El Jefe), Jose Torvay (Pablo), Margarito Luna (Pancho), Jacqueline Dalya (Flashy girl), Robert Blake (Boy selling lottery tickets), Spencer Chan (Proprietor), Julian Rivero (Barber), John Huston (Man in white), Harry Vejar (Bartender), Pat Flaherty (Customer), Clifton Young, Ralph Dunn, Jack Holt (Flophouse men), Guillermo Calleo (Mexican storekeeper), Ildefonso Vega, Francisco Islas, Alberto Valdespino (Indians), Mario Mancilla (Youth), Ann Sheridan (Streetwalker), Martin Garralaga (Railroad conductor), Ernesto Escoto (First Mexican bandit), Ignacio Villabajo (Second Mexican bandit), Roberto Canedo

(Mexican lieutenant).

SYNOPSIS: Americans Fred C. Dobbs and Curtin convince
elderly prospector Howard to help them hunt for gold in the
Mexican hills in 1925. Despite Howard's warnings about how
greed can corrupt friendship, Curtin and Fred become jealous
and suspicious as soon as they find gold in the Sierra
mountains. Howard remains rational and tries to convince the
others to put a limit on their prospecting. When a gang of
bandits attack, the trio decides to return to town with their
claim. On the way down the mountain, an Indian tribe asks
Howard to help a sick child. Howard entrusts Fred and Curtin
with most of his share. Fred loses his mind and shoots
Curtin when he thinks his friend is after his claim. Fred
leaves Curtin for dead and heads to town with all the gold.
The Indians treat Howard like a hero after he saves the boy.
When they find the wounded Curtin, they help Howard nurse
him. Howard and Curtin chase Fred to reclaim their share.
The bandits find Fred first. They kill him and steal his
burros. To lighten the load, the bandits dump the burros'
sacks, unaware there is gold inside. The bandits are
apprehended when they try to sell the burros. They are put
before the firing squad. Howard and Curtin return to town
and learn what happened to Fred and the gold. When Howard
realizes the swift wind carried the gold dust back to the
mountains, he is amused by the irony. Although Curtin
initially is depressed by their wasted efforts, he soon joins
Howard's laughter. Howard returns to the tribe to be a
medicine man. He gives Curtin what is left of his share to
buy a farm. The friends wish each other luck as they go
their separate ways.

REVIEWS:
Variety, January 7, 1948:   "The Treasure of the Sierra
Madre is not only radically different, but it's a
distinguished work that will take its place in the repertory
of Hollywood's great and enduring achievements....Except for
some incidental femmes that have no bearing on the story,
it's an all-male cast..."

Harrison's Reports, January 10, 1948:   "Though its overlong
running time could be cut to advantage to tighten up its
rambling plot, The Treasure of the Sierra Madre is a grim,
powerful melodrama, the sort that grips one's interest from
start to finish....Able performances are contributed by the
entire cast..."

New York Times, January 24, 1948:   "Greed, a despicable
passion out of which other base ferments may spawn, is seldom
treated in the movies with frank and ironic contempt that is
vividly manifested toward it in Treasure of Sierra Madre
[sic]. And certainly the big stars of the movies are rarely
exposed in such cruel light as that which is thrown on
Humphrey Bogart....Even the least perceptive patron should
find this a swell adventure film."

NOTES: The Treasure of the Sierra Madre shows how greed
can corrupt. Director/screenwriter John Huston had wanted to

film B. Traven's novel since first reading it in 1935. At
that point, he considered giving his father, Walter Houston,
the role of Fred Dobbs, which ended up being played by
Humphrey Bogart. By the time the film was made in 1948, the
younger Huston had a difficult time convincing his matinee
idol father to play the elderly prospector. Reportedly, when
Walter arrived on the set, John asked him to remove his false
teeth. The actor refused so the director and Bogart held him
down and stole them (B-431).

John Huston won Oscars for Best Direction and Best
Screenplay; Walter Huston won for Best Supporting Actor. It
marked the first time two generations of the same family won
Academy Awards. Thirty-seven years later, John's daughter
Angelica continued the family tradition by picking up the
Best Supporting Actress Oscar for Prizzi's Honor (20th
Century-Fox, 1985), which also was directed by her father.
The Treasure of the Sierra Madre boasted another father/son
team. Tim Holt portrayed Curtin, one of the prospectors,
while his father, Jack Holt, was one of the men listening to
Walter Huston's prospecting tales in the flophouse.

The movie was the first postwar film produced by a major
studio that was shot almost entirely on location. Most of
the work was done around Jungapeo, Mexico, with a few retakes
made on the Warner Bros. backlot. The location work proved
very expensive, which had mogul Jack Warner fuming. The
final cost was around $3 million. Although The Treasure of
the Sierra Madre was a critical success, it was only
through rereleases that it recouped its investment.

The cast and crew were notorious for playing practical
jokes on each other. According to several sources, Ann
Sheridan made an unbilled cameo as a prostitute in the film
as a joke for friend Humphrey Bogart. Conspiring with John
Huston, Ann donned a padded black satin dress and a dark wig
and wiggled past Bogart as he exited a Mexican bar. He did
not recognize her until she lifted her skirt, revealing a
tattoo with a butterfly, a fee, and "Annie" (B-262). It is
debatable whether Ann's footage appears in the final film.
It is obvious another actress is used in close-ups of the
prostitute, however it is possible that a long shot could be
Ann. Rudy Behlmer's book of Warner Bros. memos includes a
still of Ann in costume on the set. Behlmer reprints a memo
from assistant director Don Page, checking with the legal
department about whether the movie can use Ann in the scene.
Page calls the bit a "good-luck gesture" for Huston. Behlmer
concludes that while the long shot could be Ann, it is
possible that Huston used an alternate take with a different
actress in the final film (B-88). The Warner Bros. Archive
of Historial Papers at USC's School of Cinema-Television
includes a talent agreement for Ann's participation in the
movie, as well as a letter concerning her appearance, so
there is no dispute that she filmed the scene.

See also V-15.

F-77   Silver River   (Warner Bros., May 29, 1948)
       110 mins.

Producer: Owen Crump. Director: Raoul Walsh. Dialogue

director: Maurice Murphy. Screenplay: Stephen Longstreet
and Harriet Frank, Jr. Based on an unpublished novel by
Stephen Longstreet. Music: Max Steiner. Musical director:
Leo F. Forbstein. Orchestrations: Murray Cutter.
Photography: Sid Hickox. Montages: James Leicester.
Editor: Alan Crosland, Jr. Art direction: Ted Smith.
Sets: William G. Wallace. Costumes: William Travilla and
Marjorie Best. Sound: Francis J. Scheid. Makeup: Perc
Westmore. Special effects: William McGann and Edwin DuPar.
Technical advisor: J.G. Taylor.

CAST: Errol Flynn (Captain Mike McComb), Ann Sheridan
(Georgia Moore), Thomas Mitchell (John "Plato" Beck), Bruce
Bennett (Stanley Moore), Tom D'Andrea (Pistol Porter), Barton
MacLane (Banjo Sweeney), Monte Blue (Buck Chevigee), Jonathan
Hale (Major Spencer), Alan Bridge (Sam Slade), Arthur Space
(Major Ross), Art Baker (Major Wilson), Joe Crehan (President
Ullyses S. Grant), Norman Jolley (Scout), Jack Davis (Judge
Advocate), Harry Strang (Soldier), Norman Willis (Honest
Harry), Ian Wolfe (Deputy), Jim Ames (Barker), Lois Austin,
Gladys Turney (Ladies), Marjorie Bennett (Large woman),
Dorothy Christy, Grayce Hampton (Women), Joe Bernard
(Riverboat captain), Harry Hayden (Schaefer, the teller),
Lester Dorr (Taylor), Russell Hicks (Edwards, the architect),
Fred Kelsey (Townsman), Ben Corbett (Henchman), Leo White
(Barber), Franklyn Farnum (Officer), Bud Osborne (Posse man),
Ed Parker (Bugler), Jerry Jerome, Harry Strang, Frank
McCarroll, James H. Harrison, Bob Stephenson, Ross Ford
(Soldiers), Henry [Harry] Morgan (Tailor), Harry Woods (Card
player), Dan White, Otto Reichow (Miners).

SYNOPSIS: After Union Army captain Mike McComb is court-
martialed, he vows to live by his own rules and promote his
own interests. He opens a casino in Missouri, which
infuriates his rival, Banjo Sweeney. When Georgia and
Stanely Moore have financial difficulties, Stanley offers
Mike an interest in their Silver River mine. Georgia
dislikes Mike and is upset by the merger. After the miners
tie up their money at his casino, Mike sets up a bank,
insisting on a cut of stock from each mine company. He soon
becomes the dominant silver mine controller. Mike is
indirectly responsible for Stanley's death when he sends
Stanley to check out an expansion site in Indian territory.
Mike's lawyer, Plato Beck, accuses Mike of purposely sending
Stanley into a dangerous area so he can marry Georgia.
Despite her initial hatred of Mike, Georgia soon falls in
love with him and marries him. Mike's enemies plot to ruin
him by forming a combine. Plato runs for senator, promising
to clean up the mining industry. Georgia realizes how
ruthless Mike is when he refuses to do what is best for the
miners. She leaves him. The combine makes a run on the bank
and Mike loses everything. Banjo fatally shoots Plato to
keep him from carrying out his reforms. Mike resolves to
help the poor and downtrodden and win back his wife. He
convinces the miners to go after the combine and bring
justice to Plato's killer. Mike takes the blame for the ruin
of the town. He promises to reopen the mines and give the
combine mob a fair hearing. Proud of her reformed husband,

Georgia agrees to a reconciliation.

REVIEWS:
<u>Variety</u>, May 5, 1948: "Ingredients of western background, some rousing action, and combo of Errol Flynn and Ann Sheridan sparking ticket sales indicate grosses will be on the good side....While Miss Sheridan adds marquee advantages, she's not particularly at home in the role, but, nevertheless, gives a competent performance."

<u>Harrison's Reports</u>, May 8, 1948: "Although it is a 'big' picture from the viewpoint of production and star value, this Western saga of the rise and fall of an empire builder...is a spotty entertainment. To begin with, it is overlong....the episodic manner in which the story is presented somehow makes the hero's rise and fall, and even his romance with the heroine, never seem believable."

<u>New York Times</u>, May 22, 1948: "...all the charm Errol Flynn turns on to mask his true colors, plus all the temperament and determination that Ann Sheridan displays in the role of a hardy, pioneer beauty doesn't help much to stem the ebbing tide....The stars are not given any opportunity for acting of any consequence, but they are assured in what they do..."

<u>Rochester Democrat and Chronicle</u> [NY], June 3, 1948: "Errol Flynn, Ann Sheridan, Thomas Mitchell and Bruce Bennett found substance here on which they could take hold and turn in good, believable, interesting performances....Miss Sheridan is natural and skillful with revealing touches as the woman [Flynn] seeks though she is the wife of another."

NOTES: <u>Silver River</u> was filmed in the High Sierras, Calabasas, and Hollywood, California. It was Ann Sheridan's final film under her Warner Bros. contract. It also marked the seventh and final collaboration between Errol Flynn and director Raoul Walsh. In order to finish the picture on time, Walsh demanded that Flynn stay sober until after 5:00 P.M., when both would sit down and drink. There were rumors that both Ann and Errol were drunk throughout filming (B-88).
    <u>Silver River</u> was a disappointment to fans who had enjoyed Ann Sheridan and Errol Flynn in <u>Dodge City</u> (F-47), a bigger budget Technicolor western made at the height of Flynn's career. In a 1960s interview, Ann recalled that Jack Warner was surprised that she accepted a role in <u>Silver River</u> because the script was not very good. She explained that she welcomed another chance to work with Errol Flynn. She hoped that his box office appeal and their chemistry would improve the script. She also said that she chose the role because there were few westerns for women (B-206).

See also V-28.

F-78 <u>Good Sam</u>   (RKO, 1948)   128 mins.

Producer: Leo McCarey. Director: Leo McCarey. Assistant director: Jesse Hibbs. Screenplay: Ken Englund. Based on

a story by Leo McCarey and John Klorer. Songs: Leo McCarey
and Robert Emmet Dolan. Music: Robert Emmet Dolan.
Photography: George Barnes. Editor: James McKay. Art
direction: John B. Goodman. Sets: Darrell Silvera and
Jacques Mapes. Costumes: Travilla. Sound: John L. Cass
and Clem Portman. Special effects: Russell A. Cully.

CAST: Gary Cooper (Sam Clayton), Ann Sheridan (Lu Clayton),
Ray Collins (Reverend Daniels), Edmund Lowe (H.C. Borden),
Joan Lorring (Shirley Mae), Clinton Sundberg (Nelson),
Minerva Urecal (Mrs. Nelson), Louise Beavers (Chloe), Ruth
Roman (Ruthie), Dick Ross (Claude), Lora Lee Michel (Lulu),
Bobby Dolan, Jr. (Butch), Matt Moore (Mr. Butler), Netta
Packer (Mrs. Butler), Carol Stevens (Mrs. Adams), Todd Karns
(Joe Adams), Irving Bacon (Tramp), William Frawley (Tom),
Harry Hayden (Banker), Irmgard Dawson, Jane Allan (Girls),
Tom Dugan (Santa Claus), Sarah Edwards (Mrs. Gilmore), Ruth
Sanderson (Sam's secretary), Marta Mitrovich (Mysterious
woman), Mimi Doyle (Red Cross nurse), Franklin Parker
(Photographer), Ida Moore (Old lady), Florence Auer (Woman on
bus), Dick Wessel (Bus driver), Sedal Bennett (Woman chasing
bus), Cliff Clarke (Probation officer), Jack Gargan, Bess
Flowers (Parents), Almira Sessions (Landlady), Garry Owens
(Taxi driver), Stanley McKay (Young minister), Bert Roach
(Whispering usher), Bob Tidwell (Telegraph boy), Ann Lawrence
(Salvation Army girl), Joe Hinds, Francis Stevens (Salvation
Army workers), Joseph Crehan (Casey), William Haade (Taxi
driver), Bert Moorehouse (Man), Dick Elliott, Bert Roach
(Politicians), Louis Mason (Mr. Duffield), Effie Laird (Mrs.
Duffield).

SONGS: "Eight to Five" (McCarey), "Call to Remberance,"
"Daddy Dear" (Dolan) (B-100).

SYNOPSIS: Kindly department store manager Sam Clayton
frustrates his wife Lu with his altruism. He supports his
brother-in-law, loans money to friends, and prevents a
coworker from committing suicide, while neglecting his own
family's needs. Despite Sam's penchant for helping his
neighbors, the Claytons finally save enough to buy their own
home. While they prepare to move, Sam heads the store's
annual Christmas charity drive. On Christmas Eve, he is
accosted by a thief, who steals the money he had collected
from store employees. Sam replaces the money with his own
savings, leaving him without enough funds for the down-
payment on his new home. He unsuccessfully tries to borrow
money from his many debtors. Guilty and depressed, he goes
to a bar and gets drunk. Lu worries when he does not come
home, realizing how much she needs her husband. The
Salvation Army leads Sam home, where he is reuinted with his
family. Meanwhile, the banker decides to give Sam a loan,
saving the Claytons' dream house.

REVIEWS:
Hollywood Reporter, July 28, 1948: "Ann Sheridan supplies
vitality, curves and a loving sense of humor as the wife.
The way she tosses the glib lines is a joy to watch."

Variety, July 28, 1948: "Ann Sheridan, as something that
might have stepped out of a Christian Dior salon instead of
being an ever-lovin' wife and mother, is not always credible
in a part that's unusual for her. Domestication is hardly
Miss Sheridan's cinematic dish, no matter how authentic-
looking are her scrambled eggs. Miss Sheridan has been given
most of the gags, and much of the situational comedy payoffs
revolve around her sharp retorts."

Harrison's Reports, July 31, 1948: "Very good mass entertainment. It is a domestic comedy-drama, the sort that
captivates an audience from start to finish because of its
warm, human quality, as well as it hilarious comedy....[Ann]
Sheridan...gives one of the best performances of her career
in this role."

New York Times, September 17, 1948: "...as [Gary Cooper's]
long-suffering wife, Ann Sheridan gives a thoroughly amusing
look at a woman who accepts her husband's bigness of heart
with bitter and candid distaste. As a matter of fact, it is
the lovely and willful sarcasm in her approach - the
non-Pollyannaism - that keys the whole purpose of the film."

NOTES: After Ann Sheridan turned down several Warner Bros.
scripts, they loaned her to RKO for Good Sam. Still
discontent with the films the studio offered her, Ann bought
out the remaining six months of her contract for thirty-five
thousand dollars in 1948. Ann recalled working for eleven
weeks on Good Sam, which initially ran much longer than the
released version. Although she enjoyed working with director
Leo McCarey and longtime friend Gary Cooper, she was not
pleased with the script, the editing, or her lack of
chemistry with her co-star (B-206). Some television prints
of Good Sam have been cut to 113 minutes.

See also R-26, V-17.

F-79 I Was a Male War Bride   (20th Century-Fox, 1949)
      105 mins.

Producer: Sol C. Siegel. Director: Howard Hawks.
Screenplay: Charles Lederer, Leonard Spigelgass, and Hagar
Wilde. Based on a story by Henri Rouchard. Music: Cyril
Mockridge. Musical director: Lionel Newman.
Orchestrations: Herbert Spencer. Photography: Norbert
Brodine and O. Borradaile. Editor: James B. Clark. Art
direction: Lyle Wheeler and Albert Hogsett. Sets: Thomas
Little and Walter M. Scott. Sound: George Leverett and
Roger Herman. Makeup: Ben Nye. Special effects: Fred
Sersen.

CAST: Cary Grant (Capt. Henri Rochard), Ann Sheridan (Lt.
Catherine Gates), Marion Marshall, Randy Stuart (WACs),
William Neff (Captain Jack Rumsey), Eugene Gericke (Tony
Jowitt), Ruben Wendorf (Innkeeper's assistant), John Whitney
(Trumble), Ken Tobey (Seaman), Alfred Linder (Bartender),
David McMahon (Chaplain), Joe Haworth (Shore patrol), William
Pullen, William Self, Bill Murphy (Sergeants), Robert

Stevenson, Harry Lauter (Lieutenants), Barbara Perry (Tall
WAC), Otto Reichow, William Yetter (German policeman), Andre
Charlot (French minister), Lester Sharpe, Alex Gerry
(Waiters), Gil Herman (Naval officer), Ben Pollock (Officer),
William McLean (Expectant GI), Russ Conway (Commander
Willis), Mike Mahoney (Sailor), Kay Young (Major
Prendergast), Lillie Kann (Innkeeper's wife), Carl Jaffe
(Jail officer), Martin Miller (Schindler), Paul Hardmuth
(Burgomeister), John Serrett (French notary), Patricia Curts
(Girl in door).

SYNOPSIS: Flirtatious French army captain Henri Rochard is
sent on a mission in post-World War II occupied Germany. He
is dismayed when American WAC lieutenant Catherine Gates is
assigned as his aide and interpreter, since the two clashed
on previous assignments. During the three-day mission, Henri
and Catherine have a series of misadventures. Although Henri
confesses the case holds special importance to him, since it
is his last in the army, Catherine solves it without him. On
the way back to Heidelburg, they fall in love, despite their
initial dislike for one another. They decide to marry, but
encounter problems with army red tape. After making their
way through all the paperwork and three ceremonies, the
Rochards run into obstacles trying to consummate their
marriage. On their wedding night, Catherine receives her
sailing orders. They struggle to get Henri's passport in
order so he can accompany her to the United States. When
they find immigration quotas are filled, the American consul
suggests they fill out papers declaring Henri as a war bride,
since the army does not have a policy for officers' husbands.
Caught in the red tape of army regulations, Henri masquerades
as a WAC so he can travel with Catherine. His ruse is
discovered on the ship and the newlyweds are kept apart
again. When the captain learns of the situation, he lets
Henri sail in an isolated cabin. Henri and Catherine finally
consummate their marriage as they head for New York.

REVIEWS:
Variety, August 10, 1949: "[Cary] Grant and [Ann]
Sheridan, carrying most of the film, display some of their
best comedic thesping yet."

Harrison's Reports, August 13, 1949: "An hilariously funny
sophisticated comedy. Word-of-mouth advertising, coupled
with the popularity of the players, should make it one of the
outstanding box-office pictures of the year....The direction
is bright and snappy, and both [Cary] Grant and [Ann]
Sheridan do very good work, romping through the farcical
situations in a highly amusing way."

New York Times, August 27, 1949: "[Ann] Sheridan also does
nicely by her somewhat metallic role of the crisply efficient
lieutenant who is supposed to be dynamite. That she isn't,
precisely. Miss Sheridan is getting on. But she plays a
nice foil of feminine sangfroid to the supercharged ire of
[Cary] Grant."

Movie Stars Parade, November 1949: "Ann Sheridan gives one

of her best performances, showing a vitality too long hidden."

NOTES: I Was a Male War Bride was Ann Sheridan's first film following her release from Warner Bros. She recalled that she jumped at the chance to work with director Howard Hawks and Cary Grant and would have signed for the picture without reading the script. Much of the movie was improvised, written on the set as the actors went through the scenes. Ann praised Grant's comedic skills and tried to talk him into directing her in a film. He declined, insisting that directing was too much work (B-206).

I Was a Male War Bride was a difficult project for its stars, as both Cary Grant and Ann Sheridan were plagued by illness during location shooting in Germany and England. Grant developed hepatitis, causing weeks of delays. Ann caught pneumonia and was bothered by bronchial problems throughout the rest of her life. Some film historians have noted that it may have marked the beginning of her cancer. The balance of the movie was filmed in Hollywood. It took nearly ten months to complete because of the delays caused by the stars' illnesses.

I Was a Male War Bride is one of Ann Sheridan's best remembered films. It was the third top-grossing film of 1949, earning $4,100,000 at the box office (B-650). I Was a Male War Bride was based on Henri Rouchard's real life experiences as told in a November 1947 Reader's Digest article. The character's name is spelled "Rochard" on screen. In England, the film is known as You Can't Sleep Here, a line which refers to war husband Grant's search for a bed on his wedding night after his wife is ordered to an officers' hotel. Ann recalled that Rouchard and his wife spoke of writing a sequel, but it never materialized. She and Grant also discussed reteaming, but could not find a suitable property (B-206).

See also V-18.

F-80 Stella   (20th Century-Fox, August 1950)   83 mins.

Producer: Sol C. Siegel. Director: Claude Binyon. Screenplay: Claude Binyon. Based on the novel Family Skeleton by Doris Miles Disney. Music: Cyril Mockridge. Musical director: Lionel Newman. Orchestrations: Edward Powell. Photography: Joe MacDonald. Editor: Harmon Jones. Art direction: Lyle Wheeler and Mark-Lee Kirk. Sets: Thomas Litle and Paul S. Fox. Costumes: Edward Stevenson. Wardrobe direction: Charles LeMaire. Makeup: Ben Nye. Special effects: Fred Serser, E. Clayton Wan, and Roger Herman.

CAST: Ann Sheridan (Stella Bevins), Victor Mature (Jeff De Marco), David Wayne (Carl Granger), Frank Fontaine (Don Cary), Randy Stuart (Claire), Marion Marshall (Mary), Leif Erickson (Fred Anderson, Jr.), Evelyn Varden (Flora), Lea Penman (Mrs. Calhoun), Joyce MacKenzie (Peggy Denny), Hobart Cavanaugh (Tim Gross), Charles Halton (Mr. Beeker), Walter Baldwin (Farmer), Larry Keating (Gil Wright), Mary Bear

(Myra), Paul Harvey (Ralph Denny), Chill Wills (Officer),
Lorelie Witek (Cigarette girl).

SYNOPSIS: Harried insurance office secretary Stella Bevins
supports her mother, her uncle Joe, two married sisters, and
their lazy husbands, Carl Granger and Don Cary. Although
Stella's boss, Fred Anderson, Jr., begs her to marry him, she
is unsure of her feelings. During a picnic, Joe fatally hits
his head while fighting with Carl. Carl and Don bury him at
the picnic grounds, afraid they will be accused of foul play.
Joe's girlfriend reports his disappearance to the police.
Though the family convinces the officer that Joe is out on a
drunken binge, they confess the truth to Stella. While
insurance representative Jeff De Marco investigates Fred for
a promotion, he looks into Joe's disappearance, since Joe had
a twenty thousand dollar life insurance policy. When Don and
Carl learn they must produce a body to claim the money, they
falsely identify other corpses as Joe. Jeff falls in love
with Stella and offers to drop the case if her family stays
out of trouble. Feeling guilty, Stella tells Fred the truth.
Fred urges her to let Carl and Don collect the twenty
thousand dollars, since it will keep them from leaning on
her. However, when Fred learns Stella plans to marry Jeff,
Fred threatens to tell the police about Joe unless she
marries him instead. Stella breaks her engagement to Jeff to
protect her family. Realizing that the Bevinses are ruining
her life, Jeff vows to uncover the truth. He follows Stella
and Fred to the picnic grounds, where they try to stop her
brothers-in-law from digging up Joe's body. Jeff and the
police overhear Carl and Don arguing and learn Joe's death
was accidental. Jeff realizes that Joe is illegally buried
in an Indian cemetery and that the men will have to search
for the corpse. As Stella and Jeff head for New York to
start a new life together, Carl and Don dig for Joe's body.

REVIEWS:
Variety, July 19, 1950: "Ann Sheridan and Victor Mature
headline the cast as the stars, but neither of their roles
has any particular potency in the story-telling."

Harrison's Reports, July 22, 1950: "Stella is a comedy-
farce of questionable taste and doubtful box-office value,
mainly because of the macabre quality of its subject
matter....The acting is just fair, and the camera has not
been too kind to Ann Sheridan; she appears wan."

New York Times, August 19, 1950: "[Ann] Sheridan...gives
her usual competent performance in a part that gives her star
billing but is secondary in the development of the story.
She has a few sharp scenes with Victor Mature..."

Photoplay, October 1950: "The Bevinses are about the
daffiest family to liven up the screen in many a month....
Red-headed Ann [Sheridan] and muscle man Vic [Mature] make a
very handsome romantic couple."

NOTES: Stella was part of a two-picture deal with 20th
Century-Fox, along with I Was a Male War Bride (F-79).

However, unlike its predecessor which utilized extensive
location shootings, <u>Stella</u> was filmed entirely on the back
lot. The black comedy failed to live up to its screwball
intentions and was a disappointment at the box office. Ann
Sheridan recalled that she liked Doris Miles Disney's 1949
novel, <u>Family Skeleton</u>, but was disappointed in <u>Stella</u>.
She thought the comedy seemed forced, despite the talented
actors involved. She also noted her lack of screen chemistry
with Victor Mature (B-206).

See also S-11.

F-81 <u>Woman on the Run</u>   (Fidelity Pictures/Universal-
      International, October 1950)   77 mins.

Producer: Howard Welsch. Director: Norman Foster.
Assistant director: Maurie M. Suess. Dialogue director:
Ross Hunter. Screenplay: Alan Campbell and Norman Foster.
Based on a story by Sylvia Tate. Music: Emil Newman and
Arthur Lange. Photography: Hal Mohr, Loyal Griggs, and
Robert Hansard. Editor: Otto Ludwig. Art direction: Boris
Levin. Sets: Jacques Mapes. Costumes: Martha Bunch and
William Travilla. Sound: Fred Lau and Mac Daigleish.
Hairstylist: Vera Peterson. Production supervisor: Ben
Hersh.

CAST: Ann Sheridan (Eleanor Johnson), Dennis O'Keefe (Danny
Leggett), Robert Keith (Inspector Ferris), Ross Elliott
(Frank Johnson), Frank Jenks (Detective Shaw), John Qualen
(Maibus), J. Farrell MacDonald (Sea captain), Thomas P.
Dillon (Joe Gordon), Joan Shawlee (Blonde), Steven Geray (Dr.
Hohler), Rako Sato (Suzie), Victor Sen Yung (Sammy), Joan
Fulton, Jane Liddell, Syd Saylor.

SYNOPSIS: Artist Frank Johnson accidently witnesses a mob
killing. Frightened but unharmed, Frank promises to identify
the assassin in a line-up. When he learns the victim was
killed because he was going to testify, Frank flees and goes
into hiding. Frank's estranged wife Eleanor realizes that
she still loves him. When Inspector Ferris reveals that
Frank needs medication for his heart, she decides to search
for her husband. Tabloid reporter Danny Legett offers
Eleanor a thousand dollars if she will lead him to Frank for
an exclusive interview. After she receives a cryptic letter
from Frank, she retraces his steps to decipher it. When a
dancer reveals that Frank drew a picture of Danny, the
reporter kills her to keep her from talking to the police.
During Eleanor's search, she realizes Frank still loves her.
She admits to Ferris that their marital problems are her
fault. She decodes Frank's letter, realizing he is hiding at
a beach amusement park. Ferris follows Eleanor and Danny.
Eleanor delivers Frank's medicine and tells him she wants a
reconciliation. Frank agrees to an interview with Danny.
Ferris realizes that Danny is the killer and the police go
after him. Danny forces Eleanor on the roller coaster so he
can hide. During a horrifying ride, she realizes that Danny
is the killer. When it stops, she rushes to warn Frank about
Danny. She is relieved to find the police have already

killed Danny and rescued her husband.   The Johnsons
reconcile.

REVIEWS:
Hollywood Reporter, October 4, 1950:   "[Ann] Sheridan does
an excellent job as the wife who learns to appreciate her
husband's real worth as she frantically searches to find him.
She gets off her bitterly flippant lines with finesse, at the
same time getting over her inner discontent."

Los Angeles Daily News, October 30, 1950:   "The artist is
played by Ross Elliott.   His wife is portrayed by Ann
Sheridan, who seems to be playing Ann Sheridan rather than
anyone else."

Los Angeles Times, October 30, 1950:   "The picture...won't
chase anybody out of the theater..., but 'Annie' Sheridan
well might.   No one - and I am not excepting even Barbara
Stanwyck - can be as thoroughly nasty and disagreeable as
Annie when she sets herself to it.   Why, Annie can make
'vixen' and 'virago' sound like compliments."

New York Times, November 30, 1950:   "Among [the players]
list first Ann Sheridan, who, in shedding glamor for the role
of Eleanor Johnson, makes the wife a truly confused,
distraught and terrified figure....Woman on the Run will
not win prizes but it does make crime enjoyable."

NOTES: Woman on the Run was an independent film released
by Universal-International.   Although basically a "B"
picture, the movie was shot on location in San Francisco and
offered a quality a step above the usual backlot melodramas.
Ann Sheridan received a share of the film's profits as part
of her contract.   Woman on the Run was the subject of a
brief legal entanglement when two writers sued the production
company, claiming their story had been plagiarized.   The
matter was settled out of court.   Set decorator Jacques Mapes
frequently escorted Ann Sheridan to movie premieres in the
1950s.   At Ann's insistence, dialogue director and longtime
friend Ross Hunter produced Steel Town (F-82) and Take Me
to Town (F-84) (B-469).

See also V-19.

F-82   Steel Town   (Universal-International, March 1952)
        85 mins.   Technicolor

Producer: Leonard Goldstein. Associate producer: Ross
Hunter. Director: George Sherman. Screenplay: Gerald
Drayson Adams and Lou Breslow. Based on a story by Leonard
Freeman. Musical director: Joseph Gershenson. Photography:
Charles P. Boyle. Editor: Ted J. Kent. Art direction:
Bernard Herzbrun and Robert Clatworthy. Sets: Russell A.
Garsman and Oliver Emert. Costumes: Bill Thomas. Sound:
Leslie I Carey and Joe Lapis. Makeup: Bud Westmore.
Hairstylist: Joan St. Oegger. Technicolor consultant:
William Fritzsche.

CAST: Ann Sheridan ("Red" McNamara), John Lund (Steve Kostane), Howard Duff (Jim Denko), William Harrigan (John McNamara), Eileen Crowe (Millie McNamara), Chick Chandler (Ernie), James Best (Joe Rakich), Nancy Kulp (Dolores), Elaine Riley (Valerie), Tudor Owen (McIntosh), Frank Marlowe (Taxi driver), Robert Karnes (Intern), Herbert Lytton (Doctor), Lorin Raker (Milquetoasty man), Lois Wilde (Nurse), James McLaughlin (Helper).

SYNOPSIS: Steel worker Jim Denko takes an immediate dislike to mill heir Steve Kostane, who comes to learn the business from veteran mill worker John McNamara. Jim is jealous when Steve boards with the McNamaras, afraid Steve will steal his girlfriend Red. Jim is furious when Steve is assigned to his crew. In addition to their personal differences, Jim worries that an inexperienced worker will handicap his team in a tonnage contest. Although Red initially dislikes Steve, she finds herself attracted to him. While he is drunk, Steve admits that he loves her, but Red questions his sincerity. Steve is hung over during the last day of the tonnage contest. When John suffers chest pains on the job, Steve leaves his furnace unattended to help him. John recovers quickly, but a loss of molten metal costs Jim's crew the prize. John fears that he will be forced to retire so he asks Steve to keep his attack a secret. Steve accepts blame for losing the contest because of his drinking and becomes even less popular at the plant. A few days later, John has another attack and falls into a ladle that is about to receive molten metal from a furnace. Steve saves John's life, winning the respect of Jim and the other workers. A burned Steve proposes to Red from his hospital bed. She agrees to marry him, realizing she misjudged him.

REVIEWS:
Daily Variety, March 5, 1952: "[Ann] Sheridan delivers one of her snappy portrayals of a modern young woman with her customary verve."

Los Angeles Examiner, March 20, 1952: "You'll be glad to know that Annie is back at her Sheridan best in the role of a wise-cracking owner of a restaurant in the steel town. And, just for the record, she's added some becoming weight plus a new dark blonde hair color - a switch from her usual titian tresses, but you'll like it."

Los Angeles Times, March 20, 1952: "[Ann] Sheridan is very good in her recitation of sharp, snappy lines and gives zest to the part of a regular girl."

New York Herald Tribune, May 10, 1952: "Ann Sheridan, who can toss a wise crack with the best of them, is the girl in the case and she looks very good in Technicolor."

NOTES: Steel Town was the first in Ann Sheridan's three-picture deal with Universal-International. Although it utilizes location footage of the Kaiser Steel Plant in Fontana, California, it is a routine love triangle melodrama. The New York Times noted, "Practically the entire action is predictable after the first ten minutes or so" (May 10, 1952).

According to a report on cable network AMC (American Movie Classics), the set was a jovial place to work, with Ann Sheridan often bringing three of her poodles along for company. After Ann, Howard Duff, and John Lund continually lost their scripts, director George Sherman presented them with oversize copies for the press. Universal-International hosted a weekend press preview junket at Fontana, California. They screened the film at the Arrowhead Springs Hotel, with Ann Sheridan, John Lund, Howard Duff, and Duff's wife, Ida Lupino, in attendance. To further promote the film, the three stars were sent on a four-day personal appearance tour. They traveled to cities which boasted large steel mills, like Atlanta, Detroit, Cleveland, and Birmingham (P-12). In New York, Steel Town played on double bills with producer Leonard Goldstein's The Battle at Apache Pass (Universal-International, 1952). Both films were written in part by Gerald Drayson Adams and directed by George Sherman.

F-83   Just Across the Street   (Universal-International,
       June 1952)   78 mins.

Producer: Leonard Goldstein. Director: Joseph Pevney. Screenplay: Roswell Rogers and Joel Malone. Musical director: Joseph Gershenson. Photography: Maury Gertsman. Editor: Virgil Vogel. Art direction: Bernard Herzbrun and Emrich Nicholson.

CAST: Ann Sheridan (Henrietta Smith), John Lund (Fred Newcombe), Robert Keith (Walter Medford), Cecil Kellaway (Pop Smith), Natalie Schafer (Gertrude Medford), Harvey Lembeck (Al), Alan Mowbray (Davis), George Eldredge (John Ballanger), Burt Mustin (Ed Timens), Billie Bird (Pearl), Jack Kruchen (Character), Lou Lubin (Man in trouble), Herbert Vigran (Liquor salesman), Steve Roberts (C.L.), Fritzi Dugan (Woman in house), George "Shorty" Chirello (Flower vendor), Miles Shepard, Wally Walker (Cab drivers).

SYNOPSIS: Henrietta Smith needs a job to help support her father. While applying for a position as a social secretary at Walter and Gertrude Medford's mansion, plumber Fred Newcombe mistakes her for their spoiled daughter and lectures her on the importance of hard work. The Medfords do not hire Henrietta. Later, Henrietta answers an ad for a secretary at a plumbing shop and finds herself being interviewed by Fred. He still believes she is the banker's daughter, but hires her anyway. Fred drives her to the Medfords' house every night, unaware that she really lives across the street from the plumbing shop. When Gertrude sees Henrietta sneaking around the bushes, she suspects her husband is cheating. When Walter notices Fred prowling the grounds, he becomes suspicious of his wife. Gertrude calls her lawyer to start divorce proceedings, while Walter visits the plumbing shop. Walter offers Fred ten thousand dollars to forget his wife, confessing that she has been involved with many men. Fred, now in love with Henrietta, thinks she is the one with a past and becomes very disillusioned. Henrietta's father straightens out the confusion.   Henrietta and Fred reconcile.

REVIEWS:
Variety, May 28, 1952:   "...entertainment values are
slight....[Ann Sheridan and John Lund] give what they can to
characters that are rather trite."

Showmen's Trade Review, May 31, 1952:   "Ann Sheridan,
always attractive, gives a smooth, convincing portrayal of
the young secretary..."

The Green Sheet, June 1, 1952:   "Good acting by an expert
cast makes this trite farce seem better than it is."

New York Times, June 28, 1952:   "[Ann] Sheridan is
perfectly cast as a practical, caustic Girl Friday to a
gullible, self-made plumber, [John] Lund, no less....The
entire cast...seems to be enjoying itself....But the loud
helter-skelter climax is so crammed with slamming doors and
coy coincidence that the film becomes more of a wise accident
than a bright surprise."

NOTES: Just Across the Street is the second in Ann
Sheridan's three-picture deal with Universal-International.
Unlike most of Ann's 1940s and 1950s films, it is seldom seen
on television.

F-84   Take Me to Town   (Universal-International, June
       1953)   81 mins.   Technicolor

Producers: Ross Hunter and Leonard Goldstein. Director:
Douglas Sirk. Assistant director: Joseph E. Kenny.
Choreographer: Hal Belfer. Screenplay: Richard Morris.
Based on the story "Flame of the Timberline" by Richard
Morris. Songs: Frederick Herbert, Milton Rosen, Lester Lee,
and Dan Shapiro. Music: Joseph Gershenson. Photography:
Russell Metty. Editor: Milton Carruth. Art direction:
Alexander Golitzen and Hilyard Brown. Sets: Russell A.
Gausman and Julia Heron. Costumes: Bill Thomas. Sound:
Leslie I. Carey and Richard DeWeese. Hair stylist: Joan St.
Oegger. Makeup: Bud Westmore. Technicolor consultant:
William Fritzsche.

CAST: Ann Sheridan (Mae Madison/Vermilion O'Toole), Sterling
Hayden (Will Hall), Philip Reed (Newton Cole), Lee Patrick
(Rose), Lee Aaker (Corney), Harvey Grant (Petey), Dusty
Henley (Bucket), Larry Gates (Ed Daggett), Phyllis Stanley
(Mrs. Stoffer), Forrest Lewis (Ed Higgins), Dorothy Neumann
(Felice Pickett), Ann Tyrell (Louise Pickett), Robert
Anderson (Chuck), Frank Sully (Sammy), Lane Chandler (Mike),
Guy Williams (Hero), Alice Kelley (Heroine), Ruth Hampton,
Jackie Loughery, Valerie Jackson, Anita Ekberg (Dance hall
girls), Fess Parker (Long John), Dusty Walker (Singer),
Mickey Little, Jimmy Karath, Jerry Wayne (Boys).

SONGS: "The Tale of Vermilion O'Toole" (Herbert), "Oh, You
Redhead" (Herbert, Rosen), "Take Me to Town" (Lee, Shapiro),
"Holy, Holy, Holy" (traditional).

SYNOPSIS: Vermilion O'Toole and her boyfriend Newton Cole
escape from federal marshal Ed Daggett after they are
arrested on bunco charges. Angry at Newton for not
explaining her innocence, Vermilion becomes a dance hall girl
at a gambling palace in the northwest lumber area. Widowed
logger and preacher Will Hall struggles to raise his three
sons and fight off the attentions of widowed parishioners.
The boys decide to find their own step-mother while their
father is at logging camp. They are entranced by Vermilion,
but she gently turns down their offer. When Vermilion learns
Daggett is on her trail, she decides to hide out in the
Halls' home. Although the parishioners are quick to
criticize Vermilion, she earns Will's respect after she saves
the boys from a grizzly bear. As Vermilion gets to know
Will, she realizes that she has dated the wrong kind of men.
The parishioners shun Vermilion because of her shady past.
Will insists that they show her brotherly love and get better
acquainted with her. Vermilion confesses to Will that the
marshal is after her. Will urges her to stay and enjoy the
simple life with him and the boys. Vermilion organizes a
show to raise money for the church building fund. The boys
are thrilled when Will and Vermilion announce they will marry
when the church is finished. Daggett promises to clear
Vermilion if she leads him to Newton. Will helps Daggett
capture the con artist. Vermilion marries Will and becomes a
Sunday school teacher.

REVIEWS:
Variety, May 20, 1953: "Since [Ann] Sheridan is a saloon
singer, there is ample reason for the sight values of the
castumes [sic] she wears for display purposes. She does
justice to them, as well as furnishing the situations and
dialog [sic] with a well-charged humorous worldliness that's
a big help to the picture."

Harrison's Reports, May 23, 1953: "[Ann] Sheridan is
appealing in her part, and quite beautiful in her dance-hall
costumes....Fine for the family."

Los Angeles Daily News, June 13, 1953: "Of course, the
very capable - and curvaceous - [Ann] Sheridan is an old hand
at this type of thing, always manages to sock over a good
performance in almost any type of role, which is one of the
reasons why the red-headed actress has remained right up at
the top for so many years."

Los Angeles Examiner, June 13, 1953: "Ann Sheridan has
the kind of role that put her in the top brackets - wise-
cracking, throw-away lines, sexy, beautifully gowned,
likable - and she should do at least a dozen more in the
same vein right away....Miss S. displays some mighty fine
cheesecake in the song-and-dance routines..."

NOTES: Take Me to Town was Ann Sheridan's third and final
film under her Universal-International contract. Like the
others, it was a percentage deal, with Ann receiving a share
of the movie's profits. At Ann's insistence, the Technicolor
musical was produced by her friend Ross Hunter (B-469). Ann

performs three songs in the film. She sings "Oh, You
Redhead" as the chorus dances behind her in a number set at
Rose's Elite Opera House. Ann joins the church congregation
in the hymn "Holy, Holy, Holy." During a rehearsal for the
church benefit, Ann demonstrates "Take Me to Town" for Ann
Tyrrell and Dorothy Neumann. Take Me to Town marked one of
sex symbol Anita Ekberg's first films. Another dance hall
girl, Jackie Loughery, was Miss USA in 1952.

In 1958, producer Ross Hunter wanted to turn Take Me
to Town into a Broadway musical for Ann Sheridan. He
suggested she get some stage experience, which led to her
appearances in Kind Sir (P-16), The Time of Your Life
(P-17), and Odd Man In (P-19). The stage musical never was
produced.

Oddly, the name of Ann's character has two spellings in
the film. On a poster advertising her appearance at Rose's
Elite Opera House, Vermilion is spelled with two "l"s. In
the closing credits, it is spelled with one.

F-85   Appointment in Honduras   (RKO, October 16, 1953)
       79 mins.   Technicolor

Producer: Benedict Bogeaus. Director: Jacques Tourneur.
Assistant director: Ralph J. Slosser. Screenplay: Karen De
Wolf. Based on a story by Mario Silveira and Jack Cornall.
Script supervisor: William Orr. Music: Louis Forbes.
Music associate: Howard Jackson. Photography: Joseph
Biroc. Editor: James Leicester. Art direction: Charles D.
Hall. Sets: Alfred E. Spencer. Costumes: Izzy Bern.
Sound: Ben Winkler. Makeup: Frank Westmore and Dave
Grayson. Special effects: Lee Zavitz. Production
supervisor: William Stephens.

CAST: Glenn Ford (Steve Corbett), Ann Sheridan (Sylvia
Sheppard), Zachary Scott (Harry Sheppard), Rodolfo Acosta
(Reyes), Jack Elam (Castro), Ric Roman (Jiminez), Rico Alaniz
(Bermudez), Paul Zaramba (Luis), Stanley Andrews (Captain
McTaggart).

SYNOPSIS: It is 1910. Adventurer Steve Corbett travels on a
South American ship with Harry and Sylvia Sheppard, a
wealthy, quarrelsome couple, and a group of hispanic
prisoners, led by Reyes. Steve wants to reroute the boat so
he can deliver a large sum of money to an Honduran leader who
was deposed by revolutionists. When Steve cannot persuade
the captain to stop, he promises the prisoners their freedom
in Guatamala if they help him take over the ship. The
prisoners knock out the crew. Steve takes the Sheppards as
hostages to protect himself. In the jungle, Steve's life is
threatened by the revolutionist leader, as well as Reyes.
Harry becomes jealous of Steve's attentions to Sylvia. She
denies any feelings and plots to escape with her husband.
However, after Steve saves the Sheppards several times,
Sylvia openly shows her growing affection for Steve and her
disdain for her cowardly husband. Sylvia nurses Steve
through malaria and discovers his money belt. She bribes
Reyes to keep him from killing Steve. When Steve recovers,
he pursues Reyes and the prisoners in an effort to retrieve

the money intended for the deposed leader. In a bloody
battle, Harry, Reyes, and the prisoners are killed. As Steve
rides off to help the anti-revolutionists, he anticipates a
new life with Sylvia.

REVIEWS:
Variety, October 28, 1953: "To be most demanded of [Ann]
Sheridan is to look jungle-weary and quarrel with her
cowardly husband. [Zachary] Scott fares no better."

The Green Sheet, November 15, 1953: "What with a jungle
full of crocodiles, snakes, pumas, tiger fish and man-eating
ants, [Glenn] Ford spends most of his time saving [Ann]
Sheridan from everything but Mr. Ford. The lady, by the
way, spends most of her time in a yellow satin negligee."

Cleveland Plain Dealer [OH], November 18, 1953: "While Ann
Sheridan is required to look miserable here, I am content to
report that very, very few can do that better than she
does...and [look] lovely at the same time."

New York Times, November 19, 1953: "[Ann] Sheridan, as the
disenchanted wife, is more tired than frightened as she
staggers through the tangled greenery in torn negligee and,
later, in shirt and dungarees."

NOTES: In 1949 RKO chief Howard Hughes promised Ann Sheridan
a role in Carriage Entrance, but they got into a dispute
about her leading man when Robert Young withdrew from the
project. Ann suggested Robert Mitchum as a replacement,
while Hughes wanted contract player Mel Ferrer. Hughes ended
up making the film with Mitchum, Melvyn Douglas, and, in
Ann's role, Hughes's girlfriend Ava Gardner. Released in
1951 as My Forbidden Past, the film was a box office
failure. Despite the fate of My Forbidden Past, Ann took
Hughes to court, suing for $350,000 damages for breach of
contract. She settled for $55,162 and a role in Appointment
in Honduras. She later admitted that she took the movie
only because she was tired of fighting (B-475). Although in
1966, Ann claimed she never saw the picture, she said, "I
heard it was an absolute horror" (B-206). Film historian
Leonard Maltin best summed up Appointment in Honduras:
"Sheridan is not focal point, and a pity" (B-337).
       The film's working title was Rage of the Jungle.
During shooting, the trade papers hinted that there was
friction between co-stars Ann Sheridan and Glenn Ford,
particularly when it came to upstaging before the camera.
Ann told the Los Angeles Times that she knew her way around
those tricks, implying that she had put Ford in his place.
"I have no financial interest in this picture," she explained
(B-543). Ann also disliked the conditions she had to endure
while making Appointment in Honduras. Since most of the
movie was set in the jungle, Ann had to have her clothes
dirtied and torn. "The thing that bothered me most was that
it took the makeup people longer to dirty me up each day than
it took me to clean it off," she said (B-543). Ann refused
to let the studio retouch the photos from the film, believing
that it would look artificial for her to look too glamorous

in the jungle. "I took a beating in this film and I want
every bit of credit for it," she said (B-543). Actor Rodolfo
Acosta, who plays the leader of the prisoners, dated Ann
Sheridan for several years after the film.
     Makeup expert Frank Westmore marked the fourth of the
six Westmore brothers that Ann Sheridan worked with during
her career. Wally helmed Paramount's makeup department in
the 1930s and is credited in Limehouse Blues (F-14). Perc
was head of the makeup department at Warner Bros. during the
time she was under contract and is credited in most of her
Warners films. Bud was head of makeup at Universal and
receives credit for Steel Town (F-82), Take Me to Town
(F-84), and The Far Out West (F-89).

See also V-20.

F-86 Come Next Spring   (Republic, 1956)   92 mins.
      color

Producer: Herbert J. Yates. Director: R.G. Springsteen.
Assistant director: Herb Mendelson. Screenplay: Montgomery
Pittman. Song "Come Next Spring": Lenny Adelson and Max
Steiner. Music: Max Steiner. Photography: Jack Marta.
Editor: Tony Martinelli. Art direction: Frank Arrigo.
Sets: John McCarthy, Jr. and George Milo. Costumes: Adele
Palmer. Sound: Dick Tyler, Sr. and Howard Wilson. Makeup:
Bob Mark. Optical effects: Consolidated Film Industries.
Special effects: Howard and Theodore Lydecker.

CAST: Ann Sheridan (Bess Ballot), Steve Cochran (Matt
Ballot), Walter Brennan (Jeff Storys), Sherry Jackson (Annie
Ballot), Richard Eyer (Abraham Ballot), Edgar Buchanan (Mr.
Canary), Sonny Tufts (Leroy Hytower), Harry Shannon (Mr.
Totter), Rad Fulton (Bob Storys), Mae Clarke (Myrtle), Roscoe
Ates (Shorty Wilkins), Wade Ruby (Delbert Meaner), James Best
(Bill Jackson).

SYNOPSIS: Hard-drinking Matt Ballot returns to his Arkansas
farm and family after a nine-year absence. He hopes to prove
he has reformed to his wife Bess and their children, Annie, a
mute, and Abraham. Bess agrees to let him work the farm and
get reacquainted with his children, although she wants their
relationship to remain platonic. Matt is shunned by his old
friends. Neighbor Mr. Canary tells him that the only way he
can convince them of his reform is to remain with his family
until next spring. Bess is slow to forgive her husband,
unable to forget the pain he put her through during his
absence. Matt risks alienating the children by confessing
that his drinking caused the accident that made Annie lose
her speech. Annie forgives him. Bess realizes that she
still loves Matt, but her fear of abandonment keeps her from
reconciling. Matt proves himself during a tornado, organ-
izing the citizens and saving Annie's life. During the
annual Halloween dance, the men taunt Matt into taking a
drink. Matt loses his temper when rival Leroy Hytower flirts
with another man's date. Bess is furious about the drinking
and fighting and leaves. During the party, Annie and her dog
disappear. As Matt and the men look for her, he tells Bess

he plans to take Annie to a specialist to restore her speech.
Bess begs him to stay on the farm so they can be a real
family again. Annie falls over a cliff on her way home from
visiting her dog's new pups. She hangs perilously until her
fear forces her to scream. Matt rescues her with the help of
his friends. As her parents reconcile, Annie continues to
scream, happy to have her voice back.

REVIEWS:
Harrison's Reports, February 11, 1956: "Good family
entertainment. It is a heartwarming and poignant story....
Enhanced by a good script and understanding direction, it is
the type of tale that makes a direct appeal to the emotions
without becoming maudlin....Ann Sheridan...turns in a fine
portrayal as the wife who falls in love with [Steve] Cochran
once again but who restrains her feelings until she is sure
of his rehabilitation."

Picturegoer [England], March 10, 1956: "Equally beguiling
is Ann Sheridan, as the wife....I can't remember being so
moved in the cinema for years. The film has a quality of
warmth and humanity that is far more realistic than most of
the so-called 'realistic' shockers that have been shot at
us."

Films in Review, March 1956: "Ann Sheridan, as [Steve
Cochran's] wife, has never acted so well, and she portrays
with insight a backroad countrywoman. Her beauty has been
made down to that of an abandoned wife and worried mother."

Los Angeles Times, April 4, 1956: "[Ann] Sheridan gives a
sincere, worth-while [sic] performance of the long-suffering
wife and mother, who is torn between taking back her husband
and her fear that he hasn't completely conquered liquor."

NOTES: Filmed on location in Sacramento, California, Come
Next Spring was packaged by Republic star Steve Cochran.
Critics praised the movie's simplicity and family appeal.
Photoplay called it "an unassuming, thoroughly winning
story" (April 1956). Commonweal noted that it was a
pleasure to see an outdoor movie "without the gun slinging
and trumped-up violence" (April 13, 1956). Despite the
outstanding reviews, Republic did little to promote the
small, sensitive film and it did poorly at the box office.
Ann Sheridan recalled that Come Next Spring was supposed to
receive an "A" picture release, but Republic often delegated
it to the second feature on double bills. Since the studio
did not own the film, they accepted any booking available
(B-206). In recent years, film historians have deemed it one
of Ann Sheridan's best performances and it has become a minor
cult classic. Tony Bennett sings the title song over the
opening credits.

See also S-12.

F-87   The Opposite Sex   (MGM, October 1956)   115 mins.
        Metrocolor

Producer: Joe Pasternak. Director: David Miller.
Assistant director: George Rhain. Choreographer: Robert
Sidney. Screenplay: Fay and Michael Kanin. Based on the
play The Women by Clare Boothe. Songs: Nicholas Brodszky,
Sammy Cahn, George Stoll, and Ralph Freed. Music: Nicholas
Brodszky. Orchestrations: Albert Sendrey and Skip Martin.
Musical supervision: George Stoll. Vocal supervision:
Robert Tucker. Music coordinator: Irving Aaronson.
Photography: Robert Bronner. Editor: John McSweeney, Jr.
Art direction: Cedric Gibbons and Daniel B. Cathcart. Sets:
Edwin B. Willis and Harry Grace. Costumes: Helen Rose.
Recording supervisor: Dr. McKay O. Miller. Hairstylist:
Sydney Guilaroff. Makeup: William Tuttle. Special effects:
A. Arnold Gillespie and Warren Newcombe. Color consultant:
Charles K. Hazedorn.

CAST: June Allyson (Kay Hilliard), Joan Collins (Crystal
Allen), Dolores Gray (Sylvia Fowler), Ann Sheridan (Amanda
Penrose), Ann Miller (Gloria Doll), Leslie Nielsen (Steve
Hilliard), Jeff Richards (Buck Winston), Agnes Moorehead
(Countess Lavaliere), Charlotte Greenwood (Lucy), Joan
Blondell (Edith Potter), Sam Levene (Mike Pearl), Bill
Goodwin (Howard Fowler), Alice Pearce (Olga), Barbara Jo
Allen [Vera Vague] (Dolly), Sandy Descher (Debbie Hilliard),
Carolyn Jones (Pat), Jerry Antes (Dancer), Alan Marshal
(Ted), Jonathan Hale (Phelps Potter), Harry James (Himself),
Art Mooney (Himself), Dick Shawn (Singer in benefit number),
Jim Backus (Psychiatrist in benefit number), Celia Lovsky
(Lutsi), Harry McKenna (Hughie), Ann Moriss (Receptionist),
Dean Jones (Assistant stage manager), Kay English
(Aristocratic woman), Gordon Richards (Butler), Barrie Chase,
Ellen Ray (Benefit dancers), Gail Bonney, Maxine Sermon, Jean
Andren (Gossips), Bob Hopkins (Drunk in 21 Club), Janet Lake
(Girl on train), Jo Gilbert (Woman attendant), Donald
Dillaway (Box office man), Joe Karnes (Pianist), Juanita
Moore (Maid), Vivian Marshal (Girl), Marc Wilder (Dancer),
Marjorie Helen (Leg model), Trio Ariston (Specialty act), Jo
Ann Greer (Voice double for June Allyson on "A Perfect
Love").

SONGS: "The Opposite Sex," "A Perfect Love," "Now! Baby,
Now!," "Dere's Yellow Gold on De Trees," "Rock and Roll
Tumbleweed" (Cahn, Brodszky), "Young Man with a Horn" (Freed,
Stoll), "Jungle Red" (Brodszky).

SYNOPSIS: Playwright Amanda Penrose dislikes the catty,
back-stabbing ways of her friends, especially chief gossip
Sylvia Fowler. Although Kay Hilliard is her friend, Sylvia
cannot wait to report that Kay's producer husband Steve is
cheating with chorus girl Crystal Allen. Jealous of Kay's
happiness with Steve and daughter Debbie, Sylvia sends her to
get a manicure, knowing she also will hear the gossip.
Although Steve breaks off the affair, gold digger Crystal
vows to trap him. While Kay is away, reexamining her
marriage, Crystal tries to befriend Debbie and make another
play for Steve. He rebuffs Crystal, realizing he loves his
wife. Kay returns and resumes her marriage. When Sylvia and
Crystal imply that the affair is continuing, Kay confronts

Steve. Despite his protests of innocence, Kay goes to Reno
to get a divorce. There, she runs into Sylvia, who lost her
husband to dancer Gloria Doll. Sylvia quickly recovers,
romancing singing ranch hand Buck Winston. Amanda begs Kay
to reconcile with Steve before he gets involved with Crystal
on the rebound. Kay decides to tear up her decree, but
before she can tell Steve, he elopes with Crystal. Kay
returns to New York and resumes her singing career. Sylvia
brings Buck to New York, determined to turn him into a
successful cowboy crooner. Buck begins an affair with
newlywed Crystal. Debbie confides to Kay that Steve still
loves her and that Crystal is cheating with Buck. Kay
decides to become as catty and ruthless as Sylvia and fight
for her man. At Buck's nightclub opening, Kay enlists the
help of a columnist to reveal Buck's affair to Sylvia.
Crystal asks Steve for a divorce, sure she is set with Buck.
She is shocked when Buck rebuffs her, insisting a
relationship will ruin his image as a sex symbol. Kay
reconciles with Steve, determined not to let her friends
interfere in their happiness again.

REVIEWS:
Saturday Review of Literature, November 17, 1956: "The
ladies this time are June Allyson, Joan Collins, and Ann
Sheridan....Somewhere along the line whatever bite was in
[The Women] has been dissipated. The movie is terribly
old-fashioned, very sentimental, and a bore."

Detroit Times [MI], November 18, 1956: "[Ann] Sheridan
stands out as the moral friend determined to save June
[Allyson's] marriage."

Films in Review, November 1956: "The Kanins wrote a new
part...a successful career woman, and [it] is well played by
an actress whose future could be more distinguished than her
past - Ann Sheridan. I thought she out-glamoured everybody
else. And she has the best line of dialogue: 'Females - the
lost sex, substituting fashion for passion and the
psychoanalyst's couch for the double bed.'"

The New Yorker, December 15, 1956: "The ladies assembled
for The Opposite Sex have all the best of the acting
assignments, the men...being compelled to function as
hopelessly as male spiders. Leading the feminine pack are
June Allyson...; Joan Collins...; Ann Sheridan, who plays -
Lord knows how she got into the act - a sympathetic literary
type; and Agnes Moorehead....Collectively, they're a bit
frightening."

NOTES: The Opposite Sex is based on Clare Boothe's play
The Women, which opened on Broadway on December 26, 1936
and ran for 657 performances. MGM first filmed the comedy in
1939 with Norma Shearer, Rosalind Russell, Joan Crawford, and
Paulette Goddard in the roles taken by June Allyson, Dolores
Gray, Joan Collins, and Ann Miller in the remake. The least
gossipy of the females, originally played by Adrienne Marden
on stage and Joan Fontaine on screen, was overhauled for Ann
Sheridan. Instead of a naive newlywed, Ann plays an

unmarried career woman who is the only true friend Allyson's character has. Although many men were mentioned in Boothe's play and the original film, both employed all female casts, with the action involving the males taking place offstage. The Opposite Sex adds actors to the story.

Despite the fact that The Opposite Sex cast many musical performers in key roles, few of them were able to utilize their talents in the film. Neither Dolores Gray nor Ann Miller, best known for their singing and dancing, have the opportunity to appear in a musical number. However, an uncredited Gray can be heard singing the title song over the opening credits. Most of the songs are woven into the plot, taking place during one of Steve's shows, Kay's act, or Buck's debut. A flashback scene shows June Allyson singing "Young Man with a Horn" with Harry James. Although Allyson and James originally performed the number in Two Girls and a Sailor (MGM, 1944), new footage is used in The Opposite Sex.

The hair and nail salon where the women receive their gossip is named Sydney's, a nod to hairstylist Sydney Guilaroff, who worked on the film.

Although Ann Sheridan had appeared in remakes of many Joan Blondell films at Warner Bros., The Opposite Sex is the only time they worked together. Coincidentally, both Blondell and June Allyson were married to Dick Powell, who appeared with Ann in Cowboy from Brooklyn (F-41) and Naughty But Nice (F-48).

See also S-13, V-21.

F-88   The Woman and the Hunter   (Gross-Krasne-Phoenix, 1957)   79 mins.

Producer: George Breakston. Executive producer: Brian Robson. Associate producer: Robert V. Perkins. Director: George Breakston. Screenplay: Maurice H. Conn. Music: Phil Green. Musical director: Phil Green. Photography: E. Kyrath and Johnny Johnson. Supervising editor: Klaus Dudenhofer. Sets: Michael Boltbee. Costumes: Audrey Cooper. Sound: John R. Carter. Location manager: Vincent Navothey. Unit manager: Alan Tarlton.

CAST: Ann Sheridan (Laura Dodd), David Farrar (David Kirby), John Loder (Mitchell Gifford), Jan Merlin (Robert Gifford), Ronald Adam, Howarth Wood, Brian Epsom, Ed Johnson, John Cook.

SYNOPSIS: Greedy secretary Laura Dodd is angry when wealthy Mitchell Gifford breaks their engagement before he goes on a safari. She decides to pit Mitchell against his alcoholic son Robert and get the Gifford fortune. She convinces Robert to assert his independence by hiring David Kirby instead of the guide Mitchell prefers. Laura not only is attracted to David, but thinks she can blame him for trouble, since he lost a man on safari. In the African jungle, Robert falls in love with Laura and becomes jealous of David's attentions to her. Laura builds Robert's confidence and self respect while romancing David on the sly. Although she loves David, she

admits that she has grown used to the Giffords' wealthy
lifestyle. Motivated by greed, Laura elopes with a drunken
Robert. She flaunts her marriage to Mitchell and tries to
blackmail him. When he refuses to cooperate, Laura shoots
him in cold blood. She lies to David, claiming she killed
Mitchell in self-defense. Marriage gives Robert a new self
confidence and he looks forward to standing up to his father.
Inspector McGregor reaches the camp and reports Mitchell's
death.. McGregor suspects Robert, but David supplies a phony
alibi. At David's urging, Laura agrees to tell McGregor she
killed Mitchell in self-defense. She vows to be with David
someday. On safari, Robert saves David's life when David
panics during a lion attack. David realizes Laura is using
him to get rid of the Giffords. He accuses her of killing
Mitchell in cold blood to frame Robert and inherit his money.
When McGregor confronts Robert with the murder weapon, Robert
admits he could have shot his father during a drunken
blackout. After McGregor explains that Robert will not get
his inheritance if he is convicted, Robert decides to commit
suicide so Laura can get the Gifford fortune. David and
Laura try to stop Robert from killing himself. David
convinces Robert of his innocence. Laura is trampled by an
elephant. On her deathbed, she confesses to McGregor.

REVIEW:
Monthly Film Bulletin, April 1961: "It is a pity that two
such rarely seen stars as Ann Sheridan and John Loder should
be involved in the trite love-hate relationships which form
the mainstay of this safari melodrama. The spliced-in
action sequences carry little conviction, the photography is
squalid and the direction lacks aplomb."

NOTES: The Woman and the Hunter is a low-budget British
adventure story, shot in Africa. It marked Ann Sheridan's
last original movie and one she came to regret. Ann told
Louella Parsons that she received the script for The Woman
and the Hunter in May 1956, while finishing The Opposite
Sex (F-87). She was so excited about the film, she
accepted the producers' offer the same day (B-482). She left
Hollywood on June 3, 1956; shooting began in Africa on
June 11. Part of her reason for accepting the role was the
travel opportunity it provided. The film also offered
another incentive. Since Ann received a percentage deal, its
success could mean a financial windfall. Although Ann liked
the original script, she was angered by the way the movie was
cut. She also disliked the odd skin tones in the film,
caused by color makeup being photographed in black and white.
Ann called The Woman and the Hunter "the damnedest thing
I've ever seen in my life" (B-475).
        Although intended for theatrical release, The Woman
and the Hunter was sold directly to television in the
United States. In Great Britain, it is known as Triangle
on Safari. Jack Gross and Philip Krasne's production
company, Gross-Krasne-Phoenix, released the film, but they
are not billed.

F-89   The Far Out West   (Universal, 1967)   87 mins.
        Technicolor

Producer: Joe Connelly. Associate producer: Irving Paley.
Director: Joe Connelly. Assistant directors: Jack Doran
and Lou Watt. Screenplay: George Tibbles. Music: Jack
Elliott. Music supervisor: Stanley Wilson. Photography:
Benjamin H. Kline and Irving I. Lippman. Editors: Michael
R. McAdam and Bud S. Isaacs. Art direction: Robert Crawley,
Howard E. Johnson, Frank Arrigo, and William D. DeCinces.
Sets: John McCarthy, Audrey Blasdel, Julia Heron, and James
S. Redd. Costumes: Helen Colvig. Sound: James Tom Porter,
Frank H. Wilkinson, and Robert Bertrand. Hairstyles: Larry
Germain. Makeup: Bud Westmore. Unit production managers:
James Hogan, Jack Corrick, and Edward K. Dodds. Editorial
supervision: Richard Belding. Color coordinator: Robert
Brower.

CAST: Ann Sheridan (Henrietta "Hank" Hanks), Ruth McDevitt
(Grandma Dora), Douglas V. Fowley (Grandpa Andrew), Carole
Welles (Lucy Hanks), Gary Vinson (Sheriff Harold Sikes),
Robert Lowery (Buss Courtney), Morgan Woodward (Mark
Hangman), Lon Chaney, Jr. (Chief Eagle Shadow), Marc Cavell
(Gray Hawk), Leo Gordon (Cyrus Breach), Jay Silverheels
(Great Bear), Alex Henteloff (Little Bear), Stanley Adams
(Jed Timmons), Eleanor Audley (Mrs. Teasley), Gil Lamb (Town
drunk), Quinn O'Hara (Mary McTigue), Fred Willard (Trooper
Evans), George Murdock (First gunman), Francine Pyne
(Flossie), Bill Oberlin (Fat man), Willis Bouchey (Doctor).

SYNOPSIS: Cattleman Buss Courtney plots with justice of the
peace/real estate broker/attorney Jed Timmons to steal the
land and water rights in Wretched, Colorado in 1871. Jed
explains that their biggest obstacle is the Hanks family:
sharp-shooter Hank, her parents Dora and Andrew, and her
daughter Lucy. Buss sets out to get control of the Hankses'
land with a series of plans that backfire: provoking a
gunfight with Andrew, inciting an Indian attack, and
instigating a war between rival Indian tribes. When these
fail, Buss tries to get the Hankses' water rights by
proposing to Hank. She overhears his plan and knocks him
out. His henchmen kidnap her and ask for the ranch as
ransom. Dora rescues Hank before bumbling Sheriff Harold
Sikes can arrive. Buss pays for the damages and goes to
jail. He vows to keep fighting for the ranch, but promises
not to toy with Hank's affections again.

NOTES: After Ann Sheridan's death, Universal combined
several episodes of her television series Pistols 'n'
Petticoats (T-56) to make the telefilm The Far Out West.
Among the episodes used are the following, which are listed
in the television chapter: PnP-2, PnP-5, and PnP-11.
Although the series is seldom rerun, due to the small number
of episodes and its lack of popularity, The Far Our West
continues to be syndicated and aired on TV late shows across
the country.

RADIO

Ann Sheridan's national radio appearances are listed chronologically in this chapter. Each entry offers the name of the series, episode title, date of broadcast, network, cast, and a brief description. Selected reviews also are provided. NN indicates a non-network or syndicated series. AFRS denotes programs broadcast to servicemen over the Armed Forces Radio Service. Regional programs and those done outside the United States are not included.

R-1   The Kraft Music Hall   November 10, 1938   NBC
      60 mins.

Bing Crosby hosted this variety program sponsored by Kraft. Among the guests were Ann Sheridan, actor Brian Aherne, soprano Mafalda Favero, drummer Gene Krupa, and the Foursome Quartet. John Scott Trotter conducted the orchestra.

R-2   The Gulf Screen Guild Show   May 28, 1939   CBS
      30 mins.

Performers donated their time for the Screen Actor's Guild on this weekly anthology. Roland Young hosted this episode, a variety revue with guests Ann Sheridan, Fibber McGee and Molly (Jim and Marion Jordan), Douglas Fairbanks, Jr., and the Music Maids. Ann flirted with McGee, who called himself the Oomph Man. The program was directed by Frank Borzage and written by Eddie Moran. Gulf Oil was the sponsor.

R-3   The Gulf Screen Guild Show   "Elmer the Great"
      April 14, 1940   CBS   30 mins.

This episode of the anthology series was an adaptation of the movie Elmer the Great (Warner Bros., 1933), which had starred Joe E. Brown and Patricia Ellis. The radio version featured Bob Hope as a naive baseball player who got involved with crooks. Elvia Allman co-starred in the radio play. Although several sources list Ann Sheridan as the leading lady on this broadcast, radio expert Larry Gassman said that Rita Hayworth performed the female lead. Since the program was broadcast live, it is possible that Hayworth was a last-

minute substitution for Ann, who already was having contract
problems at Warner Bros.

R-4   The Jack Benny Show   May 3, 1942   NBC   30 mins.

To promote George Washington Slept Here (F-64), Ann
Sheridan and director William Keighley appeared as themselves
on Jack Benny's comedy program. The premise had series
regulars Mary Livingstone, Dennis Day, Phil Harris, and Eddie
"Rochester" Anderson visiting Benny on the Warner Bros. set.
They watched Benny and Ann rehearse scenes about his film
character's proposal and the couple's first quarrel. The
scenes were not part of the actual movie. Since Benny was
single on the radio show, a subplot had him flirting with Ann
when filming stopped. Ironically, Mary Livingstone suspected
a real life flirtation (B-91). The program was written by
Bill Morrow and Ed Beloin and sponsored by Jello.

R-5   Mail Call   #3   August 27, 1942   AFRS   30 mins.

Ann Sheridan, Jack Benny, Rosemary Lane, and the King's Men
performed on this half-hour variety show aimed at servicemen.

R-6   The Lady Esther Screen Guild Theatre   "Love Is News"
       June 14, 1943   CBS   30 mins.

Jack Benny, Ann Sheridan, and James Gleason starred in this
comedy about an heiress (Sheridan) and an annoying reporter
(Benny). She pretended to be engaged to him to teach him a
lesson about living life in a goldfish bowl, but ended up
falling in love with him. This episode of the anthology
series was based on a 1937 20th Century-Fox movie, which
starred Tyrone Power, Loretta Young, and Don Ameche.

R-7   Burns and Allen   September 28, 1943   CBS   30 mins.

Ann Sheridan appeared as herself on this comedy program
hosted by George Burns and Gracie Allen. The premise had Ann
going to the Burnses' house to discuss their work at a U.S.O.
canteen. When announcer Bill Goodwin fell in love with Ann,
Gracie and her friend Toots Sagwell (Bea Benaderet) tried to
"de-oomph" her. Ann finally resorted to flirting with George
to discourage the unwanted suitor. Other cast members
included tenor Jimmy Cash, Felix Mills and His Orchestra, and
the musical group the Swantet. The show was sponsored by
Swan Soap. The script for this program is part of the George
Burns-Gracie Allen Collection at the USC Cinema-Television
Library.

R-8   Command Performance   #155   January 1944   AFRS
       30 mins.

Bob Hope hosted this broadcast that was beamed to armed
forces around the globe. Guests included Ann Sheridan, Benny
Goodman and His Quartet, cartoonist Bill Mauldin, Bing
Crosby, and the Andrews Sisters. Ann clowned with Hope and
Crosby, appearing in a skit about a little boy misbehaving on
her movie set. She fulfilled a serviceman's request by

pretending to dream about him while Crosby sang Brahm's
Lullaby.

R-9   <u>George Washington Slept Here</u>· 1944   AFRS   30 mins.

The War Department syndicated this half-hour dramatization to
armed forces stations. Jack Benny and Ann Sheridan reprised
their 1942 film roles (F-64).

R-10 <u>Mail Call</u> 1944   AFRS   30 mins.

Ann Sheridan acted as mistress of ceremonies on the variety
series aimed at servicemen (B-399).

R-11 <u>Command Performance</u>   #212   circa 1944   AFRS
      30 mins.

Ann Sheridan appeared on this broadcast aimed at servicemen.

R-12 <u>The Show Goes On</u>   December 6, 1944   NBC   60 mins.

Bing Crosby and Bob Hope were the masters of ceremonies on
this all-star broadcast produced by NBC and the War
Activities Committee to increase war bond sales. The cast
included Larry Adler, Fred Astaire, Edgar Bergen, James
Cagney, Jerry Colonna, Paulette Goddard, Frances Langford,
Adolphe Menjou, Merle Oberon, Ann Sheridan, Dinah Shore, and
Meredith Willson and His Orchestra.

REVIEW:
<u>Variety</u>, December 13, 1944: "Here's a show that merited a
four-network hookup in the 'heart' of the evening....But what
happens? One of the top radio shows of the year is tucked
away in the quiet 11:30-12:30 (EWT) nighttime spot....here
was a gold-mine package of solid showmanship virtually
wasted."

R-13 <u>The Jack Benny Show</u>   January 28, 1945   NBC
      30 mins.

Ann Sheridan was a guest on the comedy program, which was
broadcast from Mitchell Field in California. An incomplete
tape of the program is in the collection at the Library of
Congress. The show was sponsored by the American Tobacco
Company (Lucky Strike cigarettes).

R-14 Unidentified shortwave broadcast   circa 1945   AFRS

According to <u>Screen Stars</u>, April 1945, Ann Sheridan and Bob
Hope appeared on a shortwave broadcast for servicemen
overseas (B-565). It is not known if the photograph was
taken at their <u>Command Performance</u> broadcast from January
1944 (R-8) or another show.

R-15 <u>Let Yourself Go</u>   May 16, 1945   CBS   30 mins.

Ann Sheridan was a guest on this radio game show hosted by
Milton Berle. Contestants and celebrities were encouraged to

release long-suppressed urges and "let themselves go" by
participating in stunts.

R-16 **The Raleigh Room with Hildegarde**   May 22, 1945   NBC
       30 mins.

Pianist/chanteuse Hildegarde hosted this musical game show
sponsored by Raleigh cigarettes. Broadcast from New York,
contestants tried to stump the band with musical questions.
Ann Sheridan and Bert Lahr were guests.

R-17 **Time to Smile** June 20, 1945   NBC   30 mins.

Ann Sheridan appeared as a Coast Guard instructor in this
comedy/variety program hosted by Eddie Cantor. This
broadcast originated from the U.S. Coast Guard Training
Station in Manhattan Beach, New York. Series regulars
included "The Mad Russian" (Bert Gordon), singer Fred
Martell, announcer Don Wilson, Leonard Seuss and His
Orchestra, and Nora Martin. The program also was known as
The Eddie Cantor Show.

R-18 **The Smiths of Hollywood**   "Cancer Fund Drive"   #6
       February 14, 1947   NN   30 mins.

This syndicated half-hour drama from Hollywood featured
Brenda Marshall, Arthur Treacher, and Harry Von Zell. Ann
Sheridan guested on an episode about a cancer fund drive.

R-19 **The Smiths of Hollywood**   #24   June 22, 1947   NN
       30 mins.

Ann Sheridan returned for another episode of this half-hour
drama with Brenda Marshall, Arthur Treacher, and Harry Von
Zell.

R-20 **Chesterfield Supper Club**   September 22, 1949   NBC
       30 mins.

Perry Como, the Fontaine Sisters, and the Mitchell Ayres
Orchestra were among the regulars on this musical program.
Although the **New York Times** lists Fibber McGee and Molly
(Jim and Marion Jordan) as guests, the NBC Radio Index at the
Library of Congress credits Ann Sheridan as "star of the
week" on the series.

R-21 **Hollywood Calling**   December 18, 1949   NBC
       60 mins.

George Murphy hosted this movie quiz program that had actors
calling listeners to test their film knowledge. According to
the NBC Radio Index, Ann Sheridan was a guest on this
episode.

R-22 **Anacin Hollywood Star Theatre**   "Experiment in
       Murder"   February 4, 1950   30 mins.

As guest of honor, Ann Sheridan introduced Jim Backus, who

had the lead role in the drama "Experiment in Murder."
Later, Ann chatted with the actor, plugging their mutual
projects. The show was sponsored by Anacin.

R-23 **Bill Stern's Colgate Sports Newsreel of the Air**
      October 13, 1950   NBC   15 mins.

Sports reporter Bill Stern told a story about a Texas
football player who loved the game, revealing at the end that
it was Ann Sheridan. In an interview, Ann recalled her
childhood as a tomboy and said her current favorite sport was
bullfighting.

R-24 **Edgar Bergen with Charlie McCarthy**   May 20, 1951
      CBS   30 mins.

Ann Sheridan played herself on this comedy program hosted by
ventriloquist Edgar Bergen and his flirtatious dummy Charlie
McCarthy. Ann traded quips with her hosts and appeared in a
skit about Little Red Riding Hood, which cast Charlie as the
wolf. Show regulars included actors Pat Patrick and Elvia
Allman, ventriloquist dummy Mortimer Snerd, and Ray Nobel and
His Orchestra. The show was sponsored by Coca-Cola. The
script for this episode is part of the Edgar Bergen
Collection at the USC Cinema-Television Library.

R-25 **The Big Show**   November 11, 1951   NBC   90 mins.

Tallulah Bankhead hosted this variety program, which featured
a melange of guests: Ann Sheridan, singers Morton Downey,
June Valli, and Sophie Tucker, comedians Jerry Lester and
Jackie Miles, and actor/raconteur Ken Murray. Ann played
Sari in a skit entitled "The Last Day of All." A tape of the
broadcast can be found at the Library of Congress.

R-26 **Stars in the Air**   "Good Sam"   March 13, 1952   CBS
      30 mins.

Ann Sheridan and David Wayne appeared in a dramatization of
Good Sam, with Wayne essaying the part played by Gary
Cooper in the 1948 film (F-78).

R-27 **The Dean Martin and Jerry Lewis Show**   April 25, 1952
      NBC   30 mins.

Ann Sheridan was a guest on this comedy show hosted by singer
Dean Martin and comedian Jerry Lewis. The program was
broadcast from Hollywood.

R-28 **The Kate Smith Show**   April 27, 1952   NBC   30 mins.

The NBC Radio Index at the Library of Congress lists Ann
Sheridan as a guest on the program.

R-29 **The Dean Martin and Jerry Lewis Show**   October 21,
      1952   NBC   30 mins.

Ann Sheridan returned to the comedy program, appearing in a

sketch entitled "Just Plain Bedlam" with hosts Dean Martin
and Jerry Lewis. The show originated from Hollywood and was
sponsored by Chesterfield cigarettes.

TELEVISION

This chapter is a chronological listing of Ann Sheridan's national television appearances. Anthology episodes broadcast on more than one series are noted under both titles. Theatrical motion pictures shown on TV, telethons, and repeats are not listed. A few regional broadcasts are noted because of their significance. Each entry includes the name of the series, the episode title, the date of broadcast, the network, and a brief synopsis of the type of series and Ann's participation. Selected reviews also are provided. NN denotes a non-network or syndicated show. Programs available on video cassette are noted by a number with the prefix "V," leading the reader to the proper entry in the videography.

T-1   The Ed Wynn Show   February 11, 1950   CBS   30 mins.

Ann Sheridan made her television debut on this Los Angeles-based variety program hosted by the legendary "perfect fool." She traded quips with Ed Wynn and appeared in a comic western sketch, pretending to replace Gary Cooper. Singer Robert Clary, best known for his later role on Hogan's Heroes (CBS, 1965-71), also was a guest. The show was broadcast live on the west coast, while kinescopes aired in the east and midwest. Usually the west received kinescopes of eastern broadcasts.

REVIEW:
Variety, February 15, 1950: "Ann Sheridan...proved again the old adage that a talented performer in any part of show business will show well on TV. She was on more than 20 minutes with [Ed] Wynn, socking across some patter and then lampooning Gary Cooper's 'yep' and 'nope' type of dramatics in a western satire."

See also V-23.

T-2   Stop the Music   October 26, 1950   ABC   60 mins.

Bert Parks, best known as the master of ceremonies of the Miss America pageant, hosted this prime time game show. Audience members and home viewers were called upon to

identify songs sung by Parks and others. Ann Sheridan
reportedly earned $3,500 for her guest spot, which included
acting in four skits and plugging her next film, Woman on
the Run (F-81). Singers Jimmy Blaine, Betty Ann Grove, and
Marion Morgan, the Variety Dancers, and the Harry Salter
Orchestra also performed on the program.

REVIEW:
Variety, November 1, 1950: "Ann Sheridan, subjecting
herself to the kind of raucous slapstick that no film
director probably would have dared to suggest to her, must
have won new fans with her guest appearance on ABC-TV's Stop
the Music....[She]...has played her quota of comedy roles in
pictures but it was a complete surprise to see her get
slapped around by a paintbrush wielded by emcee Bert Parks
and to take a rough-looking pratfall and still come up
smiling."

T-3   The Kate Smith Evening Hour   November 21, 1951   NBC
       60 mins.

Kate Smith's guests on this Thanksgiving episode of her
variety show included Ann Sheridan, comedian Myron Cohen,
actor Philip Reed, and three dancers from the New York City
Ballet. Ann appeared in a dramatic skit entitled "Beginner's
Luck," playing a divorcee who convinces a philandering
husband (Reed) to return to his wife. The listing in The
Cincinnati Enquirer erroneously heralded this appearance as
Ann's TV debut.

See also V-24.

T-4   The Colgate Comedy Hour   May 25, 1952   NBC
       60 mins.

Ben Blue hosted this episode of the variety program, which
rotated emcees each week. Guests included Ann Sheridan,
singer Peggy Lee, the dancing Step Brothers, and vocal group
The Whippoorwills. Ann and Blue appeared in a sketch about a
couple battling over their favorite television programs while
they struggled to dress for the evening.

REVIEWS:
Daily Variety, May 26, 1952: "...one sketch with guestar
[sic] Ann Sheridan became absolutely silly. It revolved
about a couple's squabbles over their favorite TV program.
While the idea may have merit, the lines handed the pair were
not laugh-provoking. Miss Sheridan was completely wasted."

Variety, May 28, 1952: "Hollywood star Ann Sheridan worked
neatly with [Ben] Blue in a boudoir bit in which both were
dressing for the opera. A TV set in the room was good for
laughs as she insisted upon tuning 'The Continental' while he
was partial to 'The Lone Ranger.' There was also mutual
confusion as both struggled to don their garb despite stuck
zippers, etc."

T-5   What's My Line?   July 20, 1952   CBS   30 mins.

Ann Sheridan was the Mystery Guest on this long-running prime
time game show moderated by John Daly. The blindfolded
panelists who tried to guess Ann's identity included Arlene
Francis, Bennett Cerf, and Dorothy Kilgallen.

T-6   The Colgate Comedy Hour   November 16, 1952   NBC
       60 mins.

Donald O'Connor hosted this episode of the variety series,
with guests Ann Sheridan, the singing Bell Sisters, and comic
actors Patti Moore, Ben Lessy, Sid Miller, Hal March, and Tom
D'Andrea. Ann played a French saleswoman in a sketch that
had O'Connor visiting her perfume shop.

REVIEWS:
Daily Variety, November 17, 1952: "Ann Sheridan was cast
as a French perfumer, whose accent was too phoney to be
funny. It would have been better had she played it straight.
Spark was missing, here, too and the film star struggled
against too many odds to make her appearance more
impressive."

Variety, November 19, 1952: "[Donald] O'Connor's top guest
star was Ann Sheridan, and Miss Sheridan was no help. She
fluffed a couple of times and failed to punch over the lines
in the sketch with the headliner, a weak piece of material in
which Miss Sheridan played a French saleswoman in a gift
shop. And Miss Sheridan had better shed some of that heft,
or was it the dress that made her look that way?"

T-7   Ford Theater   "Malaya Incident"   June 18, 1953
       NBC   30 mins.

Producer: Irving Starr. Director: John Brahm. Production
executive: Fred Briskin. Screenplay: Adele Commandini.
Photography: Gert Andersen. Art director: Rose Bellah.
Editor: Richard Fantl.

CAST: Ann Sheridan, Richard Egan, Steven Geray, Phyllis
Stanley, Margaret Blankley, Bernie Gozler, Sanders Clark,
Alec Harford.

In this episode of the dramatic anthology series, Ann
Sheridan played a woman of questionable reputation who
tricked Richard Egan into leading her out of the jungle.
Along the way, Egan battled some Communist guerrillas and the
couple fell in love. The show was filmed in Hollywood.

REVIEW:
Daily Variety, June 22, 1953: "This time the story gets a
good production dressing and okay performances from Ann
Sheridan and Richard Egan to give the rubber-locale yarn
enough bounce to satisfy....Cast toppers are both good..."

T-8   Dunninger   1953   NN   30 mins.

According to TV expert David Inman, Ann Sheridan appeared as
a guest on this syndicated program hosted by mentalist Joseph

Dunninger (B-266). No additional information is available.

T-9   Lux Video Theatre   "The Lovely Day"   August 13,
       1953   CBS   30 mins.

Producers: Jack Gross and Phil Krasne. Associate producer:
Marshall Grant. Director: Peter Godfrey. Teleplay:
Lawrence Kimble. Based on "Mother's Day" by Mildred
Masterson McNeilly. Editor: Chester Schaeffer.
Photography: Frederick Gately.

CAST: Ann Sheridan (Mrs. Russell), Robert Paige (Bill
Russell), Sandy Descher (Linto Russell), Tom Powers (Mr.
Marshall), "Scat Man" Crothers (Calhoun Johnson).

This comic episode of the anthology series revolved around
efficiency expert Bill Russell's attempts to keep his family
on a tight schedule to impress his potential boss, Mr.
Marshall. Although a new puppy wreaked havoc and Bill's wife
was less than efficient, Mr. Marshall was impressed with the
family and hired Bill. Jack Gross and Phil Krasne also
produced Ann Sheridan's last feature film The Woman and the
Hunter (F-88).

REVIEW:
Daily Variety, August 21, 1953: "A lightweight story that
rambles nowhere proves too much of a handicap even for an
actress of Ann Sheridan's talents....Despite a low-cut gown
that may have caused critical winces, Miss Sheridan frames a
glamorous picture and her acting is equally attractive."

See also V-25.

T-10   Schlitz Playhouse of Stars   "The Prize"   October 2,
        1953   CBS   30 mins.

Producer: Meridian Pictures. Associate producer: William
Self. Director: Bill Karn. Teleplay: Herman Fahlhaber.
Photography: Russ Harlan. Editors: George Amy and John
Hall. Art direction: Serge Krizman. Sound: Fred Lau.

CAST: Ann Sheridan, Walter Coy, William H. Wright, Roscoe
Ates, Myrna Dell, Mary Newton.

In this early feminist story, Ann Sheridan played a farmer
who put aside marriage to raise a prize bull. Although she
spurned the advances of a professor (Walter Coy), preferring
to be treated like the male contestants, she was angry when
judge Coy awarded another bull the prize. Her father
(William H. Wright) straightened her out, making way for a
happy ending. Although some episodes of the dramatic
anthology were broadcast live, "The Prize" was filmed.

REVIEW:
Daily Variety, October 5, 1953: "This telefilm is a trite
offering right down the line....[Ann] Sheridan, clad in an
unbecoming Mother Hubbard type of garment, seems miscast and
suffers in comparison to the others who appear in straight-

forward characterizations."

T-11 <u>All-Star Revue</u>   November 28, 1953   NBC   90 mins.

Host Phil Harris welcomed guests Ann Sheridan, actors Edward
Everett Horton and Michael O'Shea, singer Eartha Kitt,
comedians Sandra Gould and Jim Backus, the acrobatic Ramses,
and the music of Red Nichols and His Five Pennies. Ann
appeared in a sketch with Horton, O'Shea, and Harris. Alice
Faye, Harris's wife, made a surprise appearance at the end of
the program.

REVIEWS:
<u>Daily Variety</u>, November 30, 1953: "Ann Sheridan had little
to do and less to do it with. She played the head of a book-
making syndicate, who worked on Harris to pry from him the
winners he kept in a black book. This fell in with the story
line, a takeoff on <u>Three Men on a Horse</u>....For Miss
Sheridan it wasn't much of a ride."

<u>Variety</u>, December 2, 1953: Film actress Ann Sheridan was
spotted briefly as head of the bookie syndicate..."

T-12 <u>Juke Box Jury</u>   1953-54   ABC   30 mins.

Peter Potter hosted this prime time game show in which a
celebrity panel rated records and predicted their chances for
success. Ann Sheridan, Art Linkletter, Patricia Crowley, and
Robert Wagner were panelists on an episode.

T-13 <u>The Buick-Berle Show</u>   May 25, 1954   NBC   60 mins.

Ann Sheridan, George Raft, and Sig Ruman joined comedian
Milton Berle on his weekly show-within-a-show. Emanating
from California, the running plot had Berle planning to
produce and star in his own movie, with Ann as his leading
lady. The script, by veteran comedy writer Goodman Ace,
allowed Ann to perform several musical numbers with Berle and
Raft. A near calamity happened during the South American
finale, one of the perils of live TV. Ann had a brief amount
of time to change from her previous costume into a ruffled
rumba dress. "In the rush, her right breast was left out of
the ruffled top," designer Bill Jobe recalled. "Before the
dresser could check her, impetuous Uncle Miltie pulled her on
stage." The fuzzy camera work saved the day, and viewers
could not recognize the skin through the ruffles (B-174).
The series also was known as <u>The Milton Berle Show</u>.

REVIEW:
<u>Daily Variety</u>, May 26, 1954: "Both [Ann] Sheridan and
[George] Raft obviously sensed the script's shortcomings, but
went through their paces like real troupers."

T-14 <u>A Star Is Born World Premiere</u>   September 29, 1954
      NN

The star-studded premiere of Judy Garland's <u>A Star Is Born</u>
(Warner Bros., 1954) was televised live from the Los Angeles

Pantages Theatre, with hosts George Fisher, Larry Finley, and
Jack Carson trying to chat with as many celebrities as
possible. The results were a hodgepodge of actors trotting
before the camera, predicting success for the film. Ann
Sheridan and escort Jacques Mapes were interviewed briefly by
Finley. This marked the first nationally televised motion
picture premiere. According to Garland biographer Judy
Coleman, the show was so successful that it was rebroadcast
the following night (The Complete Judy Garland, Harper &
Rowe, Grand Rapids, MI, 1990). It is doubtful that it was
televised in all areas of the country.

See also P-14, V-29.

T-15   Henry Fonda Presents The Star and the Story
       "Malaya Incident" 1955   NN   30 mins.

Henry Fonda hosted this dramatic series, which mostly
rebroadcast material from other anthologies. According to TV
historian Vincent Terrace, this episode was a rerun of the
1953 Ford Theater program with Ann Sheridan (T-7).

T-16   The Eddie Cantor Comedy Theater   September 26, 1955
       NN   30 mins.

Comedian Eddie Cantor hosted this syndicated anthology, which
presented full-length comedies or variety acts. Ann Sheridan
appeared in a sketch about a female army platoon leader.

T-17   Mexican TV Shorts   filmed October 1955+

According to Variety, Ann Sheridan and Mexican actor
Rodolfo Acosta produced fifty shorts for television. The
first was due to be shot in mid-October 1955 and featured
Acosta as director and actor. The series, primarily
mysteries, had a budget of $1,250,000 (B-26). It is not
known how many actually were produced or if Ann Sheridan
acted in any of the programs.

T-18   Sneak Preview   "Calling Terry Conway"   August 14,
       1956   NBC   30 mins.

Ann Sheridan played the title role in this unsold pilot,
which co-starred Una Merkel and Philip Ober. The show
revolved around a public relations director in a plush Las
Vegas hotel. Ann later claimed that the series was not
picked up because the networks did not want to endorse
gambling (B-206).

T-19   The Steve Allen Show   September 2, 1956   NBC
       60 mins.

Ann Sheridan appeared on Steve Allen's prime time variety
show. Other guests included comedians [Joseph] Smith and
[Charles] Dale, and singers Fats Domino, Georgia Gibbs, and
Steve Lawrence. The program was broadcast live from New York
and competed with Ed Sullivan's Sunday night variety
broadcast.

T-20 I've Got a Secret   fall, 1956   CBS   30 mins.

Ann Sheridan was a guest on this prime time game show, in which panelists Faye Emerson, Jayne Meadows, Bill Cullen, and Henry Morgan tried to guess her secret. In the end, Ann revealed that she was sending cantakerous panelist Morgan to the Belgian Congo. The trip was profiled in a TV Guide article (B-370) and in Morgan's autobiography (B-371). The series was hosted by Garry Moore.

T-21 The U.S. Steel Hour   "Hunted"   December 5, 1956
      CBS   60 mins.

Director: Robert Mulligan. Teleplay: Morton Wishengrad.
Technical consultant: Leon Volkov.

CAST: Ann Sheridan, Theodore Bikel, Nehemiah Persoff, Mike Kellin.

Morton Wishengrad's story was an unusual one for the cold war era: a portrait of Russians as real people, rather than villains. Theodore Bikel played an intellectual Russian refugee whom the Communists were trying to intimidate into returning to Russia. Ann Sheridan was the promiscuous neighbor who offered to marry him so that he could remain in the United States. Nehemiah Persoff was a sympathetic Russian diplomat who prefered delicacy to violence. The show was broadcast live from New York and was produced by the Theatre Guild.

REVIEWS:
New York Times, December 6, 1956: "[Ann] Sheridan unfortunately suffered the most with a role that was taken right from the stockpile."

Variety, December 12, 1956: "Only spot in which the playwright came close to a cliche was in the depiction of [Ann] Sheridan's floozy....However, he carefully brought attractiveness to her part, as the play progressed, and Miss Sheridan, as the woman under the influence of the understanding Russian, was constant to the author's intent."

T-22 Lux Video Theatre   "The Hard Way"   May 2, 1957
      NBC   60 mins.

Director: Richard Goode. Teleplay: Sanford Barnett.

CAST: Ann Sheridan (Helen), Steve Dunne (Paul), Jack Kruschen (John Taber), Nancy Gates, Tommy Farrell.

Ann Sheridan returned to the anthology in "The Hard Way," marking her first color television broadcast. She played a domineering woman who lost her savings backing a Broadway show starring her sister (Nancy Gates). In the end, Gates traded her sister's attention for the love of Steve Dunne.

REVIEW:
Daily Variety, May 6, 1957: "[Ann] Sheridan rode through

it with calculating coldness albeit showing some flashes of
thespic adeptness."

T-23 Playhouse 90   "Without Incident"   June 6, 1957
      CBS   90 mins.

Producer: Charles Marquis Warren. Director: Charles
Marquis Warren. Teleplay: David Victor and Herbert Little,
Jr. Based on a story by Charles Marquis Warren. Editor:
Sam Gold. Photography: Joseph Biroc.

CAST: Errol Flynn (Capt. Russell Bidlack), Ann Sheridan
(Kathy), John Ireland (Sergeant Turley), Julie London
(Angela), H.M. Wynant (Private Surratt), Rodolfo Acosta
(Chaves), John Pickard (Private Rutledge), Irene Tedrow (Ma
Morgan), Dick Shannon, Bing Russell, Sheb Wooley, Dunne Gray,
Bill Hale, Jack Loman, Rush Williams, Dick Gilden, Al Wyatt.

This episode of the dramatic anthology was filmed on location
in Tucson, Arizona in March 1957. In a CBS press release
dated May 17, 1957, Ann Sheridan recalled her location antics
through the years, including backing into a cactus during the
Playhouse 90 filming. The show reunited Ann and Errol
Flynn, who had co-starred in three films at Warner Bros.
Rodolfo Acosta, who played the Indian who abducted Ann in
"Without Incident," was linked romantically with her for
several years.
     Set in 1870, the story revolved around Flynn, a U.S.
Cavalry commander who set out on a rescue mission through
dangerous Indian territory. Along the way, he saved two
sisters (Ann and Julie London), whose trader husbands were
murdered, and captured the Indian chief who killed them.
When Flynn returned to his fort, he was faced with a revolt
among his men.
     "Without Incident" was shot in twelve days, a lengthy
schedule for the period. Ann told the Detroit Times, "The
reason it was extended that long was that the horses and
ponies weren't as well rehearsed as the actors and their
scenes had to be shot several times" (B-713). After working
on the episode, she considered doing a western series with
Errol Flynn called Cavalry Patrol. The project did not
develop. Flynn died in 1959.

REVIEWS:
Daily Variety, June 10, 1957: "[Errol] Flynn, [Ann]
Sheridan and [John] Ireland are properly mournful."

Variety, June 12, 1957: "Characters, especially, are
stock-company-styled with...Ann Sheridan and Julie London as
a pair of women with a past....The acting was for the most
part undistinguished."

T-24 Ford Theater   "Cross Hairs"   June 12, 1957   ABC
      30 mins.

Producer: Lou Breslow. Director: Jack Gage. Teleplay:
Miles Tolner. Editor: Richard Brockway. Photography: Gert
Andersen.

CAST: Ann Sheridan (Mary Bartley), James Daly (Frank
Bartley), James Griffith (Mr. Harris), Elizabeth Patterson
(Mrs. Dunkel), S. John Launer (Lt. Burt Jenners), John
Beradino (Robert Jones).

Ann Sheridan played a secondary role in this episode of the
dramatic anthology series.   The tale concerned a radar
equipment foreman who was killed while investigating a
robbery at his warehouse.   Before he died, he told a coworker
(James Daly) the identity of the murderers, jeopardizing
Daly's life. Ann was Daly's worried wife.   The series was
filmed in Hollywood.

REVIEW:
Daily Variety, June 14, 1957:   "As co-star with James Daly,
the outing will do little to advance the thespic cause of Ann
Sheridan.   She has little to do other than plead for the
safety of her husband and register the proper degree of
fright....Miss Sheridan didn't seem to over-extend herself in
the anxieties of her role."

T-25   Undercurrent   "Cross Hairs"   September 20, 1957
       CBS   30 mins.

This summer replacement series for The Lineup (CBS,
1954-60) featured reruns of other anthology episodes, even
those from competing networks.   This was a rebroadcast of the
Ford Theater episode starring Ann Sheridan and James Daly
(T-24).

T-26   Bulova Showtime   "The Prize"   November 10, 1957
       30 mins.

In this rebroadcast of the 1953 Schlitz Playhouse of Stars
episode (T-10), Ann Sheridan played a glamorous farmer who
put her livestock ahead of romance.

T-27   Celebrity Playhouse   April 2, 1958   NN   30 mins.

Ann Sheridan played Peter Graves's fiancee in this little-
known anthology broadcast.   A construction boss (Robert
Lowery) found trouble when he hired a supervisor (Graves) for
a vital project in Arabia.   It is listed in the April 2, 1958
issue of the Miami News [FL], but the series is not
chronicled in most TV reference books.

T-28   The Perry Como Show   September 27, 1958   NBC
       60 mins.

Ann Sheridan, Art Linkletter, Ray Walston, and the Everly
Brothers were the guests on this musical variety show hosted
by Perry Como.   Ann sang "Guess Who I Saw Today."

T-29   Pursuit   "The Dark Cloud"   December 31, 1958   CBS
       60 mins.

Producer: Peter Kortner.   Director: James Clark.   Teleplay:
Joseph Landon.

CAST: Ann Sheridan, Gary Merrill, Darryl Hickman, James
Westerfield, Eduardo Ciannelli, Fay Spain, Mike Ross, Ann
McCrea, Glen Holzman, Bill Walker.

Each episode of this filmed dramatic anthology involved a
person or group being pursued. In "The Dark Cloud," Gary
Merrill played a police detective who was under suspicion for
associating with bookies. He was suspended when he was found
at the murder scene of a gangland prosecution witness. To
clear his name, he searched for a little black book which
held the key to a grand jury investigation of the gambling
ring. In the end, he discovered his name was in the book.
Ann Sheridan had a secondary role.

REVIEW:
Daily Variety, January 2, 1959: "...Ann Sheridan displays
faint remnants of oomph and evidence of considerable talent
as keeper of 'the book.'"

T-30   The Arthur Murray Party   February 9, 1959   NBC
        30 mins.

Songs, dance contests, and comedy sketches abounded on this
musical series hosted by dancing master Arthur Murray and his
wife Kathryn. Ann Sheridan, singer/actress Vivian Blaine,
ventriloquist Shari Lewis, and actor David Janssen were
guests on this episode.

T-31   The Arthur Murray Party   April 26, 1960   NBC
        30 mins.

Arthur and Kathryn Murray welcomed Ann Sheridan back as a
guest on their musical program. In addition to competing in
their dance contest, Ann sang some old favorites with
lyricists/librettists Betty Comden and Adolph Green. The
show was broadcast in color.

T-32   The U.S. Steel Hour   "The Imposter"   June 15, 1960
        CBS   60 mins.

Director: Paul Bogart. Teleplay: James Yaffe. Based on a
story by Michael Dyne.

CAST: Ann Sheridan (Alida Volterra), Jean Pierre Aumont
(Man), Liliane Montevecchi (Philomena), Nancy Wickwire
(Marina), John Colicos (Silvio).

Ann Sheridan and Jean Pierre Aumont starred in this dramatic
anthology. In the story, Alida had been searching for her
husband for six years, after he was reported missing in Italy
during World War II. When she found an amnesiac in the
hospital, she brought him home, despite her aunt's insistence
that he was an imposter. After Alida took the man to visit
Philomena, his former mistress, he regained his memory. He
returned to his wife, philosophizing that while Philomena
gave him back his memory, Alida gave him back his life.

REVIEWS:

Miami Beach Sun [FL], June 16, 1960: "[Ann] Sheridan
sometimes under-played her role, which made it tougher to
accept."

Variety, June 22, 1960: "James Yaffe's script...was a hack
job with little point but to woo the sentimental housfrau
viewers. [Ann] Sheridan, [Jean Pierre] Aumont, [Liliane]
Montevecchi, John Colicos and Nancy Wickwire played it
accordingly."

T-33 Celebrity Talent Scouts   August 1, 1960   CBS
      30 mins.

Sam Levenson hosted this prime time talent contest, where
celebrities introduced their proteges. Ann Sheridan brought
the Mattison Trio, ballet-tap dancers who performed to "Music
for a Pack of Hungry Cannibals." Audrey Meadows and Phil
Silvers also were guests on the premiere episode of this
summer replacement series.

REVIEW:
Hollywood Reporter, August 3, 1960: "Ann Sheridan
introduced, and made at least one viewer wish for more of her
own talents on either the large or small screen."

T-34 Wagon Train   "The Mavis Grant Story"   October 24,
      1962   ABC   60 mins.

CAST: John McIntire (Christopher Hale), Terry Wilson (Bill
Hawks), Frank McGrath (Charley Wooster), Ann Sheridan (Mavis
Grant), Parley Baer (John Maitland), Anna Karen (Hattie
Maitland), Mary Jayne Saunders (Sally Maitland), Rod Redwing
(Calli), Russ Conway (Tom Morgan), Jerry Riggio (Moca), Dee
Polluck (Gerald Morgan), J. Stanford Jolley (Willet), Jerry
Oddo (Togoc), Scott Miller (Duke Shannon), Yvonne White (Mrs.
Folsom), John McKee (Mr. Folsom).

The long-running western series revolved around a wagon train
heading west from St. Joseph, Missouri after the Civil War.
In this episode, wagonmaster Christopher Hale desperately
needed water as his caravan passed through an isolated area
where Mavis Grant's well was the only source. Mavis agreed
to share her water supply, as long as Hale and the settlers
paid her twenty-five to forty dollars a barrel. When settler
John Maitland cast off his daughter Sally, Mavis softened.
She offered Hale free water if he let Sally stay with her.
Hale made Mavis realize how her bitterness ruined her own
life. Mavis convinced John to take back Sally so she would
not turn out the way Mavis did. With a clear conscience,
Mavis sent the wagon train on its way.

REVIEW:
Miami News [FL], October 24, 1962: "[Ann] Sheridan does
quite well as the embittered woman....Unfortunately, there
are weaknesses in the supporting cast."

T-35 Talent Scouts   August 6, 1963   CBS   60 mins.

Merv Griffin briefly interviewed Ann Sheridan before she
introduced Broadway singer Maura K. Wedge on this prime time
talent show. When Griffin asked if Ann would like to do a
Broadway play or musical, she called the experience
"terrifying," but said she would like to try it. Van
Johnson, Howard Keel, Art Carney, and Monique Van Vooren also
appeared.

T-36 To Tell the Truth   September 9, 1963-September 13,
      1963   CBS   30 mins.

Ann Sheridan told Screen Facts that she guested on To
Tell the Truth many times (B-206). This marked her first
appearance as a panelist on the long-running daytime game
show hosted by Budd Collyer. Celebrities guessed which of
three contestants was being honest about their identity.
Other panelists were Barry Nelson, Robert Q. Lewis, and
Phyllis Newman.

T-37 Missing Links   October 21, 1963-October 25, 1963
      NBC   30 mins.

Ann Sheridan, Sam Levenson, and Nipsy Russell were the
panelists on this daytime game show hosted by Ed MacMahon, in
which contestants tried to predict celebrities' ability to
fill in blanks in stories previously read aloud.

T-38 To Tell the Truth   November 4, 1963-November 8, 1963
      CBS   30 mins.

Ann Sheridan returned for another week as a panelist on the
daytime game show, joining Abe Burrows, Barry Nelson, and
Phyllis Newman.

T-39 To Tell the Truth   December 23, 1963-December 27,
      1963   CBS   30 mins.

Ann Sheridan, Barry Nelson, Robert Q. Lewis, and Phyllis
Newman were panelists on this daytime version of the game
show hosted by Bud Collyer.

T-40 Burke's Law   c. 1964   60 mins.

According to Glenn Gregory, Ann played a reporter on an
episode of the mystery series (B-204). She is not listed in
TV Guide during the series' entire run, nor Larry
Gianakos's episode guide (B-186), so it is assumed her role
was a cameo.

T-41 To Tell the Truth   February 10, 1964-February 14,
      1964   CBS   30 mins.

Ann Sheridan, Douglas Fairbanks, Jr., and disc jockey William
B. Williams were among the panelists during this week of
games.

T-42 To Tell the Truth   March 30, 1964-April 3, 1964
      CBS   30 mins.

Ann Sheridan, Barry Nelson, Sam Levenson, and Nancy Dussault
attempted to eliminate the imposters in this daytime game
show hosted by Bud Collyer.

T-43 Hollywood and the Stars   "Sirens, Symbols and Glamor
      Girls"   May 11, 1964 and May 18, 1964   NBC   60 mins.

Ann Sheridan was one of the actresses seen in this two-part
documentary on sex symbols, past and present. Others
included Mary Pickford, Carole Lombard, Betty Grable, and
Marilyn Monroe. The special aired in two thirty-minute
installments.

T-44 To Tell the Truth   July 13, 1964-July 17, 1964   CBS
      30 mins.

Ann Sheridan spent another week as a panelist on this daytime
game show, joined by Phyllis Newman, Robert Alda, and Milt
Kamen.

T-45 Get the Message   July 20, 1964-July 24, 1964   ABC
      30 mins.

Ann Sheridan, Roddy McDowall, Wally Cox, and Lauren Bacall
were panelists on this daytime game show hosted by Frank
Buxton. Two celebrities provided clues to a word or phrase
which their contestant tried to guess.

T-46 The Match Game   August 31, 1964-September 4, 1964
      NBC   30 mins.

Gene Rayburn hosted this daytime game show, which pitted two
three-member teams (two celebrities and a contestant) against
each other. The object was for teammates to match answers
when they filled in a blank in a sentence. Ann Sheridan and
Robert Q. Lewis were team captains.

T-47 To Tell the Truth   September 7, 1964-September 11,
      1964   CBS   30 mins.

Ann Sheridan joined Eva Gabor, Barry Nelson, and Orson Bean
as they tried to find the imposters on this daytime game show
hosted by Bud Collyer.

T-48 To Tell the Truth   November 16, 1964-November 20,
      1964   CBS   30 mins.

Bud Collyer welcomed panelists Ann Sheridan, Phyllis Newman,
Barry Nelson, and broadcaster John Henry Faulk in this
daytime game show.

T-49 To Tell the Truth   January 4, 1965-January 8, 1965
      CBS   30 mins.

Ann Sheridan, Barry Nelson, Abe Burrows, and Phyllis Newman
were panelists on this daytime version of the game show,
which was hosted by Bud Collyer.

T-50 <u>To Tell the Truth</u>   March 22, 1965-March 26, 1965
      CBS   30 mins.

Panelists Ann Sheridan, Buddy Hackett, Peggy Cass, and Skitch
Henderson tried to determine the imposters in this daytime
version of the game show. Bud Collyer was the host.

T-51 <u>To Tell the Truth</u>   May 17, 1965-May 21, 1965   CBS
      30 mins.

This daytime edition of the popular game show featured Ann
Sheridan, Penny Fuller, Robert Q. Lewis, and Dick Shawn as
panelists. Bud Collyer was the host.

T-52 <u>The Price Is Right</u>   May 31, 1965-June 4, 1965   ABC
      30 mins.

Bill Cullen hosted this daytime game show, in which
contestants tried to guess the retail prices of various
prizes. Ann Sheridan appeared as a week-long celebrity
guest.

T-53 <u>Another World</u>   (series)   November 11, 1965-
      April 15, 1966   NBC   30 mins.

Ann Sheridan was one of the first movie stars to appear in a
soap opera, playing the recurring role of Cathryn Corning on
<u>Another World</u>. Although Ann admitted that she did not know
much about her character in the beginning, she said that
Cathryn "was a woman with a purpose" (B-332). As the plot
wore on, it was revealed that Cathryn had cheated on her
husband during World War II, resulting in a child she gave up
for adoption. Cathryn began investigating Melinda Palmer
(actress Carol Roux), who turned out to be her daughter.
    Ann signed a contract for thirteen weeks, with a
thirteen-week option. Although she was quick to praise the
daytime genre, she said she took the role to keep people from
saying she was lazy (B-206). She agreed to join the cast
with the stipulation that her appearances would be limited to
one or two a week (B-11).
    1965 was a banner year for stars appearing on soaps.
The networks increased their daytime budgets, allowing
salaries to rise to two thousand dollars a week (B-705). In
addition to Ann Sheridan, movie veterans like Macdonald Carey
and Gloria DeHaven joined serials that same season.
    Created by veteran radio writer Irna Phillips, <u>Another
World</u> was the first soap opera to have a spinoff
(<u>Somerset</u>, NBC, 1970-76) and the first to expand to an hour
in 1975. Although the show currently tapes its episodes,
during the 1960s the soap usually was broadcast live from New
York each afternoon from NBC's Brooklyn studios. As soon as
Ann's scenes were finished, she left. She told <u>TV Guide</u>,
"I get paid to act, not socialize. So I act and go home."
She traveled to and from work by limosine, which she paid for
herself, proclaiming, "I'm too old to have my teeth shaken
out in a bus" (B-222).
    Soon after Ann started on <u>Another World</u>, she received
an offer to film another pilot. In December 1965, she

returned to California to shoot "Stop Shootin' Folks,
Grandma" (T-54), the pilot for Pistols 'n' Petticoats
(T-56). So Ann's disappearance on Another World would not
leave viewers confused, she taped several segments that were
inserted in the show. When Pistols 'n' Petticoats was
picked up in the spring of 1966, Ann left the soap.

T-54   Pistols 'n' Petticoats   "Quit Shootin' Folks
       Grandma"   (unaired pilot)   30 mins.   CBS

Producers: Joe Connelly and Bob Mosher. Director: Earl
Bellamy. Teleplay: George Tibbles.

CAST: Ann Sheridan (Henrietta "Hank" Hanks), Ruth McDevitt
(Grandma Dora), Chris Noel (Lucy Hanks), Joel D. McCrea [Jody
McCrea] (Sheriff Eric), Douglas V. Fowley (Grandpa Andrew).

Filmed at Universal Studios in early December 1965, this
unaired pilot prompted the series Pistols 'n' Petticoats
(T-56). The sitcom centered around the sharp-shooting Hanks
family in 1870s Colorado. The pilot concerned the Hanks
family's efforts to put down an Indian uprising. Two casting
changes were made before the series went on the air. In the
pilot, Joel D. McCrea portrayed Sheriff Eric, a bumbling
precursor to Gary Vinson's Sheriff Sikes. Chris Noel played
daughter Lucy, but was replaced by Carole Welles in the
series. McCrea was the son of actors Joel McCrea and Frances
Dee. The pilot was picked up in March 1966.

T-55   The Tonight Show Starring Johnny Carson   January 17,
       1966   NBC   90 mins.

Ann Sheridan, actor Roger Moore, comedian Milt Kamen, and
singer Annette Sanders were interviewed on the late night
talk show hosted by Johnny Carson, which was broadcast from
New York. Ann discussed her work on Another World (T-53),
then running on NBC. She recalled that she had asked her
agent about finding her a role on a soap opera ten or twelve
years earlier, but they were all done in New York. When she
moved from Los Angeles, it all came together. She said, "I
think it's some of the hardest work I've ever done in my
life, but I've never enjoyed anything more." Ann admitted
that she was "nauseated" by the oomph tag and claimed she had
not viewed any of her movies in a long time. She and Carson
reminisced about the wonders of live TV. She was amazed that
nothing outrageous had happened on Another World's live
broadcast. When Carson asked if she was content with her
soap stardom, Ann philosophized, "I think you're happier when
you get older. You have a completely different set of values
and all. I've never been as happy in my life. I wouldn't
change it for twenty-one for anything." The show was
broadcast in color.

T-56   Pistols 'n' Petticoats   (series)   September 17,
       1966-August 26, 1967   CBS   30 mins.

Executive producer: Joe Connelly. Producer: Irving Paley.
Directors: Joe Connelly and Sid Lanfield. Teleplay: George

Tibbles and Lois Hire. Music: George Tibbles, Jack Elliott, and Stanley Wilson.

CAST: Ann Sheridan (Henrietta "Hank" Hanks), Ruth McDevitt (Grandma Dora), Douglas V. Fowley (Grandpa Andrew), Gary Vinson (Sheriff Harold Sikes), Carole Wells (Lucy Hanks), Ron Russell (Curly Bigelow), Robert Lowery (Buss Courtney), Alex Henteloff (Little Bear), Marc Cavell (Gray Hawk).

SYNOPSIS: Henrietta "Hank" Hanks was the widowed matriarch of a sharp-shooting family in Wretched, Colorado in the 1870s. In addition to Hank's parents, known as Grandma and Grandpa, and her boarding-school-bred daughter Lucy, the clan included a timberwolf named Bowser and a wildcat named Kitty. Comic situations involved the Hankses helping local citizens, the Indians, and the cowardly Sheriff Sikes, who was engaged to Lucy.

PnP-1   "A Crooked Line"   September 17, 1966
The Hankses helped a neighbor who wanted to sidestep family tradition and become something other than a thief. With Pat Buttram and Butch Patrick.

PnP-2   "No Sale"   September 24, 1966
The Hankses were determined to hang onto their land, even if it meant a gunfight, when the ruthless Buss Courtney tried to purchase all the land in Wretched.

PnP-3   no title   October 1, 1966
In an attempt to learn the whereabouts of an Irish woman, kidnapped by the Indians years ago, the Hankses invited the chief to tea. With Lon Chaney, Jr. and Jack Albertson.

PnP-4   no title   October 8, 1966
The Hankses thought a visiting British poet was helpless, unaware that he was the brains behind a stagecoach robbery.

PnP-5   no title   October 15, 1966
In hopes of preventing an intertribal war, the Hankses hosted a peace powwow. With Jay Silverheels.

PnP-6   "The Triangle"   October 22, 1966
Grandma's former sweetheart came to town to marry her, unaware that Grandpa was still alive. With Charlie Ruggles.

PnP-7   no title   October 29, 1966
The Wretched bachelors were upset when their mail-order brides were kidnapped by a neighboring town.

PnP-8   no title   November 5, 1966
Hank and Grandma mistakenly rented a spare room to a female bank robber. With Beverly Garland.

PnP-9   no title   November 12, 1966
When Hank and Grandma were suspected of selling guns to the Indians, they took jobs as hostesses at a saloon operated by a gunrunner in order to prove their innocence.

PnP-10   no title   November 19, 1966
When crafty land-grabber Buss Courtney tossed the Hankses in
jail in order to take possession of their ranch, the family
tried to break out and foil his plans.

PnP-11   no title   November 26, 1966
The Hankses tried to keep peace in Wretched, despite the
Indians' threat to go on the warpath. With Lon Chaney, Jr.

PnP-12   no title   December 3, 1966
Sheriff Sikes was aided by the aging Doc Holliday and Wyatt
Earp when a murderous band of criminals came to Wretched.

PnP-13   no title   December 10, 1966
The Hankses tactfully tried to get rid of the prim and
patronizing head of Lucy's finishing school, who was living
in their guest room. With Lurene Tuttle.

PnP-14   no title   December 17, 1966
After the Hankses performed a life-saving rescue, they were
rewarded with the services of a finicky French valet.

PnP-15   no title   December 24, 1966
Buss Courtney convinced sharpshooter Curly Bigelow that the
sheriff was the retired gunfighter he wanted to kill.

PnP-16   no title   December 31, 1966
When a pair of bankrobbers threatened to harm the Hankses'
pet wolf, Grandpa was forced into helping them.

PnP-17   no title   January 7, 1967
Grandma was jealous when a gun-wielding woman had her eye on
Grandpa. With Judy Canova.

PnP-18   no title   January 14, 1967
A fast-talking actor came to Wretched, hoping to fleece the
entire community. With Lee Bergere.

PnP-19   no title   January 21, 1967
The Hankses helped defend Little Bear after Buss Courtney
tried to frame him for cattle rustling.

PnP-20   no title   January 28, 1967
The arrival of a Bostonian land grabber, a group of Indians,
and a gunslinger torpedoed a fortuneteller's prediction that
Hank would marry the first man who came to visit. With
William Schallert.

PnP-21   no title   February 4, 1967
Three desperadoes held Lucy hostage at the Hankses' ranch.

PnP-22   "Golden Fleece"   February 11, 1967
After a hitch in prison, a con man was ready to go straight.
However, he was tempted to revert to his old ways when a
wealthy easterner came to Wretched, shopping for a goldmine.
With Pat Buttram and Judy Canova.

PnP-23   no title   February 18, 1967

When an Indian who studied medicine in Boston was rejected by his tribe, the Hankses taught him how to act like a brave.

PnP-24 no title   February 25, 1967
Hank and Grandma tried to save a neighboring town that was taken over by outlaws, forcing Grandpa to rescue them when they were captured.

PnP-25 no title   March 4, 1967
A group of Confederate soldiers, unaware that the Civil War was over, held the Hanks clan hostage.

PnP-26 "Harold's Double"   March 11, 1967
Everyone was fooled when an outlaw, who looked like the sheriff, impersonated him. But Lucy was impressed with the shy sheriff's new-found boldness.

REVIEWS:
Los Angeles Times, September 19, 1966: "Pistols 'n' Petticoats was one of the final shows to make its bow this season and it would be nice to be able to say that CBS had saved the best for last. Unfortunately, such was not the case in the premiere episode....Ann Sheridan, the movies' former Oomph girl, is turned into an Annie Oakley in this one."

Miami Herald [FL], September 20, 1966: "The years have been kind to [Ann] Sheridan and it's good to have her back. But in this project she seems detached and somewhat bemused by what in the world she's doing in it."

Variety, September 21, 1966: "Caught up in all these low, low brow shenanigans was Ann Sheridan, who deserves better....The humor was so rural that it made The Beverly Hillbillies [(CBS, 1962-71)] represent the apex of sophistication....Every season there is one show which is panned by the critics and loved the by the Nielsens. This shouldn't be it. (Nielsen willin')."

TV Guide, January 14, 1967: "This show is not so much wild 'n' woolly as it is stuff 'n' nonsense....the show stars... Miss Ann Sheridan. Miss Sheridan made her name as The Oomph Girl. In this show, however, we are afraid she isn't given much to oomph with or to oomph about."

NOTES: Ann Sheridan left Another World (T-53) to begin work on Pistols 'n' Petticoats in May 1966. The comic western, which was filmed at Universal Studios' California lot and marked one of CBS's first color series, was panned by most of the critics. In a season plagued by failing series, the Los Angeles Times said that CBS kept the show on the air only because it had run out of replacements (September 19, 1966). It aired on Saturday nights opposite the popular Get Smart (NBS, 1965-69; CBS, 1969-70) and The Lawrence Welk Show (ABC, 1955-71; NN, 1971-82).
       Shortly after the series began, Ann spoke to UPI writer Dick Kleiner about Pistols 'n' Petticoats. She told him that she had looked for a series for twelve years before

settling on a format with which she could live. She said she
chose a comedy because "Comedies stand up better on TV than
drama. I know I get bored with TV dramas. Nowadays, all I
watch are the news, documentaries and travelogues" (B-293).
If Pistols 'n' Petticoats failed, she thought about trying
to write. She did not have time to find out.

    Ann's role on Pistols 'n' Petticoats proved to be her
last. Despite suffering from terminal cancer, she completed
twenty-five of the twenty-six episodes of the series.
Reportedly, she was not scheduled to be in the last episode.
At the time of her death, she had been off for three weeks;
however, she never revealed the severity of her condition to
her colleagues. Some insensitive workers thought her wobbly
legs and disorientation were due to drunkenness. Although
producer Joe Connelly claimed he was not particularly fond of
actresses, he called her a "great, wonderful human being."
He recalled, "I asked her doctor several times [about the
severity of Ann's illness] and he would never tell me."
Connelly continued, "She worked with a lot of guts and
character. She said she wanted to see the series through"
(B-67). Longtime friend John Engstead recalled her weariness
during production stills and marvelled at how she was able to
gather her strength before the cameras (B-161). She was so
weak during the final filming that her dialogue had to be
dubbed on the last episodes.

    In 1967, several episodes were combined in a movie, The
Far Out West (F-89), which continues to be syndicated on
television. The series seldom is seen because of its lack of
popularity and low number of episodes.

T-57   Art Linkletter's House Party   September 20, 1966
       CBS   30 mins.

Ann Sheridan was a guest on the daytime variety show hosted
by Art Linkletter. He called her the most rambunctious star
Warner Bros. had, besides Bette Davis, prompting Ann to dub
herself "the suspension kid." She said she enjoyed working
at Warner Bros., despite the fights, because of the wonderful
training and good people she met. She felt sorry for young
stars who had no contract system to train them. Ann also
promoted Pistols 'n Petticoats (T-56), which was running on
CBS. She said the series was a crazy show that kept her
laughing on the set. She had rented a house in Hollywood
and planned to buy if the series was a hit.

DISCOGRAPHY

The discography includes long-playing records (LPs), compact
discs (CDs), and commercially released cassette tapes that
feature Ann Sheridan. All recordings are listed
alphabetically by title. Each entry includes format, label,
number, and songs or scenes Ann Sheridan performs. If the
track comes from one of her films, the title is noted in
parentheses.

D-1 <u>Ann Sheridan Live</u>   Amalgamated Record Company 249

Although this LP is noted in Michael Pitts's <u>Radio
Soundtracks: A Reference Guide</u> (B-519), neither Pitts nor
the Library of Congress have a copy on file to verify its
contents. It is assumed it is a bootleg recording of songs
from Ann Sheridan's films or radio appearances.

D-2 <u>Ann Sheridan/Marlene Dietrich</u>   Marsher 201

Released in 1976, this LP features songs from the soundtracks
of Ann Sheridan's films, including <u>It All Came True</u> (F-53),
<u>Navy Blues</u> (F-59), and <u>Nora Prentiss</u> (F-74). One side of
the record features songs by Marlene Dietrich. According to
film historian James Robert Parish, Ann's <u>Navy Blues</u> vocals
were dubbed (B-475). The author and Sheridan biographer Tom
Sharpley disagree.

"Gaucho Serenade" (<u>It All Came True</u>) - Ann Sheridan
"Navy Blues" (<u>Navy Blues</u>) - Ann Sheridan, Martha Raye,
  Navy Blues Sextet
"In Waikiki" (<u>Navy Blues</u>) - Ann Sheridan, Navy Blues Sextet
"You're a Natural" (<u>Navy Blues</u>) - Ann Sheridan, Herbert
  Anderson
"Would You Like a Souvenir?" (<u>Nora Prentiss</u>) - Ann
  Sheridan
"Who Cares What People Say?" (<u>Nora Prentiss</u>) - Ann Sheridan

D-3 <u>Fifty Years of Film</u>   Warner Bros. 3XX2737

To celebrate Warner Bros.'s fiftieth anniversary in 1973, the
studio issued this three-record set featuring scenes from

their movies. Ann Sheridan appears in excerpts from <u>Castle on the Hudson</u> (F-52), <u>They Drive by Night</u> (F-55), and <u>Kings Row</u> (F-61). The set also comes with a glossy, soft-bound book about the studio. A companion set salutes Warner Bros. musicals.

Scene from <u>They Drive by Night</u> - Ann Sheridan, George Raft, Roscoe Karns, George Lloyd
Scene from <u>Castle on the Hudson</u> - Ann Sheridan, John Garfield
Scene from <u>Kings Row</u> - Ann Sheridan, Ronald Reagan

D-4   <u>The Greatest Hits in the War Time</u>   S.I.A.E.

This Italian CD contains radio performances by stars like Bing Crosby, Al Jolson, and Marlene Dietrich. It also is known as <u>Songs That Sent Us to War</u>.

"As Time Goes By" - Ann Sheridan

D-5   <u>Ladies of Burlesque</u>   Legends 1000/2 (LP); Sandy Hook LSH-2019 (LP and cassette)

Songs from the soundtracks of films centering around burlesque and nightclubs are collected in this LP, first issued by Legends in 1978. It includes performances by Ann Sothern, Marilyn Monroe, and Gwen Verdon. Sandy Hook later issued LP and cassette versions.

"Would You Like a Souvenir?" (<u>Nora Prentiss</u>) - Ann Sheridan

D-6   <u>Martha Raye</u>   Legends 1000/5-6

This album of songs from Martha Raye's films was taken directly from the soundtracks.

"Navy Blues" (<u>Navy Blues</u>) - Ann Sheridan, Martha Raye, Navy Blues Sextet

D-7   <u>The Music of Arthur Schwartz, Vol. III</u>   JJA Records 19758

Released in 1975, this LP collects songs by composer Arthur Schwartz, taken directly from film soundtracks.

<u>Navy Blues</u> Finale: "Navy Blues"/"When Are We Gonna Land Abroad?"/"In Waikiki"/"You're a Natural" - Ann Sheridan, Martha Raye, Herbert Anderson, Jack Oakie, Jack Haley, Navy Blues Sextet, cast

D-8   <u>Stars for Victory</u>   Kilroy Cassettes K-1003

Radio performances are collected on this cassette tape, released in 1987.

"As Time Goes By" - Ann Sheridan

D-9   <u>Thank Your Lucky Stars</u>   Curtain Calls 100/8 (LP);

Sandy Hook LSH-2012 (LP and cassette), CDSH-2012 (CD).

Curtain Calls released the soundtrack LP of the 1943 film nearly thirty years after the musical premiered (F-59). It includes songs by Bette Davis, Eddie Cantor, Joan Leslie, and Dennis Morgan. Sandy Hook produced the soundtrack in LP, CD, and cassette versions.

"Love Isn't Born, It's Made" - Ann Sheridan, Joyce Reynolds, chorus

AWARDS AND HONORS

The following is a list of awards and honors received by Ann Sheridan. Since it is impossible to catalogue all tributes, film festivals, keys to the city., etc., the list is intended to be a representative sampling.

A-1   Search for Beauty (F-1) contest finalist, 1933. Conducted by Paramount, the international competition brought thirty winners to Hollywood for an appearance in the film of the same name. Six winners, including Clara Lou Sheridan, were given Paramount contracts after the movie.

A-2   One of six Paramount starlets named most likely to succeed by the studio, March 1935. Others honored were Grace Bradley, Katherine DeMille, Gail Patrick, Wendy Barry, and Gertrude Michael.

A-3   Made an honorary member of the Lake Arrowhead police force, 1938.

A-4   Chosen Oomph Girl at publicity banquet held by Warner Bros. on March 16, 1939 at the Los Angeles Town House. She received a certificate and a bracelet, as well as an avalanche of publicity.

A-5   Nevin-Seymour Company, Inc. insured her oomph for a million dollars, March 1939.

A-6   Chosen as the movie actress "most unlikely to succeed" by the Harvard Lampoon, March 1940.

A-7   Appointed "a daughter of New Jersey and sister of Princeton" by the New Jersey Assembly, March 11, 1940. The honor was bestowed in answer to Princeton's rival, Harvard, insulting Ann Sheridan with its "most unlikely to succeed" citation (A-6).

A-8   Named as makeup giant Max Factor's "Girl of the Year" for 1939.

A-9   Came in eighteenth in the top twenty box office
       personalities for 1940.

A-10   Chosen "Sweetheart of the U.S. Marines" by the
       Leathernecks at League Island Navy Yard in
       Philadelphia, 1941.

A-11   Named honorary editor of the Advocate, Harvard's
       literary magazine, October 1941.

A-12   Voted glamour beauty of the month, Photoplay,
       February 1942.

A-13   Received duralumin plaque naming her "Novio del Aire"
       (Sweetheart of the Air) from South American student
       pilots at Camp Francis Warren, March 1942, during
       Funzafire U.S.O. tour (P-7).

A-14   Named an honorary officer by a New Zealand fighting
       division, circa 1942.

A-15   Received the Golden Apple award from the Hollywood
       Women's Press Club, naming her the most cooperative
       actress, December 19, 1943. Bob Hope was named most
       cooperative actor.

A-16   Received the Golden Apple award from the Hollywood
       Women's Press Club, naming her the most cooperative
       actress, December 1944. Cary Grant was named most
       cooperative actor.

A-17   Named Best Dressed Woman in Motion Pictures by New
       York's Fashion Academy, 1945.

A-18   Named one of America's Ten Best Dressed Women, 1940s.

A-19   Named one of America's Ten Best Dressed Women for the
       second time, 1940s.

A-20   Named one of America's Ten Best Dressed Women for the
       third time, circa 1946.

A-21   Became honorary Mexican citizen, 1940s.

A-22   Listed as one of Warner Bros. makeup chief Perc
       Westmore's favorite stars, 1948. Ann Sheridan was
       selected for her personality.

A-23   Presented with a plaque from the Mickey Finn Youth
       Foundation for her "valuable assistance and untiring
       efforts," 1949.

A-24   Star awarded on the Hollywood Walk of Fame for her film
       work. The star is located at 7000 Hollywood Boulevard.

A-25   An Ann Sheridan film retrospective was screened at
       Chicago's Clark Theatre, April 3, 1967-April 7, 1967.
       The following films were shown: Black Legion (F-31),

<u>San Quentin</u> (F-33), <u>Alcatraz Island</u> (F-36), <u>Angels with Dirty Faces</u> (F-45), <u>They Made Me a Criminal</u> (F-46), <u>Torrid Zone</u> (F-54), <u>They Drive By Night</u> (F-55), <u>King's Row</u> (F-61), <u>Juke Girl</u> (F-62), and <u>Come Next Spring</u> (F-86).

A-26   Named "Star of the Month" on TCM (Turner Classic Movies) and honored with a month-long film festival.

SONG SHEETS

The following song sheets and song books picture Ann
Sheridan. They are listed chronologically by film release
date. Each entry includes publishing information and a brief
description. Music from Sheridan films which do not picture
her are not included.

SONG SHEETS:
S-1   San Quentin   (1937, F-33)

SONG: "How Could You?"

Pat O'Brien and Ann Sheridan are pictured embracing on this
song sheet published by Remick Music Corporation.

S-2   Naughty But Nice   (1939, F-48)

SONGS: "Hooray for Spinach," "Corn Pickin'," "I'm Happy
about the Whole Thing," "In a Moment of Weakness."

A circular headshot of Ann Sheridan towers over a still of
Gale Page and Dick Powell on the cover of this song sheet
published by Remick Music Corporation.

S-3   Winter Carnival   (1939, F-49)

SONG: "Winter Blossoms."

Ann Sheridan is pictured on the cover of this song sheet
published by Gilbert.

S-4   It All Came True   (1940, F-53)

SONGS: "Angel in Disguise" (Tams Witmark), "Gaucho Serenade"
(Remick Music Corporation).

Ann Sheridan and Jeffrey Lynn are pictured on the cover.
Publishers are noted in parentheses.

S-5   Torrid Zone   (1940, F-54)

SONG: "Mi Caballero."

Ann Sheridan, James Cagney, and Pat O'Brien are pictured on
the cover of this song sheet, which was published by Harms,
Inc.

S-6   <u>Navy Blues</u>   (1941, F-59)

SONGS: "In Waikiki," "When Are We Going to Land Abroad?,"
"You're a Natural."

Ann Sheridan, Martha Raye, Jack Oakie, and Jack Haley are
seen on the cover. All songs were published by M. Witmark &
Sons.

S-7   <u>Thank Your Lucky Stars</u>   (1943, F-66)

SONGS: "The Dreamer" (Witmark) *, "Good Night, Good
Neighbor" (Witmark), "How Sweet You Are" (Witmark) *, "Ice
Cold Katie" (Witmark), "I'm Ridin' for a Fall" (Witmark) *,
"Love Isn't Born, It's Made" (Witmark), "Thank Your Lucky
Stars" (Witmark) *, "They're Either Too Young or Too Old"
(Witmark).

The cover of the songs sheets, which were published by M.
Witmark & Sons, have a patriotic feel, with the blue title
strips alternating with white pictorial strips. Sepia
photographs of Eddie Cantor, Dinah Shore, Humphrey Bogart,
Bette Davis, Olivia de Havilland, Errol Flynn, Joan Leslie,
John Garfield, Ida Lupino, Ann Sheridan, Dennis Morgan, and
Alexis Smith grace the three white rows. The songs marked
with asterisks were reprinted by Harms, Inc.

S-8   <u>Shine On Harvest Moon</u>   (1944, F-68)

SONGS: "I Go for You," "Shine On Harvest Moon," "So Dumb But
So Beautiful," "Time Waits for No One," "When It's Apple
Blossom Time in Normandy."

A yellow tinted still of Ann Sheridan and Dennis Morgan
performing the finale graces the covers. All songs were
published by Remick Music Corporation.

S-9   <u>One More Tomorrow</u>   (1946, F-71)

SONG: "One More Tomorrow."

Dennis Morgan, Ann Sheridan, Jack Carson, and Alexis Smith
are seen twice on the cover of this Remick Music Corporation
sheet. At the top, the head shots of the two couples are
tinted blue; at the bottom, the brown-tinted, full-length
shot shows the four stars arm in arm.

S-10   <u>Nora Prentiss</u>   (1947, F-74)

SONG: "Who Cares What People Say?"

A green-tinted glamour portrait of Ann Sheridan is in the

top left, looking down on circular head shots of Robert Alda,
Bruce Bennett, and Kent Smith. The song was published by
Harms, Inc.

S-11 Stella   (1950, F-80)

SONG: "Stella."

Ann Sheridan and Victor Mature are pictured on the cover of
this Miller sheet. The song is not in the film.

S-12 Come Next Spring   (1955, F-86)

SONG: "Come Next Spring."

Ann Sheridan and Steve Cochran are pictured on the cover of
this song sheet, which was published by Frank.

S-13 The Opposite Sex   (1956, F-87)

SONGS: "Now! Baby, Now!" (Robbins), "The Opposite Sex"
(Robbins), "A Perfect Love" (Robbins), "Rock and Roll
Tumbleweed" (Robbins), "Young Man with a Horn" (Feist).

The cover includes pictures of June Allyson, Joan Collins,
Dolores Gray, Ann Sheridan, and Ann Miller. Songs were
published by Leo Feist Inc. and Robbins Music Corporation as
noted. It is not known whether the companies have different
covers.

SONG BOOKS:
S-14 Warner Bros. Song Folio, Second Edition   (1939)

Ann Sheridan, Errol Flynn, Bette Davis, Olivia de Havilland,
Rosemary Lane, and John Garfield are pictured on the cover of
this collection of songs from Warner Bros. films. Among the
twenty-five selections are "Ride, Tenderfoot, Ride" from
Cowboy from Brooklyn (F-41) and a medley from Naughty
But Nice (F-48). Two photos of Ann Sheridan are included
inside the book, which was published by Harms, Inc.

S-15 Let's Sing Grandfather's Favorites   (1947)

Warner Bros. records at the USC Cinema-Television Library,
Warner Bros. archive, list this in an Ann Sheridan file. It
is assumed that photos of Ann were included in this song
collection.

VIDEOGRAPHY

The following Ann Sheridan appearances have been released
commercially on video cassette or laserdisc. All currently
may not be available for sale or rental. Each entry lists
studio, year of initial release, filmography/TV entry number,
and distributor of the video or laserdisc. The chapter is
divided into two sections: films and miscellaneous
appearances. The films are listed chronologically, according
to their original release date, and follow the same order as
they do in the filmography. The miscellaneous appearances
are arranged alphabetically by title. They include
compilations, bloopers, and television shows.

FILMS:
V-1   Murder at the Vanities   (Paramount, 1934, F-4)
        released May 1987

        VIDEO: MCA Home Video (#80410).

V-2   Rocky Mountain Mystery   (released on video as The
        Fighting Westerner)   (Paramount, 1935, F-20)

        VIDEO: Video Yesteryear; Bridgestone Multimedia; Moore
        Video; Front Row Entertainment, Inc.

V-3   Letter of Introduction   (Universal, 1938, F-42)

        VIDEO: Budget Video; Cable Films; Congress Video Group
        (#12070); Video Yesteryear (#1024); KVC Home Video.

V-4   Angels with Dirty Faces   (Warner Bros., 1938, F-45)

        VIDEO: MGM/UA Home Video (black and white and
        colorized versions); CBS/Fox (black and white); Mike
        LeBell's Video (black and white); Warner Home Video
        (black and white).

        LASER: Image Entertainment Laser (#C4584); LaserDisc
        Corp. of America (#4584-80).

V-5   They Made Me a Criminal   (Warner Bros., 1939, F-46)

VIDEO: New York Film Annex; Congress Video Group; Film Classics VCII, Inc.; Video Signature; Northeast Video and Sound; Nostalgia Family Video; Prism Entertainment.

V-6   Dodge City   (Warner Bros., 1939, F-47)

VIDEO: MGM/UA Home Video (#M201698); Commtron (#FOX4625); CBS/Fox Video; Ingram Video (#058115-VHS, #058074-Beta); Facets Multimedia, Inc. (#S13635).

LASER: Image Entertainment (#C4625); CBS/Fox; 20th Century-Fox Video; LaserDisc Corp. of America (#4573-80).

V-7   Torrid Zone   (Warner Bros., 1940, F-54)

VIDEO: MGM/UA Home Video.

LASER: MGM/UA Home Video.

V-8   They Drive By Night   (Warner Bros., 1940, F-55)

VIDEO: MGM/UA Home Video (#M202265); CBS/Fox Video (Key Video).

LASER: MGM/UA Home Video (#ML102265).

NOTES: The laser release contains the original trailer. The MGM/UA video was released July 1991.

V-9   City for Conquest   (Warner Bros., 1940, F-56)
       released Febuary 1992

VIDEO: MGM/UA Home Video (#M202485).

V-10   The Man Who Came to Dinner   (Warner Bros., 1942, F-60)

VIDEO: MGM/UA Home Video (#M201804).

NOTE: According to Bowker's Complete Video Directory, the video was released in February 1991 in both black and white and colorized versions (B-99).

V-11   Kings Row   (Warner Bros., 1942, F-61)

VIDEO: MGM/UA Home Video (#M202438); CBS/Fox Video (Key Video).

LASER: MGM/UA Home Video (#ML102438).

NOTES: The MGM/UA video is colorized. It was released in March 1992 as part of the Screen Masterpieces Series. The laser package is a two-disc set.

V-12   George Washington Slept Here   (Warner Bros., 1942, F-64)

VIDEO: Warner Bros. Home Video; MGM/UA Home Video
(#M202629).

V-13 Edge of Darkness   (Warner Bros., 1943, F-65)

VIDEO: Warner Bros. Home Video (colorized); MGM/UA
Home Video (black and white).

V-14 Thank Your Lucky Stars   (Warner Bros., 1943, F-66)

VIDEO: MGM/UA Home Video (#M301052).

LASER: MGM/UA Home Video (#ML102341).

NOTES: The laser edition is part of a two-disc set which
includes Thank Your Lucky Stars and It's a Great Feeling
(Warner Bros., 1949), as well as the trailers for both films.
It was released in September 1991.

V-15 The Treasure of the Sierra Madre   (Warner Bros.,
1948, F-76)

VIDEO: MGM/UA Home Video (#M601587).

LASER: MGM/UA Home Video (#ML101587).

V-16 Silver River   (Warner Bros, 1948, F-77)

VIDEO: MGM/UA Home Video.

V-17 Good Sam   (RKO, 1948, F-78)

VIDEO: NTA Home Entertainment; Republic Pictures Home
Video (#1578).

V-18 I Was a Male War Bride   (RKO, 1949, F-79)

VIDEO: Fox Video.

V-19 Woman on the Run   (Universal-International, 1950,
F-81)

VIDEO: Matinee Classics/Universal-International.

V-20 Appointment in Honduras   (RKO, 1953, F-85)

VIDEO: Commtron (#DIS783); Bleak Beauty Video.

V-21 The Opposite Sex   (MGM, 1956, F-87)

VIDEO: MGM/UA Home Video (#M202134); Facets
Multimedia, Inc. (#S13308).

LASER: MGM/UA Home Video (#ML102134 or M202134).

NOTES: The laser disc is in letter-box format and contains
the original trailer. The MGM/UA video was released in
January 1991.

MISCELLANEOUS:
V-22   Bloopers from the Legends of Hollywood

   VIDEO: Parade Video (#514).

NOTES: This thirty-minute tape combines Warner Bros. footage
with outtakes from Abbott and Costello movies and the TV
series Gunsmoke (CBS, 1955-75).   It was compiled in 1989.

V-23   The Ed Wynn Show, II

   VIDEO: Shokus Video (#448).

NOTES: Four episodes of Ed Wynn's TV series are compiled on
this video, including the February 11, 1950 show with Ann
Sheridan (T-1).

V-24   The Kate Smith Evening Hour

   VIDEO: Video Resources New York Inc.

NOTES: This 1994 release compiles two episodes of Kate
Smith's variety show.   The November 21, 1951 broadcast
features Ann Sheridan, Philip Reed, and Myron Cohen (T-3).
Peg Lynch and Alan Bunce (of Ethel and Albert) and Akim
Tamiroff were guests on the February 15, 1951 show.

V-25   The Lovely Day

   VIDEO: Parasol Group/Instar Corporation.

NOTES: This 1989 video is the August 13, 1953 Lux Video
Theatre episode entitled "The Lovely Day" (T-9).   It lasts
twenty-four minutes.

V-26   The Lustre Creme Movie Star Collection, Volume 1

   VIDEO: Video Resources New York Inc. (VRNY 007).

NOTES: This sixty-minute collection of Lustre Creme Shampoo
commercials includes spots by Ann Sheridan, Joan Bennett,
Yvonne De Carlo, Barbara Stanwyck, Elizabeth Taylor, Esther
Williams, and Jane Powell.

V-27   Movie Bloopers

   VIDEO: Viking Video Classics (#VCC 812).

NOTES: Many stars are seen fluffing lines, tripping, and
breaking up in this series of outtakes from Warner Bros.
movies.   Ann Sheridan is seen cracking a vase over Allen
Jenkins's head in a clip from Cowboy from Brooklyn (F-41).
The fifty-seven-minute video was compiled in 1988.

V-28   The Return of Video Yesterbloop

   VIDEO: Video Yesteryear (#1058).

NOTES: This twenty-seven-minute tape contains three
compilations of Warner Bros. outtakes entitled <u>Blow-ups of
1941</u>, <u>Blow-ups of 1946</u>, and <u>Blow-ups of 1947</u>.   In
addition to footage from <u>Silver River</u> (F-77) with Errol
Flynn and Ann Sheridan, the tape includes shots of Humphrey
Bogart, Gary Cooper, Edward G. Robinson, and James Stewart.

V-29   <u>A Star Is Born World Premiere</u>

VIDEO: Video Yesteryear.

NOTES: The televised premiere of <u>A Star Is Born</u> (Warner
Bros., 1954, P-14 and T-14) features many celebrities
expressing high hopes for the film.

BIBLIOGRAPHY

The bibliography contains articles, reviews, and books, by
and about Ann Sheridan. Undated articles and photographs
can be found in major archives, which are noted in
parentheses. "Lincoln Center Collection" denotes clippings
from the files of the Billy Rose Theatre Collection, New
York Public Library at Lincoln Center. Those marked
"Constance McCormick Collection" can be found in two
scrapbooks at the USC Cinema-Television Library, University
of Southern California. Items from the student newspaper
Campus Chat and other undated sources can be found in the
collection at the University of North Texas.

B-1   "Actor Denies Affair with Ann Sheridan." Los
        Angeles Times. March 30, 1960.
Scott McKay denies his estranged wife Joan Morgan McKay's
allegations that he had an affair with Ann Sheridan during
the 1958 tour of Kind Sir (P-16). During the McKays'
separation suit, Scott testified that he never had an affair
with Ann. "In every instance, in every show that I was in,
there was always somebody [Joan] was jealous of," he said.
"She accused me on numerous occasions of having affairs."
Joan committed suicide in 1962; Scott married Ann in 1966.

B-2   "Actor Scott McKay Dies at 71." Los Angeles
        Times. March 20, 1987.
This obituary for Ann Sheridan's third husband briefly
mentions their marriage.

B-3   "Actress Accused of Half-Affair." Miami News [FL].
        February 24, 1960.
An attorney representing Scott McKay's estranged wife accuses
the actor of having an affair with his Odd Man In (P-19)
co-star Ann Sheridan. The lawyer requested an increase in
alimony after Joan Morgan McKay required psychiatric care
following several suicide attempts.

B-4   "Actress Ann Sheridan to Aid War Bond Drive." Los
        Angeles Examiner. circa May 1942. (Constance
        McCormick Collection.)
Ann Sheridan's participation in a war bond drive, set to

begin May 25, 1942, is discussed. Ann planned to knock on
doors, selling bonds. The article urges other citizens to
join the campaign.

B-5   "Actress Brands Report Nonsense." Miami Herald
       [FL]. February 29, 1960.
Ann Sheridan denies rumors about an affair with her Odd Man
In (P-19) co-star Scott McKay.

B-6   "Actress Enters Race for Mayor." Los Angeles
       Times. April 24, circa 1950-51. (Constance
       McCormick Collection.)
Ann Sheridan announces her candidacy for honorary mayor of
Encino, California. Her six opponents were all men:
incumbent Tom Beneman, Mickey Rooney, Mischa Auer, Jim
"Fibber McGee" Jordan, Phil Harris, and Carmen Cavallaro.

B-7   "Actress Sheridan Remembered Here." Denton
       Record-Chronicle [TX]. 1967. (University of
       North Texas collection.)
After Ann Sheridan's death, professor Floyd Graham recalls
performing with her at North Texas State Teachers College
(P-1).

B-8   "Actress Wins Salary Strike." Richmond News
       Leader [VA]. December 5, 1940.
An alleged friend reports on Ann Sheridan's motives for
holding a press conference at her home that evening about her
strike at Warner Bros. The friend claims that Ann would
return to work for $1,500 a week and other benefits.

B-9   "Actress' Father Dies." Los Angeles Times.
       May 21, 1938.
Ann Sheridan's sixty-three-year-old father, George Sheridan,
died unexpectedly at his home on May 20, 1938.

B-10   Adams, Michael. "The Unfaithful." Magill's
       Cinema Annual 1986. Salem Press. Englewood
       Cliffs, New Jersey. 1986. pp. 550-54.
Adams discusses The Unfaithful (F-75), criticizing the
casting of Ann Sheridan. "[She] is made to appear more
attractive and less mannish than usual, but she is still
hardly a femme fatale who would drive an artist mad with
desire," he writes. "She does not convey Chris's sensitivity
and pain as well as would have dozens of other actresses."

B-11   Adams, Val. "Ann Lends 'Oomph' to Soaps." New
       York Times. November 21, 1965.
Another World (T-53) star Ann Sheridan talks about her love
of soap operas. One of her conditions for taking the role
was that she would not be overexposed, only appearing once or
twice a week. Although she knew her character's history, the
writers were secretive about her future. "I haven't the
faintest idea where I'm going," Ann insists.

B-12   Agan, Patrick. "Ann Sheridan." Hollywood Studio
       Magazine. November 1985. pp. 26-9.
This biographical sketch of Ann Sheridan includes several

stills.

B-13   Albelli, Alfred. "Accuse Ann Sheridan of Over
        Co-Starring." New York Daily News. February 24,
        1960.
Albelli discusses court actions to increase Scott McKay's
alimony payments to Joan Morgan McKay, which raised
questions about whether Scott was having an affair with Odd
Man In (P-19) co-star Ann Sheridan.

B-14   _____. "His Pal Ann Gets 218G Hannagan
        Insurance." New York Daily News. July 27, 1955.
Ann Sheridan is named beneficiary of six of Steve Hannagan's
insurance policies, totaling $218,399.

B-15   "Along the Straw-Hat Trail This Week." New York
        Times. July 6, 1958.
Ann Sheridan, then starring in Kind Sir (P-16) in
Fayetteville, NY, is pictured.

B-16   "And So Now It's Mrs. Oomph." New York Post.
        January 6, 1942.
The article announces Ann Sheridan's January 5 marriage to
George Brent.

B-17   Anderson, Jack E. "The Oomph Girl Is Back." Miami
        Herald Sunday Magazine [FL]. August 7, 1966.
Ann Sheridan discusses her new series, Pistols 'n'
Petticoats (T-56), and the changes in Hollywood since her
heyday. Anderson mistakenly claims Ann was married to Steve
Hannagan.

B-18   "Ann ('Anita') Sheridan Goes to Mexico." Stardom.
        January 1944. pp. 47-48.
Ann Sheridan's Mexican vacation is chronicled in this seven-
panel pictorial.

B-19   "Ann at Ease." Miami Daily News [FL].
        November 23, 1943.
Ann Sheridan is pictured on vacation in Miami Beach. When
asked about rumors concerning her relationship with Steve
Hannagan, Ann responded, "I'm flattered at the idea of being
engaged, but don't make any bets on either engagement or
marriage, as far as I'm concerned."

B-20   "Ann Meets the Army." Movies. 1942. (Constance
        McCormick Collection.)
Ann Sheridan's week-long U.S.O. tour with the Funzafire
troupe (P-7) is chronicled in this pictorial.

B-21   "Ann Sheridan." Motion Picture. May 1938.
Ann Sheridan poses in a low-cut gown. The caption mentions
her upcoming film, Little Lady Luck, released as Little
Miss Thoroughbred (F-40).

B-22   _____. Photoplay. March 1939.
The article credits Ann Sheridan's success in Letter of
Introduction (F-42) to an incident that occurred shortly

before filming began. After attending a preview of another
of Ann's films, a friend criticized her acting and lack of
sex appeal. Ann's anger allegedly propelled her performance
in Letter of Introduction.

B-23   _____.   TV Radio Annual. 1966.
Ann Sheridan discusses her role on Another World (T-53).
"There's no time to fool around in this medium of
television," she says. "You have to learn your lines every
day, and learn you do, or else."

B-24   _____.   TV Star Annual #22. 1967.
Ann Sheridan's career is recalled in this brief profile. It
includes photos from Pistols 'n' Petticoats (T-56) and of
Ann with husband Scott McKay.

B-25   "Ann Sheridan: A Photo Interview." Screen Guide.
        June 1946. p. 24.
In a five-panel pictorial, Ann Sheridan discusses her tour to
the CBI theatre to entertain during World War II (P-9).
"It's nothing to shout about," she insists. "Lots of
Hollywood people did much more than I....But one thing I know
- a lot has happened that I'll never forget."

B-26   "Ann Sheridan, Acosta Producing Mex Shorts."
        Variety. October 12, 1955.
Ann Sheridan and Rodolfo Acosta planned to produce a series
of fifty shorts for television (T-17). Filming was set to
begin that week in Mexico City. The budget was $1,250,000.

B-27   "Ann Sheridan, Actress, 51 Dies; Career Spanned 33-
        Year Period." New York Times. January 22, 1967.
Ann Sheridan's career is recalled in this obituary.

B-28   "Ann Sheridan Adjudged Girl with Most 'Oomph.'"
        Los Angeles Examiner. March 17, 1939.
A large glamour portrait of Ann Sheridan announces her
selection as the girl with the most personality, glamour, and
oomph at a banquet the previous evening (A-4).

B-29   "Ann Sheridan and Brent Part." Los Angeles Times.
        circa September 1942. (Constance McCormick
        Collection.)
Ann Sheridan and George Brent's separation is announced.
Although a Warner Bros. spokesman insists that there were no
divorce plans, Ann filed for divorce three months later in
December 1942.

B-30   "Ann Sheridan as Lead for Kermit Maynard."
        Hollywood Reporter. March 18, 1935.
Ann Sheridan's loan-out to Ambassador for Red Blood of
Courage (F-25) is announced.

B-31   "Ann Sheridan at American." St. Louis Post-
        Dispatch [MO]. February 14, 1960.
Odd Man In (P-19) is previewed. Ann Sheridan is pictured
in a scene from the play.

B-32   "Ann Sheridan Back From Tour." New York Times.
        September 7, 1944.
Ann Sheridan's return from the China-Burma-India theatre is
announced (P-9).

B-33   "Ann Sheridan Best-Dressed Screen Star, Says
        Academy." Hollywood Citizen-News [CA]. March 20,
        1945.
New York's Fashion Academy announces the thirteen winners of
its annual awards. Ann Sheridan won a medal as best dressed
screen actress (A-17).

B-34   "Ann Sheridan Can't Return to Mexico." Exposed.
        April 1957.
Ann Sheridan's affair with Rodolfo Acosta is revealed.

B-35   "Ann Sheridan Dies At 51." Chicago Sun-Times.
        January 22, 1967.
Photos from 1947, 1958, and 1966 accompany this obituary.

B-36   _____. St. Petersburg Times [FL]. January 22,
        1967.
This obituary recalls Ann Sheridan's career.

B-37   "Ann Sheridan Dies; Movie's 'Oomph Girl.'" Fort
        Wayne Journal-Gazette [IN]. January 22, 1967.
Ann Sheridan's career is detailed.

B-38   "Ann Sheridan Dies of Cancer." New York Sunday
        News. January 22, 1967. pp. 1, 3, 70.
New York's picture newspaper devotes a lot of space to Ann
Sheridan's death. Although her obituary begins on page
three, a headline takes up a quarter of the front page. Six
photos accompany the article.

B-39   "Ann Sheridan Dies Of Cancer At 51." Denton
        Record-Chronicle [TX]. January 22, 1967.
Ann Sheridan's hometown newspaper spotlights her career.

B-40   "Ann Sheridan Dies; 'Oomph Girl' of Movies." Dayton
        News [OH]. January 22, 1967.
This obituary erroneously blames emphysema for Ann Sheridan's
death.

B-41   "Ann Sheridan Donates Blood." Los Angeles Times.
        circa 1942. (Constance McCormick Collection.)
A photo of Ann Sheridan giving blood to the American Red
Cross accompanies an article on the center. It stresses how
easy the process is, noting that Ann returned to the set of
Wings for the Eagle (F-63) after her donation.

B-42   "Ann Sheridan, 51, Dies - Oomph Girl of 1930s."
        Miami Herald [FL]. January 22, 1967.
This detailed obituary includes a 1940s portrait and a still
from Pistols 'n' Petticoats (T-56).

B-43   "Ann Sheridan Flies to Mexico to Divorce George
        Brent." Los Angeles Times. December 11, 1942.

Ann Sheridan's divorce plans are discussed. Ann is pictured
buying her plane ticket to Mexico on December 10, 1942.

B-44   "Ann Sheridan Gets Hannagan's 218G." New York
        Daily Mirror. July 27, 1955.
Ann Sheridan is announced as the beneficiary of six insurance
policies totaling $218,399 from Steve Hannagan's estate.
Other details of his will are disclosed.

B-45   "Ann Sheridan Gives Up Oomph!" Screen Guide.
        circa 1941. (Constance McCormick Collection.)
This pictorial shows the different imgages Ann Sheridan
projects in Navy Blues (F-59) and King Row (F-61). The
article features ten photographs, including costume, hair,
and makeup tests for Kings Row.

B-46   "Ann Sheridan Goes Literary." New York Morning
        Telegraph. October 12, 1941.
Ann Sheridan accepts the Harvard Advocate's invitation to
attend it's seventy-fifth anniversary "Punch" banquet on
November 20, 1941, where she would be inducted as an honorary
editor of the literary magazine (A-11).

B-47   "Ann Sheridan Handcuffed to Student Who Gulps Key."
        Los Angeles Times. 1939. (Constance McCormick
        Collection.)
An over-zealous fan's attempt to win a bet is chronicled in
this article. At a preview of It All Came True (F-53),
UCLA junior Dick Brunnenkamp handcuffed himself to Ann
Sheridan, then swallowed the key. Ann was released by a
locksmith within fifteen minutes. Brunnenkamp explained, "I
did it because the boys at the fraternity house bet me $1 I
couldn't get away with it."

B-48   "Ann Sheridan - Home Town Girl Who Made Good."
        Dallas Morning News [TX]. January 22, 1967.
This obituary focuses on Ann Sheridan's Texas roots.

B-49   "Ann Sheridan in Farce Next at American." St.
        Louis Post-Dispatch [MO]. February 7, 1960.
Odd Man In (P-19) is previewed.

B-50   "Ann Sheridan Is Press Favorite." Boston Post
        [MA]. December 20, 1943.
The Hollywood Women's Press Club names Ann Sheridan and Bob
Hope the most cooperative stars (A-15).

B-51   "Ann Sheridan Kills Love Rumor." Miami News [FL].
        February 28, 1960.
Ann Sheridan denies rumors of an affair with Odd Man In
(P-19) co-star Scott McKay.

B-52   "Ann Sheridan - Love Nest Pigeon?" Top Secret.
        June 1957.
Ann Sheridan's relationship with Rodolfo Acosta is discussed
in this scandal magazine.

B-53   "Ann Sheridan Models for a Plastic Oomph Girl."

Look. February 13, 1940. pp. 38-39.
Warner Bros. makeup chief Perc Westmore is shown casting a
plastic mask of Ann Sheridan. Ann poses with the finished
product on the cover. The article accompanies "Look Calls
on Ann Sheridan" (B-318).

B-54   "Ann Sheridan on Stand in Her Suit Against Studio."
        Los Angeles Times. 1952. (Constance McCormick
        Collection.)
Ann Sheridan's testimony in her suit against RKO is
discussed. She sued the studio over her dismissal from
Carriage Entrance, released as My Forbidden Past (RKO,
1951).

B-55   "Ann Sheridan, 'Oomph Girl' of Hollywood." London
        Daily Telegraph [England]. January 23, 1967.
This obituary summarizes Ann Sheridan's career.

B-56   "Ann Sheridan Play Opening Monday." New Orleans
        Times-Picayunne [LA]. January 10, 1960.
Odd Man In (P-19) is previewed.

B-57   "Ann Sheridan, Preferred." Look. June 18, 1940.
        pp. 54-59.
This nineteen-panel pictorial charts the rise of Ann
Sheridan's popularity after Warner Bros. began promoting her
as the Oomph Girl. The article looks at advances and
setbacks in her career, from her beginnings as a $75-a-week
stock player to her role in Torrid Zone (F-54).

B-58   "Ann Sheridan Returns." New York Times.
        September 9, 1944.
Ann Sheridan discusses her tour of the China-Burma-India
front (P-9).

B-59   "Ann Sheridan Rites Conducted Privately." Los
        Angeles Times. January 23, 1967.
Private services were held for Ann Sheridan at Pierce
Brothers Valhalla Mortuary.

B-60   "Ann Sheridan Seeks Divorce." New York Times.
        October 14, 1942.
Ann Sheridan announces her plans to divorce George Brent
after finishing her current film.

B-61   "Ann Sheridan Shows You Her New House." Motion
        Picture. November 1943.
Ann Sheridan's home is seen in this seven-panel pictorial.

B-62   "Ann Sheridan: 'So Close He Stood to Me...'"
        Sheilah Graham's Hollywood Romances #3. 1953.
Ann Sheridan's relationship with Steve Hannagan is recalled
following his death on February 5, 1953. Ann is pictured
attending his funeral.

B-63   "Ann Sheridan The 'I Don't Care' Girl."
        Suppressed. January 1956.
Ann Sheridan is profiled in this scandal magazine.

B-64   "Ann Sheridan The Oomph Girl Returns." Fort
        Lauderdale News [FL]. July 29, 1966.
Two stills from Pistols 'n' Petticoats (T-56) accompany
this profile of Ann Sheridan.

B-65   "Ann Sheridan: What She Did in Mexico!" Inside.
        June 1957. pp. 49-53.
The scandal magazine details Ann Sheridan's relationship with
Rodolfo Acosta, which led to his wife suing the actress for
criminal adultery.

B-66   "Ann Sheridan Wins $55,162 in Film Suit." Los
        Angeles Times. Febuary 7, 1951.
The results of Ann Sheridan's suit against RKO are reported.
Although Ann had sued for $350,000 damages, the jury awarded
her $55,162, her apparent salary for four months employment
in 1949.

B-67   "Ann Sheridan's Fatal Sickness Unknown to Movie
        Associates." Fort Wayne News-Sentinel [IN].
        January 23, 1967.
This obituary recounts Ann Sheridan's career, erroneously
crediting her as Grandma Hanks on Pistols 'n' Petticoats
(T-56).

B-68   "Ann Sheridan's House Has Built-in Chinese Ghost."
        Miami Sunday News [FL]. March 26, 1956.
Ann Sheridan discusses her San Fernando valley home, a former
gambling casino that allegedly was haunted by a Chinese
ghost.

B-69   "Ann Sheridan's in love." Movieland. March 1947.
Ann Sheridan's zest for life and friendship are discussed.

B-70   "Ann Sheridan's Secret Life." Movies. January
        1943. pp. 16-18.
This pictorial traces Ann Sheridan's career from Search for
Beauty (F-1) through George Washington Slept Here (F-64).

B-71   "Ann Sheridan's Shack Job South of the Border." On
        the QT. May 1957.
Ann Sheridan's relationship with Rodolfo Acosta is revealed
in this scandal magazine.

B-72   "Ann to Divorce Brent." Los Angeles Examiner.
        December 11, 1942.
Ann Sheridan's plans to obtain a Mexican divorce from George
Brent are announced in this article. Ann is pictured buying
her plane ticket.

B-73   "Annie and Friends." Movie World. October 1955.
        pp. 50-51.
Ann Sheridan shows off her poodles in this pictorial.

B-74   "Annie at Home and at Work." Screenland. February
        1947. pp. 54-55.
This nine-panel pictorial shows Ann Sheridan relaxing at her
Encino home and filming Nora Prentiss (F-74).

B-75   "Annie Gets Clipped." <u>Screen Guide</u>. July 1949.
This pictorial shows Ann Sheridan getting a haircut from
Helen Turpin. "Yikes, I feel bald," Ann says as she
examines four-inch hunks of hair.

B-76   Archerd, Army. "Just for Variety." <u>Daily</u>
         <u>Variety</u>. October 12, 1956.
Archerd announces that Ann Sheridan canceled plans to live
in Mexico and work in Hollywood, choosing to move to New
York instead.

B-77   Asher, Jerry. "I'm on the Spot." <u>Picture Play</u>.
         September 1939. pp. 24-25, 61
Ann Sheridan discusses the oomph campaign and her efforts to
overcome it.

B-78   _____. "This Is Bogart." <u>Photoplay</u>. January
         1944. pp. 20-21, 96.
Humphrey Bogart names Ann Sheridan, Barbara Stanwyck, Mary
Astor, and Ingrid Bergman as his favorite leading ladies.
"They aren't dames," he explains. "Those dames who wet their
lips and wiggle give me a pain."

B-79   Atkins, Irene Kahn. "Director's Guild of America
         Oral History - LeRoy Prinz." Academy of Motion
         Picture Arts and Sciences. 1978.
In this taped interview, director/choreographer LeRoy Prinz
recalls being a judge in the <u>Search for Beauty</u> (F-1)
contest that brought Ann Sheridan to Hollywood. To choose a
winner, he threw the finalists' photos in the air. The last
to land face up was Ann Sheridan. When he shared the story
with Ann years later, telling her she received a break
because she was the last to land on her back, Ann replied,
"Yes, you S.O.B. and I've been on my back ever since."

B-80   "Auction Costumes to Save Haulage." <u>Variety</u>.
         March 23, 1960.
The trade paper reports on an auction of the props and
costumes from <u>Odd Man In</u> (P-19).

B-81   "Autograph Collector." <u>Dallas Morning News TV</u>
         <u>Channels</u> [TX]. January 22, 1967. p. 16.
Ann Sheridan describes her autograph collection, which
included signatures of five presidents. She says, "Sometimes
an actress begins to take her press clippings too seriously.
When I feel I may be falling into that trap I just look at my
collection and I immediately regain my sense of proportion."
Coincidentally, Ann died on January 21, 1967 and the piece
ran in the same edition as her obituary.

B-82   "Autographed - Special for the S.F. Mayor."
         <u>Hollywood Citizen-News</u> [CA]. November 28, 1946.
Ann Sheridan is pictured presenting an autographed sheet of
Christmas Seals to a San Francisco stewardess, who was
supposed to deliver them to Mayor Roger Lapham. As part of
the Christmas Seal campaign, Ann planned to send seals to
other western mayors and governors.

B-83   Bailey, Margaret J. Those Glorious Glamour Years.
        Citadel Press. Secaucus, NJ. 1982. p. 73.
This pictorial book on movie fashion includes a full-page
portrait of Ann Sheridan modeling a gown by Shoup as she
sings into a microphone in Broadway Musketeers (F-44).

B-84   Barton, Ann. "Wedding Bells Didn't Ring." Motion
        Picture. November 1951. pp. 24-25, 56-57.
Barton recalls celebrity romances that did not culminate in
marriage, including Ann Sheridan's relationships with Jeff
Chandler and Steve Hannagan.

B-85   Basten, Fred E. Max Factor's Hollywood: Glamour,
        Movies, Make-Up. Central Publishing Group. Los
        Angeles. 1995. p. 163.
A full page photo of Ann Sheridan notes her as Max Factor's
"Girl of the Year" for 1939.

B-86   "The Bear Saw Pink." Silver Screen. February
        1953.
While filming a scene for Flame of the Timberline, released
as Take Me to Town (F-84), scantily-clad Ann Sheridan was
chased by a bear. Ann surmised, "I think he didn't like my
pink corset. Who would?"

B-87   Beck, Jerry and Friedwald, Will. Looney Tunes and
        Merrie Melodies. Henry Holt and Company. New
        York. 1989. pp. 116, 168.
This book on Warner Bros. cartoons includes information on
Hollywood Steps Out (F-58) and Hollywood Daffy (F-72).
Both cartoons spoof Ann Sheridan.

B-88   Behlmer, Rudy. Inside Warner Bros. (1935-1951).
        Viking. New York. 1985. pp. 84, 136-41, 199, 287.
Behlmer reprints internal memos from Warner Bros. files and
comments on their place in film history. Ann Sheridan is
mentioned in memos about Gone with the Wind (MGM, 1939),
Casablanca (Warner Bros., 1942), Juke Girl (F-62), and
The Treasure of the Sierra Madre (F-76).

B-89   Benjamin, Ruth and Rosenblatt, Arthur. Movie Song
        Catalog. McFarland & Company, Inc. Jefferson,
        North Carolina. 1993.
Benjamin and Rosenblatt present a selected listing of songs
from musical and dramatic films and the performers who sang
them.

B-90   Benny, Jack and Benny, Joan. Sunday Nights at
        Seven. Warner Books. New York. 1990.
Jack Benny and his daughter Joan share anecdotes about the
comedian's life and career, including his friendship with Ann
Sheridan.

B-91   Benny, Mary Livingstone and Marks, Hilliard, with
        Borie, Marcia. Jack Benny. Doubleday & Company,
        Inc. Garden City, New York. 1978. pp. 48-49, 139,
        220-21.
Jack Benny's wife and brother-in-law reminisce about the

comedian in this biography. Livingstone recalls her jealousy
when Ann Sheridan and Benny were filming <u>George
Washington Slept Here</u> (F-64). Marks notes that Ann was
among the many Hollywood beauties who found Benny enchanting.

B-92   "Benny's Mrs. May Get Lead in His WB Film."
          <u>Variety</u>. April 8, 1942.
Despite the headline's prediction that Mary Livingstone might
co-star with husband Jack Benny in <u>George Washington Slept
Here</u> (F-64), Ann Sheridan kept the role. The article
claims Warner Bros. considered replacing Ann because she
wanted a ten-day rest after a personal appearance tour (P-7),
which would delay the film's shooting schedule.

B-93   Berg, Louis. "Cast-Iron Annie." <u>New York Herald-
          Tribune</u>. October 3, 1948.
Berg marvels at Ann Sheridan's cast-iron stomach and her
indifference about her appearance, two rare traits in
Hollywood.

B-94   Bergan, Ronald. <u>The United Artists Story</u>. Crown
          Publishers, Inc. New York. 1986. p. 86.
A synopsis and still from <u>Winter Carnival</u> (F-49) are
included in this history of United Artists.

B-95   "Better Than 'Oomph.'" <u>Picturegoer</u> [England].
          December 31, 1949.
A reader from Bristol praises Ann Sheridan's work in <u>Good
Sam</u>, calling her "the finest comedienne on the screen
today."

B-96   Billingsley, Mary Jo. "Oomph Girl on Ice." <u>Life</u>.
          August 21, 1939.
A reader from West Los Angeles recalls Ann Sheridan's
natural behavior at a skating rink. She wore no makeup and
did not care about her awkwardness on the ice. "Despite
many falls, bumps and bruises," Billingsley reports, "She
always came up with a grin and a yell for a cigaret [sic]
before she went out to try it again."

B-97   Bilson, Hattie. "Good Time Annie." <u>Screenland</u>.
          circa 1948. pp. 28-29, 59. (Constance McCormick
          Collection.)
Bilson recalls Ann Sheridan's penchant for practical jokes
during the filming of <u>Silver River</u> (F-77). Wardrobe woman
Martha Giddings, who often traveled with Ann, discusses her
friendship with the actress. Five stills are included.

B-98   "The Birth of a Bathing-Suit." <u>Screen Guide</u>.
          January 1939.
Ann Sheridan is among the stars modeling new swimsuit styles
in Palm Springs.

B-99   Blake, Anita. "Learned in Exile." <u>Photoplay</u>.
          June 1941. pp. 43, 99-100.
Blake claims to have the true story of Ann Sheridan's salary
dispute with Warner Bros. Ann discusses the way colleagues
treated her during her suspension.

B-100   Bloom, Ken. <u>Hollywood Song</u>. Facts on File. New
         York. 1995.
This extensive three-volume set lists songs composed for film
musicals, as well as some that were cut before release.

B-101   Bogart, Humphrey with Haas, Dorothy B. "Sister
         Annie." <u>Silver Screen</u>. March 1943.
Bogart discusses co-star Ann Sheridan, a pal he thinks of as
a sister. He recalls coaching her during <u>The Great</u>
<u>O'Malley</u> (F-32), as well as her practical jokes through the
years. He concludes, calling her "the nicest girl in
Hollywood." This piece ran two months after Ann Sheridan's
article "Brother Bogie" (B-590).

B-102   Boone, Betty. "Inside the Stars' Homes."
         <u>Screenland</u>. March 1939.
Ann Sheridan fries chicken for Boone and a photographer in
this humanizing article.

B-103   <u>Bowker's Complete Video Directory</u>. R.R. Bowker.
         New York. 1995.
This reference volume lists video cassettes and laserdiscs
available.

B-104   "Box-Office Build-Up." <u>Modern Movies</u>. circa
         1939. pp. 41-42. (Constance McCormick
         Collection.)
Ann Sheridan's rise from beauty contest winner to Oomph Girl
is charted in this article, which ponders whether <u>Winter</u>
<u>Carnival</u> (F-49) would catapult Ann to "A" picture roles.
The article includes nineteen stills.

B-105   Brady, Thomas F. "Al Werker Wins Director's Prize."
         <u>New York Times</u>. January 10, 1950.
A federal judge refuses to dismiss Ann Sheridan's breach of
contract suit against RKO, but reduces her admissible damage
claim to $150,000.

B-106   _____. "Ann Sheridan Sues R.K.O. for $350,000."
         <u>New York Times</u>. November 22, 1949.
Brady details Ann Sheridan's breach of contract suit against
RKO after the studio filmed <u>Carriage Entrance</u> without her.
The movie was released as <u>My Forbidden Past</u> (RKO, 1951).

B-107   _____. "Ann Sheridan Wins $55,162 in Lawsuit."
         <u>New York Times</u>. February 7, 1951.
Brady reveals the results of Ann Sheridan's suit against RKO.

B-108   _____. "Before the Court." <u>New York Times</u>.
         November 27, 1949.
Brady discusses lawsuits in Hollywood, including Ann
Sheridan's breach of contract suit against RKO.

B-109   Brooks, Tim and Marsh, Earle. <u>The Complete</u>
         <u>Directory to Prime Time Network TV Shows, 1946-</u>
         <u>Present</u>. Ballantine Books. New York. 1985.
Many of Ann Sheridan's TV performances are listed in this
reference volume. It also mentions her non-appearance on

This Is Your Life (NBC, 1952-61).

B-110   Burr, Betty. "Betty Burr's Fan Club Corner."
        Movie Stars Parade. August 1947.
Ann Sheridan is seen accepting scrapbooks from a fan on the
set of The Unfaithful (F-75).

B-111   Busch, Noel F. "America's Oomph Girl." Life.
        July 24, 1939.
Busch labels Ann Sheridan a "second Jean Harlow" as he
reports on her rise in popularity since the oomph campaign.
Among the trivia revealed is that Ann smoked thirty
cigarettes a day and that her Warner Bros. contract included
a clause requiring her to appear at three nightclubs per
week. Ann is seen in eleven photos, as well as the magazine
cover.

B-112   "Busiest Gal in Town." Movie Stars Parade. circa
        1941. (Constance McCormick Collection.)
This pictorial stresses Ann Sheridan's hectic life,
concurrently filming The Man Who Came to Dinner (F-60) and
Kings Row (F-61).

B-113   Camlin, Edward B. "Enquirer Reader Tells How...Ann
        Sheridan Shared Her Tragic Secret with Me."
        National Enquirer. May 20, 1973.
Former stewardess Cheri McLintock won twenty-five dollars for
sharing her celebrity stories with the tabloid. Among her
memories was meeting Ann Sheridan shortly after she was
diagnosed with cancer. "Miss Sheridan was truly a great
lady," McLintock says. "I will never forget her courage and
her concern for her fans."

B-114   Candide. "Only Human." New York Daily Mirror.
        October 18, 1939.
Candide chronicles how ex-newspaperman Mitch Rawson was
inspired to mold Ann Sheridan into a glamorous star after the
death of Jean Harlow.

B-115   Canfield, Alyce. "Ann Sheridan X-Rayed!"
        Screenland. August 1944. pp. 28-29, 83-85.
Ann Sheridan recalls how she weathered disappointments in
life, including the loss of the lead in Texas Guinan. The
film biography was made as Incendiary Blonde (Paramount,
1945) with Betty Hutton in the title role.

B-116   _____. "If You Had a Date with Ann Sheridan."
        Motion Picture. August 1947. pp. 49, 80.
Canfield discusses the different aspects of Ann Sheridan's
personality: the femme fatale, the tomboy, the high-spirited
party girl, and the loyal friend.

B-117   Carpozi, Jr., George. That's Hollywood: Volume 2
        The Love Goddesses. Manor Books. New York. 1978.
        pp. 39-52.
In a chapter titled "A Firebrand With Oomph," Carpozi recalls
Ann Sheridan's life and career.

B-118   Carr, William H.A.   "La Sheridan Faces Mexico City
         Arrest as a Love Thief." New York Post.
         November 1, 1956.
Carr details an arrest warrant for Ann Sheridan in Mexico
City. Actor Rodolfo Acosta's estranged wife charged Ann with
criminal adultery, claiming Rodolfo lived with Ann, then
pressured his wife for a divorce.

B-119   Cassa, Anthony.   "Ann Sheridan - The Oomph Girl."
         Hollywood Studio Magazine.   June 1979.
Cassa recalls the hightlights of Ann Sheridan's career.

B-120   "Charm on the Farm." Movie Play. Winter, 1944.
Ann Sheridan shows off her ranch.

B-121   "Chicago Opening Today for Raintree County."
         Motion Picture Daily.   October 23, 1957.
Ann Sheridan was among the celebrities scheduled to appear at
the Chicago premiere of Raintree County (P-15).

B-122   Chierichetti, David. Hollywood Director: The
         Career of Mitchell Leisen. Curtis Books. New
         York. 1973. pp. 83-84.
Ann Sheridan's role in Behold My Wife (F-16) is noted in
this chronicle of director Mitchell Leisen's career.

B-123   Cleveland Plain Dealer [OH]. March 19, 1952.
Ann Sheridan, John Lund, and Howard Duff are pictured at a
St. Patrick's Day luncheon while in Cleveland to promote
Steel Town (P-12).

B-124   "Closest Friends Unaware Ann Sheridan Was Sick."
         Miami News [FL].   January 23, 1967.
This obituary includes an overview of Ann Sheridan's career.

B-125   "Consensus." Television Magazine. November 1966.
         pp. 52-55, 64-65, 68.
Television Magazine polls twenty-four critics about the
1966-67 TV season, which includes Pistols 'n' Petticoats
(T-56).   Sixteen of the critics rate the series "bad," noting
its resemblance to The Beverly Hillbillies (CBS, 1962-71).
Only two of the critics give Pistols 'n' Petticoats a
positive rating.

B-126   Conshise, Juan. "Why Ann Sheridan Didn't Like that
         Mexican Hayride." Uncensored Magazine. May 1957.
         pp. 38-39, 68.
Conshise chronicles Ann Sheridan's legal troubles involving
Mexican movie villain Rodolfo Acosta. The actor's estranged
wife tried to sue Ann for alienation of affection, but a
judge dismissed the charges. Ann's marriages to Edward
Norris and George Brent are recalled.

B-127   "Contest Leads to Chance for Fame." Los Angeles
         Times. November 24, 1933.
Six of the Search for Beauty (F-1) contestants are pictured
in this announcement about Paramount signing them to a
contract. While it is noted that Gwenllian Gill, Alfred

Delcambre, Julian Madison, Colin Tapley, Eldred Tidbury, and
Clara Lou Sheridan were hired, only Gill and Tidbury received
thousand-dollar bonuses for best performances.

B-128   "Contracts for Films Go to Six." Los Angeles
          Times. November 24, 1933.
Clara Lou Sheridan and five other Search for Beauty (F-1)
contestants are announced as winners of Paramount contracts.

B-129   Copeland, Elizabeth. "Ann Sheridan, 'Oomph' Girl,
          Finds Film's Title Describes Own Career." Richmond
          News Leader [VA]. April 5, 1940.
Copeland reviews Ann Sheridan's career, insisting that the
title of her current film, It All Came True (F-53), could
describe Ann's dreams of success.

B-130   _____. "Purloined Picture Makes Anne [sic]
          Sheridan Movie Star Instead of School Teacher."
          Richmond News Leader [VA]. June 6, 1940.
This trivia-filled account of Ann Sheridan's career is full
of errors, including her real name and her sister's name.

B-131   "Cowboy from Brooklyn." Screen Romances. July
          1938. pp. 20-22.
This fourteen-panel pictorial includes a still of Ann
Sheridan, Dick Powell, and Pat O'Brien in Cowboy from
Brooklyn (F-41).

B-132   Cox, Edwin. Los Angeles Times. August 7, 1939.
This cartoon of Ann Sheridan depicts her unique party
invitations, which Cox calls "Hollywood's cleverest." They
are made up of windshield stickers, illustrating the route to
her home.

B-133   "Craig, Sheridan to Appear Again with Stage Band."
          Campus Chat [Denton, TX]. March 2, 1933.
          (University of North Texas Collection).
A North Texas State Teachers College show is previewed (P-1)
in the college newspaper.

B-134   Crichton, Kyle. "Easy, Thar, with our Clara Lou."
          Collier's. July 22, 1939. pp. 18, 24.
Crichton accesses Warner Bros.'s oomph campaign and recalls
Ann Sheridan's career. He marvels at her unaffectedness,
noting, "If even after the build-up she is getting now, she
ends up doing mysteries and Westerns, it will only be what
she has always done and she won't beef."

B-135   Crisler, B.R. "Feuds and Fancies." New York
          Times. March 10, 1940.
Crisler recounts the feud between Ann Sheridan and the
Harvard Lampoon after the publication named her the actress
"most unlikely to succeed" (A-6). Ann quotes statistics
about Harvard graduates, proving she is more successful.

B-136   Crowther, Bosley. "A Definition of 'Oomph.'" New
          York Times. October 1, 1939.
During Ann Sheridan's first personal appearance tour (P-5),

Crowther recalls her career and the oomph campaign.

B-137   Culbertson, Judi and Randall, Tom. Permanent
         Californians. Chelsea Green Publishing Co.
         Chelsea, Vermont. 1989. p. 150.
This book on cemeteries which feature celebrities includes a
report on Chapel of the Pines mausoleum and crematory.
Culbertson and Randall note that Ann Sheridan's remains are
in a basement holding vault and unavailable for viewing.

B-138   "Cummings, Sheridan Go in Kings Row." Hollywood
         Reporter. April 30, 1941. p. 3.
Ann Sheridan and Robert Cummings are announced for leading
roles in Kings Row (F-61).

B-139   "Dancing Doll." Look. May 7, 1940. p. 7.
Reader Tommy Wonder submits a photo of himself with a dance
dummy that looks like Ann Sheridan. The mask was pictured
with Ann on the February 13, 1940 cover of Look.

B-140   "Death Takes Five Film Figures." Los Angeles
         Citizen-News. January 23, 1967.
This obituary for Ann Sheridan notes that private services
were held at Pierce Bros. Mortuary in North Hollywood.

B-141   Delehanty, Thornton. "Temperament - to the Public -
         Likely to be Row over Money." New York Herald
         Tribune. December 15, 1940.
Delehanty reports on a press conference at Ann Sheridan's
home, an effort to reestablish a rapport with the media
during her strike from Warner Bros.

B-142   "Dennis Morgan Opposite Ann Sheridan in WB Pic."
         Variety. November 25, 1942.
Ann Sheridan and Dennis Morgan are announced for The Time
Between, a Warner Bros. film. The movie was not made.

B-143   Denton, Charles. "Ann Sheridan Sees Big Test Due
         for Marilyn Monroe." Rochester Democrat and
         Chronicle [NY]. September 16, 1952.
Former Oomph Girl Ann Sheridan offers advice to Marilyn
Monroe and other sex symbols.

B-144   de Thuin, Richard. "Blonde bombshells and voluptuous
         vamps of the silver screen." AntiqueWeek.
         November 1, 1993.
In a column on the collectability of movie memorabilia,
de Thuin notes that posters and lobby cards of Betty Grable,
Ann Sheridan, and Lana Turner are very popular.

B-145   "Devil's Disciple Pays 2d Visit to Park; Ann
         Sheridan Stars in Comedy at Bristol."
         Philadelphia Bulletin [PA]. July 13, 1958.
Summer theatre productions playing around Philadelphia are
announced in this column, which includes notes about Ann
Sheridan's appearance in Kind Sir (P-16).

B-146   "Dietrich, Turner Tops in Sex Appeal, Says

Scientist." Hollywood Reporter. April 23, 1941.
Stanford psychiatrist Dr. Joseph Catton announces the results
of his study on film stars' "man power pull." Catton claims
Marlene Dietrich, Lana Turner, and Ann Sheridan ranked
highest, with 90%, 86%, and 85% respectively.

B-147   "Dissolved." Modern Screen. April 1943.
After a trip to Mexico to divorce George Brent, Ann Sheridan
was rumored to be dating Errol Flynn. The article insists
the stars were just friends.

B-148   Doan, Richard K. "'Oomph Girl' Ann Sheridan Cast in
         NBC Soap Opera." New York Herald Tribune. 1965.
         (Lincoln Center Collection.)
When asked about her upcoming role in Another World (T-53),
Ann Sheridan says, "I'm going to love it. There's no time
to fool around in this medium of television." Doan
mistakenly identifies Odd Man In (P-19) as Odd Man Out.

B-149   "'Dodge City' Has Dodge City Premiere That Dazzles
         Kansas and Half the West." Life. April 17, 1939.
         pp. 68-71.
The premiere of Dodge City (F-47, P-3) is chronicled in
this pictorial.

B-150   Dolven, Frank. "Ann Sheridan Deserved a Brighter
         Star." Big Reel. July 1995. pp. 154-56.
Ann Sheridan's career is recalled in this mistake-laden
profile.

B-151   "Domestic Comedy." New York Times. August 9,
         1953.
Ann Sheridan and Robert Paige are pictured in a scene from
the Lux Video Theatre production of "The Lovely Day" (T-9).

B-152   "Down Mexico Way." Movie Life. January 1953.
Ann Sheridan's weekend in Tijuana is chronicled in this
seven-photo story. She is seen attending the bullfights,
shopping at an outdoor market, and joining matador Carlos
Arruza at the jai alai games. The vacation was cut short so
she could return to Hollywood to begin filming Flame of
the Timberline, released as Take Me to Town (F-84).

B-153   "Dream Dresses." Fort Wayne News Sentinel [IN].
         November 24, 1956.
Costume sketches for The Opposite Sex (F-87) accompany a
still from the film.

B-154   Drew, Janice. "A Farmer's Market." Silver
         Screen. August 1943. pp. 54-55.
This six-panel fashion layout shows off Ann Sheridan's ranch
and promotes Thank Your Lucky Stars (F-66).

B-155   Druxman, Michael B. "Ann Sheridan: A Texan Never
         Quits." Coronet. October 1973. pp. 122-25.
Druxman looks back at Ann Sheridan's career in this brief
feature. Four stills are included.

B-156   Eames, John Douglas. The MGM Story. Crown
         Publishers, Inc. New York. 1975. pp. 120, 276.
Ann Sheridan is pictured in a still from The Opposite Sex
(F-87).

B-157   _____. The Paramount Story. Crown Publishers,
         Inc. New York. 1985. pp. 100, 105, 113.
All of Ann Sheridan's Paramount films are included in this
studio history, although she is not given credit for most of
them.

B-158   "Earlier Days in L.A." Los Angeles Herald-
         Examiner. November 8, 1969.
The paper looks back in its files to twenty-five years
earlier, November 1944. Ann Sheridan is among the stars who
paid off election bets by parading on Hollywood Boulevard in
a torn dress with burnt cork on her face.

B-159   "Election Bet Payoffs." Screen Guide. January
         1945.
This pictorial shows how celebrities paid off their election
bets. Ann Sheridan let Warner Bros.'s Perc Westmore make her
up in black face because she backed the losing Thomas Dewey.

B-160   Ellenberg, Albert. "Ann Sheridan Honeymooning."
         New York Post. June 14, 1966.
This announcement of Ann Sheridan and Scott McKay's marriage
includes the complicated history of their previous romantic
entanglements.

B-161   Engstead, John. Star Shots. E.P. Dutton. New
         York. 1978. pp. 18, 36, 112, 114-15.
Photographer Engstead shares his memories of the many stars
he worked with, including Ann Sheridan. Engstead recalls his
thirty-year friendship with Ann in words and pictures,
including a photograph from the Paramount stock company
production of Double Door (P-2), in which both were
featured, and her last publicity photos from Pistols 'n'
Petticoats (T-56).

B-162   "Estoy Muy Alegre." Picture Scope. July 1953.
Ann Sheridan's weekend trip to Tijuana for the Mexican
Independence Day is chronicled in this pictorial. Universal-
International allegedly had to postpone work on Vermilion
O'Toole to accomodate Ann's busy schedule in Mexico. The
film was released as Take Me to Town (F-84).

B-163   Evans, Delight. "The Editor's Page: An Open Letter
         to Ann Sheridan." Screenland. circa 1943-44.
         p. 19. (Constance McCormick Collection.)
The Screenland editor salutes Ann Sheridan for her ability
to change her image from Oomph Girl to dramatic actress.
Evans also praises Ann for her lack of phoniness. "You're
one star who is prouder of her farm than her form," Evans
writes. "You boast about your cow and your chickens and your
collection of Mexican records, but never about your fan
mail."

B-164   Evans, Harry. "Hollywood Diary." _Family Circle_.
        October 30, 1942.
Evans talks to Ann Sheridan and director Lewis Milestone
about their upcoming film _Edge of Darkness_ (F-65). Evans
compares Ann's personality to that of Carole Lombard. He
concludes, "Every person who has known the privilege of her
friendship will swear to this: Ann Sheridan is a grand
person, and a genuinely lovely woman." Ann also is pictured
on the cover.

B-165   "Facing the Future." _Hollywood Reporter_. June 20,
        1934. pp. 7-9.
In this three-page ad, Paramount recalls 1933-34 discoveries
and heralds sixteen new personalities for 1934-35. Clara Lou
Sheridan is among the potential stars pictured.

B-166   "Fashions." _Motion Picture_. May 1948. p. 59.
Ann Sheridan models three blouses.

B-167   Fearless. "About Stars' Tastes." _Photoplay_. June
        1942. pp. 65, 77.
The reporter, using the pseudonym "Fearless," discusses
habits of the stars, including Ann Sheridan's penchant for
tailored suits.

B-168   Fein, Irving A. _Jack Benny_. G.P Putnam's Sons.
        New York. 1976. p. 88.
Benny's agent recalls the comedian's career, including his
work in _George Washington Slept Here_ (F-64).

B-169   "Fifty Years Ago Today." _New York Post_. April 3,
        1990. p. 3.
A story from the April 3, 1940 _New York Post_ is recalled in
which a University of California student handcuffed himself
to Ann Sheridan and swallowed the key.

B-170   "Film Actress Wins Divorce." _Los Angeles Times_.
        October 6, 1938.
Ann Sheridan received her interlocutory decree of divorce
from Edward Norris on October 5, 1938.

B-171   "Film Folk." _Chicago Sunday Tribune_. June 21,
        1953.
Ann Sheridan and Glenn Ford are seen in a still from _Rage
of the Jungle_, released as _Appointment in Honduras_
(F-85).

B-172   _Film Fun_. January 1936. p. 29.
A still of Ann Sheridan and David Worth from _Fighting
Youth_ (F-28) accompanies a joke.

B-173   _Filmland_. March 1955.
Ann Sheridan and Jacques Mapes are pictured.

B-174   Fireman, Judy. _TV Book_. Workman Publishing
        Company. New York. 1977. pp. 76, 294.
Ann Sheridan's appearance on _The Buick-Berle Show_ (T-13) is
recalled by costume designer Bill Jobe.

B-175   Fletcher, Adele Whitely. "Gay Companions."
         Photoplay. March 1944. pp. 27, 87-88.
Fletcher speculates about the seriousness of Ann Sheridan and
Steve Hannagan's relationship. Although Fletcher claims Ann
was filming _Hollywood Canteeen_ (Warner Bros., 1944), she
did not appear in the movie.

B-176   Flynn, Don. "$4M Nudes Deal." _New York Daily
         News_. September 25, 1986. p. 7.
Flynn reports the results of an auction of Alberto Vargas
paintings, including a 1939 watercolor of Ann Sheridan that
sold for $100,000.

B-177   Flynn, Errol. _My Wicked, Wicked Ways_. G. P.
         Putnam's Sons. New York. 1959. p. 267.
In this autobiography, shocking for its day, Flynn implies
that he helped Ann Sheridan's career advance after they had
an affair.

B-178   Friedrich, Otto. _City of Nets_. Harper & Row,
         Publishers. New York. 1986.
This chronicle of Hollywood in the 1940s includes an anecdote
Ann Sheridan liked to tell about the frugality at Warner
Bros. While Ann was showing a young actor around the lot,
they spotted an elderly man walking slowly with his head
bowed, picking something off the ground and putting it in his
mouth. The actor asked about the man's behavior. "[He's]
doing what comes naturally," Ann responded. "He's picking up
nails. His name is Harry Warner, and he happens to be
president of the company."

B-179   Frings, Katharine Hartley. "Will the 'Oomph' Title
         Hurt Her?" _Motion Picture_. August 1939. pp. 29,
         74-75.
Frings recalls the origins of the Oomph Girl campaign and
speculates on whether the title would effect Ann Sheridan's
career. Frings implies that it was only after the Oomph Girl
contest that Warner Bros. became interested in the tag;
however, the studio arranged for Ann to be the winner.

B-180   "Funeral for Ann Sheridan Takes Place on the Coast."
         New York Times. January 23, 1967.
A private funeral service was held for Ann Sheridan in North
Hollywood on January 22, 1967. The article recalls her
career.

B-181   Gardella, Kay. "My Kingdom for _The News_ & a Horse,
         Says Sheridan." _New York Daily News_. August 30,
         1966.
Ann Sheridan discusses _Pistols 'n' Petticoats_ (T-56) and
reminisces about her career. She claims she misses reading
the _New York Daily News_ when she is in California.

B-182   "Gay Pix Stressed on Warners' Sked." _Hollywood
         Reporter_. September 8, 1939. p. 3.
Warner Bros. announces their schedule for 1939-40, which
includes _Virginia City_ (Warner Bros., 1940). Although Ann
Sheridan is listed in the cast, she was not in the film.

B-183   "George Brent-Ann Sheridan Elopement Plan Disclosed."
         Los Angeles Times. circa 1941. (Constance
         McCormick Collection.)
Capt. Harry G. Peterson, the former sailing master for George
Brent's yacht, reveals that Brent planned to elope to Mexico
with Ann Sheridan a month before this article. Peterson, who
was on trial for intoxication, told the judge that he planned
to be the actor's best man. The elopement was delayed until
January 5, 1942.

B-184   "George Brent, Bride Return." Los Angeles
         Examiner. January 11, 1942.
Ann Sheridan and George Brent are seen at the San Bernardino,
California train station, following their Florida elopement.
The couple planned to spend a week in Palm Springs for their
honeymoon.

B-185   "George Washington Slept Here." Movie Story.
         October 1942. pp. 20-22, 92-95.
An adaptation of George Washington Slept Here (F-64)
accompanies some behind-the-scenes gossip. Ann Sheridan is
seen in five stills.

B-186   Gianakos, Larry James. Television Drama Series
         Programming 1947-1959. Scarecrow Press, Inc.
         Metuchen, NJ. 1980.
Although some obituaries list Climax (CBS, 1954-58) and
Burke's Law (T-40) in Ann Sheridan's credits, she is not
mentioned in logs of these series.

B-187   Girard, James P. "I Was a Male War Bride."
         Magill's American Film Guide, vol. 3. Salem Press.
         Englewood Cliffs, New Jersey. 1983. pp. 1561-65.
Girard discusses I Was a Male War Bride (F-79), one of
director Howard Hawks's favorite films. Girard praises the
direction and script, adding, "Of course, the brightest
dialogue would be of little use without talented actors to
deliver it." He says, "[Cary] Grant and [Ann] Sheridan fill
the bill nicely," concluding, "Sheridan is a worthy
'opponent' for Grant."

B-188   _____. "I Was a Male War Bride." Magills'
         Survey of Cinema, Second Series, vol. 3. Salem
         Press. Englewood Cliffs, New Jersey. 1981.
         pp. 1098-1102.
Girard's essay on I Was a Male War Bride (F-79) is the same
as above (B-181).

B-189   "'Girl' Back in Work." Hollywood Reporter.
         December 8, 1941. p. 2.
After being blown off the Moorpark, California location by
heavy winds, the Juke Girl (F-62) company planned to resume
shooting on December 8, 1941.

B-190   "Girls Protest Sheridan 'Slur.'" Boston Post [MA].
         March 12, 1940.
After the Harvard Lampoon named Ann Sheridan as "the
actress least likely to succeed" (A-6), four Radcliffe

students staged a protest to defend her.

B-191   "Gold Stars for Pic Actors Who Tour Camps on Their
         Own." Variety. August 12, 1942.
Ann Sheridan is among the performers listed who received gold
stars by their names on a board in the Hollywood Victory
Committee office. The stars indicated actors who had
entertained the troops in their free time.

B-192   Golden, Arthur. "Whatever Happened to...George
         Brent?" National Enquirer. October 27, 1971.
This profile of George Brent mentions that he co-starred with
Ann Sheridan, but omits their marriage. Golden claims Brent
planned to write an autobiography, however it was not
published at this writing.

B-193   "Good Sam." Movie Show. August 1948. p. 29.
This eight-panel pictorial summarizes Good Sam (F-78).

B-194   Gooter, Joe. "Ann Sheridan...A Miss on a Mission."
         Movieland. December 1944. pp. 32-33, 63.
Ann Sheridan's U.S.O. tour in the China-Burma-India theatre
(P-9) is chronicled. Six photos from the front are included.

B-195   Graham, Sheilah. "Ann Sheridan Is Back." Baltimore
         Sun [MD]. April 28, 1946.
Ann Sheridan discusses her upcoming roles in The Sentence,
released as Nora Prentiss (F-74), and Serenade (MGM,
1956), a film which was made without her. Graham recalls
Ann's strike from Warner Bros. and the origin of oomph.

B-196   _____. "Ann Sheridan's Weighty Problem." New
         York Post. September 17, 1966.
Ann Sheridan discusses her inability to gain weight, the
oomph campaign, and her role on Pistols 'n' Petticoats
(T-56).

B-197   _____. "Annie, Get Your Guy." Modern Screen.
         December 1949. pp. 46-47, 74.
Graham analyzes Ann Sheridan's love life, blaming her brief
relationships on her inability to take men seriously. Ann is
seen with nine escorts, including Steve Hannagan, Bruce
Cabot, and Cesar Romero.

B-198   _____. "Ava May Get Matador Role." Miami News
         [FL]. November 4, 1957.
After reporting on Ann Sheridan's dates with Jacques Mapes,
the columnist observes that she hopes 1950s sex symbol Kim
Novak looks as good as Ann in 1975 as Ann did twenty years
after her debut.

B-199   _____. "Come Out, Annie...Here's Job Offer."
         Chicago Daily News. January 19, 1955.
Australian producer Chips Rafferty wanted to cast Ann
Sheridan and Richard Boone in The Headhunters, scheduled to
be filmed in New Guinea. Ann's relatives, friends, and agent
did not know how to contact her. No further information can
be found about the project.

B-200   _____. "Competition For Spencer Tracy." Miami
Daily News [FL]. May 31, 1957.
Graham reminds readers that Ann Sheridan helped Ross Hunter
when he was a bit player at Republic. Hunter went on to
produce several of Ann's Universal-International films.

B-201   _____. "Sheridan Rides Again at Studio."
Dallas Morning News [TX]. February 21, 1946.
This is an edited version of "Ann Sheridan Is Back" (B-189).

B-202   "Graphic." Detroit Free Press [MI]. February 24,
1952.
Ann Sheridan is seen winking at a party.

B-203   Greaves, William. "Calls Ann Sheridan the 'Other
Woman.'" New York Post. March 29, 1960.
Greaves chronicles the marital problems of Scott McKay and
his wife, Joan Morgan McKay.

B-204   Gregory, Glenn. "Whatever Happened to Ann Sheridan?
The Oomph Girl - Then and Now." Movies
Illustrated. September 1965. pp. 30-33.
Gregory recalls Ann Sheridan's movie career in this
retrospective.

B-205   "The Gripe." Newsweek. October 23, 1944.
This column recounts the complaints that were publicized in
the GI newspaper Roundup concerning celebrity camp shows in
the China-Burma-India theatre. Ann Sheridan is among the
stars mentioned who defended her trip (P-9). She is seen
hugging a soldier.

B-206   Hagen, Ray. "A Screen Facts' Interview: Ann
Sheridan." Screen Facts. #14. Vol. 3, no. 2.
1966. pp. 1-62.
This entire issue is devoted to Ann Sheridan. In addition to
an extensive interview with the actress, conducted by Hagen
in 1965, the magazine includes numerous stills, a filmography
compiled by James Robert Parish, and a fine caricature by Al
Kilgore.

B-207   Hale, Wanda. "Ann Sheridan Has New Love - It's
Africa." New York Daily News. December 2, 1956.
Ann Sheridan discusses The Opposite Sex (F-87), her home
in New York, and her newfound love of Africa.

B-208   Hall, Gladys. "Confessions of a Contest Winner."
Motion Picture. December 1938. pp. 24, 63, 65-66.
Ann Sheridan recalls the Search for Beauty (F-1) contest
which brought her to Hollywood. She complains that
contestants are not taken seriously, concluding, "Being a
contest winner gets you to Hollywood, sure, but it doesn't
keep you there."

B-209   _____. "Putting On the Heat." Modern Screen.
April 1939. pp. 42-43, 90-91.
Hall interviews Ann Sheridan about how she became a sex
symbol. Ann credits clothes and hairstyles for making her

look more glamorous. Despite the publicity, Hall insists
that Ann remained down-to-earth. She reveals that Ann wore
tennis shoes under many of her gowns during photo sessions
because they were more comfortable and her feet were not in
the pictures.

B-210   Hammond, Sally. "Ann Sheridan On Hollywood: No
        Oomph Left." New York Post. November 23, 1965.
Ann Sheridan recalls her behind-the-scenes adventures and
complains about the changes in Hollywood.

B-211   Hanson, Patricia King, executive editor. The
        American Film Institute Catalog of Motion Pictures
        Produced in the United States, Feature Films,
        1931-1940. University of California Press.
        Berkeley, California. 1993.
This set includes detailed credits, synopses, and trivia for
feature films made between 1931 and 1940.

B-212   Haranis, Chrys. "Ann Sheridan: She Had Oomph &
        Courage." Photoplay. April 1967. pp. 18, 78.
Ann Sheridan's career is recalled in this memorial tribute.
Pistols 'n' Petticoats (T-56) director/producer Joe
Connelly is quoted about her bravery during her battle with
cancer. "She had guts and courage," he says. "We all
thought somehow she'd pull through."

B-213   Harman, Bob. Bob Harman's Hollywood Panorama.
        E.P. Dutton & Co., Inc. New York. 1971. pp. 28,
        91.
Harman presents a mini history of the movies, caricaturing
many stars of the golden age. Ann Sheridan appears in a
panel with other Warner Bros. stars, hitchhiking in a scene
from They Drive by Night (F-55).

B-214   Hartley, Katharine. "Another Star Is Born."
        Picture Play. November 1938.
Several months before the oomph campaign, Hartley announces
Warner Bros.'s plans to build Ann Sheridan into the number
one glamour girl in Hollywood. Ann discusses her early
career.

B-215   "Harvard Honor to Ann Sheridan." Boston Post [MA].
        October 11, 1941.
Following Ann Sheridan's feud with the Harvard Lampoon for
naming her the star least likely to succeed (A-6), the
university awarded her an honorary editorship of the
Advocate, its literary magazine (A-11).

B-216   "Has Ann Sheridan More Than SEX APPEAL?" Screen
        Guide. circa 1939. pp. 19-21. (Constance
        McCormick Collection.)
This pictorial debates whether or not Ann Sheridan can follow
up the oomph campaign with solid roles that will prove her
acting skills. She answers critics by talking about her
acting idol, Bette Davis. "Good, bad or indifferent, I'm
trying to give my work a measure of the sincerity [Bette]
gives hers," Ann says. "I love the picture business; I hope

it can stand me for a long, long time!"

B-217   Hayes, David and Walker, Brent. The Films of the
        Bowery Boys. Citadel Press. Secaucus, New Jersey.
        1984. pp. 26-30, 32-34.
This profile of the Dead End Kids includes information on
Angels with Dirty Faces (F-45), They Made Me a Criminal
(F-46), and The Angels Wash Their Faces (F-51).

B-218   "Heavenly Hideaway." Screen Stars. December 1946.
This pictorial shows Ann Sheridan vacationing in New Milford,
Connecticut.

B-219   "Heiress." Bradenton Herald [FL]. August 1, 1955.
After an inventory was taken on Steve Hannagan's estate, Ann
Sheridan is announced as the sole beneficiary of $219,399 in
insurance policies.

B-220   Heisenfelt, Kathryn. Ann Sheridan and the Sign of
        the Sphinx. Whitman Publishing Company. Racine,
        Wisconsin. 1943.
Ann Sheridan is the star of this juvenile mystery, one of a
series that had film stars solving crimes in the manner of
Nancy Drew. A disclaimer notes that "Except for the
authorized use of the name of Ann Sheridan, all names,
events, places, and characters in this book are entirely
fictitious." Henry E. Vallely offers drawings of Ann and
other characters.

B-221   "A Helping Hand." Movie Story. September 1950.
When Ann Sheridan had trouble screaming for a roller coaster
scene in Woman on the Run (F-81), co-star Dennis O'Keefe
pinched her to get the proper effect.

B-222   Higgins, Robert. "The 'Oomph Girl' Is 51." TV
        Guide. May 21, 1966. pp. 24-27.
Higgins interviews Ann Sheridan about her career and her
appearance on Another World (T-53). Ann recalls, "As tough
as Warners could be and as tough as we could be on Warners,
the actors never fought among themselves. We worked hard and
had fun." A color portrait is included.

B-223   Higham, Charles and Greenberg, Joel. Hollywood in
        the Forties. A.S. Barnes. New York. 1968.
        pp. 31, 150-51, 161.
Higham and Greenberg discuss 1940s films, including The Man
Who Came to Dinner (F-60), Kings Row (F-61), Nora
Prentiss (F-74), and The Unfaithful (F-75). They
describe Ann Sheridan's personality as "pleasantly charming
and direct," noting that she "quickly (and all too briefly)
developed into a dramatic actress" after the oomph campaign.

B-224   Hirschhorn, Clive. The Hollywood Musical. Crown
        Publishers, Inc. New York. 1981. pp. 89, 127, 149,
        161, 193, 229, 239, 355.
Ann Sheridan is mentioned in entries for the following
movies: Murder at the Vanities (F-4), Sing Me a Love
Song (F-30), Cowboy from Brooklyn (F-41), Naughty But

Nice (F-48), Navy Blues (F-59), Thank Your Lucky Stars
(F-66), Shine On Harvest Moon (F-68), and The Opposite
Sex (F-87). Several of her early films also are included
in this chronicle of musical movies, but Ann is not credited.

B-225   _____. The Universal Story. Crown Publishers,
          Inc. New York. 1983. pp. 91, 106, 192, 206, 207,
          217.
Ann Sheridan is mentioned in the entries for the following
Universal films: Fighting Youth (F-28), Letter of
Introduction (F-42), Woman on the Run (F-81), Steel
Town (F-82), Just Across the Street (F-83), and Take
Me to Town (F-84).

B-226   _____. The Warner Bros. Story. Crown
          Publishers, Inc. New York. 1979. pp. 173, 179,
          180, 181, 182, 183, 186, 188, 190, 194, 195, 196,
          197, 199, 201, 202, 207, 211, 213, 214, 219, 220,
          225, 230, 233, 236, 237, 238, 240, 245, 246, 259,
          264, 265, 271, 274.
All of Ann Sheridan's Warner Bros. films are included in this
film history.

B-227   "Hit Film Stars Again." New York Times.
          October 20, 1944.
The army newspaper Roundup responds to criticism by Ann
Sheridan and other stars who were accused of neglecting
their work with the troops (P-9) in a Roundup editorial.

B-228   Hitchen, Brian. "Ann, The Star Who Had 'Oomph.'"
          London Daily Mirror [England]. January 23, 1967.
This obituary focuses on Ann Sheridan's Oomph Girl image and
includes a pinup pose.

B-229   Hoffman, Irving. "Unfaithful Wins Praise; Loud
          Applause for Fiesta." Hollywood Reporter.
          July 1, 1947. p. 12.
Hoffman quotes New York critics who praised Ann Sheridan's
performance in The Unfaithful (F-75).

B-230   Holiday. December 1946.
Ann Sheridan is seen rowing. The caption claims she believes
holidays are an excuse to shed formality.

B-231   Hollywood. January 1939.
After being named an honorary member of the Lake Arrowhead
police force, Ann Sheridan dons a swimsuit to show off her
regulation cap and gun.

B-232   _____. March 1942.
Ann Sheridan and George Brent pose in their wedding attire.

B-233   "Hollywood and Broadway at the Fronts." New York
          Times Magazine. September 24, 1944.
This pictorial shows celebrities entertaining for the U.S.O.
Ann Sheridan is seen helping a showgirl with her hair during
their China-Burma-India tour (P-9).

B-234   "Hollywood Earfuls." Silver Screen. June 1940.
The gossip column reveals that Ann Sheridan wears men's
shorts in Torrid Zone (F-54).

B-235   "Hollywood Life." Screen Guide. July 1944.
Ann Sheridan poses on a wooden horse.

B-236   "Hollywood Off Guard." St. Louis Post Dispatch
         [MO]. February 24, 1952.
Ann Sheridan and producer Leonard Goldstein are pictured at a
Screen Director's Guild dinner dance.

B-237   "Hollywood Reporter 40 Years Ago Today."
         Hollywood Reporter. October 24, 1974.
This retrospective column announces Ann Sheridan's casting in
The Vanishing Pioneer with Randolph Scott and Chic Sale.
The film was released as Rocky Mountain Mystery (F-20).

B-238   "Hollywood's Growing Pains." Motion Picture.
         August 1943.
Hollywood victory gardens are discussed in this article,
which includes a photo of Ann Sheridan hoeing. The piece
claims Ann not only had a cow, but a thriving chicken and egg
business.

B-239   "Hoofing in Havana." Variety. August 6, 1940.
Ann Sheridan and George Raft are announced for Maid in
Havana. The film was not produced.

B-240   Hopper, Hedda. "Ann Sheridan May Be Taking Wrong
         Road." San Francisco Chronicle [CA]. May 27,
         1940.
The columnist predicts Ann Sheridan's career will decline if
she continues copying George Brent and acting uncooperative
with reporters.

B-241   _____. "Ann Sheridan Set to Sign for Musical of
         The Women." Chicago Tribune. November 26, 1956.
Hopper announces that Ann Sheridan and Dolores Gray were cast
in The Opposite Sex (F-87). Hopper claims producer Joe
Pasternak wanted Marlene Dietrich and Miriam Hopkins for the
roles that went to Agnes Moorehead and Barbara Jo Allen.

B-242   _____. "Boomtown Remake Set." Miami News
         [FL]. July 12, 1958.
Hopper quotes producer Ross Hunter, who flew to New York to
see Ann Sheridan perform in Kind Sir (P-16). Hunter
suggested Ann do the play to prepare for a stage musical of
Take Me to Town (F-84).

B-243   _____. "Career Resumed by Ann Sheridan." Los
         Angeles Times. February 16, 1947.
Hopper announces Ann Sheridan's return to the screen after an
eighteen-month absence. In addition to The Unfaithful
(F-75), Hopper mentions two films that did not materialize.

B-244   _____. "Derek Awarded Long Contract." Miami
         Daily News [FL]. March 10, 1954.

Hopper reveals that Ann Sheridan traded her San Fernando
valley home for a Bakersfield department store. Ann planned
to buy a smaller house in Hollywood and keep her apartment in
Mexico City.

B-245   _____. "Germans to Star Jurgens in 'Rasputin.'"
         Chicago Tribune. September 23, 1959.
Hopper comments on Ann Sheridan helping her friends. Warner
Bros. designer William Travilla was set to create her
costumes for Odd Man In (P-19).

B-246   _____. "Hollywood." December 1965. (Lincoln
         Center Collection.)
Hopper reports on the pilot for Pistols 'n' Petticoats
(T-54), which starred Ann Sheridan, Chris Noel, and Jody
McCrea. "I've been working on location and got my eyeballs
sunburned," Ann told Hopper. "I'm quite a bit older than I
used to be - frankly 50 - but a little makeup helps."

B-247   _____. "Looking at Hollywood." Chicago Daily
         Tribune. February 19, 1948.
Hopper says that Ann Sheridan wore out friend Peggy Cummins
during a New York trip.

B-248   _____. "Looking at Hollywood." Los Angeles
         Times. May 24, 1948.
Ann Sheridan is announced as one of the stars participating
in a benefit involving the Ringling Brothers and Barnum &
Bailey Circus and St. John's Hospital on September 4, 1948
(P-11).

B-249   _____. "Nearby Kids, Ranch Keep Sheridan Busy."
         Los Angeles Times. 1949. (Constance McCormick
         Collection.)
Hopper reports on Ann Sheridan's trip to Europe, where she
filmed I Was a Male War Bride (F-79). During her seven-
month sojourn, Ann acquired a serious case of pneumonia,
seven crates of china, and a French poodle. Hopper describes
Ann's house, which required remodeling to accomodate the
china. Ann's charitable work with the Mickey Finn Foundation
also is discussed.

B-250   _____. "Screen City Says 'Uncle' to Sheridan."
         Chicago Tribune. July 9, 1944.
Ann Sheridan's career is recalled in this biographical
sketch, written to promote The Doughgirls (F-69).

B-251   _____. "Seek a Five Year Contract with Eva Marie
         Saint." Chicago Tribune. December 9, 1955.
Hopper reveals that Ann Sheridan had not received her bequest
from Steve Hannagan yet. The columnist also reports that Ann
wanted to buy land in Mexico City.

B-252   _____. "She's No Sister Under the Make-Up." San
         Francisco Chronicle [CA]. July 14, 1944.
Hopper recalls Ann Sheridan's career and notes her friendship
with her male colleagues.

B-253   _____. "Stack Will Leave for 'Last Voyage.'"
         Los Angeles Times. May 4, 1959.
Despite offers for summer stock, Hopper reports that Ann
Sheridan will make a TV pilot in Germany. The pilot was
canceled.

B-254   _____. "'Why Don't You Two Get Married?'" Modern
         Screen. December 1947. pp. 54-55, 98-100.
Hopper recalls Ann Sheridan and Steve Hannagan's
relationship. The columnist notes the kindness of the
couple, remembering a Thanksgiving when they ate a second
turkey dinner so Hopper would not dine alone.

B-255   Hopper's staff, Hedda. "Phyllis Kirk, Jerry Lewis
         Tops as Stars of 'Sad Sack.'" Chicago Daily
         Tribune. March 5, 1957.
Ann Sheridan's boyfriend, Rodolfo Acosta, was hired to play
the Indian who abducts her on Playhouse 90 (T-23).

B-256   Horn, John. "...As Ann Sheridan, Carey Start Their
         Soapy Serials." New York Herald Tribune.
         November 12, 1965.
Horn welcomes Ann Sheridan and Macdonald Carey to daytime
television as they begin on Another World (T-53) and Days
of Our Lives (NBC, 1965-present).

B-257   Hough, Donald. "Four-Fifths Clara Lou." New York
         Herald Tribune. March 16, 1941.
Ann Sheridan's early career is chronicled.

B-258   Houston, Paul. "Ann Sheridan, Film 'Oomph Girl,'
         Dies at 51." Los Angeles Times. January 22, 1967.
Houston erroneously casts Ann Sheridan as Grandma Hanks on
Pistols 'n' Petticoats (T-56) in this obituary. Ann's
sister, Kitty Sheridan Kent, told the paper that the family
remained close, but knew nothing of Ann's cancer. "I never
dreamed of such a thing," she says.

B-259   "How Ann Sheridan Got Oomph." Look. August 1,
         1939. pp. 16-20.
This pictorial shows Ann Sheridan in the makeup department,
on set, and relaxing. She also is pictured on the cover.

B-260   "How Ann Sheridan's Secret Romance Got Her a Bundle."
         Tip-Off. June 1956.
The scandal magazine reports on Ann Sheridan's inheritance
from Steve Hannagan.

B-261   Howe, Cliff. "Ten Favorites." Classic Images.
         October 1987.
Warner Bros. makeup chief Perc Westmore names his favorite
stars for 1948. Ann Sheridan is selected for her
personality.

B-262   Howe, Herb. "Sheridan Preferred." Photoplay.
         October 1947. pp. 58-59, 117-19.
Howe recalls Ann Sheridan's penchant for practical jokes. He
reveals her creed was "have fun and get fat."

B-263   Humphrey, Hal. "Ann Sheridan: Queen of the Pistol
         Range." _TV Times: Los Angeles Times Weekly TV
         Magazine_. January 22, 1967.
Humphrey discusses film actresses who currently were starring
on TV series, including Jean Arthur and Ann Sheridan.   Ann
appears on the cover of the magazine.   Ironically, it was in
the same edition of the _Los Angeles Times_ as Ann's
obituary.

B-264   _____. "Horseless Series for Ann Sheridan." _Los
         Angeles Times_. August 2, 1966.
Humphrey interviews Ann Sheridan about _Pistols 'n'
Petticoats_ (T-56) and her career.

B-265   "I Wish I Were..." _Photoplay_. circa 1943.
         (Constance McCormick Collection.)
Celebrities discuss their idols in this article.   Ann
Sheridan marvels at Eleanor Roosevelt's ability to make
friends, Amelia Earhart's courage, Fred Astaire's dancing
skills, and Bing Crosby's voice.

B-266   Inman, David. _The TV Encyclopedia_. A Perigree
         Book. New York. 1991. p. 704.
Inman lists TV credits for select performers, including Ann
Sheridan.

B-267   "Inside Stuff." _Movie Mirror_. December 1939.
Ann Sheridan, Lillian Lamont (Mrs. Fred MacMurray), and Mr.
and Mrs. Ray Milland greet skater Bess Ehrhardt at the Ice
Follies.

B-268   _____. _Movie Mirror_. September 1940.
George Brent helps Ann Sheridan light her cigarette at a
Warner Bros. meeting.

B-269   _____. _Photoplay_. December 1947.
Ann Sheridan is seen holding a dog at a benefit for the Damon
Runyon Cancer Fund (P-10).

B-270   "'_Intermezzo_' Tuneful 100G on B'way; '_Dust_'-
         Weems-Ann Sheridan Oomph 45G, '_U-Boat_' 16G,
         '_Quiet_' Loud 14G." _Variety_. October 11, 1939.
Box office grosses on Ann Sheridan's personal appearance
dates in New York are reported (P-5).   The trade paper
credits Ann with bringing in most of the forty-five thousand
dollars that the Strand Theatre made.

B-271   "Is It Fun to Be a Movie Star?" _Look_. January 4,
         1938.
Ann Sheridan demonstrates a shoulder exercise in a panel
about stars watching their figures.

B-272   "The 'It' Girls." _Pittsburgh Sun-Telegraph_ [PA].
         March 16, 1957.
Mamie Van Doren, Ann Sheridan, and Clara Bow are among the
stars recalled in this article on sex symbols.

B-273   "It's Still Called Oomph..." _Screen Stories_.

November 1944.   p. 41.
Ann Sheridan models four summer fashions in this layout.   The
article notes that "she gets oomphier all the time."

B-274   Jailer-Chamberlin, Mildred.   "Celebrity jewelry
         offers a glimpse into Hollywood's golden past."
         AntiqueWeek.   July 5, 1993.
This auction report on celebrity items includes details on a
gold, jeweled compact that George Raft gave to Ann Sheridan
in 1940.

B-275   Jefferson, Sally.   "Why Ann Sheridan and George
         Brent Have Separated."   Photoplay.   December 1942.
         pp. 67, 70.
Jefferson recalls the courtship and marriage of Ann Sheridan
and George Brent.   She blames their separation on their
opposite personalities.

B-276   Jerome, Jerry.   "Ann Sheridan's in Love with Living."
         circa 1947.   pp. 34-35, 98-99.   (Constance McCormick
         Collection.)
Jerome discusses Ann Sheridan's love of Mexico and animals,
as well as what she looks for in a man.   She says, "The most
important quality he could ever have would be a basic
consideration for others.   If a man has that quality, he has
a pretty good start on being pretty perfect."

B-277   Jerome, Stuart.   Those Crazy Wonderful Years When
         WE Ran Warner Bros..   Lyle Stuart Inc.   Secaucus,
         New Jersey.   1983.   pp. 33, 35-36, 52, 55, 83, 141,
         176-78, 221-25.
TV writer Stuart Jerome recalls his tenure as a Warner Bros.
messenger before World War II.   He shares stories from the
sets of Broadway Musketeers (F-44), Torrid Zone (F-54),
and Navy Blues (F-59).   Jerome is the son of M.K. Jerome,
who wrote songs for several of Ann Sheridan's films.

B-278   "Jersey Honors Snubbed Actress."   New York Times.
         March 13, 1940.
After the Harvard Lampoon named Ann Sheridan as the actress
"least likely to succeed" (A-6), the New Jersey Assembly
appointed Ann "a daughter of New Jersey and sister of
Princeton" (A-7).   To play up the rivalry between Harvard and
Princeton, the general assembly planned to escort Ann to the
Princeton-Harvard football game on November 2, 1940.

B-279   Jewell, Richard B. and Harbin, Vernon.   The RKO
         Story.   Arlington House.   New York.   1982.   pp. 55,
         232, 256, 274.
Ann Sheridan is mentioned in entries for her RKO films,
including Good Sam (F-78) and Appointment in Honduras
(F-85).

B-280   "Jimmie Fidler in Hollywood."   Screen Stories.
         January 1952.
Ann Sheridan and Jacques Mapes are pictured at the Hollywood
premiere of A Streetcar Named Desire (Warner Bros., 1951).

B-281   Johaneson, Blond. "It Was Hard Job to Really Find
          Out About 'Oomph.'" New York Daily Mirror.
          September 17, 1939.
Johaneson tries to define oomph in this comic essay.

B-282   Johansen, Arno. "Are Stars' Salaries Too High?"
          Screen Guide. June 1948.
Johansen discusses stars' salaries, including Ann Sheridan's
$161,000 earnings in 1947.

B-283   "Jolson and Harpo Got Biggest Camp Crowds."
          Variety. April 15, 1942.
Al Jolson and Harpo Marx are credited with attracting
audiences of about 60,000 in this report on celebrities who
entertained at army and navy camps under the USO-Camp Shows,
Inc. banner. It is noted that Ann Sheridan's drew 15,868
during her eight-day appearance at camps (P-7).

B-284   "Just-for-fun Days." Photoplay. July 1943.
Ann Sheridan promotes Edge of Darkness (F-65) in this
three-page fashion layout.

B-285   "Just Fur [sic] Fun." Movie Life. January 1948.
Ann Sheridan pulls a rabbit out of Keenan Wynn's hat at a
benefit for the Damon Runyon Cancer Fund at Ciro's (P-10).

B-286   Kamey, Paul. "Ann Sheridan, Who's Afraid of
          Broadway." New York Daily Compass. October 30,
          1950.
Ann Sheridan discusses Woman on the Run (F-81) and admits
her fear of performing on the stage.

B-287   Keavy, Hubbard. "Ann Sheridan Crawls into 'Shell'
          of 9 Generous Rooms." New Orleans Times-Picayune
          [LA]. January 15, 1942.
Ann Sheridan discusses the secluded home she shared with
George Brent, her disgust with drunken nightclub patrons who
ask her to dance, and the odd fan mail she received.

B-288   Kendall, Read. "Around and About Hollywood." Los
          Angeles Times. May 23, 1938.
Kendall reports that Ann Sheridan went to Denton, Texas to
attend her father's funeral.

B-289   Kilgallen, Dorothy. "Screen 'Porgy' Costs $8
          Millions [sic] Plus." Washington Post and Times-
          Herald [Washington, D.C.]. November 21, 1958.
Kilgallen notes that Ann Sheridan asked friends to toast with
gin and stout at her New York housewarming.

B-290   _____. "Tony Curtis In Big Deal." Miami News
          [FL]. January 12, 1962.
Kilgallen reports that Ann Sheridan was happy over the
casting of the Chicago production of Kind Sir (P-20).
Although Kilgallen claims favorite leading man and future
husband Scott McKay was Ann's co-star, a Stagebill from
early in the run disgarees.

B-291   "Kings Row."   Picturegoer [England].   October 16,
         1943.   p. 14.
This condensation of Kings Row (F-61) includes a still of
Ann Sheridan, Robert Cummings, and Ronald Reagan.

B-292   "Kings Row to Continue:"   Los Angeles Times.
         April 14, 1942.
Because Kings Row (F-61) was so popular with Los Angeles
audiences, its two-week run was extended.

B-293   Kleiner, Dick.   "Rumors Flying In TV Factories."
         Fort Lauderdale News [FL].   October 14, 1966.
Ann Sheridan discusses her preferences on television,
stating, "Comedies stand up better on TV than drama."   If
Pistols 'n' Petticoats (T-56) failed, she wanted to try
writing.

B-294   Knickerbocker, Cholly.   "Debs Getting Bird's-Eye
         View of Power Diplomacy."   Miami Herald [FL].
         January 12, 1956.
The columnist reports that friends expected Ann Sheridan and
Rodolfo Acosta to marry soon.

B-295   Knox, Jack.   "Hollywood's Best Kept Secret!"
         Movieland and TV Time.   April 1967.   pp. 38, 48,
         50.
Knox interviews Ann Sheridan about Pistols 'n' Petticoats
(T-56) shortly before her death.   Though Knox implies that
her illness was a secret, Ann mentions her inability to put
on weight, a hint of her cancer.   The article was printed
posthumously.

B-296   Kobal, John.   "Ann Sheridan."   Film.   December
         1974.   pp. 21-23.
In the first installment of Kobal's interview, Ann Sheridan
discusses her early career.

B-297   _____.   "Ann Sheridan, Part II."   Film.   January
         1975.   pp. 21-23.
Kobal concludes his interview with Ann Sheridan, covering the
Oomph Girl epitaph and her later career.

B-298   _____.   People Will Talk.   Alfred A. Knopf.
         New York.   1985.   pp. 212, 413-25, 456, 460, 501,
         535, 536, 542, 564, 565, 569.
Ann Sheridan discusses her film career in this 1966 interview
which originally ran in the December 1974 and January 1975
issues of Film (B-296 and B-297).   She also is mentioned in
interviews with photographer Madison Lacy, actresses Ingrid
Bergman and Ida Lupino, and directors Howard Hawks and
Vincent Sherman.

B-299   Krug, Karl.   "Auntie Mame for Stadium?"
         Pittsburgh Sun-Telegraph [PA].   June 6, 1957.
The Pittsburgh Civic Light Opera wanted to book the stage
comedy Auntie Mame for a two-week run.   It was predicted
that Ann Sheridan would replace Greer Garson in the national
company after this production.   Ann did not appear in the

play.

B-300   Kupcinet, Irv. "Kup's Column." Chicago Sun-
         Times. August 11, 1958.
Ann Sheridan renewed her friendship with restaurateur Trader
Vic during her Kind Sir tour (P-16).

B-301   Lacy, Madison S. and Morgan, Don. Leg Art.
         Citadel Press. Secaucus, New Jersey. 1981.
         pp. 65-67.
Photographer Madison Lacy reminisces about Ann Sheridan, whom
he describes as "honest, unspoiled, fearless, down-to-earth,
[and] beautiful."

B-302   "Ladies be Good!" Movie Mirror. December 1956.
This pictorial shows the stars of The Opposite Sex (F-87)
hosting a comic shower for director David Miller. Ann
Sheridan gave Miller a live midget who popped out of a huge
gift box.

B-303   "The Lady Knows All the Answers." Screen Stories.
         April 1967. pp. 28-29, 82.
Although Ann Sheridan died on January 12, 1967, the editors
of Screen Stories decided to run this interview as it was
written. In it, Ann recalls her career and promotes Pistols
'n' Petticoats (T-56). When asked why she chose a sitcom,
Ann responds, "I didn't have to do a grinding TV series, but
I like to keep busy - when I can find something that isn't
bogged down with messages." She reflects on the changes in
Hollywood. "I'm glad I was around when things were less
hectic and more glamorous," she says.

B-304   Lamparski, Richard. Lamparski's Whatever Became
         Of...? First Giant Annual. Bantam Books. New
         York. 1976. pp. 149-54.
Ann Sheridan's first husband, Edward Norris, is profiled.
Lamparski claims Norris kept a photo of Ann on his dresser
some thirty years after their divorce. "Annie was terrific,"
Norris recalls. "I don't know how she stood me that long. I
was trying to drown my disappointments with alcohol."

B-305   _____. Whatever Became Of...? Fourth Series.
         Bantam Books. New York. 1973. pp. 161-63.
A biographical sketch of Ann Sheridan's second husband,
George Brent, is included.

B-306   Lane, Lydia. "Secret of Managing Unruly Hair Told
         by Ann Sheridan." Los Angeles Times. 1950.
         (Constance McCormick Collection.)
Ann Sheridan shares beauty tips for hair, nails, and figure.

B-307   Laurent, Lawrence. "Video Season Projects New Image
         - the Same Old Rut." Los Angeles Times.
         October 3, 1966. IV: p. 28.
Laurent critiques the 1966-67 television season, including
Pistols 'n' Petticoats (T-56). He notes, "Even with [Ann]
Sheridan, the series is more 'ugh' than 'oomph.'"

B-308   Lawton, Richard. A World of Movies. Bonanza
          Books. New York. 1974. p. 194.
A full-page glamour close-up of Ann Sheridan is included in
this pictorial book.

B-309   Lax, Roger and Smith, Frederick. The Great Song
          Thesaurus. Oxford University Press. New York.
          1984.
Many of the uncredited songs from Ann Sheridan's films are
listed in this reference book.

B-310   Leary, Chuck. "Ann Sheridan's Last Interview: 'I'm
          in Love with Life...' She Said Three Weeks Before
          She Died." National Star. March 20, 1967.
Ann Sheridan discusses the changes in her personality since
her Oomph Girl days in this tabloid article, billed as her
last interview. It includes a publicity photo from Pistols
'n' Petticoats (T-56).

B-311   Leeds, Lois. "Beauty Arts." New Orleans Times-
          Picayune [LA]. November 8, 1942.
Ann Sheridan offers beauty tips.

B-312   "Legacy." Newsweek. August 8, 1955. p. 44.
Ann Sheridan is announced as the beneficiary of six insurance
policies taken out by Steve Hannagan, totaling $218,399.

B-313   "Legion Makes Flat Deal with TA." Variety.
          September 20, 1939.
The American Legion signed an agreement with the talent
agency Theatre Authority to pay the agency a flat three
thousand dollar fee for performances by its clients at the
Legion's Chicago convention. The Legion also planned to pay
for stars, like Eddie Cantor and Ann Sheridan, to appear at
a show at Soldier Field on September 24, 1939 (P-4).

B-314   "'Legit' Slate." Rochester Democrat-Chronicle
          [NY]. September 6, 1959.
The 1959-60 Rochester Broadway Theater League season is
previewed. Ann Sheridan, set to appear in Odd Man In
(P-19), is among the stars pictured.

B-315   Leonard, William Torbert. Broadway Bound.
          Scarecrow Press, Inc. Metuchen, NJ. 1983.
          pp. 343-44.
The book chronicles shows that closed before their scheduled
Broadway openings, including Odd Man In (P-19).

B-316   "Life Visits the Stork Club." Life.
          November 6, 1944. pp. 119-23.
This pictorial on New York's Stork Club shows Ann Sheridan
dining with Steve Hannagan and Cliff Edwards. The article
notes that one of the club's dishes was named Wild Duck a la
Hannagan after the publicity man.

B-317   "The Lone Star State Introduces..." Modern
          Screen. July 1957.
Ann Sheridan is among the Texas-born celebrities pictured.

B-318   "Look Calls on Ann Sheridan."   Look.
         February 13, 1940. pp.40-43.
This pictorial shows Ann Sheridan at home, while chronicling
her rise to fame. The story notés that since the oomph
banquet on March 16, 1939, Ann had become Hollywood's most
publicized person, with a potential value of $5 million to
Warner Bros. In addition to breaking records for personal
appearances, the article claims that her fan mail was topped
only by Bette Davis and Priscilla Lane. The article
accompanies "Ann Sheridan Models for a Plastic Oomph Girl"
(B-53). Ann also is pictured on the magazine cover.

B-319   Look editors. Movie Lot to Beachhead: The
         Motion Picture Goes to War and Prepares for the
         Future. Doubleday, Doran and Company. Garden
         City, New Jersey. 1945.
Ann Sheridan's war work is mentioned in this survey of the
film industry's role in World War II.

B-320   Los Angeles Citizen-News. September 10, 1966.
Ann Sheridan is seen in a publicity photo from Pistols 'n'
Petticoats (T-56) in this pictorial preview of the fall TV
season.

B-321   Los Angeles Times. circa 1943. (Constance
         McCormick Collection.)
Ann Sheridan, then appearing in Thank Your Lucky Stars
(F-66), models a gray suit and a matching coat with a
chinchilla lining.

B-322   _____. circa 1944. (Constance McCormick
         Collection.)
Ann Sheridan poses by a chicken coop as she models slacks and
a long-sleeved shirt.

B-323   _____. June 14, 1966.
The paper reveals Ann Sheridan's marriage to Scott McKay on
June 5, 1966.

B-324   Louisville Courier-Journal [KY]. June 12, 1960.
Ann Sheridan and Liliane Montevecchi are pictured in a scene
from "The Impostor" on The U.S. Steel Hour (T-32).

B-325   Lovell, James. "Dallas." Hollywood Reporter.
         April 30, 1940. p. 4.
Lovell quotes reviews of It All Came True (F-53) from Ann
Sheridan's hometown papers. Both the Dallas News and the
Dallas Journal called the film her best to date.

B-326   "The Loves of Ann Sheridan." Screen Guide.
         October 1943. p. 25.
Ann Sheridan denies rumors about romances with Errol Flynn,
Cesar Romero, and George Raft. She says, "I know some
wonderful male characters, but I'm not thinking of marriage
at present....If you know a handsome soldier who could sweep
me off my feet, send him around!"

B-327   "The Lowdown on the Flynn-Sheridan 'Romance.'"

Screen Guide. March 1943. p. 10.
Ann Sheridan denies having a romance with Errol Flynn while
in Mexico obtaining her divorce from George Brent.

B-328   Lowery, Cynthia. "Big Name Stars Clean Up in Soap
         Operas." Newark Star Ledger [NJ]. December 19,
         1965.
Lowery chronicles the trend of casting famous stars on
daytime soap operas. Ann Sheridan discusses her role on
Another World (T-53).

B-329   Lucas, Blake. "They Drive By Night." Magill's
         Cinema Annual. Salem Press. Englewood Cliffs,
         New Jersey. 1983. pp. 508-14.
Lucas discusses the significance of They Drive By Night
(F-55). He credits director Raoul Walsh with displacing the
usual male protagonist (George Raft) with two contrasting
actresses (Ida Lupino and Ann Sheridan).

B-330   McCarey, Leo. "My Love Affair with Ann Sheridan."
         Modern Screen. 1948. pp. 47, 104. (Constance
         McCormick Collection.)
Director Leo McCarey recalls how a chance encounter at the
Kentucky Derby led to Ann Sheridan being cast in Good Sam
(F-78).

B-331   McClelland, Doug. Forties Film Talk. McFarland &
         Co. Jefferson, North Carolina. 1992.
Filmmakers of the 1940s reminisce about their work in this
collection. Ann Sheridan is mentioned in anecdotes by Lew
Ayres, John Beal, James Cagney, director Raoul Walsh, and
designer William Travilla. She discusses her work in Good
Sam (F-78).

B-332   MacMinn, Aileen. "Daytime TV 'Fascinates' Ann
         Sheridan." New York Journal-American. January 15,
         1966.
Ann Sheridan discusses her role on Another World (T-53).
"Originally, I thought I was going to be an actress playing
an actress, but there's been no hint of that yet," she
confides. "The role can go any number of ways and that's
another thing that makes daytime TV so interesting."

B-333   _____. "Film Stars Clean Up in Soap Operas."
         Los Angeles Times. December 30, 1965.
This article is the same as MacMinn's piece above (B-332).

B-334   McNeil, Alex. Total Television. Penguin Books.
         New York. 1980.
This comprehensive listing of network and syndicated programs
provides data on many of Ann Sheridan's TV appearances.

B-335   MacPherson, Virginia. "Star to Continue Youth Aid."
         New York Morning Telegraph. June 15, 1950.
Ann Sheridan breaks her three-year silence about her charity
work with the Mickey Finn youth clubs to appeal for
donations.

B-336   Mackin, Tom. "Ann Had Finished Filming." <u>Newark</u>
          <u>Evening News</u> [NJ]. January 23, 1967.
Two days after Ann Sheridan's death, Mackin discusses plans
for <u>Pistols 'n' Petticoats</u> (T-56). Although Ann was not
scheduled for the unfilmed twenty-sixth episode, there was
some doubt over whether it would be made.

B-337   Maltin, Leonard. <u>Leonard Maltin's 1996 Movie and</u>
          <u>Video Guide</u>. Plume. New York. 1995.
Maltin summerizes and rates thousands of films.

B-338   _____. "MGM Shorts at the Museum of Modern Art."
          <u>Film Fan Monthly</u>. November 1974.
Maltin reviews shorts from the Museum of Modern Art,
including <u>Star Night at Coconut Grove</u> (F-21).

B-339   Mank, Gregory William. "<u>Angels with Dirty Faces</u>."
          <u>Magill's American Film Guide, vol. 1</u>. Salem
          Press. Englewood Cliffs, New Jersey. 1983.
          pp. 138-40.
Mank traces the history of <u>Angels with Dirty Faces</u> (F-45),
calling it "one of the most fondly remembered and most
frequently revived movies of the 1930s." He praises Ann
Sheridan, whom he says "works splendidly with both leading
men and brings a power to her part."

B-340   _____. "<u>Angels with Dirty Faces</u>." <u>Magill's</u>
          <u>Survey of Cinema, 1st Series</u>. Salem Press.
          Englewood Cliffs, New Jersey. 1980. pp. 72-74.
Mank's article on <u>Angels with Dirty Faces</u> (F-45) is the
same as above (B-330).

B-341   Mann, May. "All This and Ann Too." <u>New York</u>
          <u>Journal American</u>. November 6, 1942.
Mann discusses Ann Sheridan and George Brent's separation and
offers an ironic list: Ann's rules for "How to Hold a Man."

B-342   Manners, Dorothy. <u>Los Angeles Examiner</u>. 1948.
          (Constance McCormick Collection.) Manners reports on
Ann Sheridan's upcoming appearance with the Ringling
Brothers and Barnum & Bailey Circus (P-11). During a
benefit for St. John's Hospital, Ann planned to ride an
elephant.

B-343   _____. <u>Los Angeles Herald-Examiner</u>. March 3,
          1966.
Manners announces that CBS bought the pilot of <u>Pistols 'n'</u>
<u>Petticoats</u> (T-54).

B-344   Margolies, John. <u>Pump and Circumstances: Glory</u>
          <u>Days of the Gas Station</u>. Little, Brown and
          Company. Boston. 1993. p.25.
A color photograph of an Ann Sheridan decal for Signal
Gasoline is included in this gas station history.

B-345   Margulies, Edward. "Bad Movies We Love."
          <u>Movieline</u>. June 1993. p. 77.
Margulies calls <u>The Opposite Sex</u> (F-87) "the best of the

worst" in this paean to campy 1950s film musicals.

B-346   Marsh, W. Ward.   "Ann Sheridan, Howard Duff, John
         Lund Here in Behalf of 'Steel Town,' Coming to
         Hipp." Cleveland Plain Dealer [OH].   March 18,
         1952.
Marsh reports on the stars' visit to Cleveland, Ohio to
promote Steel Town (P-12).

B-347   Marshall, Jim.   "Sheridan's Ride." Collier's.
         July 19, 1947.   pp. 26, 61-62.
Marshall recaps Ann Sheridan's career, detailing many
publicity stunts.   He credits the oomph campaign to press
agent Bernie Williams.   A full-length photo of the actress
accompanies the article.

B-348   "Martha Raye, Herbert, Ann Sheridan, Pearl, Others
         Touring Camps." Variety.   March 25, 1942.
The USO-Camp Shows, Inc. announces upcoming appearances by
celebrities at army and navy camps, including Ann Sheridan's
stint with the "Funzafire" unit (P-7).

B-349   Marx, Kenneth S.   Star Stats: Who's Whose in
         Hollywood.   Price/Stern/Sloan Publishers, Inc.
         Los Angeles.   1979.
Ann Sheridan's vital statistics are included in this
print-out on celebrities.   In addition to listing her
parents, siblings, brothers-in-law, and husbands, Marx offers
some erroneous information.   He claims Ann was in Casey at
the Bat in 1927, a film made when she was still a high
school student, and that she married James Owens in 1956.
Marx was a cousin of the Marx Brothers.

B-350   "Maugham Play Due Tuesday." Atlanta Constitution
         [GA].   October 26, 1959.
A picture of Ann Sheridan in Odd Man In (P-19) accompanies
a preview of the play.

B-351   "Mexican Holiday." New York Sunday News.
         February 15, 1953.
This pictorial chronicles Ann Sheridan's Tiajuana vacation.

B-352   "Mexico Actor's Wife Accuses Ann Sheridan." Los
         Angeles Times.   November 1, 1956.
Jeanine Cohen Acosta's criminal adultery suit against her
husband, Rodolfo Acosta, and Ann Sheridan is announced.

B-353   Miami Daily News [FL].   November 25, 1951.
Ann Sheridan and Dan Dailey are pictured at a party.

B-354   Miami Herald [FL].   December 10, 1953.
The newspaper reports that Ann Sheridan was sent to Cedars of
Lebanon Hospital in Hollywood, California when her
temperature reached a dangerous level.   Her doctor said she
was threatened with pneumonia.

B-355   "Milestones: Died." Time.   January 27, 1967.
Ann Sheridan's death is announced.

B-356   Miller, Lucy Key.   "Front Views & Profiles."
        <u>Chicago Daily Tribune</u>.   August 12, 1958.
Ann Sheridan is interviewed while touring in <u>Kind Sir</u>
(P-16).   She confesses that she liked to capture her travels
on canvas.   Her realistic paintings were done during
vacations in her Mexico City apartment.

B-357   "Miss Ann Sheridan."   <u>London Times</u> [England].
        January 23, 1967.   p. 12.
This obituary notes, "Without ever quite achieving the mythic
status of a super-star, [Ann Sheridan] was always a pleasure
to watch and, as with all true stars, was never quite like
anyone else."

B-358   "Miss Oomph Is Mad; Harvard Insulted Her."   <u>New
        York Daily News</u>.   March 6, 1940.
Ann Sheridan attacks Harvard after the <u>Lampoon</u> named her
the actress least likely to succeed (A-6).

B-359   "Missed Moments of Movie Fame."   <u>USA Weekend</u>.
        March 22, 1991.   p. 22.
This weekend supplement to Gannett newspapers repeats the
myth that Ronald Reagan and Ann Sheridan were serious
contenders for the leads in <u>Casablanca</u> (Warner Bros.,
1942).

B-360   <u>Modern Screen</u>.   April 1939.
Ann Sheridan is pictured with Cesar Romero.   The caption
suggests a romance between the stars.

B-361   _____.   June 1941.
Ann Sheridan and George Brent wave from a car.

B-362   _____.   August 1943.
Ann Sheridan is seen with Bruce Cabot.   The caption notes she
developed a sinus complication from the cornflake snow used
in filming <u>The Animal Kingdom</u>, released as <u>One More
Tomorrow</u> (F-71).

B-363   _____.   February 1944.
Ann Sheridan dines with Steve Hannagan.   The caption notes
that Ann also was being courted by Oscar Brooke of Mexico.

B-364   _____.   March 1944.
Bob Hope and Ann Sheridan are pictured at a press luncheon.

B-365   _____.   November 1944.
Ann Sheridan shares a comic incident that occurred during her
U.S.O. trip to India (P-9).

B-366   _____.   April 1945.
Ann Sheridan is seen with George Brent.   The caption notes
that neither was upset by their divorce.

B-367   _____.   October 1950.
Ann Sheridan is seen with an unidentified Jacques Mapes at a
party welcoming Vic Damone to MGM.

B-368   _____. July 1951.
Ann Sheridan and Jeff Chandler are seen at the premiere of I
Was a Communist for the F.B.I. (Warner Bros., 1951).

B-369   Morella, Joe and Epstein, Edward Z. Jane Wyman: A
         Biography. Delacorte Press. New York. 1985.
         pp. 25, 28, 42, 47-48, 56, 68-69, 70-71, 90-91, 184,
         189, 190.
Morella and Epstein discuss Jane Wyman's friendship with her
co-star Ann Sheridan.

B-370   Morgan, Henry. "Bongo, Bongo, Bongo, Morgan's In
         the Congo." TV Guide. October 27, 1956.
         pp. 24-25.
I've Got a Secret panelist Henry Morgan recalls his trip to
Africa with Ann Sheridan, part of a stunt for the prime time
game show (T-20).

B-371   _____. Here's Morgan!. Barricade Books, Inc.
         New York. 1994.
In this autobiography, Morgan recalls his trip to Africa with
Ann Sheridan for an I've Got a Secret (T-20) segment, as
well as Ann's subsequent trip to London.

B-372   Morino, Marianne. The Hollywood Walk of Fame. Ten
         Speed Press. Berkeley, California. 1987. p. 362.
A short biographical sketch of Ann Sheridan is included with
the address of her star on the Hollywood Walk of Fame.

B-373   Morris, Goerge. Errol Flynn. Pyramid Books. New
         York. 1975. pp. 75, 77. 95, 97, 99.
Ann Sheridan's work with Errol Flynn in Edge of Darkness
(F-65) and Silver River (F-77) is mentioned. Morris
recalls the actors' "extraordinary rapport" in the latter
film, calling Ann "the best match for [Flynn] since Olivia de
Havilland."

B-374   Mosby, Aline. "Ann Sheridan Quits Hollywood." New
         York Morning Telegraph. July 2, 1953.
Ann Sheridan announces her plans to move to Mexico and make
films in English and Spanish.

B-375   "The Most Exciting Star Since Harlow!" Screen
         Guide. April 1939. p. 26.
At the beginning of the oomph campaign, Ann Sheridan is
compared to sex symbol Jean Harlow. Although the actresses'
appearances are contrasted, the writer notes that both were
well-liked by their movie peers. Ann is seen with Reginald
Gardiner.

B-376   Motion Picture. December 1940.
Ann Sheridan and George Brent are pictured dancing.

B-377   _____. October 1942.
Ann Sheridan is seen sewing a star on Warner Bros.'s service
flag to represent husband George Brent.

B-378   _____. February 1943.

Ann Sheridan and George Brent relax with their dogs.

B-379   _____.   June 1943.
Ann Sheridan's next film is announced as <u>Night Shift</u>.

B-380   _____.   September 1944.
A color photo of Ann Sheridan reveals an unusual hobby:
embroidering hose.

B-381   _____.   May 1947.
On the set of <u>The Unfaithful</u> (F-75), Ann Sheridan and
Zachary Scott chat with ex-governor Lehman of New York and
his son.

B-382   _____.   July 1947.
Ann Sheridan gives Zachary Scott a new tie.

B-383   _____.   April 1948.
Ann Sheridan, Zachary Scott, and Morton Downey are pictured
at the Stork Club.

B-384   _____.   July 1950.
Ann Sheridan, Jane Wyman, and Alexis Smith are seen lunching.

B-385   <u>Motion Picture Herald</u>.   August 6, 1949.
Ann Sheridan and Cary Grant are in a still from <u>I Was a</u>
<u>Male War Bride</u> (F-79).

B-386   "<u>Motion Picture's</u> Varga Girl."   <u>Motion Picture</u>.
         October 1947. pp. 48-49.
A color Alberto Vargas portrait of Ann Sheridan accompanies a
black and white photograph of the pinup artist drawing the
actress.

B-387   "<u>Movie Fan Album</u> Headliners: Ann Sheridan."
         <u>Movie Fan Album</u>. September 1947.
The writer calls Ann Sheridan "the most honest person in
pictures." Five photos range from a cheesecake shot to
publicity poses taken on her ranch.

B-388   <u>Movie Life</u>. November 1940.
Ann Sheridan and Anthony Quinn are seen doing the rumba in
<u>City for Conquest</u> (F-56).

B-389   _____.   September 1942.
Ann Sheridan and Jack Benny share a horse in <u>George</u>
<u>Washington Slept Here</u> (F-64).

B-390   _____.   January 1946.
Ann Sheridan and Steve Hannagan are pictured.

B-391   _____.   December 1952.
Former Warner Bros. contractees Ann Sheridan and Olivia de
Havilland are seen at a party with composer Jimmy McHugh.

B-392   _____.   September 1956.
The stars of <u>The Opposite Sex</u> (F-87) surround director
David Miller at a shower.

B-393   "Movie Life of Ann Sheridan." Movie Life. circa
         1940. pp. 36-39. (Constance McCormick Collection.)
This thirty-four panel pictorial traces the life of Ann
Sheridan, from childhood through Torrid Zone (F-54).

B-394   _____. Movie Life. circa 1943-44. (Constance
         McCormick Collection.)
Ann Sheridan's career and private life are recalled in over
eighty pictures.

B-395   "Movie Might-Have-Beens." American Movie Classics
         Magazine. March 1994.
Alternate casting for Casablanca (Warner Bros., 1942) is
recalled, with Ronald Reagan and George Sanders mentioned for
the Humphrey Bogart role and Ann Sheridan and Tamara
Toumanova for the part played by Ingrid Bergman.

B-396   Movie Mirror. June 1939.
Ann Sheridan is flanked by Sterling Holloway, David Niven,
Rudy Vallee, and Otto Kruger as she is named Oomph Girl at a
banquet (A-4).

B-397   _____. February 1940.
Ann Sheridan and Jean Negulesco are seen talking with Rudy
Vallee at an opening.

B-398   _____. April 1940.
In a feature superimposing stars's faces on art masterpieces,
Ann Sheridan becomes Sir Thomas Lawrence's Pinkie.

B-399   Movie Show. August 1944.
Ann Sheridan is seen receiving instructions from Capt. Tom
McKnight before she hosted Mail Call (R-10).

B-400   _____. November 1945.
Ann Sheridan is seen dining with Faye Emerson, her husband
Brig. Gen. Elliott Roosevelt, Steve Hannagan, and Cliff
"Ukelele Ike" Edwards.

B-401   Movie Stars. September 1962.
Ann Sheridan and Cary Grant are seen in a still from I Was
a Male War Bride (F-79).

B-402   Movie Stars Parade. October 1943.
Ann Sheridan dines with producer S.P. Eagle.

B-403   _____. November 1943.
Ann Sheridan, Ingrid Bergman, and Hedda Hopper are seen
making sandwiches at the Hollywood Canteen. In another
photo, Ann attends a premiere with director David Butler.

B-404   _____. May 1944.
Ann Sheridan and Joseph Cotten are seen at a party following
an NBC radio rehearsal.

B-405   _____. February 1946.
Ann Sheridan and Steve Hannagan are pictured at the opening
of Club Donroy.

B-406   _____.   February 1947.
Ann Sheridan is seen in several stills from <u>Nora Prentiss</u>
(F-74).

B-407   _____.   October 1950.
Ann Sheridan dances with Vic Damone at an MGM party.

B-408   _____.   July 1952.
Ann Sheridan, John Lund, and Howard Duff are seen promoting
<u>Steel Town</u> (F-82) at the Stork Club.

B-409   <u>Movie Story</u>.   March 1944.
Cary Grant, Bob Hope, and Ann Sheridan are pictured at a
luncheon hosted by the Hollywood Women's Press Club. The
group named Grant and Sheridan most cooperative actor and
actress (A-15).

B-410   _____.   June 1945.
Following her selection as the Best Dressed Woman in Motion
Pictures by New York's Fashion Academy (A-17), Ann Sheridan
models a gingham suit.

B-411   _____.   December 1947.
Ann Sheridan is seen collecting two white rabbits she won in
an auction for the Damon Runyon Memorial Benefit (P-10).

B-412   _____.   April 1948.
Ann Sheridan dines with Zachary Scott.

B-413   _____.   March 1949.
Ann Sheridan is pictured trying on mules.

B-414   _____.   April 1949.
Ann Sheridan tries on more mules.

B-415   <u>Movie Time</u>.   January 1952.
Ann Sheridan and June Haver attend the premiere of <u>David
and Bathsheba</u> (20th Century-Fox, 1951).

B-416   "Movie, TV Star Ann Sheridan Dies." <u>Springfield
        Sun</u> [OH].   January 21, 1967.
Ann Sheridan's career is recalled in this obituary.

B-417   <u>Movie World</u>.   January 1952.
Ann Sheridan and Dale Evans examine a school contest entry.

B-418   <u>Movieland</u>.   August 1943.
Ann Sheridan is pictured with Cully Richards. The caption
notes that Richards is almost a double for Ann's first
husband, Edward Norris.

B-419   _____.   September 1943.
Ann Sheridan and George Raft are seen dancing at the Mocambo.

B-420   _____.   April 1947.
Ann Sheridan and George Raft watch Betty Field sign an
autograph.

B-421   _____.   February 1948.
Keenan Wynn, Jackie Cooper, and Ann Sheridan are seen
preparing a puppy for a charity auction at Ciro's (P-10).

B-422   _____.   August 1953.
The column discusses Ann Sheridan's plans since Steve
Hannagan's death, including selling her San Fernando Valley
home.

B-423   Movies.   November 1939.
Ann Sheridan and director Anatole Litvak are pictured at the
premiere of When Tomorrow Comes (Universal, 1939).

B-424   _____.   October 1941.   p. 53.
Ann Sheridan receives a massage on the set of Navy Blues
(F-59).

B-425   _____.   November 1943.   p. 39.
Photos of Ann Sheridan in the early 1930s and in 1943 are
contrasted.

B-426   _____.   January 1944.
Ann Sheridan is seen wearing a corsage made of war bond
pledges.

B-427   "Movies' Cover Girl."   Movies.   May 1944."
Ann Sheridan models a costume from Shine On Harvest Moon
(F-68).   The caption notes that one hat weighed fifteen
pounds.

B-428   Mulvey, Kay.   "The Real Sheridan."   Woman's Home
         Companion.   May 1942.   p. 40.
Mulvey compares Ann Sheridan's real-life upbringing with that
of her character in Kings Row (F-61).   Ann is seen reading
with her dog.

B-429   "Musical Role Set for Ann Sheridan."   New York
         Times.   July 17, 1964.
Ann Sheridan is announced for the lead in an untitled musical
about evangelist Aimee Semple McPherson.   The show was
scheduled to open in October 1964; it was not produced.

B-430   "My Secret Dream."   Photoplay.   October 1943.
Celebrities share their aspirations.   Ann Sheridan wants to
build a home in Mexico City and return to Hollywood to make
movies.

B-431   Nash, Jay Robert and Ross, Stanley Ralph.   The
         Motion Picture Guide.   Cinebooks, Inc.   Chicago.
         1986.
Credits and synopses for most feature films are included in
this reference set.

B-432   "The New Miss Oomph!"   Screen Album.   Fall, 1953.
On the set of Take Me to Town (F-84), Ann Sheridan crowned
a new Oomph Girl, Universal-International starlet Mari
Blanchard.

B-433   New Movie. June 1934.
The magazine includes a profile of Clara Lou Sheridan, a
winner in the Search for Beauty (F-1) contest.

B-434   "New Tunes Will Be Featured in Saturday Revue."
         Campus Chat [Denton, TX]. August 11, 1933.
         (University of North Texas Collection).
Clara Lou Sheridan's appearance with the North Texas State
Teachers College Stage Band is previewed (P-1).

B-435   New York Daily News. May 12, 1958.
Ann Sheridan is seen at Ciro's with Jacques Mapes.

B-436   New York Times. September 27, 1939.
Ann Sheridan's arrival in New York is announced.

B-437   New York World-Telegram and Sun. November 10,
         1956.
A publicity still of June Allyson, Joan Collins, Dolores
Gray, Ann Sheridan, Ann Miller, and Joan Blondell promotes
the New York opening of The Opposite Sex (F-87).

B-438   Newark Evening News [NJ]. April 5, 1941.
During Ann Sheridan's 1941 strike from Warner Bros., she
amused herself by rebuilding seven abandoned cars at a
friend's garage. "No reason for it," she explains, "Except
that I like it."

B-439   "Night-Club Flashes." Photoplay. February 1942.
Ann Sheridan encountered a lot of excitement during a night
at Ciro's. After Ann was voted the glamour beauty of the
month, her necklace almost was stolen by a fan.

B-440   Nolan, Robert and Nolan, Gwendolyn. Movie
         Characters of Leading Performers of the Sound Era.
         American Library Association. Chicago. 1990.
         pp. 336-37.
The Nolans provide a brief profile of Ann Sheridan and list
her most memorable film roles.

B-441   "Nora Prentiss." Movie Show. February 1947.
This pictorial shows scenes from Nora Prentiss (F-74).

B-442   _____. Silver Screen. March 1947.
This seven-panel pictorial includes stills from Nora
Prentiss (F-74), as well as behind-the-scenes shots.

B-443   "Obituaries." Variety. May 25, 1938.
The May 20 death of Ann Sheridan's father, sixty-three-year-
old G.W. Sheridan, is announced.

B-444   _____. Variety. January 30, 1946.
Ann Sheridan's mother, sixty-eight, died January 27, 1946.

B-445   _____. Variety. August 30, 1950.
The death of Steve Hannagan's mother is announced.

B-446   _____. Variety. October 17, 1962.

Joan Morgan McKay's career and suicide are discussed in this obituary for Scott McKay's estranged wife.

B-447   _____. Variety. January 25, 1967.
This death notice recalls the highlights of Ann Sheridan's career.

B-448   _____. Variety. December 4, 1974.
Rodolfo Acosta's death is announced.

B-449   _____. Variety. May 30, 1979.
George Brent's career is recalled in this obituary.

B-450   _____. Variety. February 26, 1986.
This death notice for Rene Cummings Shonting notes that she met Ann Sheridan while working in Steve Hannagan's publicity office. Shonting later handled public realtions for Pistols 'n' Petticoats (T-56).

B-451   _____. Variety. March 18, 1987.
Scott McKay's career is recalled in this obituary.

B-452   O'Brian, Jack. "'Meg-Hello-Mania." New York
           Journal-American. November 8, 1965.
O'Brian announces that Ann Sheridan would begin appearing on Another World (T-53) on November 11, 1965.

B-453   _____. "Murphy Follows Rich Steps." Asbury Park
           Press [NJ]. February 3, 1988. p. C-10.
O'Brian reports that the Hollywood home Ann Sheridan shared with Steve Hannagan was for sale for $1.5 million.

B-454   "Off Guard in the Canteen." Movie Life. November
           1943. p. 52.
Ann Sheridan is seen signing autographs with columnist Hedda Hopper at the Hollywood Canteen (P-8).

B-455   "Oomph!" Newsweek. October 30, 1944. pp. 8, 10.
Three soldiers criticize Ann Sheridan's publicity about her China-Burma-India tour (P-9).

B-456   "Oomph Before Breakfast." New Yorker. October 7,
           1939.
The reporter describes the hysteria surrounding Ann Sheridan's arrival in New York during the oomph campaign.

B-457   "Oomph Girl." Holiday. November 1948.
Ann Sheridan is pictured smoking on a Warner Bros. set.

B-458   "'Oomph Girl' Back on Job at a 'Mere' $600 Per Week."
           New Yorking Morning Telegraph. March 15, 1941.
As Ann Sheridan returned to Warner Bros. after a six-month strike, her dispute with the studio is recalled.

B-459   "Oomph Girl Dies At 51 Of Cancer." Tallahassee
           Democrat [FL]. January 22, 1967.
A pre-oomph photo accompanies this obituary of Ann Sheridan.

B-460   "'Oomph' Girl Freed; Don't Rush Boys, She's in
         Love." New York Daily Mirror. October 7, 1939.
The article announces that Ann Sheridan received her final
divorce decree from Edward Norris on October 6, 1939.

B-461   "Oomph Girl Off to Lead Legion." Los Angeles
         Examiner. circa September 1939. (Constance
         McCormick Collection.)
Ann Sheridan is pictured leaving for the American Legion
convention in Chicago (P-4). After being chosen "Sweetheart
of the Legion" by a vote of three hundred posts, she planned
to lead a fifteen-hour parade that kicked off the Legion's
national convention and preside over Legion festivities for a
week.

B-462   "Oomph Girl Sheridan Dies at 52." Jacksonville
         Times-Union [FL]. January 22, 1967.
This error-filled obituary notes that Ann Sheridan's friend
claimed the actress died of emphysema rather than cancer.

B-463   "The Oomph Girl's Still Got It." Movie Stars.
         May 1966.
Ann Sheridan, then appearing on Another World (T-53), is
profiled.

B-464   "Oomph That Is." Movie Life. 1947. (Constance
         McCormick Collection.)
The caption on this pinup photo of Ann Sheridan says that,
despite her best dressed list honors and dramatic work in
Nora Prentiss (F-74), she "still has what it takes to fill
a swim suit [sic]."

B-465   "Oomph - with Options." New York Post.
         October 10, 1942.
This six-panel pictorial traces Ann Sheridan's career from
her beginnings at Paramount to the star of George
Washington Slept Here (F-64). A photo from one of the
Paramount workshop productions (P-2) erroneously is
identified as a still from her first film.

B-466   "Orchid to Ann." Picturegoer [England].
         November 7, 1953.
A reader awards an orchid to Ann Sheridan for her "lively
performance in the otherwise dull Take Me to Town" (F-84).

B-467   "Order Star's Arrest in Triangle Suit." New York
         Mirror. December 13, 1956.
The article reports that a Mexican D.A. issued an arrest
warrant for Ann Sheridan on December 12, 1956 after she
failed to answer several subpoenas in connection with
adultery charges. Jeanine Acosta accused the actress of
living with her husband, actor Rodolfo Acosta, in Mexico
City.

B-468   "Orphans of the War." Variety. January 14, 1942.
Ann Sheridan and Ronald Reagan are announced for the leads
in Casablanca (Warner Bros., 1942).

B-469   Osborne, Robert.   "Ross Hunter: What a wonderful
          hayride it was." _Hollywood Reporter_. March 14,
          1996.
This obituary for Ross Hunter recalls how Ann Sheridan helped
him become a producer at Universal-International.

B-470   Othman, Frederick C.   "Ann Tells of Being 'Oomph
          Queen.'" _Hollywood Citizen-News_ [CA].   circa
          1939-40. (Constance McCormick Collection.)
Ann Sheridan discusses the pros and cons of the oomph
campaign. She says, "If I had it to do over, I'm not sure
but what I'd rather remain plain Annie Sheridan of Denton,
Texas."

B-471   _____. "Oomph Girl Goes 'Private.'" _New York
          Morning Telegraph_. March 20, 1942.
Othman previews Ann Sheridan's wardrobe for her tour of army
camps.

B-472   Owczarzak, Jerry F.   "Ann Sheridan." _Films in
          Review_. March 1976. p. 190.
In this letter to the editor, Owczarzak offers biographical
information on Ann Sheridan, as well as a list of film
credits.

B-473   "Paramount Picks Its Own Baby Stars." _Hollywood
          Reporter_. March 26, 1935.
Ann Sheridan is announced as one of Paramount's proteges for
1935 (A-2). The starlets were selected by 280 studio
executives.

B-474   "Par's Experience with Its Beauty Winners Chills on
          Such Contests." _Variety_. January 16, 1934.
The trade paper reports on Paramount's problems with its
Search for Beauty (F-1) contestants. First the aspiring
stars charged outrageous expenses to the studio. When the
contest was over, many contestants refused to leave
Hollywood. Paramount signed six of the thirty finalists,
including Clara Lou Sheridan.

B-475   Parish, James Robert. _The Forties Gals_.
          Arlington House. New Rochelle, New York. 1980.
          pp. 255-322.
Parish devotes a lengthy chapter to Ann Sheridan's life and
career in this look at film actresses of the 1940s.

B-476   _____. _Hollywood's Great Love Teams_. Arlington
          House. New Rochelle, New York. 1974. pp. 17, 173,
          175, 196, 353, 354, 364, 454-72, 655.
Parish discusses the screen pairing of Ann Sheridan and James
Cagney, detailing their three films together.

B-477   Parish, James Robert and DeCarl, Lennard.
          Hollywood Players: The Forties. Arlington House.
          New Rochelle, New York. 1976. pp. 18, 126, 142,
          200, 258, 264, 308, 372, 484.
Ann Sheridan is mentioned in chapters on Robert Alda,
Marguerite Chapman, Steve Cochran, Faye Emerson, Peggy Ann

Garner, Virginia Gilmore, Wanda Hendrix, John Lund, and Kent Smith.

B-478   Parish, James Robert and Stanke, Don E. _The Debonairs_. Arlington House. New Rochelle, New York. 1975.
Ann Sheridan is mentioned in a chapter devoted to the life and career of her ex-husband, George Brent.

B-479   Parsons, Louella O. "Ann Sheridan." _Los Angeles Examiner_. circa 1947-48. (Constance McCormick Collection.)
Ann Sheridan discusses her weight, her relationship with Steve Hannagan, and her career plans. She expresses her desire to do a comedy after the heavy drama of _Nora Prentiss_ (F-74) and _The Unfaithful_ (F-75). "I would run a mile if anybody suggested I do another musical," she says. "I really despise them."

B-480   _____. "Ann Sheridan Denies Plan to Wed Flynn." _Los Angeles Examiner_. April 12, 1943.
Parsons speculates on the relationship between Ann Sheridan and Errol Flynn, both in the process of divorcing their spouses. Although Ann denies plans to marry Flynn, Parsons points out that Ann also denied serious feelings for George Brent before their elopement in 1942.

B-481   _____. "Audry [sic], Gary to Co-Star." _Detroit Times_ [MI]. August 29, 1956.
The columnist notes that Ann Sheridan was very thin following her trip to Africa to film _The Woman and the Hunter_ (F-88). Parsons hints that Ann was dating Stork Club owner Sherman Billingsley.

B-482   _____. "Big Thrill for Ann Sheridan." _Detroit Times_ [MI]. May 31, 1956.
Ann Sheridan discusses her upcoming trip to Nairobi to star in _The Woman and the Hunter_ (F-88).

B-483   _____. "Hannagan's Romance with Ann Recalled." _Miami Herald_ [FL]. February 22, 1953.
Parsons eulogizes Steve Hannagan and shares her memories of his relationship with Ann Sheridan.

B-484   _____. "Hollywood." _New York Journal-American_. April 2, 1944.
Ann Sheridan discusses her relationship with Steve Hannagan and her desire to entertain troops overseas.

B-485   _____. "Hollywood, Ann Sheridan Delight King." _Miami Herald_ [FL]. December 9, 1957.
Parsons reports on a Biltmore Bowl dinner honoring King Mohamed V of Morocco. The king was delighted to see Ann Sheridan, who had toured Morocco during the war. Ann planned to visit Morocco again in February 1958.

B-486   _____. "Louella Parsons' Good News." _Modern Screen_. October 1949.

Ann Sheridan, Cesar Romero, and Zachary Scott are seen at Romanoff's.

B-487   _____. "Mary Fickett Has Ticket to Hollywood
        Stardom." Dallas Times Herald [TX]. May 28, 1957.
Parsons reports that Ann Sheridan would tour in Auntie
Mame. Following dates in San Francisco, Los Angeles, and
around the country, Ann was supposed to replace Rosalind
Russell on Broadway in 1958. Ann did not do the tour.

B-488   _____. "Sheridan, Brent Split Up." San Diego
        Union [CA]. September 29, 1942.
Parsons tries to play peacemaker when George Brent and Ann
Sheridan announce their separation. Although Brent claims
Ann wanted her freedom, she insists the split was his idea.

B-489   "People in the News." Miami News [FL]. June 14,
        1966.
The column reveals the secret marriage of Ann Sheridan and
Scott McKay.

B-490   Photoplay. June 1935. p. 79.
Ann Sheridan is pictured with Cary Grant and five other
starlets whom Paramount named most likely to succeed in 1935.

B-491   _____. November 1939.
Ann Sheridan dances with director Anatole Litvak at the
Trocadero.

B-492   _____. August 1941.
Ann Sheridan and Rita Hayworth are seen chatting.

B-493   _____. October 1941.
Ann Sheridan, Monty Woolley, and Bette Davis talk to
Photoplay's Sara Hamilton.

B-494   _____. January 1943.
Ann Sheridan and Jack Benny pose in Roman outfits to promote
George Washington Slept Here (F-64).

B-495   _____. March 1943.
Ann Sheridan is pictured in a glittering gown.

B-496   _____. August 1943.
Ann Sheridan is seen at the Mocambo with Bruce Cabot and
Mickey Rooney.

B-497   _____. September 1943.
Ann Sheridan and Sgt. Alan Manson exchange romantic looks at
the Mocambo.

B-498   _____. January 1944. pp. 32-33.
Full-page tinted photos of Ann Sheridan and Dennis Morgan
promote Shine On Harvest Moon (F-68).

B-499   _____. February 1944.
Ann Sheridan and Steve Hannagan are seen at the Mocambo.

B-500 _____. February 1945.
Ann Sheridan is seen with Steve Hannagan and a sailor.

B-501 _____. January 1946.
Ann Sheridan and Steve Hannagan are pictured.

B-502 _____. August 1948.
Ann Sheridan and wardrobe woman Martha Giddings are seen
sewing.

B-503 _____. April 1949.
Cary Grant and Ann Sheridan are pictured in a still from I
Was a Male War Bride (F-79).

B-504 _____. July 1949.
Ann Sheridan and Clark Gable are seen at the Racquet Club in
Palm Springs.

B-505 _____. October 1949.
Ann Sheridan, Cesar Romero, and the Dana Andrewses are
pictured at a party.

B-506 _____. April 1950.
Ann Sheridan and Clark Gable are seen in a candid shot.

B-507 _____. June 1950.
Ann Sheridan and Jane Wyman, labeled "the two most eligible
bachelor girls in town," exchange stories at a party.

B-508 _____. September 1950.
Ann Sheridan buys shoes from a movie bit player in this
still.

B-509 _____. January 1951.
Ann Sheridan and director Norman Foster discuss Woman on
the Run (F-81).

B-510 Physical Culture. Feburary 1940.
Ann Sheridan plays tennis.

B-511 Picture Play. January 1940.
Ann Sheridan is included in a chart about stars' beauty
hints.

B-512 Picturegoer [England]. March 22, 1952.
Ann Sheridan, Howard Duff, and John Lund are in a scene from
Steel Town (F-82).

B-513 _____. July 11, 1953.
Ann Sheridan is seen in a tinted, full-page photo from Take
Me to Town (F-84).

B-514 "Pin-up of the Past Ann Sheridan." Films and
Filming. February 1974. p. 56.
A 1940s glamour photo of Ann Sheridan accompanies a
biographical paragraph about her career.

B-515 "A Pistol in Petticoats." TV Guide. December 24,

1966. pp. 24-26.
In this profile of Ruth McDevitt, Grandma on _Pistols 'n'_
Petticoats (T-56), Ann Sheridan's playful personality is
recalled. In addition to teasing her septegenarian co-star
on the set, Ann gave her a bawdy birthday cake.

B-516   "Pistols and [sic] Petticoats." _Movieland and TV_
         Time 1966 Album. 1966. p. 35.
Pistols 'n' Petticoats (T-56) is previewed. The magazine
notes the sitcom faced tough competition: _The Lawrence_
Welk Show (ABC, 1955-71; NN, 1972-82) and _Get Smart_ (NBC,
1965-69; CBS 1969-70).

B-517   "_Pistols 'n' Petticoats_." _TV Guide_.
         September 10, 1966. pp. 20-21.
Pistols 'n' Petticoats (T-56) is among the new series
previewed.

B-518   "Pit Orchestra to Feature Popular Medley Saturday."
         Campus Chat [Denton, TX]. April 27, 1933.
         (University of North Texas Collection.)
Sing and Dance (P-1), a North Texas State Teachers College
production, is previewed in the college newspaper.

B-519   Pitts, Michael. _Radio Soundtracks: A Reference_
         Guide. The Scarecrow Press, Inc. Metuchen, New
         Jersey. 1986. pp. 77, 238.
Records and tapes featuring film performers are listed in
this reference volume, including _Ann Sheridan Live_ (D-1).

B-520   "'Play Ball' Tonight in Charity Game." _Hollywood_
         Reporter. August 14, 1941. p. 5.
Plans for the seventh annual Comedians and Leading Men
Baseball Game (P-6) are discussed. Team captains were Ann
Sheridan and Martha Raye. The August 14 game, which was
preceded by a Parade of the Stars, raised money for Mount
Sinai Hospital and Free Medical Clinic.

B-521   Poff, Tip. "That Certain Party." _Los Angeles_
         Times. November 12, 1933.
Clara Lou Sheridan, here erroneously called Lou, attended the
opening of the Gay Nineties nightclub with Jack La Rue.

B-522   "Popular Tunes to Be Featured." _Campus Chat_
         [Denton, TX]. August 4, 1933. (University of North
         Texas Collection.)
The North Texas State Teachers College newspaper previews _A_
Revue of Music (P-1).

B-523   "The Private Life of Ann Sheridan." _Movies_.
         circa 1943-44. (Constance McCormick Collection.)
Ann Sheridan shows off her home in Encino in this pictorial.

B-524   "The Rare Bird." _Time_. February 16, 1953.
This obituary for press agent Steve Hannagan mentions that he
dated Ann Sheridan.

B-525   Rasmussen, Leon. "The Movie Front." _Movie-Radio_

<u>Guide</u>. May 9, 1942.
Rasmussen reports on Jack Benny's ad libs while filming
<u>George Washington Slept Here</u> (F-64) with Ann Sheridan.

B-526   Reagan, Ronald and Hubler, Richard G. <u>Where's the
         Rest of Me?</u> Duell, Sloan and Pierce. New York.
         1965.
Ann Sheridan's frequent co-star discusses their work in
<u>Kings Row</u> (F-61) in his autobiography.

B-527   "Red-Haired 'Ludie' Sheridan Grew Up To Become A
         Star." <u>Denton Record Chronicle</u> [TX]. February 3,
         1957.
Residents of Ann Sheridan's hometown recall the actress'
childhood in Denton, Texas.

B-528   Reid, Louis. "Ann's USO Tour of China-Burma-India."
         <u>Silver Screen</u>. January 1945. pp. 22-23, 67-68.
Reid chronicles Ann Sheridan's U.S.O. tour of the China-
Burma-India theatre (P-9). "I would have regretted it all my
days if I couldn't have had a part in helping to bring a bit
of happiness and cheer to our fighting men," Ann says.
"Every actor and actress should visit the war theatres....If
the boys can take it for months on end, we can do so for a
few short weeks."

B-529   "Remembering." <u>Screen Stories</u>. May 1952.
In this flashback to news of the 1940s, the column recalls
how Ann Sheridan mistakenly was called to active duty after
she had been made an honorary officer in a New Zealand
fighting division (A-14).

B-530   _____. <u>Screen Stories</u>. April 1953.
Anecdotes from the 1940s spotlight this column. In one, Ann
Sheridan was asked to autograph a portrait of Rita Hayworth
while vacationing in Mexico.

B-531   Rhea, Marian. "Texas Bombshell, Part I." <u>Movie
         Mirror</u>. May 1939. pp. 36-37, 72, 74.
Ann Sheridan recalls her childhood in Texas in the first
installment of Rhea's article. Several early photos are
included.

B-532   _____. "Texas Bombshell, Part II." <u>Movie
         Mirror</u>. June 1939. pp. 51, 72-75.
Rhea picks up Ann Sheridan's story with her arrival in
Hollywood to film <u>Search for Beauty</u> (F-1). The article
chronicles Ann's experiences at Paramount, her marriage to
Edward Norris, and her success at Warner Bros.

B-533   "Royalty Sees Benny." <u>Hollywood Reporter</u>.
         April 2, 1943. p. 4.
Britain's royal family joined military camps for a command
performance of <u>George Washington Slept Here</u> (F-64).

B-534   Ryon, Ruth. "Hot Property." <u>Los Angeles Times</u>.
         June 16, 1991. pp. K-1, K-11.
Director Jerome "Gerry" Cohen bought a home built for Ann

Sheridan for just under one million dollars.

B-535   Salerno, Al. "Former Oomph Girl Filming TV Comedy."
        New York World-Telegram. December 6, 1965.
Salerno announces that Ann Sheridan began filming the
Pistols 'n' Petticoats pilot (T-54) on December 3, 1965.

B-536   Schallert, Edwin. "Emil Jannings Rated Great."
        Los Angeles Times. January 16, 1934.
Schallert announces that Clara Lou Sheridan's performance in
Double Door (P-2) with the Paramount stock company led to
her being cast in Come On Marines! (F-3).

B-537   _____. "Henry Travers Leaves Stage for Davis
        Film." Los Angeles Times. May 20, 1938.
An item on Marie Wilson mentions that her next film would be
Three Girls on Broadway, released as Broadway Musketeers
(F-44).

B-538   _____. "Screen Career Resumed by Militant Ann
        Sheridan." Los Angeles Times. January 27, 1946.
Schallert discusses Ann Sheridan's return to movies in Nora
Prentiss (F-74) after a lengthy suspension.

B-539   _____. "Sextet Given New Contracts." Los
        Angeles Times. November 24, 1934.
Schallert names the six Search for Beauty (F-1) contestants
who won Paramount contracts, including Clara Lou Sheridan.

B-540   _____. "Withers to Free-Lance; 'Aloha' Goes
        Romantic." Los Angeles Times. December 22, 1941.
Ann Sheridan and Dennis Morgan are announced for Aloha
Means Goodbye, a Warner Bros. film about Japanese spy
activities in the Pacific. The movie was not made.

B-541   Scheuer, Philip K. "Ann Sheridan to Risk Oomph on
        Own Movie." Los Angeles Times. May 22, 1949.
Ann Sheridan discusses her illnesses during the filming of I
Was a Male War Bride (F-79) and her plans to make Second
Lady. She owned the rights to the latter and intended to
shoot it independently, however the project never
materialized.

B-542   Schultz, Margie. "Ann Sheridan: The Oomph Girl Who
        Died Too Soon!" Hollywood Studio Magazine. July
        1987. pp. 20-23.
Ann Sheridan's career is profiled in this biographical
sketch.

B-543   Scott, John L. "Ann Sheridan Will Settle in Mexico
        to Make Films." Los Angeles Times. circa 1953.
        (Constance McCormick Collection.)
During the filming of Appointment in Honduras (F-85), Ann
Sheridan discusses her plans to move to Mexico.

B-544   "Scrapbook Short: Ann Sheridan." Star Album.
        1949. p. 37.
Ann Sheridan's career is reviewed. The author describes the

actress as "a gal who loves a joke, who always turns in a
bright and competent job on whatever assignment she's given,
but who aims for no Oscars."

B-545   Screen Album. Summer 1947.
Ann Sheridan's vacation in rural Connecticut is discussed.

B-546   _____. Spring 1948. p. 36.
This profile reveals Ann Sheridan's penchant for practical
jokes. Incidents on the sets of Silver River (F-77) and
Good Sam (F-78) are recalled.

B-547 Screen Guide. December 1938.
A Cleveland reader's question leads the magazine to deem Ann
Sheridan "the star with the most sex appeal."

B-548   _____. August 1942.
Ann Sheridan is pictured smoking.

B-549   _____. January 1945.
Ann Sheridan is seen hugging a GI during her China-Burma-
India tour (P-9).

B-550   _____. June 1947.
Ann Sheridan and Greer Garson are seen at a party following
the Academy Awards.

B-551   _____. January 1948.
Two photos show Ann Sheridan at a party for cancer research
(P-10).

B-552   _____. June 1950.
Ann Sheridan and Jane Wyman are seen at a party on the set of
Louisa (Universal, 1950).

B-553   _____. July 1950.
Tony Curtis visits Ann Sheridan and Victor Mature on the set
of Stella (F-79).

B-554   _____. December 1950.
The article reports that during a year-long remodeling job,
Ann Sheridan and her secretary lived in a small house in
North Hollywood, California. Ann returned home only to swim.

B-555   _____. December 1951.
Ann Sheridan and Ross Hunter are seen at a charity dinner.

B-556   "A Screen Guide Cover Is Born." Screen Guide.
         June 1948. pp. 44-47.
This pictorial traces the June 1948 Screen Guide cover from
drawing board to photo session. Ann Sheridan is the cover
subject.

B-557 Screen Life. March 1940.
Ann Sheridan totes a child at a charity ball, collecting
donations.

B-558 Screen Magazine. January 1954.

The columnist shares an anecdote about Ann Sheridan's lack of vanity. Despite Ann's disheveled appearance, she refused to let the studio retouch stills from <u>Rage of the Jungle</u>. She said, "I've worked terribly hard and looked progressively worse each day and I want every bit of credit for it!" The film was released as <u>Appointment in Honduras</u> (F-85).

B-559   _____. November 1956.
Ann Sheridan and Jacques Mapes are seen at Ciro's. The two planned a TV project.

B-560   <u>Screen Romances</u>. January 1939. pp. 71-73.
Ann Sheridan models seven designs by Warner Bros.'s Orry-Kelly.

B-561   _____. August 1943.
Ann Sheridan is pictured with frequent escort Bruce Cabot and Mickey Rooney.

B-562   _____. November 1945.
A Stork Club party includes Ann Sheridan, Steve Hannagan, Faye Emerson, Brig. Gen. Elliott Roosevelt, and Cliff Edwards.

B-563   _____. July 1947.
Ann Sheridan is pictured with Steve Hannagan and Sherman Billingsley at the Stork Club.

B-564   <u>Screen Stars</u>. July 1944.
Ann Sheridan is seen chatting with Deanna Durbin.

B-565   _____. April 1945.
Ann Sheridan and Bob Hope are pictured at a rehearsal for a shortwave overseas broadcast (R-14).

B-566   _____. December 1945.
Jane Wyman and Ann Sheridan chat on the set of <u>One More Tomorrow</u> (F-71).

B-567   <u>Screen Stories</u>. December 1945.
Ann Sheridan and Jane Wyman are seen on the set of <u>One More Tomorrow</u> (F-71).

B-568   _____. August 1954.
Ann Sheridan and Jacques Mapes pose for photographers.

B-569   _____. September 1954.
Ann Sheridan and Jacques Mapes are pictured.

B-570   <u>Screenland</u>. February 1940.
Ann Sheridan hosts an ice skating party for her celebrity friends, which ended with a feast of fried chicken.

B-571   _____. September 1941.
Ann Sheridan is dressed like Martha Washington for a dream sequence in <u>George Washington Slept Here</u> (F-64).

B-572   _____. October 1941. p. 30.

Three publicity photos from <u>Navy Blues</u> (F-59) promote the
film.

B-573 _____. April 1943.
Tired of reporters' questions about Errol Flynn, Ann Sheridan
tells a persistent scribe that her stiff neck came from
trying to find Flynn in a crowd at the airport.

B-574 _____. April 1945.
Ann Sheridan mugs with Jerry Colonna and Bing Crosby.

B-575 _____. April 1946.
Ann Sheridan denies marriage rumors after Steve Hannagan
gives her diamond jewelry. The column also reveals that Ann
selected Kent Smith from twenty actors who auditioned for
<u>The Sentence</u>, released as <u>Nora Prentiss</u> (F-74).

B-576 _____. November 1948.
Ann Sheridan and Gary Cooper are seen in a still from <u>Good
Sam</u> (F-78).

B-577 _____. May 1952.
Ann Sheridan is pictured with Leonard Goldstein, producer of
<u>Just Across the Street</u> (F-83).

B-578 _____. June 1952.
The column details practical jokes that Ann Sheridan and John
Lund pulled on each other while filming <u>Steel Town</u> (F-82)
and <u>Just Across the Street</u> (F-83).

B-579   Shafer, Jack. "Clara Lou had the oomph to climb
         stairs to stardom." <u>Newark Star-Ledger</u> [NJ].
         October 23, 1966.
<u>Pistols 'n' Petticoats</u> (T-56) star Ann Sheridan discusses
her early career, including her aspirations to be a band
singer. Shafer reveals Ann's screen squint was due to poor
eyesight and that she wore thick glasses off camera.

B-580   Shaw, Joy and Jerry. "Today's Cele-Birthday."
         <u>Miami Herald</u> [FL]. February 21, 1958.
According to this profile, Ann Sheridan was named to the list
of the nation's ten best-dressed women three times. Her
favorite food was hamburger. The article includes a
caricature by Jerry Shaw that looks more like Alexis Smith
than Ann.

B-581   Sheridan, Ann. "Hollywood Divorce." <u>Liberty</u>.
         August 17, 1940. pp. 15-16.
The actress discusses the different types of divorce in this
apparently ghostwritten piece. She complains about the
public way divorce is handled in Hollywood.

B-582 _____. "I Wouldn't Marry a Perfect Man!" <u>Motion
         Picture</u>. June 1944. p. 44.
Ann Sheridan discusses the qualities she looks for in a man.

B-583 _____. "Man Traps." <u>Screen Stars</u>. December
         1949. pp. 24, 91.

Ann Sheridan recalls how a bargain on china led her to remodel her home.

B-584   _____. "Take My Word for It." Modern
         Screen. July 1953. pp. 78-80.
Ann Sheridan shares her opinions about women drivers, beds, American manners, and grooming. She also discusses the ways her family influenced her personality.

B-585   _____. "This Guy Cary Grant." Silver Screen.
         September 1949. pp. 20-21, 54-55.
Ann Sheridan discusses Cary Grant and the filming of I Was a Male War Bride (F-79). She praises his sense of humor, recalling practical jokes they pulled on each other.

B-586   _____. "Unfair to Oomph!" Liberty. May 3,
         1941. pp. 20-21, 60.
In this apparently ghostwritten article, Ann Sheridan shares her views on the salary dispute with Warner Bros. that led to her suspension.

B-587   _____. "What Does the American Way of Life Mean
         to Me?" Motion Picture. circa 1941. (Constance
         McCormick Collection.)
With World War II raging in Europe, Ann Sheridan gives a patriotic take on why she is proud to be an American.

B-588   _____. "Why Should Married Life Change Me?"
         Screen Guide. 1942. (Constance McCormick
         Collection.)
Ann Sheridan insists that her marriage to George Brent will not change her. "Now that we are successful in our careers and happy in our home life, we intend to stay that way," she says. Despite the happy portrait painted by Ann's quotes and five pictures of the Brents, they were divorced within a year of their marriage.

B-589   Sheridan, Ann as told to Canfield, Alyce. "Next
         Time I Love." Movieland. March 1943.
Canfield interviews Ann Sheridan on the set of Edge of Darkness (F-65), praising her ability to laugh at herself. Ann discusses her recent divorce from George Brent, implying that he was critical, jealous, and possessive. "George knew how I was when he married me," she says. "I thought he wanted me 'as is,' but as soon as I said 'I do,' it was different somehow."

B-590   Sheridan, Ann as told to Haas, Dorothy B. "Brother
         Bogie." Silver Screen. January 1943. pp. 22-23,
         61-62.
Ann Sheridan discusses friend and co-star Humphrey Bogart, including his penchant for practical jokes. She explains that their nicknames "Brother Bogie" and "Sister Annie" derived from their playing siblings in San Quentin (F-33). A companion piece, "Sister Annie" by Humphrey Bogart and Haas, ran two issues later (B-101).

B-591   Sheridan, Ann as told to Surmelian, Leon. "10 Ways

to Lose a Serviceman."   circa 1943-44.   pp. 42-43.
(Constance McCormick Collection.)
Ann Sheridan gives advice on what not to do while dating a
soldier.   Six comic pictures show Ann and a model acting out
her advice.

B-592   "Sheridan as Tex Guinan."   <u>Variety</u>.   May 27, 1942.
Ann Sheridan is announced as the lead in <u>Texas Guinan</u>, a
Paramount biography.   Warner Bros. planned to loan her in
exchange for Fred MacMurray's services for <u>Princess
O'Rourke</u> (Paramount, 1943).   The deal fell through.

B-593   "Sheridan Back to Work on Old Terms."   <u>Hollywood
        Reporter</u>.   March 14, 1941.   p. 1.
Warner Bros. announces that Ann Sheridan would begin filming
<u>Navy Blues</u> (F-59) on March 14, 1941 following a five-month
salary dispute and layoff.

B-594   "Sheridan-Bogart Teamed."   <u>Variety</u>.   January 11,
        1938.
Ann Sheridan and Humphrey Bogart are announced as Warner
Bros.'s newest romantic team, set to star in <u>Torchy in
Panama</u>.   The film was released as <u>Torchy Blane in Panama</u>
(Warner Bros., 1938) with Lola Lane and Paul Kelly.

B-595   "Sheridan Gets '<u>Heiress</u>.'"   <u>Hollywood Reporter</u>.
        February 20, 1937.   p. 4.
Ann Sheridan is announced to replace Patricia Ellis in <u>The
Madcap Heiress</u>, released as <u>The Footloose Heiress</u> (F-34).

B-596   "Sheridan-'<u>Life</u>' Oomph $18,500 in Wash."
        <u>Variety</u>.   October 4, 1939.
The trade paper reports on the box office receipts from Ann
Sheridan's personal appearance tour in Washington, D.C.
(P-5), where she played on a bill with <u>What a Life</u>
(Paramount, 1939), a Henry Aldrich film.

B-597   "Sheridan Meets the Boys in Burma."   <u>P.M.</u>
        October 1, 1944.
A full-page photo shows Ann Sheridan hugging a GI after he
gave her a Japanese battle flag during her tour of the
China-Burma-India theatre (P-9).

B-598   "Sheridan Tour Opening Switched to Washington."
        <u>Hollywood Reporter</u>.   September 21, 1939.   p. 18.
The article announces a change in Ann Sheridan's personal
appearance tour (P-5).

B-599   "Sheridan Was Independent."   <u>Denton Record-
        Chronicle</u> [TX].   January 23, 1967.
Ann Sheridan's hometown newspaper recalls her career in this
obituary.

B-600   Shipman, David.   <u>The Great Movie Stars: The
        Golden Years</u>.   Crown Publishers, Inc.   New York.
        1970.   pp. 492-95.
In this biographical sketch, Shipman notes that Ann Sheridan
"never quite received her due."   He says that she was "too

warm, too lush and too genuinely glamorous to compete with
the other tinny girls [on screen]."

B-601   _____. "In the Picture." Radio Times.
         January 26, 1985.
Shipman remembers Ann Sheridan's career, lamenting her
neglect by many film historians. He writes, "'Annie' they
called her on the Warner lot, and she's probably 'Annie' to
all those like me, who start missing her if too long goes by
without a Sheridan movie on television. How could we have
let her go so lightly?"

B-602   "Short Circuit." Time. October 23, 1944.
         pp. 68-70.
Time reports on the controversy surrounding performers in
the China-Burma-India theatre during World War II (P-9).
Roundup, a GI weekly, is quoted, complaining about Ann
Sheridan, Joe E. Brown, Paulette Goddard, and others. The
Hollywood Victory Comitte claims Ann's tour was curtailed
because of lack of transportation.

B-603   Shupper, Alyce. "Ann How!" Silver Screen.
         November 1938. p. 34.
Ann Sheridan's life story is recounted in this pre-oomph
profile. Shupper points out how Ann's experiences in
teachers college and singing with a band helped her with
movie roles. Despite her rising career at Warner Bros.,
Shupper maintains that Ann was still a regular girl who fried
her own chicken, answered her own telephone, and loved
playing a friendly game of poker.

B-604   Silver Screen. December 1939.
Ann Sheridan, Cesar Romero, the Fred MacMurrays, and the Ray
Millands are seen dining at the Cafe Lamaze.

B-605   _____. December 1939.
Grooming tips accompany this portrait of Ann Sheridan.

B-606   _____. March 1940.
Ann Sheridan and Una O'Connor are featured in a still from
It All Came True (F-53).

B-607   _____. August 1940.
A gossip column offers two bits about Ann Sheridan. When
producer Billy Rose offered Ann $100,000 to wear a bathing
suit at his San Francisco Aquacade, she said, "I don't feel
inclined, so that's that." In another item, a director
blames George Brent when Ann is an hour late to the set.

B-608   _____. August 1940.
Ann Sheridan, George Brent, Heather Angel, and Ralph Forbes
are seen leaving Ciro's. Coincidentally, both Brent and
Forbes were divorced from Ruth Chatterton.

B-609   _____. August 1940. p. 37.
A portrait of Ann Sheridan accompanies an item about a
waitress not recognizing the actress.

B-610 _____. December 1940.
Ann Sheridan is seen teaching Charlie Ruggles the rumba
before he taught it to her on screen in Honeymoon for
Three (F-57).

B-611 _____. September 1942.
Ann Sheridan helps two soldiers peel potatoes during a U.S.O.
tour at Fort Riley (P-7).

B-612 _____. December 1942.
A sultry photo of Ann Sheridan accompanies a note about her
surprise separation from George Brent.

B-613 _____. March 1944.
Ann Sheridan is pictured at the Stork Club with owner Sherman
Billingsley and actor Jeffrey Lynn.

B-614 _____. January 1945.
Ann Sheridan dines with Carole Landis and Pat O'Brien.

B-615 _____. August 1945.
Ann Sheridan and Warner Bros. makeup chief Perc Westmore are
pictured at a party in his honor.

B-616 _____. October 1945.
Ann Sheridan is mentioned as a recent guest on Milton Berle's
radio program (R-15).

B-617 _____. December 1947.
Travilla fits Ann Sheridan for a costume for Silver River
(F-77).

B-618 _____. July 1951.
Ann Sheridan and Steve Hannagan are pictured with Janis
Paige.

B-619 _____. August 1951.
Ann Sheridan and Jeff Chandler are seen at the premiere of I
Was a Communist for the F.B.I. (Warner Bros., 1951).

B-620 _____. April 1952.
Ann Sheridan chats with Ross Hunter and Lauren Bacall at the
premiere of Meet Danny Wilson (Universal, 1952).

B-621 _____. August 1952.
During the Steel Town promotional tour (P-12), Ann
Sheridan, Howard Duff, and John Lund are pictured at the
Stork Club.

B-622 _____. August 1952.
A photo of Ann Sheridan and her dog accompanies a caption
about Ann having few female friends.

B-623 _____. February 1953.
The columnist recalls Ann Sheridan's trouble with a bear
while filming Flame of the Timberline. Instead of chasing
his co-star, the bear ruined twelve takes, trying to hug her.
The film was released as Take Me to Town (F-84).

B-624   _____. May 1953.
Ann Sheridan is pictured after the funeral mass for Steve
Hannagan.

B-625   _____. September 1953.
The columnist announces Ann Sheridan's plans to sell her San
Fernando valley home and spend at least six months a year in
Mexico.

B-626   "Silver Screen Topics for Gossip." Silver
         Screen. July 1941. pp. 19, 21.
The column shares Ann Sheridan's tip for turning bangs into a
pompadour and shows her dancing with Cesar Romero.

B-627   Skolsky, Sidney. "Ann Prefers the Boys." New
         York Post. April 1, 1944.
Ann Sheridan's idiosyncrasies are revealed in this
biographical sketch. Among the trivia: she preferred
canned peas to fresh, she smoked a cigarette every hour on
the hour, and she slept in the nude.

B-628   _____. "Ann's a Good Guy - But Pidgeon-Toed."
         New York Post. December 12, 1942.
Skolsky reviews Ann Sheridan's career. He reveals that Bing
Crosby and Fred Astaire were two of her favorite stars and
that "she would give practically anything to be able to
dance with Fred Astaire in a picture."

B-629   _____. "Comfortable." New York Post Week-End
         Magazine. May 28, 1950.
In this biographical sketch, Skolsky reveals that Ann
Sheridan had a difficult time containing herself on the set,
always wanting to compliment, applaud, or laugh at her
co-stars' performances.

B-630   _____. "Hollywood Is My Beat." Hollywood
         Citizen-News [CA]. November 12, 1943.
Ann Sheridan is profiled in this trivia-filled column.

B-631   _____. "Hollywood Is My Beat." Hollywood
         Citizen-News [CA]. March 23, 1944.
Skolsky recalls Ann Sheridan's career and promotes her latest
film, The Doughgirls (F-69).

B-632   _____. "Just Keep Her Guessing." New York Post
         Home News Week-End Magazine. June 26, 1949.
Skolsky profiles Ann Sheridan, whom he describes as a
"regular."

B-633   _____. "Sidney Skolsky Presents..." Hollywood
         Citizen-News [CA]. circa 1939-40. (Constance
         McCormick Collection.)
Skolsky provides a trivia-filled biographical sketch of Ann
Sheridan, which is the basis for his many future columns
about the actress.

B-634   _____. "They Love That Girl." New York Post
         Week-End Magazine. February 7, 1947."

Ann Sheridan, then filming The Unfaithful (F-75), is
profiled.

B-635   Slide, Anthony. The Vaudevillians. Arlington
        House. Westport, Connecticut. 1981. pp. 6-7.
Nora Bayes and Jack Norworth's careers are recalled in this
biographical dictionary. Bayes and Norworth's lives inspired
Shine On Harvest Moon (F-68).

B-636   "Slippery Mission." Miami Herald [FL].
        October 7, 1953.
The column announces that Ann Sheridan slipped in and out of
Hollywood to inquire about selling her home in the San
Fernando valley.

B-637   Smith, Frederick James. "The Real Oomph Girl."
        Liberty. July 20, 1940. pp. 39-41.
Ann Sheridan discusses her career, her co-stars, and the
Oomph Girl campaign. She was unimpressed by the publicity,
insisting, "What I most want to do is to be a good actress.
If I can be a quarter as good as Bette Davis, I'll be happy."

B-638   "So You Won't Sing, Eh?" Screen Guide. October
        1943.
Ann Sheridan is seen in a still from Thank Your Lucky
Stars (F-66). The article notes that Warner Bros.
utilized many non-musical performers in the film.

B-639   Sothern, Ann as told to Reid, James. "My Pal, Ann
        Sheridan." Screen Life. October 1949.
        pp. 24-25, 61-63.
Actress Ann Sothern writes about her friendship with Ann
Sheridan. Sothern admits she was skeptical of Sheridan
during their first meeting, expecting the stereotypical
glamour girl. Instead, she found Sheridan to be very natural
and humble. Sothern reveals that Sheridan gave herself a
bracelet to remind her of her origins. The inscription read,
"From Clara Lou to Ann. You continue to amaze me." Sothern
claims the only thing the friends argued over was who got
Cesar Romero as a dancing partner.

B-640   "Special TV Section." See "The Lady Knows All the
        Answers" (B-295).

B-641   Speed, F. Maurice. Film Review, 1966-1968. A.S.
        Barnes and Company. New York. 1967.
A profile of Ann Sheridan is included in the obituaries. The
article erroneously claims that the Oomph Girl tag was given
to Ann by her agent during World War II.

B-642   "Spot Idea to Be Stage Show Bill Saturday Night."
        Campus Chat [Denton, TX]. February 16, 1933.
        (University of North Texas Collection.)
Spot Idea (P-1), a North Texas State Teachers College
production, is previewed in the college newspaper.

B-643   Springer, John and Hamilton, Jack. They Had Faces
        Then. Citadel Press. Secaucus, New Jersey. 1974.

pp. 221, 327
A brief biographical sketch and an assessment of Ann
Sheridan's early roles are included in this look at 1930s
actresses. Springer and Hamilton call Ann a "forthright,
hearty redhead, with few pretensions and no dishonesty, and a
fighter to the end."

B-644   Stardom's Calendar Girl...Ann Sheridan."
         Stardom. July 1943. p. 28.
A color photo of Ann Sheridan accompanies a calendar for
June, July, and August 1943.

B-645   "Stars Out in Hollywood." Cincinnati Pictorial
         Enquirer [OH]. March 2, 1952.
Ann Sheridan is seen dining with producer Leonard Goldstein
in this pictorial newspaper supplement.

B-646   "Stars' Night Out." Premiere. September 1989.
Premiere looks back at 1940s Hollywood with a candid of Ann
Sheridan and George Brent sharing a table at Ciro's with
William Powell and his wife Diana Lewis. The caption recalls
that when the nightclub opened in January 1940, the
advertisements claimed, "Everybody that's anybody will be at
Ciro's to-night! [sic]."

B-647   "Status of Sheridan." New York Times. August 22,
         1949.
The article details the initial problems between Ann Sheridan
and RKO over Carriage Entrance. Ann insisted her contract
had been violated when the studio wanted to cast an actor
without her approval. The film was released as My
Forbidden Past (RKO, 1951).

B-648   Stein, Herb. "Rambling Reporter." Hollywood
         Reporter. December 8, 1941. p. 2.
Stein reports that photographers "shot the hell" out of a
Ciro's table with George Brent, Ann Sheridan, William Powell,
and Diana Lewis on December 6, 1941.

B-649   _____. "What Hollywood's Whispering About."
         Photoplay. September 1951. p. 14.
Stein notes that Ann Sheridan dated Jeff Chandler when Steve
Hannagan was unavailable. When asked about the situation
during one of Hannagan's California visits, Chandler is
quoted, "I can't be [with her] - the top man's in town."

B-650   Steinberg, Cobbett. Reel Facts. Vintage Books.
         New York. 1982.
This book of movie records includes film grosses, festival
prizes, and award winners.

B-651   "Steve Hannagan Left $218,000 For Ann Sheridan."
         Daytona Beach News [FL]. July 27, 1955.
Following a tax appraisal of Steve Hannagan's estate, it was
announced that Ann Sheridan was the beneficiary of $218,399
worth of insurance policies.

B-652   "Stick to Oomph!" Screen Guide. March 1944.

Despite non-glamorous roles in Kings Row (F-61) and Edge of Darkness (F-65), Ann Sheridan planned to give the public the oomph they expected in future films. The article notes that she had seen other actresses fail when they tried to change their images so she wanted to please her fans.

B-653   Strauss, Theodore. "A Farewell to Oomph." New
         York Times. October 10, 1943.
Ann Sheridan insists she is a "successful personality," rather than an actress. She stresses the importance of good writing. "If it's on paper, anybody can do it," she says.

B-654   "Straw Hat Time." Chicago Daily News. May 24,
         1958.
Ann Sheridan, star of Kind Sir (P-16), is among the stars pictured who were appearing in Chicago.

B-655   Stubblebine, Donald J. Cinema Sheet Music.
         McFarland & Company, Inc. Jefferson, North Carolina.
         1991.
This reference volume lists songs sheets of movie music, along with the stars who are pictured on the cover.

B-656   "Suit Names 'Oomph' Girl." New York Daily News.
         July 25, 1939.
A cheesecake photo of Ann Sheridan accompanies an article about a director's ex-wife suing him for back alimony. Frank D. Dewar, the director, allegedly took Ann and her friend Gwendolyn Woodford to nightclubs instead of supporting his ex-wife.

B-657   Sullivan, Ed. "Why Hollywood Gets Nervous Stomachs."
         New York Daily News. January 21, 1940.
Sullivan describes how Ann Sheridan's lunch was interrupted by a string of Warner Bros. personnel.

B-658   Super-Star Information Chart. Modern Screen.
         1942.
This informational booklet, published by Modern Screen magazine, lists the stars' vital statistics, latest films, and miscellaneous trivia. The chart claims Ann Sheridan weighed 120 pounds and stood 5'5" tall. Divorced from George Brent, she was dating Sgt. Earl Oxford. The chart also reports that she was "nuts about" good books.

B-659   Taubman, Leslie. "The Treasure of the Sierra
         Madre." Magill's American Film Guide, vol. 5.
         Salem Press. Englewood Cliffs, New Jersey. 1983.
         pp. 3439-42.
Taubman discusses the history of The Treasure of the Sierra Madre (F-76), as well as its symbolism.

B-660   "Texas Tornado." Screen Guide. circa 1942.
         (Constance McCormick Collection.)
This twenty-panel pictorial traces Ann Sheridan's life and career, from childhood through George Washington Slept Here (F-64).

B-661   "This Week in Hollywood." <u>Movie-Radio Guide</u>.
          June 29, 1940. p. 10.
The columnist predicts Ann Sheridan will "raise the roof" at
Warner Bros. when she hears that Bette Davis planned to play
the lead in <u>Calamity Jane</u>. The script had been prepared
for Ann by Jerry Wald and the role had been promised to her.
The columnist notes that other factors in the feud included
Ann's relationship with former Davis beau George Brent and
the amount of publicity Ann had received.

B-662   Thomas, Bob. "Ann Sheridan Loves Mexico." <u>Miami
          Herald</u> [FL]. January 7, 1956.
Ann Sheridan discusses her home in Mexico and her desire for
a TV series.

B-663   _____. "Ann Sheridan Picks An All-American Man."
          <u>Hollywood Citizen-News</u> [CA]. February 27, 1947.
At the urging of columnist Bob Thomas, Ann Sheridan selects
the best features from various actors to come up with the
All-American Man for 1947. Co-stars Zachary Scott, Errol
Flynn, Kent Smith, and Humphrey Bogart respectively are
mentioned for best eyes, forehead, hairline, and ears. Ann
is seen studying a composite drawing by artist Mel Archer.

B-664   _____. "Pistol Packin' Role For Ann Sheridan."
          <u>Newark Evening News</u> [NJ]. July 29, 1966.
<u>Pistols 'n' Petticoats</u> (T-56) star Ann Sheridan discusses
her recent projects. She describes the TV series as "sort of
<u>Bonanza</u> [(NBC, 1959-73)] and <u>The Big Valley</u> [(ABC,
1965-69)] gone crazy." A photo shows producer Joe Connelly
welcoming Ann back to Hollywood.

B-665   Thomas, Nicholas. <u>International Dictionary of Film
          and Filmmakers</u>. St. James Press. Detroit. 1992.
          pp. 912-13.
Joseph Arkins provides a short biographical essay about Ann
Sheridan. A filmography includes her roles and directors.

B-666   Thomas, Tony. <u>Errol Flynn: The Spy Who Never Was</u>.
          Citadel Press. Secaucus, New Jersey. 1990. p. 25.
Ann Sheridan comments on Errol Flynn's personality, recalling
his ability to camouflage himself. "In all the years I knew
him," she says, "I never knew what really lay underneath, and
I doubt if many people did."

B-667   _____. <u>The Films of Ronald Reagan</u>. Citadel
          Press. Secaucus, New Jersey. 1980. pp. 49-52,
          79-81, 86-88, 128-36.
Ronald Reagan's film work is chronicled, including <u>Cowboy
from Brooklyn</u> (F-41), <u>Naughty But Nice</u> (F-48), <u>The
Angels Wash Their Faces</u> (F-51), <u>Kings Row</u> (F-61), and
<u>Juke Girl</u> (F-62).

B-668   Thomas, Tony and Solomon, Aubrey. <u>The Films of
          20th Century-Fox</u>. Citadel Press. Secaucus, New
          Jersey. 1979. pp. 200, 202, 213-14.
Ann Sheridan is mentioned in entries for <u>I Was a Male War
Bride</u> (F-79) and <u>Stella</u> (F-80).

B-669   Thomas, Tony and Terry, Jim. The Busby Berkeley
         Book. New York Graphic Society Ltd. New York.
         1973. pp. 120-21.
They Made Me a Criminal (F-46) is discussed.

B-670   Thomison, Dennis. "Kings Row." Magill's
         American Film Guide, vol. 3. Salem Press.
         Englewood Cliffs, New Jersey. 1983. pp. 1758-61.
Thomison assesses Kings Row (F-61), calling it one of the
best films produced during the war years. He mistakenly
credits the role of Louise to Jayne Meadows, rather than
Nancy Coleman. Thomison describes Ann Sheridan's performance
as the finest in the film. "[She]... demonstrates that she
did not have to rely only on her physical attributes," he
writes, "Her performance is that of a seasoned, competent
star."

B-671   _____. "Kings Row." Magill's Survey of
         Cinema, Second Series, vol. 3. Salem Press.
         Englewood Cliffs, New Jersey. 1981. pp. 1265-68.
Thomison's thesis on Kings Row (F-61) is the same as the
entry above (B-670).

B-672   Thompson, Verita with Shepherd, Donald. Bogie and
         Me. St. Martin's Press. New York. 1982.
         pp. 13-14, 17-19.
Hairdresser Verita Thompson, Humphrey Bogart's alleged former
mistress, recalls how Ann Sheridan introduced them.

B-673   "300 Boys and Girls Dine at Opening Youth Club."
         Los Angeles Times. December 19, 1952.
Ann Sheridan is pictured with policeman Mickey Finn and some
children at a holiday party celebrating the opening of new
quarters for the Mickey Finn Youth Clubs (P-13). Ann was an
active fundraiser for the recreation clubs for
underprivileged boys.

B-674   Tierney, Tom. Glamorous Stars of the Forties
         Paper Dolls. Dover Publications, Inc. New York.
         1994.
Ann Sheridan, Hedy Lamarr, Rita Hayworth, Lana Turner,
Dorothy Lamour, Veronica Lake, Gene Tierney, and Maria Montez
are immortalized in paper dolls, along with costumes from
some of their 1940s films. Ann Sheridan wears a swimsuit
from a studio publicity shot and comes with costumes from
The Man Who Came to Dinner (F-61), Kings Row (F-61), and
Shine On Harvest Moon (F-68).

B-675   "Toby Wing, Ann Sheridan, Mary Brown Freelancing."
         Hollywood Reporter. May 22, 1935.
The article notes that three Paramount starlets, including
Ann Sheridan, completed their Paramount contracts and were
freelancing.

B-676   "Transition: Died." Newsweek. January 30, 1967.
Ann Sheridan's obituary is included.

B-677   "Truth and Consequences." Photoplay. May 1953.

The reporter corrects rumors that religion prevented Ann
Sheridan and Steve Hannagan from marrying.

B-678   "Try Your Star's Favorite Dish." _Motion Picture_.
         May 1945.
Ann Sheridan contributes her recipe for "Eggs with Cheese in
Sauce," which features ingredients like eggs, Spanish sauce,
and bacon fat.

B-679   Turkel, Robin. "For Ann Sheridan It's Finally
         Broadway." _New York World-Telegram_. September 9,
         1959.
Ann Sheridan admits she searched two years before finding a
Broadway script that appealed to her. The one she chose was
Odd Man In (P-19), which closed during its try-out tour.

B-680   "TV Mailbag." _Miami News_ [FL]. September 8, 1960.
A reader's questions about Ann Sheridan prompt the columnist
to speculate that her absence from the screen was due to her
wise financial investments.

B-681   _____. _Miami News_ [FL]. October 15, 1962.
Ann Sheridan's career is recalled when a reader asks about
her background and current activities.

B-682   "20 Fascinating Facts about _Casablanca_." _Globe_.
         August 4, 1992.
To commemorate the fiftieth anniversary of _Casablanca_
(Warner Bros., 1942), the tabloid supplies twenty trivia
notes, including the rumor that Ann Sheridan originally was
cast as Ilsa.

B-683   "$25 A Word." _Hollywood Reporter_. September 6,
         1935.
A fashion editor at Universal Studio won $50 for coming up
with the title for _Fighting Youth_ (F-28).

B-684   "Two Beauties Put on the Dog." _Miami Herald_ [FL].
         March 6, 1956.
Ann Sheridan was unimpressed with co-star Dolores Gray's
seven poodles, since Ann had seventeen of her own.

B-685   "U.S. Play Opens at Fair." _New York Times_.
         October 9, 1958.
The opening of _The Time of Your Life_ is reviewed (P-17).

B-686   Valenti, Peter. _Errol Flynn: A Bio-Bibliography_.
         Greenwood Press. Westport, Connecticut. 1984.
         pp. 28-29, 42.
Valenti mentions changes in the script for _Virginia City_
(Warner Bros., 1940), which originally was scheduled to star
Ann Sheridan and Errol Flynn.

B-687   _Variety_. February 8, 1967.
The column notes that, although Warner Bros. was responsible
for Ann Sheridan's Oomph Girl nickname, the campaign hit its
peak while Ann was on loan to Walter Wanger for _Winter
Carnival_ (F-49).

B-688   "Vaude's Many Film Names." Variety. October 11,
        1939. pp. 1, 18.
The trade paper notes that studio cutbacks were making more
film stars available for stage performances. Ann Sheridan is
among those listed (P-5). In a sidebar, Pittsburgh's Stanley
Theatre and several other Warner Bros.-owned theatres were
trying to book Ann after her successful personal appearances
in New York and Washington, D.C. The studio wanted her to
return to begin filming on November 1, 1939. No further
appearances were made.

B-689   Vaughn, Stephen. Ronald Reagan in Hollywood. The
        Press Syndicate of the University of Cambridge. New
        York. 1994. p. 59.
Vaughn discusses the treatment of women in Ronald Reagan's
films, noting Ann Sheridan's role as a sex symbol at Warner
Bros.

B-690   "Victory Homes of the Stars." Stardom. July 1943.
Ann Sheridan shows off her ranch in this pictorial.

B-691   VideoHound's Golden Movie Retriever. Visible Ink
        Press. Detroit. 1995.
In addition to video reviews, this sourcebook includes the
addresses of video distributors and several detailed indexes.

B-692   Vinson, James. The International Directory of
        Films and Filmmakers, Vol. III. St. James Press.
        Chicago. 1986. p. 571.
Ann Sheridan's career is recalled in a brief essay by Joseph
Arkins. The filmography notes her roles, as well as the
directors.

B-693   "Vital Statistics." Movie Life. July 1942.
Director Lloyd Bacon gives Ann Sheridan a birthday spanking
on the set of Wings for the Eagle (F-63).

B-694   Walsh, Raoul. Each Man in His Time. Farrar,
        Straus and Giroux. New York. 1974. pp. 314-15.
In this autobiography, director Raoul Walsh explains how Ann
Sheridan's feud with Warner Bros. led to Rita Hayworth being
cast in The Strawberry Blonde (Warner Bros., 1941).

B-695   Warfield, Herbert. "Triple Oomph." Life.
        July 31, 1939.
In a letter to the editor, a New Yorker points out that Ann
Sheridan was featured in Life, Look, and Collier's in
one week. The editor notes that she probably set a record
for simultaneous publicity.

B-696   "WB-Par Swap Flivs." Variety. June 10, 1942.
Plans for Ann Sheridan's loan-out to Paramount for Tex
Guinan are canceled.

B-697   "Warners Rushes Filming of Air Hostess Story."
        Hollywood Reporter. September 21, 1939. p. 3.
Ann Sheridan, Priscilla Lane, Rosemary Lane, Jane Bryan, and
Jane Wyman are announced for Tough Angels, a film about air

hostesses and the rigorous training they receive at a Chicago
school. Warner Bros. planned to rush the low-budget film
into production. The melodrama was released as <u>Flight
Angels</u> (Warner Bros., 1940) with only Wyman remaining in
the cast.

B-698   Waterbury, Ruth. "We Say Good-bye to a Valiant
         Lady." <u>Modern Screen</u>. April 1967. pp. 8, 10,
         80, 82.
In this posthumous tribute, Waterbury reveals that Ann
Sheridan phoned her closest friends to say goodbye two days
before she died. Ann's doctor and friend Ross Hunter recall
her vibrant personality, her strength, and loyalty.
Waterbury mistakenly says Ann collapsed after the filming of
the twelfth episode of <u>Pistols 'n' Petticoats</u> (T-56).

B-699   "Way Back for Ann." <u>Variety</u>. December 9, 1942.
Ann Sheridan is announced for the lead in <u>The Gay
Nineties</u>, a nostalgic look at early show business. The
film was not made.

B-700   "We Applaud Ann Sheridan." <u>Hollywood Yearbook</u>.
         1951.
Ann Sheridan's work with the Mickey Finn Clubs is heralded.
The group helped underprivileged children.

B-701   Weller, Helen. "Annie's New Love." <u>Motion
         Picture</u>. June 1943. pp. 44, 87.
Weller recounts rumors of Ann Sheridan's romance with Errol
Flynn while Ann was in Mexico obtaining a divorce from George
Brent. In an interview, Ann refutes the rumors, insisting
her only romance is with Mexico. Ann is pictured with
Mexican film star Esther Fernandez and Walt Disney.

B-702   West, John C. "Ann Sheridan: Oomph Girl Was a
         Lady." <u>Los Angeles Times</u>. February 12, 1967.
West eulogizes Ann Sheridan, praising her ability to "hold
her own with the tough guys who dominated the screen in the
late 1930s." West quotes the actress, who says, "The only
way I've ever been like the parts I played in the movies is
that I've never been hesitant to tell any man off when I
wanted something done differently."

B-703   "What No Cream?" <u>Los Angeles Examiner</u>.
         August 14, 1949.
In this tinted photo, Ann Sheridan slices peaches, allegedly
preparing to can fruit from her ranch.

B-704   "When a Woman Could Be an Oomph." <u>New York Times</u>.
         September 12, 1988.
Reader Art Rogoff answers columnist Russell Baker's query
concerning Ann Sheridan being dubbed the Oomph Girl.

B-705   "Where Oomph Has Gone." <u>Newsweek</u>. November 29,
         1965. p. 88.
Expanding budgets on soap operas led to a star-studded
daytime lineup. Among the celebrities appearing on soaps
were Ann Sheridan, Gloria DeHaven, and Macdonald Carey.

Though some tried to elevate the status of their work, Ann
was realistic but uninvolved. "All I know is that I'm a
woman looking for a girl," she says, "And in this week's
script I repeat what I said in last week's script."

B-706   "Who Told the Story?" Life. February 23, 1948.
Ann Sheridan, Gary Cooper, and director Leo McCarey share a
laugh on the set of Good Sam (F-78).

B-707   "Who's That Girl?" Video Review. September 1987.
Movie still collector Ray Gain questions the identification
of Ann Sheridan in a photo from Murder at the Vanities
(F-4) from the July 1987 issue. Contributor Roy Hemming
presents an enlargement of the photo to prove it is Ann.

B-708   Who's Who in Hollywood. 1952.
Ann Sheridan is among the many celebrities profiled in this
magazine annual.

B-709   _____. 1963.
Who's Who in Hollywood, a magazine annual, highlights the
careers of many stars, including Ann Sheridan.

B-710   Wilkinson, Lupton A. "Nothing But Oomph?" Los
         Angeles Times This Week. circa 1944.
         (Constance McCormick Collection.)
Ann Sheridan discusses the pros and cons of the oomph
campaign. She recalls an apartment that had refused to allow
her and her dog to live there before the campaign, later
offered her a rent-free apartment if they could take
advantage of the publicity and advertise that the Oomph Girl
lived there.

B-711   Williams, Bob. "Ann Sheridan: A Fight To the Last
         Moment." New York Post. January 23, 1967.
Pistols 'n' Petticoats (T-56) producer Joe Connelly
discusses Ann Sheridan's death from cancer. He says, "I
don't think Miss Sheridan knew how sick she was until about
10 days ago. She never admitted it."

B-712   "Willys' Stockings." Look. July 4, 1939.
Ann Sheridan models a pair of stockings from Dodge City
(F-47) in this article on Willys', a famous hosiery supplier.

B-713   Wilson, Andy. "Only 1 of 6 a Hit -- Ann Sheridan."
         Detroit Times [MI]. June 6, 1957.
Ann Sheridan discusses her work in "Without Incident" on
Playhouse 90 (T-23) and a possible series with Errol Flynn
called Cavalry Patrol. The series was not produced.

B-714   Wilson, Earl. "Ann Sheridan Goes on Travel Binges."
         Miami Sunday News [FL]. October 28, 1956.
Ann Sheridan discusses trips to Africa to film The Woman
and the Hunter (F-88) and an episode of I've Got a
Secret (T-20).

B-715   _____. "Censors Relax, Permit Annie to Play a
         'Nice' Bad Girl." Los Angeles Daily News.

January 24, 1947.
Wilson interviews Ann Sheridan about her work in The
Unfaithful (F-75). He points out that it was rare for the
censors to allow her to portray an adulteress who goes
unpunished.

B-716   _____. "It Happened Last Night." Long Island
         Newsday [NY]. May 29, 1962.
Wilson spies Ann Sheridan doing a hula at New York's Hawaiian
Room.

B-717   _____. "Romance? Maybe, Says Sheridan." Miami
         Daily News [FL]. October 17, 1956.
When asked about her love life following the 1953 death of
Steve Hannagan, Ann Sheridan said, "If I find romance, I'll
take it."

B-718   _____. "She'll Take Romance If She Finds It
         Again." Pontiac Press [MI]. October 16, 1956.
Wilson's October 17 column (B-717) ran a day earlier and with
an alternate headline in Pontiac, Michigan.

B-719   _____. "Sticks Neck Out on Ties." Miami Daily
         News [FL]. December 17, 1953.
Wilson claims Ann Sheridan was set to marry an unidentified
Mexican admirer.

B-720   Wilson, Elizabeth. "'Get Sheridan.'" Screenland.
         August 1939. pp. 25, 92-93.
Wilson recalls how Warner Bros. used Ann Sheridan in a
variety of "B" roles before she began drawing attention in
1939. Wilson compares her appearance and joie de vivre to
that of Jean Harlow.

B-721   Winchell, Walter. "Ann Sheridan Enjoys Walks at 6
         A.M." Miami Herald [FL]. September 20, 1956.
Winchell reports on celebrities' activities in New York,
including Ann Sheridan's early-morning strolls.

B-722   Wittman, Robert C. "From Average Girl to Oomph
         Queen." New York Enquirer. August 8, 1955.
Wittman speculates on Steve Hannagan's relationship with Ann
Sheridan following news that Ann was beneficiary of Steve's
six insurance policies.

B-723   Wood, Veta Lee as told to Dudley, Fredda. "I Was
         the Millionth Fan." Movie Stars Parade. October
         1947. pp. 51, 91-93.
Twelve-year-old Veta Lee Wood recalls the excitement of
meeting her idol, Ann Sheridan, after winning a trip to
Hollywood for penning Ann's millionth fan letter. Three
photos show Wood at Warner Bros.

B-724   Yolanda. "Women of Hollywood." Screen Guide.
         April 1942. pp. 32, 34-35.
Jane Wyman, Ann Sheridan, Priscilla Lane, and others model
spring fashions.

B-725   York, Cal. "Inside Stuff." <u>Photoplay</u>. January
          1944.
Two Ann Sheridan items are in this gossip column. York
reveals that Ann is slightly pigeon-toed. He also notes that
Ann planned to vacation in New York with Oscar Brooke, an
employee at Warner Bros.'s Mexican office. When the studio
prohibited him from going, Ann saw New York with Steve
Hannagan.

B-726   _____. "Inside Stuff." <u>Photoplay</u>. October
          1953. p. 99-100.
York reports on the tension on the set of <u>Rage of the</u>
<u>Jungle</u>, released as <u>Appointment in Honduras</u> (F-85).
Glenn Ford was angry when Ann Sheridan's tardiness held up
production. Ann claimed Ford was afraid of being upstaged.

B-727   "You Must Remember This...20 Fascinating Facts about
          <u>Casablanca</u>." <u>Globe</u>. August 4, 1992. p. 29.
"Fact #3" is that Ann Sheridan and Hedy Lamarr initially were
cast in the role that went to Ingrid Bergman.

B-728   "Your Guide to Current Films." <u>Screenland</u>. July
          1953.
Ann Sheridan is seen in a still from <u>Take Me to Town</u>
(F-84).

B-729   Zeitlin, Ida. "I, Clara Lou, Take Thee, George."
          <u>Screenland</u>. May 1942. pp. 24-25, 58-59.
Newlyweds Ann Sheridan and George Brent share the story of
their wedding. Ann reveals, "If I'd known it was going to be
like this, I'd have done it a long time ago." The article
includes photos of the Brents with boss H.M. Warner and
relaxing at home. A third shot shows Ann surprising Brent at
the studio by replacing his co-star, Barbara Stanwyck, in a
wedding scene in <u>The Gay Sisters</u> (Warner Bros., 1942).

B-730   Zolotow, Sam. "Broadway Debut for Ann Sheridan."
          <u>New York Times</u>. June 29, 1959.
Zolotow announces Ann Sheridan's plans to star in <u>Odd Man</u>
<u>In</u> (P-19).

APPENDIX I: MAGAZINE COVERS

The following magazines picture Ann Sheridan on the cover.
The country of origin follows in brackets if the magazine was
published outside the United States. Some regional color
newspaper supplements also are included.

Screen Guide   April 1939
  Ann Sheridan in dance hall costume

Picturegoer   [England]   May 20, 1939
  Color photo of Ann Sheridan on leopard skin

Life   July 24, 1939
  Ann Sheridan in sweater

Look   August 1, 1939
  Color photo of Ann Sheridan in white dress with green trim

Screenland   August 1939
  Ann Sheridan in two-piece print bathing suit

Hollywood   September 1939

Modern Screen   October 1939
  Earl Christy sketch of Ann Sheridan on a surfboard

Look   February 13, 1940
  Color headshots of Ann Sheridan and a look-alike plastic
  mask created by Perc Westmore

Screen Guide   May 1940
  Ann Sheridan in blue gown and gold turban

Screenland   May 1940
  Ann Sheridan in ruffled skirt

Movie Mirror   June 1940

Silver Screen   August 1940
  Sketch of Ann Sheridan with hand in hair

Song Hits   September 1940
  Ann Sheridan head shot

Movie-Radio Guide   October 12, 1940
  Ann Sheridan head shot

Picturegoer   [England]   October 19, 1940

Picture Post   April 1941
  Ann Sheridan on leopard skin

Picturegoer   [England]   May 3, 1941

Movie-Radio Guide   November 15, 1941
  Ann Sheridan in fur coat

Movies   February 1942

Screen Guide   March 1942
  Ann Sheridan in red, white and blue striped blouse

Movie Life   April 1942
  Ann Sheridan and George Brent

Photoplay   June 1942

The Family Circle   October 30, 1942
  Glamour pose of Ann Sheridan, along with photos of the Mad
  Russian (Bert Gordon), Hedy Lamarr, and Walter Pidgeon

Screenland   December 1942
  Ann Sheridan in flowered snood and mittens

Movie Story   January 1943
  Ann Sheridan and Jack Benny in George Washington Slept
  Here (F-64)

Motion Picture Combined with Hollywood Magazine   May 1943
  Ann Sheridan by tree

Photoplay   November 1943

Stardom   January 1944
  Ann Sheridan aims snowball

Movieland   April 1944

Movies   May 1944

Screen Romances   June 1944
  Ann Sheridan in Shine On Harvest Moon (F-68)

Screenland   August 1944
  Ann Sheridan in blue swimsuit

Silver Screen   January 1948

Movie Story   June 1948

Color photo of Ann Sheridan and Errol Flynn in <u>Silver</u>
<u>River</u> (F-77)

<u>Picture Show</u>   [England]   August 6, 1949
Ann Sheridan and Gary Cooper in <u>Good Sam</u> (F-78)

<u>Picturegoer</u>   [England]   September 24, 1949
Ann Sheridan and Cary Grant in <u>I Was a Male War Bride</u>
(F-79)

<u>Silver Screen</u>   December 1949
Color photo of Ann Sheridan in green scarf

<u>Chicago Daily News Home and Life Magazine</u>   February 23,
1952
Sepia photo of Ann Sheridan winking

<u>Picturegoer</u>   [England]   June 28, 1952
Tinted photo of Ann Sheridan in bathing suit

<u>Chicago Sunday Tribune</u>   July 12, 1953
Color photo of Ann Sheridan in high-collared cape

<u>New York Sunday Mirror</u>   September 6, 1953
Color photo of Ann Sheridan in <u>Take Me to Town</u> (F-84)

<u>Screen Stories</u>   October 1956
Color photos of the cast of <u>The Opposite Sex</u> (F-87),
including June Allyson, Joan Blondell, Ann Miller, Ann
Sheridan, Dolores Gray, and Joan Collins

<u>Screen Facts</u>   #14   Vol. 3, no. 2.   1966
Al Kilgore caricature of Ann Sheridan

<u>Fort Lauderdale News Showtime</u> [FL]   July 29, 1966
Portrait of Ann Sheridan accompanies tinted sketch from
<u>Pistols 'n' Petticoats</u> (T-56)

<u>Miami Herald TV Preview</u> [FL]   August 7, 1966
Color photo of Ann Sheridan from <u>Pistols 'n' Petticoats</u>
(T-56)

<u>Los Angeles Herald-Examiner TV weekly</u>   August 28, 1966
Color caricature of Ann Sheridan and the cast of <u>Pistols</u>
<u>'n' Petticoats</u> (T-56)

<u>Detroit Times TV Times</u> [MI]   September 18, 1966
Photos of Ann Sheridan and Jean Arthur from their series
<u>Pistols 'n' Petticoats</u> (T-56) and <u>The Jean Arthur</u>
<u>Show</u> (CBS, 1966)

<u>Dallas Morning News TV Channels</u> [TX]   January 22, 1967
Color photo of Ann Sheridan from <u>Pistols 'n' Petticoats</u>
(T-56)

<u>Detroit Free Press TV Guide</u> [MI]   January 22, 1967
Color photo of Ann Sheridan from <u>Pistols 'n' Petticoats</u>
(T-56)

<u>Los Angeles Times TV Times</u>   January 22, 1967
  Color photo of Ann Sheridan from <u>Pistols 'n' Petticoats</u>
  (T-56)

<u>Films in Review</u>   November 1984
  Black and white still of Ann Sheridan, Bette Davis, and
  Monty Wooley in <u>The Man Who Came to Dinner</u> (F-60)

APPENDIX II: ADS

Ann Sheridan appeared in ads for the following products. Many were studio-arranged endorsements, used to publicize their actors or a particular movie. If there is a specific film promoted in the ad, it is indicated in parentheses.

Signal gasoline   1930s

House of Westmore foundation cream   1940   (Years without Days, released as Castle on the Hudson, F-52)

Lux Soap   1941

Chesterfield cigarettes   1941   (The Man Who Came to Dinner, F-60)

House of Westmore foundation cream   1942   (George Washington Slept Here, F-64)

Bates bedspreads and draperies   1943   (Thank Your Lucky Stars, F-66)

House of Westmore make-up [sic]   1944   (Shine On Harvest Moon, F-68)

Westmore beauty products   1944

Overglo   1944

Lux toilet soap   1945   (The Animal Kingdom, released as One More Tomorrow, F-71)

French's bird seed   1946

Chesterfield cigarettes   1947   (Nora Prentiss, F-74)

Westmore's cake-make-up [sic], foundation cream, overglo, and foundation face powder   1947   (The Unfaithful, F-75)

Ayds vitamin candy   1950

Ayds vitamin candy   1951

Sitrue tissues   1951   (<u>Woman on the Run</u>, F-81)

Jergens lotion   1951   (<u>Woman on the Run</u>, F-81)

Lux toilet soap   1952   (<u>Steel Town</u>, F-82)

Woodbury cold cream   1952   (<u>Steel Town</u>, F-82)

Crescent diamond rings   1953   (<u>Vermilion O'Toole</u>,
    released as <u>Take Me to Town</u>, F-84)

APPENDIX III: MISCELLANEOUS

Ann Sheridan's name or likeness was used on the following
products. Country of origin is noted if the item was
available outside the United States.

Black and white arcade card, 1940s, distributed through
   vending machines

Black and white American postcard (#3046) showing Ann
   Sheridan in a lacy jacket

Black and white French postcard (Editions P.I., #257) showing
   Ann Sheridan wearing two diamond bracelets, resting her
   head on a velvet couch, 1940s

Black and white French postcard (Editions P.I., #257) showing
   Ann Sheridan in same gown and bracelets, but in a sexier
   pose

Black and white British postcard (Picturegoer Series, #1455)
   showing Ann Sheridan in the same photo as above (Editions
   P.I. #257)

Black and white foreign postcard (DRC, #14) showing Ann
   Sheridan in a dark blouse, 1940s. Credit line reads "Echte
   foto."

Color tinted 5X7 photograph of Ann Sheridan in bathing suit,
   sold in picture frames, 1940s

Color tinted 8X10 photograph of Ann Sheridan in evening gown,
   sold in picture frames, 1940s

Black and white 8X10 photograph of Ann Sheridan on leopard
   skin, sold in picture frames, 1940s

Color photograph of Ann Sheridan in suit on cover of writing
   tablet, 1940s

Plaster Oomph Girl carnival dolls, 1940s

Blue tinted wallet-size photograph of Ann Sheridan with
identification information on the back, sold in wallets,
1940s

Mentioned in lyrics to Cole Porter's "See That You're Born in
Texas" from the Broadway musical <u>Something for the
Boys</u>, 1943

<u>Ann Sheridan and the Sign of the Sphinx</u>, juvenile novel by
Kathryn Heisenfelt, Whitman Publishing Company, #2390, 1943
(B-220)

<u>Ann Sheridan Paint Book</u>, Whitman Publishing Company, 1943

<u>Ann Sheridan Two Cut-out Dolls</u>, Whitman Publishing Company,
1944

Postcard advertising <u>Shine On Harvest Moon</u> (F-68), 1944

Hollywood Starstamps, #123, 1947

<u>El Buen Sam</u> (<u>Good Sam</u>, F-78) postcard, made in Madrid,
1948

Star Cal decals, 1950s

<u>Glamorous Stars of the Forties Paper Dolls</u>, paper doll book
by Tom Tierney, Dover Publications, Inc., 1994 (B-674)

<u>Ann Sheridan Celebrity Paper Doll Coloring Book</u> by Ralph
Hodgdon, available from the artist at 25 Speedwell Street,
Dorchester, MA 02122

<u>Your Hit Parade: The War Years</u>, a CD or cassette of 144
songs produced by Time/Life Music, uses footage from Ann
Sheridan's U.S.O. tour (P-9) in the infomercial, 1995

APPENDIX IV: ARCHIVES

Many libraries and archives contain material on Ann Sheridan.
Listed below are those with exceptional collections, along
with notes on their holdings.

Billy Rose Theatre Collection
New York Public Library at Lincoln Center
111 Amsterdam Avenue
New York, NY 10023
(212)-870-1639

In addition to a clipping file of features from the New York
newspapers, the library contains photographs, _Playbills_,
and reviews from Ann Sheridan's film and theatrical efforts.

Library of Congress
Motion Picture, Broadcasting and Recorded Sound Division
Washington, D.C. 20540

The archive includes Ann Sheridan's credits from the NBC
Radio Index, as well as continuity scripts, prints of her
films, tapes of radio shows, and a myriad of other material.

Margaret Herrick Library
Center for Motion Picture Study
Academy of Motion Picture Arts and Sciences
333 S. La Cienega Boulevard
Beverly Hills, CA 90211
(310)-247-3000

The collection includes an extensive clipping file on Ann
Sheridan, as well as clipping and photo files on many of her
films.

Society to Preserve and Encourage Radio
Drama, Variety and Comedy (SPERDVAC)
Box 1587
Hollywood, CA 90078

Members of the group can borrow tapes of radio programs, as well as literature about oldtime radio from individual collections. Their holdings include several Ann Sheridan broadcasts.

UCLA Film and Television Archive
46 Powell Library
405 Hilgard Avenue
Los Angeles, CA 90024-1517
(310)-206-5388

The library houses many films and videos, most of which are available for viewing at the archive by appointment. They include the short <u>Hollywood Extra Girl</u> (F-27) and unused footage from <u>Hearst Metrotone News</u> (F-43 and F-73).

University of North Texas
University Archives
Box 5188
Denton, TX 76203-5188
(817)-565-2411

Ann Sheridan's alma mater has a clipping file on its famous student, as well as yearbooks and college newspaper articles about her career singing with the school orchestra (P-1).

USC Cinema-Television Library
University of Southern California
Doheny Library
University Park
Los Angeles, CA 90089
(213)-743-0966

In addition to films, stills, radio scripts, and clipping files at the USC Cinema-Television Library, the University of Southern California's Warner Bros. archive houses memos, contracts, and other documents about Ann Sheridan's career.

Wisconsin Center for Film and Theater Research
Film and Photo Archive
412 Historical Society, 816 State Street
Madison, WI 53706
(608)-264-6466

The center has a large collection of photos of Ann Sheridan, as well as a clipping file.

INDEX

Entries are indexed as follows. Page numbers refer to the biography and chronology. Coded enumerations refer to individual chapters: "P" for Plays and Personal Appearances; "F" for Filmography; "R" for Radio; "T" for Television; "D" for Discography; "A" for Awards and Honors; "S" for Song Sheets; "V" for Videography; and "B" for Bibliography. The prefix "PnP" refers to episodes of Pistols 'n' Petticoats (T-56), which can be found in the Television chapter.

About the Author

MARGIE SCHULTZ is a freelance writer. Her previous books include *Ann Sothern: A Bio-Bibliography* (1990), *Irene Dunne: A Bio-Bibliography* (1991), and *Eleanor Powell: A Bio-Bibliography* (1994), all published by Greenwood Press.

Printed in the USA
CPSIA information can be obtained
at www.ICGtesting.com
CBHW061504170224
4301CB00036B/137